Microsoft® Official Academic Course

Networking with Windows Server 2016 Exam 70-741

WILEY

VP & PUBLISHER	Barry Pruett
SENIOR EXECUTIVE EDITOR	Jim Minatel
MICROSOFT PRODUCT MANAGER	Microsoft Learning
PRODUCT DATA MAINTENANCE COORDINATOR	Devon Lewis
TECHNICAL EDITOR	Ron Handlon
CHANNEL MARKETING MANAGER	Michele Szczesniak
CONTENT MANAGEMENT DIRECTOR	Lisa Wojcik
CONTENT MANAGER	Nichole Urban
PRODUCTION COORDINATOR	Nicole Repasky
PRODUCTION EDITOR	Umamaheswari Gnanamani
COVER DESIGNER	Tom Nery

COVER PHOTO: © shutterstock/wavebreakmedia

This book was set in Garamond by SPi Global and printed and bound by Quad/Graphics.
The covers were printed by Quad/Graphics.

ISBN: 9781119126980 (PBK)
ISBN: 9781119298267 (EVAL)

The inside back cover will contain printing identification and country of origin if omitted from this page. In addition, if the ISBN on the back cover differs from the ISBN on this page, the one on the back cover is correct.

V10017545_021320

Preface

Welcome to the Microsoft Official Academic Course (MOAC) program for becoming a Microsoft Certified Solutions Associate for Windows 10. MOAC represents the collaboration between Microsoft Learning and John Wiley & Sons, Inc. publishing company. Microsoft and Wiley teamed up to produce a series of textbooks that deliver compelling and innovative teaching solutions to instructors and superior learning experiences for students. Infused and informed by in-depth knowledge from the creators of Windows 10, and crafted by a publisher known worldwide for the pedagogical quality of its products, these textbooks maximize skills transfer in minimum time. Students are challenged to reach their potential by using their new technical skills as highly productive members of the workforce.

Because this knowledgebase comes directly from Microsoft, architect of the Windows operating system and creator of the Microsoft Certified Solutions Associate exams, you are sure to receive the topical coverage that is most relevant to students' personal and professional success. Microsoft's direct participation not only assures you that MOAC textbook content is accurate and current; it also means that students will receive the best instruction possible to enable their success on certification exams and in the workplace.

■ The Microsoft Official Academic Course Program

The Microsoft Official Academic Course series is a complete program for instructors and institutions to prepare and deliver great courses on Microsoft software technologies. With MOAC, we recognize that because of the rapid pace of change in the technology and curriculum developed by Microsoft, there is an ongoing set of needs beyond classroom instruction tools for an instructor to be ready to teach the course. The MOAC program endeavors to provide solutions for all these needs in a systematic manner in order to ensure a successful and rewarding course experience for both instructor and student—technical and curriculum training for instructor readiness with new software releases; the software itself for student use at home for building hands-on skills, assessment, and validation of skill development; and a great set of tools for delivering instruction in the classroom and lab. All are important to the smooth delivery of an interesting course on Microsoft software, and all are provided with the MOAC program. We think about the model below as a gauge for ensuring that we completely support you in your goal of teaching a great course. As you evaluate your instructional materials options, you may wish to use the model for comparison purposes with available products.

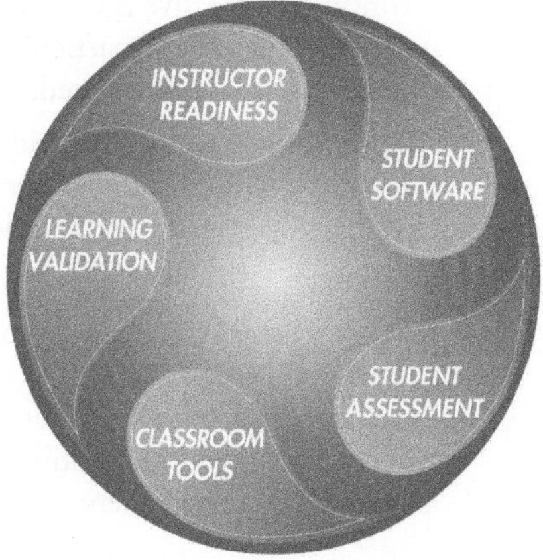

Illustrated Book Tour

Textbook Organization

This textbook is organized in twenty-one lessons, with each lesson corresponding to a particular exam objective for the 70-741 Network Windows Server 2016 Microsoft Certified Solutions Associate (MCSA) exam. This MOAC textbook covers all the learning objectives for the 70-741 MCSA certification exam. The exam objectives are highlighted throughout the textbook.

Pedagogical Features

Many pedagogical features have been developed specifically for Microsoft Official Academic Course programs.

Presenting the extensive procedural information and technical concepts woven throughout the textbook raises challenges for the student and instructor alike. The Illustrated Book Tour that follows provides a guide to the rich features contributing to Microsoft Official Academic Course program's pedagogical plan. Following is a list of key features in each lesson designed to prepare students for success on the certification exams and in the workplace:

- Each lesson begins with an overview of the skills covered in the lesson. More than a standard list of learning objectives, the overview correlates skills to the certification exam objective.
- Illustrations: Screen images provide visual feedback as students work through the exercises. The images reinforce key concepts, provide visual clues about the steps, and allow students to check their progress.
- Key Terms: Important technical vocabulary is listed at the beginning of the lesson. When these terms are used later in the lesson, they appear in bold italic type and are defined.
- Engaging point-of-use reader aids, located throughout the lessons, tell students why this topic is relevant (*The Bottom Line*), provide students with helpful hints (*Take Note*), or show cross-references to where content is covered in greater detail. Reader aids also provide additional relevant or background information that adds value to the lesson.
- Certification Ready features throughout the text signal students where a specific certification objective is covered. They provide students with a chance to check their understanding of that particular exam objective and, if necessary, review the section of the lesson where it is covered.
- Knowledge Assessments provide lesson-ending activities that test students' comprehension and retention of the material taught, presented using some of the question types that they'll see on the certification exam.
- An important supplement to this textbook is the accompanying lab work. Labs are available via a Lab Manual, and also by MOAC Labs Online. MOAC Labs Online provides students with the ability to work on the actual software simply by connecting through their Internet Explorer web browser. Either way, the labs use real-world scenarios to help students learn workplace skills associated with configuring a Windows infrastructure in an enterprise environment.

Lesson Features

70-741 EXAM OBJECTIVE — **Exam Objective**

Objective 5.1 – Implement IPv4 and IPv6. This objective may include but is not limited to the following: Configure IPv4 addresses and options; determine and configure appropriate IPv6 addresses; configure IPv4 or IPv6 subnetting; implement IPv6 stateless addressing; configure interoperability between IPv4 and IPv6 by using ISATAP, 6to4, and Teredo scenarios; *configure Border Gateway Protocol (BGP); *configure IPv4 and IPv6 routing.

Configure Border Gateway Protocol (BGP) and configure IPv4 and IPv6 routing are covered in Lesson 8.

Lesson Heading	Exam Objective
Connecting to a Network	
Implementing IPv4 and IPv6 Addressing • Exploring IPv4 Addressing • Configuring IPv4 Subnetting • Understanding Classless Interdomain Routing (CIDR) • Implementing NAT • Understanding IPv6 and IPv6 Addressing • Using the Default Gateway • Understanding Name Resolution • Configuring IPv4 and IPv6 Settings and Options • Implementing IPv6 Stateless Addressing	Configure IPv4 subnetting Determine and configure appropriate IPv6 addresses Configure IPv4 addresses and options Implement IPv6 stateless addressing
Using IPv4/IPv6 Transition Technologies • Configuring 6to4 • Configuring Intra-Site Automatic Tunnel Addressing Protocol (ISATAP) • Configuring Teredo	Configure interoperability between IPv4 and IPv6 by using ISATAP, 6to4, and Teredo scenarios

1

Key Terms

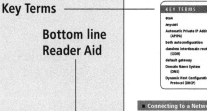

Bottom line Reader Aid

2 | Lesson **1**

KEY TERMS

6to4	**fully qualified domain names (FQDNs)**	**Network Address Translation (NAT)**
anycast	**global unicast addresses**	**network ID**
Automatic Private IP Addressing (APIPA)	**host ID**	**site-local unicast addresses**
both autoconfiguration	**Internet Protocol (IP)**	**stateful autoconfiguration**
classless interdomain routing (CIDR)	**Intra-Site Automatic Tunnel Addressing Protocol (ISATAP)**	**stateless autoconfiguration**
default gateway	**link-local addresses**	**subnetting**
Domain Name System (DNS)	**link-local unicast address**	**Teredo**
Dynamic Host Configuration Protocol (DHCP)	**multicast**	**Transmission Control Protocol/Internet Protocol (TCP/IP)**
	native IPv6 connectivity	**unicast**
		unique local addresses

■ Connecting to a Network

THE BOTTOM LINE

Designing network connectivity in today's networks requires you to make decisions about using IPv4/IPv6, designing a name resolution strategy, and understanding how to configure your wired and wireless network for security.

The most common cabling system used for wired computers is Ethernet. Most computers that use Ethernet connect with unshielded twisted-pair (UTP) cabling. Each end of the UTP cable has RJ-45 connectors. Today's servers usually come with 1 Gb/s connections for Ethernet, while some older machines only support 10 Mb/s or 100 Mb/s. To connect a server to an Ethernet network, your host connects to one end of the cable and the other end connects to a switch.

If a client cannot communicate over the network, you should first check to make sure that the cable is firmly connected to the network. You should also look at the indicator lights on the network card or interface and the lights on the switch or hub to determine what the LEDs are telling you. If you have no lights on the switch or hub, make sure that the switch or hub has power and is turned on.

If the problem only affects one computer on a subnet, the problem is most likely with the computer itself, the network interface, or the cable that connects the host to the switch or hub. To help isolate a faulty cable, you can purchase a cable tester or you can swap with a known good cable. If there is a problem with the network interface card, you should verify that you have the proper drivers loaded and that the network interface is enabled.

If the problem is affecting more than one computer, you need to look for a centralized component to those computers. For example, if the switch or hub is down, the computers connected to that switch or hub will not be able to communicate.

For wireless networks, the troubleshooting process is similar to wired networks. You must first determine if the problem is only affecting a single computer or multiple computers that are trying to access the same wireless access point. You then need to check if the wireless network has been configured properly and if the access point is turned on. Besides checking Windows to see if the network interface is enabled, you should also look for buttons or switches on laptops that can enable or disable the wireless connections. Finally, if you can connect to other hosts within the same subnet as other wireless clients but you cannot connect to wired clients or servers, you should check the network cable that connects the access point to the rest of the network.

Certification Ready Alert

6 | Lesson **1**

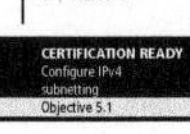

For example, you can take the 172.16.0.0/16 private IP address range and use the entire third octet as a subnet ID. This enables you to create up to 256 subnets with as many as 256 hosts on each one. The subnet masks for all the addresses on the subnets will be 255.255.255.0, and the network addresses will proceed as follows:

- 172.16.0.0/24
- 172.16.1.0/24
- 172.16.2.0/24
- 172.16.3.0/24
- . . .
- 172.16.255.0/24

Of course, when you are working on an existing network, the subnetting process will likely be more difficult. You might, for example, be given a relatively small range of addresses and be asked to create a certain number of subnets out of them. To do this, use the following procedure:

1. Determine how many subnet identifier bits you need to create the required number of subnets.
2. Subtract the subnet bits you need from the host bits and add them to the network bits.
3. Calculate the subnet mask by adding the network and subnet bits in binary form and converting the binary value to decimal.
4. Take the least significant subnet bit and the host bits, in binary form, and convert them to a decimal value.
5. Increment the network identifier (including the subnet bits) by the decimal value you calculated to determine the network addresses of your new subnets.

By using the same example from earlier in this lesson, if you take the 172.16.43.0/24 address and allocate two extra bits for the subnet ID, you end up with a binary subnet mask value of 11111111.11111111.11111111.11000000 (255.255.255.192 in decimal form, as noted earlier).

The least significant subnet bit plus the host bits gives you a binary value of 1000000, which converts to a decimal value of 64. Therefore, if we know that the network address of your first subnet is 192.168.43.0, the second subnet must be 192.168.43.64, the third 192.168.43.128, and the fourth 192.168.43.192, as shown in Table 1-3.

Table 1-3
Sample CIDR 172.16.43.0/26 Networks

Network Address	Starting IP Address	Ending IP Address	Subnet Mask
172.16.43.0	172.16.43.1	172.16.43.62	255.255.255.192
172.16.43.64	172.16.43.65	172.16.43.126	255.255.255.192
172.16.43.128	172.16.43.129	172.16.43.190	255.255.255.192
172.16.43.192	172.16.43.193	172.16.43.254	255.255.255.192

The larger subnet can be divided into 2[illegible] = 2^2 = 4 smaller subnets. For each of the smaller subnets, each subnet can hold 2[illegible] – 2 = 2^6 – 2 = 62 hosts.

Easy-to-Read Tables

Understanding Classless Interdomain Routing (CIDR)

In practical use, the IP address classes proved to be wasteful, and when the Internet first experienced a massive period of growth in the 1990s, it was feared that there might at some time be a shortage of addresses. To avoid assigning entire addresses of a particular class to networks that didn't have that many hosts, the IETF eventually published a new standard for assigning IP addresses called ***classless interdomain routing (CIDR).***

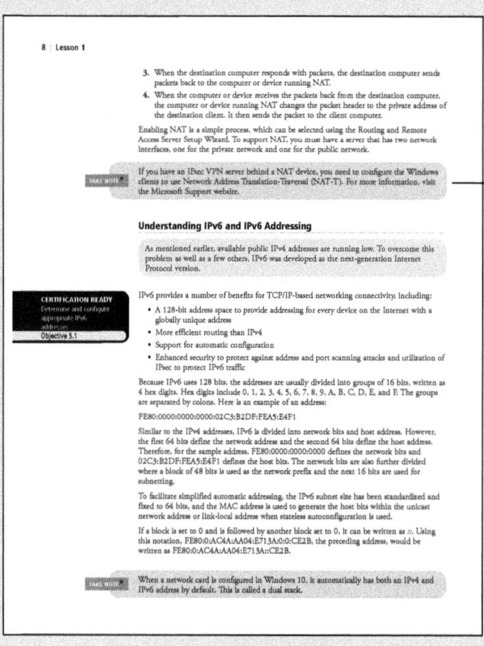

8 | Lesson 1

3. When the destination computer responds with packets, the destination computer sends packets back to the computer or device running NAT.
4. When the computer or device receives the packets back from the destination computer, the computer or device running NAT changes the packet header to the private address of the destination client. It then sends the packet to the client computer.

Enabling NAT is a simple process, which can be selected using the Routing and Remote Access Server Setup Wizard. To support NAT, you must have a server that has two network interfaces, one for the private network and one for the public network.

TAKE NOTE* If you have an IPsec VPN server behind a NAT device, you need to configure the Windows clients to use Network Address Translation-Traversal (NAT-T). For more information, visit the Microsoft Support website.

Understanding IPv6 and IPv6 Addressing

As mentioned earlier, available public IPv4 addresses are running low. To overcome this problem as well as a few others, IPv6 was developed as the next-generation Internet Protocol version.

CERTIFICATION READY
Determine and configure appropriate IPv6 addresses
Objective 5.1

IPv6 provides a number of benefits for TCP/IP-based networking connectivity, including:

- A 128-bit address space to provide addressing for every device on the Internet with a globally unique address
- More efficient routing than IPv4
- Support for automatic configuration
- Enhanced security to protect against address and port scanning attacks and utilization of IPsec to protect IPv6 traffic

Because IPv6 uses 128 bits, the addresses are usually divided into groups of 16 bits, written as 4 hex digits. Hex digits include 0, 1, 2, 3, 4, 5, 6, 7, 8, 9, A, B, C, D, E, and F. The groups are separated by colons. Here is an example of an address:

FE80:0000:0000:0000:02C3:B2DF:FEA5:E4F1

Similar to the IPv4 addresses, IPv6 is divided into network bits and host address. However, the first 64 bits define the network address and the second 64 bits define the host address. Therefore, for the sample address, FE80:0000:0000:0000 defines the network bits and 02C3:B2DF:FEA5:E4F1 defines the host bits. The network bits are also further divided where a block of 48 bits is used as the network prefix and the next 16 bits are used for subnetting.

To facilitate simplified automatic addressing, the IPv6 subnet size has been standardized and fixed to 64 bits, and the MAC address is used to generate the host bits within the unicast network address or link-local address when stateless autoconfiguration is used.

If a block is set to 0 and is followed by another block set to 0, it can be written as ::. Using this notation, FE80:0:AC4A:AA04:E713A:0:0:CE2B, the preceding address, would be written as FE80:0:AC4A:AA04:E713A::CE2B.

TAKE NOTE* When a network card is configured in Windows 10, it automatically has both an IPv4 and IPv6 address by default. This is called a dual stack.

Take Note Reader Aid

38 | Lesson 2

3. Import the NanoServerImageGenerator module by using the following Windows PowerShell `Import-Module` cmdlet:

```
Import-Module .\NanoServerImageGenerator -Verbose
```

4. Create the VHD or WIM by using the `New-NanoServerImage` cmdlet with the following syntax:

```
new-NanoServerImage -DeploymentType Guest

-Edition Standard -mediapath C:\ -Basepath c:\nano -targetpath c:\
nano\nano-svr1.vhdx

-computername NANO-SVR1 -storage -Packages
Microsoft-NanoServer-DNS-Package
```

Once the .vhd or .vhdx file is created, you need to deploy the Nano Server to Hyper-V by using the following steps:

1. Open Hyper-V Manager.
2. Create a new virtual machine with the new virtual disk file.
3. Boot the virtual machine.
4. Use Hyper-V to connect to the virtual machine.
5. Log on to the Nano Server Recovery Console using the administrator account and password.
6. Obtain the IP address for the virtual machine and connect to the Nano Server by using the remote management tools to manage the server.

MORE INFORMATION
For more information on deploying a Nano Server, refer to *70-740: Installing, Storage and Compute with Windows Server 2016*.

More Information Reader Aid

Using Root Hints

The ***root hints*** are used by DNS servers to find the root servers when performing iterative queries. The root hints are essential for DNS servers that are authoritative at lower levels of the DNS namespace when locating and finding the authoritative server for a zone.

CERTIFICATION READY
Configure root hints
Objective 1.1

The DNS Server service must be configured with root hints to resolve queries for names that it is not authoritative for or for which it contains no delegations. By default, Windows DNS contains a root hint, which contain the names and IP addresses of the DNS servers authoritative for the root zone. By default, DNS servers use a root hints file, called cache.dns, on Microsoft DNS servers. The cache.dns file is stored in the *%systemroot%*\System32\Dns folder on the server computer.

UPDATE ROOT HINTS

GET READY. To update root hints, perform the following steps.

1. On LON-DC1, log on as **adatum\administrator** with the password of **Pa$$w0rd.**
2. Click **Start** and click **Server Manager**.
3. Using Server Manager, click **Tools > DNS.**
4. If necessary, expand the DNS Manager console to a full-screen view.
5. Right-click the server and choose **Properties**. The Properties dialog box opens.
6. Select the **Root Hints** tab, as shown in Figure 2-6.

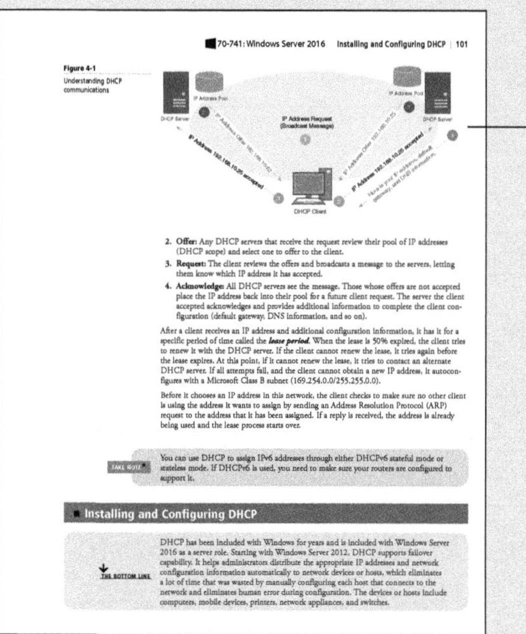

70-741: Windows Server 2016 Installing and Configuring DHCP | 101

Figure 4-1
Understanding DHCP communications

2. **Offer:** Any DHCP servers that receive the request review their pool of IP addresses (DHCP scope) and select one to offer to the client.
3. **Request:** The client reviews the offers and broadcasts a message to the servers, letting them know which IP address it has accepted.
4. **Acknowledge:** All DHCP servers see the message. Those whose offers are not accepted place the IP address back into their pool for a future client request. The server the client accepted acknowledges and provides additional information to complete the client configuration (default gateway, DNS information, and so on).

After a client receives an IP address and additional configuration information, it has it for a specific period of time called the ***lease period***. When the lease is 50% expired, the client tries to renew it with the DHCP server. If the client cannot renew the lease, it tries again before the lease expires. At this point, if it cannot renew the lease, it tries to contact an alternate DHCP server. If all attempts fail, and the client cannot obtain a new IP address, it autoconfigures with a Microsoft Class B subnet (169.254.0.0/255.255.0.0).

Before it chooses an IP address in this network, the client checks to make sure no other client is using the address it wants to assign by sending an Address Resolution Protocol (ARP) request to the address that it has been assigned. If a reply is received, the address is already being used and the lease process starts over.

TAKE NOTE* You can use DHCP to assign IPv6 addresses through either DHCPv6 stateful mode or stateless mode. If DHCPv6 is used, you need to make sure your routers are configured to support it.

Installing and Configuring DHCP

THE BOTTOM LINE

DHCP has been included with Windows for years and is included with Windows Server 2016 as a server role. Starting with Windows Server 2012, DHCP supports failover capability. It helps administrators distribute the appropriate IP addresses and network configuration information automatically to network devices or hosts, which eliminates a lot of time that was wasted by manually configuring each host that connects to the network and eliminates human error during configuration. The devices or hosts include computers, mobile devices, printers, network appliances, and switches.

Informative Diagrams

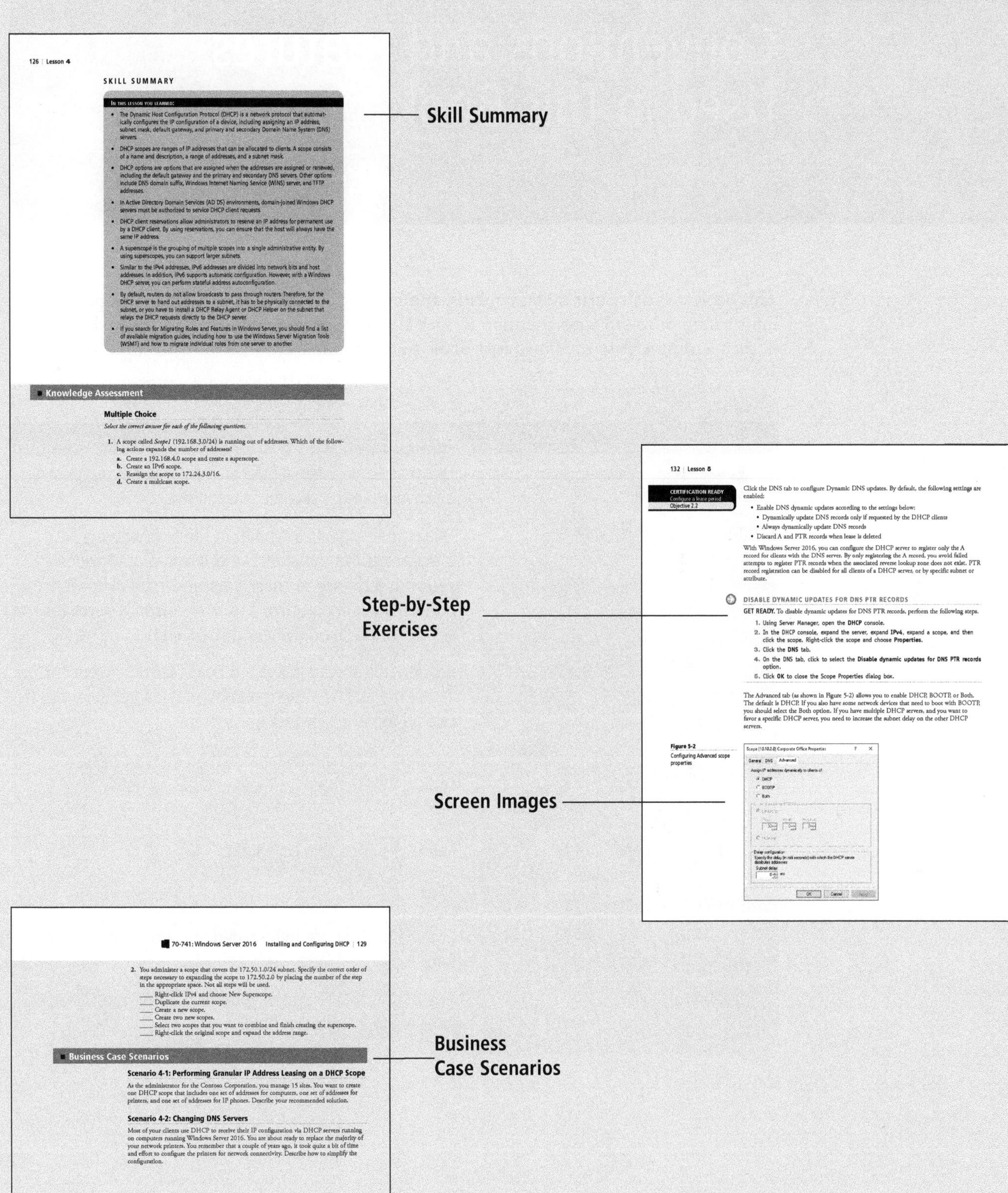
Skill Summary
Step-by-Step Exercises
Screen Images
Business Case Scenarios

Conventions and Features Used in This Book

This book uses particular fonts, symbols, and heading conventions to highlight important information or to call your attention to special steps. For more information about the features in each lesson, refer to the Illustrated Book Tour section.

CONVENTION	MEANING
↓ THE BOTTOM LINE	This feature provides a brief summary of the material to be covered in the section that follows.
CERTIFICATION READY	This feature signals the point in the text where a specific certification objective is covered. It provides you with a chance to check your understanding of that particular exam objective and, if necessary, review the section of the lesson where it is covered.
TAKE NOTE* MORE INFORMATION	Reader aids appear in shaded boxes found in your text. *Take Note and More Information* provide helpful hints related to particular tasks or topics.
WARNING	*Warning* points out instances when error or misuse could cause damage to the computer or network.
A ***shared printer*** can be used by many individuals on a network.	Key terms appear in bold italic.
`cd\windows\system32\ServerMigrationTools`	Commands that are to be typed are shown in a special font.
Click **Install Now**.	Any button on the screen you are supposed to click on or select will appear in bold.

Instructor Support Program

The Microsoft Official Academic Course programs are accompanied by a rich array of resources that incorporate the extensive textbook visuals to form a pedagogically cohesive package. These resources provide all the materials instructors need to deploy and deliver their courses. Instructor resources available at www.wiley.com/ include:

- **Instructor's Guide.** The Instructor's Guide contains solutions to all the textbook exercises as well as chapter summaries and lecture notes. The Instructor's Guide and Syllabi for various term lengths are available from the Instructor's Book Companion site.
- **Test Bank.** The Test Bank contains hundreds of questions organized by lesson in multiple-choice, best answer, build list, and essay formats and is available to download from the Instructor's Book Companion site. A complete answer key is provided.
- **PowerPoint Presentations.** A complete set of PowerPoint presentations is available on the Instructor's Book Companion site to enhance classroom presentations. Tailored to the text's topical coverage, these presentations are designed to convey key Windows Server 2012 concepts addressed in the text.
- **Available Textbook Figures.** All figures from the text are on the Instructor's Book Companion site. By using these visuals in class discussions, you can help focus students' attention on key elements of Windows 8 and help them understand how to use it effectively in the workplace.
- **MOAC Labs Online.** MOAC Labs Online is a cloud-based environment that enables students to conduct exercises using real Microsoft products. These are not simulations but instead are live virtual machines where faculty and students can perform any activities they would on a local virtual machine. MOAC Labs Online relieves the need for local setup, configuration, and most troubleshooting tasks. This represents an opportunity to lower costs, eliminate the hassle of lab setup, and support and improve student access and portability. MOAC Labs Online are available for students at an additional cost. Contact your Wiley rep about including MOAC Labs Online with your course offering.
- **Lab Answer Keys.** Answer keys for review questions found in the lab manuals and MOAC Labs Online are available on the Instructor's Book Companion site.
- **Lab Worksheets.** The review questions found in the lab manuals and MOAC Labs Online are gathered in Microsoft Word documents for students to use. These are available on the Instructor's Book Companion site.

Student Support Program

Book Companion Web Site (www.wiley.com)

The students' book companion site for the MOAC series includes any resources, exercise files, and Web links that will be used in conjunction with this course and any errata.

■ Microsoft Certification

Microsoft Certification has many benefits and enables you to keep your skills relevant, applicable, and competitive. In addition, Microsoft Certification is an industry standard that is recognized worldwide—which helps open doors to potential job opportunities. After you earn your Microsoft Certification, you have access to a number of benefits, which can be found on the Microsoft Certified Professional member site.

Microsoft Learning has reinvented the Microsoft Certification Program by building cloud-related skills validation into the industry's most recognized certification program. Microsoft Certified Solutions Expert (MCSE) and Microsoft Certified Solutions Developer (MCSD) are Microsoft's flagship certifications for professionals who want to lead their IT organization's journey to the cloud. These certifications recognize IT professionals with broad and deep skill sets across Microsoft solutions. The Microsoft Certified Solutions Associate (MCSA) is the certification for aspiring IT professionals and is also the prerequisite certification necessary to earn an MCSE. These new certifications integrate cloud-related and on-premise skills validation in order to support organizations and recognize individuals who have the skills required to be productive using Microsoft technologies.

On-premise or in the cloud, Microsoft training and certification empowers technology professionals to expand their skills and gain knowledge directly from the source. Securing these essential skills will allow you to grow your career and make yourself indispensable as the industry shifts to the cloud. Cloud computing ultimately enables IT to focus on more mission-critical activities, raising the bar of required expertise for IT professionals and developers. These reinvented certifications test on a deeper set of skills that map to real-world business context. Rather than testing only on a feature of a technology, Microsoft Certifications now validate more advanced skills and a deeper understanding of the platform.

Preparing to Take an Exam

Unless you are a very experienced user, you will need to use test preparation materials to prepare to complete the test correctly and within the time allowed. The Microsoft Official Academic Course series is designed to prepare you with a strong knowledge of all exam topics, and with some additional review and practice on your own, you should feel confident in your ability to pass the appropriate exam.

After you decide which exam to take, review the list of objectives for the exam. You can easily identify tasks that are included in the objective list by locating the exam objective overview at the start of each lesson and the Certification Ready sidebars in the margin of the lessons in this book.

To register for the MCSA exam, visit the Microsoft Certifications webpage for directions on how to register with Pearson VUE, the company that delivers the MCSA exams. Keep in mind these important items about the testing procedure:

- **What to expect.** Microsoft Certification testing labs typically have multiple workstations, which may or may not be occupied by other candidates. Test center administrators strive to provide a quiet and comfortable environment for all test takers.
- **Plan to arrive early.** It is recommended that you arrive at the test center at least 30 minutes before the test is scheduled to begin.
- **Bring your identification.** To take your exam, you must bring the identification (ID) that was specified when you registered for the exam. If you are unclear about which forms of ID are required, contact the exam sponsor identified in your registration information. Although requirements vary, you typically must show two valid forms of ID, one with a photo, both with your signature.
- **Leave personal items at home.** The only item allowed into the testing area is your identification, so leave any backpacks, laptops, briefcases, and other personal items at home. If you have items that cannot be left behind (such as purses), the testing center might have small lockers available for use.
- **Nondisclosure agreement.** At the testing center, Microsoft requires that you accept the terms of a nondisclosure agreement (NDA) and complete a brief demographic survey before taking your certification exam.

Acknowledgements

We thank the MOAC faculty and instructors who have assisted us in building the Microsoft Official Academic Course courseware. These elite educators have acted as our sounding board on key pedagogical and design decisions leading to the development of the MOAC courseware for future Information Technology workers. They have provided invaluable advice in the service of quality instructional materials, and we truly appreciate their dedication to technology education.

Brian Bridson, Baker College of Flint

David Chaulk, Baker College Online

Ron Handlon, Remington College – Tampa Campus

Katherine James, Seneca College of Applied Arts & Technology

Wen Liu, ITT Educational Services

Zeshan Sattar, Pearson in Practice

Jared Spencer, Westwood College Online

David Vallerga, MTI College

Bonny Willy, Ivy Tech State College

We also thank Microsoft Learning's Heidi Johnson, Larry Kaye, Rob Linsky, Colin Lyth, Paul Pardi, Merrick Van Dongen, Liberty Munson, Keith Loeber, Natasha Chornesky, Briana Roberts, Jim Clark, Anne Hamilton, Erika Cravens, and Jim Cochran, for their encouragement and support in making the Microsoft Official Academic Course programs the finest academic materials for mastering the newest Microsoft technologies for both students and instructors.

About the Author

Patrick Regan has been a PC technician, network administrator/engineer, design architect, and security analyst for the past 23 years. He has taught computer and network classes at Sacramento local colleges (Heald Colleges and MTI Colleges) and participated in and led many projects (Heald Colleges, Intel Corporation, Miles Consulting Corporation, and Pacific Coast Companies). For his teaching accomplishments, he received the Teacher of the Year award from Heald Colleges and he has received several recognition awards from Intel. As a senior system administrator, he supports approximately 120 servers and 1,500 users spread over 5 subsidiaries and 70 sites. He has authored a number of textbooks, including books on SharePoint 2010, Windows 7, Windows 8.1, and Windows Server 2012 for John Wiley & Sons.

Brief Contents

Contents

Implementing IPv4 and IPv6 Addressing

LESSON 1

70-741 EXAM OBJECTIVE

Objective 5.1 – Implement IPv4 and IPv6. This objective may include but is not limited to the following: Configure IPv4 addresses and options; determine and configure appropriate IPv6 addresses; configure IPv4 or IPv6 subnetting; implement IPv6 stateless addressing; configure interoperability between IPv4 and IPv6 by using ISATAP, 6to4, and Teredo scenarios; *configure Border Gateway Protocol (BGP); *configure IPv4 and IPv6 routing.

*Configure Border Gateway Protocol (BGP) and configure IPv4 and IPv6 routing are covered in Lesson 8.

Lesson Heading	Exam Objective
Connecting to a Network	
Implementing IPv4 and IPv6 Addressing • Exploring IPv4 Addressing • Configuring IPv4 Subnetting • Understanding Classless Interdomain Routing (CIDR) • Implementing NAT • Understanding IPv6 and IPv6 Addressing • Using the Default Gateway • Understanding Name Resolution • Configuring IPv4 and IPv6 Settings and Options • Implementing IPv6 Stateless Addressing	Configure IPv4 subnetting Determine and configure appropriate IPv6 addresses Configure IPv4 addresses and options Implement IPv6 stateless addressing
Using IPv4/IPv6 Transition Technologies • Configuring 6to4 • Configuring Intra-Site Automatic Tunnel Addressing Protocol (ISATAP) • Configuring Teredo	Configure interoperability between IPv4 and IPv6 by using ISATAP, 6to4, and Teredo scenarios

KEY TERMS

6to4
anycast
Automatic Private IP Addressing (APIPA)
both autoconfiguration
classless interdomain routing (CIDR)
default gateway
Domain Name System (DNS)
Dynamic Host Configuration Protocol (DHCP)
fully qualified domain names (FQDNs)
global unicast addresses
host ID
Internet Protocol (IP)
Intra-Site Automatic Tunnel Addressing Protocol (ISATAP)
link-local addresses
link-local unicast address
multicast
native IPv6 connectivity
Network Address Translation (NAT)
network ID
site-local unicast addresses
stateful autoconfiguration
stateless autoconfiguration
subnetting
Teredo
Transmission Control Protocol/Internet Protocol (TCP/IP)
unicast
unique local addresses

Connecting to a Network

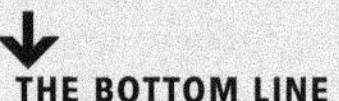

Designing network connectivity in today's networks requires you to make decisions about using IPv4/IPv6, designing a name resolution strategy, and understanding how to configure your wired and wireless network for security.

The most common cabling system used for wired computers is Ethernet. Most computers that use Ethernet connect with unshielded twisted-pair (UTP) cabling. Each end of the UTP cable has RJ-45 connectors. Today's servers usually come with 1 Gb/s connections for Ethernet, while some older machines only support 10 Mb/s or 100 Mb/s. To connect a server to an Ethernet network, your host connects to one end of the cable and the other end connects to a switch.

If a client cannot communicate over the network, you should first check to make sure that the cable is firmly connected to the network. You should also look at the indicator lights on the network card or interface and the lights on the switch or hub to determine what the LEDs are telling you. If you have no lights on the switch or hub, make sure that the switch or hub has power and is turned on.

If the problem only affects one computer on a subnet, the problem is most likely with the computer itself, the network interface, or the cable that connects the host to the switch or hub. To help isolate a faulty cable, you can purchase a cable tester or you can swap with a known good cable. If there is a problem with the network interface card, you should verify that you have the proper drivers loaded and that the network interface is enabled.

If the problem is affecting more than one computer, you need to look for a centralized component to those computers. For example, if the switch or hub is down, the computers connected to that switch or hub will not be able to communicate.

For wireless networks, the troubleshooting process is similar to wired networks. You must first determine if the problem is only affecting a single computer or multiple computers that are trying to access the same wireless access point. You then need to check if the wireless network has been configured properly and if the access point is turned on. Besides checking Windows to see if the network interface is enabled, you should also look for buttons or switches on laptops that can enable or disable the wireless connections. Finally, if you can connect to other hosts within the same subnet as other wireless clients but you cannot connect to wired clients or servers, you should check the network cable that connects the access point to the rest of the network.

Implementing IPv4 And IPv6 Addressing

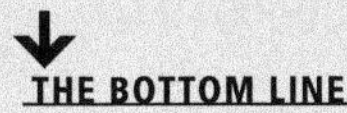

When accessing computers on a network, you typically communicate by using their host names. If you are accessing a website, you enter a friendly name such as www.microsoft.com. Every device that connects to your network or the Internet must have an Internet Protocol (IP) address. You also need a way to associate these names to their assigned IP address.

Internet Protocol (IP) is the key protocol in the TCP/IP suite. It is responsible for adding addressing information to the packets for the sender and the receiver, as well as adding data to help route and deliver the packet. Windows 10 uses TCP/IP as its default networking protocol.

Transmission Control Protocol/Internet Protocol (TCP/IP) is a set of protocols that allows computers to exchange data within a network and between networks. These protocols (or rules) manage the content, format, timing, sequencing, and error control of the messages that are exchanged between the devices. Every device that communicates over TCP/IP must have a unique IP address. Windows 10 uses a dual-layer architecture that enables it to implement both IPv4 and IPv6 address schemes. Both share the common TCP Transport layer protocol.

Before configuring TCP/IP on your network, take time to plan the implementation. For example, how big do you expect your network to be? How will your network be designed from a physical and logical standpoint?

Exploring IPv4 Addressing

Microsoft, along with other industry leaders, is working hard to make IPv6 the next standard for IP addressing. In the meantime, you have a mixture of IPv4 and IPv6 devices on your network, so you need to understand how these devices are configured and how they interact with each other.

During the 1960s, several universities and research centers needed a network to share information. To address this need, a U.S. government agency called the Advanced Research Projects Agency (ARPA) developed the ARPANET, which initially used the Network Control Protocol (NCP) to handle file transfers, remote logon, and email needs. NCP, the predecessor to TCP/IP, was first used in 1972. By 1973, the protocol no longer met the needs of its users, and research was done to find a better solution. TCP/IPv4 was introduced and standardized in 1981 and is still in use today. Microsoft and other industry leaders have been working for years to roll out a newer version: IPv6.

TAKE NOTE* IPv6 is not backward compatible with IPv4. An IPv6-only device cannot talk to an IPv4 device. Your current transition strategy should be to use both in the short term.

Many enterprise administrators are so comfortable working with IPv4 addresses that they are hesitant to change. The goal of IPv6 is to address the exhaustion of the IPv4 address space, which supports about 4 billion addresses. At the time IPv4 was created, no one considered that anything other than computers would be connected. As more computers, smartphones, tablets, and home appliances are being attached to the Internet, the IPv4 address space is quickly being exhausted.

Over the years, engineers have found ways to reduce the number of addresses needed through a process called Network Address Translation (NAT). Instead of assigning an IPv4 public address to every device on your network, you can purchase a single IPv4 address and allow all devices behind your router to share the same address. Still, as each year passes and the number of devices connected to the Internet continues to grow exponentially, IPv6 will eventually take over as the main addressing scheme. In the meantime, let's take a closer look at each of the protocols.

An IPv4 address is a 32-bit-long number assigned to a host on the network. These addresses are broken into four different sections called octets, which are 8 bits long. For example, the number 192.160.10.2 in binary is 11000000.10100000.00001010.00000010 (see Figure 1-1).

Figure 1-1
Converting binary to decimal

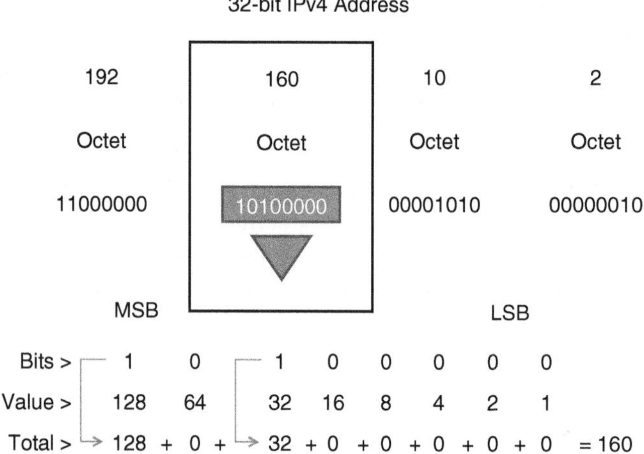

A portion of the 32 bits is associated with the network on which the computer is physically located. This portion of bits is called the ***network ID***. The remaining bits, allocated to the host, are called the ***host ID***. All computers on the same local network/subnet share the same network ID, but each computer within the local network/subnet has its own unique host ID.

A subnet mask, also 32 bits long, is used to determine which of the 32 bits represent the network ID and which represent the host ID (see Table 1-1). The class of IP address you are using determines the default subnet mask. IPv4 addresses are divided into classes based on the number in the first octet of the IP address. These classes were originally designed to support different organizational sizes. However, classful IP addressing is very wasteful and has mostly been discarded.

There are five classes of IP addresses (see Table 1-1).

Table 1-1
TCP/IPv4 Address Classes

Class	Range	Network ID (Octet)	Host ID (Octet)	Number of Networks	Number of Hosts
A	1–127*	First octet	Second, third, and fourth octets	126	16,777,214
B	128–191	First and second octets	Third and fourth octets	16,384	65,534
C	192–223	First, second, and third octets	Fourth octet	2,097,152	254
D	224–239	N/A	N/A	N/A	N/A
E	240–254	N/A	N/A	MA	N/A

*0, 127, and 255 are reserved and cannot be used for a specific host. An IP address with all 0s in the host ID describes the network, whereas 127 in the first octet is reserved for loopback testing and handling traffic to the local host. An IP address using 255s in the host ID is a broadcast transmitting to all interfaces on the specified network.

Table 1-2 shows the default subnet masks for each class along with its binary and decimal values.

Table 1-2

Default Subnet Masks for IPv4 Address Classes

Class	Binary	Decimal
A	11111111.00000000.00000000.00000000	255.0.0.0
B	11111111.11111111.00000000.00000000	255.255.0.0
C	11111111.11111111.11111111.00000000	255.255.255.0

If a host is on the same local network (has the same network ID), it can issue broadcast packets to locate other computers. To communicate with computers on a separate network, the packets have to traverse a router. To determine when a computer is on another network, your computer uses the subnet mask and a process called logical ANDing.

Because ANDing is performed using binary, you have to convert the IP address and the subnet mask to binary form. After you complete the conversions, you match up binary 1s (between the IP address and the subnet mask). If there is a 1 in the binary address of the IP and a 1 in the binary address of the subnet mask, set the binary number in the ANDing row to binary 1. After you complete the process, add up the values, as demonstrated in Figure 1-2. When you are using it for a default subnet mask, it really isn't necessary, but when your network is subnetted, the network ID is a little harder to decipher.

Figure 1-2

Using ANDing to determine network location

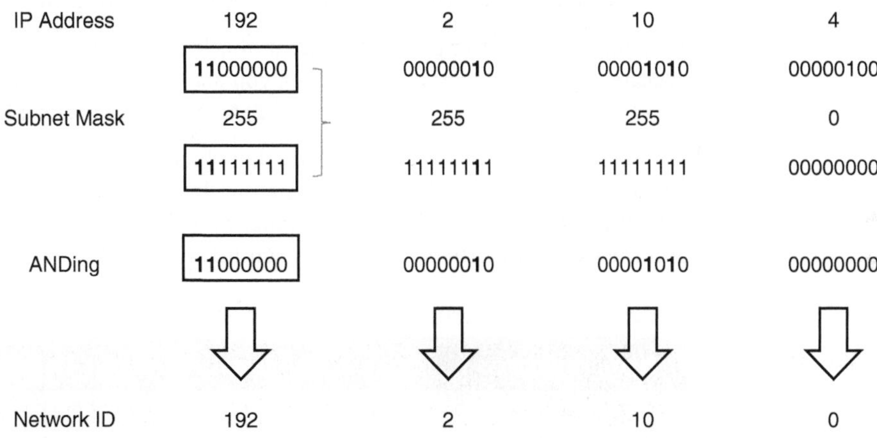

If the computer is determined to be on another network after the ANDing process is completed, the packet is sent to the default gateway configured on the computer (for example, the router's IP address). The router then uses information in its routing tables to locate and transfer your packet to the destination computer.

Configuring IPv4 Subnetting

Subnetting is the process used to break a larger network into smaller segments. For example, a Class B IP address has more than 65,000 host addresses for a single, logical segment. Adding that many computers to a single network isn't feasible. If you break the larger network into smaller segments (for example, 254 subnetworks), each can host up to 254 hosts. You accomplish subnetting by stealing bits from the host portion of an address to create a new subnet section.

CERTIFICATION READY
Configure IPv4 subnetting
Objective 5.1

For example, you can take the 172.16.0.0/16 private IP address range and use the entire third octet as a subnet ID. This enables you to create up to 256 subnets with as many as 256 hosts on each one. The subnet masks for all the addresses on the subnets will be 255.255.255.0, and the network addresses will proceed as follows:

- 172.16.0.0/24
- 172.16.1.0/24
- 172.16.2.0/24
- 172.16.3.0/24
- . . .
- 172.16.255.0/24

Of course, when you are working on an existing network, the subnetting process will likely be more difficult. You might, for example, be given a relatively small range of addresses and be asked to create a certain number of subnets out of them. To do this, use the following procedure:

1. Determine how many subnet identifier bits you need to create the required number of subnets.
2. Subtract the subnet bits you need from the host bits and add them to the network bits.
3. Calculate the subnet mask by adding the network and subnet bits in binary form and converting the binary value to decimal.
4. Take the least significant subnet bit and the host bits, in binary form, and convert them to a decimal value.
5. Increment the network identifier (including the subnet bits) by the decimal value you calculated to determine the network addresses of your new subnets.

By using the same example from earlier in this lesson, if you take the 172.16.43.0/24 address and allocate two extra bits for the subnet ID, you end up with a binary subnet mask value of 11111111.11111111.11111111.11000000 (255.255.255.192 in decimal form, as noted earlier).

The least significant subnet bit plus the host bits gives you a binary value of 1000000, which converts to a decimal value of 64. Therefore, if we know that the network address of your first subnet is 192.168.43.0, the second subnet must be 192.168.43.64, the third 192.168.43.128, and the fourth 192.168.43.192, as shown in Table 1-3.

Table 1-3

Sample CIDR 172.16.43.0/26 Networks

Network Address	Starting IP Address	Ending IP Address	Subnet Mask
172.16.43.0	172.16.43.1	172.16.43.62	255.255.255.192
172.16.43.64	172.16.43.65	172.16.43.126	255.255.255.192
172.16.43.128	172.16.43.129	172.16.43.190	255.255.255.192
172.16.43.192	172.16.43.193	172.16.43.254	255.255.255.192

The larger subnet can be divided into $2^{masked\_bits} = 2^2 = 4$ smaller subnets. For each of the smaller subnets, each subnet can hold $2^{unmasked\_bits} - 2 = 2^6 - 2 = 62$ hosts.

Understanding Classless Interdomain Routing (CIDR)

In practical use, the IP address classes proved to be wasteful, and when the Internet first experienced a massive period of growth in the 1990s, it was feared that there might at some time be a shortage of addresses. To avoid assigning entire addresses of a particular class to networks that didn't have that many hosts, the IETF eventually published a new standard for assigning IP addresses called ***classless interdomain routing (CIDR)***.

CIDR differs from traditional addressing (now called *classful addressing*) by allowing the division between the network identifier and the host identifier to fall anywhere in an IPv4 address; it does not have to fall on one of the 8-bit boundaries. For example, a subnet mask of 255.255.240.0 translates into a binary value of 11111111 11111111 11110000 00000000, meaning that the network identifier is 20 bits long and the host identifier is 12 bits long. This falls between a Class B and a Class C address, and enables ISPs to assign clients only the number of addresses they need, which conserves the IP address space.

CIDR also introduced a new syntax for IP network address references. In classful notation, an address like 172.23.0.0 was assumed to be a Class B address and used the standard 255.255.0.0 Class B subnet mask. In CIDR notation, the network address is followed by a slash and the number of bits in the network identifier. Therefore, 172.23.0.0/16 would be the CIDR equivalent of a Class B address. An address that used the 255.255.240.0 subnet mask described earlier would, therefore, look something like 172.23.0.0/20.

Implementing NAT

Although CIDR helped use the IPv4 addresses more efficiently, additional steps had to prevent the exhaustion of IPv4 addresses. ***Network Address Translation (NAT)*** is used with masquerading to hide an entire address space behind a single IP address. In other words, it allows multiple computers on a network to connect to the Internet through a single IP address.

NAT enables a local area network (LAN) to use one set of IP addresses for internal traffic and a second set of addresses for external traffic. The NAT computer or device is usually a router (including routers made for home and small-office Internet connections) or a proxy server. As a result, you can:

- Provide a type of firewall by hiding internal IP addresses.
- Enable multiple internal computers to share a single external public IP address.

The private addresses are reserved addresses not allocated to any specific organization. Because these private addresses cannot be assigned to global addresses used on the Internet and are not routable on the Internet, you must use a NAT gateway or proxy server to convert between private and public addresses. The private network addresses are expressed in RFC 1918:

- 10.0.0.0–10.255.255.255
- 172.16.0.0–172.31.255.255
- 192.168.0.0–192.168.255.255

NAT obscures an internal network's structure by making all traffic appear to originate from the NAT device or proxy server. To accomplish this, the NAT device or proxy server uses stateful translation tables to map the "hidden" addresses into a single address and then rewrites the outgoing Internet Protocol (IP) packets on exit so that they appear to originate from the router. As data packets are returned from the Internet, the responding data packets are mapped back to the originating IP address using the entries stored in the translation tables.

When NAT is used to connect a private network to a public network, the following process occurs:

1. The client on the internal private network creates an IP packet, which is forwarded to the computer or device running NAT.
2. The computer or device running NAT changes the outgoing packet header to indicate the packet originated from the NAT computer or device's external address. It then sends the remapped packet over the public network such as the Internet to its intended destination. During this process, it stores the source address and the remapped NAT information in a table so it can keep track of all source computers.

3. When the destination computer responds with packets, the destination computer sends packets back to the computer or device running NAT.
4. When the computer or device receives the packets back from the destination computer, the computer or device running NAT changes the packet header to the private address of the destination client. It then sends the packet to the client computer.

Enabling NAT is a simple process, which can be selected using the Routing and Remote Access Server Setup Wizard. To support NAT, you must have a server that has two network interfaces, one for the private network and one for the public network.

TAKE NOTE* If you have an IPsec VPN server behind a NAT device, you need to configure the Windows clients to use Network Address Translation-Traversal (NAT-T). For more information, visit the Microsoft Support website.

Understanding IPv6 and IPv6 Addressing

As mentioned earlier, available public IPv4 addresses are running low. To overcome this problem as well as a few others, IPv6 was developed as the next-generation Internet Protocol version.

CERTIFICATION READY
Determine and configure appropriate IPv6 addresses
Objective 5.1

IPv6 provides a number of benefits for TCP/IP-based networking connectivity, including:

- A 128-bit address space to provide addressing for every device on the Internet with a globally unique address
- More efficient routing than IPv4
- Support for automatic configuration
- Enhanced security to protect against address and port scanning attacks and utilization of IPsec to protect IPv6 traffic

Because IPv6 uses 128 bits, the addresses are usually divided into groups of 16 bits, written as 4 hex digits. Hex digits include 0, 1, 2, 3, 4, 5, 6, 7, 8, 9, A, B, C, D, E, and F. The groups are separated by colons. Here is an example of an address:

FE80:0000:0000:0000:02C3:B2DF:FEA5:E4F1

Similar to the IPv4 addresses, IPv6 is divided into network bits and host address. However, the first 64 bits define the network address and the second 64 bits define the host address. Therefore, for the sample address, FE80:0000:0000:0000 defines the network bits and 02C3:B2DF:FEA5:E4F1 defines the host bits. The network bits are also further divided where a block of 48 bits is used as the network prefix and the next 16 bits are used for subnetting.

To facilitate simplified automatic addressing, the IPv6 subnet size has been standardized and fixed to 64 bits, and the MAC address is used to generate the host bits within the unicast network address or link-local address when stateless autoconfiguration is used.

If a block is set to 0 and is followed by another block set to 0, it can be written as ::. Using this notation, FE80:0:AC4A:AA04:E713A:0:0:CE2B, the preceding address, would be written as FE80:0:AC4A:AA04:E713A::CE2B.

TAKE NOTE* When a network card is configured in Windows 10, it automatically has both an IPv4 and IPv6 address by default. This is called a dual stack.

IPv6 supports three address types:

- ***Unicast*** provides one-to-one transmission service to individual interfaces, including server farms sharing a single address. IPv6 supports several types of unicast addresses, including global, link-local, and unique local, terms that identify the scope of the address. Each type of unicast has a different format prefix (FP), a sequence of bits that identifies the type, just as an IPv4 address uses a sequence of bits to identify its class.
- ***Multicast*** provides one-to-many transmission service to groups of interfaces identified by a single multicast address.
- ***Anycast*** provides one-to-one-of-many transmission service to groups of interfaces, only the nearest of which (measured by the number of intermediate routers) receives the transmission. You typically use this for locating services or the nearest router.

With IPv6, you still have unicast and multicast addressing. However, unicast addressing can be divided into:

- ***Global unicast addresses***: Public addresses that are globally routable and reachable on the IPv6 portion of the Internet. They are equivalent to a registered IPv4 address and unique on the Internet.
- ***Link-local addresses***: Private nonroutable addresses confined to a single subnet. They are used by hosts when communicating with neighboring hosts on the same link, but can also be used to create temporary networks for conferences or meetings, or to set up a permanent, small LAN. Routers process packets destined for a link-local address, but they will not forward them to other links.
- ***Unique local addresses***: Meant for private addressing, with the addition of being unique, so that joining two subnets does not cause address collisions.

The structure of a global unicast address has the following parts:

- **Fixed portion set to 001**: The first three bits are set to 001. The address prefix for currently assigned global addresses is 2000::/3. Therefore, all global unicast addresses begin with either 2 or 3.
- **Global routing prefix**: This field identifies the global routing prefix for a specific organization's site, which consists of the first 3 bits and the 45-bit global routing prefix to create a 48-bit site prefix, which is assigned to an organization's individual site.
- **Subnet ID**: The subnet ID is used within an organization's site to identify subnets. The field size is 16 bits, which allows up to 65,536 subnets.
- **Interface ID**: The interface ID identifies the interface on a specific subnet within the site. This field's size is 64 bits. This is either generated randomly or assigned by DHCPv6.

In IPv6, systems that assign themselves an address automatically create a ***link-local unicast address***, which is essentially the equivalent of an APIPA address in IPv4. All link-local addresses have the same network identifier: a 10-bit FP of 1111 1110 10 followed by 54 zeros, resulting in the following network address:

```
fe80:0000:0000:0000/64
```

In its more compact form, the link-local network address is as follows:

```
fe80::/64
```

Because all link-local addresses are on the same network, they are not routable, and systems possessing them can communicate only with other systems on the same link.

TAKE NOTE*

In IPv6, the term *link* refers to the local network segment, which in IPv4 is called the *broadcast domain*. However, because IPv6 has no broadcasts, that latter term does not apply.

Unique local unicast addresses are the IPv6 equivalent of the 10.0.0.0/8, 172.16.0.0/12, and 192.168.0.0/16 private network addresses in IPv4. Like the IPv4 private addresses, unique local addresses are routable within an organization. You can also subnet them as needed to support an organization of any size.

The format of a unique local unicast address is as follows:

- **Global ID**: A 48-bit field beginning with an 8-bit FP of 11111101 in binary, or fd00::/8 in hexadecimal. The remaining 40 bits of the global ID are randomly generated.
- **Subnet ID**: A 16-bit field that organizations can use to create an internal hierarchy of sites or subnets.
- **Interface ID**: A 64-bit field identifying a specific interface on the network.

Because unique local addresses are not routable outside the organization, the global ID does not have to be unique in most cases. In fact, because part of the global ID value is randomly generated, two organizations might possibly end up using the same value. However, the IPv6 standards make every attempt short of creating a central registrar to keep these identifiers unique. This is so that addressing conflicts will not likely occur when organizations merge, when virtual private network (VPN) address spaces overlap, or when mobile computers connect to different enterprise networks.

TAKE NOTE*

Many sources of IPv6 information continue to list ***site-local unicast addresses*** as a valid type of unicast, with a function similar to that of the private IPv4 network addresses. Site-local addresses have an FP of 11111110 11 in binary, or fec0::/10 in hexadecimal. For various reasons, site-local unicast addresses have been deprecated, and although their use is not forbidden, their functionality has been replaced by unique local unicast addresses.

Although you can assign IPv6 addresses manually, IPv6 is usually configured automatically via autoconfiguration. For IPv6, there are three types of autoconfiguration:

- ***Stateless autoconfiguration***: Configuration is based on Router Advertisement messages, which include the stateless address prefixes. When you are using stateless autoconfiguration, you are using ***native IPv6 connectivity***.
- ***Stateful autoconfiguration***: Configuration is based on a stateful address configuration protocol, such as DHCPv6, to obtain addresses and other configuration options. A host will also use a stateful address configuration protocol when no routers are present on the local link.
- ***Both autoconfiguration***: Although configuration is based on Router Advertisement messages to provide stateless address prefixes, it also requests hosts to use a stateful address configuration protocol.

Using the Default Gateway

A ***default gateway*** is a device, usually a router, which connects the local network to other networks. When you need to communicate with a host on another subnet, you forward all packets to the default gateway.

The default gateway allows a host to communicate with remote hosts. Every time a host needs to send packets, it first determines if the host is local (same subnet) or if it is remote (where it has to go through a router to get to the remote host). The router then determines the best way to get to the remote subnet, and it forwards the packets to the remote subnet.

To determine if the destination address is local or remote, the router looks at the network bits of both the sending and destination hosts. If the network bits are the same, it assumes the destination host is local and sends the packets directly to the local host. If the network bits are different, it assumes the destination host is remote and sends the packets to the default gateway.

For example, you have the following:

Sending host address: 10.10.57.3
Sending host subnet mask: 255.255.255.0
Destination host address: 10.10.89.37

By isolating the network address for the sending host, you have 10.10.57.0. By isolating the network address for the destination host address, you have 10.10.89.0. Because they are different, the packet is sent to the default gateway, and the router determines the best way to get to its final destination.

Of course, if the subnet mask is wrong, the host might misidentify a host as being local or remote. If the default gateway is wrong, packets might not be able to leave the local subnet.

Understanding Name Resolution

Name resolution is the process of converting friendly names to IP addresses. The primary name resolution system is DNS.

Domain Name System (DNS) is a naming service used by the TCP/IP network, is an essential service used by the Internet, and can be integrated with other services, such as WINS, DHCP, and Active Directory. DNS servers are used to associate a computer name such as Server01.Support.contoso.com to an IP address.

Every time a user accesses a web page, the user must type a URL. Before the client communicates with the web server, the client computer needs to use DNS to retrieve the IP address of the web server, similar to someone using a phone book to find a phone number. When an enterprise client needs to communicate with a corporate server, the enterprise client also uses DNS to find the IP address of the corporate server. The DNS servers are often referred to as name servers.

DNS uses ***fully qualified domain names (FQDNs)*** to map a host name to an IP address. An FQDN describes the exact relationship between a host and its DNS domain. For example, computer1.sales.microsoft.com represents an FQDN; the computer1 host is located in the sales domain, which is located in the Microsoft second-level domain, which is located in the .com top-level domain.

DNS is a hierarchical distributed naming system used to locate computers and services on a TCP/IP network. DNS clients send queries to a DNS server and the Domain Name System receives and resolves queries such as translating a host or domain name to an IP address. Because it is so closely tied to the Internet and TCP/IP network, it is an essential service that enables the Internet and network to function and it is required by many network services, including Active Directory.

Configuring IPv4 and IPv6 Settings and Options

CERTIFICATION READY
Configure IPv4 addresses and options
Objective 5.1

Network settings can be configured either manually or automatically using DHCP. Using manual settings can introduce configuration issues that can affect communications. Using a centralized approach to IP address management requires you to have a solid understanding of DHCP.

CERTIFICATION READY
Determine and configure appropriate IPv6 addresses
Objective 5.1

Configuring TCP/IP on a Windows Server 2016 computer can be done manually or automatically. Setting up TCP/IP manually involves configuring it to use a static IP address. This involves entering an IP address, a subnet mask, and (if you need to access computers outside of the local network segment) a default gateway address. To resolve friendly names to IP addresses, you also need to configure at least one IP address for a DNS on your network.

DEFINE A STATIC IPv4 ADDRESS

GET READY. To define a static IP IPv4 address, perform the following steps.

1. On LON-SRV1, on the taskbar, right-click the **network status** icon and choose **Open Network and Sharing center.**
2. Click **Change adapter settings.**
3. Right-click a network adapter, such as **Ethernet**, and choose **Properties.**
4. In the Ethernet Properties dialog box, as shown in Figure 1-3, click **Internet Protocol Version 4 (TCP/IPv4)** and then click **Properties.**

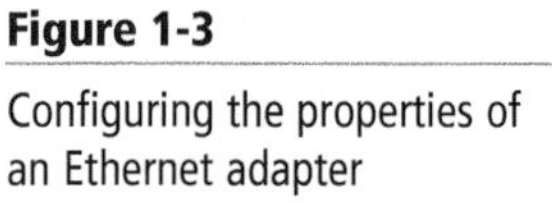

Figure 1-3
Configuring the properties of an Ethernet adapter

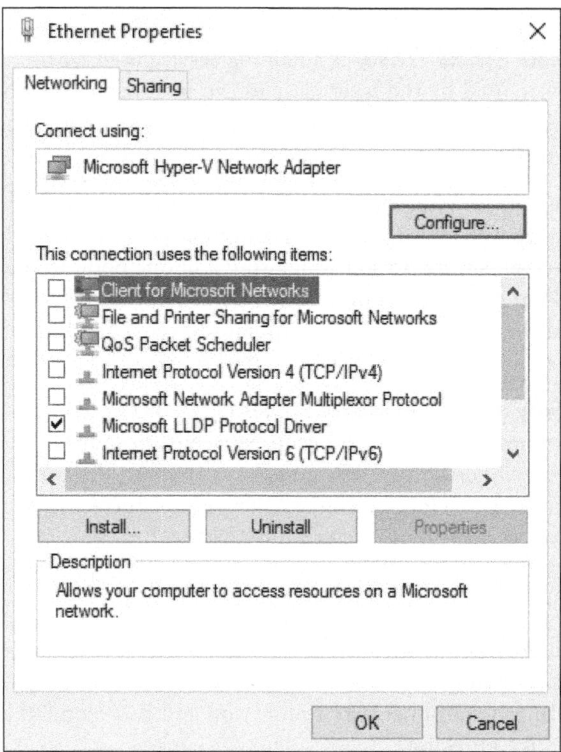

5. Select **Use the following IP address** and then type the IPv4 address, subnet mask, and default gateway you want to use, as shown in Figure 1-4.
6. Select **Use the following DNS server addresses** and then type an IP address for a preferred DNS server and an alternate DNS server.
7. Click **OK** to accept your settings and to close the Internet Protocol Version 4 (TCP/IPv4) Properties dialog box.
8. Click **Close** to close the Ethernet Properties dialog box.

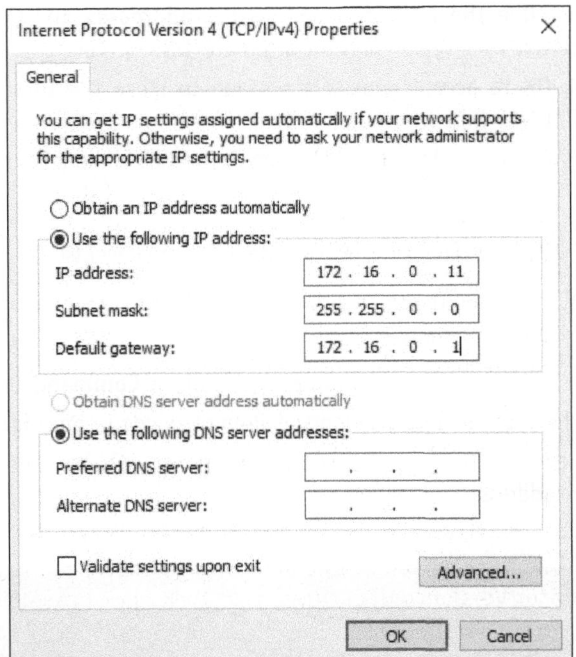

Figure 1-4

Entering a static IPv4 address

DEFINE A STATIC IPv6 ADDRESS

GET READY. To define a static IP IPv6 address, perform the following steps.

1. On the taskbar, right-click the **network status** icon and choose **Open Network and Sharing center.**
2. Click **Change adapter settings.**
3. Right-click a network adapter, such as **Ethernet**, and choose **Properties.**
4. In the Ethernet Properties dialog box, click **Internet Protocol Version 6 (TCP/IPv6)** and then click **Properties.**
5. Select **Use the following IP address** (as shown in Figure 1-5) and then type the IPv6 address, subnet prefix length, and default gateway you want to use.

Figure 1-5

Entering a static IPv6 address

6. Select **Use the following DNS server addresses** and then type an IP address for a preferred DNS server and an alternate DNS server.
7. Click **OK** to accept your settings and to close the Internet Protocol Version 6 (TCP/IPv6) Properties dialog box.
8. Click **Close** to close the Ethernet Properties dialog box.

USE CMD AND WINDOWS POWERSHELL TO VIEW IP ADDRESS INFORMATION

GET READY. To use cmd and Windows PowerShell to view your IP address configuration, perform the following steps.

1. On LON-SRV1, right-click **Start** and choose **Command Prompt (Admin)**.
2. In the Administrator: Command Prompt window, type **ipconfig** and then press **Enter**.
3. Review your settings (as shown in Figure 1-6). You should see both an IPv4 and IPv6 address.

Figure 1-6

Reviewing the IP configuration

```
Administrator: Command Prompt

C:\>ipconfig

Windows IP Configuration


Ethernet adapter vEthernet (HNS Internal NIC):

   Connection-specific DNS Suffix  . :
   Link-local IPv6 Address . . . . . : fe80::cc2f:6cf6:4228:3beb%4
   IPv4 Address. . . . . . . . . . . : 172.18.240.1
   Subnet Mask . . . . . . . . . . . : 255.255.240.0
   Default Gateway . . . . . . . . . :

Ethernet adapter vEthernet (Microsoft Hyper-V Network Adapter - Virtual Switch):

   Connection-specific DNS Suffix  . : hsd1.ca.comcast.net.
   Link-local IPv6 Address . . . . . : fe80::e4df:81cd:7ec1:f429%6
   IPv4 Address. . . . . . . . . . . : 192.168.3.148
   Subnet Mask . . . . . . . . . . . : 255.255.255.0
   Default Gateway . . . . . . . . . : 192.168.3.1

Tunnel adapter isatap.{2833E2BE-2D84-4B9A-8293-5179DBC0294F}:

   Media State . . . . . . . . . . . : Media disconnected
   Connection-specific DNS Suffix  . :

Tunnel adapter isatap.hsd1.ca.comcast.net.:

   Media State . . . . . . . . . . . : Media disconnected
   Connection-specific DNS Suffix  . : hsd1.ca.comcast.net.

C:\>
```

4. Type **exit** and then press **Enter** to close the cmd shell.
5. Click **Start** and then type **PowerShell**.
6. Type `Resolve-DNSName` *`<website address>`* (for example, `Resolve-DNSName www.microsoft.com`) and then press **Enter**.
7. Review the address records returned.
8. Does the site support IPv6?
9. Type `Resolve-DNSName www.msn.com` and then press **Enter**.
10. Review the address records returned.

    Does the site support IPv6?

If you select the Validate settings upon exit option after configuring IP settings, Windows Server 2016 performs a network diagnostics test to check your settings for any problems and offers to help fix them. If you click the Advanced button, you could make additional configurations to your TCP/IP configuration. For example, in Windows Server 2016, you can configure multiple gateways. When you do this, a metric is used to determine which gateway to use. Multiple gateways are used to provide fault tolerance so if one router goes down, the computer defaults to the other gateway. You can configure additional gateways and DNS settings in the Advanced TCP/IP Settings dialog box (see Figure 1-7):

Figure 1-7

Reviewing advanced TCP/IP setting options

- **DNS server addresses, in order of use**: You can specify multiple DNS servers to use for name resolution. The order listed determines the sequence in which your client attempts to resolve host names. If the first server does not respond to a name resolution request, the client contacts the next one in the list.
- **Append primary and connection-specific DNS suffixes**: This is selected by default. If you attempt to access a computer named FileServer1, and the parent name is contoso.com, the name resolves to FileServer1.contoso.com. If the FQDN does not exist in the domain, the query fails. The parent name used (contoso.com) is configured on the System Properties/Computer Name tab.
- **Append parent suffixes of the primary DNS suffix**: This is selected by default. It works as follows: If the computer FS2 is in the eastcoast.contoso.com domain, DNS attempts to resolve the name to FS2.eastcoast.contoso.com. If this doesn't work, it tries FS2.contoso.com.
- **Append these DNS suffixes (in order)**: Use this option when you want to specify DNS suffixes to use other than resolving names through your parent domain.
- **DNS suffix for this connection**: This setting overrides DNS names that are already configured for this connection. This is typically configured through the System Properties/Computer Name tab by clicking the More button.
- **Register this connection's addresses in DNS**: This option, selected by default, automatically enters the FQDN in DNS records.
- **Use this connection's DNS suffix in DNS registration**: If this option is selected, all IP addresses for this connection are registered in DNS at the parent domain.

When you assign static IP addresses (IPv4 or IPv6) to your clients, you run the risk of duplicating IP addresses on your network or misconfiguring the settings, which can result in communication problems. A better approach is to dynamically assign your TCP/IP configurations from a central pool of IP addresses. This is done by using the ***Dynamic Host Configuration Protocol (DHCP)*** server. The DHCP server can also be configured to provide the default gateway, primary, and secondary DNS information; WINS server; and DNS domain name.

Automatic Private IP Addressing (APIPA) is the name assigned by Microsoft to a DHCP failover mechanism used by all current Microsoft Windows operating systems. On Windows computers, the DHCP client is enabled by default. If, after several attempts, a system fails to locate a DHCP server on the network, APIPA takes over and automatically assigns an address on the 169.254.0.0/16 network to the computer. The system then uses the Address Resolution Protocol (ARP) to ensure that no other computer on the local network is using the same address.

For a small network that consists of only a single LAN, APIPA is a simple and effective alternative to installing a DHCP server. However, for installations consisting of multiple LANs, with routers connecting them, you must take more positive control over the IP address assignment process. This usually means deploying one or more DHCP servers in some form.

Implementing IPv6 Stateless Addressing

To enable native IPv6 functionality, you need to configure the router to support native IPv6 connectivity. To advertise the default route, use the Windows PowerShell `Set-NetIPInterface` cmdlet with the `-advertiseDefaultRoute` enabled option.

CERTIFICATION READY
Implement IPv6 stateless addressing
Objective 5.1

When a Windows computer starts, it initiates the stateless address autoconfiguration process, during which it assigns each interface a link-local unicast address. This assignment always occurs, even when the interface is to receive a global unicast address later. The link-local address enables the system to communicate with the router on the link, which provides additional instructions.

The steps of the stateless address autoconfiguration process are as follows:

1. **Link-local address creation**: The IPv6 implementation on the system creates a link-local address for each interface by using the fe80::/64 network address and generating an interface ID, either using the interface's MAC address or a pseudorandom generator.
2. **Duplicate address detection**: Using the IPv6 Neighbor Discovery (ND) protocol, the system transmits a Neighbor Solicitation message to determine if any other computer on the link is using the same address and listens for a Neighbor Advertisement message sent in reply. If there is no reply, the system considers the address to be unique on the link. If there is a reply, the system must generate a new address and repeat the procedure.
3. **Link-local address assignment**: When the system determines that the link-local address is unique, it configures the interface to use that address. On a small network consisting of a single segment or link, this may be the interface's permanent address assignment. On a network with multiple subnets, the primary function of the link-local address assignment is to enable the system to communicate with a router on the link.
4. **Router advertisement solicitation**: The system uses the ND protocol to transmit Router Solicitation messages to the *all routers* multicast address. These messages compel routers to transmit the Router Advertisement messages more frequently.
5. **Router advertisement**: The router on the link uses the ND protocol to transmit Router Advertisement messages to the system, which contain information on how the autoconfiguration process should proceed. The Router Advertisement messages typically supply a network prefix, which the system will use with its existing interface ID to create a global or unique local unicast address. The messages might also instruct the system to initiate a

stateful autoconfiguration process by contacting a specific DHCPv6 server. If there is no router on the link, as determined by the system's failure to receive Router Advertisement messages, the system must attempt to initiate a stateful autoconfiguration process.

6. **Global or unique local address configuration**: Using the information it receives from the router, the system generates a suitable address—one that is routable, either globally or within the enterprise—and configures the interface to use it. If so instructed, the system might also initiate a stateful autoconfiguration process by contacting the DHCPv6 server specified by the router and obtaining a global or unique local address from that server, along with other configuration settings.

IPv6 is automatically installed and enabled on a Windows-based host. However, to use native IPv6, an IPv6 router on the local subnet must begin advertising.

CONFIGURE NATIVE IPv6 CONNECTIVITY

GET READY. To configure native IPv6 connectivity, perform the following steps.

1. Log on to EU-RTR as **adatum\administrator** with the password of **Pa$$w0rd.**
2. On EU-RTR, on the taskbar, click the **Windows PowerShell** icon.
3. In the Windows PowerShell window, execute the following Windows PowerShell command:

```
Set-NetIPInterface -AddressFamily ipv6

-InterfaceAlias "London_Network" -Advertising enabled
-AdvertiseDefaultRoute enabled
```

4. In the Windows PowerShell window, execute the following Windows PowerShell command:

```
Set-NetIPInterface -AddressFamily ipv6

-InterfaceAlias "NA_WAN" -Advertising enabled

-AdvertiseDefaultRoute enabled
```

5. In the Windows PowerShell window, execute the following Windows PowerShell command:

```
New-NetRoute -InterfaceAlias "London_Network"

-DestinationPrefix 2001:db8::/64 -Publish Yes
```

6. In the Windows PowerShell window, execute the following Windows PowerShell command:

```
New-NetRoute -InterfaceAlias "NA_WAN"

-DestinationPrefix 2001:db8:0:2::/64 -Publish Yes
```

7. In the Windows PowerShell window, execute the following Windows PowerShell command:

```
Get-NetIPAddress
```

8. In the Windows PowerShell window, record the link-local IPv6 address of the London_Network adapter.
9. In the Windows PowerShell window, execute the following Windows PowerShell command:

```
New-NetRoute -InterfaceAlias "London_Network"

-DestinationPrefix ::/0 -NextHop <link-local_address_of_EU-RTR
"London_Network"> interface -Publish yes
```

where the *<link-local_address_of_EU-RTR>* is the address that you recorded in Step 8.

10. In the Windows PowerShell window, execute the following Windows PowerShell command:

    Get-NetIPAddress

    Notice the new IPv6 address starting with 2001:db8:: assigned to the London_Network interface and the address starting with 2001:db8:0:2 assigned to the NA_Network interface.
11. Log on to LON-SVR1 as **adatum\administrator** with the password of **Pa$$w0rd.**
12. On LON_SVR1, on the taskbar, click the **Windows PowerShell** icon.
13. In the Windows PowerShell window, execute the following Windows PowerShell command:

    Get-NetIPAddress

    Notice the new IPv6 address starting with 2001:db8:: and the default gateway of EU-RTR link-local address.
14. Log on to LON-DC1 as **adatum\administrator** with the password of **Pa$$w0rd.**
15. Click **Start** and click **Server Manager.**
16. In Server Manager, open the **Tools** menu and click **DNS.**
17. In the DNS console, expand **DNS\LON-DC1\Forward Lookup Zones\Adatum.com,** and refresh the information in the DNS console to verify that there are new AAAA records registered.
18. Log on to TOR-SVR1 as **adatum\administrator** with the password of **Pa$$w0rd.**
19. On TOR-SVR1, on the taskbar, click the **Windows PowerShell** icon.
20. In the Windows PowerShell window, execute the following Windows PowerShell command:

    ipconfig /flushdns
21. To show connectivity, in the Windows PowerShell window, execute the following Windows PowerShell command:

    Test-NetConnection LON-DC1

■ Using IPv4/IPv6 Transition Technologies

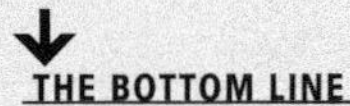

The transition from IPv4 to IPv6 is expected to take several more years. In the meantime, expect to see a mix of IPv4, IPv4/IPv6 (dual stack), and IPv6-only networks. To help with the transition from IPv4 to IPv6, several methods were developed, including 6to4, Teredo, and Intra-Site Automatic Tunnel Addressing Protocol (IPv6).

CERTIFICATION READY
Configure interoperability between IPv4 and IPv6 by using ISATAP, 6to4, and Teredo scenarios
Objective 5.1

The IPv4 to IPv6 transition technologies that Windows supports are:

- 6to4
- ISATAP
- Teredo

Figure 1-8 shows the tail end of the IPConfig/all command, which shows a Windows system using IPv4/IPv6 transition technology.

Figure 1-8

Displaying the IPv6 transition technology addresses using the IPConfig /all command

```
Select Administrator: Command Prompt

Tunnel adapter Teredo Tunneling Pseudo-Interface:

   Connection-specific DNS Suffix  . :
   Description . . . . . . . . . . . : Teredo Tunneling Pseudo-Interface
   Physical Address. . . . . . . . . : 00-00-00-00-00-00-00-E0
   DHCP Enabled. . . . . . . . . . . : No
   Autoconfiguration Enabled . . . . : Yes
   IPv6 Address. . . . . . . . . . . : 2001:0:9d38:6abd:4e2:257:3f57:fc36(Preferred)
   Link-local IPv6 Address . . . . . : fe80::4e2:257:3f57:fc36%5(Preferred)
   Default Gateway . . . . . . . . . : ::
   DHCPv6 IAID . . . . . . . . . . . : 134217728
   DHCPv6 Client DUID. . . . . . . . : 00-01-00-01-1F-FC-CA-11-00-15-5D-03-C8-1E
   NetBIOS over Tcpip. . . . . . . . : Disabled

Tunnel adapter isatap.{F294E95C-257E-47FC-B661-22804BEC12D5}:

   Media State . . . . . . . . . . . : Media disconnected
   Connection-specific DNS Suffix  . :
   Description . . . . . . . . . . . : Microsoft ISATAP Adapter #2
   Physical Address. . . . . . . . . : 00-00-00-00-00-00-00-E0
   DHCP Enabled. . . . . . . . . . . : No
   Autoconfiguration Enabled . . . . : Yes

C:\Windows\system32>_

BPA results    BPA results    BPA results
```

Configuring 6to4

The ***6to4*** transition mechanism allows IPv6 packets to be transmitted over an IPv4 network, such as the current Internet. Instead of configuring an explicit tunnel, you define the IPv4 addresses in IPv6 format and then encapsulate IPv6 traffic into IPv4 packets. Because IPv4 is the underlying technology, you must have a global IPv4 address connected. The sending host and receiving host run both IPv4 and IPv6. The sending host is responsible for encapsulating outgoing IPv6 packets and the receiving host is responsible for encapsulating incoming 6to4 packets. A router could be configured as the sending or receiving host, which would then forward packets to other clients.

The 6to4 address is formed by combining the prefix 2002::/16 with the 32 bits of a public IPv4 address of the node, forming a 48-bit prefix. Therefore, if you have an IPv4 address (written in decimal format) of 157.54.176.7, when you convert the values to hexadecimal:

157 = 9d

54 = 36

176 = b0

7 = 07

You get:

`9d36:b007`

The last 16 bits of the 64-bit prefix define the subnet and interface behind the same 6to4 router. Because the 6to4 IPv6 address will begin with 2002, the entire 64-bit prefix is:

`2002:9d36:b007:`*`subnetID`*`:`*`interfaceID`*

Because most IPv6 networks use autoconfiguration, the IPv6 host will have a unique 64-bit portion.

CONFIGURE THE 6TO4 TRANSITION MECHANISM

GET READY. To configure the 6to4 transition mechanism, perform the following steps.

1. Log on to EU-RTR as **adatum\administrator** with the password of **Pa$$w0rd.**
2. On EU-RTR, on the taskbar, click the **Windows PowerShell** icon.
3. In Windows PowerShell, execute the following Windows PowerShell command:

   Set-Net6to4Configuration -State enabled
4. In the Windows PowerShell window, execute the following Windows PowerShell command:

   Set-NetIPInterface -InterfaceAlias "6to4 Adapter" -Forwarding enabled
5. In the Windows PowerShell window, execute the following Windows PowerShell command:

   Set-NetIPInterface -InterfaceAlias "London_Network" -Forwarding enabled
6. Log on to INET1 as **adatum\administrator** with the password of **Pa$$w0rd.**
7. On INET1, open **Server Manager.** In Server Manager, open the **Tools** menu and then click **DNS.**
8. In the DNS console, right-click **Forward Lookup Zones**, choose **New Zone**, and then click **Next.**
9. On the Zone Type page, click **Next.**
10. On the Zone Name page, in the Zone name box, type **ipv6.microsoft.com** and then click **Next.**
11. On the Zone File page, click **Next.**
12. On the Dynamic Update page, click **Do not allow dynamic updates**, click **Next**, and then click **Finish.**
13. In the DNS console, in the console tree, right-click the **ipv6.microsoft.com** zone and choose **New Host (A or AAAA).**
14. In the New Host dialog box, in the Name box, type **6to4.** In the IP address box, type **131.107.0.10**, click **Add Host**, click **OK**, and then click **Done.**
15. On EU-RTR, in the Windows PowerShell window, execute the following Windows PowerShell command:

    Get-NetIPAddress

    Notice the 2002:836b:a::836b:a IPv6 address assigned to the 6TO4 Adapter. This is a 6to4 address that EU-RTR automatically assigns based on the public IPv4 address 131.107.0.10, which is assigned to the Internet interface.
16. Log on to LON-CL1 as **adatum\administrator** with the password of **Pa$$w0rd.**
17. On LON-CL1, right-click **Start** and choose **Control Panel.**
18. In Control Panel, click **Network and Internet**, and then click **Network and Sharing Center.**
19. In the Network and Sharing Center window, click **Change adapter settings.**
20. Right-click **London_Network** and choose **Disable.**
21. Right-click **Internet** and choose **Enable.**
22. Close the Network Connections window. In the Networks pane, click **Yes.**

23. On LON-CL1, in the Windows PowerShell window, type `Get-NetIPAddress` and then press **Enter.** The address starting with 2002:836b: is assigned to the 6TO4 Adapter, which corresponds to its public IPv4 address. Also notice that the default gateway for the 6TO4 Adapter is set to 2002:836b:a::836b:a, a 6to4 address assigned to EU-RTR.
24. On EU-RTR, in the Windows PowerShell window, type `Get-NetIPAddress` and then press **Enter.** Notice and record the address starting with 2001:db8:: assigned to the London_Network interface.
25. On LON-DC1, in the Windows PowerShell window, type `Get-NetIPAddress` and then press **Enter.** Notice and record the address starting with 2001:db8:: assigned to the Ethernet interface.
26. On LON-CL1, in the Windows PowerShell window, execute the following Windows PowerShell command:

    Test-NetConnection EU-RTR IPv6 <Recorded_address>

    where the *<Recorded_address>* is the IPv6 address for EU-RTR on the London_ Network adapter you recorded earlier.
27. Execute the following Windows PowerShell command:

    Test-NetConnection LON-DC1 <Recorded_address>

    where *<Recorded_address>* is the IPv6 address for LON-DC1 on the Ethernet adapter you recorded earlier.

Configuring Intra-Site Automatic Tunnel Addressing Protocol (ISATAP)

Intra-Site Automatic Tunnel Addressing Protocol (ISATAP) is an automatic tunneling protocol used by the Windows workstation operating systems, which allows you to use IPv6 applications on an IPv4 network by emulating an IPv6 link using an IPv4 network. The ISATAP address consists of a valid 64-bit unicast address prefix and the interface identifier, such as a link-local address prefix (FE80::/64), site-local prefix, or global prefix. The last 64 bits are ISATAP addresses, which are the locally administered interface ID ::0:5EFE:w.x.y.z, where *w.x.y.z* is any unicast IPv4 address in hexadecimal form.

For example, the IPv4 address 157.54.176.7 would have the following as its ISATAP address:

`fe80:0000:0000:0000:0000:5efe:9d36:b007`

In compressed form, the address appears as follows:

`fe80::5efe:9d36:b007`

ISATAP hosts perform their own tunneling to other ISATAP hosts by using the link-local ISATAP addresses if they are on the same logical IPv4 subnet. If you want to communicate with other ISATAP hosts on other subnets, you communicate using ISATAP-based global addresses through an ISATAP router.

The ISATAP router is a key component of the ISATAP solution. The ISATAP hosts on the network will be able to query the router for IP addressing information, which is used to configure the ISATAP adapter on the ISATAP host. Modern Windows clients and servers have their ISATAP adapters enabled by default and use DNS to resolve the name ISATAP to an ISATAP router. The clients and servers connect to the router and automatically configure their ISATAP interfaces.

If there are IPv6-only hosts, the ISATAP router also unpacks IPv6 packets. ISATAP hosts send packets to the IPv4 address of the ISATAP router. If there are no IPv6-only hosts, the ISATAP router advertises the IPv6 prefix that ISATAP clients use, which the ISATAP interface on client computers is configured to use.

ISATAP does not support multicasting. Therefore, for an ISATAP host to find ISATAP routers, the host compiles a potential routers list (PRL) using DNS queries and sends Router Discovery messages to them on a regular basis, using Internet Control Message Protocol version 6 (ICMPv6).

CONFIGURE ISATAP ROUTING – SIDE A

GET READY. To configure ISATAP for Side A, perform the following steps.

1. Log on to LON-DC1 as **adatum\administrator** with the password of **Pa$$w0rd.**
2. On LON-DC1, click **Start** and search for **PowerShell.** From the results, click **Windows PowerShell.**
3. On LON-DC1, to remove ISATAP from the default global query block list, execute the following Windows PowerShell command:

   ```
   dnscmd /config /globalqueryblocklist wpad
   ```
4. Using Server Manager, click **Tools > DNS.**
5. In the DNS console, right-click **LON-DC1** and choose **All Tasks > Restart.**
6. Expand the **DNS\LON-DC1** node and click to expand **Forward Lookup Zones.**
7. Right-click **Adatum.com** and choose **New Host (A or AAAA).**
8. In the New Host dialog box, in the Name box, type **isatap.** In the IP address box, type **172.16.0.1**, click **Add Host**, click **OK**, and then click **Done.**
9. Log on to EU-RTR as **adatum\administrator** with the password of **Pa$$w0rd.**
10. On EU-RTR, click **Start** and then click **Windows PowerShell.**
11. In the Windows PowerShell window, execute the following Windows PowerShell command:

    ```
    Set-NetIsatapConfiguration -Router 172.16.0.1
    ```
12. In the Windows PowerShell window, execute the following Windows PowerShell command:

    ```
    Get-NetIPAddress | Format-Table InterfaceAlias,InterfaceIndex,
    IPv6Address
    ```
13. Record the InterfaceIndex of the ISATAP interface that has an IPv6 address that includes 172.16.0.1. Alternatively, you can save the InterfaceIndex information to a file on the C drive, the Results.txt file, with the following Windows PowerShell command:

    ```
    Get-NetIPAddress | Format-Table InterfaceAlias,InterfaceIndex,
    IPv6Address > C:\Results.txt
    ```
14. To show that forwarding is enabled for the interface and that advertising is disabled, in the Windows PowerShell window, execute the following Windows PowerShell command:

    ```
    Get-NetIPInterface -InterfaceIndex <IndexYouRecorded> -
    PolicyStore ActiveStore | Format-List
    ```
15. To enable forwarding and advertising, in the Windows PowerShell window, execute the following Windows PowerShell command:

    ```
    Set-NetIPInterface -InterfaceIndex IndexYouRecorded -Advertising
    Enabled
    ```

16. To create a new IPv6 network that will be used for the ISATAP network, in the Windows PowerShell window, execute the following Windows PowerShell command:

    New-NetRoute -InterfaceIndex IndexYouRecorded

    -DestinationPrefix 2001:db8:0:2::/64 -Publish Yes
17. To view the IP address configuration for the ISATAP interface, in the Windows PowerShell window, execute the following Windows PowerShell command:

    Get-NetIPAddress -InterfaceIndex <IndexYouRecorded>
18. Verify that an IPv6 address is listed on the 2001:db8:0:2::/64 network, and then close the Windows PowerShell window.

CONFIGURE ISATAP ROUTING – SIDE B

GET READY. To configure ISATAP for Side B, perform the following steps.

1. Log on to TOR-SVR1 as **adatum\administrator** with the password of **Pa$$w0rd.**
2. On TOR-SVR1, click **Start** and then click **Windows PowerShell.**
3. In the Windows PowerShell window, execute the following Windows PowerShell command:

    Get-NetIPAddress

    Verify that the Tunnel adapter has received an IPv6 address starting with 2001.
4. Log on to LON-SVR1 as **adatum\administrator** with the password of **Pa$$w0rd.**
5. On LON-SVR1, click **Start** and then click **Windows PowerShell.**
6. In the Windows PowerShell window, execute the following Windows PowerShell command:

    Get-NetIPAddress

    Verify that the Tunnel adapter has received an IPv6 address starting with 2001.
7. Log on to LON-DC1 as **adatum\administrator** with the password of **Pa$$w0rd.**
8. On LON-DC1, click **Start** and then click **Server Manager**.
9. In Server Manager, click **Tools** > **DNS.**
10. In the DNS management console tree, expand **DNS\LON-DC1** and then expand **Forward Lookup Zones.**
11. Click **Adatum.com** and then click the **Refresh** button to verify that there are new AAAA records registered.
12. On TOR-SVR1, to verify a connection to LON-SVR1, in the Windows PowerShell window, execute the following Windows PowerShell command:

    Test-NetConnection 2001:db8:0:2:0:5efe:172.16.0.11

    Notice that the message Ping Succeeded: True is received from LON-SVR1 tunnel ISATAP adapter's IPv6 address.

Configuring Teredo

Teredo, an IPv4 Network Address Translation-Traversal (NAT-T) for IPv6, is an address assignment and automatic tunneling technology that provides unicast IPv6 connectivity across the IPv4 Internet by encapsulating IPv6 packets within User Datagram Protocol (UDP) datagrams. One advantage of Teredo is that it will function even when the IPv6/IPv4 hosts are located behind one or multiple IPv4 NATs.

For a Teredo client to function as a tunnel endpoint, it must have access to a Teredo server, which is connected to both the IPv4 and IPv6 networks. The Teredo server exchanges Router Solicitation and Router Advertisement messages to determine whether the client is located behind a NAT router.

Teredo addresses use the following format:

- **Prefix**: A 32-bit field that identifies the system as a Teredo client. Windows clients use the prefix value 2001:0000, or 2001::/32.
- **Server IPv4**: A 32-bit field containing the IPv4 address of the Teredo server the client uses.
- **Flags**: A 16-bit field, the first bit of which is the Cone flag, set to 1 when the NAT device providing access to the Internet is a cone NAT, which stores the mappings between internal and external addresses and port numbers. The second bit is reserved for future use. The seventh and eighth bits are the Universal/Local and Individual/Group flags, which are both set to 0. The Teredo standard calls for the remaining 12 bits to be set to 0, but Windows assigns a random number to these bits, to prevent attackers from attempting to discover the Teredo address.
- **Port**: A 16-bit field that specifies the external UDP port that the client uses for all Teredo traffic, in obscured form. The obscuration of the port number (and the following IPv4 address) is to prevent the NAT router from translating the port as it normally would as part of its packet processing. To obscure the port, the system runs an exclusive OR (XOR) with the value ffff.
- **Client IPv4**: A 32-bit field that specifies the external IPv4 address that the client uses for all Teredo traffic, in obscured form. As with the Port field, the obscuration is the result of converting the IPv4 address to hexadecimal and running an XOR with the value ffffffff.

If, for example, the IPv4 address and port of the Teredo client are 192.168.31.243:32000, the Teredo server uses the address 157.54.176.7, and the client is behind a cone NAT router, the Teredo address, in standard format, would consist of the following elements:

2001:0000: Standard Teredo prefix

9d36:b007: Server IPv4 address (157.54.176.7) converted to hexadecimal

8000: Flags field with first bit set to 1 and all others 0

82ff: Client UDP port number (32000), converted to hexadecimal (7d00) and XORed with ffff

3f57:e00c: Client IPv4 address (192.168.31.243), converted to hexadecimal (C0a8:1ff3) and XORed with ffffffff

Thus, the final Teredo address is as follows:

```
2001:0000:9d36:b007:8000:82ff:3f57:e00c
```

Several public Teredo servers are available for use on the Internet. Windows operating systems use the Microsoft-provided Teredo server at teredo.ipv6.microsoft.com by default. By using the `Netsh` command, you can configure Teredo servers other than the default servers on teredo.ipv6.microsoft.com.

You can configure a computer running Windows Server 2016 as a Teredo client, a Teredo relay, or a Teredo server. To configure Teredo, use the Windows PowerShell cmdlet `Set-NetTeredoConfiguration` with the `-type` option.

Type `<Type>`

where <*Type*> is:

- **Disabled**: Disables the Teredo service
- **Client**: Enables the Teredo client
- **Enterpriseclient**: Skips the managed network detection
- **Server**: Enables the Teredo server
- **Relay**: Configures the interface as a relay
- **Automatic**: Sets the interface to automatically configure

The default configuration for Teredo is client.

When a computer is configured as a Teredo client, Teredo is disabled when the computer is attached to a domain network. To enable Teredo on the domain network, you must configure the computer as an enterprise client.

SKILL SUMMARY

IN THIS LESSON YOU LEARNED:

- When accessing computers on a network, you typically communicate by using their host names. If you are accessing a website, you enter a friendly name such as www.microsoft.com. Every device that connects to your network or the Internet must have an Internet Protocol (IP) address. You also need a way to associate these names to their assigned IP address.
- Subnetting is the process used to break a larger network into smaller segments. For example, a Class B IP address has more than 65,000 host addresses for a single, logical segment.
- Available public IPv4 addresses are running low. To overcome this problem as well as a few others, IPv6 was developed as the next-generation Internet Protocol version: a 128-bit address space to provide addressing for every device on the Internet with a globally unique address.
- To enable native IPv6 functionality, you must configure the router to support native IPv6 connectivity.
- The transition from IPv4 to IPv6 is expected to take several more years. In the meantime, expect to see a mix of IPv4, IPv4/IPv6 (dual stack), and IPv6-only networks. To help with the transition from IPv4 to IPv6, several methods were developed, including 6to4, Teredo, and Intra-Site Automatic Tunnel Addressing Protocol (IPv6).

Knowledge Assessment

Multiple Choice

Select the correct answer for each of the following questions.

1. Which of the following statements are true?
   a. IPv4 uses 32-bit addressing.
   b. IPv4 uses 128-bit addressing.
   c. IPv4 consists of a network ID and MAC address.
   d. IPv4 consists of a host ID and MAC address.

2. How many bits does a standard IPv6 unicast address use to represent the network ID?
   a. 32
   b. 64
   c. 128
   d. 10
3. Which of the following is the default CIDR notation for a Class C subnet?
   a. /8
   b. /12
   c. /16
   d. /24
4. Which IPv6 transition technology starts with the FE80:/64 prefix and includes the IPv4 address in hexadecimal form at the end of the IPv6 address?
   a. 6to4
   b. ISATAP
   c. Teredo
   d. NAT-T
5. Which of the following is an example of a valid IPv4 address?
   a. 192.168.42.1
   b. 21cd:0053:0000:0000:e8bb:04f2:003c:c394
   c. 192.256.1.42
   d. 21cd:53::e8bb:4f2:3c:c394
6. Which of the following is an example of a valid IPv6 address?
   a. 192.168.42.1
   b. 21cd:0053:0000:0000:e8bb:04f2:003c:c394
   c. 192.256.1.42
   d. 21cd:53::::e8bb:4f2:3c:c394
7. Which of the following is (are) the class(es) of IPv4 addresses used to provide support for networks?
   a. Class A
   b. Classes A and B
   c. Classes A, B, and C
   d. Classes A, B, C, and D
8. How does classless interdomain routing (CIDR) help reduce waste of IP addresses?
   a. CIDR uses a subnetting method also called variable length subnet masking.
   b. CIDR uses a subnetting method that divides between network bits and host bits anywhere, not just between octets.
   c. CIDR uses Network Address Translation.
   d. CIDR converts between IPv4 and IPv6.
9. Which of the following is the stateless address autoconfiguration process, during a Windows computer start?
   a. The computer assigns itself an anycast address.
   b. The computer pings for an DHCP address.
   c. The computer assigns itself 192.168.0.1.
   d. The computer assigns itself a link-local unicast address.
10. Which IPv6 transition technology is based on an automatic tunneling technology that functions behind one or multiple IPv4 NATs?
    a. ISAPI
    b. Teredo
    c. 6to4
    d. IPsec

Best Answer

Choose the letter that corresponds to the best answer. More than one answer choice may achieve the goal. Select the BEST answer.

1. When communicating with a server on another subnet, which of the following settings is used to determine which direction it needs to go to get to its final destination?
   a. Subnet mask
   b. Default gateway
   c. DNS
   d. IP address
2. Which of the following is the primary reason IPv6 has not completely replaced IPv4?
   a. Administrators are hesitant and reluctant to change.
   b. Stopgap technologies such as Network Address Translation (NAT) and classless interdomain routing (CIDR) alleviate the lack of registered IPv4 addresses.
   c. IPv4 addresses have only been depleted since early 2011.
   d. IPv6 has already replaced IPv4 on the Internet.
3. Which of the following describes Intra-Site Automatic Tunnel Addressing Protocol (ISATAP)?
   a. ISATAP converts IPv4 addresses for an IPv6 network just as 6to4 offers.
   b. ISATAP emulates an IPv6 link for use on an IPv4 network.
   c. ISATAP is a method of multicasting for IPv6 networks.
   d. ISATAP translates between IPv4 and IPv6 networks without client configuration.

Build List

1. Specify the correct order of steps necessary to calculating an IPv4 subnet mask.
   a. Calculate the subnet mask by adding the network and subnet bits in binary form and converting the binary value to decimal.
   b. Take the least significant subnet bit and the host bits, in binary form, and convert them to a decimal value.
   c. Determine how many subnet identifier bits you need to create the required number of subnets.
   d. Subtract the subnet bits you need from the host bits and add them to the network bits.
   e. Increment the network identifier (including the subnet bits) by the decimal value you calculated to determine the network addresses of your new subnets.
2. Specify the correct order of steps necessary to configuring IP address settings.
   a. Select the Internet Protocol Version 4 (TCP/IPv4) component and click Properties. The Internet Protocol Version 4 (TCP/IPv4) Properties dialog box opens.
   b. In the Properties dialog box, click the Ethernet hyperlink. The Network Connections window opens.
   c. Right-click the Ethernet icon and choose Properties. The Ethernet Properties dialog box opens.
   d. In the left pane of the Server Manager window, click the Local Server icon.
   e. Specify the preferred and alternate DNS server address.
   f. Set the IP address, subnet mask, and default gateway.

Business Case Scenarios

Scenario 1-1: Calculating IPv4 Subnets

As the enterprise administrator, you have assigned Arthur the network address 172.16.85.0/25 for the branch office network that he is constructing. Arthur calculates that this gives him 126 (27) IP addresses, which is enough for his network, but he has determined that he needs six subnets with at least 10 hosts on each one. How can Arthur subnet the address he has been given to satisfy his needs? Which IP addresses and subnet masks will the computers on his branch office network use?

Scenario 1-2: Expanding the Network

You are an administrator with a network address of 172.16.0.0/24. Currently, you are responsible for 40 sites; each site has between 20 and 100 users. However, soon, you will be creating corporate and regional offices that need to hold 500 users. Each of the sites are connected through NAT devices. Many users will be using multiple computer devices and you will be hosting many servers. You want to make sure you do not run out of addresses any time soon. So, you decide to implement IPv6. What will you need to do so that you can start using IPv6 with IPv4 until the transition is complete?

Installing and Configuring DNS Servers

LESSON 2

70-741 EXAM OBJECTIVE

Objective 1.1 – Install and configure DNS servers. This objective may include but is not limited to the following: Determine DNS installation requirements; determine supported DNS deployment scenarios on Nano Server; install DNS; configure forwarders; configure root hints; *configure delegation; implement DNS policies; implement DNS global settings using Windows PowerShell; configure Domain Name System Security Extensions (DNSSEC); configure DNS socket pool; configure cache locking; enable Response Rate Limiting; configure DNS-based Authentication of Named Entities (DANE); configure DNS logging; configure delegated administration; configure recursion settings; *implement DNS performance tuning; configure global settings using Windows PowerShell.

*Configure delegation and implement DNS performance tuning are discussed in Lesson 3.

Objective 1.2 – Create and configure DNS zones and records. This objective may include but is not limited to identifying and resolving issues related to the following: configure round robin; configure Zone Scopes; configure records in Zone Scopes; configure policies for zones.

LESSON HEADING	EXAM OBJECTIVE
Understanding DNS • Understanding DNS Names and Zones • Understanding the Address Resolution Mechanism • Understanding Split DNS	
Planning and Installing DNS Servers • Determining DNS Installation Requirements • Installing DNS • Determining Supported DNS Deployment Scenarios on Nano Server • Using Root Hints • Configuring Forwarders • Implementing Advanced Settings, Including Configuring Recursion Settings • Implementing DNS Global Settings Using Windows PowerShell • Implementing DNS Policies	Determine DNS installation requirements Install DNS Determine supported DNS deployment scenarios on Nano Server Configure root hints Configure forwarders Configure round robin Configure recursion settings Implement DNS global settings using Windows PowerShell Configure global settings using Windows PowerShell Implement DNS policies Configure policies for zones Configure Zone Scopes Configure records in Zone Scopes

LESSON HEADING	EXAM OBJECTIVE
Configuring Security for DNS	
• Configuring DNSSEC	Configure Domain Name System Security Extensions (DNSSEC)
• Configuring DNS Socket Pool	Configure DNS socket pool
• Configuring DNS Cache Locking	Configure cache locking
• Enabling Response Rate Limiting	Enable Response Rate Limiting
• Configuring DNS-Based Authentication of Named Entities (DANE)	Configure DNS-based Authentication of Named Entities (DANE)
• Configuring DNS Logging	Configure DNS logging
• Configuring Delegated Administration	Configure delegated administration

KEY TERMS

automated key rollover
debug logging
DNS policies
DNS Security Extensions (DNSSEC)
DNS-based Authentication of Named Entities (DANE)
DNSSEC resource records
forwarder
host
iterative query
Key Signing Key (KSK)
Name Resolution Policy Table (NRPT)
name servers
netmask ordering
resource record (RR)
Response Rate Limiting (RRL)
root hints
round robin
second-level domains
signing the zone
socket pool
split DNS
top-level domains
trust anchor
Zone Signing Key (ZSK)
Zone Signing Parameters

■ Understanding DNS

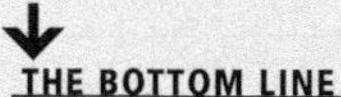
THE BOTTOM LINE

Domain Name System (DNS) is a naming service that is used by the TCP/IP network and is an essential service used by the Internet. Every time a user accesses a web page, the user must type a URL. Before the client communicates with the web server, the client computer needs to use DNS to retrieve the IP address of the web server, similar to how someone uses a phone book to find a phone number. When an enterprise client needs to communicate with a corporate server, the enterprise client also uses DNS to find the IP address of the corporate server. The DNS servers are often referred to as ***name servers***.

The Transmission Control Protocol/Internet Protocol (TCP/IP) is the most popular networking protocol suite used in the world and is the same protocol used with the Internet. Of course, the Internet is a worldwide network that links billions of computers. For a client computer or host to communicate on a TCP/IP network, a client must have an IP address.

Traditional IP addresses based on IPv4 were based on a 4-byte address written in a four-octet format. Each octet ranges from 0 to 255. An example of an IP address is 24.64.251.189 or 192.168.1.53. Most users would have difficulty remembering hundreds of telephone numbers and hundreds of IP addresses. Naming resolution enables an administrator to assign logical names to a server or network resource by IP address and translates a logical name to an IP address.

With early TCP/IP networks, name resolution was done with hosts files, which were stored locally on each computer. The hosts files were simple text files with a host name and IP address on each line (see Figure 2-1). In Windows, the hosts file is located in the C:\Windows\System32\Drivers\etc folder. The disadvantage of using hosts files is that every time you need to add a new entry, you need to add or modify the hosts file on every computer in your organization, which is not a practical way to provide up-to-date name resolution.

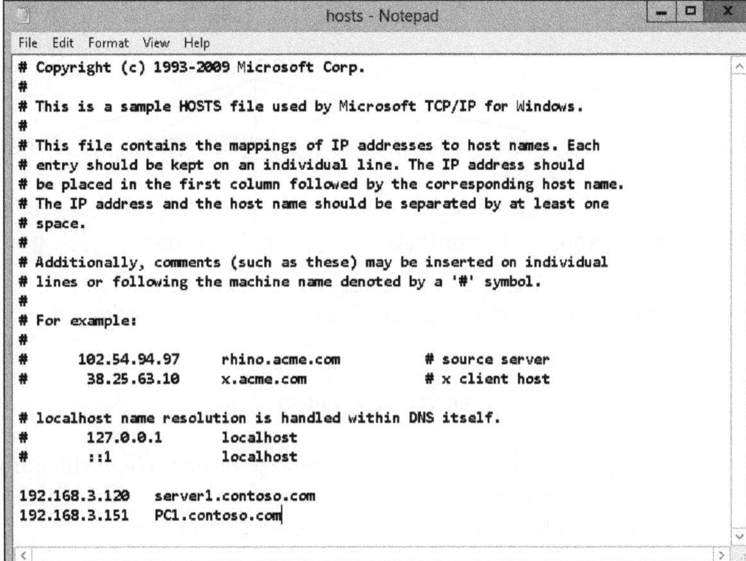

Figure 2-1

Viewing an example hosts file

DNS was developed as a system and a protocol to provide up-to-date name resolution. The benefits of DNS include the following:

- **Ease of use and simplicity:** Allows users to access computers and network resources with easy-to-remember names
- **Scalability:** Allows the workload of name resolution to be distributed across multiple servers and databases
- **Consistency:** Allows the IP addresses to be changed while keeping the host names consistent, making network resources easier to locate

A DNS resolver is a service that uses the DNS protocol to query for information about DNS servers using UDP and TCP port 53.

Understanding DNS Names and Zones

DNS uses fully qualified domain names (FQDNs) to map a host name to an IP address. An FQDN describes the exact relationship between a host and its DNS domain. For example, computer1.sales.microsoft.com represents an FQDN; the computer1 host is located in the sales domain, which is located in the Microsoft second-level domain, which is located in the .com top-level domain.

DNS is a hierarchical distributed naming system used to locate computers and services on a TCP/IP network. DNS clients send queries to a DNS server and the Domain Name System receives and resolves queries such as translating a host or domain name to an IP address.

Because it is so closely tied to the Internet and TCP/IP network, it is an essential service that enables the Internet and network to function and it is required by many network services, including Active Directory.

DNS is known as a distributed naming system because the information stored with DNS is not found on a single DNS server. Instead, the information is distributed among multiple DNS servers, all of which are linked into a hierarchical structure.

The DNS is a hierarchical system consisting of a tree of domain names. At the top of the tree is the root zone (see Figure 2-2). The tree can then be divided into zones, each served by a name (DNS) server. Each zone can contain one domain or many domains. The administrative responsibility over any zone can be delegated or divided by creating a subdomain, which can be assigned to a different name server and administrative entity.

Figure 2-2

Distributing domain names through the DNS hierarchy system

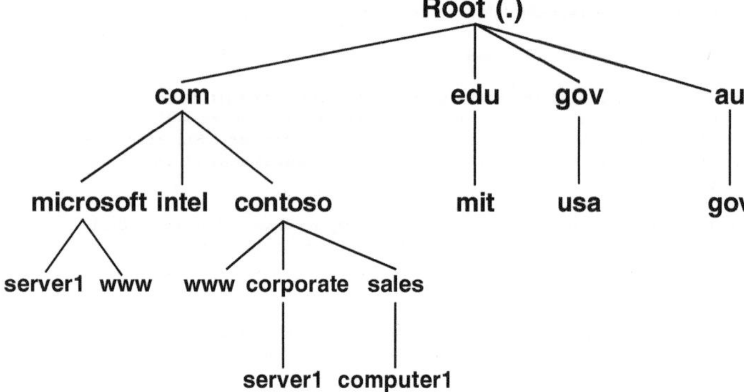

Each node or leaf in the tree is a ***resource record (RR)***, which holds information associated with the domain name. The most common resource record is the host address (A or AAA), which lists a host name and the associated IP address.

A domain name consists of one or more labels. Each label can be up to 63 characters. The full domain name cannot exceed a total length of 253 characters.

The rightmost label designates the top-level domain. For example, *microsoft.com* consists of two labels. The top-level domain is .com. The hierarchy of domains descends from right to left. Each label to the left specifies a subdomain of the domain or label on the right. Therefore, in our example, *microsoft* is a subdomain of the *.com* domain.

Traditionally, ***top-level domains*** consist of generic top-level domains and international country codes (such as *us* for United States, *uk* for United Kingdom, *de* for Germany, and *jp* for Japan). Traditional generic top-level domains include the following:

.com	Commercial
.org	Organization (originally intended for nonprofit organizations)
.edu	Educational
.gov	U.S. governmental entities
.net	Network (originally intended for the portal to a set of smaller websites)

Over the years, many other generic domains have been added, such as .aero, .biz, .coop, .info, .int, .jobs, .name, and .pro. More recently, organizations can purchase their own top-level domains.

Second-level domains are registered to individuals or organizations. Examples include:

microsoft.com	Microsoft Corporation domain
mit.edu	Massachusetts Institute of Technology
gov.au	Australian government

Second-level DNS domains can have many subdomains, and any domain can have hosts.

A ***host*** is a specific computer or other network device in a domain. For example, *computer1.sales.contoso.com* is the host called *computer1* in the sales subdomain of the *contoso.com* domain. A host has at least one IP address associated with it. For example, www.microsoft.com represents a particular address.

If you have *server1.corporate.contoso.com*, *.com* is the top domain. *contoso* is a subdomain of .com, and corporate is a subdomain of *contoso*. In the *corporate* domain, you find one or more addresses assigned to *server1*, such as 192.168.1.53. So as a result, when you type *server1.corporate.contoso.com* into your browser, the client sends a query to a DNS server asking what the IP address is for *server1.corporate.contoso.com*. The DNS server responds back with the 192.168.1.53 address. The client then communicates with the server with the address of 192.168.1.53.

Understanding the Address Resolution Mechanism

Every time a user accesses a network resource by a domain or host name, and the name has to be resolved to an IP address, the name and IP address are added to a cache so that you don't have to repeatedly contact the DNS server to resolve the IP address. If the name is not in the cache, the client contacts the first DNS server specified in the system's IP configuration. If the DNS server is available and it cannot determine the address, the client does not ask another DNS server. However, because DNS is a distributed hierarchical system, the local DNS server might need to contact other DNS servers to resolve the IP address.

The DNS client is known as the DNS resolver. Because a client computer or server depends on a DNS server to resolve IP addresses and identify certain network services, a client computer and servers alike can be DNS clients.

Before a DNS client queries a DNS server, it first checks its own local name. It then checks the hosts files. Next, it checks its own DNS cache to see if it has recently performed the same query and it already knows the resolved name.

When a DNS client queries a DNS server, it performs a recursive query, where the host asks the DNS server to respond with the requested data or it responds that the domain does not exist. The DNS server can perform a recursive query with another DNS server if it is configured to forward requests to another DNS server when it does not know the answer (see Figure 2-3).

Figure 2-3

Using a recursive query, which performs DNS forwarding when needed

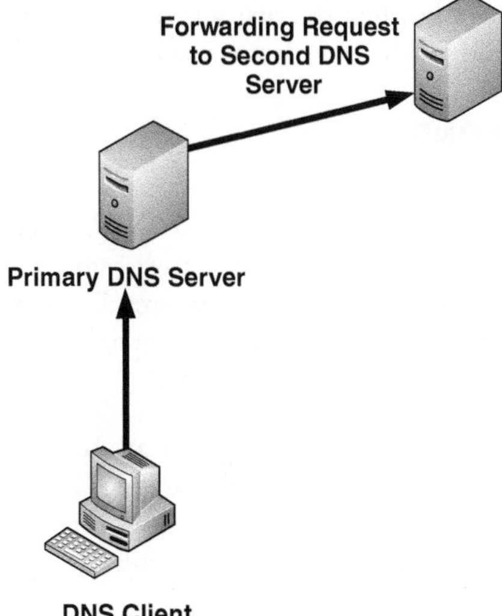

When the DNS server receives the response, it first checks its own cache. It then checks to see whether it is the authority for the requested domain. If it knows the answer, it responds with the answer.

If the client DNS server does not know the answer and it is not configured to forward requests to another DNS server, the client DNS server uses the DNS hierarchy to determine the correct answer. Instead of performing a recursive query, the client DNS server performs an ***iterative query***, which gives the best current answer back if it does not know the exact answer.

For example, when a user types support.contoso.com in her browser, and the client DNS server does not know the answer, the client DNS server contacts one of the root DNS servers to determine the addresses of a *.com* name server. The client DNS server then contacts the *.com* name server to get the name server for *contoso.com*. The DNS server contacts the *contoso .com* name server to get the IP address of *support.contoso.com*. The client DNS server responds to the client with the resolved IP address. In addition, it adds the address to its cache for future queries. Figure 2-4 shows an iterative query.

Figure 2-4

Performing an iterative query

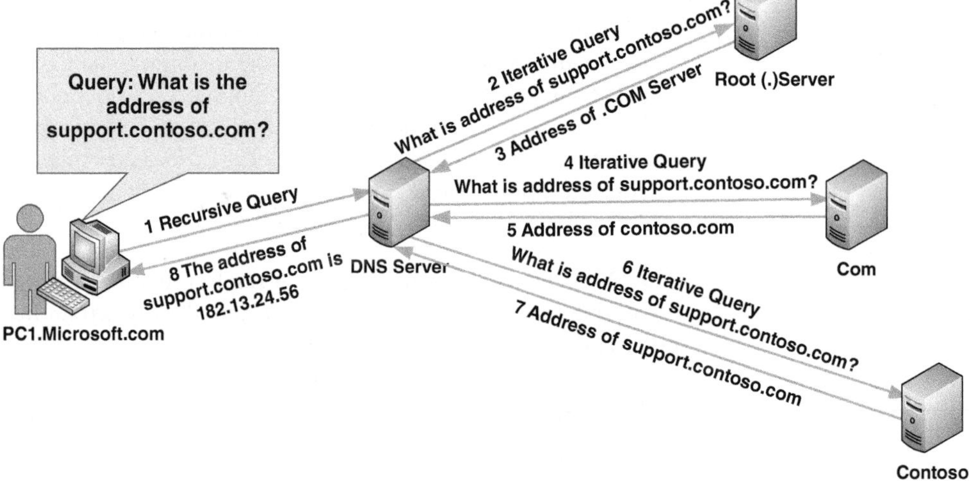

In some instances, the client DNS server does not know the answer and it cannot determine the answer, so the client DNS server responds to the client that the answer cannot be found or the query is a nonexistent domain.

Most DNS clients are configured with two or more DNS servers. The second DNS server is contacted for DNS queries only when the first server is not available. If the first server cannot answer the query, the second DNS server is not used.

Understanding Split DNS

For security reasons, most organizations use ***split DNS***, where DNS is divided into internal and external DNS. The internal DNS must remain separate from the external DNS and must be inaccessible from outside the firewall. In addition, external DNS records of servers and services must be accessible internally.

Internal clients are configured with the IP address of an Active Directory–integrated DNS server, which is also a domain controller. All DNS queries from internal clients go to the internal DNS servers. When a client needs to access resources on the Internet, the requests are then forwarded to the Internet-facing DNS server zones.

The Internet-facing DNS servers are usually deployed in the perimeter network or DMZ between the firewalls. Although they have the same domain name as the Active Directory–integrated DNS servers, the Internet-facing DNS servers do not store the same data. The resource records created on the Internet-facing DNS servers are created manually, and they usually contain records for themselves and other servers that are located in the perimeter network and that need to be accessed from the Internet.

To prevent external access to the internal DNS servers, the firewalls need to be configured to reject all DNS (UDP port 53) queries from the perimeter to the internal network, while still allowing DNS replies.

Many organizations use a subdomain of the internal DNS. For example, externally, you might use contoso.com, but internally, you might use local.contoso.com.

Planning and Installing DNS Servers

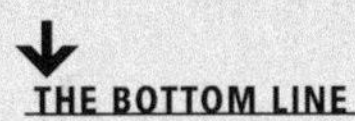

DNS is an essential service used by the Internet and can be integrated with other services, such as WINS, DHCP, and Active Directory. DNS servers are used to associate a computer name such as Server01.Support.contoso.com to an IP address. Without DNS, you are extremely limited on what you can do on the network, including finding and connecting to resources.

Before you can use DNS within your organization, you need to determine how you are going to plan out your DNS infrastructure, including determining how many DNS servers you need and determining where to place the DNS servers. Fortunately, DNS can be installed on Windows Server 2016 with Desktop Experience, Windows Server Core, and Windows Nano Server.

The five basic steps in deploying DNS are:

1. Install DNS on one or more servers.
2. Configure the DNS servers.
3. Create forward and reverse lookup zones.
4. Add resource records to the forward and reverse lookup zones that you just created.
5. Configure clients to use DNS servers.

Installing and configuring the DNS servers is discussed in this lesson. Creating forward and reverse lookup zones and adding resource records are discussed in Lesson 3.

Determining DNS Installation Requirements

Before you can start using DNS, you have to install DNS. As you do with other Windows Server roles, use Server Manager to deploy DNS.

CERTIFICATION READY
Determine DNS installation requirements
Objective 1.1

Most DNS installations do not require a lot of resources to operate, unless they need to support thousands of requests each minute. Therefore, most systems only need a 1.4-GB, 64-bit processor; 512 MB of RAM; and 32 GB of free disk space. For performance, a DNS server should be available at each site, and you should have multiple DNS servers for redundancy.

Installing DNS

Installing DNS is a very easy and quick process that can be completed using Server Manager or Windows PowerShell.

CERTIFICATION READY
Install DNS
Objective 1.1

As with any server role, before you deploy DNS, you need to plan your infrastructure. Some of the considerations involve how busy the servers are, what kind of fault tolerance is needed, what kind of performance is required, and what kind of security is needed.

INSTALL DNS

GET READY. To install DNS on Windows Server 2016, perform the following steps.

1. Click **Start** and click **Server Manager.**
2. At the top of Server Manager, click **Manage > Add Roles and Features.**
3. On the Before You Begin page, click **Next.**
4. Click **Role-based or feature-based installation** and then click **Next.**
5. Click **Select a server from the server pool**, click the name of the server to install DNS to, and then click **Next.**
6. Click **DNS Server.**
7. In the Add Roles and Features Wizard dialog box, select **Add Features** and then click **Next.**
8. On the Select Features page, click **Next.**
9. On the DNS Server page, click **Next.**
10. On the Confirm Installation Selections page, click the **Install** button.
11. When the installation is finished, click **Close.**

When DNS is installed, you use the DNS Manager console (see Figure 2-5). To open the DNS Manager console, perform one of the following:

- Open Server Manager, click Tools > DNS.
- Open Administrative Tools and double-click DNS.
- Open the run option or a command prompt and execute the `dnsmgmt.msc` command.

Alternatively, you can install the DNS Server role using an elevated Windows PowerShell console and executing the following Windows PowerShell command:

```
Install-WindowsFeature -Name DNS

-IncludeAllSubFeature -IncludeManagementTools
```

Determining Supported DNS Deployment Scenarios on Nano Server

There are many scenarios where you could take advantage of the Nano Server. For example, if you require higher security, or require a smaller hardware footprint, you should check to see if the Nano Server can run your services and applications.

Figure 2-5

Viewing the DNS Manager console

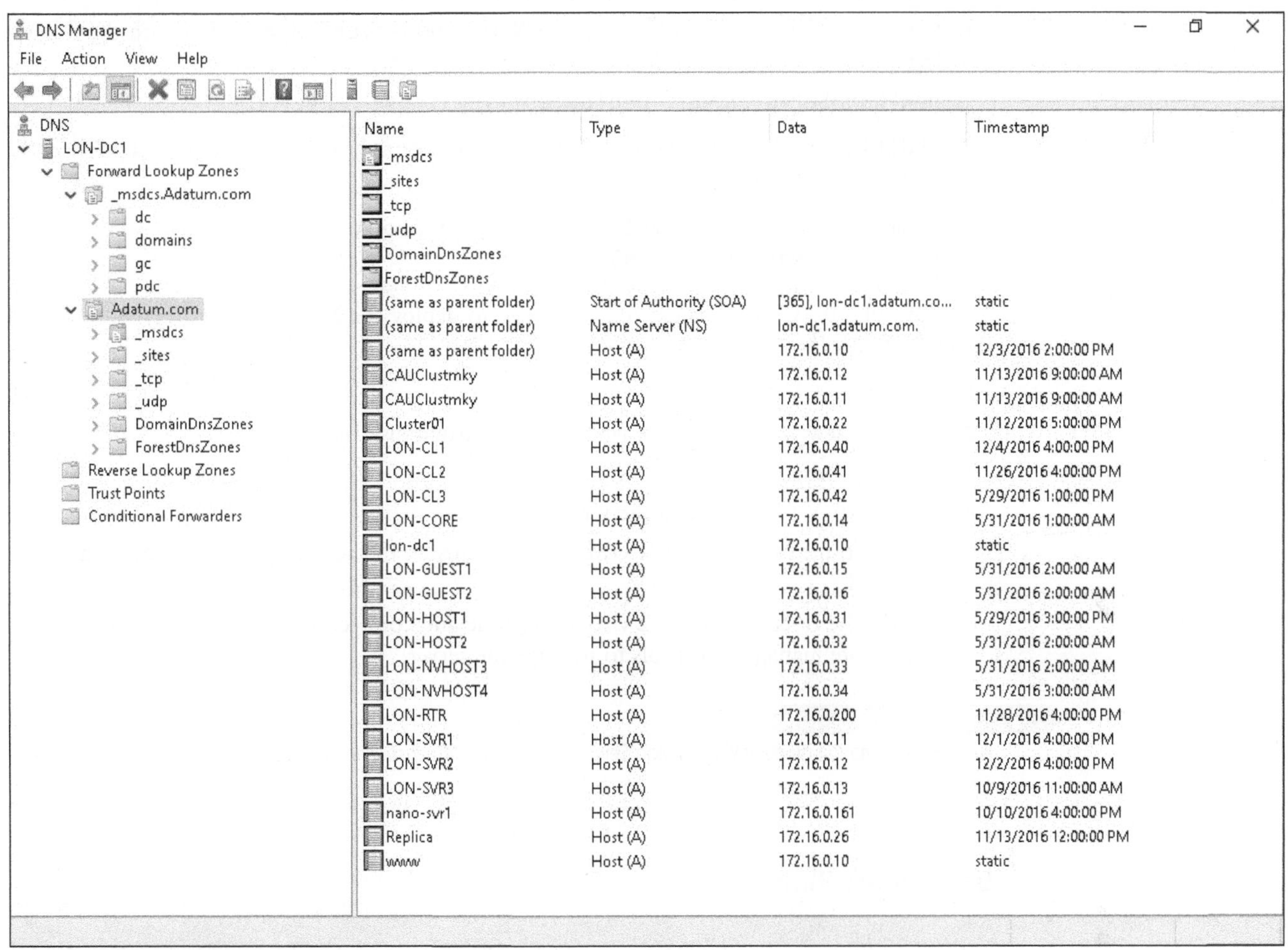

CERTIFICATION READY
Determine supported DNS deployment scenarios on Nano Server
Objective 1.1

Because of its smaller hardware footprint and higher security, if you need to place the DNS server on the DMZ, the Nano Server is an excellent choice. To install the Nano Server, you need a server running Windows Server 2016 and 800 MB of free disk space. Of course, you might need additional disk space to store data and additional processors and memory for the load that the Nano Server is running.

Nano Server is installed using one of three methods:

- Deploying a VHD image that will be hosted as a virtual machine on a Hyper-V host
- Deploying a VHD as a bootable drive on a physical computer
- Deploying a Nano Server WIM file on a physical computer

To create the Nano Server image, use the Windows PowerShell cmdlet `New-NanoServerImage`. The steps to create an image include the following:

1. Copy the NanoServerImageGenerator folder from the NanoServer folder on the Windows Server 2016 installation media to a folder on your local machine.
2. Start Windows PowerShell as an administrator and change the directory to the NanoServerImageGenerator folder on your local drive.

3. Import the NanoServerImageGenerator module by using the following Windows PowerShell `Import-Module` cmdlet:

```
Import-Module .\NanoServerImageGenerator -Verbose
```

4. Create the VHD or WIM by using the `New-NanoServerImage` cmdlet with the following syntax:

```
new-NanoServerImage -DeploymentType Guest

-Edition Standard -mediapath C:\ -Basepath c:\nano -targetpath c:\
nano\nano-svr1.vhdx

-computername NANO-SVR1 -storage -Packages
Microsoft-NanoServer-DNS-Package
```

Once the .vhd or .vhdx file is created, you need to deploy the Nano Server to Hyper-V by using the following steps:

1. Open Hyper-V Manager.
2. Create a new virtual machine with the new virtual disk file.
3. Boot the virtual machine.
4. Use Hyper-V to connect to the virtual machine.
5. Log on to the Nano Server Recovery Console using the administrator account and password.
6. Obtain the IP address for the virtual machine and connect to the Nano Server by using the remote management tools to manage the server.

MORE INFORMATION

For more information on deploying a Nano Server, refer to *70–740: Installing, Storage and Compute with Windows Server 2016.*

Using Root Hints

The ***root hints*** are used by DNS servers to find the root servers when performing iterative queries. The root hints are essential for DNS servers that are authoritative at lower levels of the DNS namespace when locating and finding the authoritative server for a zone.

CERTIFICATION READY
Configure root hints
Objective 1.1

The DNS Server service must be configured with root hints to resolve queries for names that it is not authoritative for or for which it contains no delegations. By default, Windows DNS contains a root hint, which contain the names and IP addresses of the DNS servers authoritative for the root zone. By default, DNS servers use a root hints file, called cache.dns, on Microsoft DNS servers. The cache.dns file is stored in the *%systemroot%*\System32\Dns folder on the server computer.

UPDATE ROOT HINTS

GET READY. To update root hints, perform the following steps.

1. On LON-DC1, log on as **adatum\administrator** with the password of **Pa$$w0rd.**
2. Click **Start** and click **Server Manager.**
3. Using Server Manager, click **Tools > DNS.**
4. If necessary, expand the DNS Manager console to a full-screen view.
5. Right-click the server and choose **Properties.** The Properties dialog box opens.
6. Select the **Root Hints** tab, as shown in Figure 2-6.

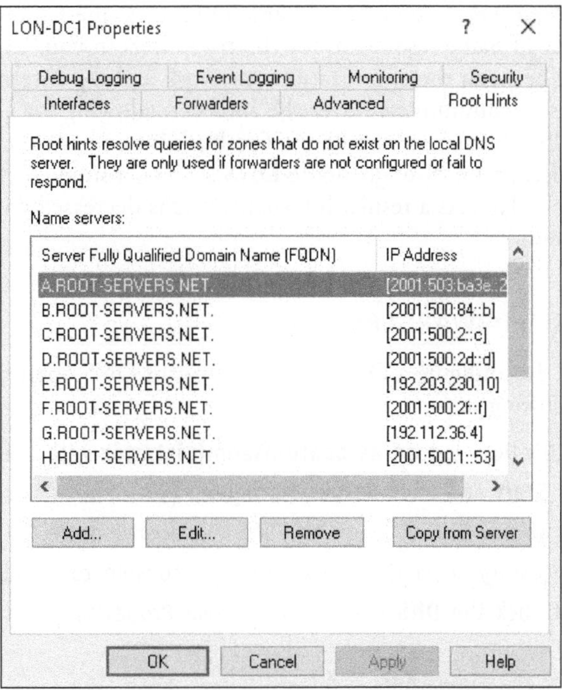

Figure 2-6
Managing root hints

7. Select one of the following options:
   - To add a root server to the list, click **Add** and then specify the name and IP address of the server to be added to the list.
   - To modify a root server in the list, click **Edit** and then specify the name and IP address of the server to be modified in the list.
   - To remove a root server from the list, select it in the list and then click **Remove.**
   - To copy root hints from a DNS server, click **Copy from server** and then specify the IP address of the DNS server from which you want to copy a list of root servers to use in resolving queries. These root hints will not overwrite any existing root hints.
8. Click **OK** to close the Properties dialog box.

Configuring Forwarders

By default, when a client contacts a DNS server and the DNS server does not know the answer, it performs an iterative query to find the answer, which means it first contacts the root domain and additional DNS servers until it finds the authoritative DNS server for the zone. However, DNS servers can be configured to be forwarded to another DNS server or a conditional forwarder based on the domain name queried.

CERTIFICATION READY
Configure forwarders
Objective 1.1

Many organizations have multiple levels of DNS servers. For example, an organization can have multiple DNS servers for its internal users and multiple DNS servers for Internet access, which provide addresses for external websites and other network services. Another example is an organization that has one level of DNS servers for internal users and an Internet service provider (ISP) that DNS services. In either of these two cases, you can configure the internal DNS servers to forward the DNS queries to the external DNS servers or the ISP servers. As a result, clients and the internal DNS servers perform recursive queries, and the external or ISP DNS performs iterative queries.

By using a ***forwarder***, you control name resolution queries and traffic, which can improve the efficiency of name resolution for the computers in your network. You can manage the DNS traffic between the organization's network and the Internet by allowing only internal DNS servers to communicate over the Internet, allowing for a more secure environment because DNS information can be used to hack into a network. In addition, by having all DNS traffic going through single DNS servers, a single server can build a larger cache of DNS data. As a result, Internet traffic is decreased and clients receive faster response times.

CONFIGURE FORWARDERS

GET READY. To configure a DNS server to forward DNS queries to another DNS server, perform the following steps.

1. On LON-DC1, log on as **adatum\administrator** with the password of **Pa$$w0rd.**
2. Click **Start** and click **Server Manager.**
3. Click **Tools > DNS** to open the DNS Manager console.
4. If necessary, expand the DNS Manager console to a full-screen view.
5. Right-click the **DNS server** and choose **Properties.** The server Properties dialog box opens.
6. Select the **Forwarders** tab.
7. Click the **Edit** button. The Edit Forwarders dialog box opens (see Figure 2-7).

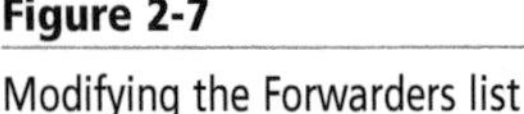

Figure 2-7

Modifying the Forwarders list

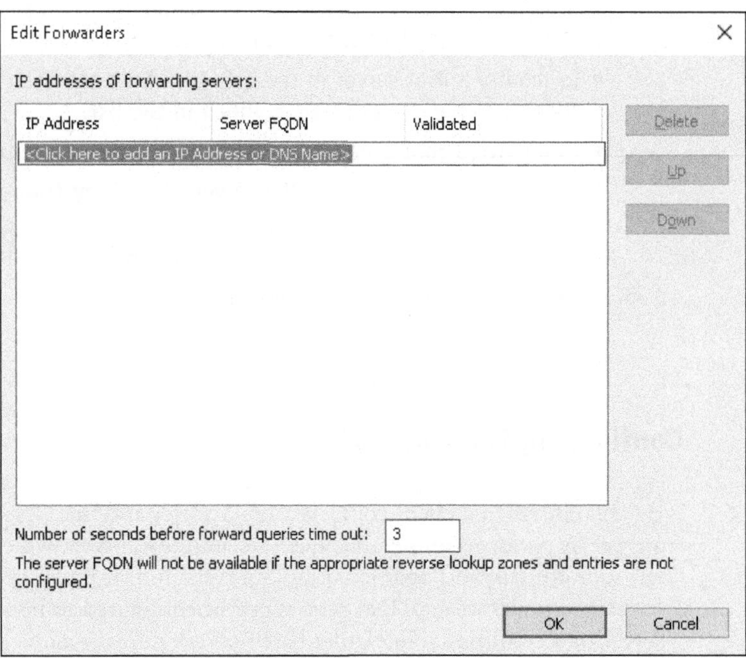

8. In the IP Address column, type the IP address of the DNS server that you want to forward DNS queries to and press **Enter.**
9. Click **OK** to close the Edit Forwarders dialog box.
10. Click **OK** to close the server Properties dialog box.
11. When the installation is finished, click **Close.**

Implementing Advanced Settings, Including Configuring Recursion Settings

CERTIFICATION READY
Configure recursion settings
Objective 1.1

The DNS server Properties Advanced options tab is used to configure common server options, including enabling or disabling recursion, round robin, netmask ordering, and secure cache against pollution option. By default, the round robin, netmask ordering, and secure cache pollution options are enabled.

CERTIFICATION READY
Configure round robin
Objective 1.2

Typically, DNS queries involve iterative queries to a root server, followed by additional DNS servers until it finds the authoritative servers for the domain name being resolved. As mentioned in the previous section, a forwarder sends a recursive query to the forwarder. Another way to stop recursive queries is to disable recursion, which disables forwarders. By default, the *Disable recursion* option is deselected.

Round robin is a DNS balancing mechanism that distributes network load among multiple servers by rotating resource records retrieved from a DNS server.

By default, DNS uses round robin to rotate the resource records returned in a DNS query where multiple resource records of the same type exist for a query's DNS host name.

For example, you can create the following host records, for webserver.contoso.com:

192.168.3.151	webserver.contoso.com
192.168.3.152	webserver.contoso.com
192.168.3.153	webserver.contoso.com

When the first client queries for webserver.contoso.com, the client gets back 192.168.3.151. When the second client queries for webserver.contoso.com, the client gets back 192.168.3.152. The third client gets back 192.168.3.153. When the fourth client accesses the web server, the client gets 192.168.3.151. If one of these clients tries to access the web server a second time before the TTL time expires, the client goes back to the same address because that address is within its DNS cache.

Round robin can be enabled or disabled by opening the server properties within the DNS Manager console. If round robin is disabled, the order of the response for these queries is based on a static ordering of RRs as they are stored in the zone.

It is common for a DNS zone to hold more than one A record for a particular host name. The ***netmask ordering*** feature allows the DNS server to return the record that is most local to the client requesting the IP address.

As an example, the FQDN AddressBook.adatum.com has several instances throughout the network and has several A resource records associated with it. Each subnet has a copy of this address book that rarely changes.

It makes sense that a DNS server always provides the most local copy for a client to access. Because the subnet identifies the location or site in which a client resides, it is easy to identify where the query was originated and thereby to provide the client with the correct A resource record in response. The alternative to this method is to provide a round-robin type of response each time the FQDN is requested, regardless of the location of the client. This method increases network traffic and is not as efficient.

ANOTHER WAY

You can use the dnscmd command-line tool to configure netmask ordering. From an elevated command prompt, enter the following dnscmd and press Enter:

```
Dnscmd /Config /LocalNetPriorityNetMask
```

The *Secure Cache Against Pollution* option specifies that the DNS server ignores DNS resource records that come from servers that are not authoritative for them. Although it can cause extra DNS queries to figure out the resource record, the additional security makes sure that those entries are not falsely injected into your DNS server cache.

CONFIGURE ADVANCED SETTINGS

GET READY. To configure advanced settings, perform the following steps.

1. On LON-DC1, log on as **adatum\administrator** with the password of **Pa$$w0rd.**
2. Click **Start** and click **Server Manager.**
3. Click **Tools > DNS.** The DNS Manager console opens.
4. If necessary, expand the DNS Manager console to a full-screen view.
5. Right-click the **DNS server** and choose **Properties.** The Properties dialog box opens.
6. Select the **Advanced** tab, as shown in Figure 2-8.

Figure 2-8

Configuring DNS advanced settings

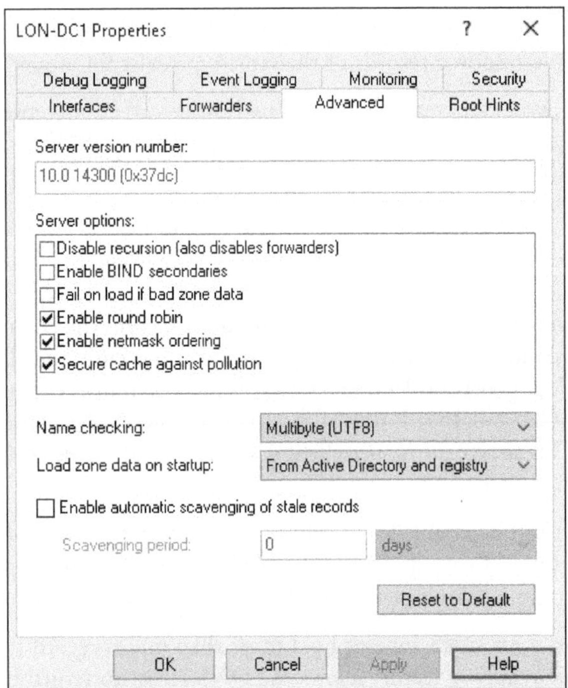

7. To disable an option (Enable round robin, Enable netmask ordering, or Secure cache against pollution), deselect the option. To enable an option, select the option.
8. Click **OK** to close the Properties dialog box.

Implementing DNS Global Settings Using Windows PowerShell

CERTIFICATION READY
Implement DNS global settings using Windows PowerShell
Objective 1.1

When configuring DNS settings, some settings are applied to the network adapters and others are applied globally. Global settings apply to all network adapters on the server. The global settings are configured with the Windows PowerShell `DNSClientGlobalSettings` cmdlet.

The `Set-DnsClientGlobalSettings` cmdlet sets the global, non-interface-specific DNS client settings that are global and are not associated with a specific interface. It can be used

CERTIFICATION READY
Configure global settings using Windows PowerShell
Objective 1.1

to configure the DNS suffix search order. For example, to configure the default suffix search order, use the following command:

```
Set-DnsClientGlobalSetting -SuffixSearchList
@("<List_of_DNS_domains>")
```

For example, to include the corp.contoso.com, na.corp.contoso.com, and servers.contoso.com, use the following command:

```
Set-DnsClientGlobalSetting -SuffixSearchList @("corp.contoso.com",
"na.corp.contoso.com", servers.contoso.com)
```

Implementing DNS Policies

CERTIFICATION READY
Implement DNS policies
Objective 1.1

CERTIFICATION READY
Configure policies for zones
Objective 1.2

CERTIFICATION READY
Configure Zone Scopes
Objective 1.2

CERTIFICATION READY
Configure records in Zone Scopes
Objective 1.2

DNS Policy is a new feature introduced in Windows Server 2016. ***DNS policies*** are used to manipulate how a DNS server handles queries based on different parameters. For example, you can redirect users to a specific server based on application high availability, traffic management, time of day, or if they are internal or external. You can also filter or block DNS queries, and you can redirect DNS clients to a non-existent or incorrect system instead of the computer they are trying to reach.

When you configure DNS policies, you must identify groups of records in a zone, groups of clients on a network, or other elements that tie the DNS clients together:

- **Client subnet:** Represents the IPv4 or IPv6 subnet from which queries are sent to a DNS server.
- **Recursion scope:** Represents unique instances of a group of settings that control if the system will use recursion or not for a given set of queries.
- **Zone scopes:** Specifies the same resource records across multiple scopes, with different IP addresses depending on the scope. You can also specify zone-transfer policies, which define zone transfers.

You can apply both policy types at the server or zone level. As you define multiple policies, the different defined values will determine processing order.

DNS policies are created and managed with the following Windows PowerShell cmdlets:

- **`Add-DnsServerClientSubnet`**: Adds a client subnet to a DNS server
- **`Add-DnsServerQueryResolutionPolicy`**: Adds a policy for query resolution to a DNS server
- **`Add-DnsServerRecursionScope`**: Adds a recursion scope on a DNS server
- **`Add-DnsServerResourceRecord`**: Adds a resource record of a specified type to a specified DNS zone
- **`Add-DnsServerZoneScope`**: Adds a zone scope to an existing zone
- **`Remove-DnsServerClientSubnet`**: Deletes a client subnet to a DNS server
- **`Remove-DnsServerQueryResolutionPolicy`**: Deletes a policy for query resolution to a DNS server
- **`Remove-DnsServerRecursionScope`**: Deletes a recursion scope on a DNS server
- **`Remove-DnsServerZoneScope`**: Deletes a zone scope to an existing zone
- **`Set-DnsServerClientSubnet`**: Updates the IP addresses in a client subnet
- **`Set-DnsServerQueryResolutionPolicy`**: Updates settings of a query resolution policy on a DNS server
- **`Set-DnsServerRecursionScope`**: Updates a recursion scope on a DNS server
- **`Set-DnsServerResourceRecord`**: Changes a resource record in a DNS zone

You use Windows PowerShell version 5.0 or higher to create and manage DNS policies. In the following example, you create traffic management policies to direct the client name resolution requests from a certain subnet in the New York data center and from another subnet to a San Francisco data center. You do this by first defining the client subnets and zone scopes. You then define the resource records in the zone and configure DNS server query resolution policies:

```
Add-DnsServerClientSubnet -Name "NewYorkSubnet" -IPv4Subnet
"172.21.33.0/24"

Add-DnsServerClientSubnet -Name "SanFranciscoSubnet" -IPv4Subnet
"172.10.44.0/24"

Add-DnsServerZoneScope -ZoneName "Contoso.com" -Name
"NewYorkZoneScope"

Add-DnsServerZoneScope -ZoneName "Contoso.com" -Name
"SanFranciscoZoneScope"

Add-DnsServerResourceRecord -ZoneName "Contoso.com" -A -Name "www"
-IPv4Address "172.10.97.97" -ZoneScope "SanFranciscoZoneScope"

Add-DnsServerResourceRecord -ZoneName "Contoso.com" -A -Name "www"
-IPv4Address "172.21.21.21" -ZoneScope "NewYorkZoneScope"

Add-DnsServerQueryResolutionPolicy -Name "NewYorkPolicy" -Action ALLOW
-ClientSubnet "eq,NewYorkSubnet" -ZoneScope "NewYorkZoneScope,1"
-ZoneName "Contoso.com"

Add-DnsServerQueryResolutionPolicy -Name "SanFranciscoPolicy"
-Action ALLOW -ClientSubnet "eq, SanFranciscoSubnet" -ZoneScope
"SanFranciscoZoneScope,1" -ZoneName "contoso.com"
```

Configuring Security for DNS

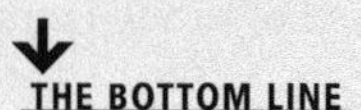

Windows Server 2016 includes a number of domain naming system (DNS) security features. Securing the DNS server and DNS records prevents false records from being added and prevents clients from receiving incorrect DNS query responses, which can lead them to visit phishing sites or worse. To prevent DNS from being used to attack systems, DNS Security Extensions (DNSSEC), cache locking, and other security measures can be implemented.

After you learn how to deploy DNS servers and configure them successfully, the need arises to secure the DNS servers and caches from spoofing, man-in-the-middle, and cache-poisoning attacks. In the modern world, it is a sad fact that securing all areas of functionality is a necessity. DNS is a common area for attack by interception and tampering.

Configuring DNSSEC

DNS Security Extensions (DNSSEC) is a suite of protocols defined by the Internet Engineering Task Force (IETF) for use on IP networks. DNSSEC provides DNS clients, or resolvers, with proof of identity of DNS records and verified denial of existence. DNSSEC does *not* provide availability or confidentiality information.

CERTIFICATION READY
Configure Domain Name System Security Extensions (DNSSEC)
Objective 1.1

A client that uses DNS to connect is always vulnerable to redirection to an attacker's servers unless the zone has been secured using DNSSEC. The process for securing a zone using DNSSEC is called ***signing the zone***. Once signed, any queries on the signed zone return digital signatures along with the normal DNS resource records. The digital signatures are verified using the public key of the server or zone from the ***trust anchor***. DNSSEC uses trust anchors represented by public keys that define the top of a chain of trust. The trust anchor verifies that a digital signature and associated data are valid.

Once this public key has been obtained, the resolver or client is able to validate the responses it receives. The trust anchor is the most important link in this chain. The server, resolver, or zone must be configured with this trust anchor. Once this is achieved, the client will be able to confirm that the DNS information it receives came from a valid server, was unchanged, and does or does not actually exist.

DNSSEC can be enabled on an Active Directory–integrated (ADI) zone or on a primary zone. As with all security measures and particularly advanced implementations, planning is important. Which zones do you want to secure? Who has access to the zone? Who has access to the server and the administration of the server security? The answers to these and lots of other questions always depend on the security requirements of your organization. By the time you are ready to implement DNSSEC on your DNS server, the security documentation should have already been created and approved.

DNSSEC is installed as part of the DNS Server role. To enable DNSSEC, Windows Server 2016 provides a DNSSEC Zone Signing Wizard. This wizard is run from the DNS Manager console and configures the ***Zone Signing Parameters*** with the settings required for ensuring the zone is signed correctly and securely. Follow the instructions to configure DNSSEC for the Adatum.com ADI zone.

Once a zone is signed, there are a number of new ***DNSSEC resource records*** available. These records are in addition to the standard A, NS, and SRV records in an unsigned zone. These DNSSEC resource records include DNSKEY, RRSIG, and NSEC. DNSKEY records are used to sign the records. The RRSIG record is returned to the client in response to a successful query along with the A record. The NSEC record is returned to positively deny that the requested A record exists in the zone.

DNSSEC uses a series of keys to secure the server and the zones. These include the ***Key Signing Key (KSK)*** and the ***Zone Signing Key (ZSK)***. The KSK is an authentication key that signs all the DNSKEY records at the root of the zone, and it is part of the chain of trust. The ZSK is used to sign zone data.

Automated key rollover is the process by which a DNSSEC key management strategy for key management is made easier with automated key regeneration.

CONFIGURE DNSSEC ON AN ACTIVE DIRECTORY–INTEGRATED ZONE

GET READY. Log on to the computer where you installed the DNS Server role and the Adatum.com ADI zone, with administrative privileges. To configure DNSSEC on an Active Directory–integrated zone, perform the following steps.

1. On LON-DC1, log on as **adatum\administrator** with the password of **Pa$$w0rd.**
2. Click **Start** and then click **Server Manager.**
3. Expand the **DNS server** by clicking the **arrow** to the left of the server name.
4. Expand **Forward Lookup Zones** by clicking the **arrow** to the left of Forward Lookup Zones.
5. Click and then right-click the **Adatum.com** zone and choose **DNSSEC>Sign the Zone.**
6. When the DNSSEC Zone Signing Wizard opens, click **Next.**
7. On the Signing Options page, as shown in Figure 2-9, there are three options to define the parameters used to sign the zone. Select **Customize zone signing parameters** and then click **Next.**
8. On the Key Master page, the default is the current server. Click **Next.**

Figure 2-9

Selecting the signing options

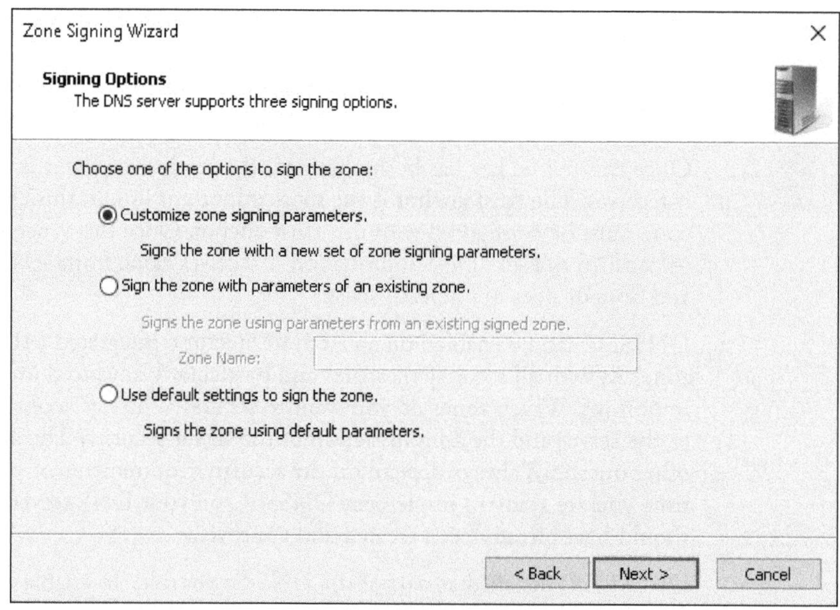

9. On the Key Signing Key (KSK) page, click **Next.**
10. In the Key Signing Key (KSK) dialog box, click **Add.** The New Key Signing Key (KSK) dialog box opens, as shown in Figure 2-10.

Figure 2-10

Creating a new Key Signing Key (KSK)

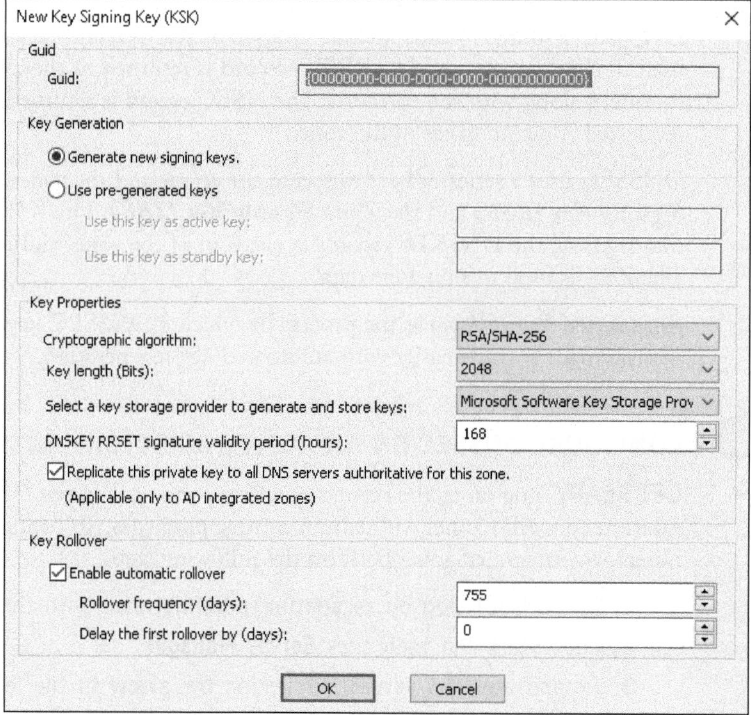

11. Make the Key Signing Key property selections. Settings include the algorithm, key length, replication, and auto rollover. Click the desired options and then click **OK.** Click **Next** and then click **Next** again.

TAKE NOTE*

The greater the key length (in bits), the more secure the DNSSEC keys will be. A long key requires more server resources to encrypt and decrypt. This overhead can be noticeable if the key length is set too long.

TAKE NOTE*

To set automatic key rollover for DNS servers that are not part of a domain, select the Enable automatic rollover check box on this screen. The frequency and initial delay is also set here.

12. In the Zone Signing Key (ZSK) dialog box, click **Add** and then make the Zone Signing Key property selections. Settings include the algorithm, key length, key storage provider, validity period of the keys, and auto rollover. When you are finished, click **OK** and then click **Next.**
13. An NSEC record provides authenticated denial of existence. If a DNS client requests a record that does not exist, the server provides an authoritative denial and the NSEC or NSEC3 record verifies this as genuine. On the Next Secure (NSEC) page, the options (see Figure 2-11) are for NSEC or NSEC3. NSEC3 is the default. Click **Next.**

Figure 2-11

Selecting the NSEC record format

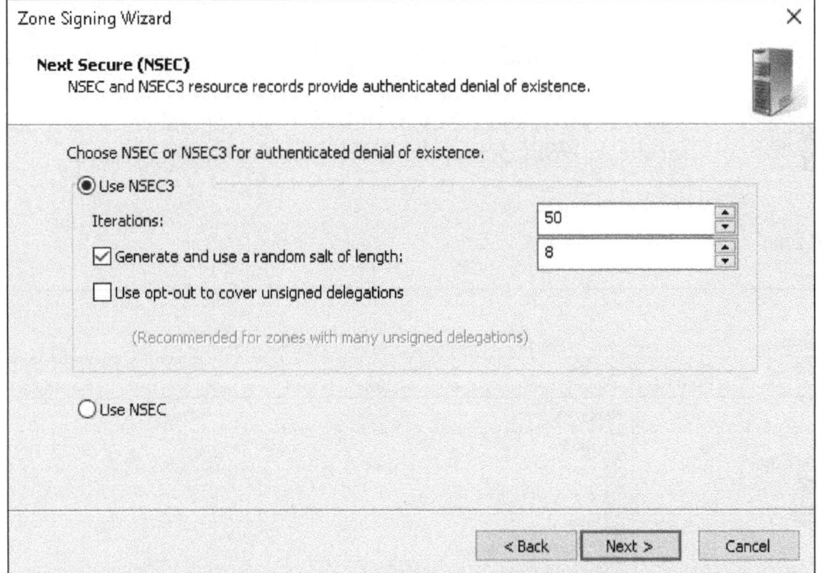

14. On the Trust Anchors (TAs) page, you configure the distribution of trust anchors and rollover keys. If the DNS server is also a domain controller, when the *Enable the distribution of trust anchors for this zone* option is enabled, every other DNS server that is also a domain controller in the forest will receive the trust anchors for the zone. This speeds up the key retrieval. When the *Enable automatic update of trust anchors on key rollover (RFC 5011)* option is enabled, automatic key rollover should be set if trust anchors are required on non-domain-joined computers. Click **Next.**
15. On the Signing and Polling Parameters page (see Figure 2-12), Signing and Polling Parameters allows for the configuration of the delegation key record algorithm (DS record) and the polling intervals for the delegated zones. Accept the defaults by clicking **Next** twice. The wizard signs the zone.
16. When the zone is signed, click **Finish**. The new DNSSEC records can now be seen in the DNS Manager console. If they do not show immediately, press the F5 key to refresh the list.

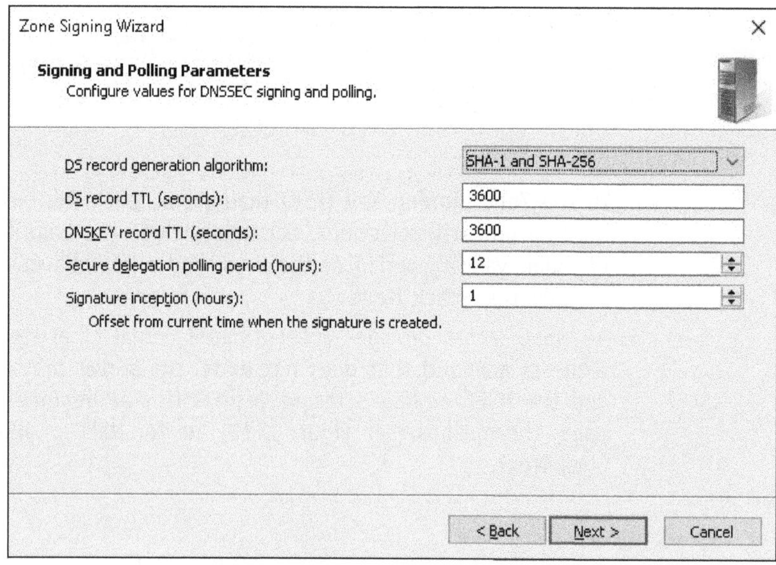

Figure 2-12

Selecting the Signing and Polling Parameters

Note that the padlock at the root of the Adatum.com zone (see Figure 2-13) shows the zone is signed. Also, note the additional records visible in the zone: DNSKEY (Public Key for the zone), RRSIG, and NSEC3. Indeed, each original entry now has four records: the A, RRSIG for the A, NSEC3, and the RRSIG for the NSEC3 record.

Figure 2-13

Displaying the signed zone

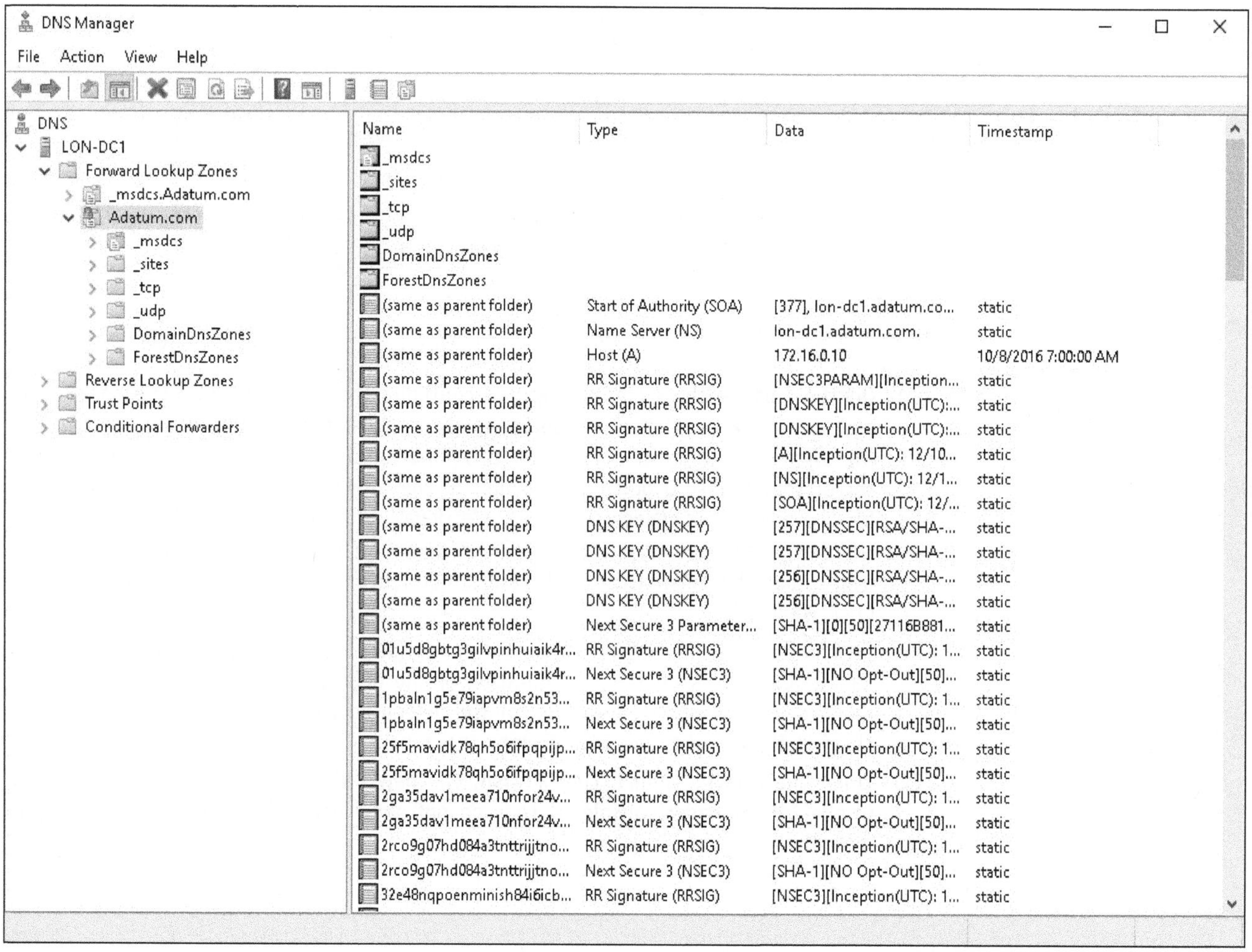

Name	Type	Data	Timestamp
_msdcs			
_sites			
_tcp			
_udp			
DomainDnsZones			
ForestDnsZones			
(same as parent folder)	Start of Authority (SOA)	[377], lon-dc1.adatum.co...	static
(same as parent folder)	Name Server (NS)	lon-dc1.adatum.com.	static
(same as parent folder)	Host (A)	172.16.0.10	10/8/2016 7:00:00 AM
(same as parent folder)	RR Signature (RRSIG)	[NSEC3PARAM][Inception...	static
(same as parent folder)	RR Signature (RRSIG)	[DNSKEY][Inception(UTC):...	static
(same as parent folder)	RR Signature (RRSIG)	[DNSKEY][Inception(UTC):...	static
(same as parent folder)	RR Signature (RRSIG)	[A][Inception(UTC): 12/10...	static
(same as parent folder)	RR Signature (RRSIG)	[NS][Inception(UTC): 12/1...	static
(same as parent folder)	RR Signature (RRSIG)	[SOA][Inception(UTC): 12/...	static
(same as parent folder)	DNS KEY (DNSKEY)	[257][DNSSEC][RSA/SHA-...	static
(same as parent folder)	DNS KEY (DNSKEY)	[257][DNSSEC][RSA/SHA-...	static
(same as parent folder)	DNS KEY (DNSKEY)	[256][DNSSEC][RSA/SHA-...	static
(same as parent folder)	DNS KEY (DNSKEY)	[256][DNSSEC][RSA/SHA-...	static
(same as parent folder)	Next Secure 3 Parameter...	[SHA-1][0][50][27116B881...	static
01u5d8gbtg3gilvpinhuiaik4r...	RR Signature (RRSIG)	[NSEC3][Inception(UTC): 1...	static
01u5d8gbtg3gilvpinhuiaik4r...	Next Secure 3 (NSEC3)	[SHA-1][NO Opt-Out][50]...	static
1pbaln1g5e79iapvm8s2n53...	RR Signature (RRSIG)	[NSEC3][Inception(UTC): 1...	static
1pbaln1g5e79iapvm8s2n53...	Next Secure 3 (NSEC3)	[SHA-1][NO Opt-Out][50]...	static
25f5mavidk78qh5o6ifpqpijp...	RR Signature (RRSIG)	[NSEC3][Inception(UTC): 1...	static
25f5mavidk78qh5o6ifpqpijp...	Next Secure 3 (NSEC3)	[SHA-1][NO Opt-Out][50]...	static
2ga35dav1meea710nfor24v...	RR Signature (RRSIG)	[NSEC3][Inception(UTC): 1...	static
2ga35dav1meea710nfor24v...	Next Secure 3 (NSEC3)	[SHA-1][NO Opt-Out][50]...	static
2rco9g07hd084a3tnttrijjtno...	RR Signature (RRSIG)	[NSEC3][Inception(UTC): 1...	static
2rco9g07hd084a3tnttrijjtno...	Next Secure 3 (NSEC3)	[SHA-1][NO Opt-Out][50]...	static
32e48nqpoenminish84i6icb...	RR Signature (RRSIG)	[NSEC3][Inception(UTC): 1...	static

If you right-click the zone and choose DNSSEC, two more options are available on the zone DNSSEC context menu: Properties and Unsign the Zone. The Properties dialog box contains the settings you configured in the wizard (see Figure 2-14). Unsign the Zone removes all the records and disables DNSSEC for this zone.

Figure 2-14
Displaying the DNSSEC zone options

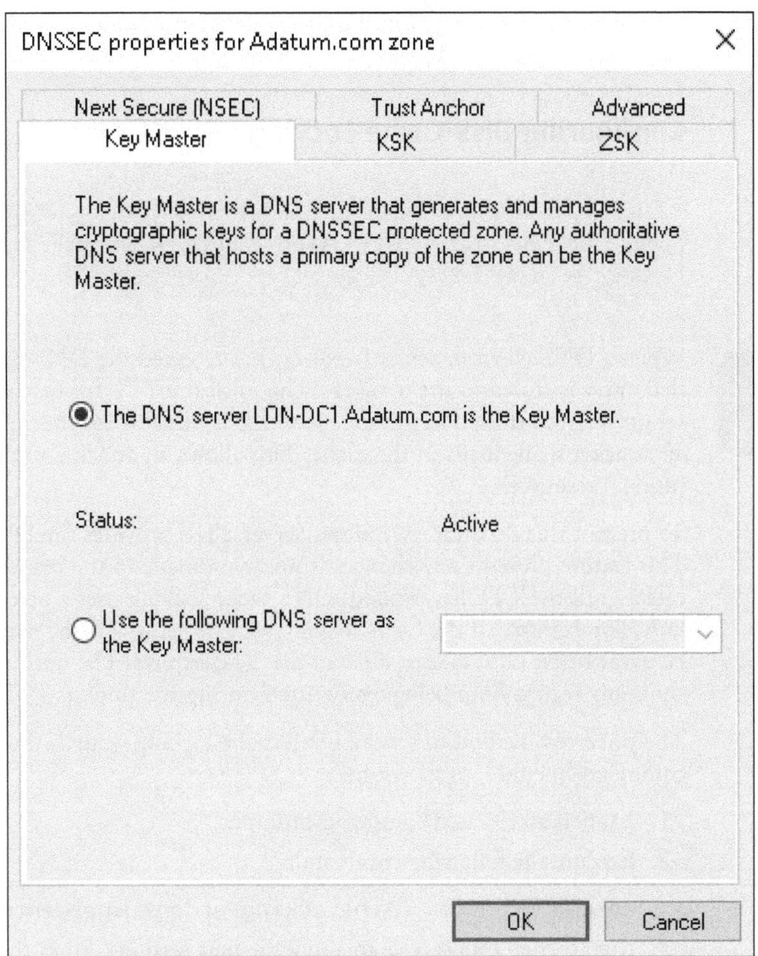

TAKE NOTE*
Once signed, a zone cannot be removed from the Active Directory unless it is unsigned first.

The ***Name Resolution Policy Table (NRPT)*** contains a list of rules for DNS client access and response to the DNS server. For example, a DNSSEC rule prompts the client computer to check for validation of the response for a particular DNS domain suffix. NRPT is normally set through Group Policy when a zone is signed using DNSSEC.

Configuring DNS Socket Pool

The DNS ***socket pool*** is a tool used to allow source port randomization for DNS queries, which reduces the chances of an attacker guessing which IP address and port (socket) the DNS traffic uses.

CERTIFICATION READY
Configure DNS socket pool
Objective 1.1

The DNS socket pool protects against DNS spoofing attacks. To be able to tamper with DNS traffic, an attacker needs to know the correct socket and the randomly generated transaction ID. DNS socket pooling is enabled by default in Windows Server 2016. The default size of the DNS socket pool is 2,500, and the available settings range from 0 to 10,000. The larger the number of ports available to the pool, the more secure the communication.

Windows Server 2016 also allows for an exclusion list to be created. The preferred method to set the socket pool size is through the use of the `dnscmd` command-line tool, as shown here:

1. Launch an elevated command prompt.
2. Execute the following command:

   ```
   dnscmd /Config /SocketPoolSize <value>
   ```

   The value must be between 0 and 10,000.

Configuring DNS Cache Locking

DNS cache locking prevents an attacker from replacing records in the resolver cache while the Time to Live (TTL) is still in force. When cache locking is enabled, records cannot be overwritten.

CERTIFICATION READY
Configure cache locking
Objective 1.1

When a DNS client or server (resolver) has received the DNS record of a requested resource, that entry is stored in the resolver cache until the TTL for that record expires. (The TTL is set on the record itself at the zone level.) It is possible for this information to be altered by an attacker while it sits in the cache. This allows an attacker to divert the client to a different (unsafe) resource.

To prevent this situation, Windows Server 2016 provides the DNS cache-locking feature. This feature prevents any changes from being made to the contents of a record in the resolver cache until the TTL has expired. DNS cache locking uses a percentage of the TTL to set the lock. For example, if the cache locking value is set to 75, the record would not be available to be overwritten until at least 75% of the TTL expires. The optimum setting is 100; this prevents any record from being overwritten during the time its TTL is valid.

The preferred method to set the DNS cache locking value is through the use of the `dnscmd` command-line tool, as shown here:

1. Launch an elevated command prompt.
2. Execute the following command:

   ```
   dnscmd /Config /CacheLockingPercent <percent>
   ```

3. Restart the DNS service to apply the new settings. From the command prompt, enter `net stop DNS`, wait for the service to stop, and then enter `net start DNS`.

USING POWERSHELL

To change the cache locking value using PowerShell, run the following cmdlet from a PowerShell window:

```
Set-DnsServerCache -LockingPercent 100
```

Enabling Response Rate Limiting (RRL)

A DNS amplification attack is when the attackers forge the IP address of the victim network and send a lot of queries to the DNS servers. As a result, the network and server become congested, causing a denial of service attack (DoS). To prevent this type of attack, DNS servers starting in Windows Server 2016 provide an option to enable ***Response Rate Limiting (RRL)***, which helps identify the potential malicious queries. If a lot of queries originate from a single source asking for similar names within a specified time window, it causes the DNS server to not respond to those queries or respond with a truncation, which reverts back to TCP, which uses a three-way handshake for validation. Overall, with RRL enabled, the Windows DNS server puts an upper limit to the number of similar responses that it will send to clients from the same subnet.

CERTIFICATION READY
Enable Response Rate Limiting
Objective 1.1

To enable RRL on a DNS server, use the Windows PowerShell `Set-DnsServerResponseRateLimiting` cmdlet. For example, you can use the following command:

```
Set-DnsServerResponseRateLimiting -WindowInSec 7 -LeakRate 4
-TruncateRate 3 -ErrorsPerSec 8 -ResponsesPerSec 8
```

- The `-WindowInSec 7` option specifies the period (in seconds) over which rates are measured and averaged for RRL.
- The `-LeakRate 4` option specifies the rate at which the server responds to dropped queries. In this example, if LeakRate is 4, the server responds to one in every four queries. The allowed range for LeakRate is 2 to 10. If LeakRate is set to 0, then no responses are leaked by RRL. The default value for LeakRate is 3.
- The `-TruncateRate 3` option specifies the rate at which the server responds with truncated responses. For queries that meet the criteria to be dropped due to RRL, the DNS server still responds with truncated responses once per the number set for TruncateRate queries. For example, if TruncateRate is 2, one in every two queries receives a truncated response. The allowed range for TruncateRate is 2 to 10. If it is set to 0, this behavior is disabled. The default value is 2.
- The `-ErrorsPerSec 8` option specifies the maximum number of times that the server can send an error response to a client within a one-second interval. The error responses include: REFUSED, FORMERR, and SERVFAIL.
- The `-ResponsesPerSec 8` option specifies the maximum number of times that the server sends a client the same response within a one-second interval.

To reset the RRL parameters on the DNS server to the default values, execute the following Windows PowerShell command:

```
Set-DnsServerResponseRateLimiting -ResetToDefault
```

Configuring DNS-Based Authentication of Named Entities (DANE)

DNS-based Authentication of Named Entities (DANE) is a protocol that uses X.509 digital certificates to be bound to the DNS name using DNSSEC. It can be used to authenticate Transport Layer Security (TLS) client and server entities without a certificate authority (CA). DANE is used to prevent man-in-the-middle attacks where a user may be directed to a fake website. It specifically prevents corruption of a DNS cache that points to a website, which uses a fake certificate that is issued from a different CA.

CERTIFICATION READY
Configure DNS-based Authentication of Named Entities (DANE)
Objective 1.1

DANE informs a DNS client which CA should have provided a certificate for a specified domain. DANE is implemented by adding a resource record using the Windows PowerShell `Add-DnsServerResourceRecord -TLSA` cmdlet. For example, to create a DNS resource record TLSA for ms1.dnslab.adatum.com, you would execute the following command:

```
add-dnsserverresourcerecord -TLSA -CertificateAssociationData
"25d645a7bd304ae552c629ca5e7061a70f921afc4dd49c1ea0c8f22de6595be7"
-CertificateUsage DomainIssuedCertificate -MatchingType Sha256Hash -
Selector FullCertificate -ZoneName ms1.dnslab.adatum.com -Name 25.
tcp.ev1-exch.ms1.dnslab.adatum.com.
```

MORE INFORMATION
For more information on creating resource records, refer to Lesson 3.

Configuring DNS Logging

DNS logging is a troubleshooting tool to allow for detailed, file-based analysis of all DNS packets and messages. The full title is DNS ***debug logging***. There is a processing and storage overhead in the use of debug logging.

CERTIFICATION READY
Configure DNS logging
Objective 1.1

Event Viewer is an essential tool in the successful management and troubleshooting of a DNS server. Windows Server 2016 provides a specific DNS server application log. This log records events such as starting and stopping the DNS service, changes to DNS configurations, warnings, and other events. In addition, the DNSSEC zone signing and zone loading events are recorded. There are, however, many occasions when more detailed logging of events, packets, and protocols is required. To facilitate this, Windows Server provides file-based debug logging.

Dns.log contains the debug logging activity. By default, this is located in the %SYSTEMROOT%\System32\Dns folder.

Debug logging is enabled at the server level and is accessed through the DNS Server Properties dialog box.

CONFIGURE DNS DEBUG LOGGING

GET READY. Log on with administrative privileges to the computer where you installed the DNS Server role. Ensure that the Adatum.com ADI zone is present. To configure DNS debug logging, perform the following steps.

1. Open **Server Manager** and click **Tools > DNS.** This loads the DNS Manager console.
2. Expand the **DNS server** by clicking the **arrow** to the left of the server name.
3. Right-click the **LON-DC1** server and choose **Properties.** Click the **Debug Logging** tab and then select the **Log packets for debugging** check box (see Figure 2-15).

Figure 2-15

Enabling DNS debug logging and options

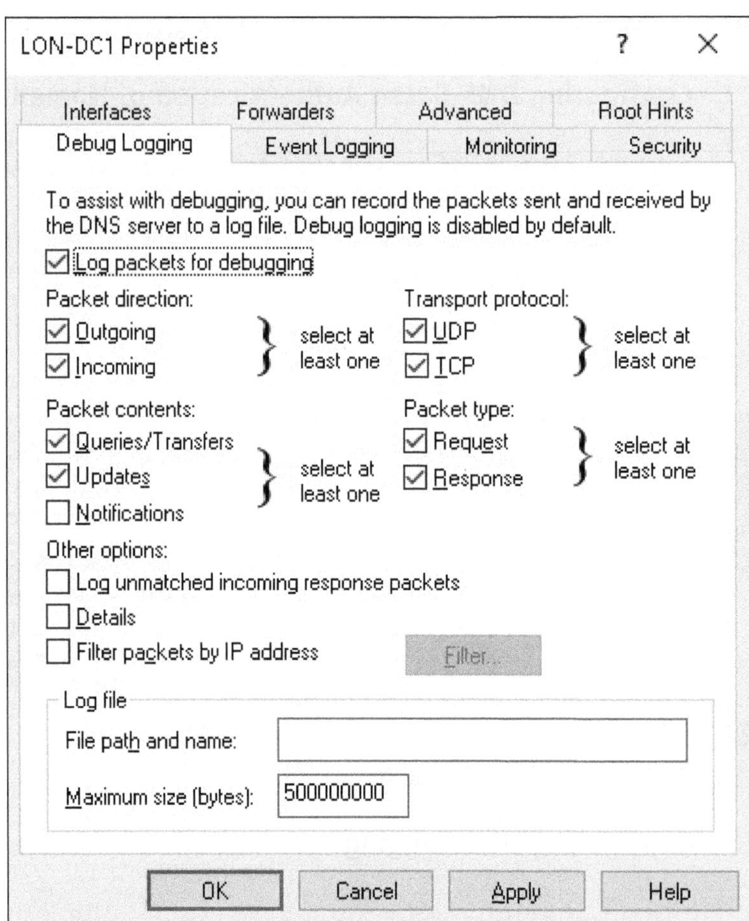

The following DNS debug logging options are available:

- **Direction of packets:** Send packets sent by the DNS server are logged in the DNS server log file. Receive packets received by the DNS server are logged in the log file.
- **Content of packets:** Queries specify that packets containing standard queries (per RFC 1034) are logged in the DNS server log file. Updates specify that packets containing dynamic updates (per RFC 2136) are logged in the DNS server log file.
- **Notifications:** This option specifies that packets containing notifications (per RFC 1996) are logged in the DNS server log file.
- **Transport protocol:** UDP specifies that packets sent and received over UDP are logged in the DNS server log file. TCP specifies that packets sent and received over TCP are logged in the DNS server log file.
- **Type of packet:** Request specifies that request packets are logged in the DNS server log file (a request packet is characterized by a QR bit set to 0 in the DNS message header). Response specifies that response packets are logged in the DNS server log file (a response packet is characterized by a QR bit set to 1 in the DNS message header).
- **Enable filtering based on IP address:** This option provides additional filtering of packets logged in the DNS server log file. This option allows logging of packets sent from specific IP addresses to a DNS server, or from a DNS server to specific IP addresses.
- **File name:** This field allows you to specify the name and location of the DNS server log file.
- **Log file maximum size limit:** This option allows you to set the maximum file size for the DNS server log file. When the specified maximum size of the DNS server log file is reached, the DNS server overwrites the oldest packet information with new information. If left unspecified, the DNS server log file's size can take up a large amount of hard disk space.

Debug logging can be highly resource-intensive and can impact the performance of the DNS server itself. It is recommended that debug logging be used as a temporary measure to gain detailed information regarding DNS server performance, only when it is required. For this reason, the debug logging is disabled by default. The debug logging settings allow for granular control of the types of events or DNS messages that are logged, which reduces the impact to a degree.

Configuring Delegated Administration

DNS is a key service within your network. Administration of the service should be restricted to those who really need it. The principle of least privilege should always apply to DNS administration.

CERTIFICATION READY
Configure delegated administration
Objective 1.1

Domain Admins have full permissions by default to manage all aspects of the DNS server, but only in the domain where the Domain Admins security group is located. A member of the Enterprise Admins group has similar permissions but throughout the entire forest.

To delegate administrative privileges to a specific user or security group, you add that user or group to the DNS Admins security group. Members of this group can view and modify all DNS data, settings, and the configuration of DNS servers within their home domain. The DNS Admins group is a Domain Local security group. By default, this group is empty.

TAKE NOTE*

It is best practice to add individual users to the Global or Universal group and then to add the Global or Universal groups to the Domain Local Groups (such as the DNS Admins Group).

If you need to assign permissions to a DNS object (scope or resource record), you can open the DNS Admin console, right-click the DNS object, and choose Properties. Then, from the Properties dialog box, click the Security tab (as shown in Figure 2-16) to add a group or user to the Access Control List (ACL), and then modify the access control entry (ACE) to provide the necessary permissions to the group or user.

Figure 2-16

Configuring security of a DNS object

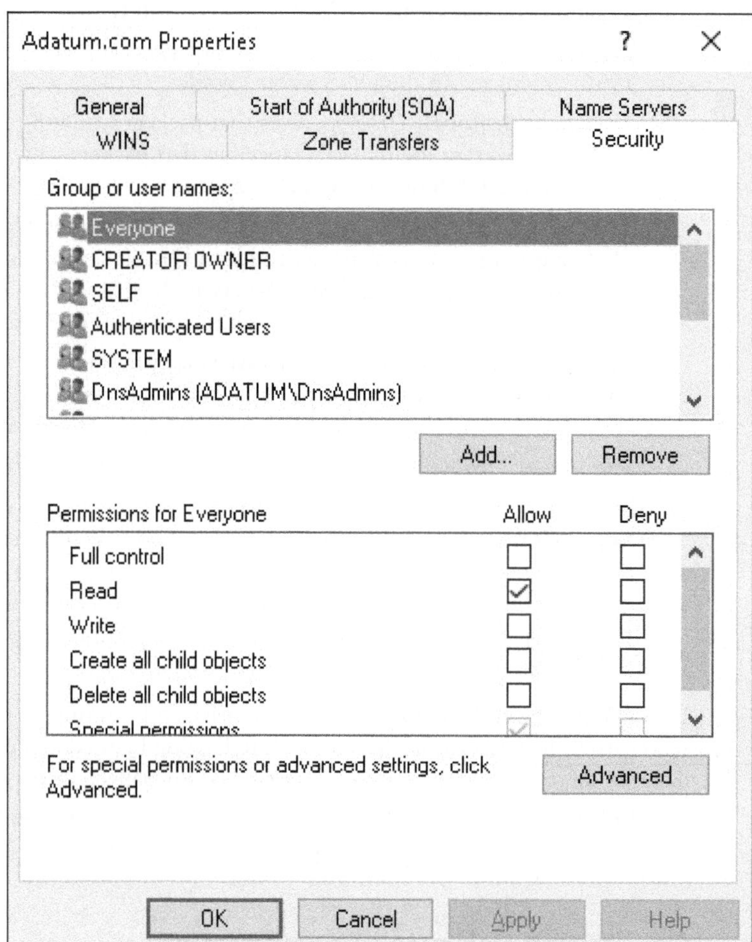

CONFIGURE THE SECURITY OF A DNS OBJECT

GET READY. To configure the security of a DNS object, perform the following steps.

1. Open **Server Manager** and click **Tools > DNS**. This loads the DNS Manager console.
2. Click and then right-click the DNS object and choose **Properties**.
3. Click the **Security** tab.
4. To add a group or user to the ACL, click **Add**.
5. In the Select Users, Computers, Service Accounts, or Groups dialog box, in the Enter the object names to select text box, type the name of the group or user, and click **OK**.
6. To modify the ACE, select the group or user, and then select or deselect the permissions.
7. To close the Properties dialog box, click **OK**.

SKILL SUMMARY

IN THIS LESSON YOU LEARNED:

- Domain Name System (DNS) is a naming service that is used by the TCP/IP network and is an essential service used by the Internet. The DNS servers are often referred to as name servers.
- DNS is a hierarchical distributed naming system used to locate computers and services on a TCP/IP network. DNS clients send queries to a DNS server and the Domain Name System receives and resolves queries, such as translating a host or domain name to an IP address.
- For security reasons, most organizations use split DNS, where DNS is divided into internal and external DNS. The internal DNS must remain separate from the external DNS and must be inaccessible from outside the firewall. In addition, external DNS records of servers and services must be accessible internally.
- By default, when a client contacts a DNS server and the DNS server does not know the answer, it performs an iterative query to find the answer, which means it first contacts the root domain and additional DNS servers until it finds the authoritative DNS server for the zone. However, DNS servers can be configured to be forwarded to another DNS server or a conditional forwarder based on the domain name queried.
- DNS policies are used to manipulate how a DNS server handles queries based on different parameters. For example, you can redirect users to a specific server based on application high availability, traffic management, time of day, or if they are internal or external. You can also filter or block DNS queries, and you can redirect DNS clients to nonexistent systems or incorrect systems instead of the computer they are trying to reach.
- Windows Server 2016 has a number of features of domain naming system (DNS) security. Securing the DNS server and DNS records prevents false records from being added and prevents clients from receiving incorrect DNS query responses, which can lead them to visit phishing sites or worse. To prevent DNS from being used to attack systems, DNS Security Extensions (DNSSEC), cache locking, and other security measures are implemented.

■ Knowledge Assessment

Multiple Choice

Select the correct answer for each of the following questions.

1. How many primary zones can a zone have?
   a. 1
   b. 2
   c. 3
   d. Unlimited
2. Which of the following are often known as name servers?
   a. DNS servers
   b. Active Directory servers
   c. Domain controllers
   d. Translation servers

3. Each node or leaf in the DNS tree is referred to as which of the following?
   a. Setting
   b. Resource record
   c. Property
   d. Row
4. Which types of keys are used in DNSSEC? (Chose two answers)
   a. KSK
   b. PLK
   c. ZSK
   d. VFK
5. When a client asks a DNS server for name resolution, which type of query is it?
   a. Iterative query
   b. Recursive query
   c. Root hint query
   d. Split query
6. Which of the following is an advantage of DNS running on a Nano Server versus DNS running on a Windows Server with Desktop Experience?
   a. More scalable
   b. Better performance
   c. More secure
   d. Costs more
7. When a DNS server does not know the answer and it must use the DNS servers on the Internet to resolve a name query, which of the following is used to determine the next DNS server to contact?
   a. DNSSEC
   b. DANE
   c. NRPT
   d. Root hints
8. If a DNS server does not know the answer to a name query, how can the DNS server be forced to go to the ISP DNS server?
   a. Use root hints.
   b. Use a forwarder.
   c. Use host files.
   d. Use netmask ordering.
9. Which of the following can be used to limit how many DNS queries a DNS server responds to so that it will reduce the effect of a denial of service attack?
   a. Netmask ordering
   b. DANE
   c. Response Rate Limiting
   d. Round robin
10. Which of the following uses a digital certificate to ensure that a user is not being directed to a fake website because the DNS cache was corrupted?
    a. Netmask ordering
    b. DANE
    c. DNSSEC
    d. Round robin

Best Answer

Choose the letter that corresponds to the best answer. More than one answer choice may achieve the goal. Select the BEST answer.

1. Which security group provides the privileges required for managing DNS within a single domain?
   a. Enterprise Admins
   b. DNS Admins
   c. Power Users
   d. Domain Admins

2. Which DNS cache locking setting should be selected?
   a. 30%
   b. 0%
   c. 100%
   d. 50%

3. To provide location-specific name resolution for DNS clients, which of the following should be enabled?
   a. DNS round-robin
   b. Hardware load-balancing cluster
   c. Netmask ordering
   d. Microsoft Network Load Balancing cluster

Matching and Identification

1. Identify which of the following is a benefit of DNS. (Not all answers will be used.)
   ____ Durability
   ____ Scalability
   ____ Strong fault tolerance
   ____ Fast modifications
   ____ Ease of use
   ____ Consistency

2. For each of the following message exchanges that can occur during a DNS name resolution procedure, specify whether the sending computer generates an iterative query or a recursive query:
   ____ Resolver to designated DNS server
   ____ Designated DNS server to top-level domain server
   ____ Designated DNS server to forwarder
   ____ Designated DNS server to second-level domain server
   ____ Forwarder to root name server

Build List

1. Specify the correct order of steps necessary to deploying DNS. Not all steps will be used.
   ____ Configure the DNS server.
   ____ Configure the clients to use DNS servers.
   ____ Add resource records to the forward and reverse lookup zones.

____ Migrate resource records from a database.
____ Install DNS on one or more servers.
____ Configure sequence numbers.
____ Create forward and reverse lookup zones.

■ Business Case Scenarios

Scenario 2-1: Deploying DNS Servers

Harold is a freelance networking consultant who has designed a network for a small company with a single location. The owner of the company wants to use an Active Directory domain, so Harold installs a Windows Server 2016 domain controller with the Active Directory Domain Services and DNS Server roles. Harold also uses DHCP to configure all of the workstations on the network to use the DNS services provided by the domain controller.

Soon after the installation, Harold notices that the DNS server queries are consuming a large amount of bandwidth when performing recursive queries. What can he do to reduce the amount of DNS traffic passing over the Internet connection?

Scenario 2-2: Managing Web Servers

You manage the network infrastructure for a large company that has around 30 sites throughout the United States. You have four primary web servers that are used by the employees to manage their employee records and such. You need to ensure that those employees visit their closest web server. What can you do?

Scenario 2-3: Distributing Traffic Web Servers

You just installed three web servers, which are used to serve your company's web page on the Internet. You want to ensure that web requests are evenly distributed to the three web servers. What do you need to do and what are the steps you need to perform to accomplish this?

Creating and Configuring DNS Zones and Records

LESSON 3

70-741 EXAM OBJECTIVE

Objective 1.2 – Create and configure DNS zones and records. This objective may include but is not limited to the following: Create primary zones; configure Active Directory integration of primary zones; create and configure secondary zones; create and configure stub zones; configure a GlobalNames zone; analyze zone-level statistics; create and configure DNS resource records (RR), including A, AAAA, PTR, SOA, NS, SRV, CNAME, and MX records; configure zone scavenging; configure record options, including Time to Live (TTL) and weight; *configure round robin; configure secure dynamic updates; configure unknown record support; use DNS audit events and analytical (query) events for auditing and troubleshooting; *configure Zone Scopes; *configure records in Zone Scopes; *configure policies for zones.

*Configure round robin, configure policies for zones, configure Zone Scopes, and configure records in Zone Scopes are discussed in Lesson 2.

Objective 1.1 – Install and configure DNS servers. This objective may include but is not limited to the following: Configure delegation; implement DNS performance tuning.

LESSON HEADING	EXAM OBJECTIVE
Configuring and Managing DNS Zones • Configuring Primary and Secondary Zones • Configuring Active Directory–Integrated Zones • Configuring Zone Delegation • Creating and Configuring Stub Zones • Configuring Conditional Forwarding • Configuring Zone Transfers • Using the DNSCMD Command to Manage Zones • Using Windows PowerShell Cmdlets to Manage Zones • Configuring Secure Dynamic Updates • Configuring Zone Scavenging	Create primary zones Create and configure secondary zones Configure Active Directory integration of primary zones Create and configure stub zones Configure delegation Configure secure dynamic updates Configure zone scavenging
Configuring DNS Record Types • Creating and Configuring DNS Resource Records • Configuring Resource Record Options	Create and configure DNS resource records (RR), including A, AAAA, PTR, SOA, NS, SRV, CNAME, and MX records Configure unknown record support Configure record options, including Time to Live (TTL) and weight

LESSON HEADING	EXAM OBJECTIVE
Using the DNSCMD and Windows PowerShell Commands to Manage Resource Records	
Configuring a GlobalNames Zone	Configure a GlobalNames zone
Analyzing Zone-Level Statistics and Implementing DNS Performance Tuning	Analyze zone-level statistics Implement DNS performance tuning
Troubleshooting DNS Problems	Use DNS audit events and analytical (query) events for auditing and troubleshooting

KEY TERMS

Active Directory–integrated zone	**GlobalNames**	**scavenging**
aging	**Host (A and AAAA) record**	**secondary name servers**
Canonical Name (CNAME) record	**incremental zone transfer (IXFR)**	**secondary zone**
conditional forwarding	**Mail Exchanger (MX) record**	**secure dynamic updates**
dnscmd.exe	**Name Server (NS) record**	**Service Location (SRV) record**
DNS Notify	**Performance Monitor**	**Start of Authority (SOA) record**
DNS zone database	**Pointer (PTR) record**	**stub zone**
dynamic updates	**primary name servers**	**subdomain**
forward lookup zone	**primary zone**	**Unknown Record**
full zone transfer (AXFR)	**reverse lookup zone**	**zone transfers**

Configuring and Managing DNS Zones

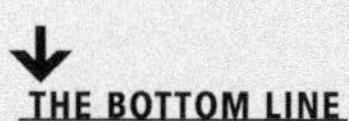

To provide DNS services, you first need to deploy DNS. Then, after you install DNS servers, you need to create each zone and then add resource records to each zone. Because DNS is an essential service for a network, you should give some thought to planning your DNS before deploy it.

The steps in deploying DNS include the following:

1. Install DNS on one or more servers.
2. Configure the DNS server, if necessary.
3. Create forward and reverse lookup zones.
4. Add resource records to the forward and reverse lookup zones.
5. Configure the clients to use the DNS servers.

Installing and configuring the DNS servers was discussed in Lesson 2.

Configuring Primary and Secondary Zones

CERTIFICATION READY
Create primary zones
Objective 1.2

On DNS original implementation, the DNS server would host either a primary or secondary zone or both. The ***primary zone*** provides an authoritative, read-write copy of the zone, whereas the ***secondary zone*** provides an authoritative, read-only copy of the primary zone.

CERTIFICATION READY
Create and configure secondary zones
Objective 1.2

When you need to make changes to the DNS zone, make the changes on the primary zone and the changes are replicated to the secondary zone. The secondary DNS zone enables the administrator to offload DNS query traffic and provide redundancy for name resolution queries. You then need to configure replication between the primary servers and the secondary servers.

Originally, the DNS was stored on a local file. By default, the primary zone file is named *zone_name.dns*, which is located in the *%systemroot%*\System32\DNS folder. By default, the *%systemroot%* is in the C:\Windows folder.

A server can host all primary zones, all secondary zones, or a mix of primary and secondary zones. Sometimes, servers that host primary zones are referred to as ***primary name servers*** and servers that host secondary zones are referred to as ***secondary name servers***.

When creating zones, there are two types of lookup zones to create:

- Forward lookup zone
- Reverse lookup zone

A ***forward lookup zone*** contains most of the resource records for a domain. Of course, as the name indicates, a forward lookup zone is used primarily to resolve host names to IP addresses. A ***reverse lookup zone*** is used to resolve IP addresses to host names. In the next two exercises, you create a standard primary zone and a secondary zone for contoso.com.

CREATE A STANDARD FORWARD LOOKUP PRIMARY ZONE

GET READY. To create a standard forward lookup primary zone, perform the following steps.

1. Open **Server Manager.**
2. Click **Tools > DNS** to open the DNS Manager console.
3. If necessary, expand the DNS Manager console to a full-screen view.
4. Expand the server so that you can see the Forward Lookup Zones and Reverse Lookup Zones folders.
5. Click and then right-click **Forward Lookup Zones** and choose **New Zone.**
6. On the Welcome to the New Zone Wizard page, click **Next.**
7. On the Zone Type page, select the **Primary zone** radio button (see Figure 3-1). Deselect the **Store the zone in Active Directory** check box and then click **Next.**

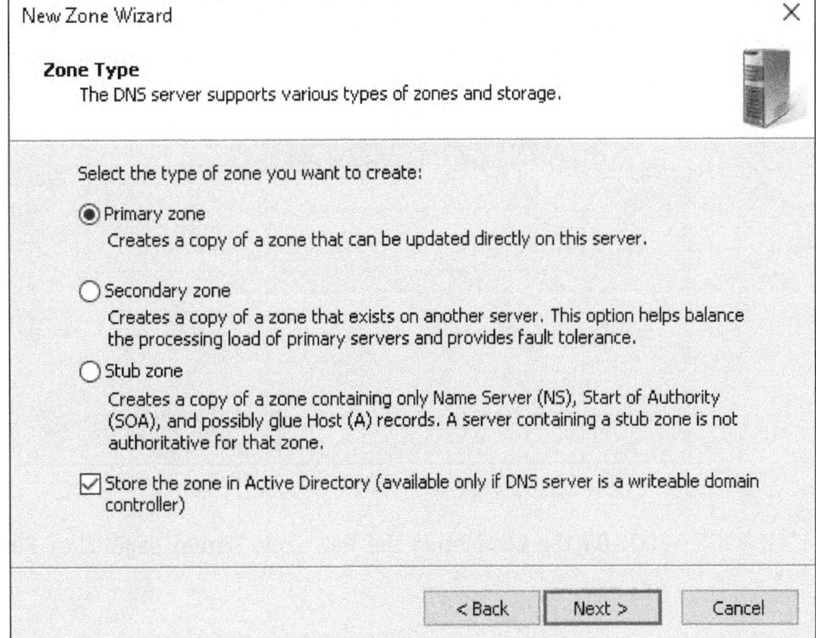

Figure 3-1
Selecting the zone type

8. On the Zone Name page, in the Zone name text box, enter the name of the domain, such as **contoso.com**, and then click **Next**.
9. On the Zone File page, ensure that the **Create a new file with this file name** radio button is selected and then click **Next**.
10. On the Dynamic Update page, ensure that the **Do not allow dynamic updates** radio button is selected and then click **Next**.
11. On the Completing the New Zone Wizard page, click **Finish**.

CREATE A STANDARD FORWARD LOOKUP SECONDARY ZONE

GET READY. To create a standard forward lookup secondary zone, perform the following steps.

1. Open **Server Manager**.
2. Click **Tools > DNS** to open the DNS Manager console.
3. If necessary, expand the DNS Manager console to a full-screen view.
4. Expand the server so that you can see the Forward Lookup Zones and Reverse Lookup Zones folders.
5. Right-click **Forward Lookup Zones** and then choose **New Zone**.
6. On the Welcome to the New Zone Wizard page, click **Next**.
7. On the Zone Type page, select the **Secondary zone** radio button and click **Next**.
8. On the Zone Name page, in the Zone name text box, enter the name of the domain, such as **subdomain.contoso.com**, and then click **Next**.
9. On the Master DNS Servers page (see Figure 3-2), type the IP address of the server that hosts the primary record and then press **Enter**. Click **Next**.

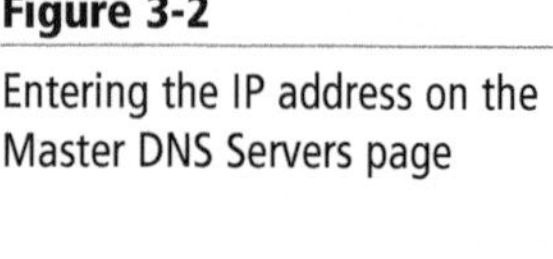

Figure 3-2

Entering the IP address on the Master DNS Servers page

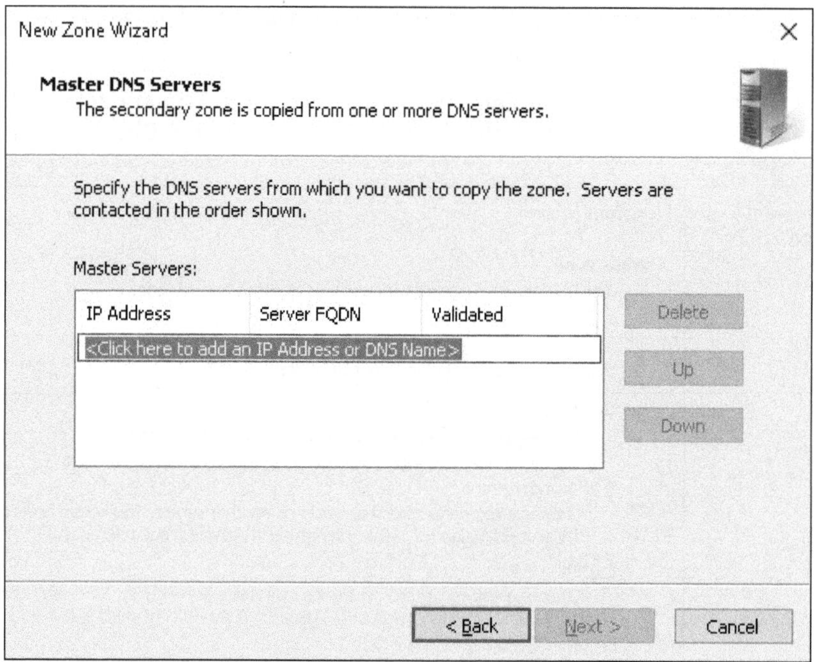

10. On the Completing the New Zone Wizard page, click **Finish**.

Because a forward lookup zone is used to look up IP addresses based on domain name and host names, you specify the name of the domain when you create the forward lookup zone. Because a reverse lookup zone is used to look up a host name based on an IP address, you have to specify the subnet that the zone covers. In the next two exercises, you create a standard reverse lookup primary zone and a standard reverse lookup secondary zone.

CREATE A STANDARD REVERSE LOOKUP PRIMARY ZONE FOR AN IPv4 SUBNET

GET READY. To create a standard reverse lookup primary zone for an IPv4 subnet, perform the following steps.

1. Open **Server Manager.**
2. Click **Tools > DNS** to open the DNS Manager console.
3. If necessary, expand the DNS Manager console to a full-screen view.
4. Expand the server so that you can see the Forward Lookup Zones and Reverse Lookup Zones folders.
5. Right-click **Reverse Lookup Zones** and choose **New Zone.**
6. On the Welcome to the New Zone Wizard page, click **Next.**
7. On the Zone Type page, select the **Primary zone** radio button. Deselect the **Store the zone in Active Directory** check box and click **Next.**
8. On the first Reverse Lookup Zone Name page, select **IPv4 Reverse Lookup Zone.** Click **Next.**
9. On the second Reverse Lookup Zone Name page, type in the subnet prefix. For example, if you have a subnet of 192.168.1.0 (with a subnet mask of 255.255.255.0), type **192.168.1** (see Figure 3-3). Click **Next.**

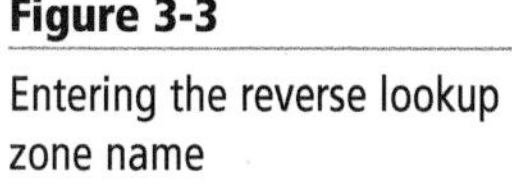

Figure 3-3

Entering the reverse lookup zone name

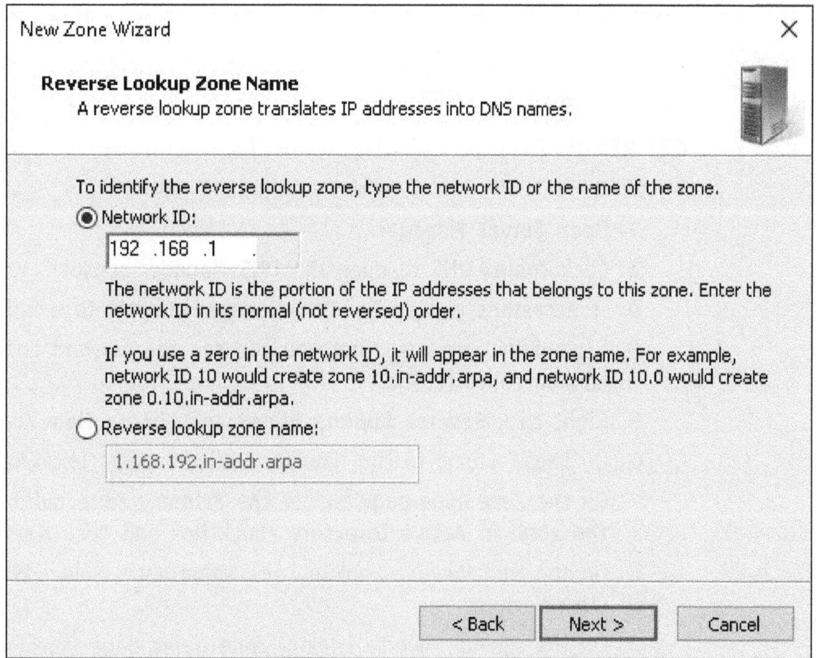

10. On the Zone File page (see Figure 3-4), accept the default value by clicking **Next.**

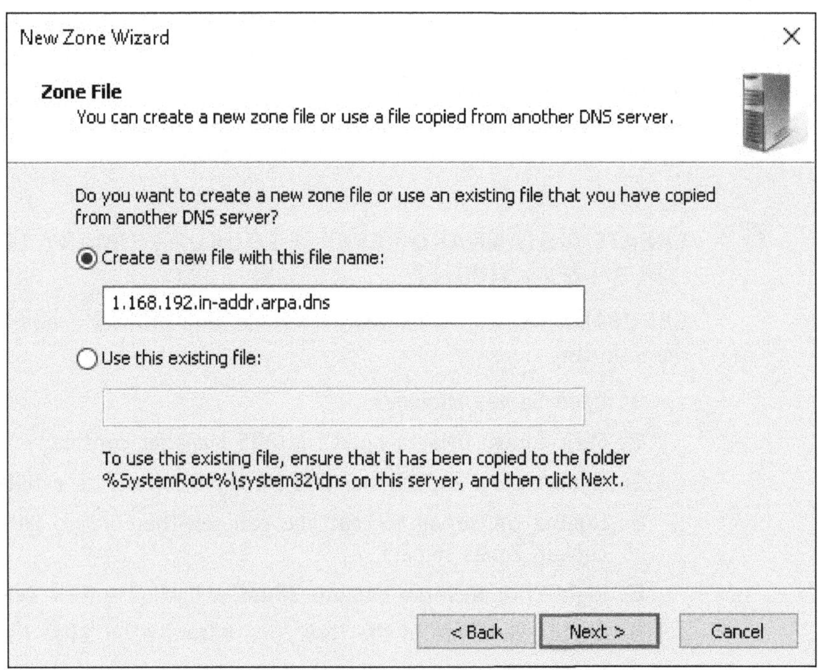

Figure 3-4
Specifying the Zone File page

11. On the Dynamic Update page, ensure that the **Do not allow dynamic updates** radio button is selected and then click **Next.**
12. On the Completing the New Zone Wizard page, click **Finish.**

When the zone is created, the zone will be defined in reverse notation. For example, if you create the 192.168.1 zone, it is stored as 1.168.192.

CREATE A STANDARD REVERSE LOOKUP PRIMARY ZONE FOR AN IPv6 SUBNET

GET READY. To create a standard reverse lookup primary zone for an IPv6 subnet, perform the following steps.

1. Open **Server Manager.**
2. Click **Tools > DNS** to open the DNS Manager console.
3. If necessary, expand the DNS Manager console to a full-screen view.
4. Expand the server so that you can see the Forward Lookup Zones and Reverse Lookup Zones folders.
5. Right-click **Reverse Lookup Zones** and choose **New Zone.**
6. On the Welcome to the New Zone Wizard page, click **Next.**
7. On the Zone Type page, select the **Primary zone** radio button. Deselect the **Store the zone in Active Directory** check box and click **Next.**
8. On the first Reverse Lookup Zone Name page, select **IPv6 Reverse Lookup Zone.** Click Next.
9. On the second Reverse Lookup Zone Name page (see Figure 3-5), type in the subnet prefix. End the prefix with::/<*number of -bits masked*>. For example, if you have a 64-bit prefix of 2001:0db8:ac10:fe01, type **2001:0db8:ac10:fe01::/64.** Click **Next.**

Figure 3-5

Specifying the reverse lookup zone name for IPv6

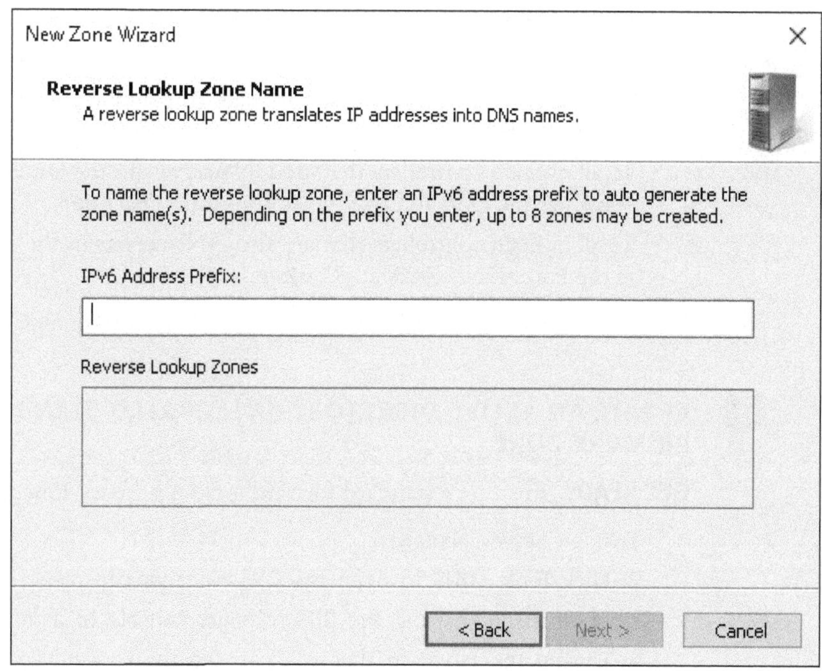

10. On the Zone File page, accept the default value by clicking **Next.**
11. On the Dynamic Update page, ensure that the **Do not allow dynamic updates** radio button is selected and then click **Next.**
12. On the Completing the New Zone Wizard page, click **Finish.**

Configuring Active Directory–Integrated Zones

Today, DNS can be stored in and replicated with Active Directory, as an ***Active Directory–integrated zone***. By using Active Directory–integrated zones, DNS follows a multimaster model, where each server enables all DNS servers to have authoritative read-write copies of the DNS zone. When a change is made on one DNS server, it is replicated to the other DNS servers.

CERTIFICATION READY
Configure Active Directory integration of primary zones
Objective 1.2

Microsoft recommends using Active Directory to store DNS and for good reason. The benefits include:

- **Fault tolerance:** Because each server is an authoritative read-write copy of DNS, you have the DNS information stored on multiple servers. In addition, you can update the DNS records from any DNS server.
- **Security:** Zone transfers are securely replicated as part of Active Directory. In addition, similar to Active Directory objects, you can manage who can access which records by using Discretionary Access Control Lists (DACLs). Finally, you can configure secure dynamic updates, which allow records to be updated only by the client that first registered the record.
- **Efficient replication:** Zone transfers are replicated more efficiently when using Active Directory, especially if the information has to be replicated over slow WAN links.

Three different replication scopes are available for Active Directory–integrated zones. They include:

- To all domain controllers in the domain (the only replication scope available in Windows 2000)
- To all domain controllers that are DNS servers in the local domain (default), which is known as the DomainDNSZones application partition
- To all domain controllers that are also DNS servers in the entire forest, which is known as the ForestDNSZones application

In the following exercise, you create an Active Directory–integrated zone.

CREATE AN ACTIVE DIRECTORY–INTEGRATED STANDARD FORWARD LOOKUP PRIMARY ZONE

GET READY. To create a standard forward lookup primary zone, perform the following steps.

1. Open **Server Manager.**
2. Click **Tools > DNS** to open the DNS Manager console.
3. If necessary, expand the DNS Manager console to a full-screen view.
4. Expand the server so that you can see the Forward Lookup Zones and Reverse Lookup Zones folders.
5. Right-click **Forward Lookup Zones** and choose **New Zone.**
6. On the Welcome to the New Zone Wizard page, click **Next.**
7. On the Zone Type page, select the **Primary zone** radio button.
8. Make sure the **Store the zone in Active Directory** check box is selected and click **Next.**
9. On the Active Directory Zone Replication Scope page, make sure that the **To all DNS servers running on domain controllers in this domain** radio button is selected (see Figure 3-6) and click **Next.**

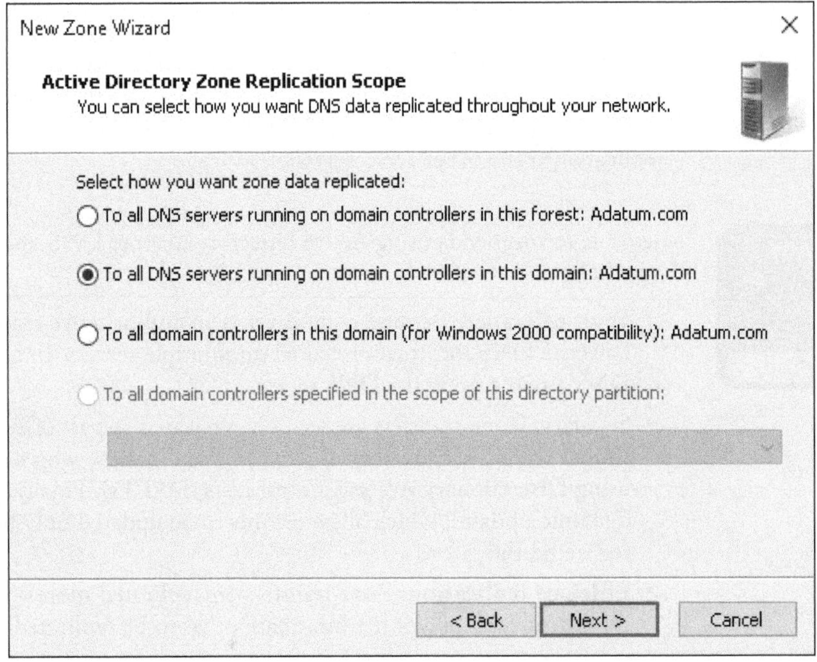

Figure 3-6
Specifying the Active Directory zone replication scope

10. On the Zone Name page, in the Zone name text box, enter the name of the domain, such as **contoso.com**, and then click **Next.**

11. On the Zone File page, ensure that the **Create a new file with this file name** radio button is selected and then click **Next.**
12. On the Dynamic Update page, ensure that the **Do not allow dynamic updates** radio button is selected and then click **Next.**
13. On the Completing the New Zone Wizard page, click **Finish.**

Configuring Zone Delegation

A DNS ***subdomain*** is a child domain that is part of a parent domain and has the same domain suffix as the parent domain. Subdomains allow you to assign unique names to be used by a particular department, subsidiary, function, or service within the organization. However, you can create a different zone for the subdomain, which can be stored on another server. As a result, you can increase performance for the DNS zones as the traffic is delegated to multiple servers.

CERTIFICATION READY
Configure delegation
Objective 1.2

Subdomains allow you to break up larger domains into smaller, more manageable domains. For example, if you have *contoso.com*, you can create a *sales* subdomain and a *support* subdomain. After doing so, you would have the parent domain *contoso.com* and two subdomains: *sales.contoso.com* and *support.contoso.com*.

In the following exercise, you learn how to create a subdomain.

CREATE A SUBDOMAIN

GET READY. To create a subdomain, perform the following steps.

1. Open **Server Manager.**
2. Click **Tools > DNS** to open the DNS Manager console.
3. If necessary, expand the DNS Manager console to a full-screen view.
4. Expand the server so that you can see the Forward Lookup Zones and Reverse Lookup Zones folders.
5. Right-click a forward lookup zone and choose **New Domain.** The New DNS Domain dialog box opens.
6. Type the name of the subdomain in the text box and then click **OK** to close the New DNS Domain dialog box.

When you delegate a DNS zone, you add subdomains within a domain, except the subdomain is stored in another zone. If the subdomain is placed on another server, you can distribute the DNS traffic among multiple servers, allowing for better performance.

DELEGATE A DNS DOMAIN

GET READY. To delegate a DNS domain on Windows Server 2016, perform the following steps.

1. Open **Server Manager.**
2. Click **Tools > DNS** to open the DNS Manager console.
3. If necessary, expand the DNS Manager console to a full-screen view.
4. Expand the server so that you can see the Forward Lookup Zones and Reverse Lookup Zones folders.
5. Right-click a forward lookup zone and choose **New Delegation.**
6. On the Welcome to the New Delegation Wizard page, click **Next.**
7. Type the name of the delegated subdomain in the delegated domain text box and then click **Next.**

8. On the Name Servers page (see Figure 3-7), click **Add** and enter the IP addresses (). Click **OK** to close the New Name Server record. Click **Next**.

Figure 3-7

Specifying name servers for the delegated zone

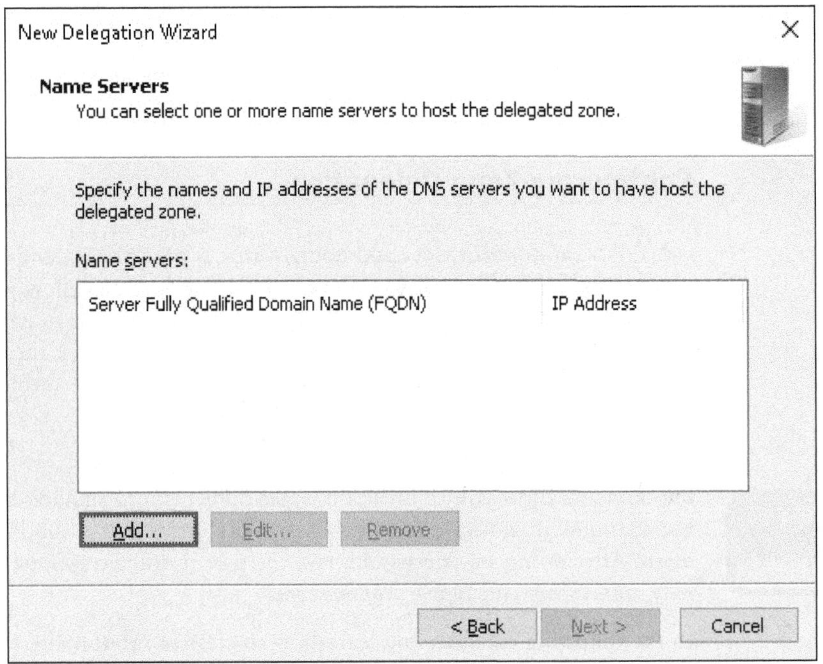

9. When the wizard is complete, click **Finish**.

Creating and Configuring Stub Zones

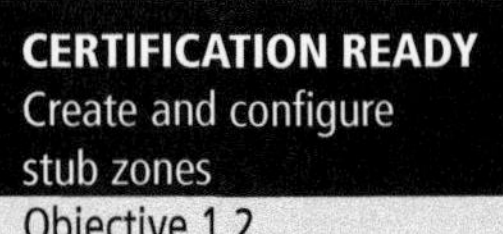

CERTIFICATION READY
Create and configure stub zones
Objective 1.2

A ***stub zone*** is a copy of a zone that contains only necessary resource records (Start of Authority [SOA], Name Server [NS], and Address/Host [A] records) in the master zone and acts as a pointer to the authoritative name server. The stub zone allows the server to forward queries to the name server that is authoritative for the master zone without going up to the root name servers and working its way down to the server. Although a stub zone can improve performance, it does not provide redundancy or load sharing.

In the following exercise, you learn how to create a stub zone.

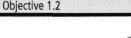

CREATE A STUB ZONE

GET READY. To create a stub zone, perform the following steps.

1. Open **Server Manager**.
2. Click **Tools > DNS** to open the DNS Manager console.
3. If necessary, expand the DNS Manager console to a full-screen view.
4. Expand the server so that you can see the Forward Lookup Zones and Reverse Lookup Zones folders.
5. Right-click a forward lookup zones and choose **New Delegation**.
6. On the Welcome to the New Zone Wizard page, click **Next**.
7. On the Zone Type page, select the **Stub zone** radio button and click **Next**.
8. If the Active Directory Zone Replication Scope page appears, click **Next**.
9. On the Zone Name page, in the Zone name text box, enter the domain name, such as **contoso.com**, and then click **Next**.

10. On the Master DNS Servers page, type the IP address of the server that hosts the primary record and press **Enter**. Click **Next**.
11. On the Completing the New Zone Wizard page, click **Finish**.

Configuring Conditional Forwarding

Conditional forwarding expands on the idea of forwarding, where you forward those queries to other DNS servers based on the DNS domain names in the query. Therefore, if you have a partner organization where you connect with a VPN tunnel, you can forward those requests to the partner's DNS when you try to access a network resource on the partner network. Of course, coordination is needed between the two organizations because firewalls have to be configured to allow DNS traffic to traverse the VPN tunnel.

The *conditional forwarder* setting consists of the following:

- The domain names for which the DNS server forwards queries
- One or more DNS server IP addresses for each domain name specified

CONFIGURE CONDITIONAL FORWARDERS

GET READY. To configure a DNS server to forward DNS queries to another DNS server, perform the following steps.

1. Open **Server Manager**.
2. Click **Tools > DNS** to open the DNS Manager console.
3. If necessary, expand the DNS Manager console to a full-screen view.
4. Expand the server so that you can see the Conditional Forwarders node.
5. Right-click the **Conditional Forwarders** node and choose **New Conditional Forwarder** (see Figure 3-8). The New Conditional Forwarder dialog box opens.

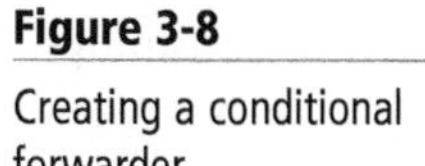

Figure 3-8

Creating a conditional forwarder

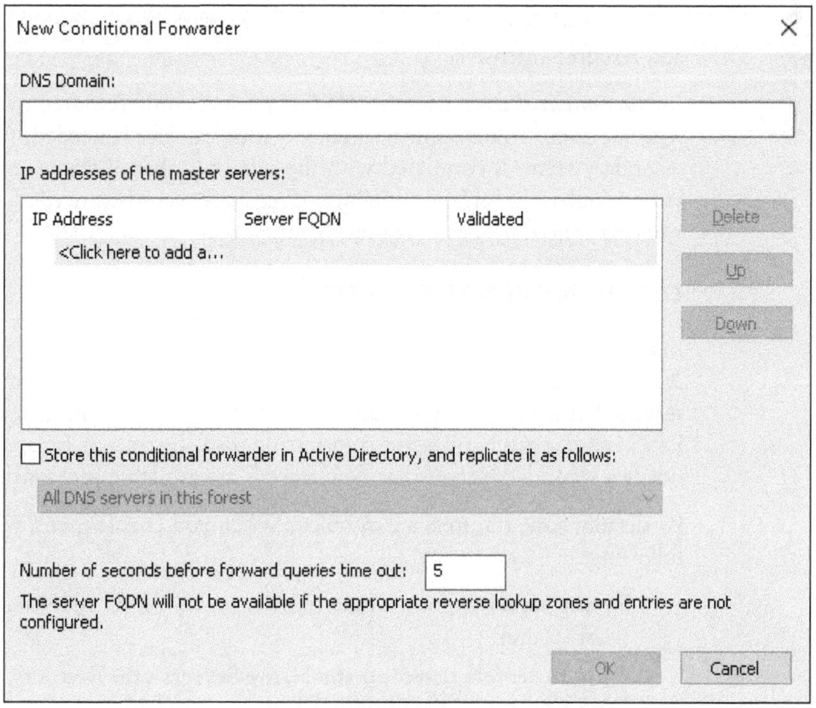

6. In the DNS Domain text box, type the name of the DNS domain included in DNS queries that you want to forward.
7. In the IP Address column, type the IP address of the DNS server that you want to forward to and then press **Enter**.
8. Click **OK** to close the New Conditional Forwarder dialog box. The zone displays under Conditional Forwarders.

Configuring Zone Transfers

Zone transfers are the complete or partial transfer of DNS data from a zone on a DNS server to another DNS server. After the initial zone transfer, the primary DNS server notifies the secondary DNS server that changes have occurred. The secondary servers then request for the records to be transferred and the changes are then replicated to all the secondary DNS servers using zone transfers.

The following events trigger a zone transfer:

- The initial transfer occurs when a secondary zone is created.
- The zone refresh interval expires.
- The DNS Server service is started at the secondary server.
- The master server notifies the secondary server that changes have been made to a zone.

There are three types of transfers:

- Full transfer
- Incremental transfer
- DNS Notify

UNDERSTANDING FULL AND INCREMENTAL TRANSFERS

A ***full zone transfer (AXFR)***, which copies the entire zone, is used when you first add a new DNS secondary server for an existing zone. With large zones, AXFRs can be time consuming and resource-intensive.

An ***incremental zone transfer (IXFR)*** retrieves only resource records that have changed within a zone. To determine whether a zone transfer is needed, the serial number on the secondary server is compared with the serial number of the primary server. If the primary server database is higher, a transfer of resource records is needed. Because the IXFR does only a partial zone transfer, it uses less bandwidth.

CONFIGURING NOTIFY SETTINGS

Instead of the secondary zone servers polling the primary server for serial numbers, the ***DNS Notify*** method allows the primary DNS server to use a "push" mechanism to notify secondary servers that it has been updated and that the resource records need to be transferred. The DNS is not a mechanism for transferring data. Instead, it is used with AXFR and IXFR to notify a secondary server that new records are available for transfer.

By default, zone transfers are disabled. When you enable them, you can choose one of the following:

- **To any server:** Allows a data transfer to any server that asks for a zone transfer (least secure)
- **Only to servers listed on the Name Servers tab:** Restricts zone transfers to secondary DNS servers as defined with NS resource records

- **Only to the following servers:** Restricts zone transfers to those servers specified in the accompanied list

In the following exercise, you enable and configure a zone transfer.

CONFIGURE ZONE TRANSFER SETTINGS

GET READY. To enable and configure zone transfer settings, perform the following steps.

1. Open **Server Manager.**
2. Click **Tools > DNS** to open the DNS Manager console.
3. If necessary, expand the DNS Manager console to a full-screen view.
4. Expand the server so that you can see the Forward Lookup Zones and Reverse Lookup Zones folders.
5. Right-click the forward or reverse lookup zone that you want to configure and choose **Properties.** The Properties dialog box opens.
6. Click the **Zone Transfers** tab (see Figure 3-9).

Figure 3-9

Viewing the Zone Transfers tab

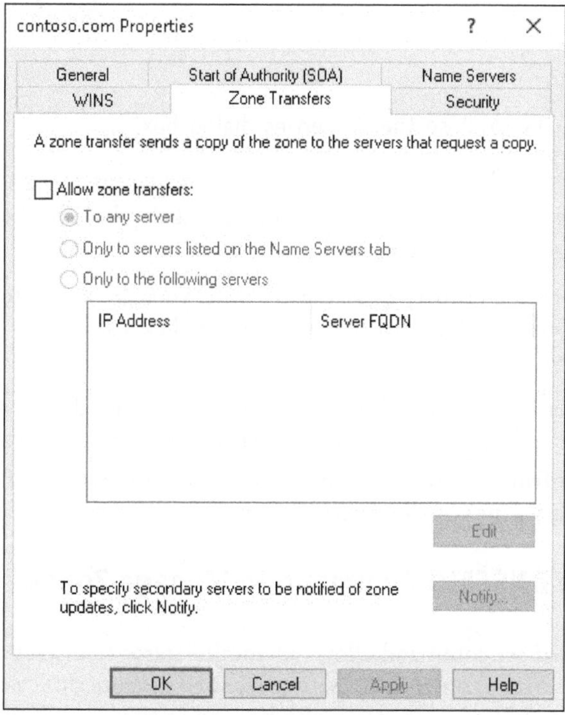

7. Select the **Allow zone transfers** check box.
8. Select the type of zone transfer:
   - To any server
   - Only to servers listed on the Name Servers tab
   - Only to the following servers

   If you select **Only to the following servers**, click the **Edit** button to specify the addresses to which you want to perform zone transfers.
9. To configure the Notify options, click the **Notify** button to display the Notify dialog box (see Figure 3-10). Then, select the **Servers listed on the Name Servers tab** radio button or select **The following servers** radio button and specify which servers you want to notify. Click **OK** to close the Notify dialog box.

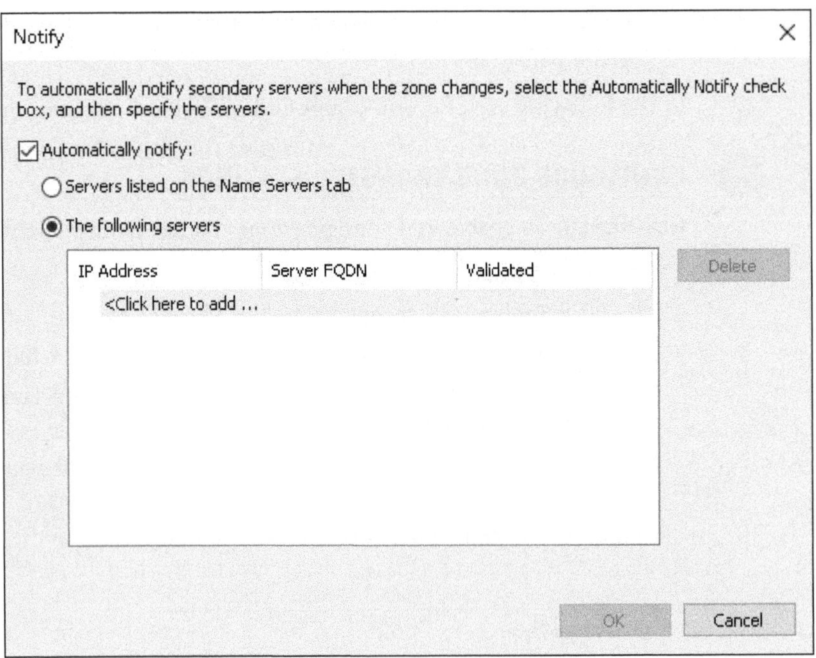

Figure 3-10

Configuring Notify options in the Notify dialog box

10. Click **OK** to close the Properties dialog box.

To configure notifications, open the Properties dialog box for the zone and click the Notify button on the Zone Transfers tab.

If you right-click a primary or secondary zone, you can choose to *Reload*, which reloads the secondary zone from local storage. If you right-click a secondary zone, you can also choose one of following options:

- **Transfer from Master:** Determines whether the local secondary zone serial number has expired and then pulls a zone transfer from the master server
- **Reload from Master:** Performs a zone transfer regardless of the serial number in the secondary zone's SOA resource records

Using the DNSCMD Command to Manage Zones

The ***dnscmd.exe*** command allows an administrator to display and change properties of the DNS servers, zones, and resource records. Because `dnscmd.exe` can be executed at the command prompt, it can also be used in script batch files to help automate the management and updates of existing DNS server configurations.

The `dnscmd.exe` command was introduced with Windows Server 2008. With it, you can perform the following:

- Create, delete, and view zones and records.
- Reset server and zone properties.
- Perform zone maintenance operations, such as updating the zone, reloading the zone, refreshing the zone, writing the zone back to a file or to Active Directory, and pausing or resuming the zone.
- Clear the cache.
- Stop and start the DNS service.
- View statistics.

For example, to view the zones on a DNS server called server1.contoso.com, execute the following command:

```
dnscmd server1.contoso.com /enumzones
```

To add an Active Directory–integrated primary zone called support.contoso.com on server1.contoso.com, execute the following command:

```
dnscmd server1.contoso.com /zoneadd support.contoso.com /dsprimary
```

To create a secondary zone called support.contoso.com on server1.contoso.com, execute the following command from the primary zone located at 10.0.0.2:

```
dnscmd server1.contoso.com /zoneadd support.contoso.com /secondary
10.0.0.2
```

To delete the secondary zone called support.contoso.com, execute the following command:

```
dnscmd server1.contoso.com /zonedelete support.contoso.com
```

To create an Active Directory conditional forwarder called lucernpublishing.com to the server2.lucernpublishing.com server while setting the replication scope to All DNS servers in this forest, execute the following command:

```
dnscmd server1.contoso.com /zoneadd lucernpublishing.com /dsforwarder
server2.lucernpublishing.com /forest
```

To force a secondary DNS zone for support.contoso.com to update from the master zone, execute the following command:

```
dnscmd server1.contoso.com /zonerefresh support.contoso.com
```

Using Windows PowerShell Cmdlets to Manage Zones

Over the last few years, Microsoft has emphasized using Windows PowerShell to perform many of the management tasks. As long as you have the DNS management tools installed on the system, you will be able to use the Windows PowerShell DNS cmdlets.

The following Windows PowerShell cmdlets are available to create DNS zones:

- **Add-DnsServerConditionalForwarderZone:** Adds a conditional forwarder
- **Add-DnsServerForwarder:** Adds a traditional forwarder
- **Add-DnsServerPrimaryZone:** Creates a primary zone
- **Add-DnsServerSecondaryZone:** Creates a secondary zone
- **Add-DnsServerStubZone:** Creates a stub zone
- **Add-DnsServerZoneDelegation:** Creates a zone delegation

For example, to create a primary zone (contoso.com), execute the following command:

```
Add-DnsServerPrimaryZone - Name "contoso.com" -ZoneFile "contoso1.com
.dns"
```

To create an Active Directory–integrated forward lookup zone called west01.contoso.com with forestwide replication scope, execute the following command:

```
Add-DnsServerPrimaryZone -Name "west.contoso.com" -ReplicationScope
"Forest" -PassThru
```

To create a DNS secondary zone, execute the following command:

```
Add-DnsServerSecondaryZone -Name "contoso.com" -ZoneFile "contoso
.com"- MasterServers 10.11.1.5
```

Configuring Secure Dynamic Updates

DNS supports ***dynamic updates***, where resource records for the clients are automatically created and updated at the host's primary DNS server. For Active Directory–integrated zones, these records are automatically replicated to the other DNS servers. However, because standard dynamic updates are insecure, Microsoft added secure dynamic updates.

CERTIFICATION READY
Configure secure dynamic updates
Objective 1.2

For years, Windows DNS has supported dynamic updates, where a DNS client host registers and dynamically updates the resource records with a DNS server. If a host's IP address changes, the resource record (particularly the A record) for the host is automatically updated, while the host utilizes the DHCP server to dynamically update its Pointer (PTR) resource record. Therefore, when a user or service needs to contact a client PC, it can look up the IP address of the host. With larger organizations, this becomes an essential feature, especially for clients that frequently move or change locations and use DHCP to automatically obtain an IP address. For dynamic DNS updates to succeed, the zone must be configured to accept dynamic updates, as shown in Figure 3-11.

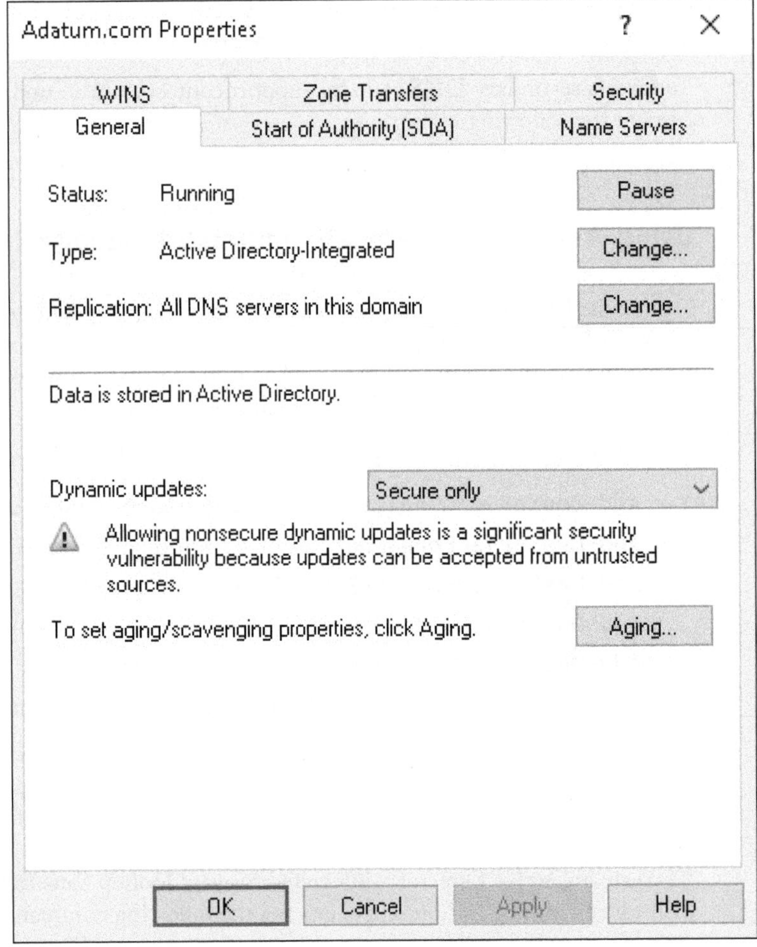

Figure 3-11
Enabling secure dynamic updates

Unfortunately, standard dynamic updates are not secure because any one can update a standard resource record. However, if you enable ***secure dynamic updates***, only updates from the same computer can update a registration for a resource record.

Configuring Zone Scavenging

By default, Windows updates its own resource record at startup time and every 24 hours after startup. This is to ensure the records are up to date and to help guard against accidental deletion. However, as some records become stale and are not removed or updated, the DNS database becomes outdated and provides some inaccurate information to clients. To help with stale data, you can configure zone scavenging to clean up the stale records. ***Aging*** in DNS is the process of using time stamps to track the age of dynamically registered resource records. ***Scavenging*** is the mechanism to remove stale resource records.

CERTIFICATION READY
Configure zone scavenging
Objective 1.2

Typically, stale DNS records occur when a computer is permanently removed from the network. Mobile users who abnormally disconnect from the network can also cause stale DNS records. To help manage stale records, Windows adds a time stamp to dynamically added resource records in primary zones where aging and scavenging are enabled. Manually added records are time-stamped with a value of 0, and they are automatically excluded from the aging and scavenging process.

To enable aging and scavenging, you must do the following:

- Resource records must either be dynamically added to zones or manually modified to be used in aging and scavenging operations.
- Scavenging and aging must be enabled both at the DNS server and on the zone.

Scavenging is disabled by default.

TAKE NOTE*

For the exam, be sure to remember that scavenging and aging must be enabled at the DNS server and on the zone.

DNS scavenging depends on the following two settings:

- **No-refresh interval:** The time between the most recent refresh of a record time stamp and the moment when the time stamp can be refreshed again. When scavenging is enabled, this is set to *7 days* by default.
- **Refresh interval:** The time between the earliest moment when a record time stamp can be refreshed and the earliest moment when the record can be scavenged. The refresh interval must be longer than the maximum record refresh period. When scavenging is enabled, this is set to *7 days* by default.

A DNS record becomes eligible for scavenging after both the no-refresh and refresh intervals have elapsed. If the default values are used, this is a total of 14 days.

WARNING!

Be careful when enabling scavenging because it can accidentally remove records that you want to keep. As a result, users cannot resolve certain DNS queries, making some network services unavailable.

ENABLE AGING/SCAVENGING AT THE SERVER

GET READY. To enable aging/scavenging at the server, perform the following steps.

1. Open **Server Manager**.
2. Click **Tools > DNS** to open the DNS Manager console.
3. If necessary, expand the DNS Manager console to a full-screen view.

4. Right-click the **DNS server** and choose **Set Aging/Scavenging for all Zones**. The Server Aging/Scavenging Properties dialog box opens (see Figure 3-12).

Figure 3-12

Opening the Server Aging/Scavenging Properties dialog box

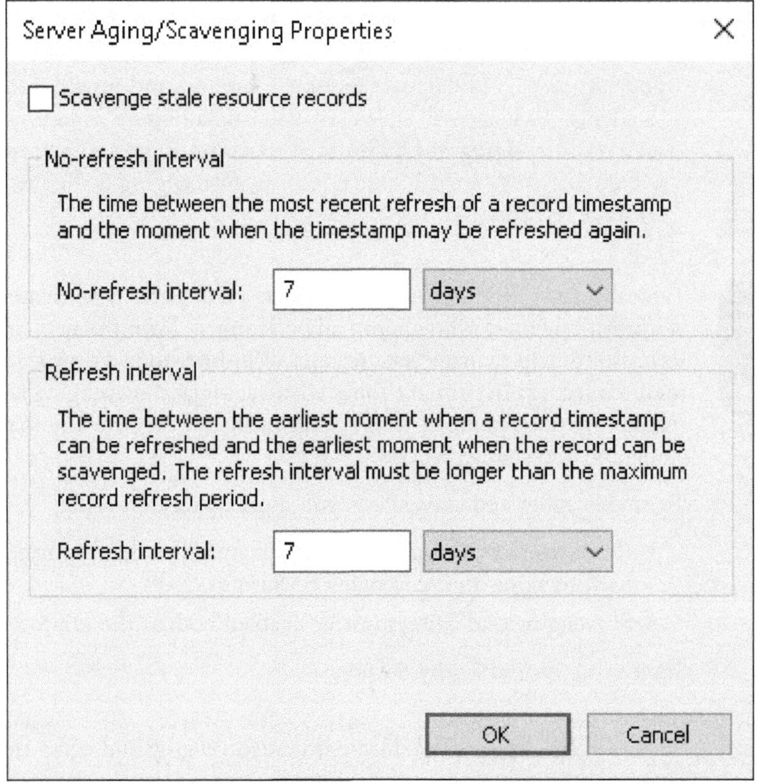

5. Click the **Scavenge stale resource records** check box.
6. Modify the **No-refresh interval** and **Refresh interval** settings as needed.
7. Click **OK** to close the Server Aging/Scavenging Properties dialog box.
8. If you want the aging/scavenging settings to apply to all existing Active Directory–integrated zones, select the **Apply these settings to the existing Active Directory-integrated zones** option. Click **OK** to close the Server Aging/Scavenging Confirmation dialog box.

TAKE NOTE*

It is best that you enable scavenging on only one DNS server. This gives you better control of the aging/scavenging settings and more control when scavenging occurs and how often.

ENABLE AGING/SCAVENGING AT THE ZONE

GET READY. To enable aging/scavenging at the zone, perform the following steps.

1. Open **Server Manager.**
2. Click **Tools > DNS** to open the DNS Manager console.
3. If necessary, expand the DNS Manager console to a full-screen view.
4. Expand the server so that you can display the Forward Lookup Zones and Reverse Lookup Zones folders.
5. Right-click the zone and choose **Properties.**
6. On the General tab, click the **Aging** button. The Zone Aging/Scavenging Properties dialog box opens.

7. Click the **Scavenge stale resource records** check box.
8. Modify the **No-refresh interval** and **Refresh interval** settings as needed.
9. Click **OK** to close the Server Aging/Scavenging Properties dialog box.
10. When you are prompted to apply aging/scavenging settings to the Standard Primary zone, click **Yes.**
11. Click **OK** to close the Properties dialog box.

Configuring DNS Record Types

A ***DNS zone database*** is made up of a collection of resource records, which are used to answer DNS queries. Each resource record (RR) specifies information about a particular object. Each record has a type, an expiration time limit, and some type-specific data.

On an organization's network, many of the resource records are automatically created. For example, the clients or the DHCP servers create the Host and Pointer (PTR) records. When you install a DNS server, NS records are usually created. When you install domain controllers, Service Location (SRV) records are created.

Creating and Configuring DNS Resource Records

When you create a user account, certain properties define the user account, such as first name, last name, and logon name. When you define a printer in Active Directory, you define a name of the printer and a location. A printer does not have a first name or a last name. Just as you have different types of objects in Active Directory, you also have different types of resource records in DNS, with different fields.

CERTIFICATION READY
Create and configure DNS resource records (RR), including A, AAAA, PTR, SOA, NS, SRV, CNAME, and MX records
Objective 1.2

When you create a new zone, two types of records are automatically created:

- ***Start of Authority (SOA) record***: Specifies authoritative information about a DNS zone, including the primary name server, the email of the domain administrator, the domain serial number, and the expiration and reload timers of the zone
- ***Name Server (NS) record***: Specifies an authoritative name server for the host

You have to add additional resource records as needed. Figure 3-13 shows a zone with common resource records. The most common resource records are:

- ***Host (A and AAAA) record***: Maps a domain/host name to an IP address
- ***Canonical Name (CNAME) record***: Sometimes referred to as an Alias, maps an alias DNS domain name to another primary or canonical name
- ***Pointer (PTR) record***: Maps an IP address to a domain/host name
- ***Mail Exchanger (MX) record***: Maps a DNS domain name to the name of a computer that exchanges or forwards email for the domain
- ***Service Location (SRV) record***: Maps a DNS domain name to a specified list of host computers that offer a specific type of service, such as Active Directory domain controllers

The PTR records are in the reverse lookup zone and all of the other record types are in the forward lookup zone.

Figure 3-13

Viewing the zone with common resource records

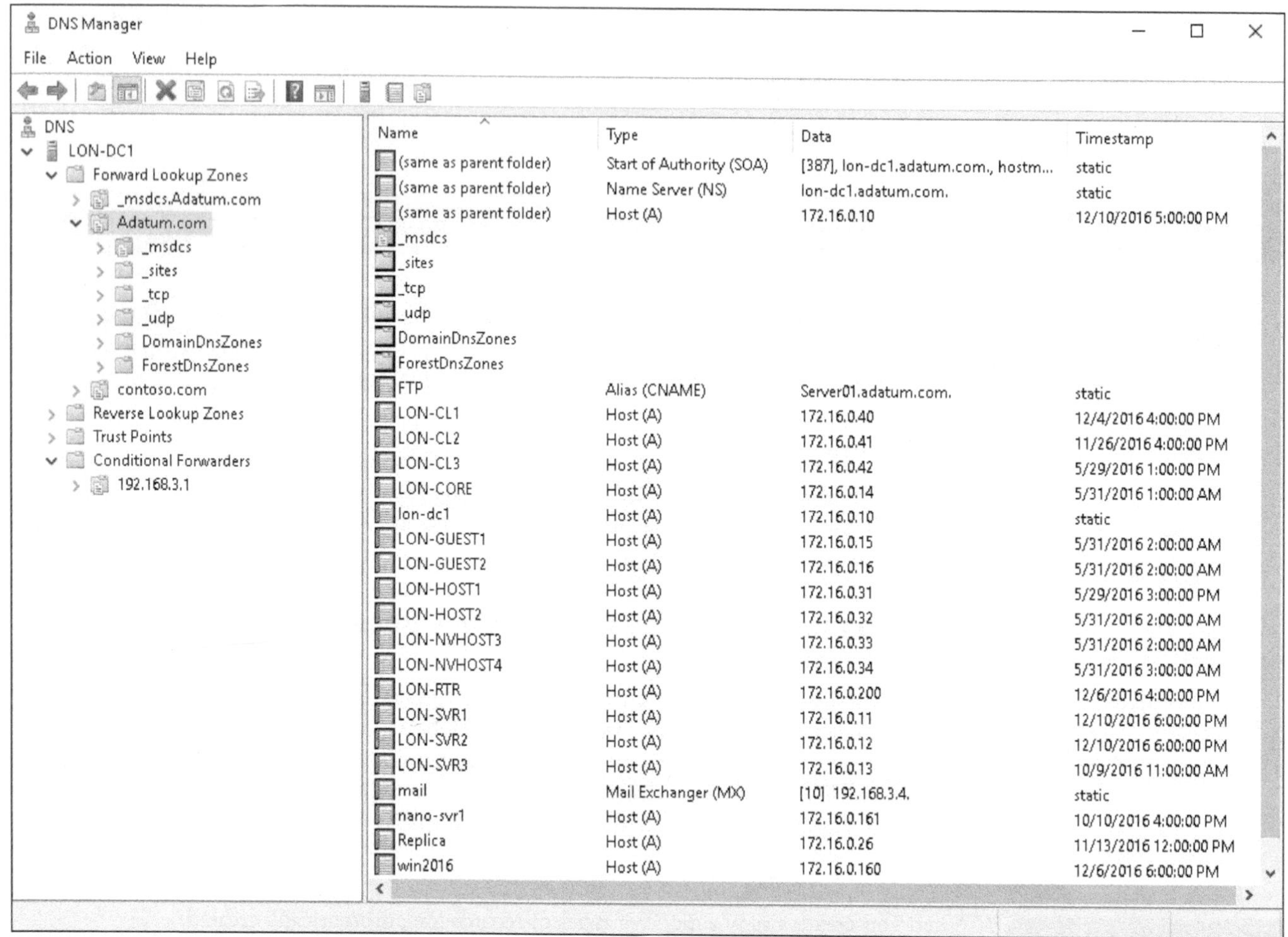

START OF AUTHORITY (SOA) RECORDS

The SOA record specifies authoritative information about the zone. Therefore, there is only one SOA record for a zone. It includes the following fields:

TAKE NOTE* The Properties dialog box labels these values differently, uses different units, and does not show the serial number.

- **Authoritative server:** Contains the name of the primary DNS server authoritative for the zone.
- **Responsible person:** Shows the email address of the administrator who is responsible for the zone. Instead of using the at (@) symbol, it uses a period (.).
- **Serial number:** Shows the version or how many times the zone has been updated. As explained previously, it is used to determine whether the zone's secondary server needs to initiate a zone transfer with the master server. If the serial number of the master server is higher, the secondary server initiates a zone transfer.
- **Refresh shows:** Determines how often the secondary server for the zone checks to see whether the zone data is changed.

- **Retry:** After sending a zone transfer request, determines how long (in seconds) the zone's secondary server waits before sending another request.
- **Expire:** After a zone transfer, determines how long (in seconds) the zone's secondary server continues to respond to zone queries before discarding its own zone as invalid.
- **Minimum TTL:** Specifies a default Time to Live (TTL) value, which defines the default time. A resource record remains in a DNS cache after a DNS query has retrieved a record. If a resource record has its own TTL value, the TTL value of the resource record is used instead of the TTL defined in the SOA record.

Figure 3-14 shows the SOA resource record.

Figure 3-14

Viewing the SOA resource record

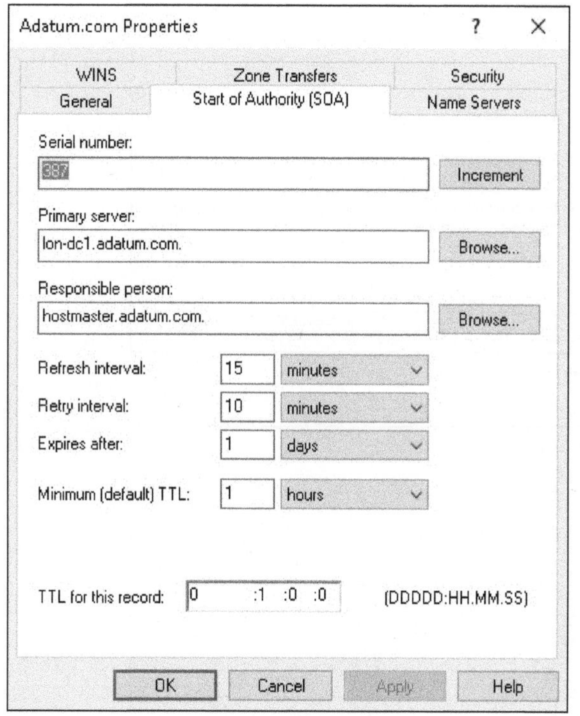

NAME SERVER (NS) RECORDS

The Name Server (NS) resource record identifies a DNS server that is authoritative for a zone, including the primary and secondary copies of the DNS zone. Because a zone can be hosted on multiple servers, there is a single record for each DNS server hosting the zone. The Windows Server DNS Server service automatically creates the first NS record for a zone when the zone is created. Figure 3-15 shows the NS resource record.

HOST (A AND AAAA) RECORDS

The most common resource records found in DNS are the Host (A and AAAA) records. The A stands for address. The A record maps a domain/host name to an IPv4 address; the AAAA record maps a domain/host name to an IPv6 address.

For example, the following A resource record is located in the zone *server1.sales.contoso.com* and maps the fully qualified domain name (FQDN) of a server to an IP address of 192.168.3.41:

```
LON-CL1.Adatum.com. IN A 172.16.0.40
```

Figure 3-16 shows the Host resource record.

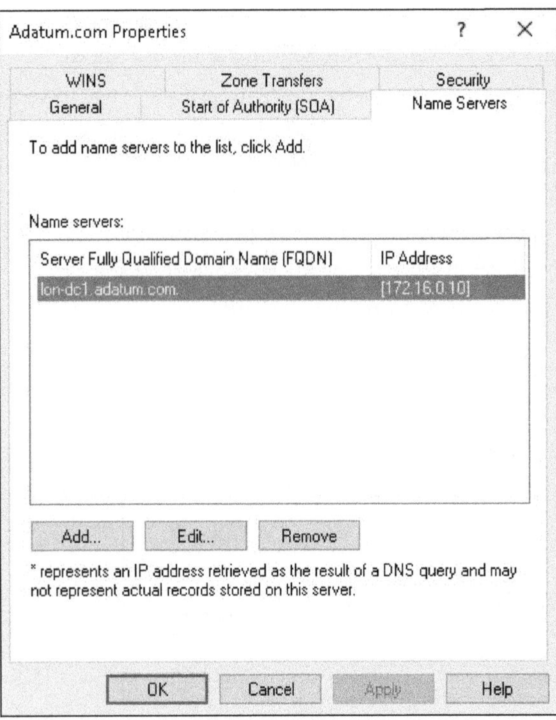

Figure 3-15
Viewing the NS resource record

Figure 3-16
Viewing the Host resource record

CANONICAL NAME (CNAME) RECORDS

The Canonical Name (CNAME) resource record is an alias for a host name. It is used to hide the implementation details of your network from the clients that connect to it, particularly if you need to make changes in the future.

For example, instead of creating a Host record for www, you can create a CNAME that specifies the web server that hosts the www websites for the domain. If you need to change servers, you just point the CNAME to another server's Host record. Of course, you need to have Host records that specify the IP address. Figure 3-17 shows the CNAME resource record.

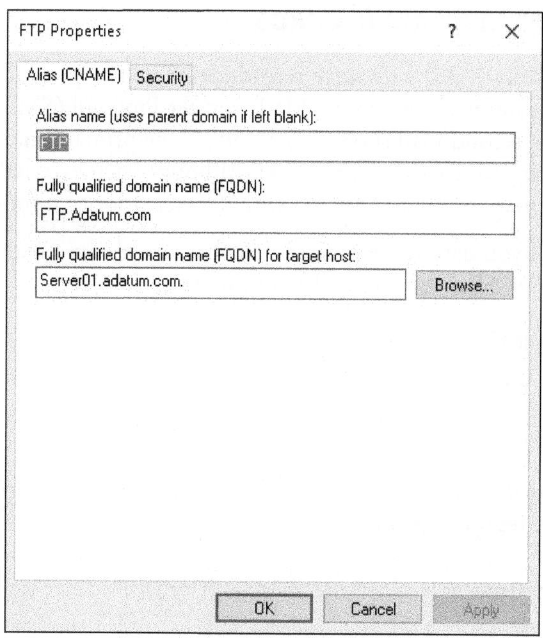

Figure 3-17

Viewing the CNAME resource record

POINTER (PTR) RECORDS

The Pointer records (PTR) are opposite to Host records. They resolve host names from an IP address. Different from the Host record, the IP address is written in reverse. For example, the IP address 192.168.3.41 that points to server1.sales.contoso is recorded as:

```
2.1.168.192.in-addr.arpa. IN PTR server2.adatum.com.
```

Figure 3-18 shows the PTR resource record.

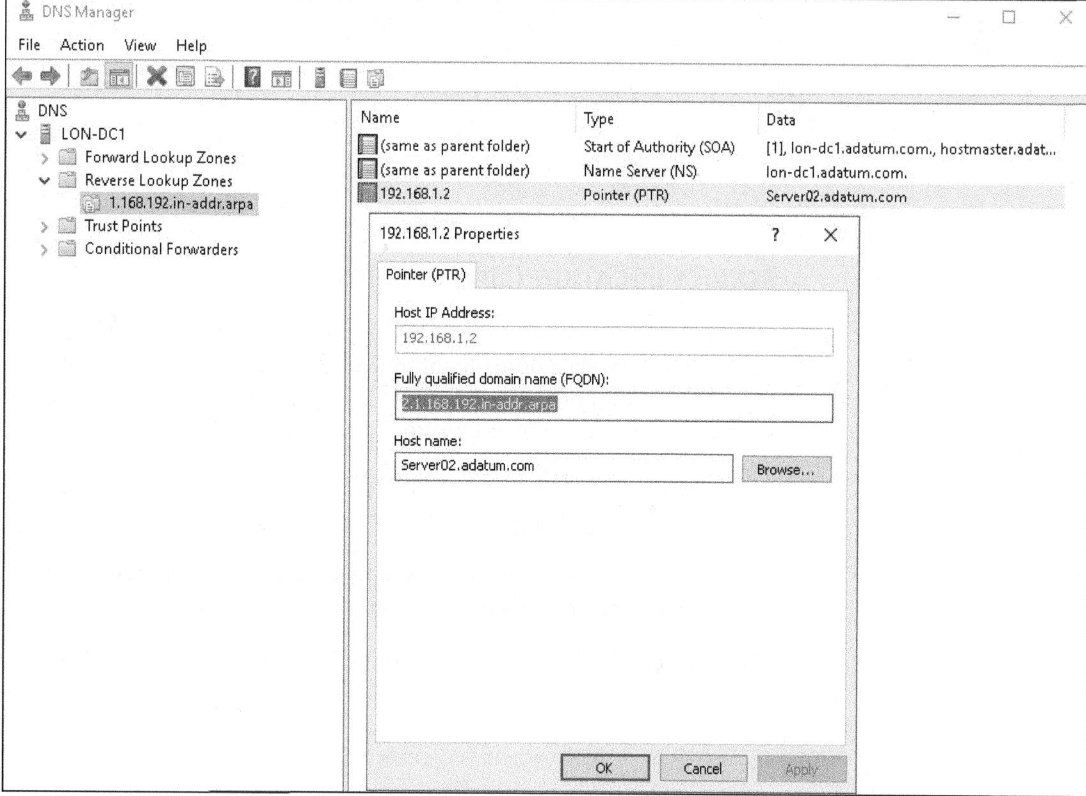

Figure 3-18

Viewing the PTR resource record

MAIL EXCHANGER (MX) RECORDS

The Mail Exchanger (MX) resource record specifies an organization's mail server, service, or device that receives mail via Simple Mail Transfer Protocol (SMTP). For fault tolerance, you can designate a second mail server. Therefore, if the primary mail server is not available, the email can be sent to the secondary server. Although each external mail server requires an MX record, the primary server is designed with a lower priority number.

For example, if you have three mail servers that can receive email over the Internet, you would have three MX records for the contoso.com domain:

```
@ IN MX 10 mail.adatum.com.
@ IN MX 10 mail2.adatum.com.
@ IN MX 10 mail3.adatum.com.
```

The primary mail server is the first one because it has a lower priority number. Figure 3-19 shows the MX resource record

Figure 3-19

Viewing the MX resource record

SERVICE LOCATION (SRV) RECORDS

SRV resource records are used to find specific network services. For example, when you install Active Directory via a domain controller, SRV records are automatically added to the DNS zone. If users cannot connect to DNS services or the SRV records are not in the zone, users cannot log on to the Active Directory domain.

The format for an SRV record is as follows:

```
Service_Protocol.Name [TTL] Class SRV Priority Weight Port Target
```

For example, to log on with Lightweight Directory Access Protocol (LDAP), you could have the following SRV records for two domain controllers:

```
_ldap._tcp.dc._msdcs.contoso.com SRV 100 0 389dc1.contoso.com.
```

```
_ldap._tcp.dc._msdcs.contoso.com SRV 100 0 389dc2.contoso.com.
```

To find global catalogs, you would use:

```
_ldap._gc._tcp.adatum.com. SRV 100 0 3268 LON-DC.adatum.com.
```

Because these examples do not specify a TTL, the DNS client uses the minimum TTL specified in the SOA resource record. Figure 3-20 shows the SRV resource record for a domain controller, specifically to find the global catalog.

Figure 3-20
Viewing the SRV record

TAKE NOTE* With SRV records, for the domain to be added to a DNS zone, the zone must allow dynamic updates.

UNKNOWN RECORDS

CERTIFICATION READY
Configure unknown record support
Objective 1.2

An ***Unknown Record*** is a resource record whose RDATA format is not known to the DNS server. Starting with Windows Server 2016, you can add unsupported record types to Windows DNS, so that DNS can still access these records although it does not understand the format of the data. When you create an unknown record, you need to include the `-RecordData` parameter, which includes the System string of necessary information for the resource record.

Configuring Resource Record Options

Managing resources is easy with Windows servers because the DNS Manager console provides a GUI interface.

Before you can create resource records, you need to first create the appropriate forward lookup zones and reverse lookup zones.

CREATE A HOST RECORD

GET READY. To create a Host record, perform the following steps.

1. Open **Server Manager.**
2. Click **Tools > DNS** to open the DNS Manager console.
3. If necessary, expand the DNS Manager console to a full-screen view.
4. Expand the server to display the Forward Lookup Zones and Reverse Lookup Zones folders.
5. Right-click the zone that you want to create a Host resource record for and choose **New Host (A or AAAA)**. The New Host dialog box opens.
6. In the Name text box, type the name of the host.
7. In the IP address text field, type the IP address (IPv4 or IPv6).
8. If you want to also create a PTR record, click the **Create associated pointer (PTR) record** option.
9. Click **Add Host.**
10. If you need to create additional Host records, add the appropriate host names and IP addresses. If you do not want to create more, click the **Done** button.

If the reverse lookup zone does not exist to store the PTR record, a message appears warning that the associated Pointer (PTR) record cannot be created.

To change a resource record, you just double-click the resource record to display the Properties dialog box, and then you make the appropriate changes. Of course, when you create resource records or change resource records, it takes time to replicate the resource records to the other DNS servers for the domain.

CERTIFICATION READY
Configure record options, including Time to Live (TTL) and weight
Objective 1.2

By opening the View menu and selecting the Advanced option in the DNS Manager console, administrators can see additional options when managing and configuring the resource records, including the TTL for the resource record. To view the TTL settings for individual resource records, you need to use the DNS Manager console in Advanced mode.

MODIFY THE TTL VALUE FOR A RESOURCE RECORD

GET READY. To modify the Time to Live (TTL) value for a resource record, perform the following steps.

1. Open **Server Manager.**
2. Click **Tools > DNS** to open the DNS Manager console.
3. If necessary, expand the DNS Manager console to a full-screen view.
4. Expand the server to display the Forward Lookup Zones and Reverse Lookup Zones folders.
5. To view additional options, click **View > Advanced.**
6. To modify a record, double-click a resource record. The Properties dialog box opens, as shown in Figure 3-21.
7. Type the TTL using the DDDDD:HH.MM.SS format, where DDDDD is days, HH is hours, MM is minutes, and SS is seconds.
8. Click **OK** to close the Properties dialog box.

As mentioned before, many records can have multiple records assigned with the same name. For example, you can have multiple A or AAAA records that have the same name or you can have multiple MX records for the same domain. With A and AAAA records, you don't define a weight to each record. Instead, each record is equal. With MX records, you must define a weight or priority (lowest number takes priority), so that it knows which SMTP server an email should be sent to first. If that one is not available, it tries the second SMTP server listed with the next lowest priority.

Figure 3-21

Viewing the record time stamps

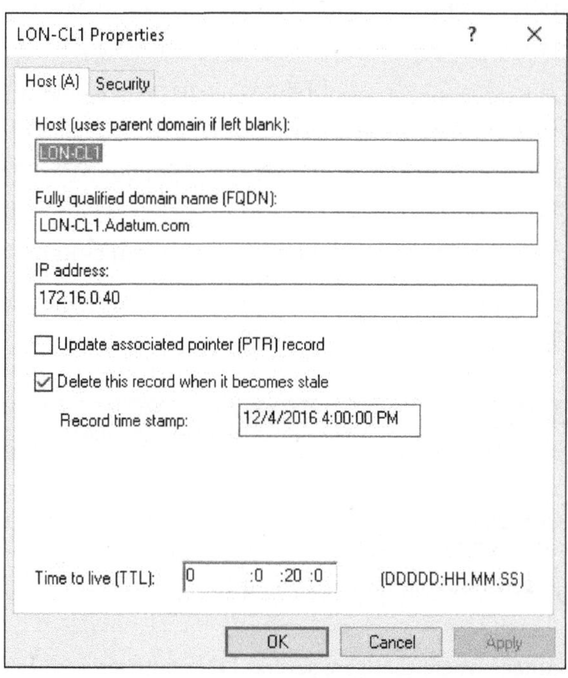

Using the DNSCMD and Windows Powershell Command to Manage Resource Records

THE BOTTOM LINE

In the previous lesson, you were introduced to the `dnscmd` command to create zones. You can also use the `dnscmd` command to manage resource records.

To add a Host record for webserver with an IPv4 address of 10.0.0.5 on server1.contoso.com, execute the following command:

```
dnscmd server1.contoso.com /recordadd contoso.com webserver A 10.0.0.5
```

To delete the same record, execute the following command:

```
dnscmd server1.contoso.com /recorddelete contoso.com webserver a
```

Because you are deleting a record, you are prompted to confirm whether you want to delete the record. If you do not want to be prompted, you can add the `/f` parameter:

```
dnscmd server1.contoso.com /recorddelete contoso.com webserver a /f
```

MORE INFORMATION

For more information about the `dnscmd` command, execute the `dnscmd.exe /?` command to show the available options. In addition, you can perform a search for *dnscmd* at the TechNet website.

You can also create Host records by using the following Windows PowerShell cmdlets for DNS:

- **Add-DnsServerResourceRecord:** Creates any resource record, specified by type
- **Add-DnsServerResourceRecordA:** Creates a type A resource record
- **Add-DnsServerResourceRecordCNAME:** Creates a CNAME alias resource record
- **Add-DnsServerResourceRecordMX:** Creates an MX resource record
- **Add-DnsServerResourceRecordPtr:** Creates a PTR resource record

For example, to create a Host record for Server01, you would use the Add-DNSServerResourceRecordA cmdlet:

```
Add-DNSServerResourceRecordA -Name "Server01" -ZoneName "Adatum.com" -
IPv4Address "172.16.0.24"
```

Alternatively, you can use the Add-DnsServerResourceRecord cmdlet:

```
Add-DnsServerResourceRecord -ZoneName "contoso.com" -A -Name Server01
-IPv4Address 172.16.0.24 -CreatePtr
```

Configuring a Globalnames Zone

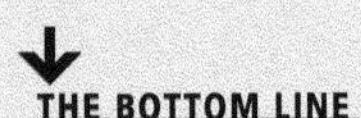

Windows Server 2016 DNS provides support for single-label names without the need for NETBIOS or WINS. This allows a large multi-DNS environment to support a single name, such as addressbook, rather than an FQDN, such as addressbook.adatum.com.

CERTIFICATION READY
Configure a GlobalNames zone
Objective 1.2

In an environment where there are several DNS suffixes such as contoso.com, adatum.com, and fabrikam.net, it is necessary to manually create a ***GlobalNames*** zone within DNS to allow a single-label name to be resolved.

As an example, the company address book is accessed throughout the enterprise by entering *addressbook* into an Internet Explorer address bar.

Without the use of a GlobalNames zone, in this scenario, the name would not be resolved. In an environment with a single DNS suffix such as contoso.com, the suffix would be appended automatically and the name would be resolved.

The only other method for achieving this would be the use of a Windows Internet Naming Service (WINS) server. This is a deprecated technology and GlobalNames zone is now the preferred method for achieving single-label name resolution.

Windows Server 2016 provides built-in support for a GlobalNames zone; however, it must be manually configured and enabled in several steps, as shown in the following section.

CONFIGURE A GLOBALNAMES ZONE

GET READY. Log on with administrative privileges to the computer where you installed the DNS Server role. Ensure that the Adatum.com ADI zone is present.

Then, to configure a GlobalNames zone, perform the following steps.

1. From the start screen, type **PowerShell.** Then right-click **Windows PowerShell** and choose **Run As administrator.**
2. In the Windows PowerShell window, execute the following command:

   Set-DnsServerGlobalNameZone -Enable $True -PassThru
3. Close the command window and repeat Steps 1 and 2 on every DNS server in the forest.
4. Open **Server Manager** and click **Tools>DNS.** The DNS Manager console opens.

5. Expand the **DNS server** by clicking the **arrow** to the left of the server name.
6. Right-click the **LON-DC1** server and choose **New Zone** to start the New Zone Wizard. Click **Next** four times. This creates a new primary forward lookup zone replicated to all DNS servers in the domain.
7. Enter the name **GlobalNames** (this is not case sensitive) and then click **Next.**
8. Select **Do not allow dynamic updates.** Because all entries in this zone will be manually created, this is not required and would be a security loophole. Click **Next** and then click **Finish.** The GlobalNames will appear in the DNS Manager console, as shown in Figure 3-22.

Figure 3-22

Displaying GlobalNames zone—DNS Manager

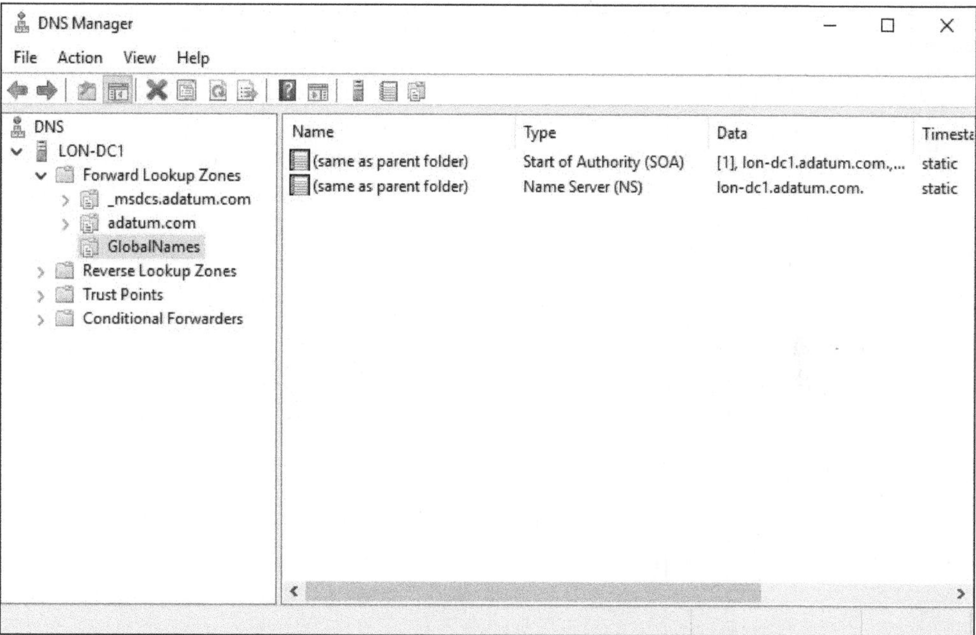

To access the addressbook, create a CNAME record in the GlobalNames zone that points to any records that already exist in the other zones on the forest DNS servers.

In this instance, a single CNAME record of addressbook in the zone pointing to addressbook .adatum.com would allow any client to resolve this FQDN by entering the label addressbook.

Analyzing Zone-Level Statistics and Implementing DNS Performance Tuning

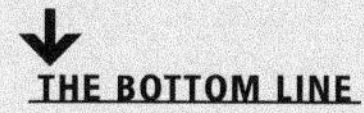

To monitor DNS performance, you can use Performance Monitor to view the performance of the DNS server and the name resolution mechanism. Besides looking at the normal processor memory, disk, and network performance metrics, Performance Monitor has numerous counters to monitor various aspects of DNS. By understanding the performance counters, you can determine if you have any bottlenecks, and you can determine if you have to add additional resources to the DNS server or reduce the load of the DNS server.

CERTIFICATION READY
Analyze zone-level statistics
Objective 1.2

Performance Monitor is an MMC snap-in that provides tools for analyzing system performance. It is included in the Computer Management console and it can be opened as a stand-alone console from Administrative Tools. It can also be started by executing the `perfmon` command. From a single console, you can monitor application and hardware performance

CERTIFICATION READY
Implement DNS performance tuning
Objective 1.2

in real time, specify which data you want to collect in logs, define thresholds for alerts and automatic actions, generate reports, and view past performance data in a variety of ways.

Performance Monitor (see Figure 3-23) provides a visual display of built-in Windows performance counters, either in real time or as a way to review historical data.

Figure 3-23

Viewing Performance Monitor

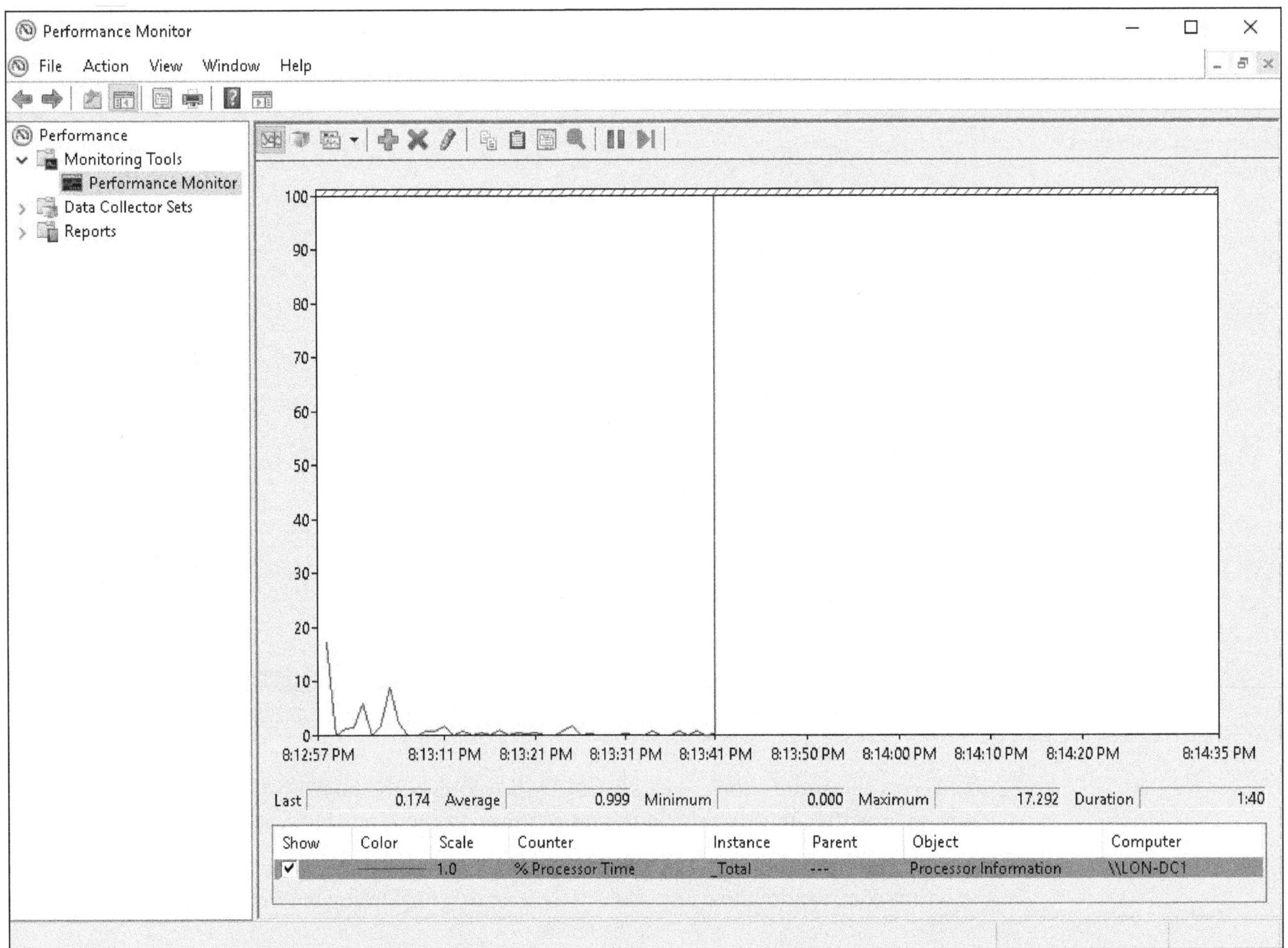

You can add performance counters to Performance Monitor by right-clicking the main pane and choosing Add Counters. Another way to add performance counters is to create and use custom Data Collector Sets. Figure 3-24 shows the Add Counters dialog box with the Show description check box already selected.

Some of these performance counters include the following:

- **Dynamic Update Received/sec:** Shows the average number of dynamic update requests received by the DNS server in each second
- **Recursive Queries/sec:** Shows the average number of recursive queries received by the DNS server in each second
- **Recursive Query Failure/sec:** Shows the average number of recursive query failures in each second
- **Secure Update Received/sec:** Shows the average number of secure update requests received by the DNS server in each second
- **TCP Query Received/sec:** Shows the average number of TCP queries received by the DNS server in each second

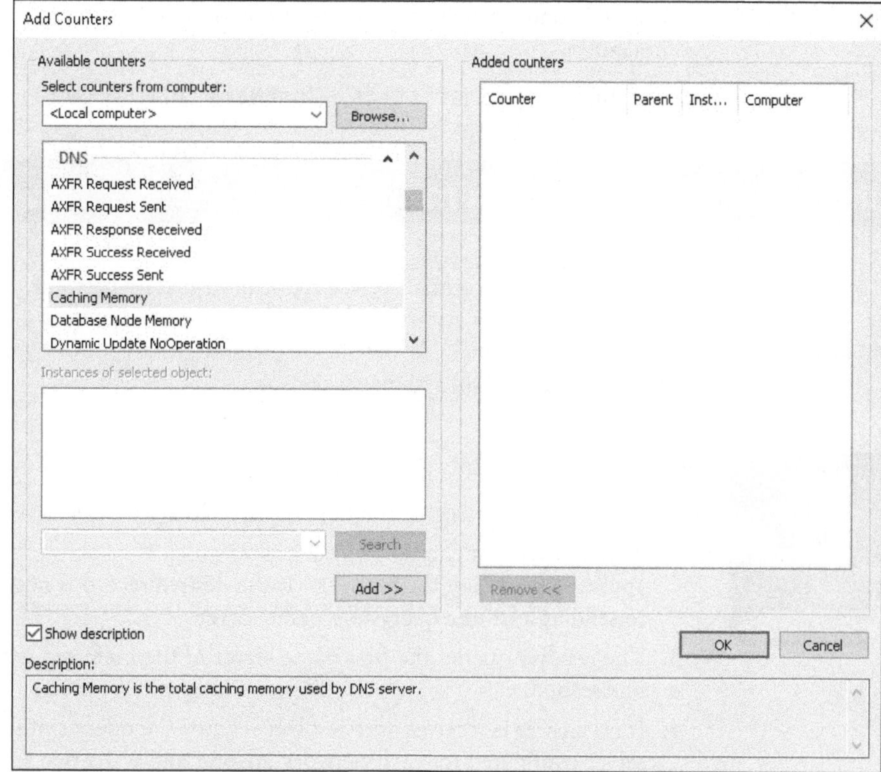

Figure 3-24

Adding counters to Performance Monitor

- **TCP Response Sent/sec:** Shows the average number of TCP responses sent by the DNS server in each second
- **Total Query Received/sec:** Shows the average number of queries received by the DNS server in each second
- **Total Response Sent/sec:** Shows the average number of responses sent by the DNS server in each second
- **UDP Query Received/sec:** Shows the average number of UDP queries received by the DNS server in each second
- **UDP Response Sent/sec:** Shows the average number of UDP responses sent by the DNS server in each second

In addition to using Performance Monitor, you can get the following statistics on every authoritative zone the server hosts:

- Zone Query Statistics
- Zone Transfer Statistics
- Zone Update Statistics

To get the complete zone-level statistics, you can use the Windows PowerShell `Get-DnsServerStatistics` cmdlet with a `ZoneName` option.

For example, to get the statistics for adatum.com, execute the following:

```
Get-DnsServerStatistics -ZoneName adatum.com
```

Alternatively, you can use the following commands to break up the statistics:

```
$statistics = Get-DnsServerStatistics -ZoneName Adatum.com
$statistics.ZoneQueryStatistics
$statistics.ZoneTransferStatistics
$statistics.ZoneUpdateStatistics
```

The administrator can reset the current zone-level statistics counter using the following command:

```
clear-DnsServerStatistics -ZoneName adatum.com
```

Troubleshooting DNS Problems

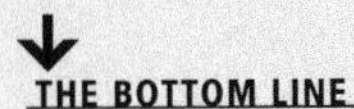

Because DNS is an essential service that can bring any network down when it is not available, you need to know how to troubleshoot it. Microsoft provides several tools to help you troubleshoot DNS problems, including the `ipconfig` command, the `nslookup` command, and the DNS Manager console.

CERTIFICATION READY
Use DNS audit events and analytical (query) events for auditing and troubleshooting
Objective 1.2

When a system attempts to resolve a name, it performs the following steps:

1. It first checks entries in the host file located at C:\Windows\System32\drivers\etc\hosts.
2. The resolver first checks its local cache, which is systemwide (and therefore shared by all applications calling the resolver). If the desired record is not in the cache, the resolver has to send at least one query to a name server.
3. The resolver queries the first name server of the preferred network adapter and waits just one second.
4. If no answer is received, the resolver resends the query simultaneously to the first name server configured for each network adapter and waits two seconds. If the host has only one network adapter, this step is skipped.
5. If no answer is received, the resolver resends the query simultaneously to all name servers configured for all adapters and waits two seconds.
6. If no answer is received, the resolver resends the query simultaneously to all name servers configured for all adapters and waits four seconds.
7. If no answer is received, the resolver resends the query simultaneously to all name servers configured for all adapters and waits eight seconds.
8. If after all this time no name server has returned an answer, the resolver gives up and an error is returned to the application.

When a client cannot access a resource, the problem is with the client or the server. As with any problem, you should quickly determine the scope of the problem. Does the problem affect only the one computer or does it affect multiple computers? If it affects just the one user, the problem most likely resides on the client's computer or it is user error. If the problem affects multiple users, the problem is most likely with the server hosting the network resource or service, a network connectivity problem, or a DNS issue.

If you suspect a DNS issue, you can use the `ipconfig` command to verify the IP configuration of the client. Used without parameters, `ipconfig` displays the IP address, subnet mask, and default gateway for all adapters. When you execute `ipconfig /all`, it displays the full TCP/IP configuration for all adapters including host name, DNS servers, and the physical address (or MAC address).

If you find problems with the DNS, the `ipconfig` command can be used in certain situations:

- **`ipconfig /flushdns`:** Flushes and resets the contents of the DNS client resolver cache.
- **`ipconfig /displaydns`:** Displays the contents of the DNS client resolver cache, which includes both entries preloaded from the local hosts file and any recently obtained resource records for name queries resolved by the computer.

- **`ipconfig /registerdns`:** Initiates manual dynamic registration for the DNS names and IP addresses that are configured at a computer. You can use this parameter to troubleshoot a failed DNS name registration or resolve a dynamic update problem between a client and the DNS server without rebooting the client computer.

If you used the `nslookup` command to test DNS resolution and found a problem with name resolution, you can fix the problem at the DNS server. Unfortunately, previous DNS results that your system processes, such as when you access a web page using a browser, are cached in your memory. Therefore, if you correct the problem, you might need to flush your DNS cache using the `ipconfig /flushdns` command so that it can query and obtain the corrected values.

Windows Server 2016 also includes Windows PowerShell cmdlets that you can use for DNS client and server management. Some of the most commonly used cmdlets are as follows:

- **`Clear-DNSClientCache`:** Clears the client cache, similar to the `ipconfig/flushdns` command
- **`Get-DNSClient`:** Displays the details of the network interfaces
- **`Get-DNSClientCache`:** Displays the content of the local DNS client cache
- **`Register-DNSClient`:** Registers all of the IP addresses on the computer onto the configured DNS server
- **`Resolve-DNSName`:** Performs a DNS name resolution for a specific name, similar to the way `nslookup` works
- **`Set-DNSClient`:** Sets the interface-specific DNS client configurations on the computer
- **`Test-DNSServer`:** Tests that a specified computer is a functioning DNS server

If you determine that old information is cached on the local DNS server, you can wait until the DNS data expires or you can clear the cache on the local DNS server. The following steps show you how to clear the cache from a DNS server.

CLEAR THE DNS CACHE

GET READY. To clear the DNS cache on a DNS server, perform the following steps.

1. Open **Server Manager**.
2. Click **Tools > DNS** to open the DNS Manager console.
3. If necessary, expand the DNS Manager console to a full-screen view.
4. Right-click the server and choose **Clear Cache**.

`Nslookup.exe` is a command-line administrative tool for testing and troubleshooting DNS name resolution. Entering *hostname* in `nslookup` provides a forward lookup of the host name to IP address. Entering *IP_Address* in `nslookup` performs a reverse lookup of IP address to host name (see Figure 3-25).

If you type `nslookup` without any parameters, you start `nslookup.exe` in interactive mode. You can use the `help` or `?` to generate a list of available commands (see Figure 3-26). To exit `nslookup` interactive mode, use the `quit` command.

While in interactive mode, by default, if you type a host name, the `nslookup` command displays the IP address. If you type an IP address, you get back the host name.

To look at the different data types in the domain namespace, use the `set type` command. For example, to look at MX records for a domain, you need to use the `set type=mx` command, and then you can perform your query for MX records (see Figure 3-27).

By default, when you use the `nslookup` command in interactive mode, it queries the client's DNS server. If you need to check the name resolution of another server, you can use the

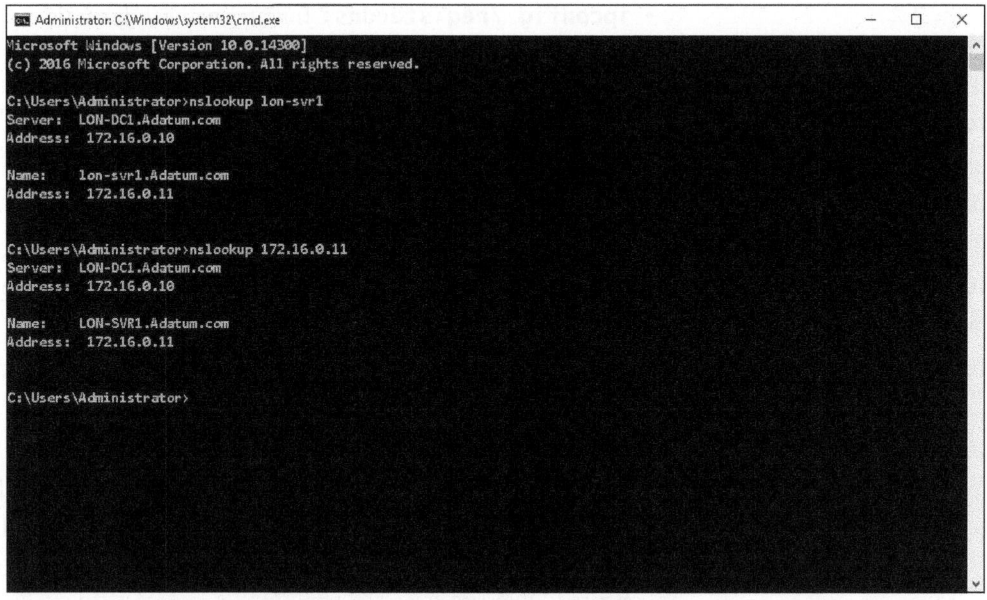

Figure 3-25

Using the `Nslookup` command

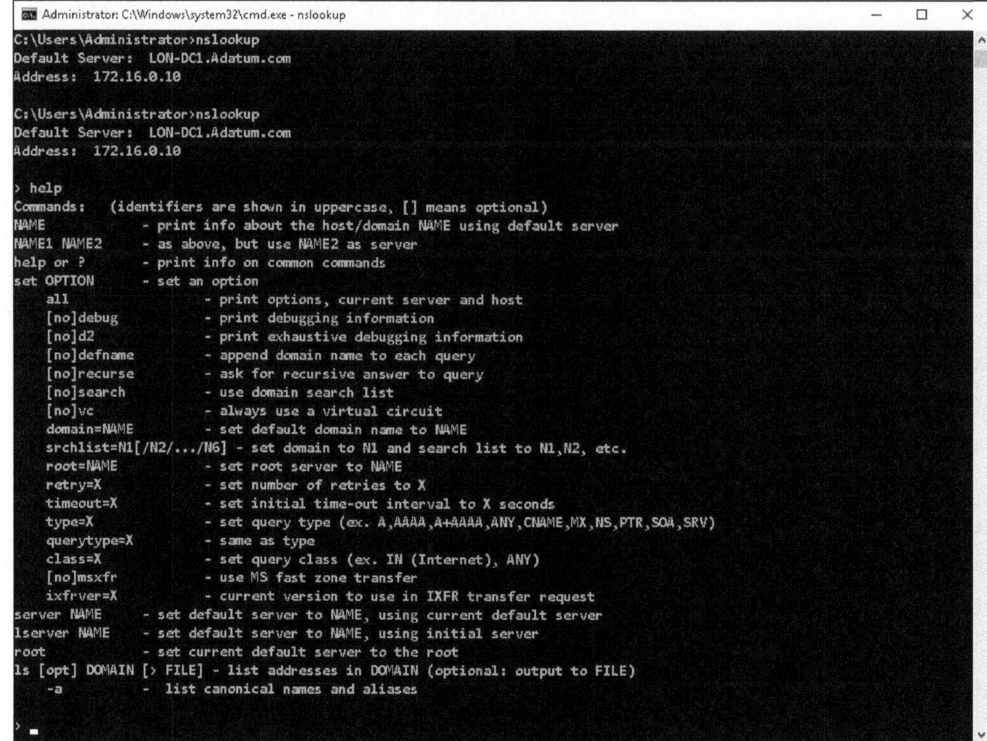

Figure 3-26

Using `Nslookup help`

`server` command. For example, if you want to jump to another DNS server (such as one that has an IP address of 4.2.2.2), execute the following command:

```
server 4.2.2.2
```

If you cannot connect to a remote server, you need to check any firewalls between the client and the remote DNS server, specifically over UDP and TCP port 53.

Finally, you can use the DNS Manager console to help troubleshoot DNS problems, specifically if the server can perform a simple query against the DNS server or a recursive query to other DNS servers.

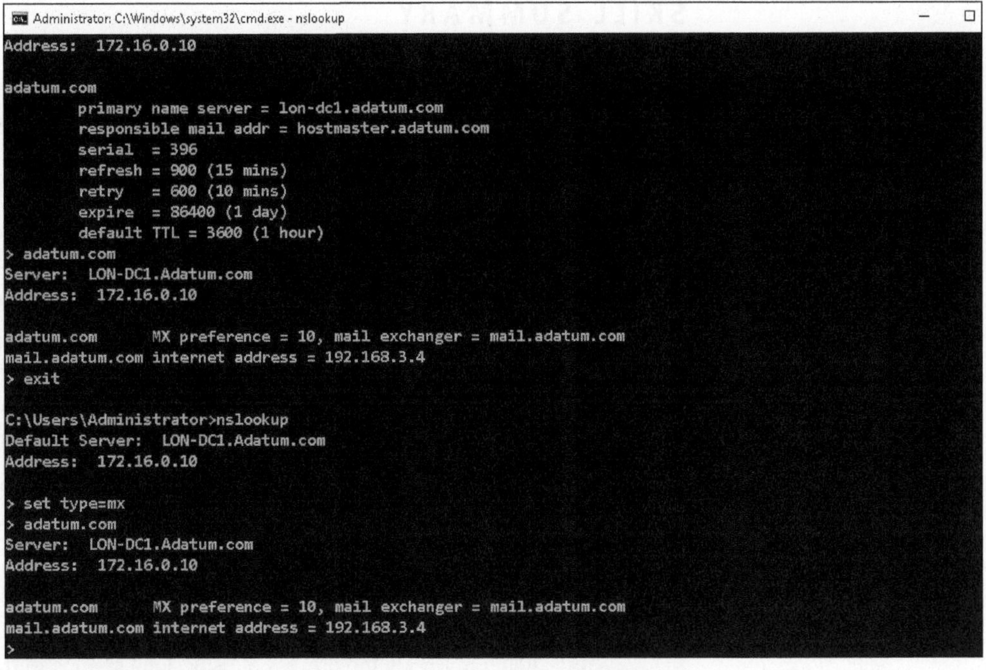

Figure 3-27

Showing MX records in `Nslookup` interactive mode

TEST A DNS SERVER

GET READY. To test a DNS server, perform the following steps.

1. Open **Server Manager** and then click **Tools > DNS** to open the DNS Manager console. If necessary, expand the DNS Manager console to a full-screen view.
2. Right-click the server and choose **Properties**. The Properties dialog box opens.
3. Click the **Monitoring** tab.
4. Select the **A simple query against this DNS server** and **A recursive query to other DNS servers** check boxes .
5. Click the **Test Now** button. (Figure 3-28 shows the test has been performed).
6. When you are finished, click **OK**.

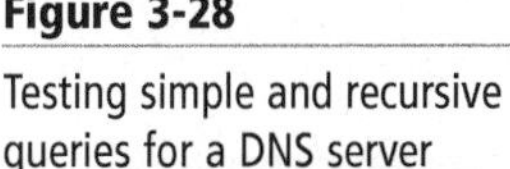

Figure 3-28

Testing simple and recursive queries for a DNS server

SKILL SUMMARY

IN THIS LESSON YOU LEARNED:

- To provide DNS services, you first need to deploy DNS. Then, after you install DNS servers, you need to create each zone and add resource records to each zone.
- On DNS original implementation, the DNS server would host either a primary or secondary zone or both. The primary zone provides an authoritative, read-write copy of the zone, whereas the secondary zone provides an authoritative, read-only copy of the primary zone.
- Today, DNS can be stored in and replicated with Active Directory, as an Active Directory–integrated zone. By using Active Directory–integrated zones, DNS follows a multimaster model, where each server enables all DNS servers to have authoritative read-write copies of the DNS zone. When a change is made on one DNS server, it is replicated to the other DNS servers.
- A DNS subdomain is a child domain that is part of a parent domain and has the same domain suffix as the parent domain. Subdomains allow you to assign unique names to be used by a particular department, subsidiary, function, or service within the organization.
- To help with stale data, you can configure zone scavenging to clean up the stale records. Aging in DNS is the process of using time stamps to track the age of dynamically registered resource records. Scavenging is the mechanism to remove stale resource records.
- A DNS zone database is made up of a collection of resource records, which are used to answer DNS queries. Each resource record (RR) specifies information about a particular object. Each record has a type, an expiration time limit, and some type-specific data.
- In an environment where there are several DNS suffixes, such as contoso.com, adatum.com, and fabrikam.net, it is necessary to manually create a GlobalNames zone within DNS to allow a single-label name to be resolved.
- Because DNS is an essential service that can bring any network down when it is not available, you need to know how to troubleshoot it. Microsoft provides several tools to help you troubleshoot DNS problems, including the `ipconfig` command, the `nslookup` command, and the DNS Manager console.

■ Knowledge Assessment

Multiple Choice

Select the correct answer for each of the following questions.

1. Which zone is used to translate host names to IP addresses?
   a. Forward lookup zone
   b. Reverse lookup zone
   c. Primary zone
   d. Secondary zone
2. Which of the following is used to automatically create and update the host's primary DNS server?
   a. Master client
   b. Dynamic updates

c. Secondary zone
d. Active Directory client

3. Which zone contains only the necessary resource records that act as an authoritative name server?
   a. Forwarding zone
   b. Conditional forwarding zone
   c. Secondary zone
   d. Stub zone
4. Which of the following forwards queries to other DNS servers based on the DNS domain name in the query?
   a. Stub forwarding
   b. Dynamic forwarding
   c. Conditional forwarding
   d. Intelligent forwarding
5. Which of the following sends DNS information from a zone on a DNS server to another DNS server?
   a. Zone lookup
   b. Dynamic transfer
   c. Resource record synchronization
   d. Zone transfer
6. Which command is used to create a zone to a DNS on a DNS server?
   a. `dnscmd /create`
   b. `dnscmd /zoneadd`
   c. `dnscmd /zonerefresh`
   d. `dnscmd /start`
7. To provide single name resolution, which of the following should be enabled?
   a. WINS
   b. NETBIOS
   c. GlobalNames support
   d. Netmask ordering
8. When you create a reverse lookup zone, how is the zone stored for the 172.25.0.0 subnet (subnet mask of 255.255.0.0)?
   a. 172.25
   b. 172.25.0.0
   c. 25.172
   d. 0.0.25.172
9. How many primary zones can a zone have?
   a. 1
   b. 2
   c. 3
   d. Unlimited
10. Which zone is used to translate IP addresses to host names?
    a. Forward lookup zone
    b. Reverse lookup zone
    c. Primary zone
    d. Secondary zone

11. Which of the following should be used when creating a reverse lookup zone for the 172.25.0.0 subnet (subnet mask of 255.255.0.0)?
    a. 172.25
    b. 172.25.0.0
    c. 25.172
    d. 0.0.25.172
12. Which records are automatically created when you create a zone? (Choose all that apply.)
    a. SOA
    b. SRV
    c. NS
    d. MX
13. Which DNS resource record is used to map a host name to an IP address?
    a. A record
    b. PTR record
    c. MX record
    d. SRV record
14. Which record do you use to specify an organization's mail server?
    a. A record
    b. PTR record
    c. SRV record
    d. MX record
15. To scavenge DNS records, where must you enable scavenging and aging? (Choose two answers.)
    a. DHCP server
    b. DNS server
    c. Each resource record
    d. Zone

Best Answer

Choose the letter that corresponds to the best answer. More than one answer choice may achieve the goal. Select the BEST answer.

1. Which of the following should be used to send name resolution queries to another DNS server?
    a. Primary zone
    b. Forwarding zone
    c. Conditional zone
    d. Secondary zone
2. Which type of transfer copies the entire zone to another DNS server?
    a. Full transfer
    b. Incremental transfer
    c. Standard transfer
    d. Notify transfer
3. Which setting enables the notification of secondary name servers when a zone has been updated and the resource records that need to be transferred are listed?
    a. `forward` command
    b. Primary transfer

c. Secondary transfer
d. DNS Notify

4. Which of the following should be used if an administrator wants several DNS servers to each act as a master for a zone?

a. Primary zone
b. Secondary zone
c. Active Directory–integrated zone

Matching and Identification

1. Identify the benefits of using Active Directory–integrated zones. (Not all answers will be used.)

____ Security
____ Self-healing
____ Customized selected replication
____ Fault tolerance
____ Efficient replication

2. Which of the following triggers a zone transfer? (Not all answers will be used.)

____ The zone refresh interval expires.
____ Initial transfer occurs when a secondary zone is created.
____ The fail-safe mechanism has been triggered.
____ DNS Server service is started at the secondary server.
____ WINS has an update for DNS.
____ The master server notifies the secondary server that changes have been made to the zone.
____ The Jet database service is restarted.

3. Identify the type of resource record (A, AAAA, PTR, SOA, NS, MX, and SRV) in the description or scenario given. Resource records may be repeated.

____ Defines the email address of the administrator for a zone
____ Used to convert a host name to an IPv4 address
____ Used to convert an IPv6 address to a host name
____ Defines the incoming email servers
____ Used to identify the DNS servers for a zone
____ Used to convert a host name to an IPv6 address
____ Used to convert an IPv4 address to a host name
____ Defines the default TTL for a zone
____ Used to identify the domain controllers
____ Shows the number of times a DNS zone has been updated

4. Identify whether the resource record should be placed in the forward lookup zone or the reverse lookup zone.

____ A
____ AAAA
____ PTR
____ SOA
____ NS
____ MX
____ SRV

Build List

1. Specify the correct order of steps necessary to enabling zone scavenging for the contoso.com zone. Not all tasks will be used.

    ____ Enable round robin.
    ____ Enable the scavenging agent.
    ____ Enable dynamic update or secure dynamic update for the contoso.com zone.
    ____ Change the refresh interval to 0 for each resource record.
    ____ Enable scavenging and aging on the DNS server.
    ____ Enable scavenging and aging on the contoso.com zone.

■ Business Case Scenarios

Scenario 3-1: Implementing DNS

You administer three large sites in your organization: the corporate office, the engineering site, and the manufacturing site. You want to make sure that you install DNS so that all of the zones have fault tolerance while still allowing changes on any DNS server and for the best performance possible. Describe your recommended solution and why you recommend this particular solution.

Scenario 3-2: Controlling DNS Updates

You are an administrator at an organization that often enables visitors to connect to the organization's network. You are worried that a visitor might modify a DNS record to hijack a computer name. What can you use to prevent this and how do you implement it?

Scenario 3-3: Configuring DNS Time to Live (TTL)

Describe where the default Time to Live (TTL) information is defined and explain how to override the default TTL for individual records.

Installing and Configuring DHCP

LESSON 4

70-741 EXAM OBJECTIVE

Objective 2.1 – Installing and configuring DHCP. This objective may include but is not limited to identifying and resolving issues related to the following: Install and configure DHCP servers; authorize a DHCP server; create and configure scopes; create and configure superscopes and multicast scopes; configure a DHCP reservation; configure DHCP options; configure DNS options from within DHCP; configure policies; configure client and server for PXE boot; configure DHCP Relay Agent; implement IPv6 addressing using DHCPv6; perform export and import of a DHCP server; perform DHCP server migration.

Lesson Heading	Exam Objective
Understanding DHCP Basics	
Installing and Configuring DHCP	Install and configure DHCP servers
• Deploying a DHCP Server	Authorize a DHCP server
• Authorizing a DHCP Server	Create and configure scopes
• Creating a DHCP Scope	Configure DHCP options
• Configuring DHCP and DNS Options	Configure DNS options from within DHCP
• Creating a DHCP Reservation	Configure a DHCP reservation
• Creating and Configuring Superscopes	Create and configure superscopes and multicast scopes
• Creating and Configuring Multicast Scopes	
• Implementing DHCPv6 Scopes	Implement IPv6 addressing using DHCPv6
• Configuring DHCP Policies	Configure policies
• Configuring DNS Registration	Configure client and server for PXE boot
• Configuring Client and Server for PXE Boot	Configure DHCP Relay Agent
• Configuring the DHCP Relay Agent	Perform export and import of a DHCP server
• Performing DHCP Server Migration Using Export and Import	Perform DHCP server migration
• Using the Windows Server Migration Tools	

KEY TERMS

Bootstrap Protocol (BOOTP)
broadcast
DHCP client reservations
DHCP console
DHCP database
DHCP Helper
DHCP options
DHCP policies
DHCP Relay Agent
DHCP scopes
DHCP server service
lease period
multicast scopes
Routing and Remote Access (RRAS)
superscope
Windows Server Migration Tools (WSMT)

■ Understanding DHCP Basics

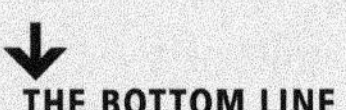

The Dynamic Host Configuration Protocol (DHCP) is a network protocol that automatically configures the IP configuration of a device, including assigning an IP address, subnet mask, default gateway, and primary and secondary Domain Name System (DNS) servers. Most clients and some servers that connect to a network receive their address from a DHCP server, including home routers/modems and office networks. In addition, the DHCP technology and protocol has become a necessary component of Windows Deployment Services (WDS) to deploy Windows to a client.

DHCP is based heavily on the ***Bootstrap Protocol (BOOTP)***, which was one of the early network protocols used to obtain an IP address from a configuration server. Although the DHCP server functions as a BOOTP server, DHCP is a more advanced protocol and includes additional functionality, including the ability to reclaim allocated addresses that are no longer used. DHCP is an open, industry-standard protocol defined by the Internet Engineering Task Force (IETF) in Request for Comments (RFCs) 2131 and 2132.

Assuming that a host is configured to use DHCP during startup, the host performs an IP broadcast in its subnet to request IP configuration from any DHCP server that receives the request. Because broadcasts are generally restricted to the local subnet, a DHCP server must be on the subnet, or a Relay Agent or IP helper grabs the broadcast and forwards it directly to a DHCP server on a remote subnet using unicast packets.

DHCP allocates IP addresses using a lease. The default lease time for a wired client is eight days. When the DHCP lease has reached 50% of the lease time, the client attempts to renew the lease. If the DHCP server is down or unreachable, the client tries again from time to time (at 75% and at 87.5%), When the DHCP server comes back up or becomes reachable again, the DHCP client will succeed in contacting it and renew its lease.

When you assign static IP addresses (IPv4 or IPv6) to your clients, you run the risk of duplicating IP addresses on your network or misconfiguring the settings, which can result in communication problems. A better approach is to dynamically assign your TCP/IP configurations from a central pool of IP addresses. This is done by using the Dynamic Host Configuration Protocol (DHCP) server. The DHCP server can also be configured to provide the default gateway, primary, and secondary DNS information; WINS server; and DNS domain name.

Figure 4-1 shows how DHCP communications work.

Here is a high-level overview of what happens with DHCP-enabled clients (sometimes referred to as DORA):

1. **Discovery:** The DHCP-enabled client starts and broadcasts a request for an IP address over the network.

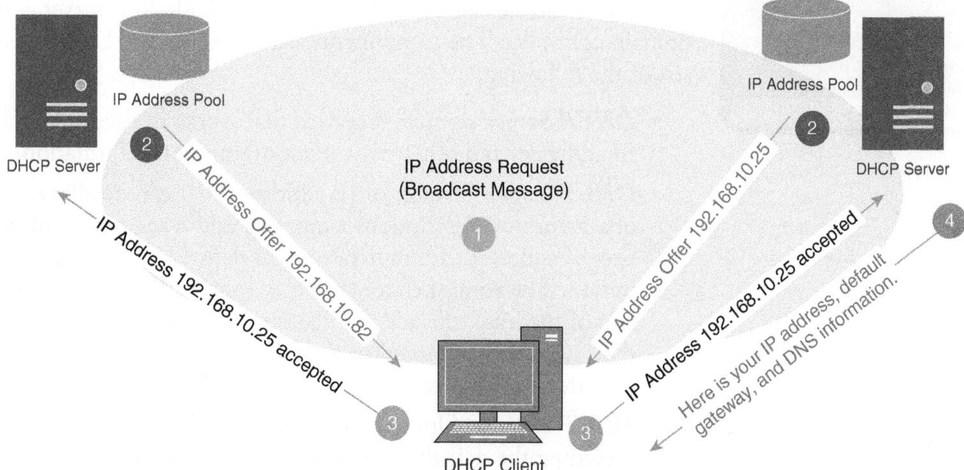

Figure 4-1

Understanding DHCP communications

2. **Offer:** Any DHCP servers that receive the request review their pool of IP addresses (DHCP scope) and select one to offer to the client.
3. **Request:** The client reviews the offers and broadcasts a message to the servers, letting them know which IP address it has accepted.
4. **Acknowledge:** All DHCP servers see the message. Those whose offers are not accepted place the IP address back into their pool for a future client request. The server the client accepted acknowledges and provides additional information to complete the client configuration (default gateway, DNS information, and so on).

After a client receives an IP address and additional configuration information, it has it for a specific period of time called the ***lease period***. When the lease is 50% expired, the client tries to renew it with the DHCP server. If the client cannot renew the lease, it tries again before the lease expires. At this point, if it cannot renew the lease, it tries to contact an alternate DHCP server. If all attempts fail, and the client cannot obtain a new IP address, it autoconfigures with a Microsoft Class B subnet (169.254.0.0/255.255.0.0).

Before it chooses an IP address in this network, the client checks to make sure no other client is using the address it wants to assign by sending an Address Resolution Protocol (ARP) request to the address that it has been assigned. If a reply is received, the address is already being used and the lease process starts over.

TAKE NOTE*

You can use DHCP to assign IPv6 addresses through either DHCPv6 stateful mode or stateless mode. If DHCPv6 is used, you need to make sure your routers are configured to support it.

Installing and Configuring DHCP

THE BOTTOM LINE

DHCP has been included with Windows for years and is included with Windows Server 2016 as a server role. Starting with Windows Server 2012, DHCP supports failover capability. It helps administrators distribute the appropriate IP addresses and network configuration information automatically to network devices or hosts, which eliminates a lot of time that was wasted by manually configuring each host that connects to the network and eliminates human error during configuration. The devices or hosts include computers, mobile devices, printers, network appliances, and switches.

CERTIFICATION READY
Install and configure DHCP servers
Objective 2.1

You can install the DHCP Server role on a stand-alone server, a domain member server, or a domain controller. The components that make up the DHCP technology and protocol consist of the following:

- ***DHCP Server service*:** A service that works in the background on a server. It distributes IP addresses and other network configuration information.
- ***DHCP scopes*:** A range of IP addresses that can be allocated to clients. A scope consists of a name and description, a range of addresses, and a subnet mask. To ease the allocation of addresses, administrators can define IP addresses that are excluded from distribution. The administrators can also specify the duration of the IP address leases. By the end of the lease, the address needs to be renewed or it is released back into the pool so that it can be reallocated to another host. After a scope is created, the scope has to be activated before it can allocate addresses.
- ***DHCP options*:** Options that are assigned when the addresses are assigned or renewed, including the default gateway and the primary and secondary DNS servers. Other options include DNS domain suffix, Windows Internet Naming Service (WINS) server, and TFTP addresses. Based on how you configure the DHCP options, you can assign the options globally (all scopes), specific to a particular scope, to specific clients based on a Class ID values, or to clients that have specific IP address reservations configured.
- ***DHCP database*:** A database that contains the configuration for the DHCP server, the IP addresses that it has distributed, their current lease time, and the IP addresses that the server still has to distribute. The database uses the Microsoft Jet Database Engine, which is stored in the %systemroot%\System32\Dhcp folder.
- ***DHCP console*:** The Microsoft Management Console (MMC) that allows you to manage the DHCP server and the scopes. Figure 4-2 shows the DHCP console.

Figure 4-2
The DHCP console

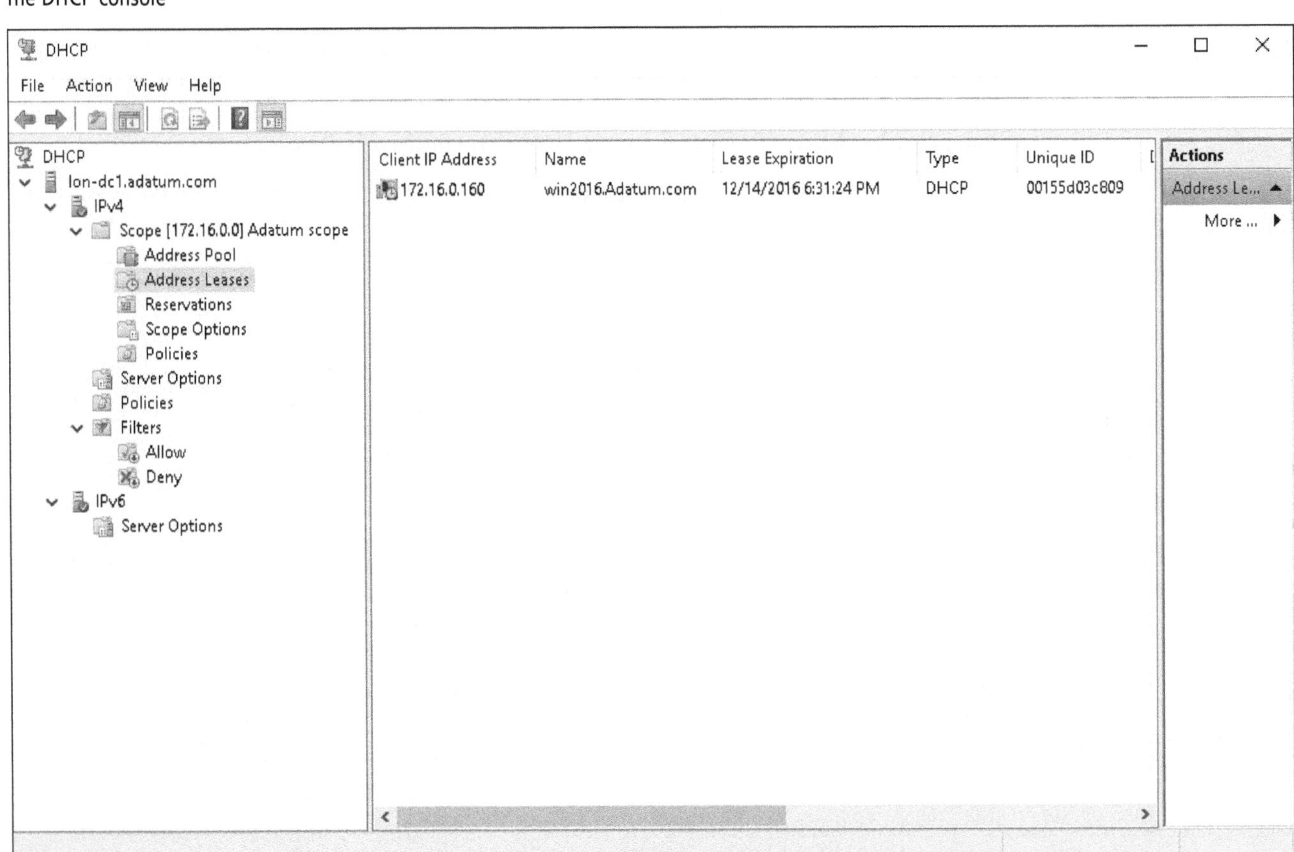

Deploying a DHCP Server

DHCP servers operate independently, so you must install the service and configure scopes on every computer that will function as a DHCP server.

The DHCP Server service is packaged as a role in Windows Server 2016, which you can install using the Add Roles and Features Wizard, accessible from the Server Manager console.

TAKE NOTE* A DHCP server should not be an active DHCP client as well. Before you install the DHCP Server role, be sure to configure the target server with a static IP address.

DEPLOY A DHCP SERVER

GET READY. To install the DHCP Server service on a Windows Server 2016 computer with Server Manager, perform the following steps.

1. Log on to a server running Windows Server 2016 as **adatum\administrator** with the password of **Pa$$w0rd**.
2. Click **Start** and click **Server Manager**.
3. Click **Manage > Add Roles and Features**. The Add Roles and Features Wizard starts, displaying the Before You Begin page.
4. Click **Next**. The Select Installation Type page appears.
5. Leave the **Role-based or feature-based installation** radio button selected and click **Next**. The Select Destination Server page appears.
6. Select the server on which you want to install the roles and/or features and click **Next**. The Select Server Roles page appears.
7. Select the **DHCP Server** check box. An Add features that are required for DHCP Server dialog box opens.
8. Click **Add Features**. Then, click **Next**. The Select Features page appears.

TAKE NOTE* If your computer does not have a static IP address, a message box appears, recommending that you reconfigure the TCP/IP client with a static address before you install the DHCP Server role.

9. Click **Next**. The DHCP Server page appears.
10. Click **Next**. The Confirm Installation Selections page appears.
11. Click **Install**. The Installation Progress page appears as the wizard installs the role.
12. Click **Close**. The wizard closes.

After the DHCP Server role is installed, you need to run the DHCP Post-Install Configuration Wizard, which will create the DHCP Administrators and DHCP Users groups and authorize the DHCP server if the server is joined to a domain. To run the wizard, use Server Manager, click the yellow triangle with the black exclamation point, and click Complete DHCP configuration. When you run the wizard, you are prompted to provide domain administrator credentials to authorize the DHCP server, which includes restarting the DHCP service.

Authorizing a DHCP Server

In Active Directory Domain Services (AD DS) environments, domain-joined Windows DHCP servers must be authorized to service DHCP client requests. By forcing DHCP servers to be authorized, clients are protected from rogue domain-joined Windows DHCP servers that might maliciously affect network clients. This authorization does not prevent rogue access points, non-domain-joined devices, or other devices from issuing addresses. Those types of devices must be restricted through the use of port security.

CERTIFICATION READY
Authorize a DHCP server
Objective 2.1

Unidentified machines entering the network, clients becoming unhealthy with viruses and malware, and even clients turning into rogue DHCP servers will always be risks. If a domain client becomes a rogue DHCP server because of malicious software that has been installed, it can then service clients and spread viruses and worms throughout the network. A rogue DHCP server can point clients to a poisoned DNS cache server and cause havoc throughout the enterprise. Clients cannot authenticate and will be vulnerable to external and internal risks, and network traffic might come to a standstill. This is where DHCP AD DS authorization comes in.

As a security measure in AD DS environments, domain-joined Windows DHCP servers must be authorized against Active Directory to ensure that a rogue DHCP server cannot lease addresses to domain clients.

When a DHCP server in a domain environment is brought online in an AD DS environment, it is checked to see whether it is authorized. If it is not authorized, it is identified as an unauthorized DHCP server and will not lease IP addresses to DHCP clients.

To authorize a DHCP server, the DHCP Server role must be installed on a domain member server or on a domain controller.

Additional considerations for AD DS interoperability include the following:

- The user authorizing the server to AD DS must be a member of the Enterprise Admins group.
- If DHCP is installed on a domain controller, the DHCP server is authorized at the time of role installation.
- The FQDN of the DHCP server cannot exceed 64 characters. If this is the case, you can authorize the server by using its IP address instead of the FQDN.

AUTHORIZE A DHCP SERVER IN AN AD DS ENVIRONMENT

GET READY. To authorize a DHCP in an AD DS environment, perform the following steps.

1. Log on to a server running Windows Server 2016 as **adatum\administrator** with the password of **Pa$$w0rd**.
2. Click **Start** and click **Server Manager.**
3. Log on to DHCP Manager as a member of the Enterprise Admins group.
4. Right-click the server and choose **Authorize** (see Figure 4-3).
5. In the Authorize DHCP Server dialog box, type the FQDN or IP address of the DHCP server to be authorized and then click **OK.**
6. In the Confirm Authorization dialog box, verify that the DHCP server name and IP address are correct. Click **OK.**

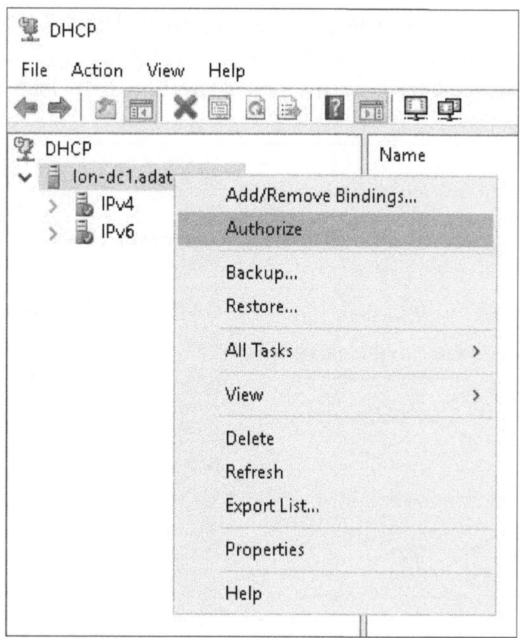

Figure 4-3
Authorizing a DHCP server

7. In the Manage Authorized Servers dialog box, verify that the newly authorized DHCP server is listed as an authorized DHCP server. Click **Close**.
8. Close the remaining windows and snap-ins.

Creating a DHCP Scope

A DHCP scope is a range of IP addresses on a particular subnet that are selected for allocation by a DHCP server. After you install the DHCP role, you can then create a scope using the DHCP snap-in for Microsoft Management Console (MMC).

CERTIFICATION READY
Create and configure scopes
Objective 2.1

A DHCP scope is the consecutive range of possible IP addresses that the DHCP server can lease to clients on a subnet. It is usually defined as a single physical subnet on your network to which DHCP services are offered. Scopes are used to manage distribution and assignment of IP addresses and any related configuration parameters to DHCP clients on the network.

CREATE A DHCP SCOPE

GET READY. To create a DHCP scope, perform the following steps.

1. Log on to a server running Windows Server 2016 as **adatum\administrator** with the password of **Pa$$w0rd.**
2. Click **Start** and click **Server Manager.**
3. Click **Tools > DHCP.**
4. Expand the **server** node and the **IPv4** node.
5. Right-click the **IPv4** node and choose **New Scope.**
6. In the New Scope Wizard, on the Welcome to the New Scope Wizard page, click **Next.**
7. On the Scope Name page, in the Name text box, type a descriptive name and click **Next.**

8. On the IP Address Range page (as shown in Figure 4-4), in the Start IP address text box, type the first in the range of addresses you want to assign. In the End IP address text box, type the last address in the range.

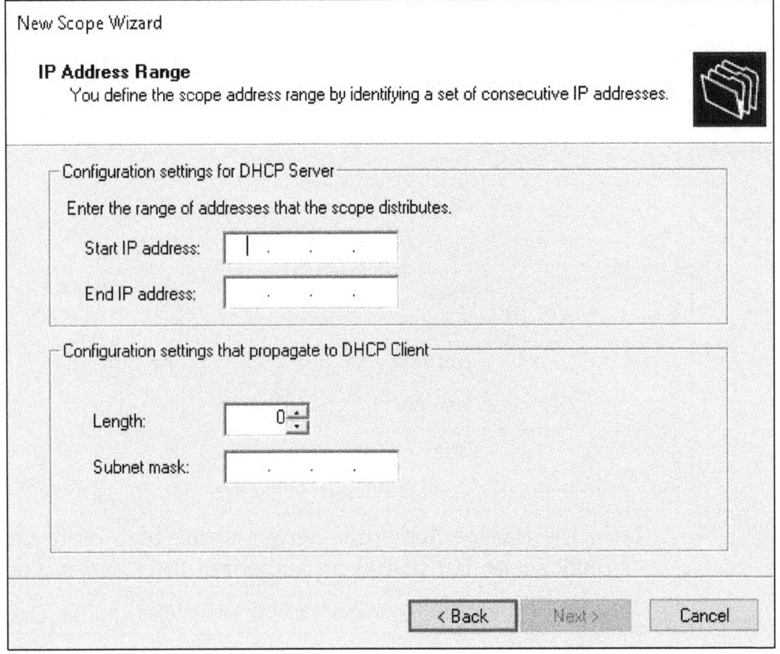

Figure 4-4

The IP Address Range page in the New Scope Wizard

9. In the Subnet mask text box, type the mask value for the subnet on which the scope will operate and click **Next.**

10. On the Add Exclusions and Delay page (as shown in Figure 4-5), in the Start IP address and End IP address text boxes, specify a range of addresses you want to exclude from the scope. You can also specify a delay interval between the server's receipt of DHCPDISCOVER messages and its transmission of DHCPOFFER messages. Then, click **Next.**

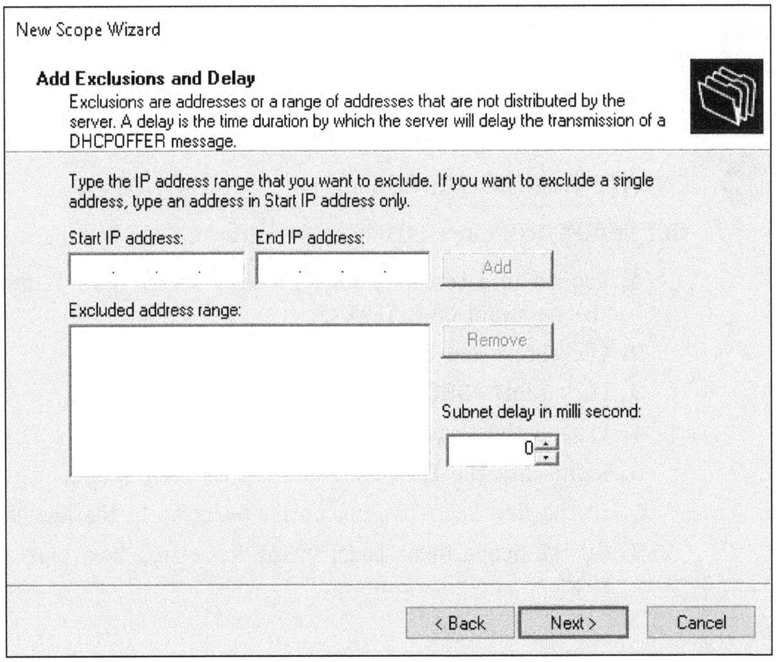

New Scope Wizard

Add Exclusions and Delay

Exclusions are addresses or a range of addresses that are not distributed by the server. A delay is the time duration by which the server will delay the transmission of a DHCPOFFER message.

Type the IP address range that you want to exclude. If you want to exclude a single address, type an address in Start IP address only.

Start IP address: End IP address: Add

Excluded address range: Remove

Subnet delay in milli second: 0

< Back Next > Cancel

Figure 4-5

The Add Exclusions and Delay page in the New Scope Wizard

11. On the Lease Duration page, specify the length of the leases for the addresses in the scope. The default lease duration is set to 8 days. Click **Next.**
12. On the Configure DHCP Options page, select **Yes, I want to configure these options now** and click **Next.**
13. On the Router (Default Gateway) page, as shown in Figure 4-6, in the IP address text box, specify the address of a router on the subnet served by the scope and click **Add.** Then, click **Next.**

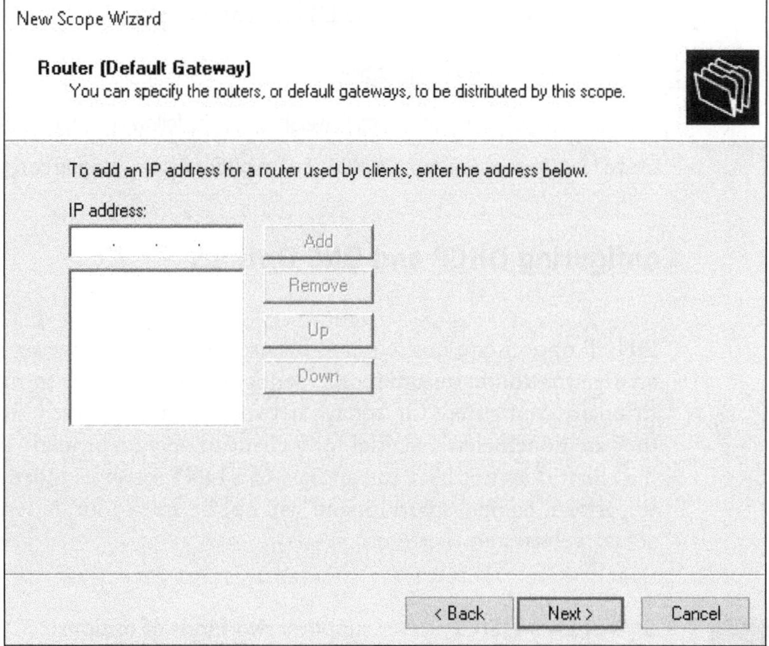

Figure 4-6

The Router (Default Gateway) page in the New Scope Wizard

14. On the Domain Name and DNS Servers page (as shown in Figure 4-7), in the Server name text box, type the name of a DNS server on the network and click **Resolve**, or type the address of a DNS server in the IP address text box and click **Add.** Then, click **Next.**

New Scope Wizard
Domain Name and DNS Servers
The Domain Name System (DNS) maps and translates domain names used by clients on your network.
You can specify the parent domain you want the client computers on your network to use for DNS name resolution.
Parent domain: Adatum.com
To configure scope clients to use DNS servers on your network, enter the IP addresses for those servers.
Server name:
IP address:
Add
Resolve
172.16.0.10
Remove
Up
Down
< Back
Next >
Cancel

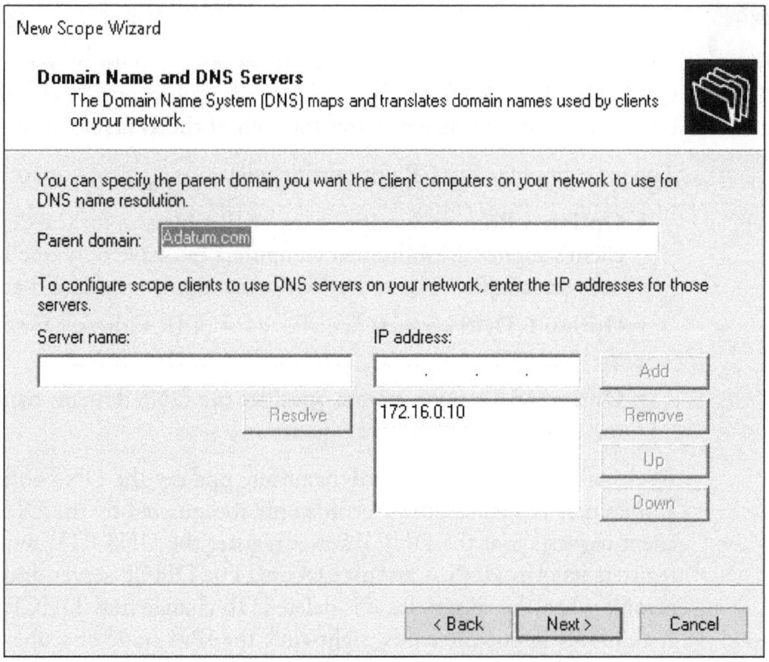

Figure 4-7

The Domain Name and DNS Servers page in the New Scope Wizard

15. On the WINS Servers page, click **Next.**
16. On the Activate Scope page, select **Yes, I want to activate this scope now** and click **Next.** The Completing the New Scope Wizard page appears.
17. Click **Finish.** The wizard closes.

Once the role installation is completed, all of the DHCP clients on the subnet identified in the scope you created can obtain their IP addresses and other TCP/IP configuration settings via DHCP. You can also use the DHCP console to create additional scopes for other subnets.

USING POWERSHELL

To install the DHCP Server role using PowerShell, use the following syntax:

```
Install-WindowsFeature DHCP [-ComputerName <computer_name>]
```

Configuring DHCP and DNS Options

DHCP options are not required for use by DHCP. However, they can be essential to an organization to automatically configure these options so that they do not have to be manually configured. On today's networks, some of these options are taken for granted; they are nonetheless essential for a client to operate properly on a network. For example, if a client does not have the address of a DNS server assigned, the client will not be able to perform name resolution, and will not be able to locate resources on the network or access websites on the Internet.

CERTIFICATION READY
Configure DHCP options
Objective 2.1

CERTIFICATION READY
Configure DNS options from within DHCP
Objective 2.1

The Windows DHCP server supports two kinds of options:

- **Scope options:** Options supplied only to DHCP clients receiving addresses from a particular scope.
- **Server options:** Options supplied to all DHCP clients receiving addresses from the server. However, the scope options can overwrite the server options.

All of the options supported by the Windows DHCP server can be either scope or server options, and the process of configuring them is basically the same. To configure a scope option, you right-click the Scope Options node and, from the context menu, choose Configure Options. The Scope Options dialog box opens, as shown in Figure 4-8. The dialog box provides appropriate controls for each of the available options.

The most popular DHCP options include:

- **Option 3 Router:** Specifies a list of IP addresses for the default gateway or router on the client's subnet. Multihomed computers can have only one list per computer, not one per network adapter. The router option is usually configured at the scope level.
- **Option 6 DNS servers:** Specifies a list of IP addresses for DNS name servers available to the client.
- **Option 15 Domain name:** Specifies the DNS domain name that the client should use for DNS computer name resolution.

By default, the DHCP server dynamically updates the DNS address Host (A) resource records and Pointer (PTR) resource records only if requested by the DHCP clients. By default, the client requests that the DHCP server register the DNS PTR resource record, while the client registers its own DNS A resource record. The DHCP server discards the A and PTR resource records when the client's lease is deleted. To change how DHCP registers and deletes DNS A and PTR resource records, right-click the IPv4 node or scope, choose Properties, and then click the DNS tab (as shown in Figure 4-9).

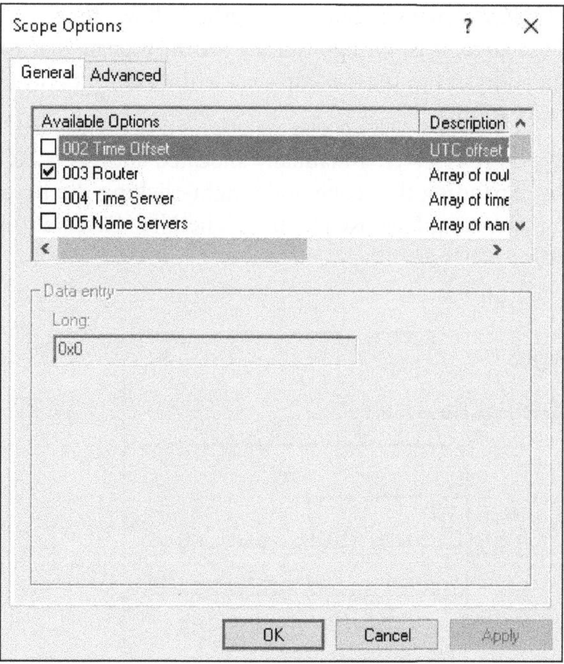

Figure 4-8

Configuring scope options

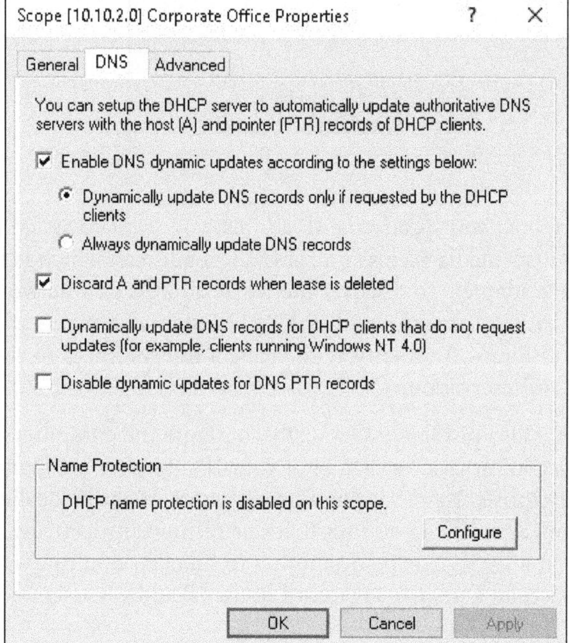

Figure 4-9

Configuring DHCP scope DNS options

Creating a DHCP Reservation

DHCP client reservations allow administrators to reserve an IP address for permanent use by a DHCP client. By using reservations, you can ensure that the host will always have the same IP address. As with any other lease, when a client receives a reserved address, the client also receives all assigned options, such as addresses of the default gateway and DNS servers. If these options are changed, they are automatically updated on the client when the lease is renewed.

CERTIFICATION READY
Configure a DHCP reservation
Objective 2.1

Because the DHCP dynamic allocation method allows for the possibility that a computer's IP address could change, it is not appropriate for these particular roles. However, it is still possible to assign addresses to these computers with DHCP by using manual allocation, instead of dynamic allocation.

In a Windows DHCP server, a manually allocated address is called a *reservation*. You create a reservation by expanding the scope node, right-clicking the Reservations node, and, from the context menu, choosing New Reservation. The New Reservation dialog box opens, as shown in Figure 4-10.

Figure 4-10

A DHCP server's New Reservation dialog box

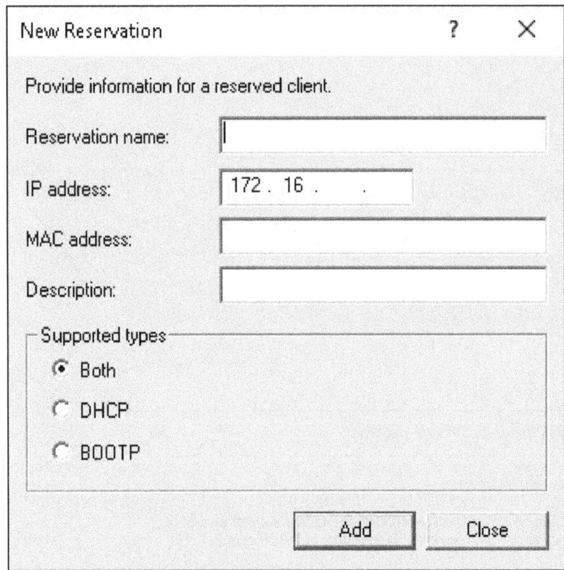

In this dialog box, you specify the IP address you want to assign and associate it with the client computer's media access control (MAC) address, which is hard-coded into its network interface adapter. To discover the MAC address of a network interface adapter, run the `Ipconfig.exe` program with the `/all` parameter, where the MAC address appears as the Physical Address. Another way to create a reservation is to right-click a current lease and choose Add to Reservation.

Of course, it is also possible to manually configure the computer's TCP/IP client, but creating a DHCP reservation ensures that all of your IP addresses are managed by your DHCP servers. In a large enterprise, where various administrators might be dealing with DHCP and TCP/IP configuration issues, the IP address that one technician manually assigns to a computer might be included in a DHCP scope by another technician, resulting in potential addressing conflicts. Reservations create a permanent record of the IP address assignment on the DHCP server.

Creating and Configuring Superscopes

A ***superscope*** is the grouping of multiple scopes into a single administrative entity. By using superscopes, you can support larger subnets.

CERTIFICATION READY
Create and configure superscopes and multicast scopes
Objective 2.1

A superscope can be used if a scope runs out of addresses and you cannot add more addresses from the subnet. Instead, you can add a new subnet to the DHCP server. You then perform multinetting, where you lease addresses to clients in the same physical network, but the clients will be in a separate network logically by subnet. Once you add a new subnet, you must configure routers to recognize the new subnet so that you ensure local communications in the physical network.

You can also use superscopes to move clients gradually into a new IP number scheme. Having both numbering schemes coexist at the same time allows you to move clients into the new subnet. When you renew all client leases in the new subnet, you can retire the old subnet.

You can only create a superscope when you have two or more IP scopes already created in DHCP. You can use the New Superscope Wizard to select the scopes that you want to combine together to create a superscope.

CREATE A SUPERSCOPE FROM TWO SCOPES

GET READY. To create a superscope out of two scopes, perform the following steps.

1. Log on to a server running Windows Server 2016 as **adatum\administrator** with the password of **Pa$$w0rd.**
2. Click **Start** and click **Server Manager.**
3. In Server Manager, click **Tools > DHCP.**
4. In the DHCP console, click a DHCP server, such as **LON-DC1.adatum.com.** Right-click **IPv4** and choose **New Scope.**
5. When the New Scope Wizard opens, click **Next.**
6. In the Name text box, type **Scope1** and click **Next.**
7. On the IP Address Range page, set the Start IP address to **172.24.20.50** and the End IP address to **172.24.20.240.** For the Subnet mask, type **255.255.255.0.** Click **Next.**
8. On the Add Exclusions and Delay page, click **Next.**
9. On the Lease Duration page, change the duration to **3** days and then click **Next.**
10. On the Configure DHCP Options page, click **Next.**
11. On the Router (Default Gateway) page, type the address of **172.24.20.1** and click **Add.** Click **Next.**
12. On the Domain Name and DNS Servers page, the Parent domain should already be set to **adatum.com** and the DNS server should already be defined. Click **Next.**
13. On the WINS Servers page, click **Next.**
14. On the Activate Scope page, click **Next.**
15. When the wizard is complete, click **Finish.**
16. Right-click **IPv4** and choose **New Scope.**
17. When the New Scope Wizard opens, click **Next.**
18. In the Name text box, type **Scope2** and click **Next.**
19. On the IP Address Range page, set the Start IP address to **172.24.21.50** and the End IP address to **172.24.21.240.** For the Subnet mask, type **255.255.255.0.** Click **Next.**
20. On the Add Exclusions and Delay page, click **Next.**
21. On the Lease Duration page, change the duration to **3** days and click **Next.**
22. On the Configure DHCP Options page, click **Next.**
23. On the Router (Default Gateway) page, type the address of **172.24.21.1** and click **Add.** Click **Next.**
24. On the Domain Name and DNS Servers page, the Parent domain should already be set to **adatum.com** and the DNS server should already be defined. Click **Next.**
25. On the WINS Servers page, click **Next.**
26. On the Activate Scope page, click **Next.**
27. When the wizard is complete, click **Finish.**
28. Right-click **IPv4** and choose **New Superscope.**
29. When the New SuperScope Wizard opens, in the Name text box, type **Super1** and click **Next.**

30. On the Select Scopes page, press the **Control** key and hold it down. Then, click **Scope1** and **Scope2** (see Figure 4-11). Release the **Control** key. Click **Next.**

Figure 4-11

Selecting scopes for a superscope

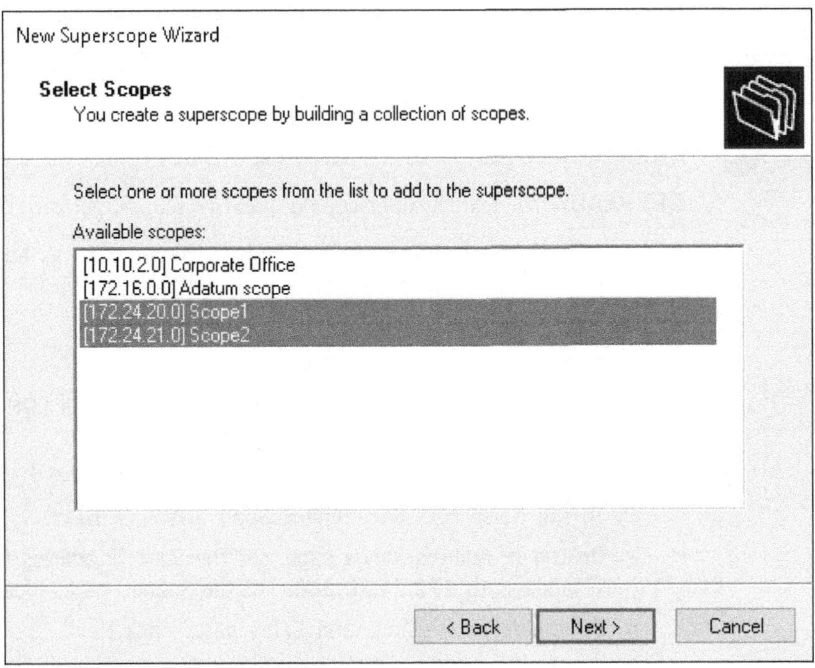

31. Click **Finish.** The superscope shows in the DHCP console (see Figure 4-12).

Figure 4-12

Viewing a superscope in the DHCP console

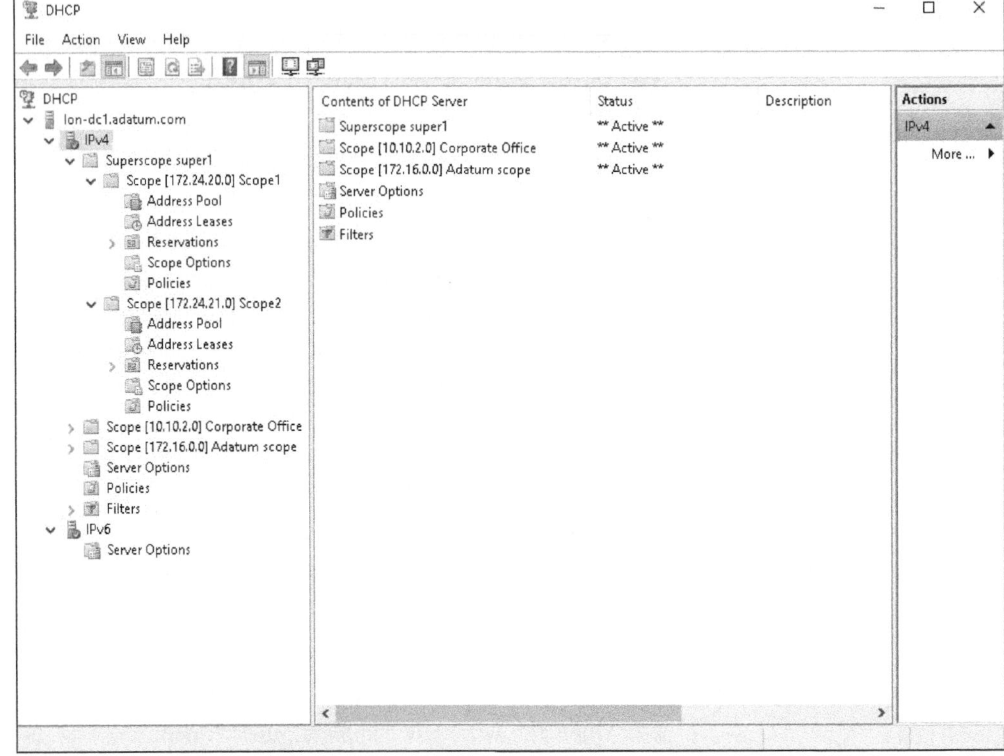

Creating and Configuring Multicast Scopes

When a host sends packets to a single host (single point to single point), the communication is *unicast*. ***Broadcast*** is sent from one host to all other hosts (one point to all other points). *Multicast* is when packets are sent from one host to multiple hosts (one point to a set of other points). Multicasting delivers the same packet simultaneously to a group of clients, which results in less bandwidth usage. For example, if you have to send a live video to 100 computers, instead of sending 100 sets of packets (unicast), you would send one set of packets. When multicast packets reach a router, the packets are forwarded only to the networks that have receivers for the packets. Besides live video or audio transmissions, it can also be used in some instances when deploying multiple computers at the same time—you only need to send one set of packets to multiple computers.

CERTIFICATION READY
Create and configure superscopes and multicast scopes
Objective 2.1

Classful networks include Class A, Class B, and Class C networks. The first octet is the following:

- **Class A:** 0–127 with a default subnet mask of 255.0.0.0
- **Class B:** 128–191 with a default subnet mask of 255.255.0.0
- **Class C:** 192–223 with a default subnet mask of 255.255.255.0

Class D addresses are defined from 224.0.0.0 to 239.255.255.255 and are used for multicast addresses.

In DHCP, ***multicast scopes*** (commonly known as *Multicast Address Dynamic Client Allocation Protocol [MADCAP] scopes*) allow applications to reserve a multicast IP address for data and content delivery. For Applications that use multicasting request addresses from the scopes, the applications need to support the MADCAP application programming interface (API).

Creating and managing a multicast scope is similar to creating and managing a normal scope; however, multicast scopes cannot use reservations and you cannot set additional options such as DNS and routing. In addition, because multicast is shared by groups of computers, the default duration of a multicast scope is 30 days.

CREATE A MULTICAST SCOPE

GET READY. To create a multicast scope, perform the following steps.

1. Log on to a server running Windows Server 2016 as **adatum\administrator** with the password of **Pa$$w0rd.**
2. Click **Start** and click **Server Manager.**
3. In Server Manager, click **Tools > DHCP**. The DHCP console opens.
4. In the DHCP console, click the DHCP server, such as **LON-DC1.adatum.com.** Right-click **IPv4** and choose **New Multicast Scope.**
5. In the New Multicast Scope Wizard, click **Next.**
6. In the Name text box, type **Multicast Scope1** and click **Next.**
7. On the IP Address Range page, set the Start IP address to **224.0.0.0** and the End IP address to **224.255.255.255** (see Figure 4-13). Click **Next.**
8. On the Add Exclusions and Delay page, click **Next.**
9. On the Lease Duration page, and click **Next.**
10. On the Activate Scope page, click **Next.**
11. When the installation is complete, click **Finish.**

Figure 4-13

Specifying the IP address range for a multicast scope

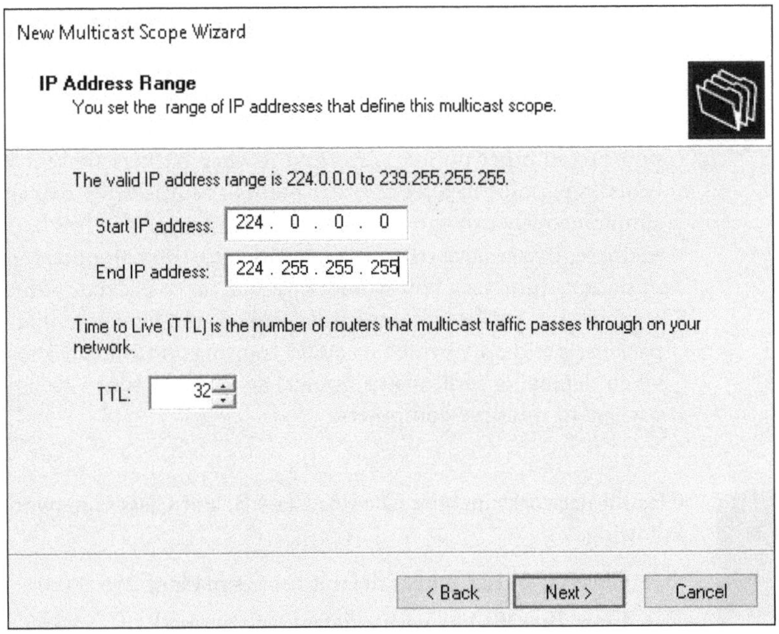

New Multicast Scope Wizard

IP Address Range
You set the range of IP addresses that define this multicast scope.

The valid IP address range is 224.0.0.0 to 239.255.255.255.

Start IP address: 224 . 0 . 0 . 0

End IP address: 224 . 255 . 255 . 255

Time to Live (TTL) is the number of routers that multicast traffic passes through on your network.

TTL: 32

< Back | Next > | Cancel

Implementing DHCPv6 Scopes

Similar to the IPv4 addresses, IPv6 addresses are divided into network bits and host addresses. In addition, IPv6 supports automatic configuration. However, with a Windows DHCP server, you can perform stateful address autoconfiguration.

CERTIFICATION READY
Implement IPv6 addressing using DHCPv6
Objective 2.1

The first 64 bits of an IPv6 address define the network address, and the second 64 bits define the host address. For example:

FE80:0000:0000:0000:02C3:B2DF:FEA5:E4F1

Therefore FE80:0000:0000:0000 defines the network bits and 02C3:B2DF:FEA5:E4F1 defines the host bits. The network bits are also further divided where 48 bits are used for the network prefix and the next 16 bits are used for subnetting. The remaining host bits are 64 bits.

If you recall from Lesson 1, with IPv6, unicast addressing can be divided into the following:

- **Global unicast addresses:** Public addresses that are globally routable and reachable on the IPv6 portion of the Internet.
- **Link-local addresses:** Private, nonroutable addresses confined to a single subnet. These addresses are used to communicate with neighboring hosts on the same link and are equivalent to the automatic private IP addresses (169.254.x.x) used by IPv4 when a DHCP server cannot be contacted. Although they can be used to set up permanent small LANs, link-local addresses can also be used to create temporary networks or ad hoc networks. Although routers process packets sent to a link-local address, they do not forward the packets to other links.
- **Unique local addresses:** Intended private addressing, so that you can join two subnets together without creating any addressing problems.

An IPv6 host addresses can be configured with stateful or stateless mode. Because the two address configuration modes are independent of each other and will not trample over each other, a host can use both stateless and stateful address configuration.

The stateless mechanism is used to configure both link-local addresses and additional non-link-local addresses based on Router Solicitation and Router Advertisement messages with neighboring routers. With stateless autoconfiguration, the MAC address is used to generate the host bits. When using stateless configuration, the address is not assigned by a DHCP server. However, a DHCP server can still assign other IPv6 configuration settings.

Stateful configuration has the IPv6 addresses and additional IPv6 configuration, assigned by a DHCPv6 server.

When you create IPv6 scopes, you define the following properties:

- **Prefix:** Defines the network portion of the IP address.
- **Preference:** Defines the values assigned to a DHCP scope that indicate the preferred DHCP server to use when an organization has multiple DHCP servers. The scope with the lowest preference value is used first.
- **Exclusions:** Defines single addresses or blocks of addresses that will not be offered for lease.
- **Valid and preferred lifetimes:** Defines how long leased addresses are valid. The preferred lifetime is the preferred amount of time the lease should be valid. The valid lifetime is the maximum amount of time the lease is valid.
- **DHCP options:** Defines IPv6 options such as DNS servers and the default gateway.

CREATE A DHCP IPv6 SCOPE

GET READY. To create a DHCP IPv6 scope, perform the following steps.

1. Log on to a server running Windows Server 2016 as **adatum\administrator** with the password of **Pa$$w0rd.**
2. Click **Start** and click **Server Manager.**
3. In Server Manager, click **Tools > DHCP.** The DHCP console opens.
4. Right-click **IPv6** and choose **New Scope.**
5. In the New Scope Wizard, click **Next.**
6. In the Name text box, type a name, such as **IPv6Scope1.** Click **Next.**
7. On the Scope Prefix page (see Figure 4-14), specify the Prefix, such as **FEC0::**. In addition, specify the Preference value, such as **0.**

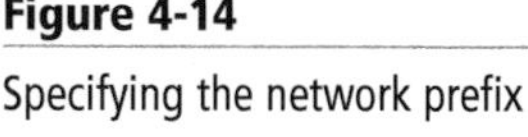

Figure 4-14

Specifying the network prefix

New Scope Wizard
Scope Prefix
You have to provide a prefix to create the scope. You also have the option of providing a preference value for the scope.
Enter the IPv6 Prefix for the addresses that the scope distributes and the preference value for the scope.
Prefix
/64
Preference
0
< Back
Next >
Cancel

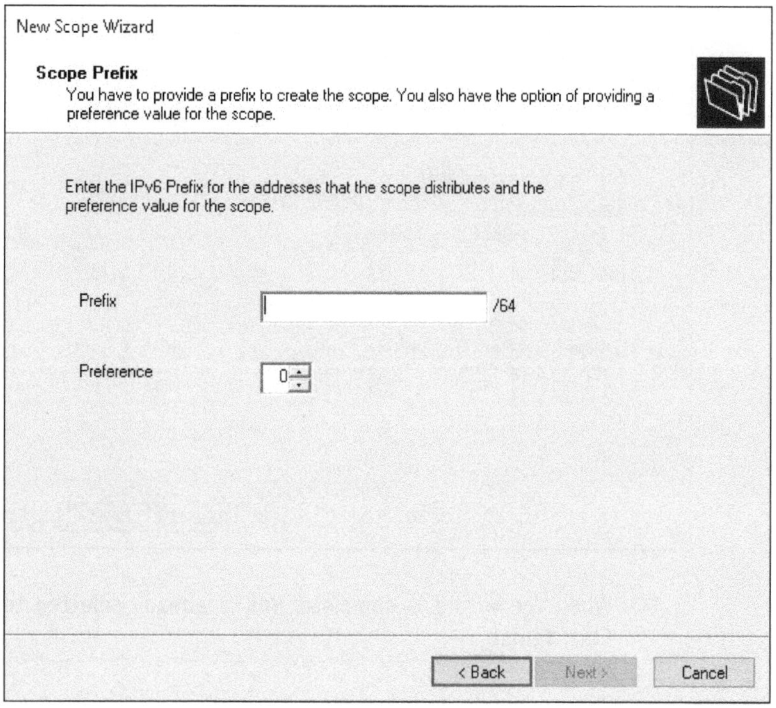

8. On the Add Exclusions page (see Figure 4-15), click **Next.**

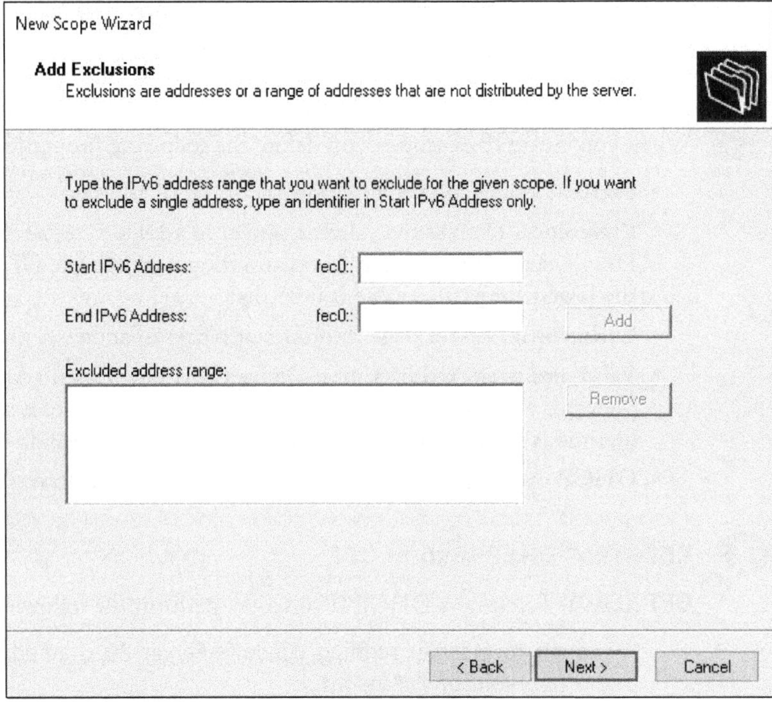

Figure 4-15
Specifying the exclusion addresses for the scope

9. On the Scope Lease page (see Figure 4-16), specify the preferred life time and valid life time for the host. Change the Preferred Life Time to **1** day and the Valid Life Time to **10** days. Click **Next.**

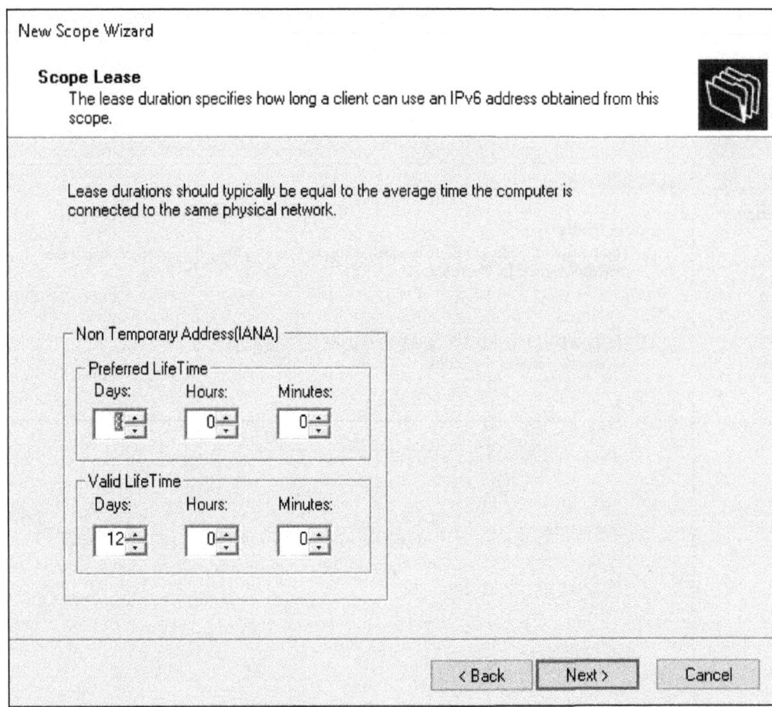

Figure 4-16
Specifying the scope lease

10. When the wizard is complete, **Yes** is already selected to activate the scope. Click **Finish.**

DHCP IPv6 options can be assigned at the server level or the scope level. To configure the options at the server level, right-click IPv6 and choose Set Predefined Options. To configure the options at the scope level, expand the scope, right-click Scope Options, and choose Configure Options. The options available include:

- **00021 SIP Server Domain Name List:** Specifies a list of the domain names of the Session Initiation Protocol (SIP) outbound proxy servers for the client to use.
- **00022 SIP Servers IPv6 Address List:** Specifies a list of IPv6 addresses indicating SIP outbound proxy servers available to the client. If an organization has more than one server, the server with the highest preference is used.
- **00023 DNS Recursive Name Server IPv6 Address:** Specifies the DNS server used for DNS queries. If an organization has more than one DNS server, the server with the highest preference is used.
- **00024 Domain Search List:** Specifies the domain search list the client is to use when resolving host names with DNS.
- **00027 NIS IPv6 Address List:** Specifies a list of IPv6 addresses indicating Network Information Services (NIS) servers available to the client.
- **00028 NIS + IPv6 Address List:** Specifies a list of IPv6 addresses indicating Network Information Services v2 (NIS +) servers available to the client.
- **00029 NIS Domain List:** Conveys the client's list of NIS Domain Name information to the client.
- **00030 NIS + Domain Name List:** Conveys the client's list of NIS+ Domain Name information to the client.
- **00031 SNTP Servers IPv6 Address List:** Provides a list of one or more IPv6 addresses of SNTP servers so clients can perform time synchronization with the SNTP server.

Configuring DHCP Policies

Starting with Windows Server 2012, by using ***DHCP policies***, you can give granular control over scopes to allow you to assign different IP addresses or different options based on the device type, or its role. Policies are applicable for a specific scope with a defined processing order. The options can be configured at the scope or inherited from server-wide policies.

CERTIFICATION READY
Configure policies
Objective 2.1

A DHCP policy can support the following scenarios:

- If you have different types of clients (for example, desktop computers, printers, and IP phones) on the same subnets, you can assign different IP address ranges within the subnet.
- If you have a mix of wired and mobile computers, you can assign shorter lease durations for mobile computers and longer lease durations to wired computers.
- You can control who gets access to your network based on MAC address for a subnet.

A DHCP policy consists of conditions and settings. A condition allows you to identify and group clients based on whether a specified criteria is equal or not equal to a specified value. The criteria include:

- MAC address
- Vendor class
- User class
- Client identifier
- Relay Agent information, such as remote ID, circuit ID, and subscriber ID

Every DHCP client request is evaluated against the conditions in a policy. If a client request matches the conditions in the policy, the specified settings (IP address and options) assigned to the policy are applied to the DHCP client. For example, you can identify the type of device, so that wired clients are in one group and mobile computers are in another group. You can also use a trailing wildcard with MAC address, vendor class, user class, and client identifier conditions to perform a partial match. A client that does not match conditions is leased an IP address from the remaining IP addresses of the scope that are not declared to a policy and are assigned the specified server options assigned to the scope.

You can configure more than one policy within a scope or server wide. When a client makes a DHCP request, each policy is evaluated and the settings are combined. If there is a conflict for a specific option, the policy higher up in the processing order overrides the previous option.

Every policy has an assigned processing order. While processing client requests, the DHCP server evaluates the client requests against the conditions in the different policies based on the processing order of the policy—with the processing order 1 policy processed first. Scope-level policies are processed first by the DHCP server followed by server-wide policies.

Depending on your needs, you might need to first build a vendor class. In the first exercise, you create a vendor class for the Nortel IP phone and the HP Jet Direct, which is the primary network interface used for HP network printers. Then, in the following exercise, you create a DHCP policy based on the vendor class.

CREATE VENDOR CLASSES

GET READY. To create a vendor class, perform the following steps.

1. Log on to a server running Windows Server 2016 as **adatum\administrator** with the password of **Pa$$w0rd.**
2. Click **Start** and click **Server Manager.**
3. In Server Manager, click **Tools > DHCP**. The DHCP console opens.
4. In the DHCP console, right-click **IPv4** or **IPv6** and choose **Define Vendor Class.**
5. In the DHCP Vendor Classes dialog box, click **Add.** The New Class dialog box opens (see Figure 4-17).

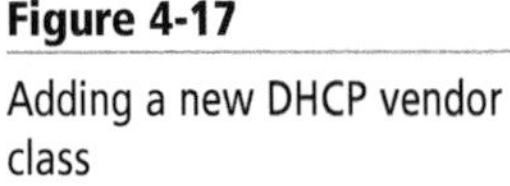

Figure 4-17

Adding a new DHCP vendor class

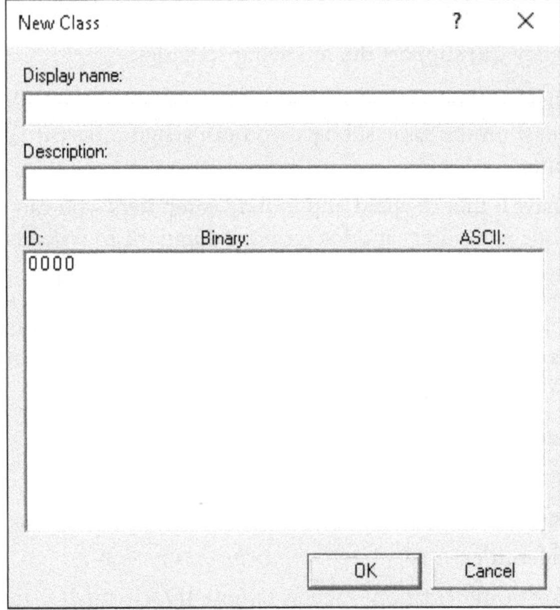

6. In the Display name text box, type **Nortel Phones.** In the Description text box, type **Desk phone.**
7. Click under the ASCII field name and type **Nortel-i 2004-A**. Click **OK.**
8. Click **Add** again.
9. In the Display name text box, type **HP Printer.**
10. Click under the ASCII field name and type **Hewlett-Packard JetDirect.** Click **OK.**
11. Click **Close** to close the DHCP Vendor Classes dialog box.

CREATE A DCHP POLICY FOR A SCOPE

GET READY. To create a DHCP policy for a scope, perform the following steps.

1. Log on to a server running Windows Server 2016 as **adatum\administrator** with the password of **Pa$$w0rd.**
2. Click **Start** and click **Server Manager.**
3. In Server Manager, click **Tools > DHCP.** The DHCP console opens.
4. In the DHCP console, right-click **IPv4** and choose **New Scope.**
5. In the New Scope Wizard, click **Next.**
6. On the Scope Name page, in the Name text box, type **NormalScope** and click **Next.**
7. On the IP Address Range page, type **172.24.25.50** for the Start IP address and type **172.24.25.200** for the End IP address. For the subnet mask, type **255.255.255.0**. Click **Next.**
8. On the Add Exclusions and Delay page, click **Next.**
9. On the Lease Duration page, click **Next.**
10. On the Configure DHCP Options page, click **Next.**
11. On the Router (Default Gateway) page, type **172.24.25.1** for the IP address and click **Add.** Click **Next.**
12. On the Domain Name and DNS Servers page, click **Next.**
13. On the WINS Servers page, click **Next.**
14. On the Activate Scope page, click **Next.**
15. When the wizard is complete, click **Finish.**
16. Under the NormalScope scope, right-click the **Policies** node and choose **New Policy.**
17. In the DHCP Policy Configuration Wizard, type **Policy1** for the Policy name and click **Next.**
18. On the Configure Conditions for the Policy page, click **Add.**
19. In the Add/Edit Condition dialog box (see Figure 4-18), select the following and click **Add:**

    Criteria: **Vendor Class**

    Operator: **Equals**

    Value: **Nortel Phones**
20. Click **OK** to close the Add/Edit Condition dialog box.
21. Back on the Configure Conditions for the Policy page, click **Next.**
22. On the Configure Settings for the Policy page (see Figure 4-19), in the Start IP address text box, type **172.24.25.50.** In the End IP address text box, type **172.24.25.99**. Click **Next.**

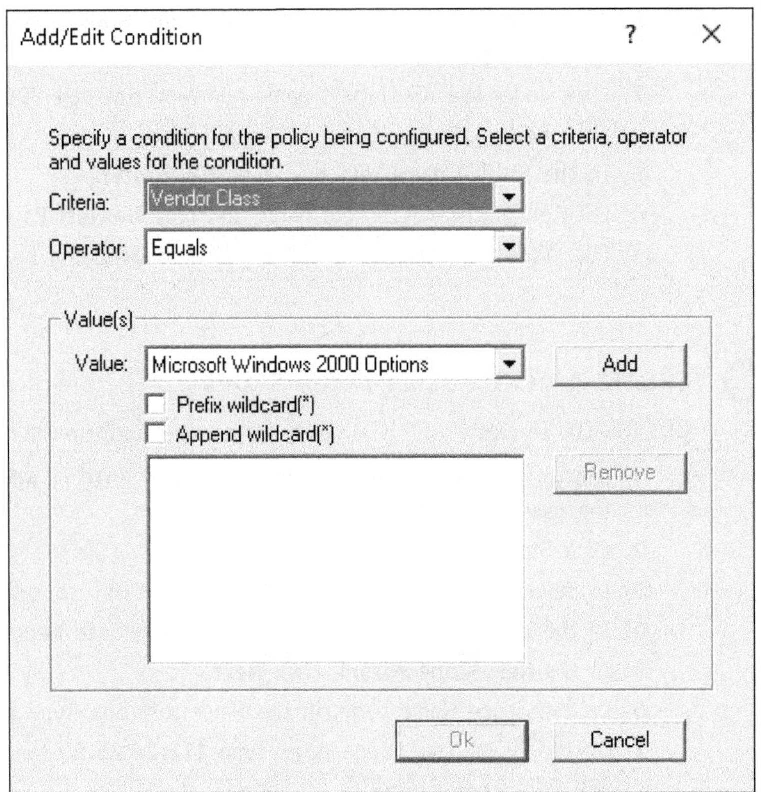

Figure 4-18
Specifying a condition

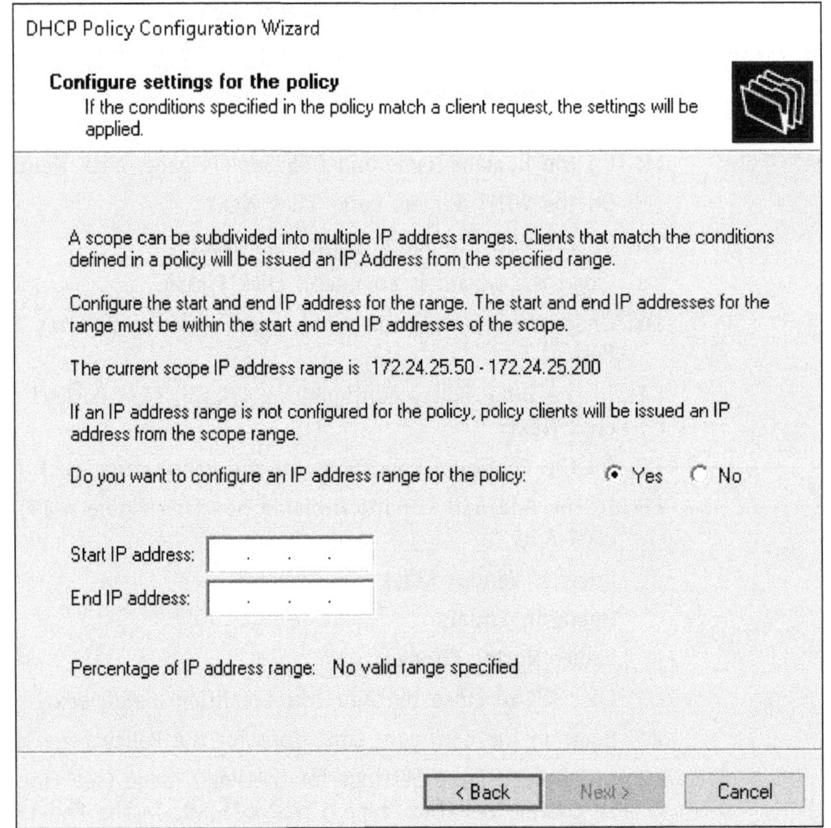

Figure 4-19
Specifying settings for a policy

23. If you need different options for the Nortel Phones, you would specify them. For now, click **Next.**
24. On the Summary page, click **Finish.**
25. Right-click **Policy1** and choose **Properties.**
26. In the Properties dialog box, click to select the **Set lease duration for the policy** option.
27. Change the lease time to **7** days. Click **OK.**

Configuring DNS Registration

Starting with Windows Server 2012 R2, by using the proper FQDN-based condition and a DNS suffix, you can use DHCP policies to fully control DNS registration for computers and devices on the network, including workgroup computers, guest devices, or clients with a specific attribute.

With Windows Server 2016, you can use DHCP policies to allow users to configure conditions based on the fully qualified domain name (FQDN) of the client. In addition, DHCP policies can be configured to register DHCP clients using a specific DNS suffix, overriding the DNS suffix that is already configured on the client.

CONFIGURE A POLICY BASED ON THE FQDN

GET READY. To configure a policy based on the FQDN, perform the following steps.

1. Using Server Manager, open the DHCP console.
2. In the DHCP console, expand the **server**, expand **IPv4**, expand a **scope**, and then click the **Policies** node. Right-click the **Policies** node and choose **New Policy.**
3. When the DHCP Policy Configuration Wizard opens, on the Policy based IP Address and Option Assignment page, in the Policy Name text box, type a name of the policy. In the Description text box, type a description for the policy. Click **Next.**
4. On the Configure Conditions for the Policy page, click **Add.**
5. In the Add/Edit Condition dialog box, for Criteria, select **Fully Qualified Domain Name.** The Operator is already set to **Equals.**
6. In the Value text box, type a domain name, such as **adatum.com** and click **Add.** If desired, you can select the **Prefix wildcard(*)** option or the **Append wildcard (*)** option. Click **OK.**
7. On the Configure Conditions for the Policy page, click **Next.**
8. On the Summary page, click **Finish.**

Configuring Client and Server for PXE Boot

Preboot Execution Environment (PXE) allows a client to boot from a server over the network. PXE-enabled network cards add the DHCP option 60 to their DHCP discover packets. Normally, DHCP clients send a DHCP option 67 packet, and then DHCP servers return a DHCP 68 option offer. The ports that DHCP uses also are used by the Windows Deployment Services PXE server function. Therefore, if you deploy DHCP and a PXE server on the same machine, you must set DHCP to make offers that also include the 60 option. A DHCP server then makes the DHCP 60 offer back to the client. You need to set DHCP options 60 (PXE Client), 66 (Boot Server Host Name), and 67 (Bootfile Name). You can set options 66 and 67 in the Scope Options window in the DHCP console, but you must set the 60 option via the command line.

CERTIFICATION READY
Configure client and server for PXE boot
Objective 2.1

If you are using Windows Deployment Services (WDS) to deploy Windows to a remote client computer, you would use a DHCP server. However, for most organizations, the WDS server is not going to be the DHCP server. Therefore, you need to configure the DHCP server to boot the computer from the WDS server.

CONFIGURE A CUSTOM DHCP OPTION

GET READY. To configure a custom DHCP option, perform the following steps.

1. Log on to a server running Windows Server 2016 as **adatum\administrator** with the password of **Pa$$w0rd**.
2. Click **Start** and click **Server Manager**.
3. In Server Manager, click **Tools > DHCP**. The DHCP console opens.
4. Expand the **server** node and the **IPv4** node.
5. Right-click the **IPv4** node and choose **Set Predefined Options**.
6. In the Predefined Options and Values dialog box, click **Add**. The Option Type dialog box opens, as shown in Figure 4-20.

Figure 4-20

The Option Type dialog box

Option Type ? ×
Class: Global
Name:
Data type: Byte ☐ Array
Code:
Description:
OK Cancel

7. In the Name text box, type **PXEClient**.
8. From the Data type drop-down list, select **String**.
9. In the Code text box, key **060**.
10. Click **OK**.
11. Click **OK** again to close the Predefined Options and Values dialog box.
12. In the scope pane, right-click the **Server Options** node and choose **Configure Options**. The Server Options dialog box opens.
13. In the Available Options list box, scroll down and select the **060 PXEClient** option you just created.
14. In the String Value text box, key the name or IP address of your WDS server. Then, click **OK**.

This procedure adds the 060 custom option value you defined to all of the DHCPOFFER packets the DHCP server sends out to clients. When a client computer boots from a local device, such as a hard drive or CD-ROM, the 060 option has no effect. However, when a client performs a network boot, after receiving and accepting an offered IP address from the DHCP server, it connects to the WDS server specified in the 060 PXEClient option and uses it to obtain the boot image file it needs to start.

Configuring the DHCP Relay Agent

By default, routers do not allow broadcasts to pass through routers. Therefore, for the DHCP server to hand out addresses to a subnet, it has to be physically connected to the subnet, or you have to install a ***DHCP Relay Agent*** or ***DHCP Helper*** on the subnet that relays the DHCP requests to the DHCP server. The DHCP Relay Agent could be a Windows server or workstation or built into a router or switch.

CERTIFICATION READY
Configure DHCP Relay Agent
Objective 2.1

The ***Routing and Remote Access (RRAS)*** is an administrative tool used to create a virtual private network (VPN) gateway for clients, provide routing functionality, and provide a DHCP Relay Agent.

MORE INFORMATION
Installing and configuring RRAS is discussed in Lesson 8.

The Relay Agent is already installed for IPv4. If you need it for IPv6, right-click the General node under IPv6 and choose New Routing Protocol. When the New Routing Protocol dialog box opens, DHCP v6 Relay Agent is already highlighted. Click OK.

CONFIGURE THE DHCP RELAY AGENT

GET READY. To configure the DHCP Relay Agent, perform the following steps.

1. Log on to a server running Windows Server 2016 as **adatum\administrator** with the password of **Pa$$w0rd.**
2. Click **Start** and click **Server Manager.**
3. Click **Tools > Routing and Remote Access.**
4. Expand the **server** node and the **IPv4** node.
5. Right-click **DHCP Relay Agent** and choose **Properties.** The DHCP Relay Agent Properties dialog box opens (see Figure 4-21).

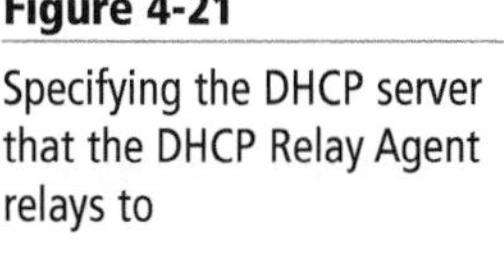

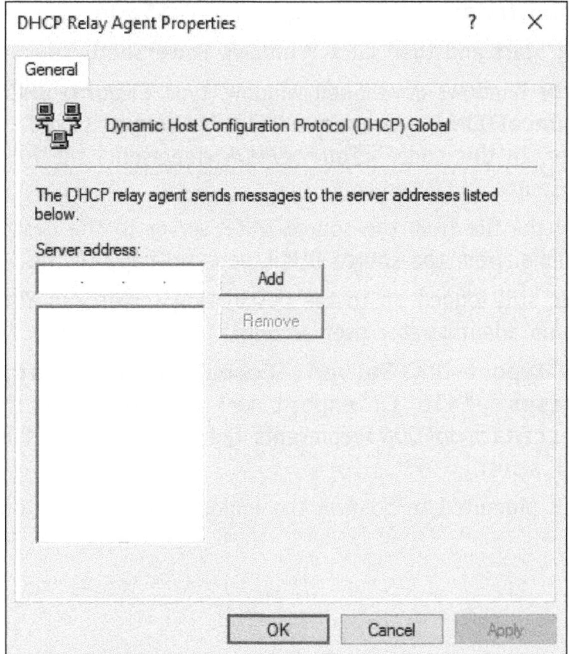

Figure 4-21
Specifying the DHCP server that the DHCP Relay Agent relays to

6. In the Server address text box, type in the address of the DHCP server and click **Add.**
7. Click **OK** to close the DHCP Relay Agent Properties dialog box.

Performing DHCP Server Migration Using Export and Import

Migrations are recommended when moving from a previous version of Windows Server to a new version, but can also be used to move from one system to another that are running the same operating system.

CERTIFICATION READY
Perform export and import of a DHCP server
Objective 2.1

To perform a migration between Windows Server 2008, Windows Server 2008 R2, Windows Server 2012, Windows Server 2012 R2, and Windows Server 2016, use the following high-level steps:

1. Install the DHCP Server role on the computer that will be the new DHCP server.
2. Stop the DHCP service on the current DHCP server.
3. Export the DHCP data from the current server.
4. Copy the DHCP data to the new server (or make it available on the network).
5. Import the DHCP data to the new server.

To export and import the data, use the following Windows PowerShell cmdlets with their required switches:

- **From the source server:** `Export-DhcpServer`
- **From the destination server:** `Import-DhcpServer`

PERFORM A DHCP SERVER MIGRATION WITH WINDOWS POWERSHELL

GET READY. With the migration prerequisites ready, and with Windows Server Migration Tools installed on both the source server and destination server, perform the following steps.

1. Log on to a source DHCP server running Windows Server 2016 as **adatum\administrator** with the password of **Pa$$w0rd.**
2. Click **Start** and then click **Windows PowerShell.**
3. In the Windows PowerShell window, type **Export-DHCPServer -ComputerName <SourceFQDN> -Leases -File C:\export.xml -verbose** and then press **Enter.** In this code, *<SourceFQDN>* represents the fully qualified domain name of the source DHCP server.
4. Copy the file from the source DHCP server to the destination DHCP server. For example, from the source DHCP, you can copy to the \\<TargetDHCPSErver>\C$.
5. While still logged on to the destination server, run Windows PowerShell under a domain administrator user account.

   Type **Import-DHCPServer -ComputerName <DestinationFQDN> -Leases -File C:\export.xml -verbose** and then press **Enter.** *<DestinationFQDN>* represents the fully qualified domain name of the destination DHCP server.
6. When prompted to confirm the import, press **Y** then press **Enter.**

Using the Windows Server Migration Tools

Many roles included with Windows Server 2016 involve a lot of configuring. A particular role might require policies, security, or other settings that you must configure before it can be used. Therefore, when you want to migrate such roles, you want to find a way that can migrate them and all their configuration settings to another server quickly and easily without having to install and configure the role from the beginning. If you search for *Migrating Roles and Features in Windows Server*, you should find a list of available migration guides, including how to use the ***Windows Server Migration Tools (WSMT)*** and how to migrate individual roles from one server to another.

CERTIFICATION READY
Perform DHCP server migration
Objective 2.1

WSMT installation and preparation can be divided into the following stages:

1. Identify the source and destination servers.
2. Install WSMT on destination servers that run Windows Server 2016.
3. Install all critical updates to the source server.
4. Prepare a migration store file location that source and destination servers can both access.
5. Register WSMT on source servers.
6. Perform the actual migration.

When you perform the actual migration, you export the configuration to the migration store by using the Windows PowerShell cmdlet `Export-SmigServerSettings`, and you import the configuration from the migration store by using the cmdlet `Import-SmigServerSettings`.

USE WINDOWS SERVER MIGRATION TOOLS

GET READY. To migrate the DHCP server from one server to another, perform the following steps.

1. On the source server, using Server Manager, click **Tools > Services.**
2. In the Services console, right-click **DHCP Server service** and choose **Stop.**
3. On the source server, using Server Manager, click **Tools > Windows Server Migration Tools > Windows Server Migration Tools.**
4. In the Windows Server Migration Tools window, execute the following command:

```
Export-SmigServerSetting -featureID DHCP -User All -Group
-IPConfig -path \\LON-DC1\software -Verbose
```

5. When prompted for a password, type **Pa$$w0rd** and press **Enter.**
6. On the target server, using Server Manager, click **Tools > Services.**
7. Right-click **DHCP Server service** and choose **Stop.**
8. On the target server, using Server Manager, click **Tools > Windows Server Migration Tools > Windows Server Migration Tools.**
9. From the Windows Server Migration Tools window, execute the following command:

```
Import-SmigServerSetting -featureID DHCP -User All -Group
-IPConfig -SourcePhysicalAddress "00-15-5D-01-32-24" -
TargetPhysicalAddress "00-15-5D-01-32-1F" -path \\LON-DC1\soft-
ware -Verbose
```

10. Back on the Services console, right-click **DHCP Server service** and choose **Start.**

SKILL SUMMARY

IN THIS LESSON YOU LEARNED:

- The Dynamic Host Configuration Protocol (DHCP) is a network protocol that automatically configures the IP configuration of a device, including assigning an IP address, subnet mask, default gateway, and primary and secondary Domain Name System (DNS) servers.
- DHCP scopes are ranges of IP addresses that can be allocated to clients. A scope consists of a name and description, a range of addresses, and a subnet mask.
- DHCP options are options that are assigned when the addresses are assigned or renewed, including the default gateway and the primary and secondary DNS servers. Other options include DNS domain suffix, Windows Internet Naming Service (WINS) server, and TFTP addresses.
- In Active Directory Domain Services (AD DS) environments, domain-joined Windows DHCP servers must be authorized to service DHCP client requests.
- DHCP client reservations allow administrators to reserve an IP address for permanent use by a DHCP client. By using reservations, you can ensure that the host will always have the same IP address.
- A superscope is the grouping of multiple scopes into a single administrative entity. By using superscopes, you can support larger subnets.
- Similar to the IPv4 addresses, IPv6 addresses are divided into network bits and host addresses. In addition, IPv6 supports automatic configuration. However, with a Windows DHCP server, you can perform stateful address autoconfiguration.
- By default, routers do not allow broadcasts to pass through routers. Therefore, for the DHCP server to hand out addresses to a subnet, it has to be physically connected to the subnet, or you have to install a DHCP Relay Agent or DHCP Helper on the subnet that relays the DHCP requests directly to the DHCP server.
- If you search for Migrating Roles and Features in Windows Server, you should find a list of available migration guides, including how to use the Windows Server Migration Tools (WSMT) and how to migrate individual roles from one server to another.

■ Knowledge Assessment

Multiple Choice

Select the correct answer for each of the following questions.

1. A scope called *Scope1* (192.168.3.0/24) is running out of addresses. Which of the following actions expands the number of addresses?
   a. Create a 192.168.4.0 scope and create a superscope.
   b. Create an IPv6 scope.
   c. Reassign the scope to 172.24.3.0/16.
   d. Create a multicast scope.

2. Which type of communication sends a single set of packets to multiple hosts at the same time?
   a. Unicast
   b. Broadcast
   c. Multicast
   d. Anycast
3. Which type of IPv6 address mechanism is used to generate link-local addresses using the MAC address?
   a. Stateless
   b. Stateful
   c. Prefix-based
   d. Multicast
4. Which of the following is the default DHCP failover mode?
   a. Stateless
   b. Stateful
   c. Load Sharing
   d. Hot Standby
5. When adding a DHCP reservation for a printer, which components should be included in the reservation? (Choose two answers.)
   a. The MAC address
   b. The default gateway
   c. The printer server name
   d. The IP address
6. After just installing a new DHCP server, you try to start the DHCP service, but it will not start. Which of the following actions should be performed?
   a. Restart the server.
   b. Configure a scope.
   c. Activate the scope.
   d. Authorize the server in Active Directory.
7. A server is running Windows Server 2016. You want to assign the same IP address from the DHCP server to the server every time. Which of the following is the next course of action?
   a. Create a DHCP policy.
   b. Create an exclusion policy.
   c. Create a single scope with the specified address.
   d. Create a reservation.
8. You manage a 192.168.1.0/24 subnet. Using DHCP, you want IP phones to be assigned addresses 192.168.1.51-100 and desktop computers assigned addresses 192.168.1.101-155. How should you proceed while keeping the administrative effort to a minimum?
   a. Create a multicast scope.
   b. Create a superscope.
   c. Use DHCP policies.
   d. Create multiple standard scopes.
9. You manage the following DHCP scope: 192.168.1.0/24 and you need to migrate the clients to 172.24.1.0/16. Which type of scope should be created to perform the migration?
   a. A multicast scope
   b. A superscope
   c. A split scope
   d. An IPv6 scope

10. A server is running Windows Server 2016 with five networks. Two teams are created, each with two NICs. You want to use reservations to always assign the same IP addresses to the interfaces. How many reservations are needed on the DHCP server?
    a. 2
    b. 3
    c. 4
    d. 5
11. When performing a DHCP server migration from Windows Server 2012 R2 to Windows Server 2016, which command is used on the source server?
    a. `NETSH`
    b. `Export-SmigServerSetting`
    c. `Export-DHCPServer`
    d. `Copy-Item`
12. In which of the following dialog boxes would the PTR record registration for a single IP range be disabled?
    a. DHCP Server Properties
    b. IPv4 Properties
    c. Scope Properties
    d. DHCP Policies

Best Answer

Choose the letter that corresponds to the best answer. More than one answer choice may achieve the goal. Select the BEST answer.

1. Which setting blocks a range of MAC addresses from being issued DHCP server addresses?
    a. MAC filters
    b. DHCP policies
    c. Reservations
    d. Server options

Build List

1. Specify the correct order of steps necessary to allocating a different range of IP addresses to network HP printers within a scope and a different lease period by placing the number of the step in the appropriate space. Not all steps will be used.
    ____ Create a scope.
    ____ Set the lease duration for the policy.
    ____ Create a policy.
    ____ Create a client identifier.
    ____ Create a user class.
    ____ Create a vendor class.
    ____ Configure a condition.

2. You administer a scope that covers the 172.50.1.0/24 subnet. Specify the correct order of steps necessary to expanding the scope to 172.50.2.0 by placing the number of the step in the appropriate space. Not all steps will be used.
    ____ Right-click IPv4 and choose New Superscope.
    ____ Duplicate the current scope.
    ____ Create a new scope.
    ____ Create two new scopes.
    ____ Select two scopes that you want to combine and finish creating the superscope.
    ____ Right-click the original scope and expand the address range.

■ Business Case Scenarios

Scenario 4-1: Performing Granular IP Address Leasing on a DHCP Scope

As the administrator for the Contoso Corporation, you manage 15 sites. You want to create one DHCP scope that includes one set of addresses for computers, one set of addresses for printers, and one set of addresses for IP phones. Describe your recommended solution.

Scenario 4-2: Changing DNS Servers

Most of your clients use DHCP to receive their IP configuration via DHCP servers running on computers running Windows Server 2016. You are about ready to replace the majority of your network printers. You remember that a couple of years ago, it took quite a bit of time and effort to configure the printers for network connectivity. Describe how to simplify the configuration.

Managing and Maintaining DHCP

70-741 EXAM OBJECTIVE

Objective 2.2 – Manage and maintain DHCP. This objective may include but is not limited to the following: Configure a lease period; back up and restore the DHCP database; configure high availability using DHCP failover; configure DHCP Name Protection; troubleshoot DHCP.

Lesson Heading	Exam Objective
Managing and Maintaining DHCP • Configuring Scope Properties, Including Configuring the Lease Period • Configuring DHCP Name Protection • Performing a DHCP Database Backup • Compacting and Reconciling the DHCP Database	Configure a lease period Configure DHCP Name Protection Back up and restore the DHCP database
Configuring High Availability for DHCP • Configuring Split Scopes • Configuring DHCP Failover	Configure high availability using DHCP failover
Troubleshooting DHCP	Troubleshoot DHCP

KEY TERMS

DHCP failover **DHCP Name Protection** **split scopes**

Managing and Maintaining DHCP

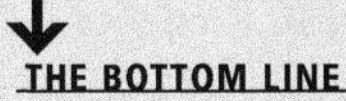

Database maintenance will keep your DHCP solution running smoothly and provide proactive measures in preparing for server failure or inconsistencies.

As with any other server or service, you must know how to run and maintain active backups and store them in a location separate from the DHCP server itself.

Along with understanding how to create a backup, it is also important to test the backup by performing routine restores of the production database into a lab environment. By maintaining and consistently practicing good backup and restore processes and testing, you provide your enterprise a well-planned and resilient environment.

Another routine maintenance task is monitoring database growth compared to actual usage. If the database begins to approach or grows over 30 MB, it is recommended to compact the database to free up white space and maintain the integrity of the database.

There are also chances of inconsistencies within the database that must be resolved by reconciling the database.

Configuring Scope Properties, Including Configuring the Lease Period

In Lesson 4, you learned how to create scopes, including defining the lease period. Right-click any DHCP scope and choose Properties to open the Properties dialog box, as shown in Figure 5-1. Then, from the Properties dialog box, you can change the lease duration of the scope. You can also change the start IP address and end IP address and change the scope name. Ideally, all scopes should have the same lease duration, particularly if you are using scavenging.

Figure 5-1

Configuring Scope properties

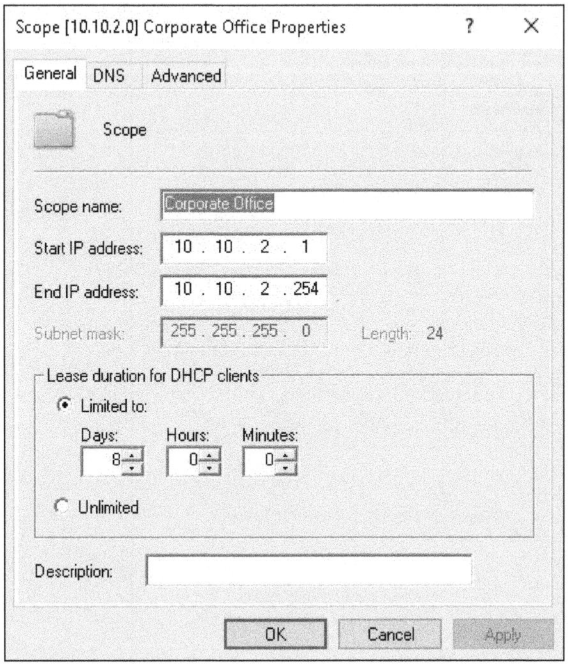

CERTIFICATION READY
Configure a lease period
Objective 2.2

Click the DNS tab to configure Dynamic DNS updates. By default, the following settings are enabled:

- Enable DNS dynamic updates according to the settings below:
  - Dynamically update DNS records only if requested by the DHCP clients
  - Always dynamically update DNS records
- Discard A and PTR records when lease is deleted

With Windows Server 2016, you can configure the DHCP server to register only the A record for clients with the DNS server. By only registering the A record, you avoid failed attempts to register PTR records when the associated reverse lookup zone does not exist. PTR record registration can be disabled for all clients of a DHCP server, or by specific subnet or attribute.

DISABLE DYNAMIC UPDATES FOR DNS PTR RECORDS

GET READY. To disable dynamic updates for DNS PTR records, perform the following steps.

1. Using Server Manager, open the **DHCP** console.
2. In the DHCP console, expand the server, expand **IPv4**, expand a scope, and then click the scope. Right-click the scope and choose **Properties.**
3. Click the **DNS** tab.
4. On the DNS tab, click to select the **Disable dynamic updates for DNS PTR records** option.
5. Click **OK** to close the Scope Properties dialog box.

The Advanced tab (as shown in Figure 5-2) allows you to enable DHCP, BOOTP, or Both. The default is DHCP. If you also have some network devices that need to boot with BOOTP, you should select the Both option. If you have multiple DHCP servers, and you want to favor a specific DHCP server, you need to increase the subnet delay on the other DHCP servers.

Figure 5-2

Configuring Advanced scope properties

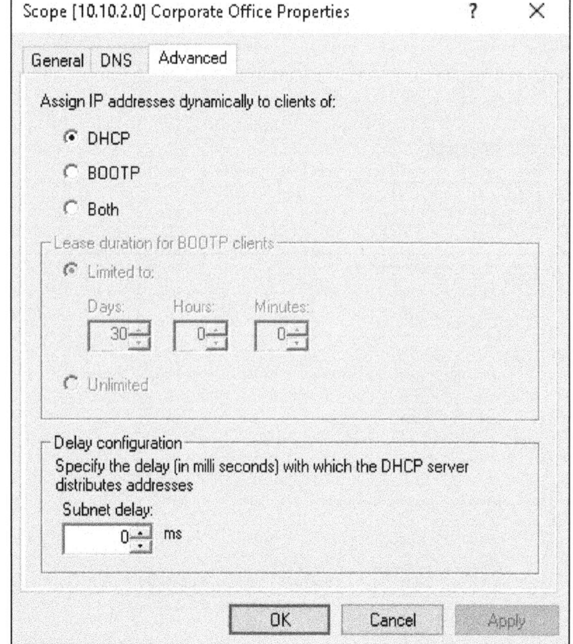

Configuring DHCP Name Protection

If an organization uses only Windows systems that are part of an Active Directory domain, each computer will have its own unique computer name, which DHCP registers in DNS on behalf of the client. Name squatting is when a non-Windows-based computer registers a name in DNS that is already registered to a Windows-based computer. To prevent non-Microsoft systems from overwriting systems that use static addresses, Windows Server 2012 introduced ***DHCP Name Protection*** to prevent these conflicts.

CERTIFICATION READY
Configure DHCP Name Protection
Objective 2.2

When one client registers a name with DNS, but the name is already used by another client, the original machine can become inaccessible. DHCP Name Protection addresses uses a resource record known as a *Dynamic Host Configuration Identifier (DHCID)* to track which machines originally requested which names. When DHCP assigns or renews an address, the DHCP server refers to the DHCID in DNS to verify that the machine that is requesting the name is the original machine that used the name. If it is not the same machine, the DNS resource record is not updated.

Name Protection can be used for both IPv4 and IPv6 and can be configured at the server level or at the scope level. However, configuring DHCP Name Protection at the server level applies only to newly created scopes.

ENABLE DHCP NAME PROTECTION FOR AN IPv4 OR IPv6 NODE

GET READY. To enable DHCP Name Protection for an IPv4 or IPv6 node, perform the following steps.

1. Open **Server Manager**, open the **Tools** menu, and click **DHCP**. The DHCP console opens.
2. Right-click **IPv4** or **IPv6** and choose **Properties**.
3. In the Properties dialog box, click the **DNS** tab.
4. Click the **Configure in the Name Protection** section. The Name Protection dialog box opens (see Figure 5-3).

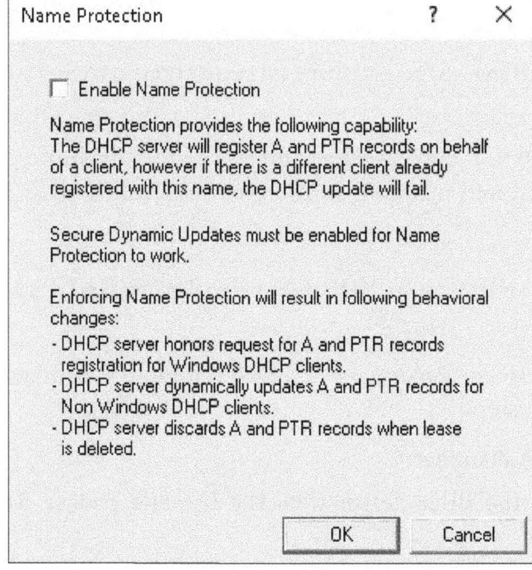

Figure 5-3
Enabling DHCP Name Protection

5. Click to select the **Enable Name Protection** option.
6. Click **OK** to close the Name Protection dialog box and click **OK** to close the Properties dialog box.

ENABLE DHCP NAME PROTECTION FOR A SCOPE

GET READY. To enable DHCP Name Protection for a scope, perform the following steps.

1. Open **Server Manager** and click **Tools > DHCP**. The DHCP console opens.
2. Right-click the scope and choose **Properties**.
3. In the Properties dialog box, click the **DNS** tab.
4. Click **Configure** in the Name Protection section. The Name Protection dialog box opens.
5. Click to select the **Enable Name Protection** option.
6. Click **OK** to close the Name Protection dialog box and click **OK** to close the Properties dialog box.

Performing a DHCP Database Backup

It is also critical to know how to perform a manual backup and restore of the database in the event of a disaster. It can be beneficial to separate the backup path from the default DHCP database location. If a disk were to fail that contained both the DHCP database and the backup database, then the design of DHCP resiliency was not properly planned for.

CERTIFICATION READY
Back up and restore the DHCP database
Objective 2.2

The dhcp.mdb file automatically backs up synchronously every 60 minutes by default. To change the interval of automatic backups, you can modify the following registry REG_DWORD:

```
HKEY_LOCAL_MACHINE\SYSTEM\CurrentControlSet\Services\DHCPServer\
Parameters\BackupInterval
```

The dhcp.mdb file can also be manually or synchronously backed up from the DHCP console or by using PowerShell. To perform a backup of the DHCP database using the console or PowerShell, the user performing the command or action must be a member of the DHCP Administrators group on the DHCP server.

Both the manual and automated backup processes described previously back up the entire database, all scopes, superscopes, multicast scopes, reservations, leases, all options, and all keys and settings found in:

```
HKEY_LOCAL_MACHINE\SYSTEM\CurrentControlSet\Services\DHCPServer\
Parameters
```

A backup of the DHCP database does not store DNS dynamic update credentials. These settings need to be restored manually in the event of a full DHCP database restore.

PERFORM A MANUAL BACKUP OF THE DHCP DATABASE FROM DHCP MANAGER

GET READY. To perform a manual backup of the DHCP database from DHCP Manager, perform the following steps.

1. Open **DHCP Manager**.
2. Right-click the DHCP server from the list and choose **Backup**. The Browse for Folder window opens.
3. Navigate to and select the desired destination path to save the backup to and then click **OK**.
4. To verify the backup, open Windows Explorer, navigate to the destination path chosen in the previous step, and then verify DHCP.cfg exists.
5. After the file has been verified and is in the correct location, close all open windows and snap-ins.

Though backups occur automatically, every 60 minutes by default, it is beneficial to take a manual backup and store it in a safe location prior to any changes to a DHCP production environment.

PERFORM A MANUAL BACKUP OF THE DHCP DATABASE USING POWERSHELL

GET READY. To perform a manual backup of the DHCP database using PowerShell, perform the following steps.

1. Identify the destination file path where the backup will be stored. This will be used as the *<Destination>* in Step 2. Open **PowerShell.**
2. At the PowerShell prompt, type **Backup-DHCPServer -Path <Destination>** and then press **Enter.**
3. To verify the backup, open Windows Explorer, navigate to the destination path chosen in the previous step, and then verify DHCP.cfg exists.
4. After the file has been verified and is in the correct location, close all open windows and snap-ins.

Though backups occur automatically, every 60 minutes by default, it is beneficial to take a manual backup and store it in a safe location prior to any changes to a DHCP production environment.

Performing a restore of the DHCP database restores those settings backed up during the backup process, including all scopes, superscopes, multicast scopes, reservations, leases, all options, and all keys and settings found in the aforementioned registry path.

A restore can be completed from within the DHCP console or by using PowerShell.

Again, if a restore is performed, the DNS dynamic update credentials must be entered again once the restore has completed.

During the restore process, if the DHCP server being restored is serving clients, they will be unable to receive an address until the DHCP service is started when the restore process has completed.

PERFORM A RESTORE OF THE DHCP DATABASE USING DHCP MANAGER

GET READY. To perform a manual restore of the DHCP database using DHCP Manager, perform the following steps.

1. Open **DHCP Manager.**
2. Right-click the DHCP server from the list and choose **Restore.** The Browse for Folder window opens.
3. Navigate to and select the desired source path from which to restore the backup and click **OK.** Click **Yes** to stop and restart DHCP service.
4. When the DHCP successful restore message appears, click **OK.**
5. Close all open windows and snap-ins.

PERFORM A RESTORE OF THE DHCP DATABASE USING POWERSHELL

GET READY. To perform a manual restore of the DHCP database using PowerShell, perform the following steps.

1. Identify the destination file path where the backup is stored. This will be used as the *<Source>* in Step 2. Open **PowerShell.**
2. At the PowerShell prompt, type **Restore-DHCPServer -Path <Source>** and then press **Enter.** The following message appears:

   Confirm

   The DHCP server database will be restored from the file<Source>. Do you want to perform this action?

[Y] Yes [N] No [S] Suspend [?] Help (default is "Y"):

WARNING: Please restart the DHCP server for the restored database to take effect.

3. Press **Enter**.
4. Restart the DHCP Server service by issuing the following command: **Restart-Service "DHCP Server"**. Press **Enter**.

Compacting and Reconciling the DHCP Database

Compacting the DHCP database will be required if the database becomes too large. During the compaction process, the DHCP database is copied to a temporary database and compacted, the original DHCP database is deleted, and the temporary database is migrated to be the live database. The temporary database is then removed.

Compacting the DHCP database requires the use of jetpack.exe, which is installed when the WINS Server feature is installed on the DHCP server. Therefore, you will need to install WINS to get access to jetpack.exe and compact the DHCP database.

COMPACT THE DHCP DATABASE

GET READY. To compact the DHCP database using PowerShell, perform the following steps.

1. Install the WINS Server feature on the DHCP server, but do not configure it.
2. Open a command prompt, type **cd %SYSTEMROOT%\System32\dhcp**, and then press **Enter**.
3. Type **net stop dhcpserver** and then press **Enter**.
4. Type **jetpack dhcp.mdb temp.mdb** and then press **Enter**. The compaction process begins.
5. When compaction has completed, type **net start dhcpserver** and then press **Enter**, as shown in Figure 5-4.

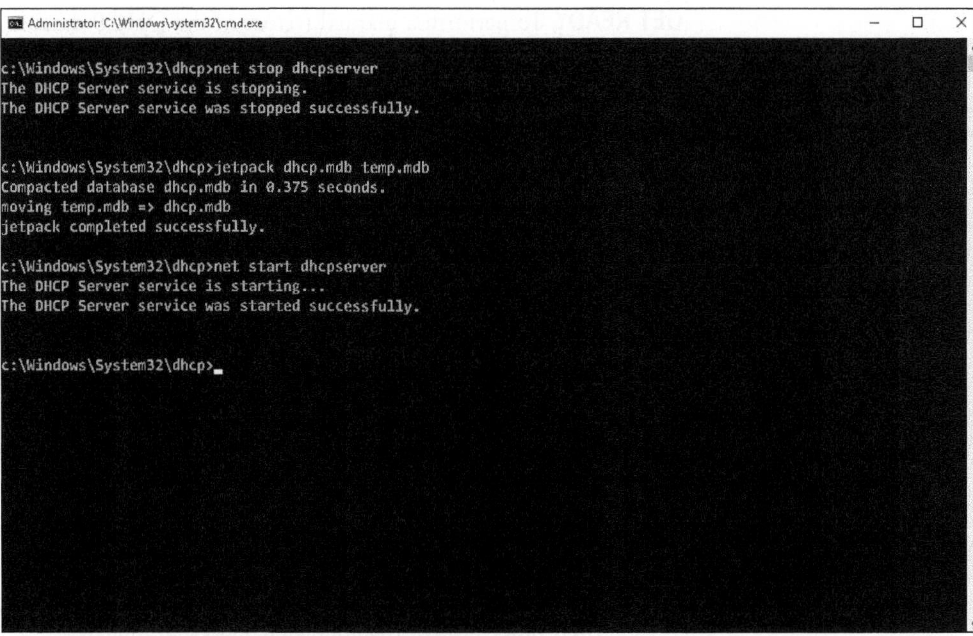

Figure 5-4
Running jetpack.exe

6. Close the Command Prompt window.

Reconciling the DHCP database checks for inconsistencies between lease records in the registry and the DHCP database. If there are inconsistencies found, the lease is reassigned to the client or a new lease is created until the client performs a DHCP discovery again.

RECONCILE THE DHCP DATABASE USING DHCP MANAGER

GET READY. To reconcile the DHCP database using DHCP Manager, perform the following steps.

1. Open **DHCP Manager.** Expand the DHCP server.
2. Right-click **IPv4** and choose **Reconcile All Scopes.** The Reconcile All Scopes window opens.
3. Click **Verify** to begin the scope repair procedure. Any inconsistencies found are displayed.
4. In the DHCP window, the following message appears: *The database is consistent.* Click **OK.**
5. After the file has been verified and is in the correct location, close all open windows and snap-ins.

RECONCILE THE DHCP DATABASE USING POWERSHELL

GET READY. To reconcile the DHCP database using PowerShell, perform the following steps.

1. Open **PowerShell.**
2. At the PowerShell prompt, type **Get-DhcpServerv4Scope | Repair-DhcpServerv4IPRecord** and then press **Enter.** When prompted to check for consistencies, for each scope press **Enter** to confirm.
3. When completed, close PowerShell.

Configuring High Availability for DHCP

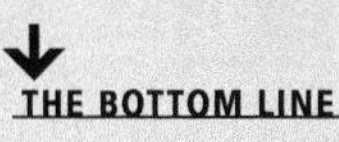

DHCP is an essential service that allows most clients and some servers to communicate on the network. As clients are turned on, or when a client renews a lease, the DHCP server must be available to assign or renew the lease. Therefore, you need to take steps to ensure that DHCP services are available.

To make DHCP highly available, you can use one of the following methods:

- ***Split scopes:*** Uses two DHCP servers to assign IP addresses. Eighty percent of the available addresses are assigned on the primary server, and 20% of the available addresses are assigned to a secondary server. When the primary server is down, the secondary server can assign IP addresses long enough for you to fix or replace the primary server.
- **Server cluster:** Uses a failover cluster to host the DHCP server. For more information about failover clustering, see the 70-740 textbook.
- ***DHCP failover:*** Replicates lease information between two DHCP servers. DHCP failover was introduced in Windows Server 2012.
- **Standby server:** Uses a hot standby DHCP server with identical scopes and options as the production DHCP server.

If you restore a DHCP database server from backup, you need to make sure that DHCP clients do not receive IP addresses that are currently in use on the network. This can be accomplished by opening the Properties of an IPv4 node, clicking the Advanced tab, and then setting the Conflict Detection value to 2.

Configuring Split Scopes

For years, if you wanted high availability, you would use a split-scope configuration, also known as the 80/20 configuration. Split-scope configuration uses two DHCP servers, with the same scopes and options. However, the scopes have complementary exclusion ranges, so that there is no overlap in the addresses that they lease clients. You do not want the two servers to hand out the same address to different clients.

It is known as the *80/20 configuration* because the primary server is assigned 80% of the available addresses, whereas the secondary server is assigned 20% of the available addresses. The secondary server is configured to respond after a delay, giving the primary server the first opportunity to hand out addresses. Because the local server responds first, it leases the address to the clients. If the primary server is not available, the secondary server will respond and lease an address.

To simplify the configuring of split scopes, Windows Server 2016 includes a DHCP Split-Scope Configuration Wizard. To access this wizard, you need to have two DHCP servers that are authorized. Then, after you create a scope, on one of the servers, you can access the DHCP Split-Scope Configuration Wizard.

USE THE DHCP SPLIT-SCOPE CONFIGURATION WIZARD

GET READY. To use the DHCP Split-Scope Configuration Wizard, perform the following steps.

1. Open **Server Manager** and click **Tools > DHCP.** The DHCP console opens.
2. Right-click a scope that you created on the DHCP server and choose **Advanced > Split-Scope.**
3. When the DHCP Split-Scope Configuration Wizard starts, click **Next.**
4. On the Additional DHCP Server page (see Figure 5-5), type the name of the secondary DCHP server and then click **Next.**

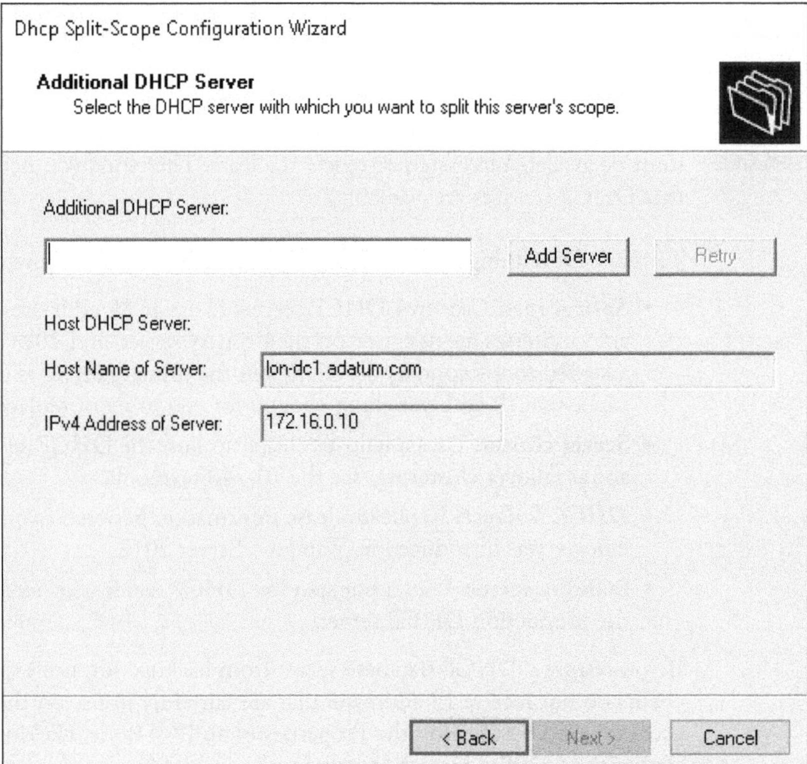

Figure 5-5

Adding a secondary DHCP server

5. On the Percentage of Split page (see Figure 5-6), the slider bar is already set at **80**. Click **Next**.

Figure 5-6

Specifying the 80-20 split

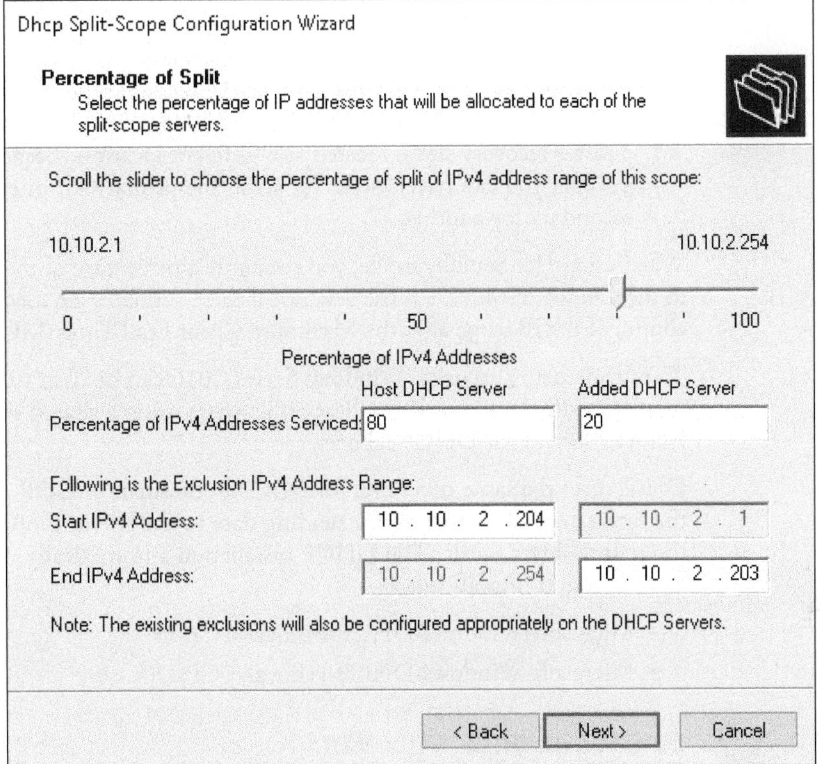

6. On the Delay in DHCP Offer page, the host DHCP server and the added DHCP server have a delay of 0 milliseconds. Change the delay of the added DHCP server to **500**. Click **Next**.
7. When the wizard is complete, click **Finish**.
8. On the Summary of Split-Scope page, click **Close**.

Configuring DHCP Failover

In the past, DHCP failover was not possible because each DHCP server had its own database. So, when a lease was granted to a client, the other DHCP server would not be aware of the other lease. So if you assigned the same pool of addresses, you would have the same address assigned to two different hosts, causing an IP address conflict. You can use clustering, which requires some manual configuration and monitoring.

CERTIFICATION READY
Configure high availability using DHCP failover
Objective 2.2

Starting with Windows Server 2012, DHCP can replicate lease information between two DHCP servers for IPv4 scopes and subnets. If one DHCP server fails or becomes overloaded, the other server services the clients for the entire subnet.

DHCP failover establishes a failover relationship between the two DHCP servers. Each relationship has a unique name, which is exchanged during configuration. A single DHCP server can have multiple failover relationships with other DHCP servers as long as each relationship has a unique name.

DHCP failover is time sensitive. The time between partners must be no greater than one minute. If the time is greater, the failover process will halt with a critical error.

DHCP failover supports two modes:

- **Load Sharing:** Both servers simultaneously supply IP configuration to clients. By default, the load is distributed evenly, 50:50. However, you can adjust the ratio if you prefer one server to another. Load Sharing is the default mode.
- **Hot Standby:** One server is the primary server that actively assigns IP configuration for the scope or subnet, and the other is the secondary server that assumes the DHCP role if the primary server becomes unavailable. Hot Standby mode is best suited when the disaster recovery site is located at a different location. Because the failover is defined for a scope, you can have one server act as the primary for one scope or subnet, and be the secondary for another.

When using Hot Standby mode, you configure a percentage of the scope addresses to be assigned to the standby server (5% is the default). If these addresses are used, the secondary server takes control of the IP scope after the Maximum Client Lead Time (MCLT) interval has passed.

To provide better security, Windows Server 2016 can be used to authenticate the failover message traffic between the replication partners using a shared secret in the Configuration Failover Wizard for DHCP failover.

DHCP uses the same two ports for BOOTP: destination UDP port 67 for sending data to the server and UDP port 68 for sending data to the client. DHCP uses TCP port 647 to listen for failover traffic. The DHCP installation automatically creates the following inbound and outbound firewall rules:

- Microsoft-Windows-DHCP-Failover-TCP-In
- Microsoft-Windows-DHCP-Failover-TCP-Out

CONFIGURE DHCP FAILOVER

GET READY. To configure DHCP failover, perform the following steps.

1. Open **Server Manager** and click **Tools > DHCP**. The DHCP console opens.
2. Expand **IPv4**.
3. To configure a single scope, right-click the scope and choose **Configure Failover.** To configure failover for all scopes, right-click **IPv4** and choose **Configure Failover.**
4. After the Configure Failover Wizard starts (see Figure 5-7), all scopes will be selected by default. To select only one scope, deselect the **Select all** option and click the scope that you want to configure. Click **Next.**

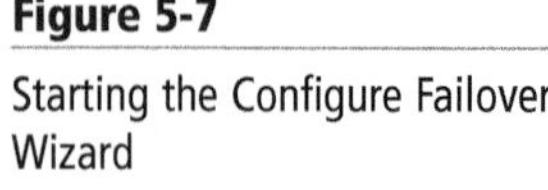

Figure 5-7

Starting the Configure Failover Wizard

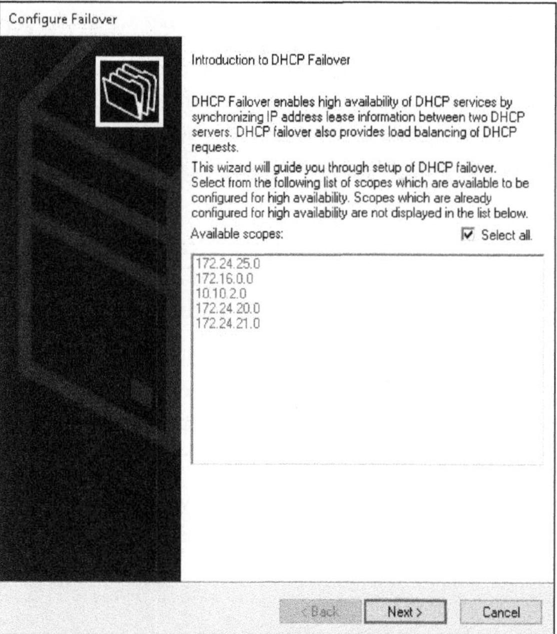

5. On the Specify the Partner Server to Use for Failover page, type the name of the partner DHCP server and click **Next.**
6. On the Create a New Failover Relationship page (see Figure 5-8), specify the Maximum Client Lead Time, the Mode, the Load Balance Percentage, and the State Switchover Interval.

Figure 5-8

Creating a new failover relationship

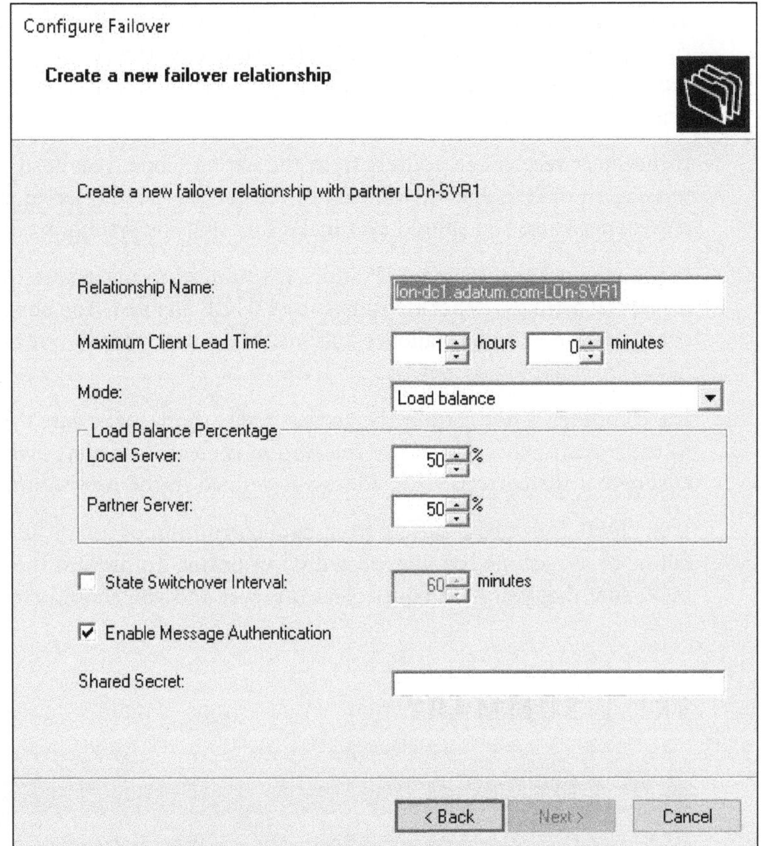

7. By default, Enable Message Authentication is enabled. Type a shared secret such as **Pa$$w0rd.** Click **Next.**
8. To complete the wizard, click **Finish.**
9. When the configuration is done, click **Close.**

Troubleshooting DHCP

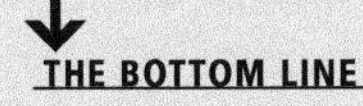

THE BOTTOM LINE

DHCP is usually one of those services that many people don't think much about until it breaks. However, when it breaks for an organization, it could be catastrophic as clients and servers cannot get their IP configuration. When this happens, you need to know how to troubleshoot DHCP.

CERTIFICATION READY
Troubleshoot DHCP
Objective 2.2

In Lesson 1, you learned that when a DHCP client cannot connect to a DHCP server to get an IP address, the system automatically assigns itself an address on the 169.254.0.0/16 network. If a client has an APIPA address, you should first check to see if the computer is connected to the network. Be sure the network adapter is connected to a network cable that is connected to an active switch or check to see if the wireless interface is turned on and connected to an active wireless access point. If the problem occurs with more than one client, it is most likely a switch problem, a network problem, or the DHCP server. You should also make sure that the DHCP relay agent or IP helper is running and is pointed to the DHCP server and make sure that you have not run out of IP addresses for the specific scope.

To see the statistics of a scope, including how many IP addresses are available in a scope, right-click a scope and choose Display Statistics. If a scope is depleted, you need to remove some of the leases or expand the scope. A temporary fix could be to reduce the lease time.

If the client receives an address from the wrong scope, you need to make sure that the DHCP relay agent or IP helper is pointing to the correct DHCP server and it is connected to the correct network. You should also make sure that the system is configured for DHCP.

If two clients have the same IP address, you need to make sure that both systems have the correct IP settings, either IP address or DHCP enabled. You should also look at your scope configuration and your failover options. Make sure you do not have two DHCP servers having overlapping scopes.

If a computer is not getting the correct reservation, make sure the computer is connected to the correct network and the reservation is created on the correct scope. You also need to ensure that the correct MAC address is defined in the reservation.

If the DHCP database suffers from data corruption or loss, it is usually caused by hardware failure or a machine has unexpectedly lost power. To prevent these situations, you should make sure that you have fault-tolerant power and you should create backups on a regular basis.

SKILL SUMMARY

IN THIS LESSON YOU LEARNED:

- Database maintenance will keep your DHCP solution running smoothly and will provide proactive measures in preparing for server failure or inconsistencies.
- Windows Server 2012 introduced DHCP Name Protection in order to prevent non-Microsoft systems from overwriting systems that use static addresses.
- It is also critical to know how to perform a manual backup and restore of the database in the event of a disaster. It can be beneficial to separate the backup path from the default DHCP database location. If a disk were to fail that contained both the DHCP database and the backup database, then the design of DHCP resiliency was not properly planned for.
- DHCP is an essential service that allows most clients and some servers to communicate on the network. As clients are turned on, or when a client renews a lease, the DHCP server must be available to assign or renew the lease. Thus, you need to take steps to ensure that DHCP services are available. To make DHCP highly available, you can use one of the following methods: split scopes, server cluster, DHCP failover, and standby server.
- When a DHCP client cannot connect to a DHCP server to get an IP address, the system automatically assigns itself an address on the 169.254.0.0/16 network.

Knowledge Assessment

Multiple Choice

Select the correct answer for each of the following questions.

1. Which of the following is used to prevent non-Windows systems from overwriting DNS information for systems that use static addresses?
   a. Dynamic Protection
   b. Stateful Protection
   c. Stateless Protection
   d. DHCP Name Protection

2. Which ports are required for DHCP failover?
   a. 20–21
   b. 67–68
   c. 101–102
   d. 140–141

3. Two DHCP servers, Server1 and Server2, are running Windows Server 2016. As the administrator, you create a scope called *Scope1*. Server1 is the primary DHCP server. Which of the following best describes the easiest way to assign 80% of the addresses to Server1 and 20% to Server2?
   a. On Scope1, run the DHCP Split-Scope Configuration Wizard.
   b. Create a multicast scope.
   c. Create a DHCP policy.
   d. Create a superscope.

4. As an administrator for the Contoso Corporation, your primary office is in Sacramento and your data recovery site in Las Vegas. You want to install a DHCP server at both locations to provide high availability. Which configuration should be used?
   a. NLB cluster
   b. Failover cluster
   c. Load Sharing mode failover partner
   d. Hot Standby mode failover partner

5. A DHCP server has been replaced due to hardware failure. The server has been restored from a backup. As the administrator, you want to ensure that DHCP clients do not receive IP addresses that are currently in use on the network. Which of the following best describes the recommended course of action?
   a. Set the Conflict Detection value to 2.
   b. Add the DHCP server option 60.
   c. Add the DHCP server option 44.
   d. Enable the Retry option.

Best Answer

Choose the letter that corresponds to the best answer. More than one answer choice may achieve the goal. Select the BEST answer.

1. Which high-availability option allows full communication and replication between two DHCP servers?
   a. DHCP failover cluster
   b. Windows Cluster Services
   c. DHCP failover
   d. DHCP split-scope

Build List

1. Specify the correct order of steps necessary to configuring a split scope by placing the number of the step in the appropriate space. Not all steps will be used.

   ____ Create the scope on the primary server.
   ____ Increase the delay for the primary server.
   ____ Increase the delay for the secondary server.
   ____ Specify the percentage of split.
   ____ Create the scope on the secondary server.
   ____ Run the DHCP Split-Scope Configuration Wizard.

■ Business Case Scenarios

Scenario 5-1: Running JetPack.exe

A DHCP database has grown to more than 50 MB in size, and various, random issues have been happening. Attempting to run `jetpack dhcp.mdb temp.mdb` from C:\Windows\System32\dhcp does not work. You realize that jetpack.exe can be found only within the subdirectories of C:\Windows\WinSxS\. You copy jetpack.exe from within that subdirectory and place it into the C:\Windows\System32\dhcp folder and attempt to run `jetpack dhcp.mdb temp.mdb` again, only to find a different error arises. Describe how to successfully run the jetpack executable with the least amount of headache.

Scenario 5-2: Configuring DHCP High Availability

You are the administrator for the Contoso Corporation. Recently, the DHCP server failed. To fix the problem, you had to fix the server and restore from backup. You want to make the server fault tolerant in case it fails again in the future. In addition, you want to ensure that you add additional sites, and you want to allow the servers to handle a bigger load. Describe your recommended solution.

Installing and Configuring IP Address Management (IPAM)

LESSON 6

70-741 EXAM OBJECTIVE

Objective 3.1 – Install and configure IP Address Management (IPAM). This objective may include but is not limited to the following: Provision IPAM manually or by using Group Policy; configure server discovery; create and manage IP blocks and ranges; monitor utilization of IP address space; migrate existing workloads to IPAM; configure IPAM database storage using SQL Server; determine scenarios for using IPAM with System Center Virtual Machine Manager for physical and virtual IP address space management.

Lesson Heading	Exam Objective
Installing and Configuring IPAM	Provision IPAM manually or by using Group Policy
• Installing IPAM	Configure IPAM database storage using SQL Server
• Provisioning IPAM Manually or by Using Group Policy	Configure server discovery
• Configuring IPAM Database Storage	Create and manage IP blocks and ranges
• Configuring Server Discovery	Migrate existing workloads to IPAM
• Creating and Managing IP Blocks and Ranges	Monitor utilization of IP address space
• Migrating Existing Workloads to IPAM	Determine scenarios for using IPAM with System Center Virtual Machine Manager for physical and virtual IP address space management
• Monitoring Utilization of IP Address Space	
• Determining Scenarios for Using IPAM with System Center Virtual Machine Manager	

KEY TERMS

IP address block
IP Address Management (IPAM)
IP address range
IP addresses
System Center Virtual Machine Manager (VMM)

■ Installing and Configuring IPAM

THE BOTTOM LINE

IP Address Management (IPAM) is a feature introduced in Windows Server 2012 that provides an administrator with the ability to plan, manage, track, and audit the use of all IP addresses and the DNS services within the network. IPAM is *not* a new network function. Planning, managing, tracking, and auditing of IP addresses have been a thorn in every network administrator's side for many years. The only method of managing such facilities prior to Windows Server 2012 was by the Dynamic Host Configuration Protocol (DHCP) and Domain Name Service (DNS) management consoles; third-party databases; or applications, spreadsheets, or in some cases even scraps of paper with details of every network node recorded. The advent of IPAM in Windows Server 2012, Windows Server 2012 R2, and Windows Server 2016 removes the necessity for all of these alternative methods.

IPAM provides a single point of administration for all DNS and IP management features within an Active Directory forest. A number of key terms need to be clearly understood prior to implementing IPAM. In addition, a number of requirements and functional limitations need to be taken into consideration:

- ***IP address block:*** IP address blocks are the highest-level conceptual entities in an IP address space. They are marked with a starting and ending IP address. For public IP addresses, the address block is assigned by the Internet Registry (for smaller ranges, this is delegated by your Internet service provider). Network administrators split address blocks into address ranges, which is the basis of DHCP scopes. An administrator can use IPAM to add, import, edit, and delete IP address blocks. IPAM automatically tracks the address ranges belonging to an address block. Figure 6-1 shows a hierarchical representation of the address block.
- ***IP address range:*** IP address ranges are the next hierarchical level of an IP address space, beneath the address block. Typically, an address range is a subnet marked by a starting and ending address, using a subnet mask. An IP address range normally maps to a DHCP scope. IP address ranges can be added or imported by IPAM.
- ***IP addresses:*** IP addresses are the individual addresses that are contained in an IP address range. IPAM allows complete end-to-end management of both IPv4 and IPv6 IP addresses. IPAM automatically maps IP addresses to the correct range by using the starting and ending addresses of a range. IP addresses can be added manually or imported by IPAM from external sources.

Figure 6-1 shows the whole IP address space and how each component fits in the hierarchical model.

Figure 6-1

Displaying the IP address space

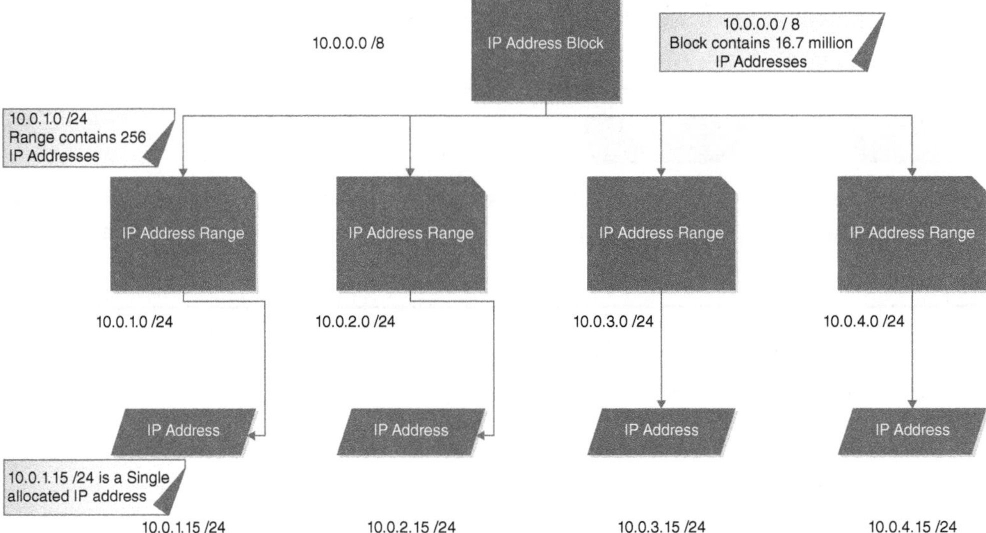

To successfully deploy IPAM, the following general requirements should be met:

- An IPAM server *must* be a domain member but *cannot* be a domain controller.
- The IPAM server should be a single-purpose server. It is not recommended to install DHCP, DNS, or any other roles on the IPAM server.
- The IPAM server can manage the IPv6 address space if IPv6 is enabled on that server.
- Always log on to the IPAM server with a domain account, *not* a local account.
- Ensure that the IPAM administrator is a member of the correct local IPAM security group on the IPAM server.
- To use IPAM to track and audit IP addresses, ensure that the *Log events on all domain controllers and NPS servers* option is enabled.

For an IPAM server to be deployed in Windows Server 2016, it must meet the following hardware requirements:

- A dual-core processor of at least 2.0 GHz
- 4 GB or more of RAM
- 80 GB of free hard disk space

To be able to manage the Windows Server 2008 DHCP and DNS roles using IPAM on Windows Server 2016, the following requirements should be installed on the Windows Server 2008 or Windows Server 2008 R2 systems:

- Service Pack 2 on Windows Server 2008
- .NET Framework 4.0 full installation
- Windows Management Framework (WMF) 3.0, which provides PowerShell 3.0
- Windows Remote Management (WinRM) must be enabled

Windows Server IPAM can manage only one Active Directory forest. IPAM can be deployed in one of three topologies:

- **Centralized:** A single IPAM server is deployed for the whole forest.
- **Distributed:** An IPAM server is deployed to every site in the forest.
- **Hybrid:** A central IPAM server and dedicated site-based IPAM servers are deployed at some sites.

Figure 6-2 shows the distributed deployment.

There are a number of published specifications for the IPAM feature, which are listed here:

- It is important to understand that an IPAM server never communicates with another IPAM server. For example, they will maintain their own IP address spaces and not share that information within their databases. To effectively manage multiple IPAM servers within a forest, it is necessary to manually configure the discovery scope of each server.
- IPAM manages only Microsoft DHCP and DNS services; no third-party solutions can be managed using Windows Server 2016 IPAM.
- IPAM supports only domain-joined DNS, DHCP, and NPS servers.
- IPAM supports the Windows Internal Database or Microsoft SQL Server. MYSQL, or any other third-party solution are not supported.
- A single IPAM server supports a maximum of 150 DHCP servers and 500 DNS servers.
- A single IPAM server supports up to 6,000 DHCP scopes and 150 DNS zones.
- IPAM stores up to three years of forensic IP data (IP address leases, MAC address details, and logon and logoff details) for up to 100,000 users.

Figure 6-2
IPAM distributed deployment

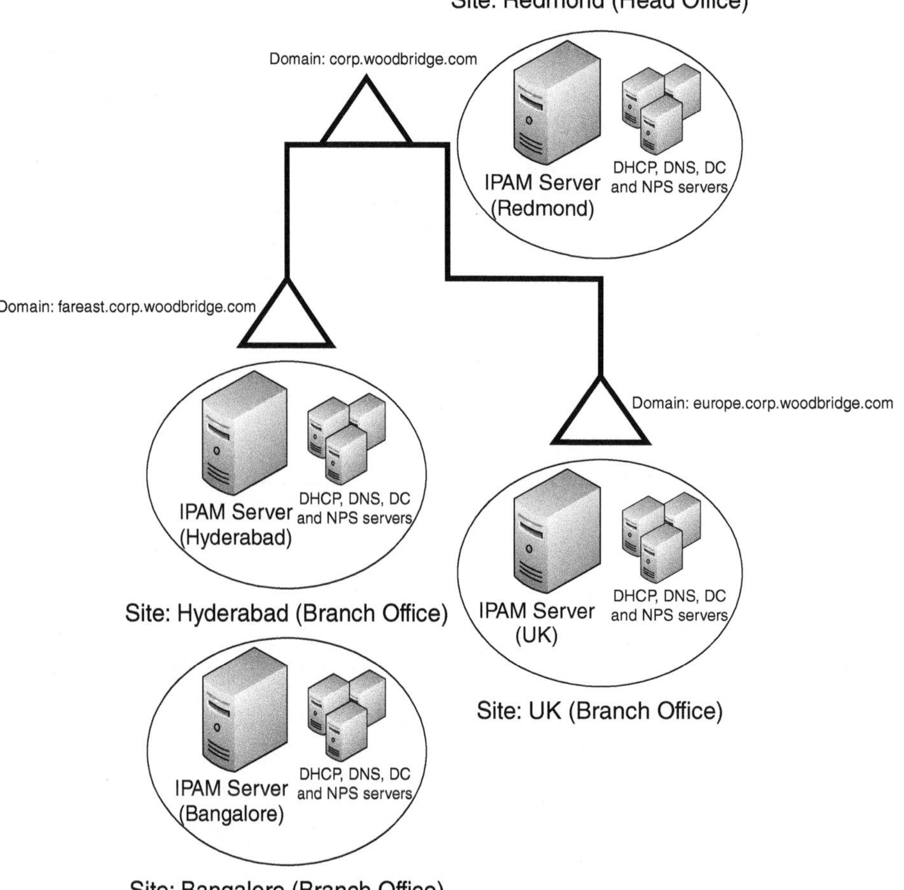

Installing IPAM

IPAM requires several steps to successfully configure the server, discovery, and address space management. The planning stage is fairly simple, but the servers, services, and administrators must all be configured carefully to ensure the feature adds full value.

There are two main components within IPAM:

- **IPAM server:** Collects data from the managed DNS and DHCP servers within the discovery scope. The IPAM server also manages the Windows Internal Database, if used. The server also provides the Role-Based Access Control (RBAC) for the IPAM installation. All the IPAM security groups and roles are managed from the IPAM server.
- **IPAM client:** Provides the interface with which the IPAM administrator manages and configures the server. The client interfaces with the server and invokes the PowerShell commands to carry out DHCP and DNS tasks along with as any remote management functions. The IPAM client is automatically installed on the IPAM server when the IPAM feature is installed. It is also possible to install the IPAM client on an alternative Windows Server 2016 without the IPAM server feature. Finally, it is also possible to manage IPAM using the IPAM client from a Windows 10 client with the Remote Server Administration Tools (RSAT) installed.

INSTALL IPAM ON A MEMBER SERVER

GET READY. Log on to the domain-joined computer where you want to install the IPAM feature, with administrative privileges. To install the IPAM feature, perform the following steps.

1. On LON-SVR1, open **Server Manager** and click **Manage > Add Roles and Features.** The Add Role Wizard begins.
2. Click **Next** four times, until the Select Features dialog box opens.
3. Select the **IP Address Management (IPAM) Server** check box. The Add Required Features dialog box opens.
4. Click **Add Features**, click **Next**, and then click **Install.** Once the installation begins, click **Close.**

Once the installation is complete, the IPAM feature appears on the main screen of Server Manager. You now have several tasks to complete in order to configure IPAM (see Figure 6-3).

Figure 6-3
Displaying IPAM server tasks

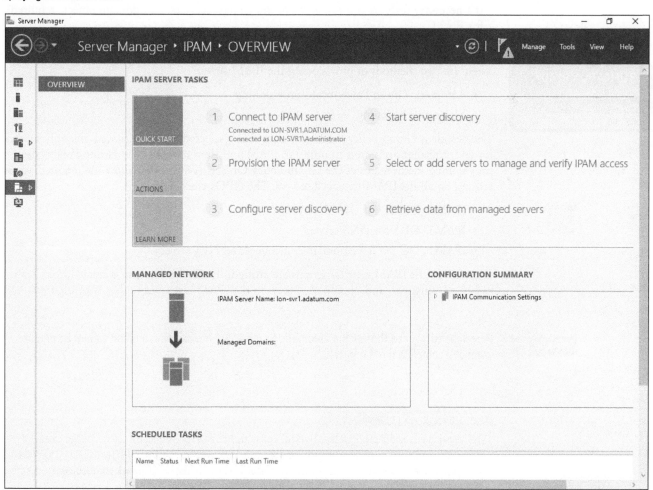

TAKE NOTE* When installing an IPAM server, the computer must be a domain member, not a domain controller.

Once the IPAM server has been installed, a number of steps are required to configure it successfully. These are all shown on the main IPAM client screen (refer to Figure 6-3).

The following IPAM tasks are required to configure the IPAM server installation:

1. Connect to IPAM server
2. Provision the IPAM server
3. Configure server discovery
4. Start server discovery
5. Select or add servers to manage and verify IPAM access
6. Retrieve data from managed servers

The Connect to IPAM server step is automatically carried out when the client is running on an IPAM server. If the client is running from a remote server (not an IPAM server), the administrator needs to connect to the chosen IPAM server.

Provisioning IPAM Manually or by Using Group Policy

IPAM provisioning is the process of allowing the IPAM server to configure and manage the necessary features and functions of the servers, services, and domain objects required for IPAM.

CERTIFICATION READY
Provision IPAM manually or by using Group Policy
Objective 3.1

There are two methods of provisioning the IPAM server:

- Automatic Group Policy-based provisioning
- Manual provisioning

The default is Group Policy-based and once this is selected and provisioned, the only method for reversing that decision is to uninstall IPAM and then reinstall. The Group Policy-based provisioning method creates the Group Policy Objects (GPOs) that allow the required access settings on all the IPAM managed servers. The GPOs created are:

- IPAM1_DHCP for DHCP servers
- IPAM1_DNS for DNS servers
- IPAM1_DC_NPS for domain controllers and NPS servers

In addition, the IPAM security groups are created, the IPAM database is created, role-based access is configured, and, finally, the access to the IPAM tasks and folders is configured.

WARNING! Remember that once chosen, the automatic Group Policy provisioning method cannot be undone without a complete IPAM reinstall.

USING POWERSHELL

The following example shows how the `Invoke-IpamGpoProvisioning` cmdlet can be used to create IPAM provisioning GPOs. In this example, three GPOs are created (IPAM1_DHCP, IPAM1_DNS, and IPAM1_DC_NPS) and linked to the contoso.com domain. These GPOs enable access for the server **ipam1.contoso.com** using the domain administrator account **user1**. In this example, the host name of the IPAM server is used as a GPO prefix; however, this is not required.

```
Invoke-IpamGpoProvisioning -Domain contoso.com -GpoPrefixName IPAM1
-IpamServerFqdn ipam1.contoso.com -DelegatedGpoUser user1
```

PROVISION THE IPAM SERVER

GET READY. To install and configure IPAM on a server running Windows Server 2016, perform the following steps.

1. On LON-SVR1, log on as **adatum\administrator** with the password of **Pa$$w0rd.**
2. Click **Start** and click **Windows PowerShell.**
3. Execute the following command in the Windows PowerShell window:

   ```
   Invoke-IpamGpoProvisioning -Domain adatum.com
   -GpoPrefixName IPAM1 -IpamServerFqdn LON-SVR1.adatum.com
   ```

   When prompted to confirm that you want to perform this action, type **Y** and press **Enter.**
4. Close the Windows PowerShell window.
5. On LON-SVR1, in Server Manager, click **IPAM.** If IPAM is not shown, press **F5.**
6. Because the IPAM server is already connected to LON-SVR1, click Step 2: **Provision the IPAM server.**
7. In the Provision IPAM Wizard, on the Before You Begin page, click **Next.**
8. On the Configure Database page, **Windows Internal Database (WID)** is already selected. Click **Next.**
9. On the Select Provisioning Method page, **Group Policy Based** is already selected. In the GPO name prefix text box, type **IPAM1** and click **Next.**
10. On the Summary page, click **Apply.**
11. After IPAM is provisioned, click **Close.**
12. Log on to LON-DC1 as **adatum\administrator** with the password of **Pa$$w0rd.**
13. In Server Manager, click **Tools > Active Directory Users and Computers.**
14. Expand **adatum.com** and click the **Users** container.
15. Double-click the **IPAMUG** group.
16. On the Member Of tab, click **Add.** In the text box, type **Enterprise admin; Event Log Readers** and then click **OK.** Click **OK** to close the IPAMUG Properties dialog box.
17. Close the Active Directory Users and Computers console.
18. Reboot **LON-DC1.** Wait until LON-DC1 finishes booting.

Configuring IPAM Database Storage

With Windows Server 2016, during the IPAM provisioning process, you can use Windows Internal Database (WID), as shown in Figure 6-4, or you can select Microsoft SQL Server so that you can use a dedicated SQL server. By using an external database, you have additional scalability, disaster recovery, and reporting.

CERTIFICATION READY
Configure IPAM database storage using SQL Server
Objective 3.1

During provisioning, the WID is selected by default and the database is stored in the C:\Windows\System32\IPAM\Database folder. However, if necessary, you can migrate the database from WID to SQL after IPAM has been provided by using the `Move-IpamDatabase` and `Set-IpamDatabase` Windows PowerShell cmdlets.

Figure 6-4

Configuring databases for IPAM

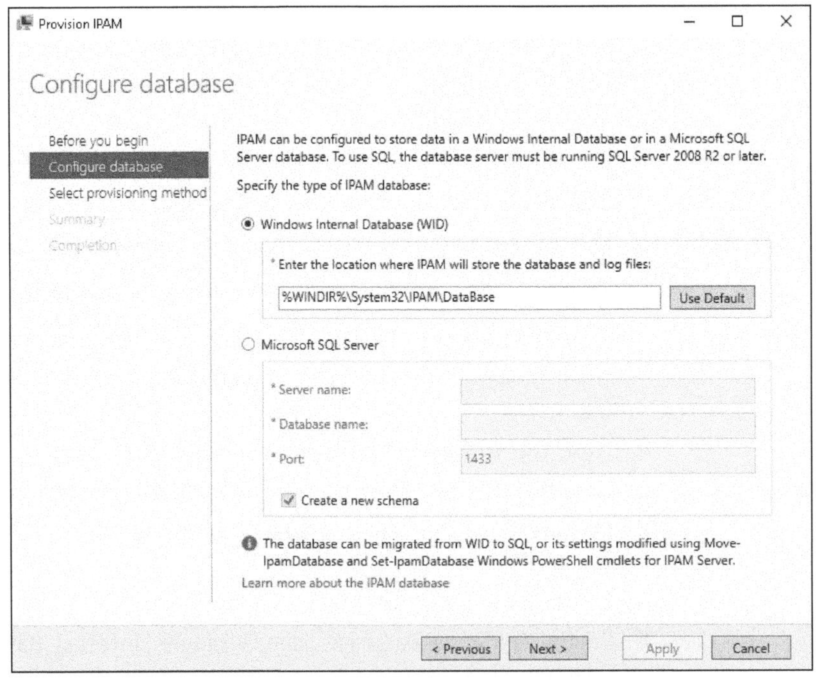

Configuring Server Discovery

Having installed and provisioned the IPAM server, the next two steps are to configure server discovery and start server discovery. Server discovery is the process of defining which domains in the forest that contain servers will be managed by this IPAM server. Then, when you start the server discovery, IPAM retrieves a list of all domain controllers, DNS servers, and DHCP servers from Active Directory.

CERTIFICATION READY
Configure server discovery
Objective 3.1

Once the IPAM discovery is complete, the IPAM administrator can select which servers, roles, and services will be managed from the list in server inventory. This final task launches various data collection tasks on the IPAM server to collect data from all the servers managed by this IPAM server. Once the IPAM server tasks are complete, the IPAM server creates a schedule of tasks to repeat at various intervals. These tasks are listed in Table 6-1.

Table 6-1

IPAM Server Scheduled Tasks

Task Name	Description	Default Frequency
AddressExpiry	Tracks IP address expiry state and logs notifications	1 day
AddressUtilization	Collects IP address space usage data from DHCP servers to display current and historical utilization	2 hours
Audit	Collects DHCP and IPAM server operational events; also collects events from domain controllers, NPS, and DHCP servers for IP address tracking	1 day
ServerAvailability	Collects service status information from DHCP and DNS servers	15 minutes
ServerConfiguration	Collects configuration information from DHCP and DNS servers for display in IP address space and server management functions	6 hours
Server Discovery	Automatically discovers the domain controllers, DHCP servers, and DNS servers in the domains you select	1 day
Service Monitoring	Collects DNS zone status events from DNS servers	30 minutes

CONFIGURE SERVER DISCOVERY

GET READY. To configure server discovery on a server running Windows Server 2016, perform the following steps.

1. On LON-SVR1, using Server Manager, on the IPAM Overview page, click Step 3: **Configure server discovery.**
2. In the Configure Server Discovery dialog box, the forest root domain (Adatum.com) is already selected. Click **Add.** The (root domain) adatum.com appears, as shown in Figure 6-5.

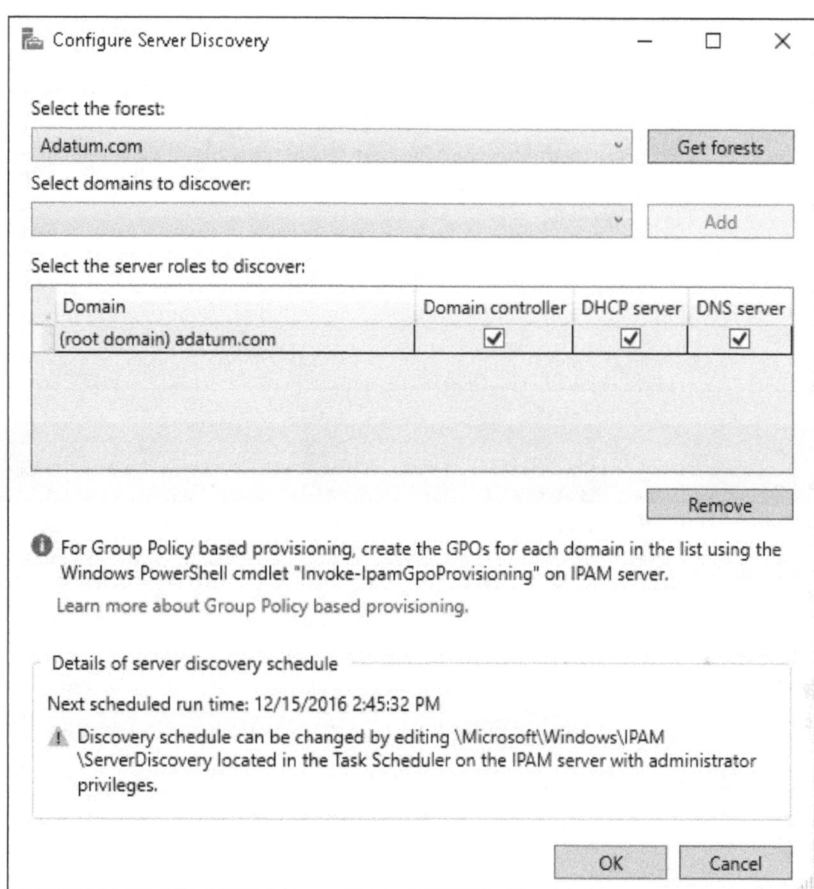

Figure 6-5

Configuring server discovery

TAKE NOTE* This might take up to 10 minutes. If the domain does not appear after 10 minutes, click Step 3 again and then click the Get Forest button and wait another 10 minutes.

3. Click **OK** to close the Configure Server Discovery dialog box.
4. On the IPAM Overview page, click Step 4: **Start server discovery.** Wait until server discovery is done; this might take 5–10 minutes. Under Scheduled Tasks at the bottom of the screen, the server discovery status should display *Ready.*
5. On the IPAM Overview screen, click Step 5: **Select or add servers to manage and verify IPAM access.**

6. On the IPv4 page, LON-DC1 is blocked. Right-click **LON-DC1** and choose **Edit Server**.
7. On the Add or Edit Server page, change the Manageability status from *Unspecified* to **Managed**. Also, make sure that **DC**, **DNS server**, and **DHCP server** are selected. Click **OK**.
8. Right-click the **LON-DC1** server and choose **Refresh Server Access Status**. If a status dialog box opens, click **OK**. When the list is refreshed, click **F5** to refresh the screen.
9. Click **Overview** again in the left pane.
10. Click Step 6: **Retrieve data from managed servers**. Again, this might take a few minutes.

Having completed the IPAM server tasks, the full server inventory will now appear (after a refresh) in the Server Manager IPAM console. The server inventory contains a list of managed servers and a panel containing the full relevant details for the selected server (see Figure 6-6).

Figure 6-6

Displaying the IPAM server inventory

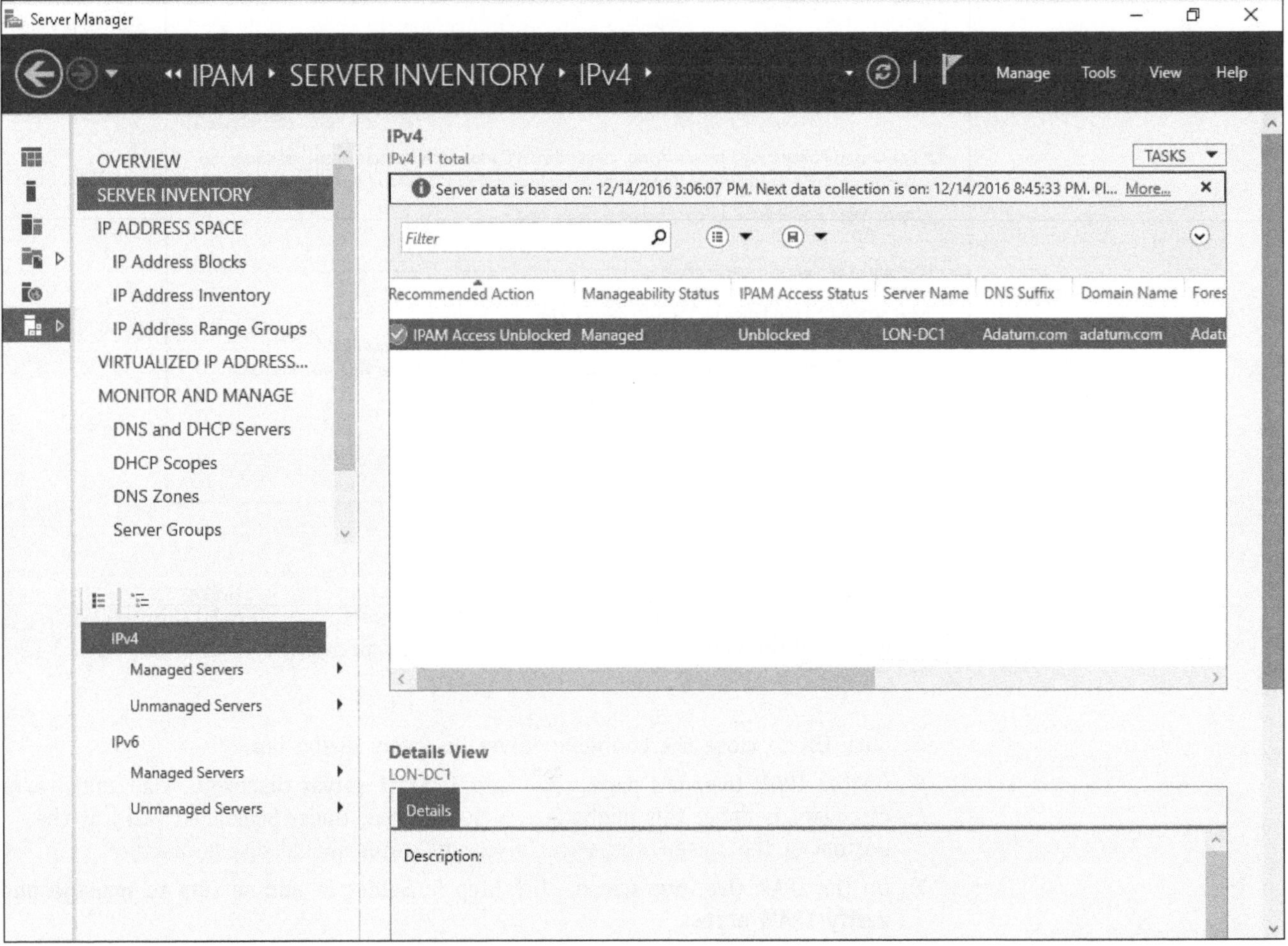

Creating and Managing IP Blocks and Ranges

Having installed and configured the IPAM server, an IPAM administrator needs to monitor the utilization of IP addresses within his scope of control. IPAM has many monitoring tools available to make this task easier, preventing ranges from running out of available addresses or blocks running out of ranges.

CERTIFICATION READY
Create and manage IP blocks and ranges
Objective 3.1

The IPAM Server console provides a dedicated Monitor and Manage section. Within this section, there are four categories:

- DNS and DHCP Servers
- DHCP Scopes
- DNS Zones
- Server Groups

The DHCP Scopes section provides a detailed breakdown of the level of utilization of all dynamic IP addresses. The utilization column is the first column of every console panel where IP addresses are listed.

To provide a more granular control of utilization, the IP Address Space section of the console provides a number of utilization tools.

The IP Address Blocks section allows the IPAM administrator to review block utilization by Public, Private, or All IP address blocks. IPAM summarizes all utilization statistics and trends at the address block level, based on the address ranges assigned to that block.

The IP Address Inventory section of the console enables complete end-to-end utilization management and displays any duplicate addresses as well as any expired or unexpectedly unallocated addresses.

IPAM allows the configuration of thresholds for the percentage of the IP address space that is utilized. IPAM then uses the preset thresholds to determine under- and overutilization of IP address blocks, ranges, and range groups.

The starting point for the configuration of IP address blocks and IP address ranges is the main IPAM screen, which is reached through Server Manager. Having reviewed the IP address space details previously in Figure 6-6, the first stage is to allocate IP address blocks for the server to track and manage.

CREATE AN IP ADDRESS BLOCK

GET READY. Log on to the IPAM server, with administrative privileges. To create an IP address block, perform the following steps.

1. Open **Server Manager** and click **IPAM > IP Address Blocks** (see Figure 6-7).
2. Click **Task > Add IP Address Block.** The Add or Edit IPv4 Address Block dialog box opens (see Figure 6-8).

Figure 6-7

Creating IP address blocks

Figure 6-8

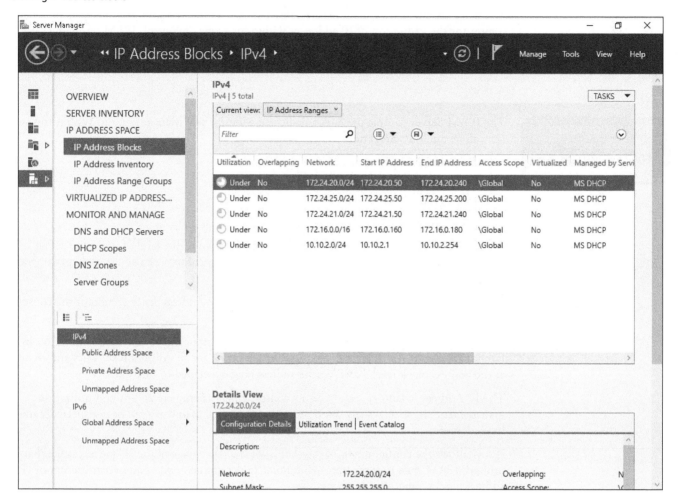

Adding an IP address block

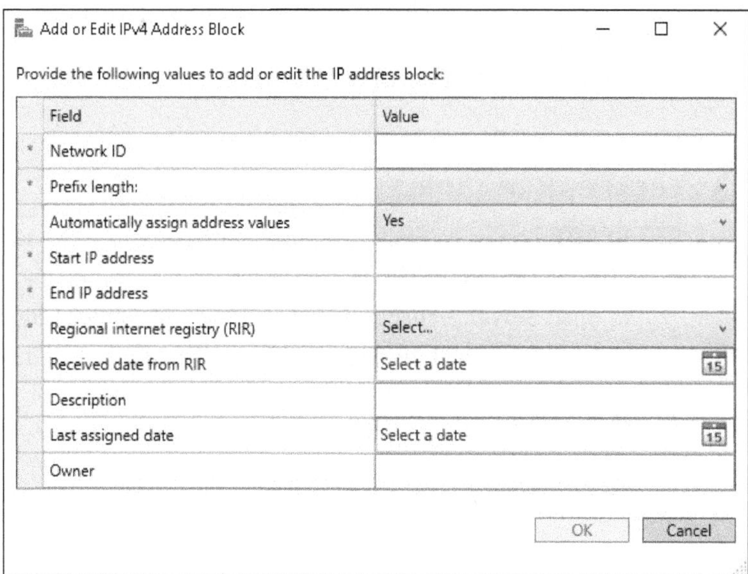

3. Complete the dialog box fields with the required IP block data and then click **OK.**

The newly added IP address block is now listed in the top panel and the configuration details are listed in the bottom panel of the IPAM IP Address Blocks section of the console.

After you create the IP address block, the next stage is to create IP address subnets, and split the IP address block into IP address ranges. This procedure is also done through the IPAM console in Server Manager.

CREATE AN IP ADDRESS SUBNET

GET READY. Log on to the IPAM server, with administrative privileges. To create an IP address subnet, perform the following steps.

1. Open **Server Manager** and click **IPAM> IP Address Blocks.**
2. Click **Task>Add IP Address Subnet.** The Add IPv4 Address Subnet dialog box opens.
3. In the Name text box, type a descriptive name for the subnet. Then, in the Network ID text box, type the network address, such as **172.24.0.0.**
4. In the Prefix length (0 - 32) text box, type the number of network bits, such as **16.** Click **OK.**

CREATE AN IP ADDRESS RANGE

GET READY. Log on to the IPAM server, with administrative privileges. To create an IP address range, perform the following steps.

1. Open **Server Manager** and click **IPAM> IP Address Range Groups.**
2. Click **Tasks>Add IP Address Range.** The Add or Edit IPv4 Address Range dialog box opens.
3. Complete the dialog box fields with the required basic IP range configuration data (see Figure 6-9).

Figure 6-9

Adding an IP address range

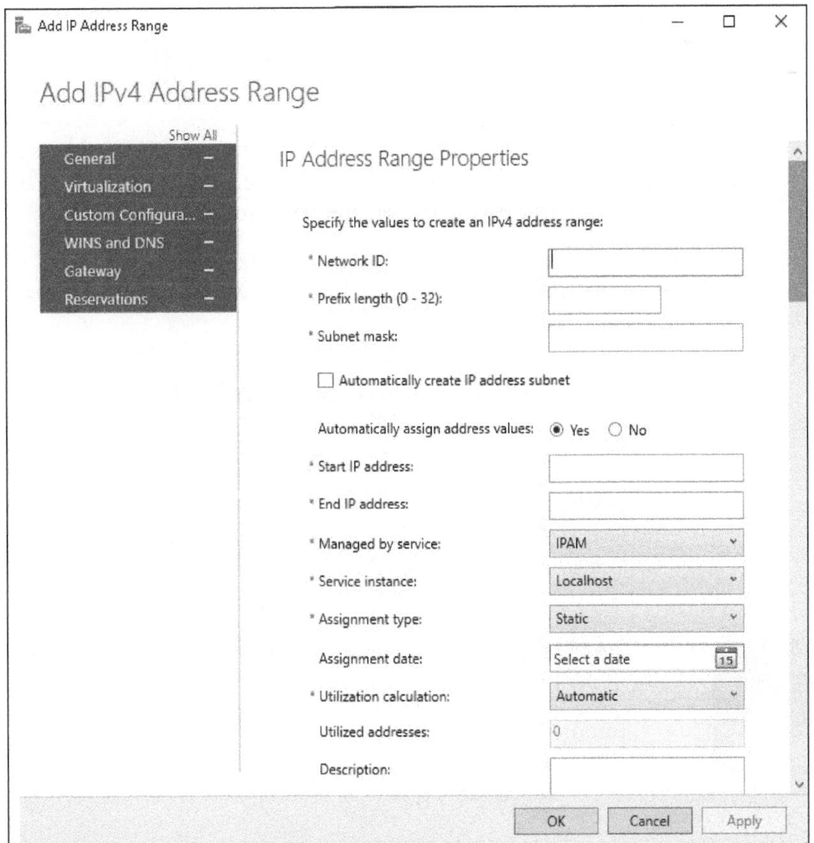

4. In this instance, there are additional custom configuration options to be made. This section allows the IPAM administrator to associate the IP address range with a number of selectable criteria (AD Site, country, region, type of network, and so on). It is possible to select several user-entered values. Click **Add**; then, select the chosen options, entering the required user data; and then click **OK**.

   Creating these attributes assists in the tracking and monitoring of IP address range utilization.

5. Click **OK** to finish the creation of the IP address range.

Now that the IP configuration is complete, the IPAM server can maintain accurate records of utilization and allocations. If the IPAM server manages several IP address ranges, the custom configuration proves most useful to reducing clutter in the console.

From the IP Address Range Groups console page, you can carry out a number of actions on each range, such as modifying a DHCP scope or adding a DHCP reservation. These options significantly reduce the workload of an IPAM administrator. Remotely logging on to a DHCP server and querying the data directly is not required.

The IPAM client console options for importing IP address data from a comma-separated value (CSV) file include the following:

- Import IP Address Block
- Import IP Address Ranges
- Import IP Addresses
- Import and Update IP Address Ranges

When you open the Add or Edit Ipv4 Address Range dialog box, use the Managed By Service drop-down list to select how the address block or range is being managed. Choices include:

- IPAM (as shown)
- Non-Microsoft DHCP solution
- Microsoft Virtual Machine Manager (VMM)
- Another method

By selecting the correct option, you can import the IP address space within IPAM but still have the assigned address managed by the current method. When ready, the IP address can be moved under IPAM management as appropriate.

An export option exports all IP address data to a user-selected CSV file. Also consider that when the IPAM server is backed up, the Windows Internal Database must also be backed up to secure the IPAM data.

Migrating Existing Workloads to IPAM

Most IP address space management is currently carried out using a mixture of spreadsheets, third-party applications, and printed materials. Having installed the IPAM feature and configured the provisioning and discovery, an IPAM administrator might choose to migrate all the IP address space data into the IPAM database.

CERTIFICATION READY
Migrate existing workloads to IPAM
Objective 3.1

The IPAM client console options for importing IP address data from a comma-separated value (CSV) file include the following:

- Import IP Address Block
- Import IP Address Ranges

- Import IP Addresses
- Import and Update IP Address Ranges

There is also an export option, which exports all IP address data to a user selected .csv file. It is important to also consider that when backing up the IPAM server, the Windows Internal Database must be backed up to secure the IPAM data.

TAKE NOTE* To ensure you format the .csv file correctly, prepare an export to capture the header information required to import IP address data into the database.

IMPORT IP ADDRESS INFORMATION

GET READY. To import IP address information, log on to the IPAM server (with administrative privileges) and then perform the following steps.

1. Open **Server Manager** and click **IPAM > IP Address Blocks.**
2. Click the **Tasks** menu and then click one of the following:
   Import IP Address Blocks
   Import IP Address Subnets
   Import IP Address Ranges
   Import IP Addresses
3. In the Open dialog box, navigate to and click the CSV file and then click the **Open** button.

Monitoring Utilization of IP Address Space

After you have configured IPAM to collect the necessary information, you can use IPAM to look at utilization trends to show you how many IP addresses are being used. For example, you can select IP Address Blocks, IP Address Inventory, or IP Address Range. You can then look at Configuration Details or Utilization Trend, as shown in Figure 6-10.

CERTIFICATION READY
Monitor utilization of IP address space
Objective 3.1

As you learned in the last section, you can create logical groups of IP address ranges so that you can visualize the address space. You can group the IP address ranges based on location, or by department. IPAM then automatically arranges IP address ranges into a hierarchy based on the grouping criteria.

Determining Scenarios for Using IPAM with System Center Virtual Machine Manager

CERTIFICATION READY
Determine scenarios for using IPAM with System Center Virtual Machine Manager for physical and virtual IP address space management
Objective 3.1

System Center Virtual Machine Manager (VMM) is a management solution for virtualized data centers, including Microsoft Hyper-V and VMware ESXi. You can integrate IPAM and Virtual Machine Manager (VMM) so that IP address settings associated with the logical networks and the virtual machine networks are stored in the IPAM server. You can then use the IPAM server to monitor the usage of VM networks that have been configured or changed in VMM. However, you still must configure the VM networks with VMM.

Figure 6-10

Viewing the utilization trends for IP address block

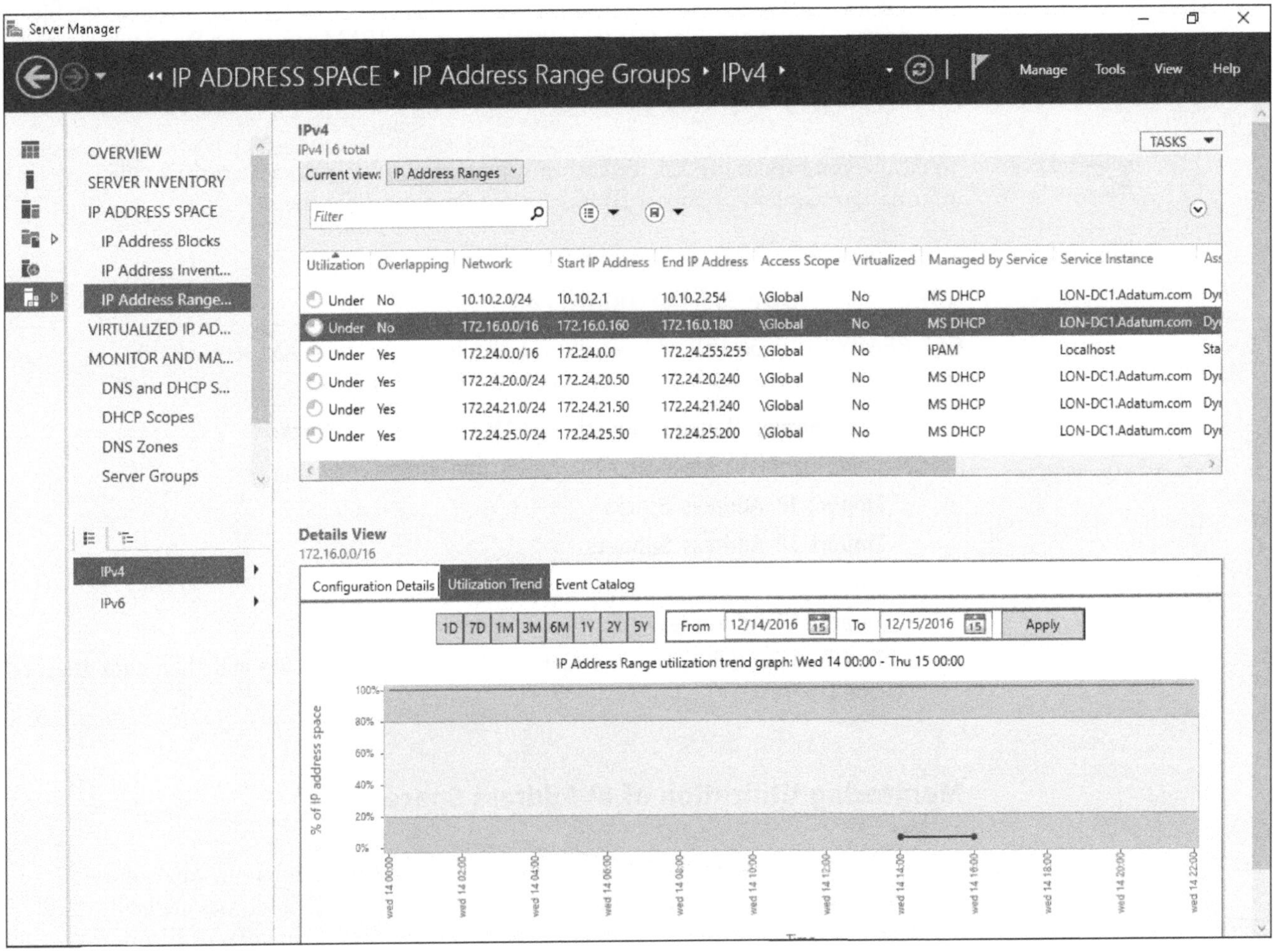

When you configure IPAM, you should use a service account that is a member of IPAM ASM Administrators or Remote Management Users. Make sure that the IPAM server and the VMM are kept in time synchrony.

ADD AN IPAM SERVER IN VMM

GET READY. To add an IPAM server to System Center 2016 Virtual Machine Manager, perform the following steps.

1. Open the VMM console and then open the **Fabric** workspace.
2. On the Home tab, in the Show group, click **Fabric Resources**.
3. In the Fabric pane, expand **Networking**, and then click **Network Service**. Network services include gateways, virtual switch extensions, network managers (which include IPAM servers), and top-of-rack (TOR) switches.
4. On the Home tab, in the Add group, click **Add Resources** and then click **Network Service**.

5. In the Add Network Service Wizard (see Figure 6-11), on the Name page, in the Name and Description text boxes, type a name and optional description, and then click **Next.**

Figure 6-11

Adding a network service in VMM

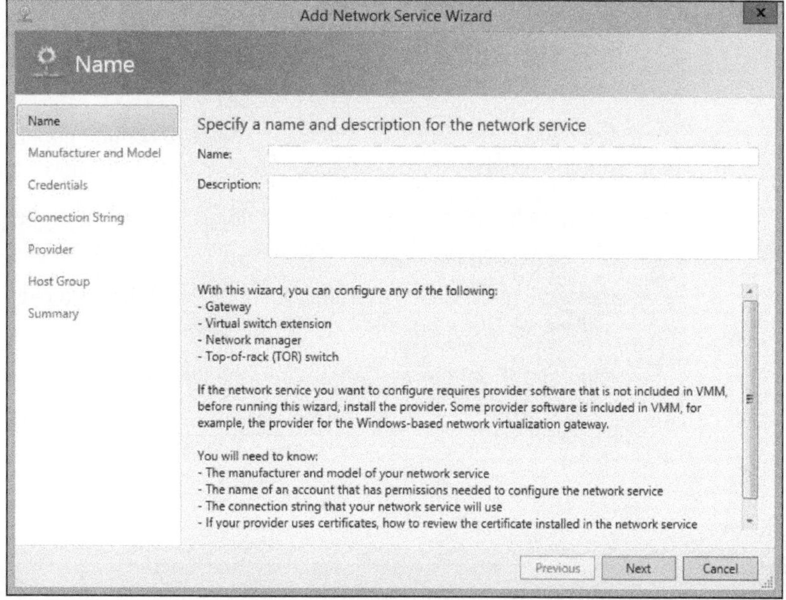

6. On the Manufacturer and Model page, in the Manufacturer list, click **Microsoft.** In the Model list, click **Microsoft Windows Server IP Address Management.** Then, click **Next.**
7. On the Credentials page, click **Browse.** In the Select a Run As Account dialog box, specify the service account. If the account is not created, click **Create Run As Account** to create a new Run As account. Click **Next.**
8. On the Connection String page, in the Connection string text box, type the fully qualified domain name (FQDN) of the IPAM server, and then click **Next.**
9. On the Provider page, in the Configuration provider list, select **Microsoft IP Address Management Provider**, and then click **Test** to run basic validation tests with the provider. If tests indicate that the provider works as expected with the IPAM server, click **Next.**
10. On the Host Group page, select one or more host groups for which you want integration between the IPAM server and the VMM server. Click **Next.**
11. On the Summary page, review and confirm the settings, and then click **Finish.**
12. Confirm that the IPAM server is listed under Network Services. Whenever you want to send or receive the latest settings to and from the IPAM server, you can right-click the listing for the IPAM server and choose **Refresh.**

SKILL SUMMARY

IN THIS LESSON YOU LEARNED:

- An installation of an IPAM server and the IPAM feature have specific hardware, software, and infrastructure requirements.
- The correct procedure for installing, configuring, and provisioning the IPAM feature in Windows Server 2016 uses the automatic Group Policy provisioning option.

- Once an IPAM server is provisioned using the automatic Group Policy option, the only way to undo this is to uninstall and reinstall the IPAM feature.
- Once an IPAM server is installed, there are several postinstallation IPAM server tasks to successfully implement the IPAM feature.
- To delegate administration of IPAM features and IPAM servers, it is necessary to use the correct IPAM server local security group.
- The IPAM client console is the correct place to configure and manage server discovery. The console provides the quick-start selections in the overview pane.
- The correct procedure for creating, managing, tracking, and editing IP address blocks, IP address ranges, and IP addresses uses the IPAM client console.
- Using the IPAM client console to monitor the under- and overutilization of address ranges and scopes is carried out on the DHCP scopes pane.
- Importing IP data from CSV files into the IPAM database is the way to migrate legacy IP address data.

■ Knowledge Assessment

Multiple Choice

Select the correct answer for each of the following questions.

1. Which IPAM servers should be installed on Windows Server 2016?

a. Domain controller
b. Non-domain-joined
c. DNS server
d. Domain-joined sole purpose

2. Which of the following functions does IPAM *not* carry out?

a. Planning
b. Auditing
c. Tracking
d. Monitoring

3. IPAM can be administered from which of the following operating systems?

a. Windows 8.1
b. Windows Server 2008 R2 SP1
c. Windows 10
d. Windows Server 2008 SP2

4. Which of the following GPOs is *not* created when IPAM is provisioned using the automatic Group Policy method?

a. IPAM1_DHCP
b. IPAM1_DNS
c. IPAM1_NPS
d. IPAM1_DC_NPS

5. How many DNS servers can be managed from a single IPAM server?
   a. 25
   b. 500
   c. 250
   d. 50
6. How much RAM is required to install an IPAM server?
   a. 1 GB
   b. 2 GB
   c. 4 GB
   d. 8 GB
7. Which PowerShell cmdlet commences the automatic Group Policy provisioning on an IPAM server?
   a. `Invoke-IpamGpoProvisioning`
   b. `Start-IpamGpoProvisioning`
   c. `Start-IpamAutoGpoProvisioning`
   d. `Invoke-IpamAutoGpoProvisioning`
8. Which of the following devices can be managed with IPAM? (Choose all that apply.)
   a. Windows Server 2008 R2 DNS server
   b. Windows Server 2003 DCHP server
   c. Cisco DHCP device
   d. Windows Server 2016 NPS server
9. Which of the following are IPAM collection tasks? (Choose all that apply.)
   a. AddressExpiry
   b. Audit
   c. Service Monitoring
   d. ServerConfiguration

Best Answer

Choose the letter that corresponds to the best answer. More than one answer choice may achieve the goal. Select the BEST answer.

1. On which Windows Server should the IPAM feature be installed?
   a. Windows Server 2008 R2 Domain Controller
   b. Windows Server 2016 DHCP Server
   c. Windows Server 2016 Domain Controller
   d. Windows Server 2016 File Server
2. Which of the following IPAM provisioning methods should be used?
   a. Manual
   b. Group Policy
   c. Automatic Group Policy
   d. Active Directory
3. Which of the following methods should be used alter a DHCP scope using IPAM?
   a. DHCP Scopes console in Server Manager
   b. Directly on the DHCP console on the DHCP server
   c. Directly via PowerShell on the DHCP server
   d. Remotely via PowerShell

Matching and Identification

1. Identify which of the following are IPAM server tasks.
   ____ AuditTracking
   ____ IPAM discovery
   ____ DNSDataCollection
   ____ ServerConfiguration
   ____ GPOCollection
   ____ Audit
   ____ DHCPDataCollection
   ____ ForestCollection
   ____ ServerAvailability
   ____ EFS recovery
   ____ AddressExpiry

Build List

1. Specify the correct order of steps necessary to executing IPAM postconfiguration tasks. Not all steps will be used.
   ____ Select or add servers to manage.
   ____ Start forest discovery.
   ____ Provision the IPAM server.
   ____ Create templates.
   ____ Configure server discovery.
   ____ Start server discovery.
   ____ Perform AD discovery.
   ____ Connect to the IPAM server.
   ____ Retrieve data from managed servers.

2. Specify the correct order of steps necessary to executing IP address management. Not all steps will be used.
   ____ Create IP addresses (static).
   ____ Create DHCP scopes.
   ____ Create IP address blocks.
   ____ Create DNS zones.
   ____ Collect all IP data from servers.
   ____ Create IP address ranges.

3. Specify the correct order of steps necessary to creating an IP address block. Not all steps will be used.
   ____ Run Server Manager and select IPAM.
   ____ Select tasks and add IP address blocks.
   ____ Select IP address ranges.
   ____ Add the IP address block data and click OK.
   ____ Select IP address blocks.

Business Case Scenarios

Scenario 6-1: Planning IPAM Deployment

You are an administrator of the Contoso Corporation, which has a forest root domain called contoso.com. There are subdomains in three trees: Eu.Contoso.com, US.contoso.com, and adatum.com. The CTO has asked you to recommend an IPAM deployment option but wants each domain administrator to have full control of the infrastructure in her own domain. Describe your recommended course of action.

Scenario 6-2: Configuring a Library Computer

You are setting up an IPAM solution for your Active Directory forest that contains a single domain (adatum.com). All domain controllers are currently running Windows Server 2012 or Windows Server 2016. The forest and domain functional levels are at Windows Server 2012. Your CTO has asked you to ensure that you can manage all DHCP and DNS servers from the IPAM server. Describe your recommended course of action.

Managing and Using IPAM

70-741 EXAM OBJECTIVE

Objective 3.2 – Manage DNS and DHCP using IPAM. This objective may include but is not limited to the following: Manage DHCP server properties using IPAM; configure DHCP scopes and options; configure DHCP policies and failover; manage DNS server properties using IPAM; manage DNS zones and records; manage DNS and DHCP servers in multiple Active Directory forests; delegate administration for DNS and DHCP using Role-Based Access Control (RBAC).

Objective 3.3 – Audit IPAM. This objective may include but is not limited to the following: Audit the changes performed on the DNS and DHCP servers; audit the IPAM address usage trail; audit DHCP lease events and user logon events.

Lesson Heading	Exam Objective
Managing DNS and DHCP Using IPAM • Managing DHCP Server Properties, Scopes, and Policies Using IPAM • Managing DNS Zones and Records • Managing DNS and DHCP Servers in Multiple Active Directory Forests	Manage DHCP server properties using IPAM Configure DHCP scopes and options Configure DHCP policies and failover Manage DNS server properties using IPAM Manage DNS zones and records Manage DNS and DHCP servers in multiple Active Directory forests
Delegating Administration for DNS and DHCP Using Role-Based Access Control (RBAC)	Delegate administration for DNS and DHCP using Role-Based Access Control (RBAC)
Auditing IPAM	Audit the changes performed on the DNS and DHCP servers Audit the IPAM address usage trail Audit DHCP lease events and user logon events

KEY TERMS

DNS Record Administrator
IP Address Record Administrator
IPAM Administrator
IPAM ASM Administrator
IPAM DHCP Administrator
IPAM DHCP Reservations Administrator
IPAM DHCP Scope Administrator
IPAM DNS Administrator
IPAM IP Audit Administrator
IPAM MSM Administrator
IPAM Users
Role-Based Access Control (RBAC)
trusts
two-way trust

Managing DNS and DHCP Using IPAM

THE BOTTOM LINE

IPAM can monitor DHCP and DNS servers from any physical location in the organization, as well as simultaneously manage multiple DHCP servers or scopes that exist among multiple DHCP servers.

CERTIFICATION READY
Manage DHCP server properties using IPAM
Objective 3.2

CERTIFICATION READY
Configure DHCP scopes and options
Objective 3.2

CERTIFICATION READY
Configure DHCP policies and failover
Objective 3.2

You can use IPAM to view and check the status and health of selected sets of Windows Server DNS and DHCP servers from a single console. It can also display recent configuration events. Based on your needs, you can also organize the managed servers into logical server groups.

Managing DHCP Server Properties, Scopes, and Policies Using IPAM

You can open Server Manager IPAM\MONITOR AND MANAGE\DNS and DHCP Servers to manage the DNS and DHCP server properties by right-clicking the server (as shown in Figure 7-1) and choosing the desired option.

Figure 7-1

Managing DHCP server with IPAM

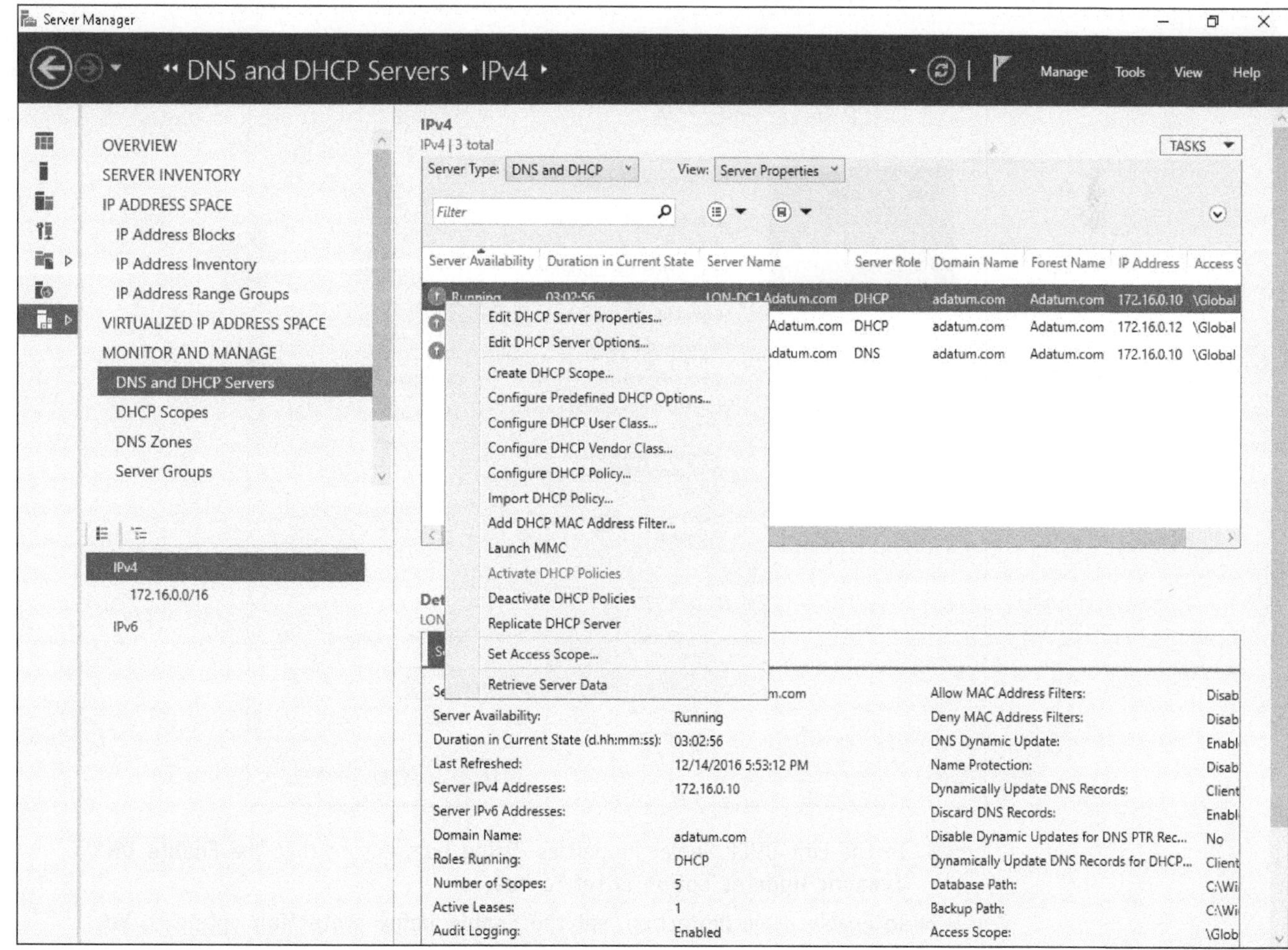

CERTIFICATION READY
Manage DNS server properties using IPAM
Objective 3.2

For DHCP servers, you track the various server settings, server options, number of scopes, and number of active leases configured on the server. From the IPAM console, you can perform the following actions:

- Edit DHCP server properties.
- Edit DHCP server options.
- Create DHCP scopes.
- Configure predefined options and values.
- Configure the user class across multiple servers simultaneously.
- Create and edit new and existing user classes across multiple servers simultaneously.
- Configure the vendor class across multiple servers simultaneously.
- Start the management console for a selected DHCP server.
- Retrieve server data from multiple servers.

CONFIGURE DHCP SERVER PROPERTIES

GET READY. To configure DHCP Server Properties, perform the following steps.

1. Log on to LON-SVR1 as **adatum\administrator** with the password of **Pa$$w0rd.**
2. Click **Start** and click **Server Manager.**
3. In Server Manager, click **IPAM > MONITOR AND MANAGE > DNS and DHCP Servers.**
4. Right-click the **LON-DC1.Adatum.com DHCP** server and choose **Edit DHCP Server Properties.**
5. In the Edit DHCP Server Properties dialog box, click the **Show All** option, as shown in Figure 7-2.

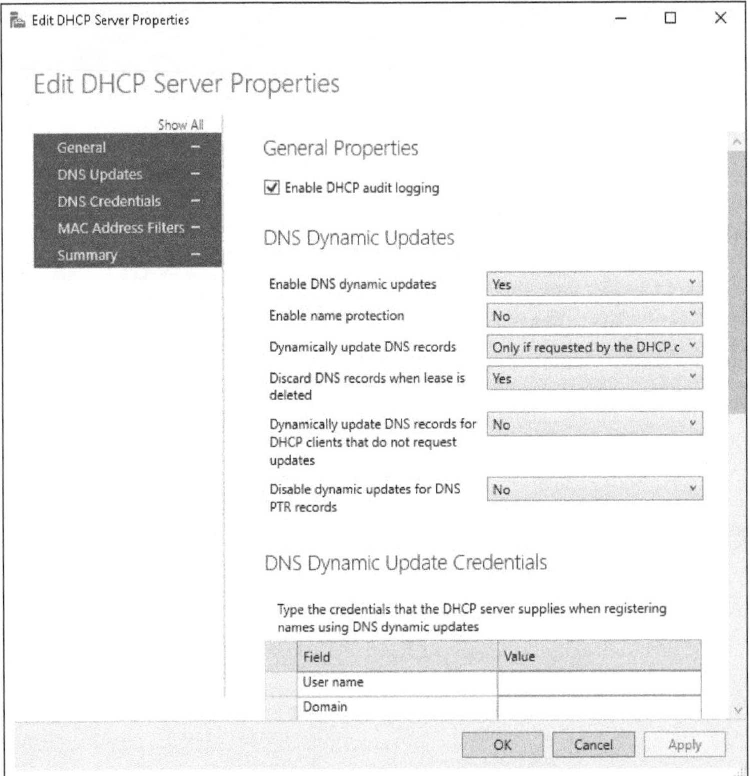

Figure 7-2
Editing DHCP Server Properties

6. In the Edit DHCP Server Properties dialog box, ensure that the **Enable DNS dynamic updates** option is set to **Yes.**
7. To enable name protection, set the **Enable name protection** option to **Yes.**
8. Click **OK** to close the Edit DHCP Server Properties dialog box.

CREATE AND CONFIGURE A DHCP SCOPE

GET READY. To create and configure a DHCP scope, perform the following steps.

1. Log on to LON-SVR1 as **adatum\administrator** with the password of **Pa$$w0rd.**
2. Click **Start** and then click **Server Manager.**
3. In Server Manager, click **IPAM > MONITOR AND MANAGE > DNS and DHCP Servers.**
4. Right-click the **LON-DC1 DHCP** server and choose **Create DHCP Scope.**
5. In the Create DHCP Scope dialog box (as shown in Figure 7-3), click **Show All.**

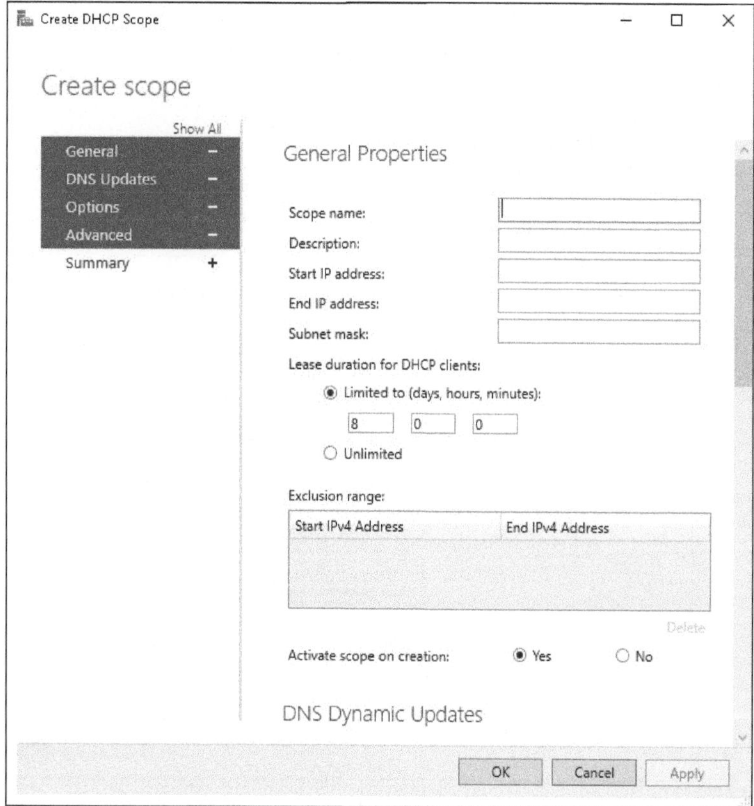

Figure 7-3
Creating a DHCP scope

6. In the Scope name text box, type **IPAMScope.**
7. In the Start IP address text box, type **192.168.2.1.** In the End IP address text box, type **192.168.2.254.**
8. Change the lease duration to **3** days.
9. Click **OK** to close the Create DHCP Scope dialog box.
10. Right-click the **LON-DC1 DHCP** server and choose **Launch MMC.**
11. In the DHCP console, expand **LON-DC1.Adatum.com > IPv4** and verify the IPAM-Scope is displayed.
12. Close the DHCP console.
13. Under MONITOR AND MANAGE, click **DHCP Scopes** and click the **IPAMScope.**
14. Right-click the **IPAMScope** and choose **Edit DHCP scope.**
15. In the Edit DHCP Scope dialog box, click the **Advanced** node. Change the subnet delay to **50** milliseconds.
16. Click **OK** to close the Edit DHCP Scope dialog box.

CONFIGURE DHCP FAILOVER

GET READY. To configure DHCP failover, perform the following steps.

1. Log on to LON-SVR1, as **adatum\administrator** with the password of **Pa$$w0rd.**
2. Click **Start** and then click **Server Manager.**
3. In Server Manager, click **IPAM > MONITOR AND MANAGE > DHCP Scopes.**
4. Right-click a scope and choose **Configure DHCP Failover.**
5. In the Configure DHCP Failover Relationship dialog box (as shown in Figure 7-4), for the Partner server option, select a second DHCP server.

Figure 7-4

Configuring DHCP failover

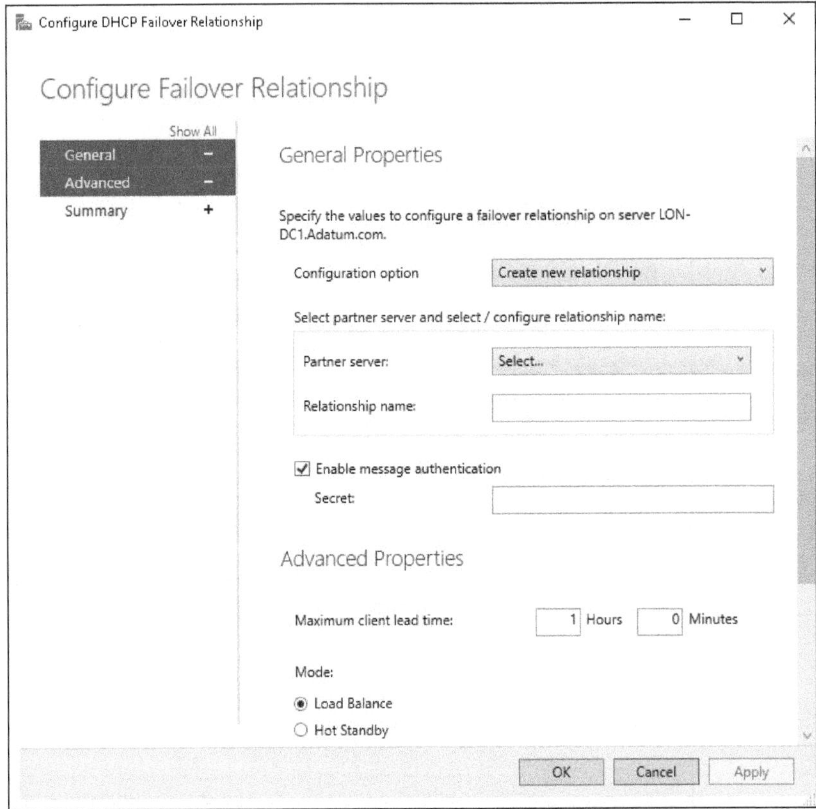

6. In the Relationship name text box, type **IPAM DHCP Failover.**
7. In the Secret text box, type **Pa$$w0rd.**
8. Click **OK** to close the Configure DHCP Failover Relationship dialog box.

CREATE A DHCP RESERVATION

GET READY. To create and configure a DHCP reservation, perform the following steps.

1. Log on to LON-SVR1 as **adatum\administrator** with the password of **Pa$$w0rd.**
2. Click **Start** and then click **Server Manager.**
3. In Server Manager, click **IPAM > MONITOR AND MANAGE > DHCP Scopes.**
4. Right-click a scope and choose **Create DHCP Reservation.**
5. In the Create DHCP Reservation dialog box (as shown in Figure 7-5), in the Name text box, type the name of the desired computer.
6. In the IP address text box, type an address, such as **10.10.2.60.**
7. In the Client ID text box, type the physical/MAC address.
8. Click **OK** to close the Create DHCP Reservation dialog box.

Figure 7-5

Configuring DHCP reservation with IPAM

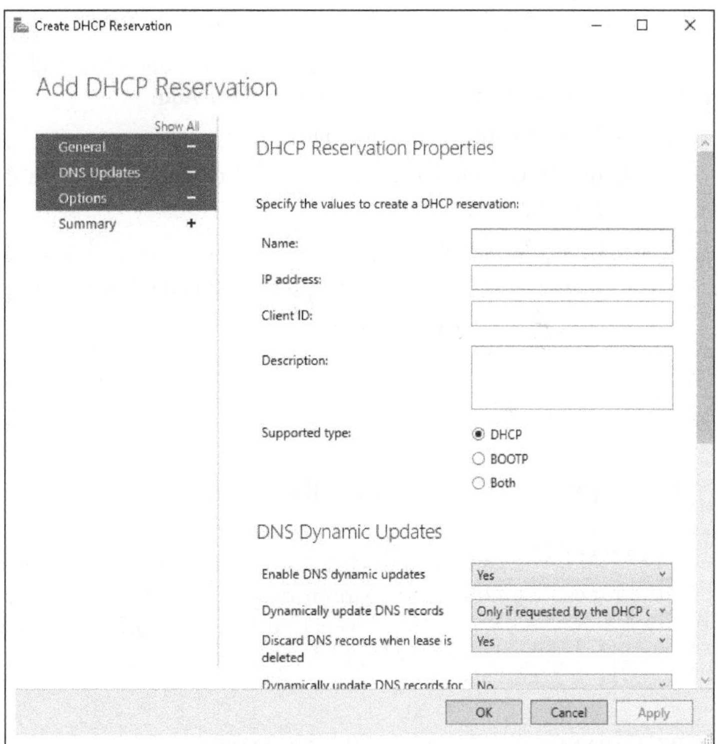

CREATE A DHCP POLICY

GET READY. To create a DHCP policy, perform the following steps.

1. Log on to LON-SVR1 as **adatum\administrator** with the password of **Pa$$w0rd.**
2. Click **Start** and then click **Server Manager.**
3. In Server Manager, click **IPAM > MONITOR AND MANAGE > DHCP Scopes.**
4. Right-click a scope and choose **Configure DHCP Policy.**
5. In the Create DHCP Policy dialog box (as shown in Figure 7-6), in the Name text box, type a name of a policy (such as **IPAMPolicy**).

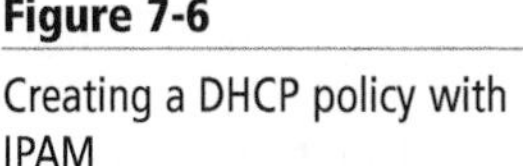

Figure 7-6

Creating a DHCP policy with IPAM

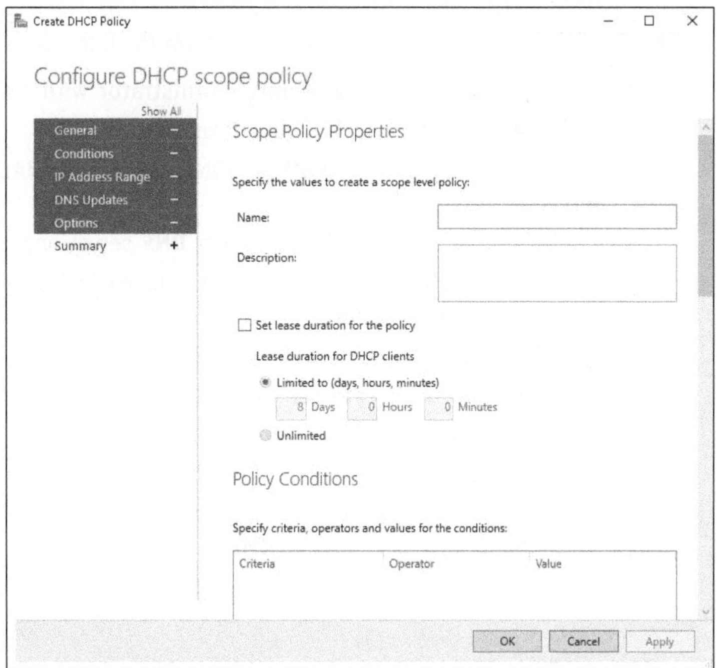

6. In the Policy Conditions section, click the **New** button.
7. In the New Condition section, Criteria, Operator, and Value are already set to Vendor Class Equals HP Printer. Click **Add.**
8. Click the **Add Condition** button.
9. In the Configured Ranges section, click to select the **Configure IP address range for this policy** option.
10. Click the **New** button.
11. In the Add IP address dialog box, specify a Start IP address and End IP address.
12. Click the **Add Range** button.
13. Click **OK** to close the Create DHCP Policy dialog box.

Managing DNS Zones and Records

For DNS, you can track all configured zones, the zone type details, and the health of the zones. The DNS Zone Monitoring view displays all the forward lookup and reverse lookup zones on all DNS servers that IPAM is currently managing. For the forward lookup zones, IPAM also displays all servers that are hosting the zone.

CERTIFICATION READY
Manage DNS zones and records
Objective 3.2

With IPAM, you can do the following DNS functions:

- View DNS servers and zones.
- Create new zones.
- Open the DNS console.
- Create DNS records.
- Manage conditional forwarders.

To view the zones, you just have to click the Server Manager IPAM\MONITOR AND MANAGE\DNS Zones.

CREATE A NEW DNS ZONE

GET READY. To create a new DNS zone, perform the following steps.

1. Log on to LON-SVR1 as **adatum\administrator** with the password of **Pa$$w0rd.**
2. Click **Start** and then click **Server Manager.**
3. In Server Manager, click **IPAM > MONITOR AND MANAGE > DNS and DHCP Servers.**
4. Right-click the **LON-DC1.Adatum.com DNS** server and choose **Create DNS zone.**
5. In the Create DNS zone dialog box (as shown in Figure 7-7), in the Zone name text box, type **IPAM.com.**
6. Click **OK** to close the Create DNS zone dialog box.
7. Right-click the **IPAM.com** zone and choose **Add DNS resource record.**
8. In the Add DNS resource records dialog box (as shown in Figure 7-8), click the **New** button.
9. For the Resource record type, select the **A** record.
10. In the Name text box, type **IPAMPC.**

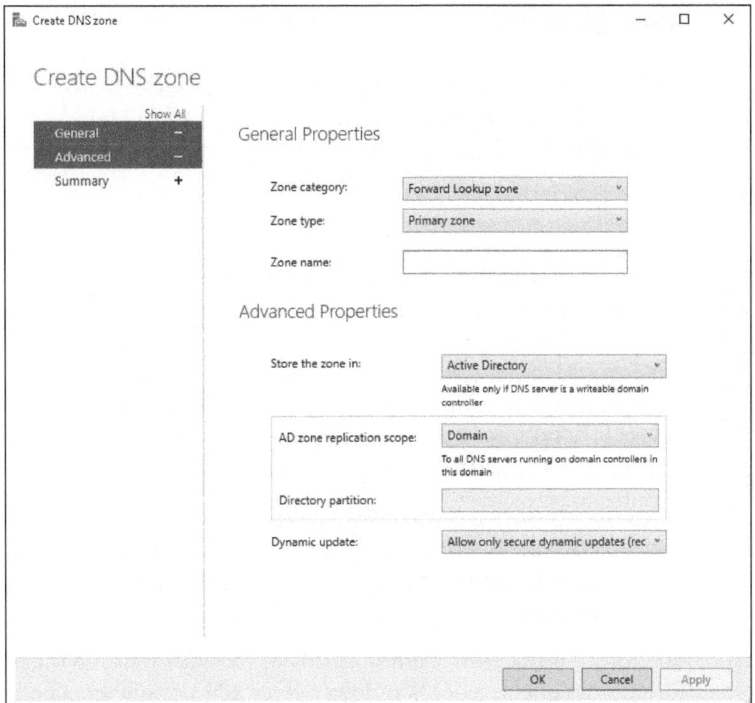

Figure 7-7

Creating a DNS zone

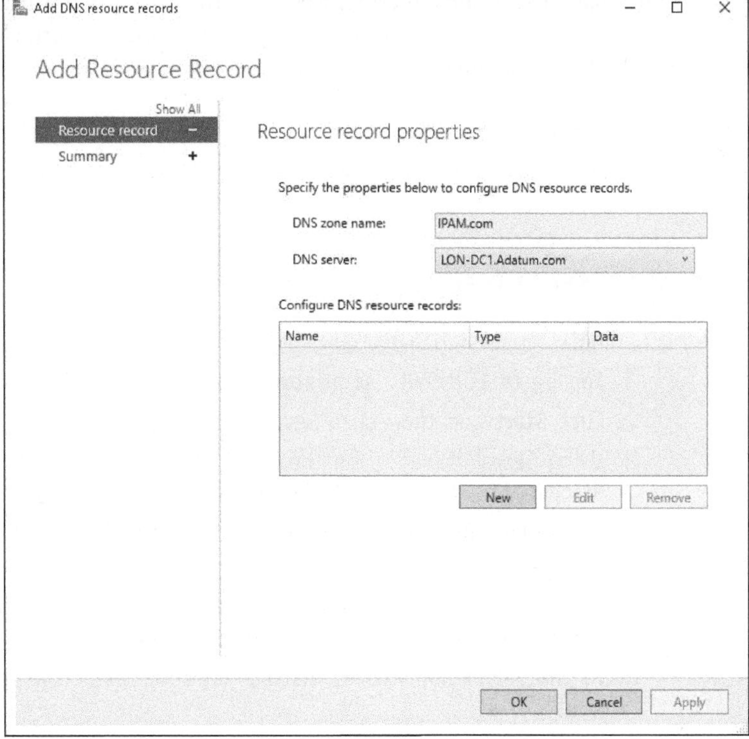

Figure 7-8

Adding a resource record

11. In the IP address text box, type **192.168.1.5**.
12. Click to select the **Create associated pointer (PTR) record** option.
13. Click the **Add resource record** option.
14. Click **OK** to close the Add DNS resource records dialog box.

Managing DNS and DHCP Servers in Multiple Active Directory Forests

With Windows Server 2016, IPAM can manage resources in its current Active Directory forests, as well as remote Active Directory forests. However, to manage remote DNS and DHCP servers, you need to have a two-way trust with the forest where IPAM is installed.

CERTIFICATION READY
Manage DNS and DHCP servers in multiple Active Directory forests
Objective 3.2

Trusts are relationships between domains or forests that enable a user to be authenticated by domain controllers from another domain. Through trusts, users can access and share resources across security boundaries. Domain controllers authenticate users via either Kerberos v5 or NT LAN Manager (NTLM). Kerberos v5 is the default protocol, but NTLM is still available when Kerberos is not possible. Clients using Kerberos v5 must obtain their ticket-granting tickets (TGTs) from a domain controller in their domain and present it to the domain controller in the trusting domain. If the client uses NTLM, the server that contains the resource must contact the domain controller in the user's domain to validate the credentials.

A ***two-way trust*** is a trust that goes in both directions. Domain A is trusted by Domain B, and Domain B is trusted by Domain A. Users in each domain can access resources in each other's domains.

To create a forest trust, both domains of the trust must be the forest root domain and have a forest functional level of Windows Server 2003 or higher. The DNS infrastructure must be able to accommodate DNS requests between forests. You must be a member of the Domain Admins group, Enterprise Admins group, or have been delegated the authority with the appropriate permissions to create the trust. To create a two-way trust, you need an account in the external domain with the appropriate permissions or work closely with the other Domain Administrator or Enterprise Administrator to complete the two-way trust.

MORE INFORMATION
More information about creating trust relationships is provided in the 70-742 book.

ADD A SECOND FOREST TO IPAM

GET READY. To add a second forest to IPAM, perform the following steps.

1. Log on to LON-SVR1 as **adatum\administrator** with the password of **Pa$$w0rd.**
2. Click **Start** and then click **Server Manager.**
3. Using Server Manager, on the IPAM Overview page, click Step 3: **Configure server discovery.**
4. In the Configure Server Discovery dialog box, the root domain (**Adatum.com**) is already selected.
5. If the two-way trust is created, under the Select the forests option, select the remote forests. If the remote forests are not available, click **Get forests.**
6. In the Select domains to discover option, select the remote domain and click **Add.**
7. Click **OK** to close the Configure Server Discovery dialog box.

After the domains have been added, you can then configure server discovery and start server discovery. After IPAM displays the DNS and DHCP servers, you can then select or add servers to manage and verify IPAM access.

Delegating Administration for DNS and DHCP Using Role-Based Access Control (RBAC)

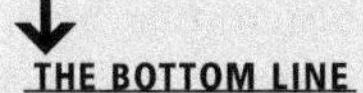

THE BOTTOM LINE

Network administration is a vast topic with many varied and differing roles required to carry it out successfully. Within IP address management are several sets of tasks that might require separate staff to carry them out. For this reason, IPAM relies on Role-Based Access Control (RBAC) to provide the necessary delegated administrative features.

CERTIFICATION READY
Delegate administration for DNS and DHCP using Role-Based Access Control (RBAC)
Objective 3.2

Role-Based Access Control (RBAC) is a method of granting access to computer or network resources based on the roles of individual users within an organization. Access allows an individual user to perform specific tasks, such as read or create a file, and open a database.

When the IPAM feature is installed, the provisioning process (if you selected automatic Group Policy–based provisioning) creates the RBAC roles to enable simple delegated administration of the entire IPAM infrastructure.

Some of the roles are controlled by security groups on the IPAM server. These groups allow delegation of tasks to individuals whom you do not want to have full administrative access to your IPAM server and data. Simply place the necessary users or groups in the correct Local group on the IPAM server:

- ***IPAM Users*:** Users who are members of this group can view server discovery, IP address space, and server management information. Group members can also view IPAM and DHCP server operational events, but they cannot view IP address tracking information.
- **IPAM MSM Administrators:** Members of this group have IPAM Users privileges and can perform common IPAM multi-server management (MSM) tasks and server management tasks.
- **IPAM ASM Administrators:** Members of this group have IPAM Users privileges and can perform common IPAM address space management (ASM) tasks and IP address space tasks.
- ***IPAM IP Audit Administrators*:** Members of this group have IPAM Users privileges and can perform common IPAM management tasks and can view IP address tracking information.
- **IPAM Administrators:** Members of this group have the privileges to view all IPAM data and perform all IPAM tasks.

To add a user to one of these roles, open the Computer Manager console and navigate to the Local Users and Groups > Groups node. Double-click the desired group and then click the Add button to add new users.

The IPAM console provides the following roles:

- ***DNS Record Administrator*:** Manages DNS resource records
- ***IP Address Record Administrator*:** Manages IP addresses but not IP address spaces, ranges, blocks, or subnets
- ***IPAM Administrator*:** Possesses the privileges to view all IPAM data and perform all IPAM tasks
- ***IPAM ASM Administrator*:** Possesses IPAM Users privileges and can perform common IPAM address space management (ASM) tasks and IP address space tasks
- ***IPAM DHCP Administrator*:** Completely manages DHCP servers
- ***IPAM DHCP Reservations Administrator*:** Manages DHCP reservations

- ***IPAM DHCP Scope Administrator*:** Manages DHCP scopes
- ***IPAM DNS Administrator*:** Completely manages the DNS server
- **IPAM MSM Administrator:** Possesses IPAM Users privileges and can perform common IPAM multi-server management (MSM) tasks and server management tasks

You can view the built-in roles and the allowed operations through Server Manager > IPAM > ACCESS CONTROL, as shown in Figure 7-9. You can create additional roles from the Tasks menu by selecting Add User Role. To assign a role to a user, create an access policy.

Figure 7-9

Viewing the IPAM roles

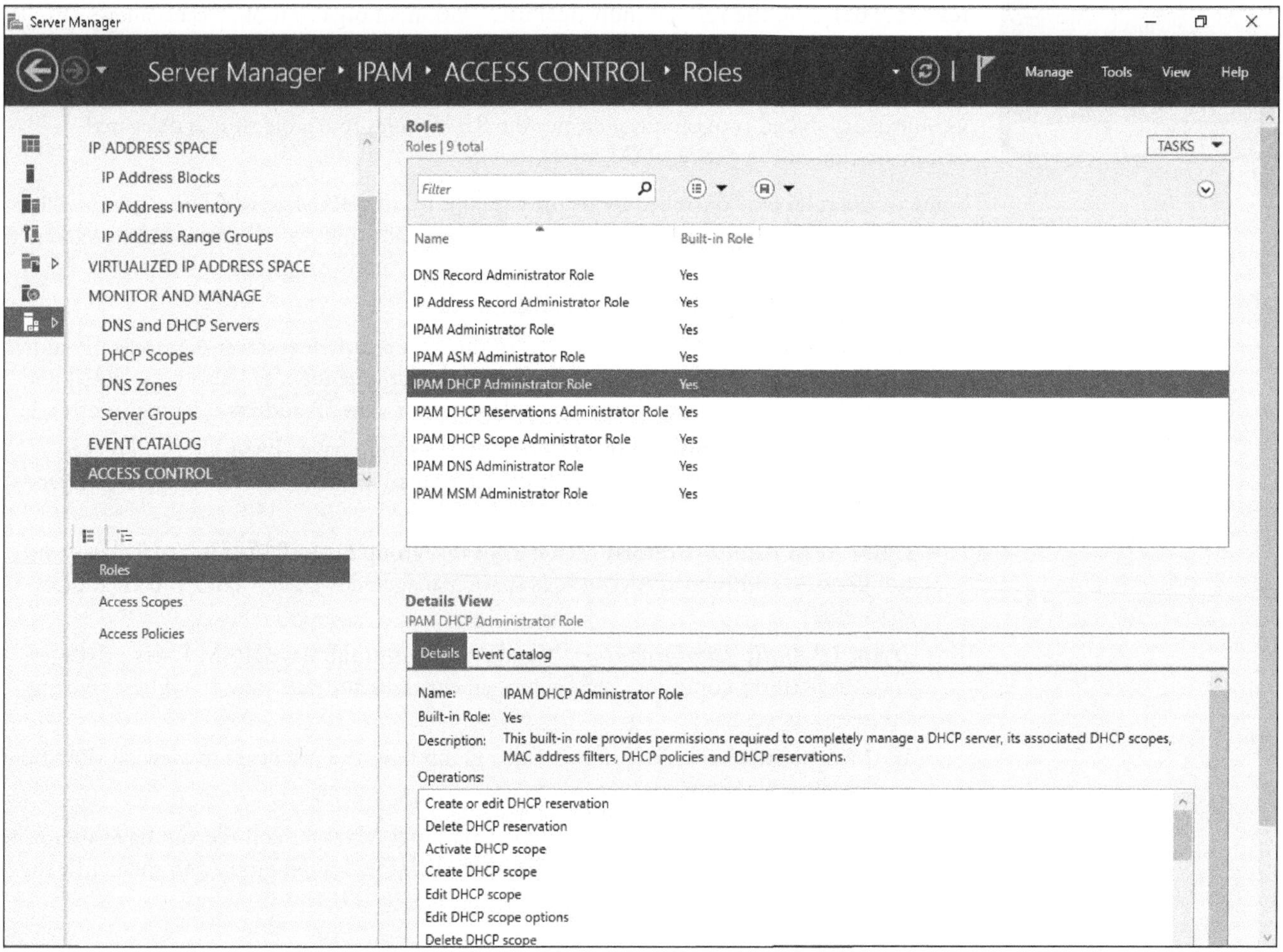

CREATE AN ACCESS POLICY

GET READY. To create an access policy in IPAM, perform the following steps.

1. Log on to LON-SVR1 as **adatum\administrator** with the password of **Pa$$w0rd.**
2. Click **Start** and click **Server Manager.**
3. In Server Manager, click **IPAM > MONITOR AND MANAGE > ACCESS CONTROL.**
4. Click **Tasks > Add Access Policy.**

Figure 7-10
Assigning users to IPAM roles

5. In the Add Access Policy dialog box (as shown in Figure 7-10), for the User alias, click **Add.**
6. In the Select User or Group dialog box, if you need to select the domain user, click the **Locations** button. Then, in the Locations dialog box, select **Entire Directory** and click **OK.**
7. In the Enter the object name to select text box, type the name of the user or group, and click **OK.**
8. In the Access Settings section, click the **New** button.
9. In the New Settings section, for the Select role section, select the appropriate role and click the **Add Settings** button.
10. Click **OK** to close the Add Access Policy dialog box.

Auditing IPAM

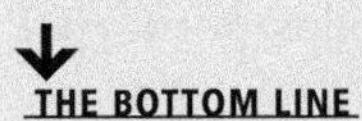

You can use IPAM to audit address utilization, policy compliance, and other information based on the type of servers IPAM is managing. To perform IPAM auditing tasks, click the Event Catalog (see Figure 7-11), open the TASKS menu, and click either Purge Event Catalog Data or Retrieve Event Catalog Data.

Figure 7-11

Viewing the IPAM configuration events

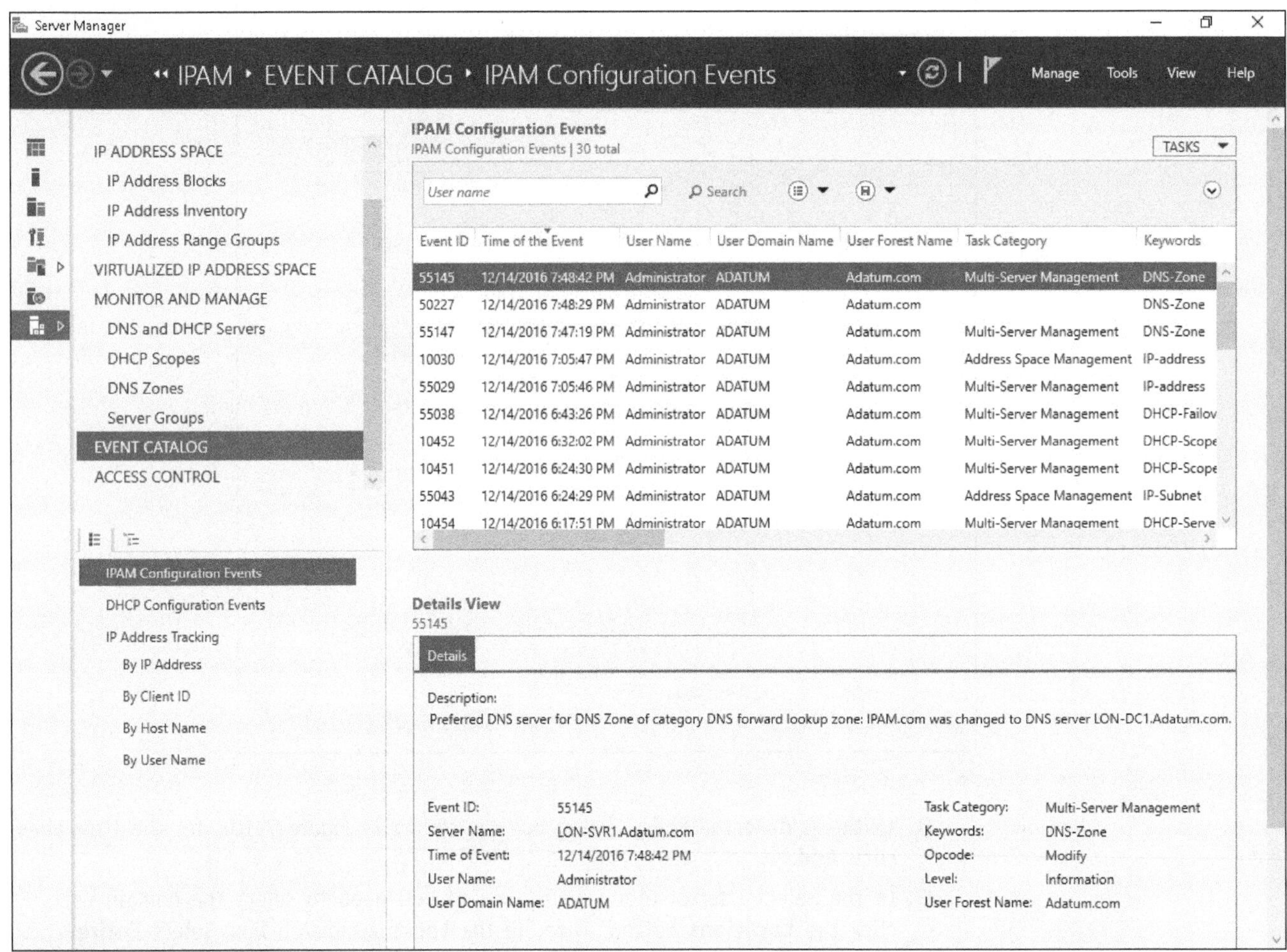

CERTIFICATION READY
Audit the changes performed on the DNS and DHCP servers
Objective 3.3

By default, the IPAM configuration events are shown. However, you can configure IPAM to show other events as well as create reports using the data stored within the database. Also, IPAM provides a query tool and search box, and criteria can be added to a query filter. After the data is retrieved, it can be exported to a comma-separated value (CSV) file. Under the Event Catalog, you can click DHCP Configuration Events to show what changes have been done on the DHCP server.

CERTIFICATION READY
Audit the IPAM address usage trail
Objective 3.3

IPAM collects user information from the DHCP servers, DNS servers, and domain controllers. The information includes the user's assigned IP address, host name, and client identifier (MAC address for IPv4 or DUID for IPv6). As a result, you can use the IP addressing tracking to view an address usage trail.

CERTIFICATION READY
Audit DHCP lease events and user logon events
Objective 3.3

With IPAM, you can easily check the status and health of selected sets of Windows Server DNS and DHCP servers from a single IPAM administrative interface. You can also use the monitoring view to organize managed servers into logical server groups. For DHCP servers, you can track the various server settings, server options, number of scopes, number of active leases that are configured on a server, and overall zone health. For DNS servers, you display all the forward and reverse lookup zones and the aggregate health of the zone access for all of the servers.

SKILL SUMMARY

IN THIS LESSON YOU LEARNED:

- IPAM can monitor DHCP and DNS servers from any physical location in the organization, as well as simultaneously manage multiple DHCP servers or scopes that exist among multiple DHCP servers.
- For DNS, you can track all configured zones, the zone type details, and the health of the zones. The DNS Zone Monitoring view displays all the forward lookup and reverse lookup zones on all DNS servers that IPAM is currently managing. For the forward lookup zones, IPAM also displays all servers that are hosting the zone.
- With Windows Server 2016, IPAM can manage resources in its current Active Directory forests, as well as remote Active Directory forests. However, to manage remote DNS and DHCP servers, you need to have a two-way trust with the forest where IPAM is installed.
- Within IP address management are several sets of tasks that might require separate staff to carry them out. For this reason, IPAM relies on Role-Based Access Control (RBAC) to provide the necessary delegated administrative features.

Knowledge Assessment

Multiple Choice

Select the correct answer for each of the following questions.

1. In Windows Server 2016, which of the following are methods to create DNS resource records? (Choose all that apply.)
   a. DNS Manager console
   b. Windows PowerShell
   c. IPAM Tools Set
   d. Server Manager IPAM
2. Instead of using the DNS Manager console, which of the following tools can be used to create a DHCP scope?
   a. Scope Manager
   b. Server Manager IPAM
   c. IPAM MMC
   d. Computer Management console
3. In Server Manager, in which of the following locations is a DHCP policy configured?
   a. IPAM > DHCP Scopes
   b. IPAM > MONITOR AND MANAGE > DHCP Policy
   c. IPAM > MONITOR AND MANAGE > DHCP Scopes
   d. IPAM > DHCP Scopes > DHCP Policy
4. Which of the following is needed for IPAM to manage DNS and DHCP servers in another forest?
   a. A two-way trust relationship
   b. Adding a DHCP Relay Agent on the remote forest
   c. Adding an IPAM agent on the remote forest
   d. A one-way trust relationship

Best Answer

Choose the letter that corresponds to the best answer. More than one answer choice may achieve the goal. Select the BEST answer.

1. Which of the following is the minimal role that is needed to view IP address space without seeing IP address tracking information?
   a. IPAM Audit Administrator
   b. IPAM DNS Administrator
   c. IP Address Record Administrator
   d. IPAM Users

Matching and Identification

1. Match the tool with the tasks it can perform:
   ____ a. IPAM Administrator
   ____ b. IPAM ASM Administrator
   ____ c. IPAM DHCP Administrator
   ____ d. IPAM DNS Administrator
   ____ e. IPAM MSM Administrator
   ____ f. IPAM Address Administrator
   1. Possess IPAM Users privileges and can perform common IPAM address space management (ASM) tasks and IP address space tasks
   2. Completely manage DNS servers
   3. Manage IP addresses but not IP address spaces, ranges, blocks, or subnets.
   4. Completely manage DHCP servers
   5. Possess the privileges to view all IPAM data and perform all IPAM tasks
   6. Possess IPAM Users privileges and can perform common IPAM multi-server management (MSM) tasks and server management tasks

■ Business Case Scenarios

Scenario 7-1: Using Windows To Go

You are an administrator at Contoso Corporation and you need to assign various users to use IPAM to manage your network resources. You want to allow help desk personnel to manage DHCP reservations. You want the server team to manage the DHCP, DNS, and IPAM servers. You also need the audit team to make sure that there are no security issues. Describe your recommended course of action.

Implementing Network Connectivity Solutions

LESSON 8

70-741 EXAM OBJECTIVE

Objective 4.1 – Implement network connectivity solutions. This objective may include but is not limited to the following: Implement Network Address Translation (NAT); configure routing.

Objective 5.1 – Implement IPv4 and IPv6 addressing. This objective may include but is not limited to the following: Configure Border Gateway Protocol (BGP); configure IPv4 and IPv6 routing.

Lesson Heading	Exam Objective
Configuring IPv4 and IPv6 Routing	Configure routing
• Installing and Configuring the Remote Access Role	Configure IPv4 and IPv6 routing
• Configuring Routing	Configure Border Gateway Protocol (BGP)
• Managing Static Routes	Implement Network Address Translation (NAT)
• Configuring Routing Information Protocol (RIP)	
• Configuring Border Gateway Protocol (BGP)	
• Implementing Network Address Translation (NAT)	
• Disabling Routing and Remote Access	

KEY TERMS

Border Gateway Protocol (BGP)
hop count
remote access server (RAS)
RIP version 2 (RIPv2)
routers
routing
Routing Information Protocol (RIP)
routing metric
routing table
static routes

Configuring IPv4 and IPv6 Routing

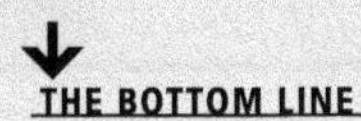

THE BOTTOM LINE

Routing is the process of selecting paths in a network where data will be sent. Routing is required to send traffic from one subnet to another within an organization, and it is required to send traffic from one organization to another. A computer running Windows can act as a router and include its own routing table, so that you can specify which direction data is sent toward its final destination.

CERTIFICATION READY
Configure routing
Objective 4.1

Routers operate at the OSI reference model Layer 3, Network layer. Therefore, they are sometimes referred to as Layer 3 devices. Routers join subnets together to form larger networks and join networks together over extended distances or WANs. They can also connect dissimilar LANs, such as an Ethernet LAN to a Fiber Distributed Data Interface (FDDI) backbone.

CERTIFICATION READY
Configure IPv4 and IPv6 routing
Objective 5.1

Installing and Configuring the Remote Access Role

Today, it is common for an organization to use a ***remote access server (RAS)***. A RAS enables users to connect remotely to a network using various protocols and connection types. By connecting to the RAS over the Internet, users can connect to their organization's network so that they can access data files, read email, and access other applications just as if they were sitting at work.

To provide RAS, Microsoft includes Routing and Remote Access Service (RRAS), which provides the following functionality:

- A virtual private network (VPN) gateway where clients can connect to an organization's private network using the Internet
- The ability to connect two private networks using a VPN connection across the Internet
- A dial-up remote access server, which enables users to connect to a private network using a modem
- Network Address Translation (NAT), which enables multiple users to share a single public network address
- Routing functionality, which can connect subnets and control where packets are forwarded based on the destination address
- Basic firewall functionality, which can allow or disallow packets based on addresses of source and/or destination and protocols

An early method to connect to an organization's network is over an analog phone line or ISDN line using a modem. Because the modem creates a dedicated connection to the server, the connection does not typically need to be encrypted. However, by today's networking standards and bandwidth requirements, the phone and ISDN system do not have the bandwidth needed. Therefore, this method typically is not used today.

Before you can use RRAS, you need to first add the Remote Access role. Then, you need to initially configure RRAS so that you can specify which options are available with it.

To install the Remote Access role, use Server Manager to install the proper role. Because the remote access computer is used to connect an organization's internal private network with the Internet, the server should have two network cards.

INSTALL THE REMOTE ACCESS ROLE

GET READY. To install the Remote Access role, perform the following steps.

1. Log on to LON-RTR as **adatum\administrator** with the password of **Pa$$w0rd.**
2. Click **Start** and then click **Server Manager.**
3. At the top of Server Manager, click **Manage > Add Roles and Features.** The Add Roles and Features Wizard opens.
4. On the Before You Begin page, click **Next.**
5. Click **Role-based or feature-based installation** and then click **Next.**
6. Click **Select a server from the server pool**, click the name of the desired server, and then click **Next.**
7. On the Server Roles page, scroll down and click **Remote Access** and then click **Next.**
8. On the Features page, click **Next.**
9. On the Remote Access page, click **Next.**
10. On the Role Services page, click **Routing** and click **Next.**
11. When you are prompted to add features required for routing, click **Add Features.** DirectAccess and VPN (RAS) will automatically be selected.
12. Back on the Role Services page, click **Next.**
13. On the Confirmation page, click **Install.**
14. When the installation is complete, click **Close.**

After you install RRAS, you need to enable the server and configure RRAS. When you start the RRAS Setup Wizard, you can use the wizard to automatically configure RRAS for specific applications or you can configure the service manually.

The wizard offers five basic options for configuring RRAS:

- **Remote access (dial-up or VPN)**: Sets up the server to accept incoming remote access connections (dial-up or VPN)
- **Network Address Translation (NAT)**: Sets up the server to provide NAT services to clients on the private network that need to access the Internet
- **Virtual private network (VPN) access and NAT**: Sets up the server to support incoming VPN connections and to provide NAT services
- **Secure connection between two private networks**: Sets up a demand-dial or persistent connection between two private networks
- **Custom configuration**: Enables you to choose individual services, including NAT, LAN routing, and VPN access

Configuring Routing

As larger networks are formed, there may be multiple pathways to get from one place to another. As WAN traffic travels multiple routes, the router chooses the fastest or cheapest route between the source and destination, while sometimes taking consideration of the current load.

Routing can also be performed by a Layer 3 switch. ***Layer 2 switches*** (which operate at Layer 2 of the OSI model) are used to connect a host to a network by performing packet switching that allows traffic to be sent only to where it needs to be sent based on mapping MAC addresses of local devices. ***Layer 3 switches*** can perform Layer 2 switching, but can also perform routing based on IP addresses within an organization. Different from a router, Layer 3 switches cannot be used for directly connecting WAN connections.

A server running Windows can have multiple network cards, with each network card connecting to a different subnet. To allow packets to be sent from one subnet to another subnet through the server, you need to configure routing on the server.

A ***routing table*** is a data table that is stored in a router or networked computer that lists the routes of particular network distances and the associated metrics or distances associated with those routes. A ***routing metric*** is a unit calculated by a routing algorithm to determine the optimal route for sending network traffic. A simple metric is the number of hops or routers from one point to another. The routing tables are manually created with ***static routes***, or are dynamically created with routing protocols such as Routing Information Protocol (RIP), based on the current routing topology.

Microsoft Windows supports the Routing Information Protocol through RRAS. RIP has been a popular distance-vector routing protocol for small organizations. RIP uses broadcasts where the entire routing table is sent to the other routers within the network. To determine the distance or cost between networks, RIP uses the metric of hop count, which is the count of routers. The maximum number of hops allowed for RIP is 15. The hop count of 16 is considered an infinite distance, and, therefore, it is considered unreachable.

RIP was improved with RIP version 2 (RIPv2) by using multicasts to send the entire routing table to all adjacent routers at the address of 224.0.0.9 instead of using broadcast. It also incorporates classless routing, which includes the network mask to allow classless routing advertisement. Finally, RIPv2 uses authentication to ensure that routes being distributed throughout the network are coming from authorized sources.

TAKE NOTE*

Windows Server 2016 functions as a software-based router that can be used for lightly trafficked subnets on a small network. For more complex networks with heavy network traffic, you should use a hardware-based router, which provides more reliability and improved network performance.

Routing can be enabled using RRAS. You will use RRAS to configure RIP or define static routes. You can also define static routes using the `Route` command.

CONFIGURE ROUTING

GET READY. To configure routing on Windows Server 2016, perform the following steps.

1. Log on to LON-RTR as **adatum\administrator** with the password of **Pa$$w0rd.**
2. On LON-RTR, click **Start** and click **Server Manager.**
3. Click **Tools > Routing and Remote Access.** The Routing and Remote Access console opens.
4. Right-click the server and choose **Configure and Enable Routing and Remote Access.**

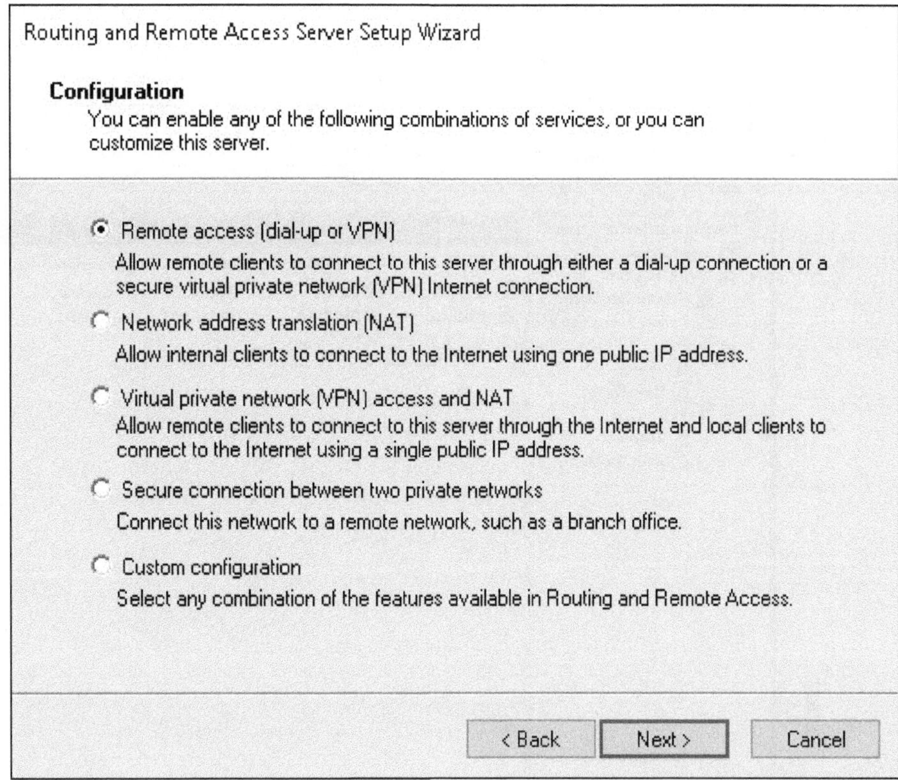

Figure 8-1
Configuring Routing and Remote Access

5. In the Routing and Remote Access Server Setup Wizard, click **Next.**
6. On the Configuration page (as shown in Figure 8-1), click **Custom configuration** and click **Next.**
7. On the Custom Configuration page, click **LAN routing** and click **Next.**
8. On the Completing the Routing and Remote Access Server Setup Wizard page, click **Finish.**
9. When the Routing and Remote Access Service is ready to use, click the **Start service** button.

Managing Static Routes

Static-routed IP networks are best suited for small, single paths that don't change much. To view the IP routing table using RRAS, expand the server node, expand the IPv4 or IPv6 nodes, right-click the static routes node, and choose Show IP Routing Table (see Figure 8-2).

When you define routes, you specify the network address of the destination, the network mask, and the local router or next hop to get to its destination. When the packet reaches the local router, the router then uses its routing table to determine the next hop that the packet needs to be sent to. The process continues until the packet reaches the destination network, where the packets are then sent to the destination host.

Figure 8-2

Displaying static routes using RRAS

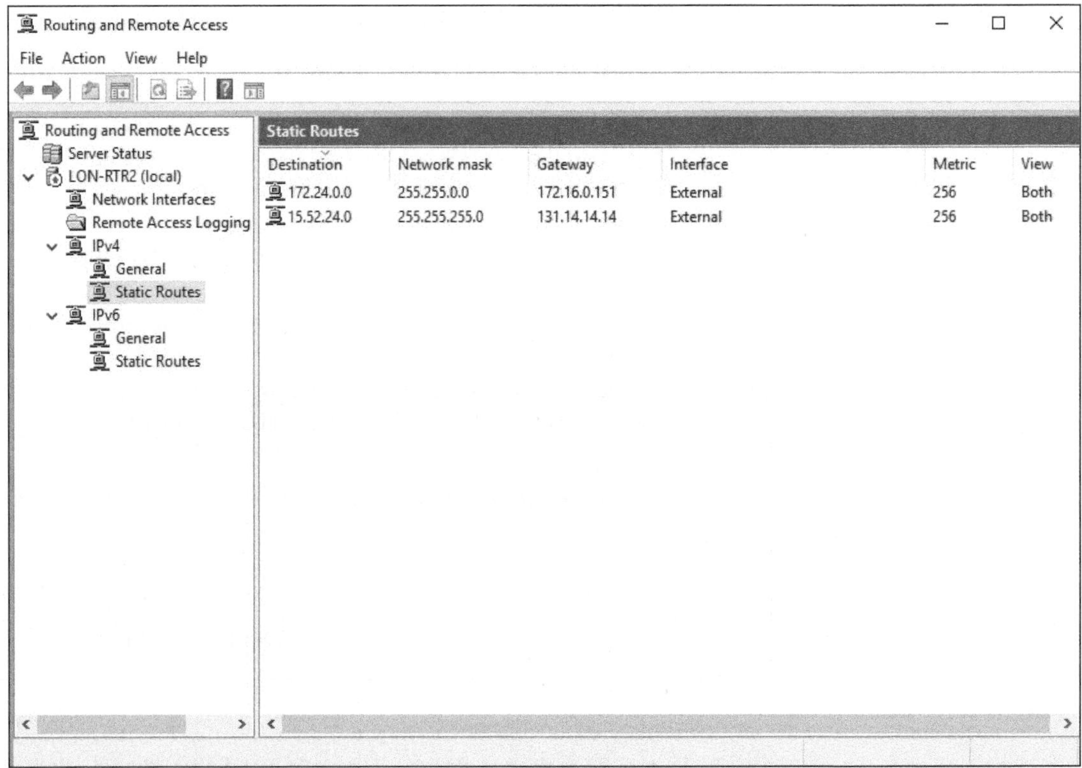

CREATE A NEW STATIC ROUTE USING RRAS

GET READY. To create a new static route using RRAS, perform the following steps.

1. Log on to LON-RTR as **adatum\administrator** with the password of **Pa$$w0rd**.
2. On LON-RTR, click **Start** and then click **Server Manager**.
3. Click **Tools > Routing and Remote Access**.
4. Expand the server node and expand the **IPv4** node.
5. Right-click the **Static Routes** node and choose **New Static Route**.
6. In the IPv4 Static Route dialog box (see Figure 8-3), specify the Interface that you want to assign the static route.
7. For the Destination, type the network address, such as **172.24.0.0** or **192.168.5.0**. You can also specify a single address.

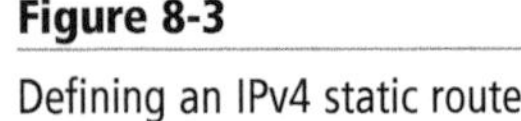

Figure 8-3

Defining an IPv4 static route

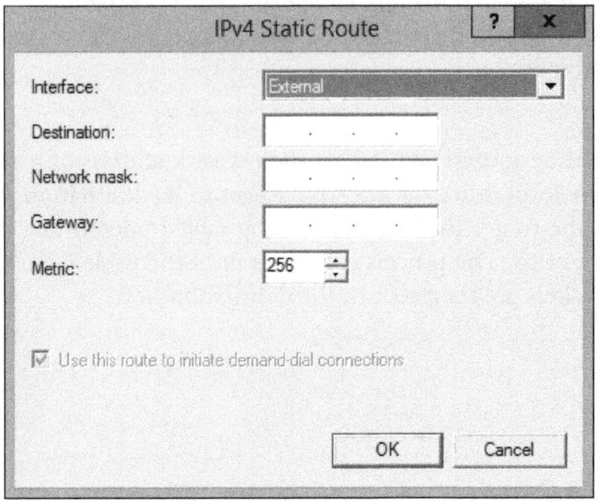

8. Specify the Network mask for the network, such as **255.255.00** or **255.255.255.0.** If you define a single address for the destination, specify **255.255.255.255.**
9. For the Gateway, specify the router that is the next hop toward the final destination.
10. Specify a Metric for the specified route.
11. Click **OK.**

To view or configure the routing table from the command line, use the `route.exe` command-line utility, as shown in Figure 8-4. The `route.exe` utility syntax is as follows:

```
route [-f] [-p] [Command [Destination] [mask Netmask]
[Gateway] [metric Metric] [if Interface]
```

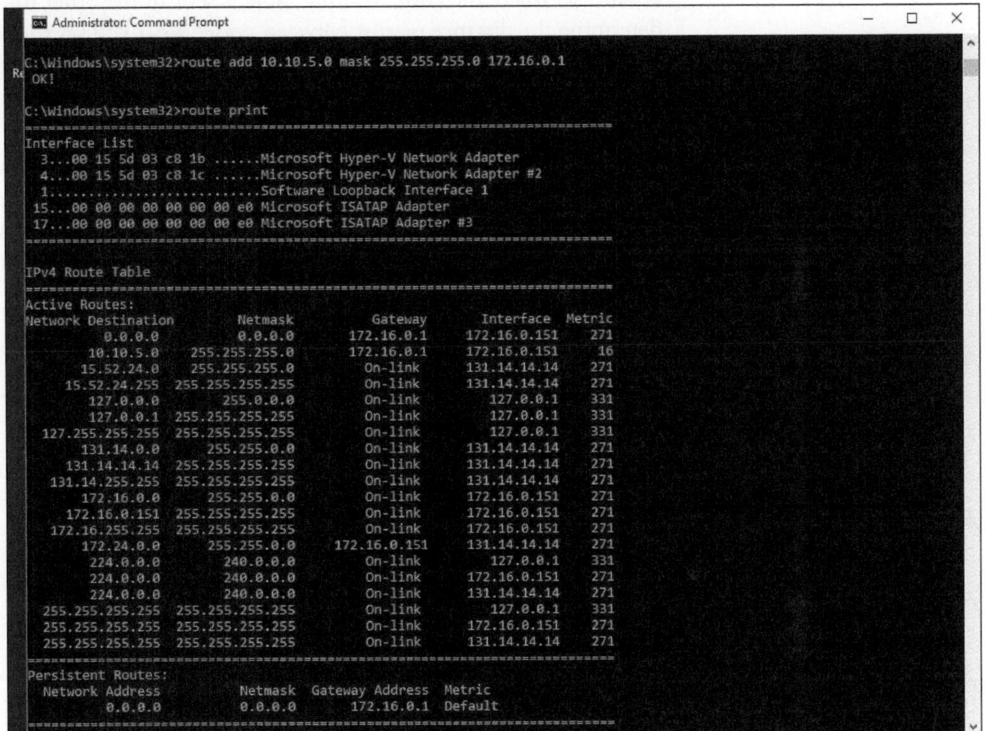

Figure 8-4

Route command

The `route` command-line utility commands are:

- **`print`**: Displays the routing table.
- **add**: Adds a route to the routing table. To make routes persistent, which will be available after the server is rebooted, you must also use the `-p` switch.
- **change**: Modifies an existing route.
- **`delete`**: Deletes an existing route.

To display the routing table, execute the following command:

```
route print
```

To add a route to 10.10.5.0 network, which will be sent to the 192.168.1.20 router, execute the following command:

```
route add 10.10.5.0 mask 255.255.255.0 192.168.1.20
```

To add a route to 10.10.5.0 network, which will be sent to the 192.168.1.20 router and make the route persistent, execute the following command:

```
route add 10.10.5.0 mask 255.255.255.0 192.168.1.20
-p
```

To change the 10.10.5.0 route to use the 192.168.1.21 router, execute the following command:

```
route change 10.10.5.0 mask 255.255.255.0
192.168.1.21
```

To delete the 10.10.5.0 route, execute the following command:

```
route delete 10.10.5.0
```

Configuring Routing Information Protocol (RIP)

Microsoft Windows supports the ***Routing Information Protocol (RIP)*** through RRAS. RIP has been a popular distance-vector routing protocol for small organizations. RIP uses broadcasts where the entire routing table is sent to the other routers within the network. To determine the distance or cost between networks, RIP uses the metric of ***hop count***, which is the count of routers. The maximum number of hops allowed for RIP is 15. The hop count of 16 is considered an infinite distance, and, therefore, it is considered unreachable.

RIP was improved with ***RIP version 2 (RIPv2)*** by using multicasts to send the entire routing table to all adjacent routers at the address of 224.0.0.9, instead of using broadcasts. It also incorporates classless routing, which includes the network mask to allow classless routing advertisement. Lastly, RIPv2 uses authentication to ensure that routes being distributed throughout the network are coming from authorized sources.

CONFIGURE ROUTING

GET READY. To configure RIP on Windows Server 2016, perform the following steps.

1. Log on to LON-RTR as **adatum\administrator** with the password of **Pa$$w0rd.**
2. Open **Server Manager.**
3. Click **Tools > Routing and Remote Access.**
4. Expand the server node and expand **IPv4.**
5. Right-click the **General** node and choose **New Routing Protocol.** The New Routing Protocol dialog box opens (see Figure 8-5).
6. Select **RIP Version 2 for Internet Protocol.**
7. Click **OK** to close the New Routing Protocol dialog box. An RIP node will appear under IPv4.

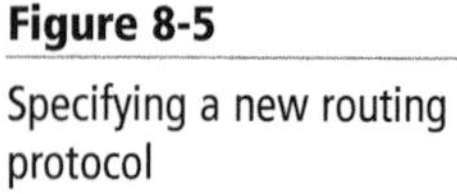

Figure 8-5

Specifying a new routing protocol

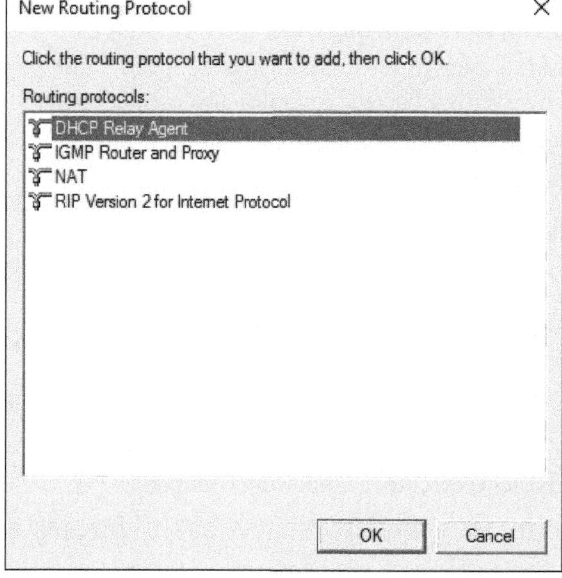

8. Right-click the **RIP** node and choose **New Interface.** The New Interface for RIP Version 2 for Internet Protocol dialog box opens.
9. Select the interface that you want to use RIP on.
10. Click **OK** to close the New Interface for RIP Version 2 for Internet Protocol dialog box. The RIP Properties dialog box opens (see Figure 8-6).

Figure 8-6

Configuring the RIP Properties

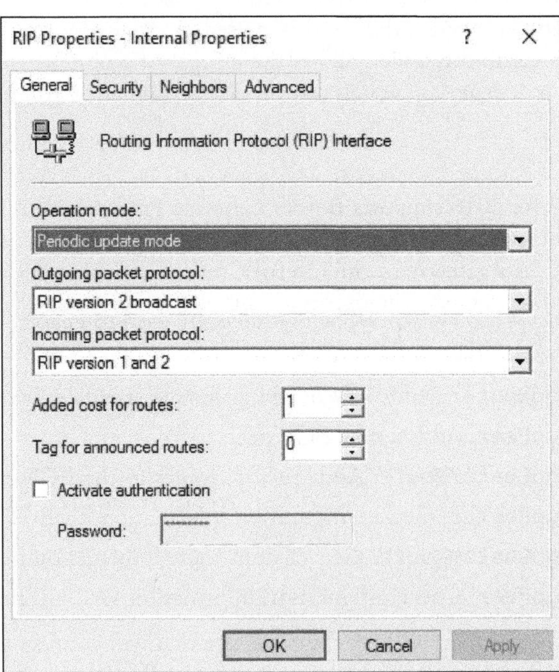

11. Click **OK** to close the RIP Properties dialog box.

If you need to configure RIP, right-click the RIP node and choose Properties. For example, if you want to specify which routes to accept, right-click a RIP interface, and select the Security tab. When you right-click an RIP interface and choose Properties, you can use the Neighbors tab to specify the neighbors that the RRAS router interfaces with (as shown in Figure 8-7).

Figure 8-7

Configuring the RIP Security and Neighbors tabs

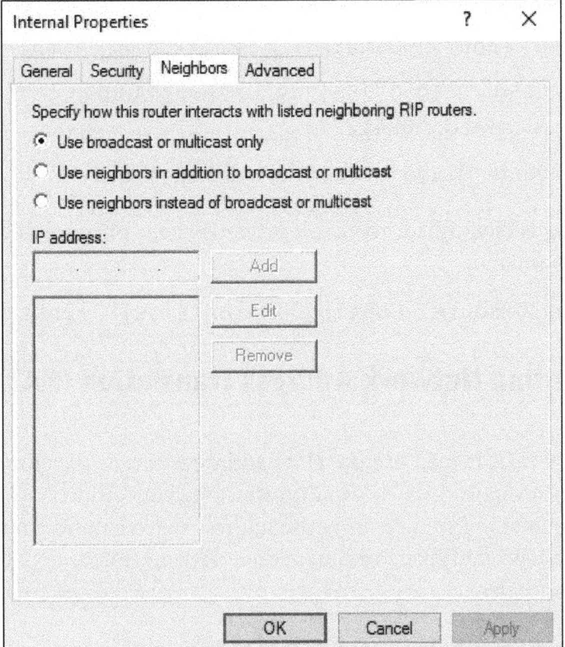

Configuring Border Gateway Protocol (BGP)

Border Gateway Protocol (BGP) is a standardized exterior gateway protocol that exchanges routing and reachability information among autonomous systems (AS) between edge routers on the Internet. Traffic that is routed within a single network AS is referred to as internal BGP. It is used by most Internet service providers to establish routing between one another, and it is used internally by very large private IP networks. It provides scalability, which allows the joining of a number of large AS areas, and it allows for multihoming, which can provide redundancy. Among routing protocols, BGP is unique in using TCP as its transport protocol.

CERTIFICATION READY
Configure Border Gateway Protocol (BGP)
Objective 5.1

Windows Server 2016 supports Border Gateway Protocol (BGP), which enables dynamic distribution and learning of routes by site-to-site (S2S) interfaces of RRAS. By adding BGP, the server can act as a gateway to the Internet, tenant premises, and tenant virtual networks.

The following Windows PowerShell cmdlets are used to enable, disable, or configure BGP in Windows Server 2016:

- **`Add-BgpRouter`**: Adds a BGP router for the specified Tenant ID
- **`Add-PgpPeer`**: Adds a new BGP peer
- **`Add-BgpCustomRoute`**: Adds custom routes to the BGP routing table
- **`Get-BgpRouter`**: Gets configuration information for BGP routers
- **`Get-BgpCustomRoute`**: Gets custom route information from the BGP router
- **`Get-BgpPeer`**: Gets configuration information for BGP peers

For example, to enable BGP for the Site1 site that will connect to the Site2 site and has an ASN of 65412 and an IPv4 address of interface IfWi1 (local address 10.0.254.249), execute the following Windows PowerShell command:

```
Add-BgpPeer -RoutingDomain "Site1" -Name "Site2"

-LocalIPAddress "10.0.254.249" -PeerIPAddress "10.1.0.1" -PeerASN
"65413" -LocalASN "65412"

-OperationMode Mixed -PeeringMode Automatic
```

You would then run similar commands at the Site2.

You would then add a BGP Peering. For example, at Site1, execute the following command:

```
Add-BgpPeer -RoutingDomain "Site1" -Name "Site2"

-LocalIPAddress "10.0.254.249" -PeerIPAddress "10.1.0.1" -PeerASN
"65413" -LocalASN "65412"

-OperationMode Mixed -PeeringMode Automatic
```

After peering is established, to enable advertisement of route 10.0.0.0/24 in Site1, execute the following command:

```
Add-BgpCustomRoute -RoutingDomain "site1" -Interface IfWe1
```

Implementing Network Address Translation (NAT)

Although CIDR helped use the IPv4 addresses more efficiently, additional steps had to prevent the exhaustion of IPv4 addresses. Network Address Translation (NAT) is used with masquerading to hide an entire address space behind a single IP address. In other words, it allows multiple computers on a network to connect to the Internet through a single IP address.

CERTIFICATION READY
Implement Network Address Translation (NAT)
Objective 4.1

NAT enables a local area network (LAN) to use one set of IP addresses for internal traffic and a second set of addresses for external traffic. The NAT computer or device is usually a router (including routers made for home and small-office Internet connections) or a proxy server. As a result, you can:

- Provide a type of firewall by hiding internal IP addresses.
- Enable multiple internal computers to share a single external public IP address.

The private addresses are reserved addresses not allocated to any specific organization. Because these private addresses cannot be assigned to global addresses used on the Internet and are not routable on the Internet, you must use a NAT gateway or proxy server to convert between private and public addresses. The private network addresses are expressed in RFC 1918:

- 10.0.0.0–10.255.255.255
- 172.16.0.0–172.31.255.255
- 192.168.0.0–192.168.255.255

NAT obscures an internal network's structure by making all traffic appear to originate from the NAT device or proxy server. To accomplish this, the NAT device or proxy server uses stateful translation tables to map the "hidden" addresses into a single address and then rewrites the outgoing Internet Protocol (IP) packets on exit so that they appear to originate from the router. As data packets are returned from the Internet, the responding data packets are mapped back to the originating IP address using the entries stored in the translation tables.

When NAT is used to connect a private network to a public network, the following process occurs:

1. The client on the internal private network creates an IP packet, which is forwarded to the computer or device running NAT.
2. The computer or device running NAT changes the outgoing packet header to indicate the packet originated from the NAT computer or device's external address. It then sends the remapped packet over the public network such as the Internet to its intended destination. During this process, it stores the source address and the remapped NAT information in a table so it can keep track of all source computers.
3. When the destination computer responds with packets, the destination computer sends packets back to the computer or device running NAT.
4. When the computer or device receives the packets back from the destination computer, the computer or device running NAT changes the packet header to the private address of the destination client. It then sends the packet to the client computer.

Enabling NAT is a simple process, which can be selected using the Routing and Remote Access Server Setup Wizard. To support NAT, you must have a server that has two network interfaces, one for the private network and one for the public network.

TAKE NOTE* If you have an IPsec VPN server behind a NAT device, you need to configure the Windows clients to use Network Address Translation-Traversal (NAT-T). For more information, search this topic on the Microsoft web site.

ENABLE NAT

GET READY. To enable NAT on Windows Server 2016, perform the following steps.

1. Log on to LON-RTR as **adatum\administrator** with the password of **Pa$$w0rd.**
2. Open **Server Manager.**
3. Click **Tools > Routing and Remote Access.**
4. Expand the server node, expand **IPv4,** and then right-click **NAT** and choose **Properties.**

5. If you do not have a DHCP server on the private network, you can use the RRAS server to respond to DHCP address requests. To do this, click the **Address Assignment** tab and select the **Automatically assign IP addresses by using the DHCP allocator** check box.
6. To allocate addresses to clients on the private network by acting as a DHCP server, in IP address text box and the Mask text box, configure a subnet address from which the addresses are assigned. For example, if you enter 192.168.0.0 and a subnet mask of 255.255.255.0, the RRAS server responds to DHCP requests with address assignments from 192.168.0.1 through 192.168.0.254.
7. Click **OK** to close the NAT Properties dialog box.
8. To add the public interface to the NAT configuration, right-click **NAT** and choose **New Interface.**
9. In the Network Interface for Network Address Translation (NAT) dialog box, select the interface connected to the public network/external/Internet and then click **OK.**
10. In the Network Address Translation Properties – public network/external/Externet Properties dialog box, on the NAT tab, click the **Public interface connected to the Internet** radio button, select the **Enable NAT on this interface** check box (as shown in Figure 8-8), and then click **OK.**

Figure 8-8

Enabling NAT

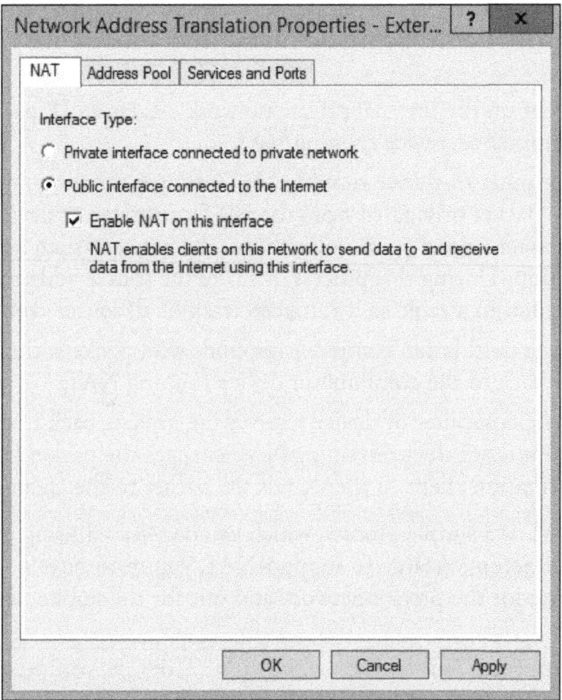

11. To add the private interface to the NAT configuration, right-click **NAT** and choose **New Interface.**
12. In the New Interface for Network Address Translation (NAT) dialog box, select the interface connected to the private network and then click **OK.**
13. In the Network Address Translation Properties – Internal Properties dialog box, on the NAT tab, click **Private interface connected to private network** and then click **OK.**

Disabling Routing and Remote Access

When you do not want a server to host Routing and Remote Access Services, or you when need to change which specific services are available through RRAS, you need to remove the Routing and Remove Access configuration and disable the Routing and Remote Access service. Then, if needed, you can rerun the Configure and Enable Routing and Remote Access wizard to reconfigure the Routing and Remote Access services.

To disable the Routing and Remote Access configuration, right-click the server and choose Disable Routing and Remote Access. However, this option is not available if you configured DirectAccess. If you configured DirectAccess, you must remove the DirectAccess configuration before you can disable Routing and Remote Access.

DISABLE ROUTING AND REMOTE ACCESS

GET READY. To disable Routing and Remote Access, perform the following steps.

1. Log on to LON-RTR as **adatum\administrator** with the password of **Pa$$w0rd.**
2. Open **Server Manager.**
3. Click **Tools > Routing and Remote Access.**
4. Right-click the server and choose **Disable Routing and Remote Access.**
5. When you are prompted to confirm whether you want to continue, click **Yes.**

SKILL SUMMARY

IN THIS LESSON YOU LEARNED:

- Routing is the process of selecting paths in a network where data will be sent. Routing is required to send traffic from one subnet to another within an organization, and it is required to send traffic from one organization to another. A computer running Windows can act as a router and include its own routing table, so that you can specify which direction data is sent toward its final destination.
- Today, it is common for an organization to use a remote access server (RAS). A RAS enables users to connect remotely to a network using various protocols and connection types. By connecting to the RAS over the Internet, users can connect to their organization's network so that they can access data files, read email, and access other applications just as if they were sitting at work.
- The routing tables are manually created with static routes, or are dynamically created with routing protocols such as Routing Information Protocol (RIP), based on the current routing topology.
- Border Gateway Protocol (BGP) is a standardized exterior gateway protocol that exchanges routing and reachability information among autonomous systems (AS) between edge routers on the Internet. Traffic that is routed within a single network AS is referred to as internal BGP. It is used by most Internet service providers to establish routing between one another, and it is used internally by very large private IP networks.
- Although CIDR helped use the IPv4 addresses more efficiently, additional steps had to prevent the exhaustion of IPv4 addresses. Network Address Translation (NAT) is used with masquerading to hide an entire address space behind a single IP address. In other words, it allows multiple computers on a network to connect to the Internet through a single IP address.

■ Knowledge Assessment

Multiple Choice

Select the correct answer for each of the following questions.

1. Which of the following can be found in RRAS? (Choose all that apply.)
   a. Routing
   b. OSPF
   c. RIP
   d. NAT
2. Which tab in the RIP properties dialog box can be used to prevent routes being received from a router located on 10.10.10.10?
   a. General
   b. Security
   c. Neighbors
   d. RIP Nodes
3. Which option should be used with the `Route` command when creating a static route that will ensure the route is still available if the computer is rebooted?
   a. `/consistent`
   b. `/save`
   c. `-p`
   d. `-s`
4. Which Windows Server 2016 services and applications offer IPv6 support?
   a. Nearly all server roles provide IPv6 support.
   b. Few offer IPv6 support, but they are expected soon.
   c. All offer IPv6 support in Windows Server 2016.
   d. Remote Access supports IPv6 routing and advertising, and the DHCP Server role can allocate IPv6 addresses.
5. Which of the following should be used to enable NAT?
   a. Services for Network File System (NFS)
   b. Wireless LAN Service
   c. Network Load Balancing (NLB)
   d. Routing and Remote Access Service (RRAS)
   e. Health Registration Authority (HRA)
   f. Simple TCP/IP Services
   g. Connection Manager Administration Kit (CMAK)
   h. Network Policy Server (NPS)
   i. Windows System Resource Manager (WSRM)
6. Which command can be used to create a static route on a server running Windows Server 2016?
   a. `ipconfig`
   b. `route`
   c. `netstat`
   d. `Add-Bgprouter`
7. Which metric is used by RIP to determine the optimal route?
   a. Hops
   b. Latency
   c. Ping time
   d. Distance

8. Which of the following is the largest number of hops supported by RIP?
   a. 4
   b. 10
   c. 15
   d. 16
9. Which of the following should be used to manage BGP on Windows Server 2016?
   a. Remote Access console
   b. Routing and Remote Access
   c. `Netsh` command
   d. PowerShell cmdlets
10. Which of the following is used to translate between private addresses and public addresses?
    a. Metric table
    b. RIP
    c. BGP
    d. NAT

Matching and Identification

1. Identify the routing protocols supported by Windows Server 2016.

   ____ a. RIP v2 for Internet Protocol
   ____ b. IGMP Router and Proxy
   ____ c. OSPF
   ____ d. BGP
   ____ e. NAT

Business Case Scenarios

Scenario 8-1: Configuring Routing

You are an administrator at a corporate office with 12 remote sites. Each remote site has a site server that also acts as a router. When you look at each of the servers, you realize that the previous administrator used the `route` command to specify static routes. However, as you have had to perform maintenance and move some of the network connections, you find it difficult to modify all of the servers to reflect the changes. In addition, you will be adding four more sites over the next six months. Describe the recommendation you will propose to management to avoid purchasing additional network equipment.

Implementing Virtual Private Network (VPN) and DirectAccess Solutions

70-741 EXAM OBJECTIVE

Objective 4.2 – Implement virtual private network (VPN) and DirectAccess solutions. This objective may include but is not limited to the following: Implement remote access and site-to-site (S2S) VPN solutions using remote access gateway; configure different VPN protocol options; configure authentication options; configure VPN Reconnect; create and configure connection profiles; determine when to use remote access VPN and site-to-site VPN and configure appropriate protocols; install and configure DirectAccess; implement server requirements; implement client configuration; troubleshoot DirectAccess.

Lesson Heading	Exam Objective
Implementing Virtual Private Network (VPN) • Configuring Different VPN Protocol Options • Configuring Authentication Options • Implementing Remote Access and Site-to-Site (S2S) VPN Solutions Using Remote Access Gateway • Configuring VPN Connections • Configuring VPN Reconnect	Determine when to use remote access VPN and site-to-site VPN and configure appropriate protocols Configure different VPN protocol options Configure authentication options Implement remote access and site-to-site (S2S) VPN solutions using remote access gateway Configure VPN Reconnect
Creating and Configuring Connection Profiles • Creating a VPN Connection Using the Set Up a Connection or Network Wizard • Using Connection Manager (CM) and the Connection Manager Administration Kit (CMAK) • Configuring Split Tunneling • Troubleshooting Remote Access Problems	Create and configure connection profiles
Installing and Configuring DirectAccess • Understanding the DirectAccess Connection Process • Implementing DirectAccess Requirements • Running the DirectAccess Getting Started Wizard • Running the Remote Access Setup Wizard • Preparing for DirectAccess Deployment • Troubleshooting DirectAccess	Install and configure DirectAccess Implement server requirements Implement client configuration Troubleshoot DirectAccess

KEY TERMS

authentication
Challenge Handshake Authentication Protocol (CHAP)
Connection Manager (CM)
Connection Manager Administration Kit (CMAK)
data encryption
data integrity
DirectAccess
encapsulation
Extensible Authentication Protocol (EAP)
Internet Key Exchange v2 (IKEv2)
Layer 2 Tunneling Protocol (L2TP) with IPsec
Microsoft CHAP version 2 (MS-CHAP v2)
Network Connectivity Assistant (NCA)
Network Location Server (NLS)
Password Authentication Protocol (PAP)
Point-to-Point Tunneling Protocol (PPTP)
Protected Extensible Authentication Protocol (PEAP)
Secure Socket Tunneling Protocol (SSTP)
site-to-site VPN connection
split tunnel
virtual private networks (VPNs)

■ Implementing Virtual Private Networks (VPNS)

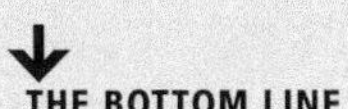

Virtual private networks (VPNs) link two computers or network devices through a wide area network (WAN) such as the Internet. Because the Internet is a public network and is considered insecure, the data sent between the two computers or devices is encapsulated and encrypted.

CERTIFICATION READY
Determine when to use remote access VPN and site-to-site VPN and configure appropriate protocols
Objective 4.2

VPN connections provide the following:

- ***Encapsulation***: Encapsulates or places private data in a packet with a header containing routing information that allows the data to traverse the transit network such as the Internet.
- ***Authentication***: Proves the identity of the user or computer that tries to connect.
- ***Data encryption***: Ensures data remains private by encrypting it prior to transmission, preventing unauthorized users from accessing it.. When it is received, the intended recipient decrypts it. Of course, the encryption and decryption depend on the sender and receiver. Both must have a common or related encryption key; larger keys offer better security.
- ***Data integrity***: Verifies that the data sent over the VPN connection has not been modified in transit. This is usually done by using a cryptographic checksum that is based on an encryption key known only to the sender and receiver. When the data is received, the same checksum calculation is performed and the value is compared to the one that was calculated before the data was sent. If the values match, the data has not been tampered with.

VPN can be used in the following scenarios:

- A client connects to the remote access server (RAS) to access internal resources from off-site.
- Two remote sites connect to each other by creating a VPN tunnel between RAS servers located at each site.
- Two different organizations create a VPN tunnel so users from one organization can privately access the resources in the other organization.

Configuring Different VPN Protocol Options

When selecting the appropriate VPN protocol to use, you must take into consideration operating systems, authentication requirements, and limitations.

CERTIFICATION READY
Configure different VPN protocol options
Objective 4.2

The following types of tunneling protocols are used with a VPN/RAS server running on Windows Server 2016:

- Point-to-Point Tunneling Protocol (PPTP)
- Layer 2 Tunneling Protocol (L2TP) with Internet Protocol Security (IPsec)
- Internet Key Exchange v2 (IKEv2)
- Secure Socket Tunneling Protocol (SSTP)

When selecting the appropriate VPN protocol to use, you must take into consideration the following:

- Operating systems you will be using
- The client's need—and ability—to traverse firewalls, NAT devices, and web proxies
- Authentication requirements, for computers as well as users
- Implementations, such as site-to-site VPN or a remote access VPN

In most situations, using VPN Reconnect (also referred to as IKEv2) should provide you the best option for security and uninterrupted VPN connectivity. You can then use SSTP for your VPN solution as a fallback mechanism.

UNDERSTANDING POINT-TO-POINT TUNNELING PROTOCOL (PPTP)

Point-to-Point Tunneling Protocol (PPTP) has widespread support with nearly all versions of Windows. It is a VPN protocol based on the legacy Point-to-Point (PPP) protocol used with modems. PPTP uses a Transmission Control Protocol (TCP) connection for tunnel management and a modified version of Generic Route Encapsulation (GRE) to encapsulate PPP frames for tunneled data. PPTP uses TCP port 1723 and IP protocol ID 47.

Payloads of the encapsulated PPP frames can be encrypted, compressed, or both. The PPP frame is encrypted with Microsoft Point-to-Point Encryption (MPPE) with RC4 (128-bit key) by using encryption keys that are generated by the MS-CHAPv2 or EAP-TLS authentication process. PPTP is easy to set up but has weak encryption technology.

PPTP provides confidentiality, meaning that it prevents the data from being viewed but does not provide data integrity (proof that the data was not modified in transit) or data origin authentication (proof that the data was sent by the authorized user). In other words, it does not protect the packet from being intercepted and modified.

TAKE NOTE*

You can encrypt data with PPTP only if you use MS-CHAPv2 and EAP-TLS as the authentication protocols. PPTP is supported natively by Windows client operating systems (Windows XP and later) and Windows server operating systems (Windows Server 2003 and later). It is used typically for remote access and site-to-site VPNs; works with IPv4; and uses Network Address Translation (NAT), which is supported via PPTP-enabled NAT routers. It uses PPP for user authentication and RC4 for data confidentiality.

UNDERSTANDING LAYER 2 TUNNELING PROTOCOL (L2TP) WITH IPSEC

Whereas PPTP supports authentication of the user only, ***Layer 2 Tunneling Protocol (L2TP) with IPsec*** requires that the computers mutually authenticate themselves to each other. The computer-to-computer authentication takes place before the user is authenticated. L2TP provides the tunneling while IPsec provides the security.

L2TP is the industry standard when setting up secure tunnels. L2TP provides a support mechanism for pre-shared keys, digital certificates, or Kerberos for mutual authentication. Pre-shared keys are basically passwords and should be used only on test networks when you do not want to set up a public key infrastructure (PKI). Digital certificates, which are stored in a format that cannot be modified, offer a more secure option. They are issued by certification authorities that you trust. Kerberos is the native authentication protocol for Windows Server 2003 and later and provides the easiest way to secure VPN connections in a domain-based environment.

By using IPsec, L2TP/IPsec VPN connections provide data confidentiality, data integrity, and data authentication. IPsec provides mutual authentication, anti-replay, and nonrepudiation just like digital certificates. Kerberos can be used only when both computers involved in the L2TP tunnel are in the same forest. L2TP uses IPsec to encrypt the PPP packets.

The L2TP message is encrypted with either Advanced Encryption Standard (AES) or Triple Data Encryption Standard (3DES) by using encryption keys that the IKE negotiation process generates. L2TP uses UDP port 500, UDP port 1701, UDP port 4500, and IP protocol ID 50.

TAKE NOTE*

L2TP/IPsec is supported by Windows client operating systems (Windows XP and later) and Windows server operating systems (Windows Server 2003 and later). It is used typically for remote access and site-to-site VPNs; works over IPv4 and IPv6; and supports NAT. It uses IPsec with 3DES (168-bit key) and uses UDP ports (500, 1701, 4500). It uses IPsec for machine authentication followed by PPP for user authentication.

UNDERSTANDING SECURE SOCKET TUNNELING PROTOCOL (SSTP)

Secure Socket Tunneling Protocol (SSTP) improved on the PPTP and L2TP/IPsec VPN tunneling protocols. It works by sending PPP or L2TP traffic through a Secure Sockets Layer (SSL) 3.0 channel.

The SSTP protocol uses SSL and TCP port 443 to relay traffic. TCP port 443 will work in network environments in which other VPN protocols might be blocked when traversing firewalls, Network Address Translation (NAT) devices, and web proxies. SSTP uses a 2,048-bit certificate for authentication and implements stronger encryption, which makes it the most secure VPN protocol.

TAKE NOTE*

SSTP is supported by Windows client operating systems (Windows Vista SP1 and later) and Windows server operating systems (Windows Server 2008 and later). It is designed for remote access VPN, works over IPv4 and IPv6 networks, and traverses NAT, firewalls, and web proxies. SSTP uses a generic port that firewalls rarely block. It uses PPP for user authentication and RC4/AES for data confidentiality.

TAKE NOTE*

If you need to use a VPN connection behind a firewall that allows only HTTPS, SSTP is your only option.

UNDERSTANDING INTERNET KEY EXCHANGE V2 (IKEV2)

Internet Key Exchange v2 (IKEv2) consists of three protocols: IPsec tunnel mode, Encapsulating Security Payload (ESP), and IKEv2 Mobility and Multihoming (MOBIKE). IPsec uses IKEv2 for key negotiations, ESP for securing the packet transmissions, and MOBIKE for switching tunnel endpoints. MOBIKE ensures that if a break occurs in connectivity, the user can continue without restarting the connection. Therefore, the VPN connection is more resilient when moving from one wireless hotspot to another or switching from wireless to a wired connection. IKEv2 is supported only on Windows 7, Windows Server 2008 R2, and later operating systems.

VPN Reconnect (also known as IKEv2) is a feature introduced with Routing and Remote Access Services (RRAS) in Windows Server 2008 R2 and Windows 7. It is designed to provide users with consistent VPN connectivity and automatically reestablishes a VPN when users temporarily lose their Internet connection.

VPN Reconnect was designed for those remote workers who are sitting in the coffee shop, waiting at the airport for their next plane to arrive, trying to submit that last expense report from their hotel room, or working at any location where Internet connections are less than optimal.

It varies from other VPN protocols in that it will not drop the VPN tunnel associated with the session. Instead, VPN Reconnect keeps the connection alive for 30 minutes by default after it is dropped. This allows you to reconnect automatically without having to go through the process of reselecting your VPN connection and reauthenticating yourself.

TAKE NOTE*

You can find the IKEv2 setting (network outage) in the RRAS console by right-clicking the RRAS server and choosing Properties > IKEv2 tab.

TAKE NOTE*

Designed for remote access VPN, it works well over IPv4 and IPv6 networks and traverses NAT. It also supports user or machine authentication via IKEv2 and uses 3DES and AES for data confidentiality.

Configuring Authentication Options

Authentication is a major component to virtual private networks because it is used to prove the identity of the user or computer that tries to connect.

CERTIFICATION READY
Configure authentication options
Objective 4.2

Authentication for VPN connections takes one of the following forms:

- **User-level authentication by using Point-to-Point Protocol (PPP) authentication:** User-level authentication is usually user name and password. With a VPN connection, if the VPN server authenticates, the VPN client attempts the connection using a PPP user-level authentication method and verifies that the VPN client has the appropriate authorization. If the method uses mutual authentication, the VPN client also authenticates the VPN server. By using mutual authentication, clients are ensured that the client does not communicate with a rogue server masquerading as a VPN server.
- **Computer-level authentication that uses IKE to exchange either computer certificates or a pre-shared key:** Microsoft recommends using computer-certificate authentication because it is a much stronger authentication method. Computer-level authentication is performed only for L2TP/IPsec connections.

When using VPNs, Windows 10 and Windows Server 2016 support the following forms of authentication:

- ***Password Authentication Protocol (PAP)***: Uses plaintext (unencrypted passwords). PAP is the least secure authentication and is not recommended.
- ***Challenge Handshake Authentication Protocol (CHAP)***: Based on a challenge-response authentication that uses the industry standard MD5 hashing scheme to encrypt the response. CHAP was an industry standard for years and is still quite popular.
- ***Microsoft CHAP version 2 (MS-CHAP v2)***: Provides two-way authentication (mutual authentication). MS-CHAP v2 provides stronger security than CHAP. Finally, MS-CHAP v2 is the only authentication protocol that Windows Server 2016 provides that allows you to change an expired password during the connection process.
- ***Extensible Authentication Protocol (EAP)***: A universal authentication framework that allows third-party vendors to develop custom authentication schemes, including retinal scans, voice recognition, fingerprint identifications, smart cards, Kerberos, and digital certificates. It also provides a mutual authentication method that supports password-based user or computer authentication. It is often combined with MS-CHAPv2.
- ***Protected Extensible Authentication Protocol (PEAP)***: Encapsulates the EAP with an encrypted and authenticated Transport Layer Security (TLS) tunnel.

TAKE NOTE* If you want to use smart cards for remote connections, you must use Extensible Authentication Protocol (EAP).

It is always best to use EAP-MS-CHAPv2 or MS-CHAPv2 whenever possible. However, Windows 10 and Windows Server 2016 can negotiate MSCHAP v2, EAP-MS-CHAPv2, and PEAP with MSCHAPv2.

If you have multiple remote access servers, you can choose to use a RADIUS server. A RADIUS server provides authentication, authorization, and accounting for the remote access clients. RADIUS servers are discussed in detail in Lesson 10.

Implementing Remote Access and Site-to-Site (S2S) VPN Solutions Using Remote Access Gateway

A ***site-to-site VPN connection*** connects two private networks. Site-to-site VPN connections can be used to connect branch offices to an organization's primary site, or to connect one organization to the network of another organization. This VPN connection allows routed connections to the remote site or network while helping to maintain secure communications over the Internet. When networks are connected over the Internet, a VPN-enabled router forwards packets to another VPN-enabled router across a VPN connection.

CERTIFICATION READY
Implement remote access and site-to-site (S2S) VPN solutions using remote access gateway
Objective 4.2

To control who can connect to the VPN server, the calling VPN server or router must authenticate itself to the answer server or router. To ensure that the calling server or router is talking to the correct VPN server (mutual authentication), the remote server must authenticate itself to the calling device.

CONFIGURE AND ENABLE ROUTING AND REMOTE ACCESS

GET READY. To configure and enable Routing and Remote Access, perform the following steps.

1. Log on to LON-RTR as **adatum\administrator** with the password of **Pa$$w0rd.**
2. Click **Start** and click **Server Manager.**
3. In Server Manager, click **Tools > Routing and Remote Access.**
4. Right-click the server and choose **Configure and Enable Routing and Remote Access.**
5. In the Routing and Remote Access Server Setup Wizard, on the Welcome page, click **Next.**
6. On the Configuration page, select **Secure connection between two private networks.** Click **Next.**
7. On the Demand-Dial Connections page, click **Next.**
8. On the IP Address Assignment page, click **From a specified range of addresses.** Click **Next.**
9. On the Address Range Assignment page, click **New.**
10. In the New IPv4 Address Range dialog box, type the following:

    Start IP address: **192.168.1.201**

    End IP address: **192.168.1.205**

    Then, click **OK.**
11. Back on the Address Range Assignment page, click **Next.**
12. On the Completing the Routing and Remote Access Server Setup Wizard page, click **Finish.** The Demand-Dial Interface Wizard opens. Leave the wizard open for the next exercise.

CONFIGURE A DEMAND-DIAL INTERFACE

GET READY. To configure a demand-dial interface, perform the following steps.

1. With the Demand-Dial Interface Wizard already open, on the Welcome page, click **Next.**
2. On the Interface Name page, *Remote Router* is the default interface name. Type a descriptive name for this interface and click **Next.**
3. On the Connection Type page, the Connect using virtual private networking (VPN) option is already selected. Click **Next.**
4. On the VPN Type page (as shown in Figure 9-1), select the appropriate VPN type, and then click **Next.**
5. On the Destination Address page, enter the IP address or name of the VPN server or device (such as **131.17.0.10**). Click **Next.**
6. On the Protocols and Security page, the Route IP packets on this interface option is already selected. Select **Add a user account so a remote router can dial in** so that a remote router can dial in.
7. On the Static Routes for Remote Networks page, click **Add.**
8. In the Static Route dialog box (see Figure 9-2), in the Destination text box, type the destination network address. In the Network Mask text box, type the subnet mask for the network. In the Metric text box, type a metric or cost for the router. Click **OK.**
9. Back on the Static Routes for Remote Networks page, click **Next.**
10. On the Dial-in Credentials page, *Remote Router* is the default user name. In the Password and Confirm password text boxes, enter a password such as **Pa$$w0rd.**
11. On the Dial-Out Credentials page, in the Username and Domain text boxes, enter a user name and domain. Then, in the Password and Confirm password text boxes, enter a password such as **Pa$$w0rd.** Click **Next.**

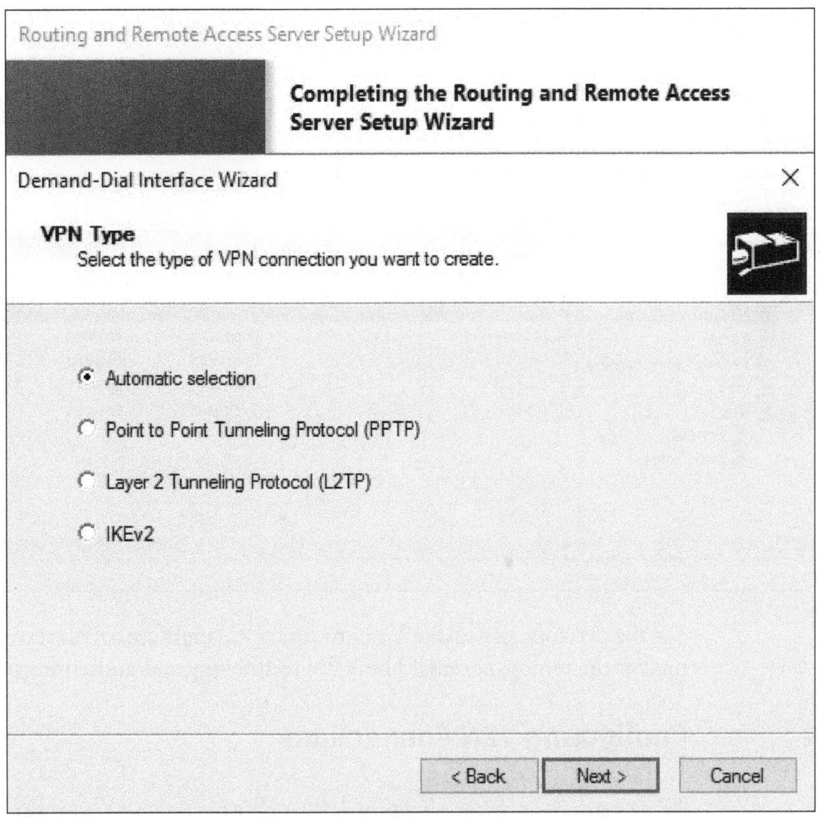

Figure 9-1
Selecting a VPN type

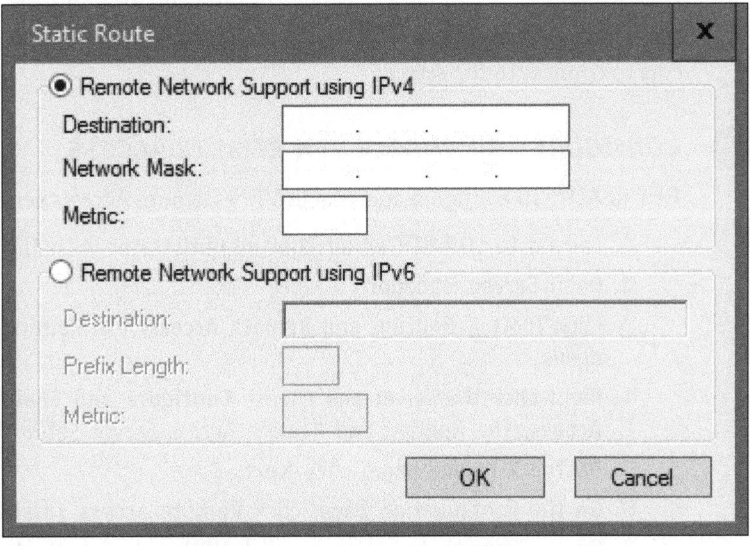

Figure 9-2
Configuring a static route

12. On the Completing the Demand-Dial Interface Wizard page, click **Finish**.

The demand-dial interface appears in the Network Interfaces list, as shown in Figure 9-3. Also, the Remote Router account appears as a local user on the computer, which has been created to allow access for the Network Access Permission.

Figure 9-3

Viewing the demand-dial interface

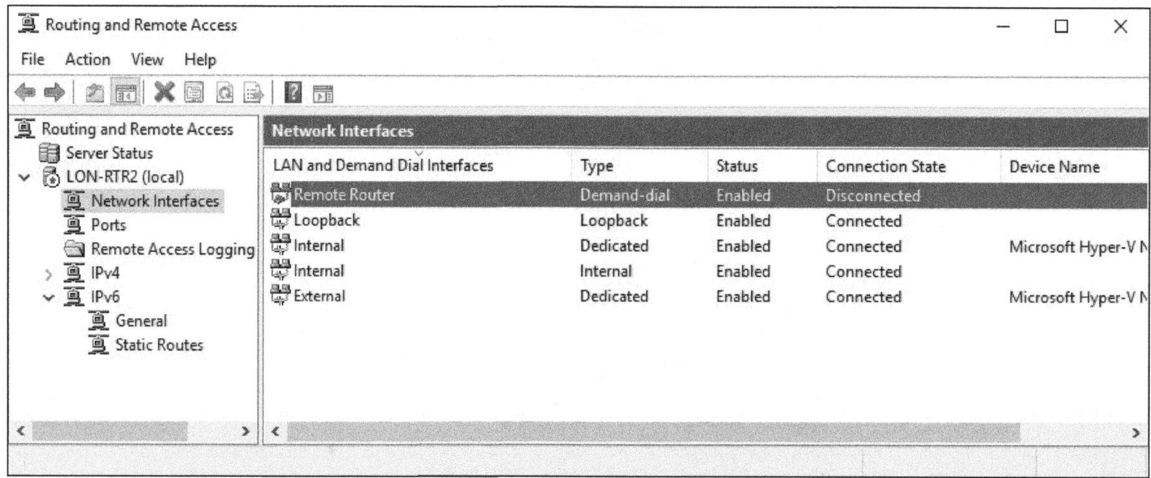

For the previous site-to-site VPN to function, a remote access server must be installed and configured at the remote address. The VPN technology and authentication must match on both sides.

Configuring VPN Connections

The remote access (dial-up or VPN) allows clients to connect to this server through a secure virtual private network connection.

For users to a remote access server, you need to first install and configure Router and Remote Access Server and configure and enable VPN Remote Access. You will then configure the clients to connect to the server.

CONFIGURE AND ENABLE VPN REMOTE ACCESS

GET READY. To configure and enable VPN Remote Access, perform the following steps.

1. Log on to LON-RTR as **adatum\administrator** with the password of **Pa$$w0rd.**
2. Open **Server Manager.**
3. Click **Tools > Routing and Remote Access.** The Routing and Remote Access console opens.
4. Right-click the server and choose **Configure and Enable Routing and Remote Access.** The Routing and Remote Access Server Setup Wizard opens.
5. On the Welcome page, click **Next.**
6. On the Configuration page, click **Remote access (dial-up or VPN)** and click **Next.**
7. On the Remote Access page, click **VPN** and click **Next.**
8. On the VPN Connection page (see Figure 9-4), select the external network card that is connected to the Internet.
9. On the IP Address Assignment page, click **from a specified range of addresses** and click **Next.**
10. On the Address Range Assignment page, click **New.**
11. In the New IPv4 Address Range dialog box, in the Start IP address and End IP address text boxes, enter the starting and ending IP addresses. Click **OK.**
12. Back on the Address Range Assignment page, click **Next.**
13. On the Managing Multiple Remote Access Servers page, if you have a RADIUS server, click **Yes, set up this server to work with a RADIUS server** and then click **Next.**

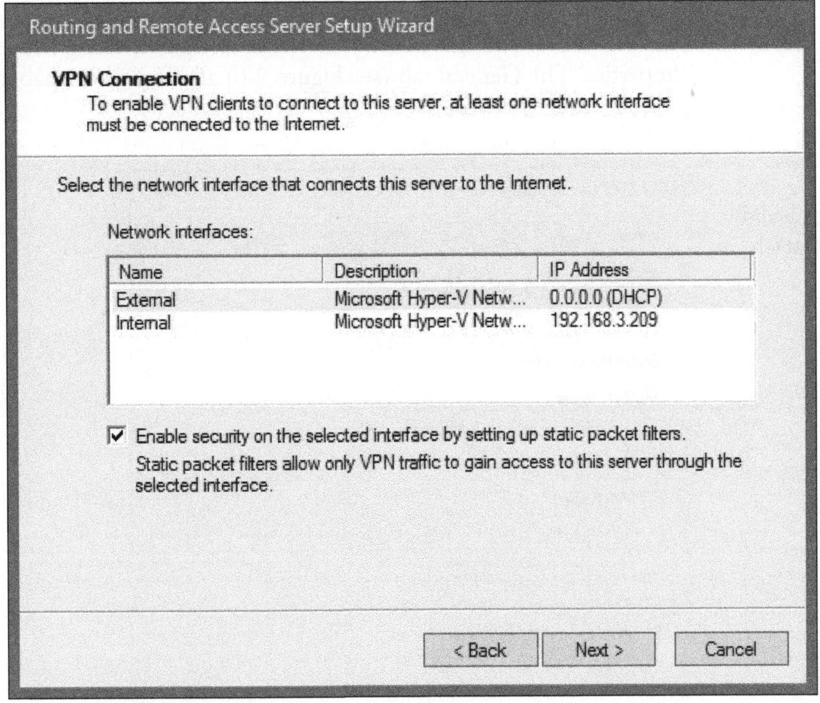

Figure 9-4

Configuring and enabling routing and remote access

Routing and Remote Access Server Setup Wizard

RADIUS Server Selection

You can specify the RADIUS servers that you want to use for authentication and accounting.

Enter the primary and alternate RADIUS servers that this server will use for remote authentication and accounting.

Primary RADIUS server:

Alternate RADIUS server:

Type the shared secret (password) that is used to contact these RADIUS servers.

Shared secret:

< Back | Next > | Cancel

Figure 9-5

Specifying the RADIUS servers on the RADIUS Server Selection page

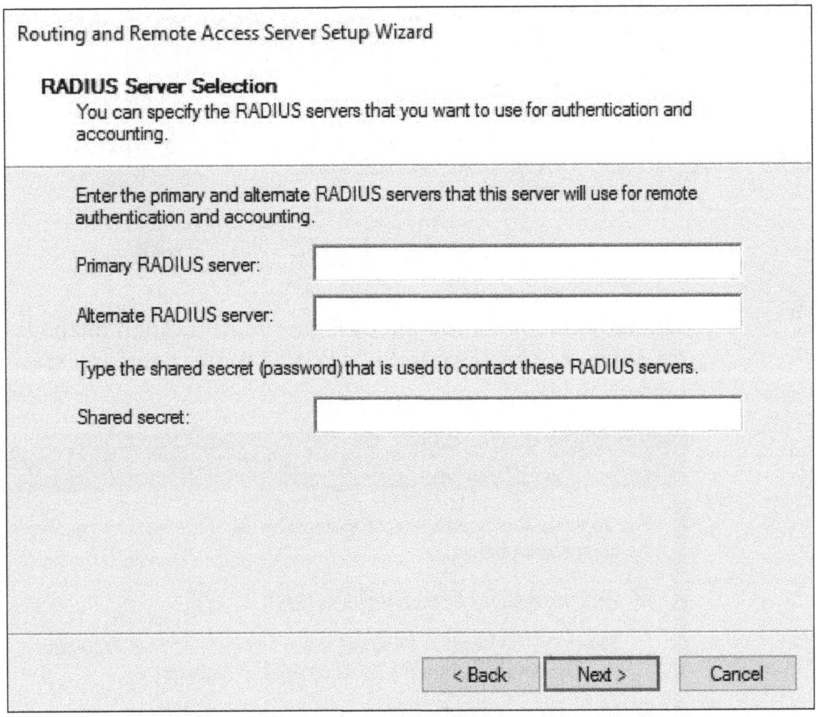

14. On the RADIUS Server Selection page (see Figure 9-5), in the Primary RADIUS server and Alternate RADIUS server text boxes, enter the primary and alternate RADIUS servers. Then, in the Shared secret text box, type the shared secret password. Click **Next.**
15. If you do not have a RADIUS server, click **No, use Routing and Remote Access to authenticate connection requests.** Click **Next.**
16. On the Completing the Routing and Remote Access Server Setup Wizard page, click **Finish.**
17. When you are prompted to support the relaying of DHCP messages from remote access clients, click **OK.**

After the VPN server is configured using Routing and Remote Access Server Setup Wizard, you can further configure the VPN server by right-clicking the server in RRAS and choosing Properties. The General tab (see Figure 9-6) allows you to enable routing and remote access without using the wizard.

Figure 9-6

Enabling routing and remote access with the General tab

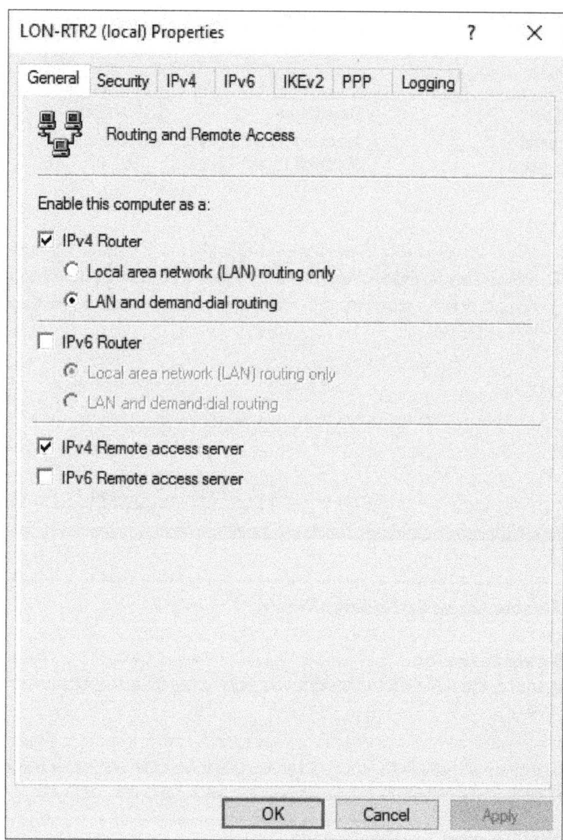

On the Security tab, you can configure authentication methods (see Figure 9-7), specify the pre-shared key for IPsec and L2TP/IKv2 connections, and specify the SSL certificate that is used by SSTP.

Figure 9-7

Using the Security tab

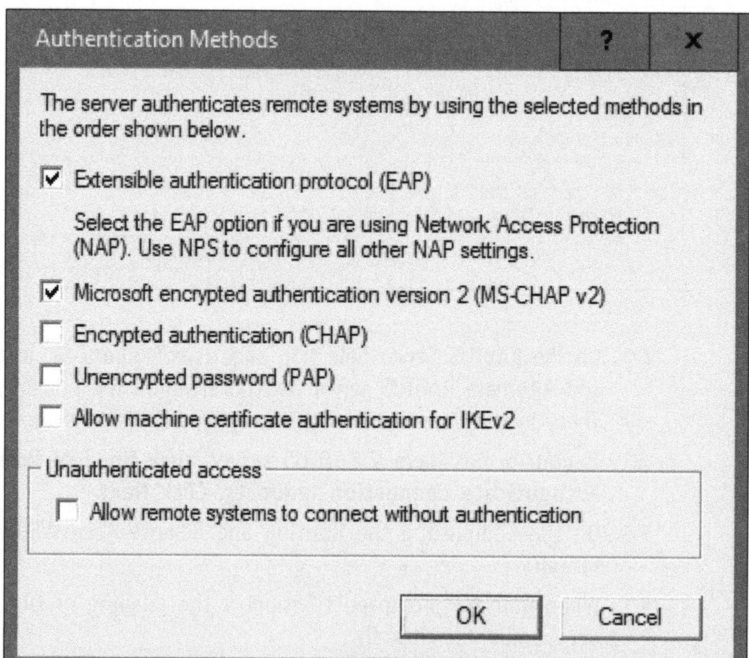

On the IPv4 tab, you can configure the IPv4 address assignments (see Figure 9-8). On the IPv6 tab, you can specify the IPv6 prefix assignment. On the IKEv2 tab, you can configure IKEv2 parameters, such as idle-timeout and network outage time.

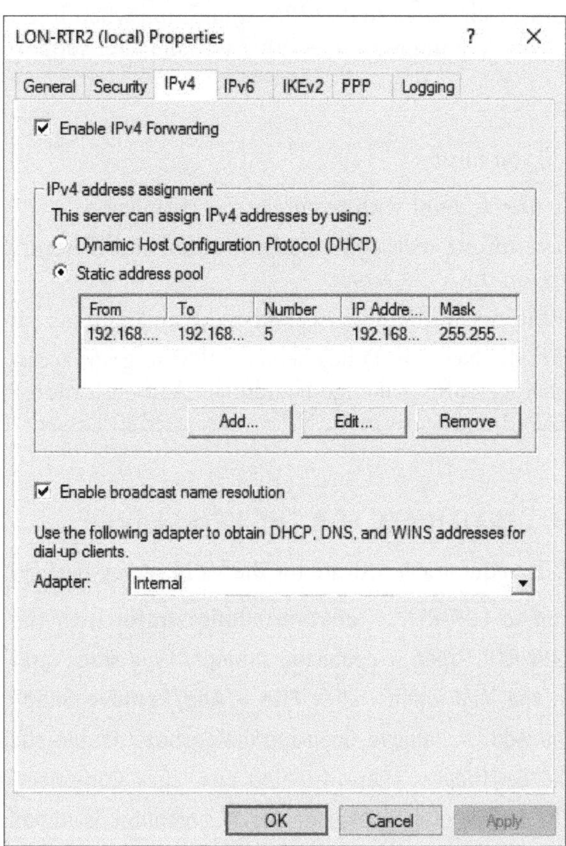

Figure 9-8
Using the IPv4 tab

By default, RRAS allows up to 128 ports for each of the VPN protocol types. If you want to change the number of ports, right-click Ports and choose Properties. You can then click the Configure button to open the Configure Device – WAN Miniport dialog box so that you can specify the maximum number of ports (see Figure 9-9).

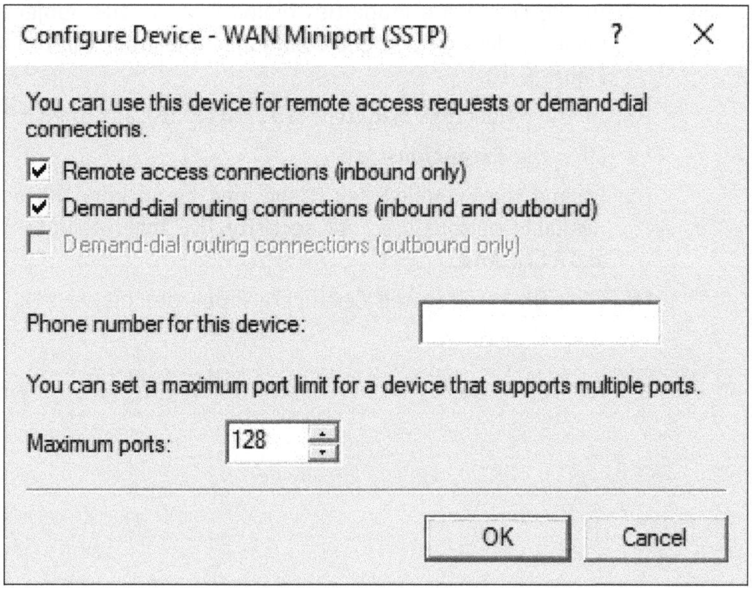

Figure 9-9
Specifying the number of ports

Configure Device - WAN Miniport (SSTP)
You can use this device for remote access requests or demand-dial connections.
Remote access connections (inbound only)
Demand-dial routing connections (inbound and outbound)
Demand-dial routing connections (outbound only)
Phone number for this device:
You can set a maximum port limit for a device that supports multiple ports.
Maximum ports: 128
OK
Cancel

Configuring VPN Reconnect

To provide constant connectivity, you use Internet Key Exchange version 2 (IKEv2), which automatically establishes a VPN connection when Internet connectivity is available. Only Windows 7, Windows Server 2008 R2, and later support VPN Reconnect.

CERTIFICATION READY
Configure VPN Reconnect
Objective 4.2

On the server, you must:

1. Create a user account with remote access permission.
2. Install a certificate with server authentication and IP security IKE intermediate extended key usage on the VPN server.
3. Install Routing and Remote Access Service and configure it as a VPN server.
4. Configure the Network Policy Server (NPS) to grant access for Extensible Authentication Protocol-Microsoft Challenge-Handshake Authentication Protocol version 2 (EAP-MSCHAPv2) authentication. NPS is discussed in Lesson 10.

REQUEST A CERTIFICATE FOR THE VPN SERVER

GET READY. To request a certificate for the VPN server, perform the following steps.

1. Log on to LON-RTR as **adatum\administrator** with the password of **Pa$$w0rd.**
2. On LON-RTR, open a command prompt, type **mmc**, and then press **Enter.**
3. When the MMC opens, click **File > Add/Remove Snap-in.**
4. In the Add or Remove Snap-ins dialog box, double-click **Certificates.**
5. In the Certificates snap-in dialog box, click **Computer account** and click **Next.**
6. On the Select Computer page, Local computer is already selected. Click **Finish.**
7. Expand the **Certificates** node and click **Personal.**
8. Right-click the **Personal** node and choose **All Tasks > Request New Certificate.**
9. In the Certificates Enrollment Wizard, on the Before You Begin page, click **Next.**
10. On the Select Certificate Enrollment Policy page, click **Next.**
11. On the Request Certificates page, click the **Adatum Web Certificate** and then click **More information is required to enroll for this certificate.**
12. In the Certificate Properties dialog box, on the Subject tab, under Subject name, under Type, select **Common name** from the drop-down list, as shown in Figure 9-10.
13. In the Value text box, type **131.107.0.10** and then click **Add.**
14. Click the **Extensions** tab.
15. Expand the Extended Key Usage area by clicking the down arrow. Then, under Available options, click **IP security IKE intermediate** (as shown in Figure 9-11) and click **Add.**
16. Click **OK** to close the Certificate Properties dialog box.

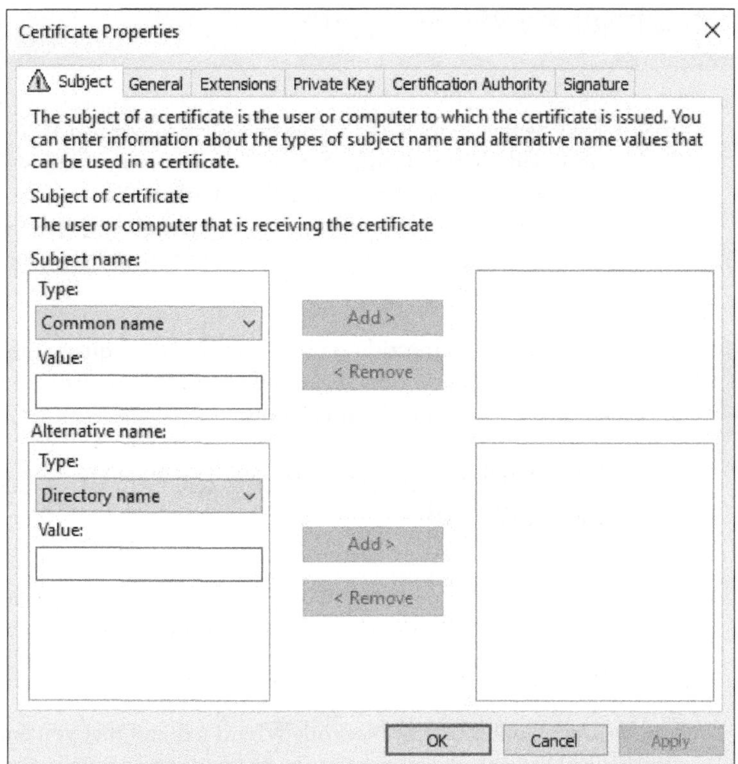

Figure 9-10
Requesting a certificate

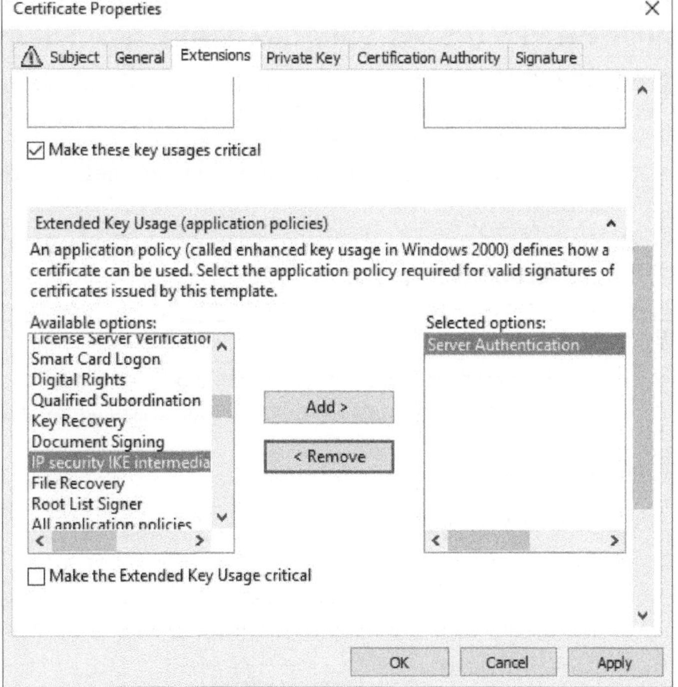

Figure 9-11
Adding Extended Key Usage options

17. On the Certificates Enrollment page, click **Enroll** and then click **Finish**.
18. Close the MMC. When you are prompted to save the settings, click **No**.

MORE INFORMATION
Certificate authorities are covered in the 70-742 book.

Creating and Configuring Connection Profiles

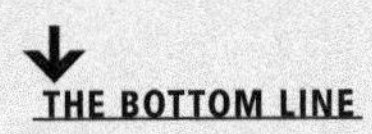

THE BOTTOM LINE

In Windows Server 2016, there are several ways to create a VPN connection. They include the Network and Sharing Center Set Up a Connection or Network Wizard, the Windows Server 2016 Settings, and the Connection Manager Administration Kit (CMAK). This book focuses on the Network and Sharing Center and CMAK because you cannot configure all of the options using the Windows Server 2016 Settings.

CERTIFICATION READY
Create and configure connection profiles
Objective 4.2

Using the Set Up a Connection or Network Wizard requires the most knowledge for the user who is creating the connection because the user must specify all necessary options. CMAK is the easiest and quickest for the user to install.

Creating a VPN Connection Using the Set Up a Connection or Network Wizard

When you create a connection using the Set Up a Connection or Network Wizard, you are manually creating a VPN connection that will allow you to connect to a VPN server. This method also gives you more control of the VPN options.

The Set Up a Connection or Network Wizard requires that you enter the server information and then it auto-discovers the authentication methods and tunneling protocols during the initial connection process.

CREATE A VPN TUNNEL USING NETWORK AND SHARING CENTER

GET READY. To create a VPN connection, perform the following steps.

1. Log on to LON-RTR as **adatum\administrator** with the password of **Pa$$w0rd.**
2. Open **Control Panel**, click **Network and Internet**, and click **Network and Sharing Center.**
3. From the Network and Sharing Center (see Figure 9-12), click **Set up a new connection or wizard.**

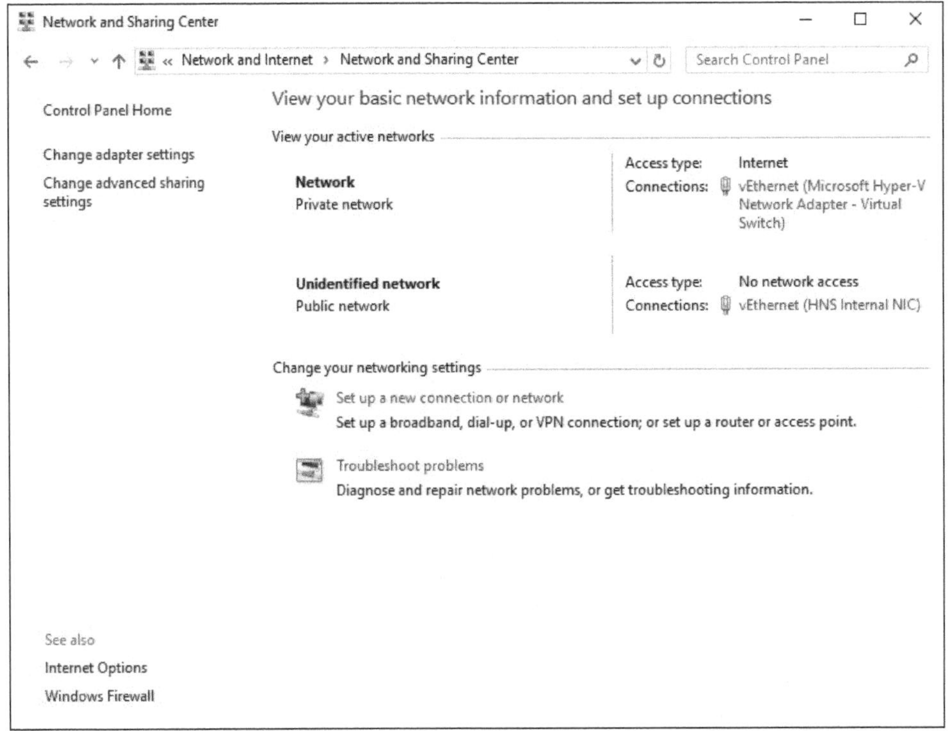

Figure 9-12
Opening the Network and Sharing Center

4. On the Set Up a Connection or Network page, click **Connect to a workplace**. Click **Next**.
5. On the Connect to a Workplace page, answer the question, "How do you want to connect?" Click the **Use my Internet connection (VPN)** option.
6. Next, you are prompted to type the Internet address to connect to (see Figure 9-13). In the Internet address text box, type the DNS name or IP address of the VPN server on the Internet. In the Destination name text box, type a meaningful name for the VPN connection. Click **Create**.

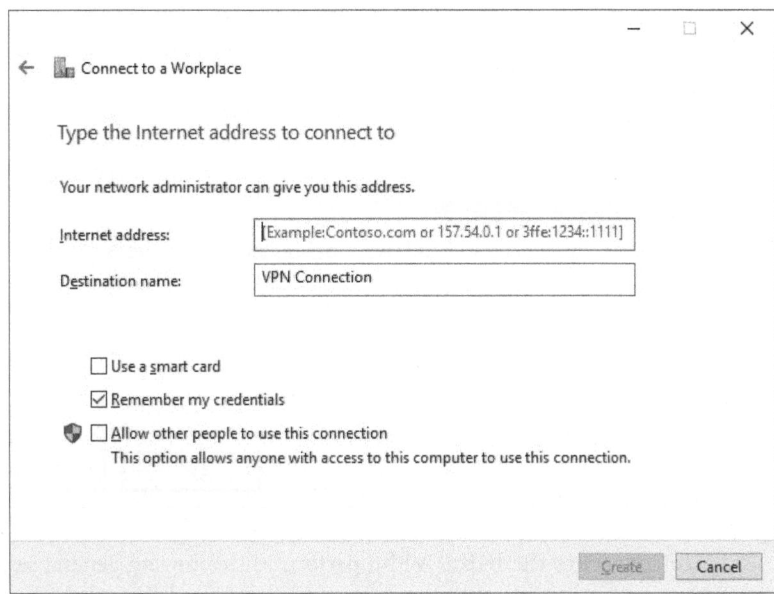

Figure 9-13
Entering the Internet address and destination name

When the connection is created, it shows under Network Connections, which is accessed by clicking the Change adapter settings option. To use the VPN client, you still need to configure the VPN connection. To configure the client, you need to right-click the VPN connection you just created and choose Properties. On the General tab, you can change the host name or IP address of the VPN server, as shown in Figure 9-14.

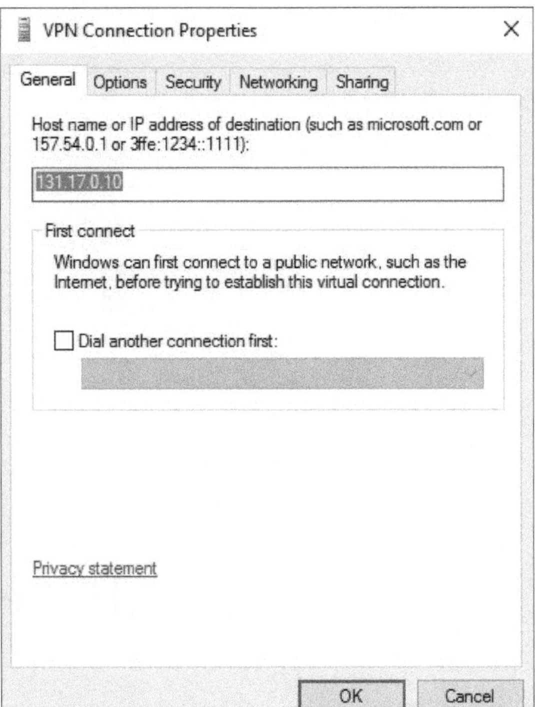

Figure 9-14
Specifying the host name or IP address of the VPN server on the General tab

On the Options tab, you can specify if the VPN connection remembers your credentials or not and how much idle time it waits before the VPN connection hangs up (disconnects).

On the Security tab, you can specify the type of VPN, whether data encryption is required, and the type of authentication. If you use L2TP, click the Advanced settings button to specify the pre-shared key used for authentication or if you are to use a digital certificate (as shown in Figure 9-15).

Figure 9-15

Configuring Security options

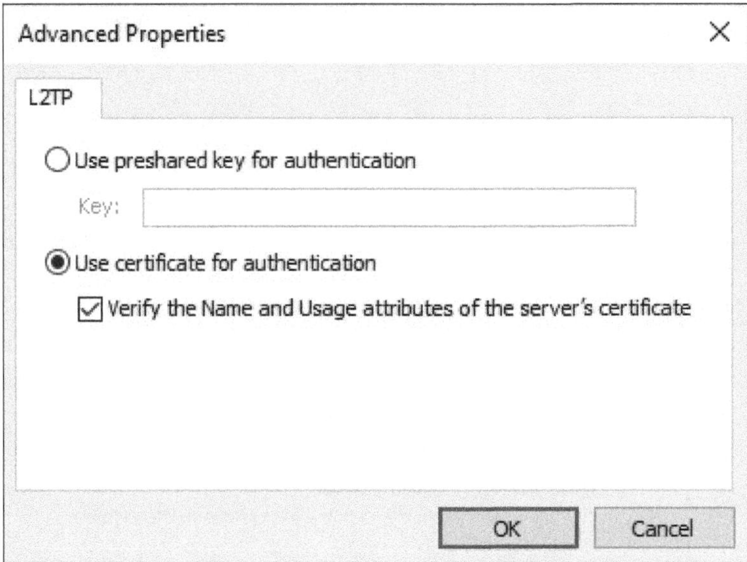

To connect to the IKEv2 VPN, perform the following general steps on the client:

1. Specify the VPN server address or host name when configuring the VPN connection properties.
2. When you specify the VPN tunnel type, in the Type of VPN list, select IKEv2 and select the level of encryption and the authentication method. VPN Reconnect supports two types of Authentication: Extensible Authentication Protocol (EAP) and X.509 Machine Certificates.
3. By default, the Mobility check box is enabled for VPN Reconnect in Advanced properties, as shown in Figure 9-16.

Figure 9-16

Configuring VPN Connection Properties for IKEv2

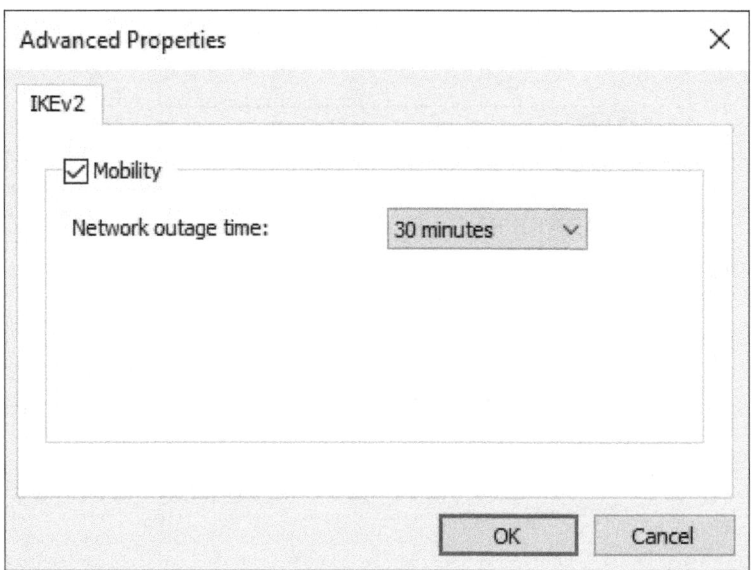

4. On the Networking tab, you can select IPv4, IPv6, or both protocols.
5. After the VPN connection is established, you can view the connection status on the Details tab of the Connection Status page.

To connect using the VPN once the VPN connection is created and configured, open the Network and Sharing Center and click Change adapter settings. Then, right-click your VPN connection and choose the Connect/Disconnect option. Alternatively, you can click the network status icon on the taskbar and then click the VPN connection. In the Settings window, click VPN, click the VPN connection, and then click Connect. You will then be prompted to log on, as shown in Figure 9-17.

Figure 9-17

Logging in to a VPN connection in Windows Server 2016

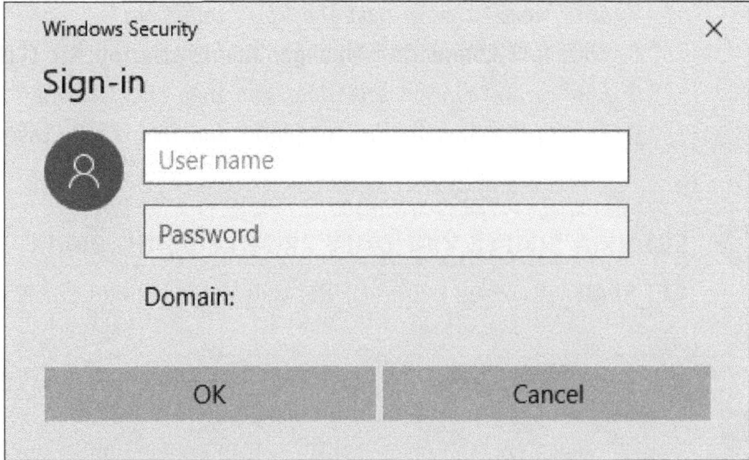

Using Connection Manager (CM) and the Connection Manager Administration Kit (CMAK)

If you have to configure multiple clients to connect to a remote server, it can be a lot of work and it can be easy to make an error. To help simplify the administration of the VPN client into an easy-to-install executable, you can use the RAS Connection Manager Administration Kit (CMAK), which can also be installed as a feature in Windows Server 2016. After an executable file is created that includes all of the VPN settings, the executable file is deployed on the client computers.

Connection Manager (CM) is a client network connection tool that helps administrators simplify the management of their remote connections. CM uses profiles that consist of settings that allow connections from the local computer to a remote network.

You use the ***Connection Manager Administration Kit (CMAK)*** to create and customize the profiles for CM and to distribute them to users. The profile, once completed, contains all the settings necessary for the user to connect, including the IP address of the VPN server.

CM supports different features in a profile depending upon the operating system that is running on the client computer. You must create a connection profile on a computer that uses the same architecture (32/64-bit) as the clients on which you will install the profile.

When running the CMAK Wizard, you will be prompted to specify the operating system on which the Connection Manager profile will be run. Options include:

- Windows Vista or above
- Windows Server 2003, Windows XP, or Windows 2000

INSTALL CMAK ON WINDOWS SERVER 2016

GET READY. To install CMAK on Windows Server 2016, perform the following steps.

1. Log on to LON-RTR as **adatum\administrator** with the password of **Pa$$w0rd**.
2. Open **Server Manager**.
3. Click **Manage > Add Roles and Features**.
4. Click **Next**.
5. Click **Role-based or feature-based installation**.
6. Select a server from the server pool and then click **Next**.
7. Click **Next** to move past the Roles selection.
8. Click **RAS Connection Manager Administration Kit (CMAK)** and then click **Next**.
9. Confirm installation selections and then click **Install**.
10. Confirm the installation completes and then click **Close**.

SET UP A SIMPLE VPN-ONLY PROFILE USING CMAK

GET READY. To set up a simple VPN-only profile using CMAK, perform the following steps.

TAKE NOTE* This activity is designed to expose the features and options available when creating a Connection Manager profile using CMAK from Windows Server 2016. As you walk through each step, be sure to read the explanation behind it to gain more insight into how CMAK could be used in your specific network environment.

1. Log on to LON-RTR as **adatum\administrator** with the password of **Pa$$w0rd**.
2. Start Connection Manager by opening **Server Manager** and then clicking **Tools > Connection Manager Administration Kit**.
3. After reading the Welcome message, click **Next**.
4. On the Select the Target Operating System page, click **Windows Vista or above** and then click **Next**.
5. On the Create or Modify a Connection Manager Profile page, click **New Profile** and then click **Next**.
6. On the Specify the Service Name and the File Name page, in the Service name text box and the File name text box, type **MyVPN** and then click **Next**.
7. On the Specify a Realm Name page, click **Do not add a realm name to the user name** and then click **Next**.
8. On the Merge Information from Other Profiles page, where you could merge information from an existing profile, click **Next**. If you had an additional profile, you could merge phone book information, access numbers, and VPN host address information.
9. On the Add Support for VPN Connections page, click **Phone book from this profile**. Then, in the Always use the same VPN server text box, type **RemoteServer.adatum.com** and then click **Next**.
10. On the Create or Modify a VPN Entry page, click **Edit** to view the settings that can be configured for this VPN profile (Figure 9-18 shows the Security tab, which allows you to configure the VPN strategy, encryption, and authentication options).

Figure 9-18

Configuring VPN settings

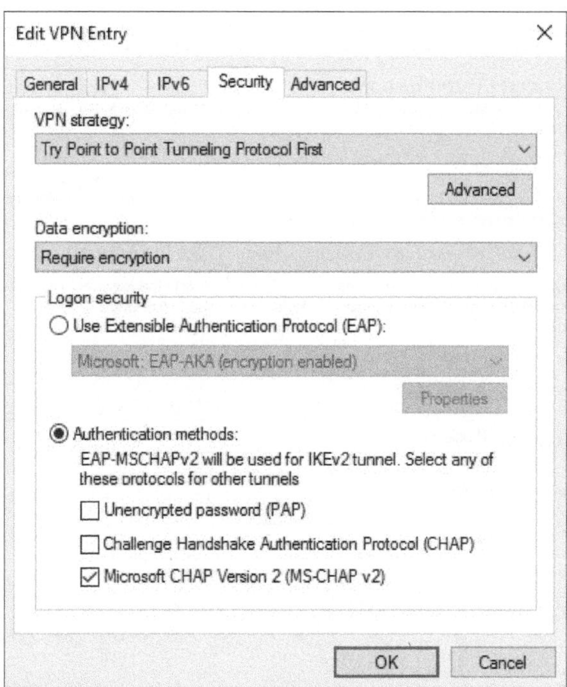

11. Click **OK** to close the Edit VPN Entry dialog box.
12. Back on the Create or Modify a VPN Entry page, click **Next**.
13. On the Add a Custom Phone Book page, deselect the **Automatically download phone book updates** option and then click **Next**.
14. On the Configure Dial-Up Networking Entries page, click **Next**.
15. On the Specify Routing Table Updates page, make sure the **Do not change the routing tables** option is selected and then click **Next**.
16. On the Configure Proxy Settings for Internet Explorer page, make sure the **Do not configure proxy setting** option is selected and then click **Next**.
17. On the Add Custom Actions page, click **Next** to *not* add any custom actions.
18. On the Display a Custom Logon Bitmap page, click **Next** to display a default graphic or select one of your own.
19. On the Display a Custom Phone Book Bitmap page, click **Next** to display a default graphic as a custom phone book.
20. On the Display Custom Icons page, click **Next** to use default icons for the Connection Manager user interface.
21. On the Include a Custom Help File page, click **Next** to use the default help file.
22. On the Display Custom Support Information page, add any text you want to appear in the logon dialog box and then click **Next**. (For example, type **Contact Support at 800-123-1234**.)
23. On the Display a Custom License Agreement page, enter the path to a text file containing a custom license agreement and then click **Next**.
24. On the Install Additional Files with the Connection Manager Profile page, specify any additional files that the Connection Manager profile will require and then click **Next**.
25. On the Build the Connection Manager Profile and Its Installation Program page, click the **Advanced customization** option and then click **Next**.

Figure 9-19

Performing advanced customization of the profile

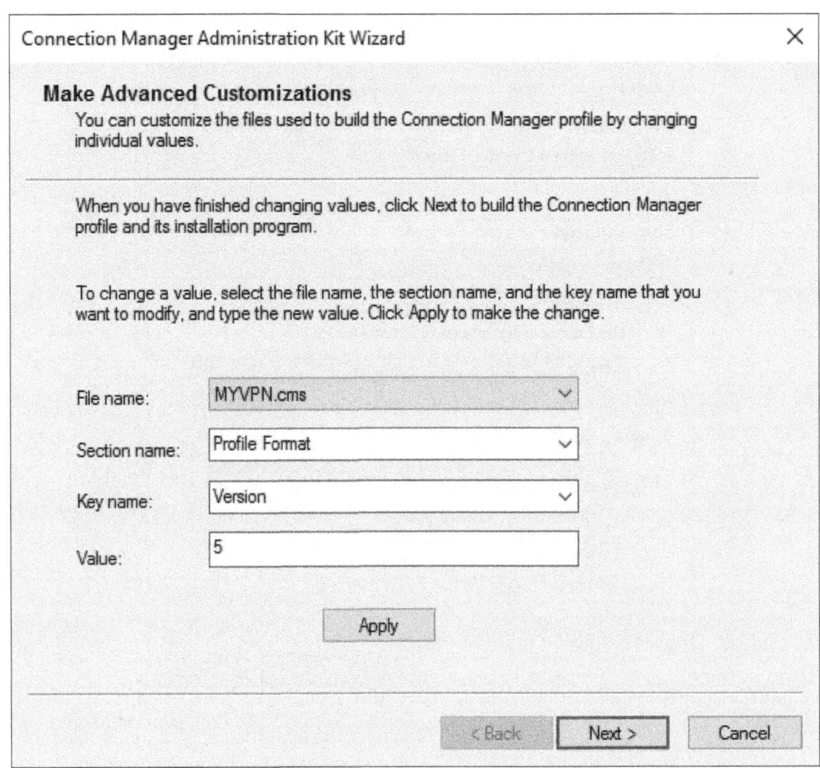

26. On the Make Advanced Customizations page, if necessary, set the values shown in Figure 9-19 and then click **Apply.** Click **Next.**
27. Make a note of the location where the profile will be saved. By default, this will be:

    ```
    c:\Program Files\CMAK\Profiles\Windows Vista and above\MyVPN\MyVPN.exe
    ```
28. Click **Finish.**

On the Add Support for VPN Connections page, you can specify the VPN server name or IP address. If you select the Allow the user to choose a VPN server before connecting option, you can provide a text file that lists the VPN servers from which the user can choose. The following provides you with an example that can be created and modified within Notepad:

```
[Settings]
default=Adatum CorpHQ
UpdateURL=http://remoteusers.adatum.com/MyVPNfile.txt
Message=Select a server that is closest to your location.
[Adatum VPN Servers]
Adatum Computers CorpHQ=remoteusers.adatum.com
Adatum Computers Los Angeles=LA.remoteusers.adatum.com
Adatum Computers Austin=Austin.remoteusers.adatum.com
```

By using Phone Book Administrator, which is included with Connection Point Services (CPS), you can create a phone book file that contains a list of multiple access numbers that can be used to connect to a remote dial-up network. CPS consists of a Phone Book Service (PBS) and the Phone Book Administrator (PBA). PBS is an extension to the Internet Information Services extension. The PBA allows you to create and edit up to 100 unique phone books. Each phone book is a collection of Points of Presence (POPs) or dial-up entries. The PBA allows you to associate POPs with the network configurations you define in the Connection Manager profile.

Configuring Split Tunneling

By default, when you connect to a VPN using the previous configuration, all web browsing and network traffic goes through the default gateway on the remote network unless you are communicating with local home computers. Having this option enabled helps protect the corporate network because all traffic also goes through firewalls and proxy servers, which prevent a network from being infected or compromised.

If you want to route your Internet browsing through your home Internet connection rather than going through the corporate network, you can disable the Use Default Gateway on Remote Network option. Disabling this option is called using a ***split tunnel***.

ENABLE A SPLIT TUNNEL

GET READY. To enable a split tunnel, perform the following steps.

1. Log on to LON-RTR as **adatum\administrator** with the password of **Pa$$w0rd.**
2. Right-click the **network status** icon on the taskbar and choose **Open Network and Sharing Center.**
3. Click **Change adapter settings.**
4. Right-click a VPN connection and choose **Properties.**
5. Click the **Networking** tab.
6. Double-click **Internet Protocol Version 4 (TCP/IPv4).**
7. In the Internet Protocol Version 4 (TCP/IPv4) Properties dialog box, click the **Advanced** button.
8. In the Advanced TCP/IP Settings dialog box, deselect the **Use default gateway on remote network** check box (as shown in Figure 9-20).

Figure 9-20

Enabling split tunneling by enabling the Use Default Gateway on Remote Network option

9. Click **OK** to close the Advanced TCP/IP Settings dialog box.
10. Click **OK** to close the Internet Protocol Version 4 (TCP/IPv4) Properties dialog box.
11. Click **OK** to close the VPN Connection Properties dialog box.

Troubleshooting Remote Access Problems

When troubleshooting remote access problems, follow basic troubleshooting techniques where you determine the scope of the problem, gather symptoms, come up with a list of possible causes, and make a plan to solve the problem. Then, use the normal Windows and network troubleshooting tools and any tools available specifically for remote access.

With network connectivity problems, you need to make sure that you are connected to the network and that name resolution works properly. If your VPN connection is to operate over the Internet, make sure that you have Internet access. To troubleshoot network connectivity problems, check Event Viewer and use `ipconfig`, `ping`, `tracert`, and `nslookup`.

Routing and Remote Access does have built-in logging, if it is enabled. To enable logging, open the Routing and Remote Access console, right-click the server, choose Properties, and then click the Logging tab. You can then select one of the following logging levels:

- Log errors only
- Log errors and warnings
- Log all events
- Do not log any events

By default, the logs are located in the C:\Windows\Tracing folder/.

Alternatively, you can enable logging with one of the following methods:

- Execute the following command:
  ```
  Netsh ras set tracing * enabled
  ```
- Set the following registry value:
  HKEY_LOCAL_MACHINE\SOFTWARE\Microsoft\Tracing\ EnableFileTracing = 1

WARNING! Because logging uses system resources, you should disable logging when you have solved the problem.

When troubleshooting VPN problems, you should perform the following:

- Use the `ping` or `nslookup` command to verify that the correct IP address is being returned for the host name. Don't always expect to have a successful ping because many firewalls on the Internet can block Internet Control Message Protocol (ICMP) packets.
- Verify that the user is using the correct user name, password, and domain name.
- Verify that the user account is not locked, expired, or disabled.
- Verify that the user is not affected by logon hour restrictions.
- Verify that the correct VPN protocol and authentication are selected.
- If used, verify that you have the correct and valid digital certificate. The certificate must be issued with a valid date, must be trusted, and must not be revoked. The certificate must also have a valid digital certificate.
- Some certificates need to be checked to see whether they have been revoked or not. Therefore, make sure that the Certificate Revocation List (CRL) is available over the Internet.

- Verify that the Routing and Remote Access Service runs on the VPN server.
- Verify that the VPN server is enabled for remote access on the General tab in the VPN Server Properties dialog box.
- Verify the appropriate ports (PPTP, L2TP, SSTP, and IKEv2) are enabled and available on the VPN server.
- Verify that the user in Active Directory Users and Computers is allowed to connect. If the connection is based on network policies, verify that the user is allowed to connect. A user network access permission can be configured by opening user properties in Active Directory Users and Computers and clicking the Dial-in tab to allow access, deny access, or control access through NPS Network Policy. Network policies are covered in Lessons 10.
- Verify that the connection's parameters have permission through network policies.
- Make sure that a firewall is not blocking any necessary packets or protocols, such as IKE. Also remember that RRAS static packet filters will block ICMP packets that are used by `ping` and `tracert`.
- If you have NAT in between the client and the VPN server, you need to configure Windows client to support IPsec NAT-Traversal (NAT-T).

If you receive an error message, the error message might give you some indication of where to look for the cause of the error. Common errors are listed in Table 9.1.

Table 9.1

Common VPN Errors

Error	Description
Error 800: VPN Server is unreachable	For whatever reason, the PPTP, L2TP, SSTP, or IKEv2 packets cannot get to the VPN server. Verify that the appropriate ports are open on all relevant firewalls, including host firewalls (on the client and server).
Error 721: Remote Computer is Not Responding	For whatever reason, GRE traffic (part of PPTP) is not getting to the VPN. Therefore, check that standard ports are open on all relevant firewalls, including host firewalls (on the client and server) for PPTP.
Error 741 or 742: Encryption Mismatch Error	These errors occur if the VPN client requests an invalid encryption level or the VPN server does not support an encryption type that the client requests. On the client, check the VPN connection properties (Security tab) to verify that the proper encryption is selected. If you are using NPS, check the encryption level in the network policy in the NPS console or check the policies on other RADIUS servers. Finally, check the server to verify that the correct encryption level is enabled.
0x80092013: The revocation function was unable to check revocation because the revocation server was offline	The client is failing the certificate revocation check. Ensure the CRL check servers on the server side are exposed on the Internet.

MORE INFORMATION

For more information on troubleshooting specific error messages, search for the error messages on the TechNet website.

Installing and Configuring Directaccess

THE BOTTOM LINE

DirectAccess is a feature introduced with Windows 7 and Windows Server 2008 R2 that provides seamless intranet connectivity to DirectAccess client computers when they are connected to the Internet. Different from the traditional virtual private network (VPN) connections, DirectAccess connections are automatically established and they provide always-on seamless connectivity.

CERTIFICATION READY
Install and configure DirectAccess
Objective 4.2

DirectAccess overcomes the limitations of VPNs by automatically establishing a bidirectional connection from client computers to the organization's network using IPsec and Internet Protocol version 6 (IPv6). For organizations that have not deployed IPv6, you can use transition mechanisms such as 6to4 and Teredo IPv6 transition technologies for connectivity across the IPv4 Internet and the Intra-Site Automatic Tunnel Addressing (ISATAP) IPv6 transition technology, so that DirectAccess clients can access IPv6-capable resources across your IPv4-only intranet. As a result, remote client computers are automatically connected to the organization's network so that they can be easily managed and kept up to date with critical updates and configuration changes.

Understanding the DirectAccess Connection Process

A DirectAccess connection to a target intranet resource is initiated when the DirectAccess client connects to the DirectAccess server through IPv6. IPsec is then negotiated between the client and server. Finally, the connection is established between the DirectAccess client and the target resource.

This general process can be broken down into the following specific steps:

1. The DirectAccess client computer running Windows 10 Enterprise, Windows 8/8.1 Enterprise, Windows 7 Enterprise, or Windows 7 Ultimate detects that it is connected to a network.
2. The DirectAccess client computer determines whether it is connected to the intranet. If the client is connected to the intranet, it does not use DirectAccess.
3. The DirectAccess client connects to the DirectAccess server by using IPv6 and IPsec.
4. If the client is not using IPv6, it tries to use 6to4 or Teredo tunneling to send IPv4-encapsulated IPv6 traffic.
5. If the client cannot reach the DirectAccess server using 6to4 or Teredo tunneling, the client tries to connect using the Internet Protocol over Secure Hypertext Transfer Protocol (IP-HTTPS) protocol. IP-HTTPS uses a Secure Sockets Layer (SSL) connection to encapsulate IPv6 traffic.
6. As part of establishing the IPsec session for the tunnel to reach the intranet DNS server and domain controller, the DirectAccess client and server authenticate each other using computer certificates for authentication.
7. When the user logs on, the DirectAccess client establishes a second IPsec tunnel to access the resources of the intranet. The DirectAccess client and server authenticate each other using a combination of computer and user credentials.
8. The DirectAccess server forwards traffic between the DirectAccess client and the intranet resources to which the user has been granted access.

The Name Resolution Policy Table (NRPT) is used to determine the behavior of the DNS clients when issuing queries and processing so that internal resources are not exposed to the public via the Internet and to separate traffic that isn't DirectAccess Internet traffic from DirectAccess Internet traffic. By using the NRPT, the DirectAccess clients use the intranet DNS servers for internal resources and Internet DNS for name resolution of other resources. The NRPT is managed using group policies, specifically, Computer Configuration\Policies\Windows Settings\Name Resolution Policy.

Implementing DirectAccess Requirements

Compared with other forms of remote access, DirectAccess is more complex, which has more required components. Of course, with the complexity, you get much more functionality than you do with other remote access technologies.

CERTIFICATION READY
Implement server requirements
Objective 4.2

Besides installing DirectAccess on the VPN server, you need to make sure that you prepare the network, the server, and the clients. A little planning also goes a long way when implementing DirectAccess.

UNDERSTANDING DIRECTACCESS SERVER REQUIREMENTS

To use DirectAccess, the DirectAccess server requires the following:

- The server must be part of an Active Directory domain.
- The DirectAccess server must have at least one network adapter connected to the domain network. You should deploy the DirectAccess server in one of the following network topologies:
  - **Edge:** Connects to the edge or DMZ with the firewall where firewall software is deployed on the edge computer. The edge computer must have two network adapters: one network adapter that connects to the internal network and the other network adapter that connects to the Internet.
  - **Behind the firewall with two network adapters:** Uses the edge device as a firewall solution. In this scenario, the DirectAccess server is located in a perimeter network, behind the edge device. The DirectAccess server must have two network adapters: one network adapter that connects to the internal network and the other network adapter that connects to the perimeter network.
  - **Behind the firewall with one network adapter:** Uses the edge device as a firewall solution where the DirectAccess server has one network adapter connected to the internal network.
- You must enable Windows Firewall for all profiles. Turning off the Windows Firewall will disable DirectAccess connectivity.
- The DirectAccess server cannot be a domain controller.
- You can deploy Windows Server 2016 DirectAccess behind a NAT support, which avoids the need for additional public addresses. However, only IP over HTTPS (IP-HTTPS) is deployed, allowing a secure IP tunnel to be established using a secure HTTP connection.
- With Windows Server 2016, you can use Network Load Balancing (up to eight nodes) to achieve high availability and scalability for both DirectAccess and RRAS.

In addition, you need the following in your network infrastructure:

- An Active Directory domain that runs a minimum of Windows Server 2008 R2 domain functional level must be available.
- Group Policy for central administration and deployment of DirectAccess client settings must be enabled.
- One domain controller running Windows Server 2008 SP2, or later, must be available.

- Public key infrastructure (PKI) must be available to issue computer certificates. The SSL certificates installed on the DirectAccess server must have a Certificate Revocation List (CRL) distribution point that is reached from the Internet. Finally, the certificate Subject field must contain the fully qualified domain name (FQDN) that can be resolved to a public IPv4 address assigned to the DirectAccess server by using DNS on the Internet.
- DirectAccess must utilize IPsec policies that are configured and administered with Windows Firewall with Advanced Security.
- Internet Control Message Protocol version 6 (ICMPv6) Echo Request traffic must be allowed. You must create separate inbound and outbound rules that allow ICMPv6 Echo Request messages. DirectAccess clients that use Teredo for IPv6 connectivity to the intranet use the ICMPv6 message when establishing communication.
- IPv6 and transition technologies such as ISATAP, Teredo, and 6to4 must be available for use on the DirectAccess server. For each DNS server running Windows Server 2008 or later, you need to remove the ISATAP name from the global query block list.

UNDERSTANDING DIRECTACCESS CLIENT REQUIREMENTS

To use DirectAccess, the clients must be Windows 7 Enterprise Edition, Windows 7 Ultimate Edition, Windows 8/8.1 Enterprise Edition, Windows 10 Enterprise Edition, Windows Server 2008 R2, Windows Server 2012, Windows Server 2012 R2, and Windows Server 2016. You will not be able to deploy DirectAccess for Windows Vista or earlier or Windows Server 2008 or earlier. Finally, the client must be joined to an Active Directory domain.

Running the DirectAccess Getting Started Wizard

To configure DirectAccess itself, you use the newly created Remote Access Management console. By using the Remote Access Management console, you can configure DirectAccess using a visual step-by-step wizard or wizards.

The Remote Access Management console includes two wizards. The Run the Getting Started Wizard allows you to quickly configure DirectAccess with the default recommended settings.

ENABLE DIRECTACCESS

GET READY. To perform a quick configuration of DirectAccess, using the Enable DirectAccess Wizard, perform the following steps.

1. Log on to LON-RTR as **adatum\administrator** with the password of **Pa$$w0rd.**
2. Start **Server Manager.**
3. Click **Tools > Remote Access Management.** In the Remote Access Management console, in the left pane, click **VPN** (see Figure 9-21).
4. Under Tasks, click the **Enable DirectAccess** link.
5. In the Enable DirectAccess Wizard, on the Introduction page, click **Next.**
6. On the Select Groups page, click **Add.** In the Select Groups dialog box, type a name of the group that contains client computers that will access the network through DirectAccess, and click **OK.** Back on the DirectAccess Client Setup page, click **Next.**

Figure 9-21

Opening the VPN node in the Remote Access Management console

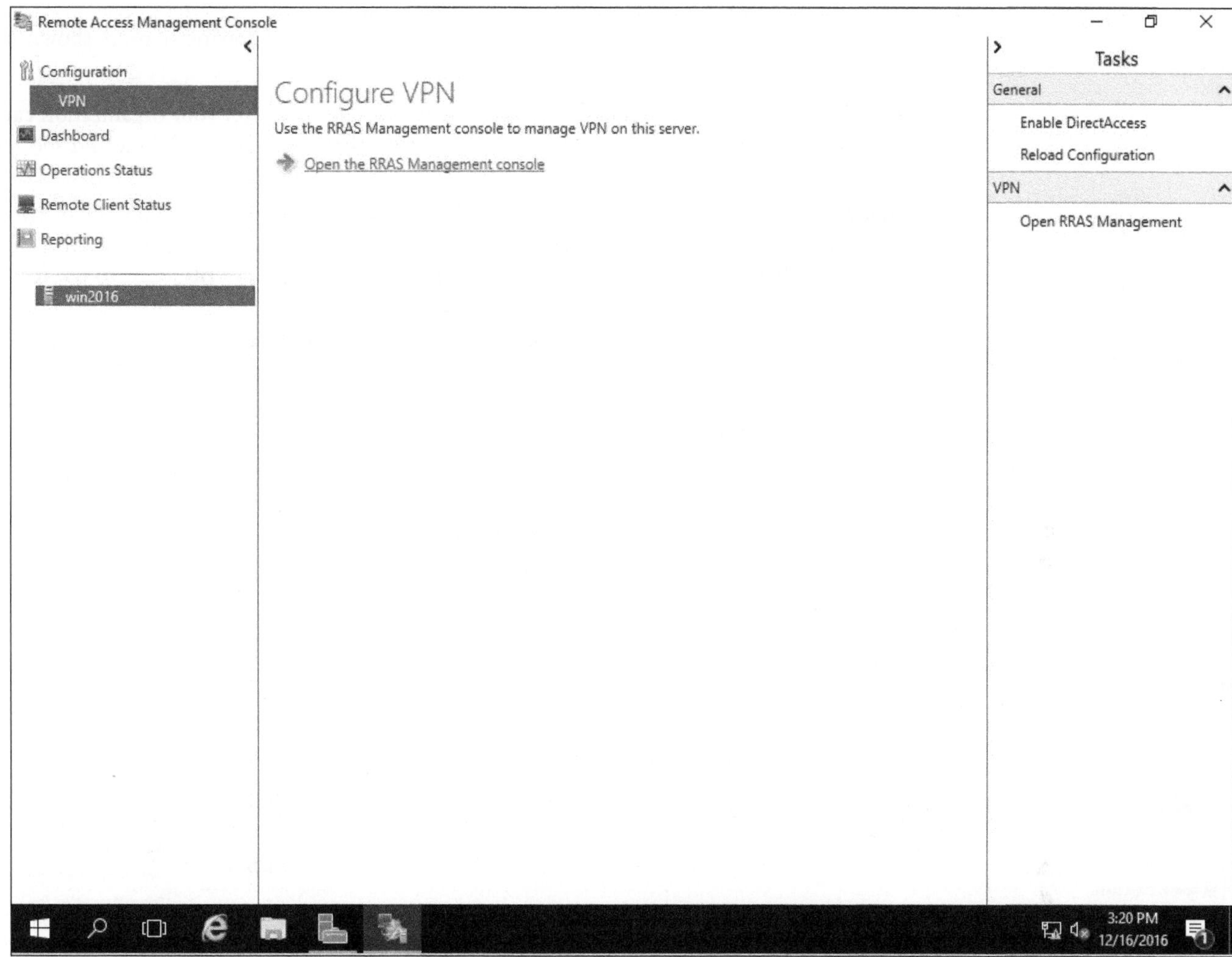

7. On the Network Topology page, click one of the following topologies:
   - **Edge**
   - **Behind an edge device (with two network adapters)**
   - **Behind an edge device (with a single adapter)**
8. In the Type the public name or IPv4 address used by clients to connect to the Remote Access server text box, type the name that users will use to access the corporate network from the Internet. Click **Next.**
9. On the DNS Suffix Search List page, select the **Configure DirectAccess clients with DNS client suffix search list** option. The primary domain DNS suffix will already appear in the list. Click **Next.**
10. On the GPO Configuration page, the DirectAccess Client Settings GPO and the DirectAccess Server Settings GPO are already specified. Click **Next.**
11. On the Summary page, click **Finish.** When the configuration settings are applied, click **Close.**

Running the Remote Access Setup Wizard

For more control, you can run the Remote Access Setup wizard instead.

The Remote Access Setup Wizard breaks the installation into the following steps, as shown in Figure 9-22:

Step 1: Remote Clients: Allows you to specify which clients within your organization can use DirectAccess. You specify the computer groups that you want to include and specify if you want to include Windows 7 clients.

Step 2: Remote Access Server: Configures the network connections based on one or two network cards and which adapters are internal and which adapters are external. You can also specify the use of smart cards and specify the certificate authority (CA) to use for DirectAccess to provide secure communications.

Step 3:Infrastructure Servers: Allows you to configure how the clients access the core infrastructure services, such as Active Directory domain controllers and DNS servers. You also specify an internal web server that can provide location services for infrastructure components to your DirectAccess clients.

Step 4: Application Servers: Allows you to configure your end-to-end authentication and security for the DirectAccess components. It also allows you to provide secure connections with individual servers that you want to establish secure connections with.

Figure 9-22

Using the Remote Access Setup Wizard

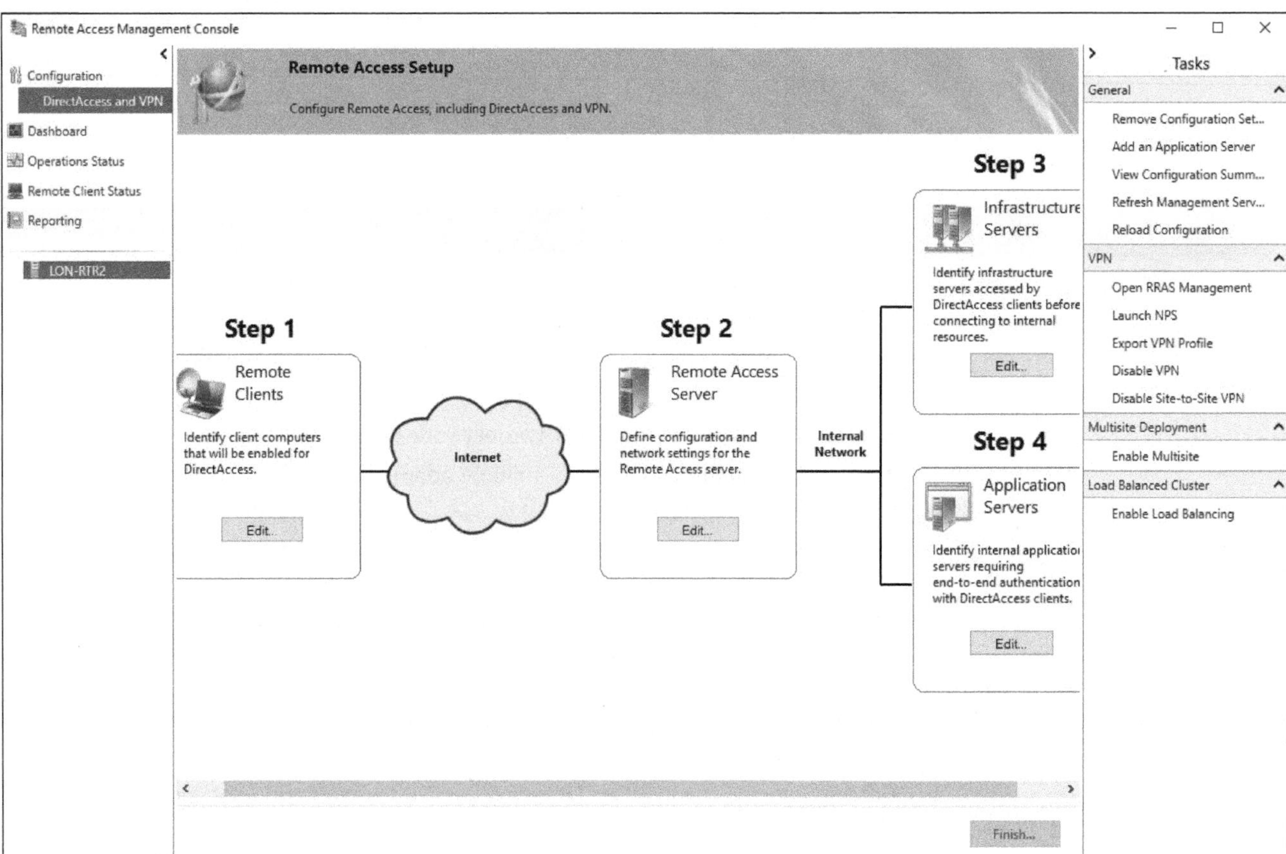

USING WINDOWS POWERSHELL

You can manage services using Windows PowerShell by using the following cmdlets:

- **Add-DAAppServer:** Adds a new application server security group to the DirectAccess (DA) deployment, adds an application server to an application server security group that is already part of the DirectAccess deployment, and adds or updates an application server Group Policy Object (GPO) in a domain.
- **Add-DAClient:** Adds one or more client computer security groups (SGs) to the DirectAccess (DA) deployment, adds one or more DA client Group Policy Objects (GPOs) in one or more domains, adds one or more SGs of down-level clients to the DA deployment in a multi-site deployment, or adds one or more down-level DA client GPOs in one or more domains in a multi-site deployment.
- **Add-DAClientDnsConfiguration:** Adds the specified DNS suffix, DNS server addresses, or proxy server set to the Name Resolution Policy Table.
- **Add-DAEntryPoint:** Adds an entry point to a multi-site deployment.
- **Add-DAMgmtServer:** Adds the specified Management Servers to the DirectAccess deployment.
- **Disable-DAMultiSite:** Disables a multi-site deployment that contains a single entry point.
- **Disable-DAOtpAuthentication:** Disables one-time password authentication for DirectAccess users.
- **Enable-DAMultiSite:** Enables and configures a multi-site deployment, and adds the first entry point.
- **Enable-DAOtpAuthentication:** Enables and configures one-time password authentication for DirectAccess users.
- **Get-DAAppServer:** Displays the list of application server security groups that are part of the DirectAccess deployment and the properties of the connections made to the groups.
- **Get-DAClient:** Displays the list of client security groups that are part of the DirectAccess deployment and the client properties.
- **Get-DAClientDnsConfiguration:** Displays all the Name Resolution Policy Table entries and the local name resolution property.
- **Get-DAEntryPoint:** Displays the settings for an entry point.
- **Get-DAEntryPointDC:** Retrieves a list of entry points and the associated domain controllers.
- **Get-DAMgmtServer:** Displays the configured Management Servers. *Management Server* here refers to update servers, domain controllers, and other servers.
- **Get-DAMultiSite:** Retrieves global settings applied to all entry points in a multi-site deployment.
- **Get-DANetworkLocationServer:** Displays the detailed Network Location Server configuration.
- **Get-DAOtpAuthentication:** Displays one-time password authentication settings for DirectAccess.
- **Get-DAServer:** Displays the properties of the DirectAccess server.
- **Remove-DAAppServer:** Removes the specified list of application server security groups (SGs) from the DirectAccess (DA) deployment, removes the specified application servers from the specified DA application server SG, and removes the application server Group Policy Objects in the specified domains.
- **Remove-DAClient:** Removes one or more client computer security groups (SGs) from the DirectAccess (DA) deployment, removes one or more DA client Group Policy Objects (GPOs) from domains, removes one or more SGs of down-level clients (down-level clients can connect only to the specified site) from the DA deployment in a multi-site deployment, and removes one or more down-level DA client GPOs from domains in a multi-site deployment.
- **Remove-DAClientDnsConfiguration:** Removes the Name Resolution Policy Table (NRPT) entry corresponding to the specified DNS suffix from the NRPT.
- **Remove-DAEntryPoint:** Removes an entry point from a multi-site deployment.
- **Remove-DAMgmtServer:** Removes the specified Management Servers from the DirectAccess deployment.
- **Set-DAClient:** Configures the properties related to a DirectAccess client.
- **Set-DAClientDnsConfiguration:** Configures the DNS server and proxy server addresses of a Name Resolution Policy Table entry and configures the local name resolution property.
- **Set-DAEntryPoint:** Configures settings for the entry point.
- **Set-DAEntryPointDC:** Modifies domain controller settings for the entry point.
- **Set-DAMultiSite:** Configures global settings for all entry points in a multi-site deployment.
- **Set-DANetworkLocationServer:** Configures the Network Location Server.
- **Set-DAOtpAuthentication:** Configures one-time password authentication settings for DirectAccess.
- **Set-DAServer:** Sets the properties specific to the DirectAccess server.
- **Update-DAMgmtServer:** Updates the list of Management Servers of the DirectAccess deployment.

IMPLEMENTING CLIENT CONFIGURATION

CERTIFICATION READY
Implement client configuration
Objective 4.2

For the clients to use DirectAccess, the clients must be joined to an Active Directory domain. In Windows 8/8.1 and 10, the ***Network Connectivity Assistant (NCA)*** determines if the client computer is connected to the corporate intranet or the Internet. It also provides tools to help users reconnect if a problem occurs, and it can provide diagnostics used by the help desk. When DirectAccess is installed and configured, GPOs are created that will configure the clients to use DirectAccess.

A DirectAccess client uses a ***Network Location Server (NLS)*** to determine its location. If a client computer can securely connect to a Network Location Server by using HTTPS, the client computer assumes it is on the intranet, and the DirectAccess policies are not enforced. If the Network Location Server cannot be contacted, the client assumes it is on the Internet.

The Network Location Server can be installed on the DirectAccess server with the Web Server role. The URL for the Network Location Server is distributed by using a Group Policy Object (GPO).

When DirectAccess is configured, a GPO configures the clients to use the DirectAccess server for DNS anytime they are not connected to the intranet. The ***Name Resolution Policy Table (NRPT)*** contains the settings used by the DNS client on the computer that determines what happens to DNS queries.

CONFIGURE DIRECTACCESS REMOTE CLIENTS

GET READY. To configure the DirectAccess remote clients, perform the following steps.

1. Log on to LON-RTR as **adatum\administrator** with the password of **Pa$$w0rd.**
2. Start **Server Manager.**
3. Click **Tools > Remote Access Management.** The Remote Access Management console opens.
4. Click the **Run the Remote Access Setup Wizard** link.
5. On the Configure Remote Access page, click **Deploy DirectAccess only.**
6. Under Step 1, Remote Clients, click **Configure.** The DirectAccess Client Setup Wizard opens. If you are changing the current configuration, click **Edit.**
7. On the Deployment Scenario page, click **Deploy full DirectAccess for client access and remote management.**
8. On the Select Groups page, select **Add.** Type the name of the group of computers that you want to include as DirectAccess clients and click **OK.**
9. Back on the Select Groups page, if Forefront UAG is configured to use force tunneling for DirectAccess clients, select **Use force tunneling.** Click **Next.**
10. On the Network Connectivity Assistant page (see Figure 9-23), double-click a blank resource space.
11. In the Configure Corporate Resources for NCA dialog box (see Figure 9-24), specify **HTTP** or **ping** and specify a URL or FQDN in the text box. Click **Add.**
12. In the Helpdesk email address text box, specify an address to the organization's help desk.
13. By default, the DirectAccess connection name is Workplace Connection. If you want to change it, do so.
14. If you want DirectAccess clients to use local DNS servers for name resolution, select the **Allow DirectAccess clients to use local name resolution** check box.

Figure 9-23

Configuring the Network Connectivity Assistant

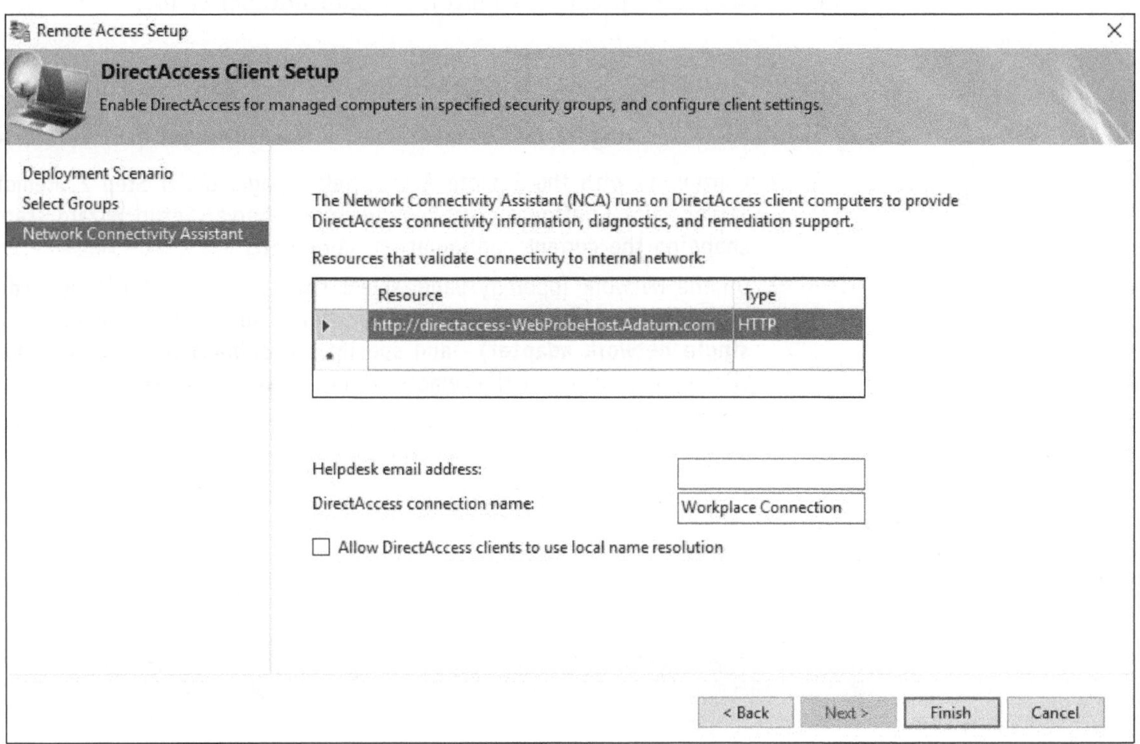

Figure 9-24

Configuring corporate resources for NCA

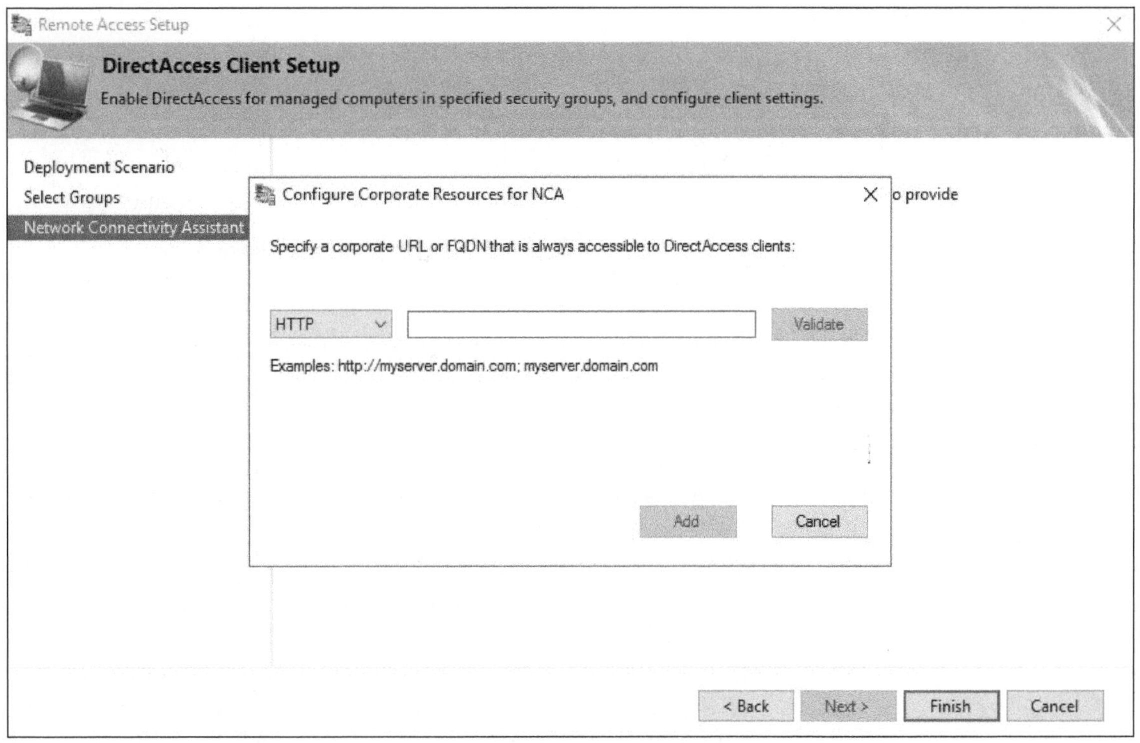

15. Click **Finish**.

IMPLEMENTING DIRECTACCESS SERVER

Using the Remote Access Server Setup Wizard, you can configure the DirectAccess server. It also allows you to specify which method of authentication to use.

CONFIGURE THE DIRECTACCESS REMOTE ACCESS SERVER

GET READY. To configure the DirectAccess remote access server, perform the following steps.

1. Continuing with the Remote Access Setup page, under Step 2, Remote Access Server, click **Configure.** The Remote Access Server Setup Wizard starts. If you are changing the current configuration, click **Edit.**
2. On the Network Topology page, select the appropriate topology—**Edge**, **Behind an edge device (with two network adapters)**, and **Behind an edge device (with a single network adapter)**—and specify the public name or IPv4 address used by clients to connect to the remote access server. Click **Next.**
3. On the Network Adapters page (see Figure 9-25), make sure that the appropriate network adapters are selected for the external and internal networks.

Figure 9-25

Configuring the network adapters

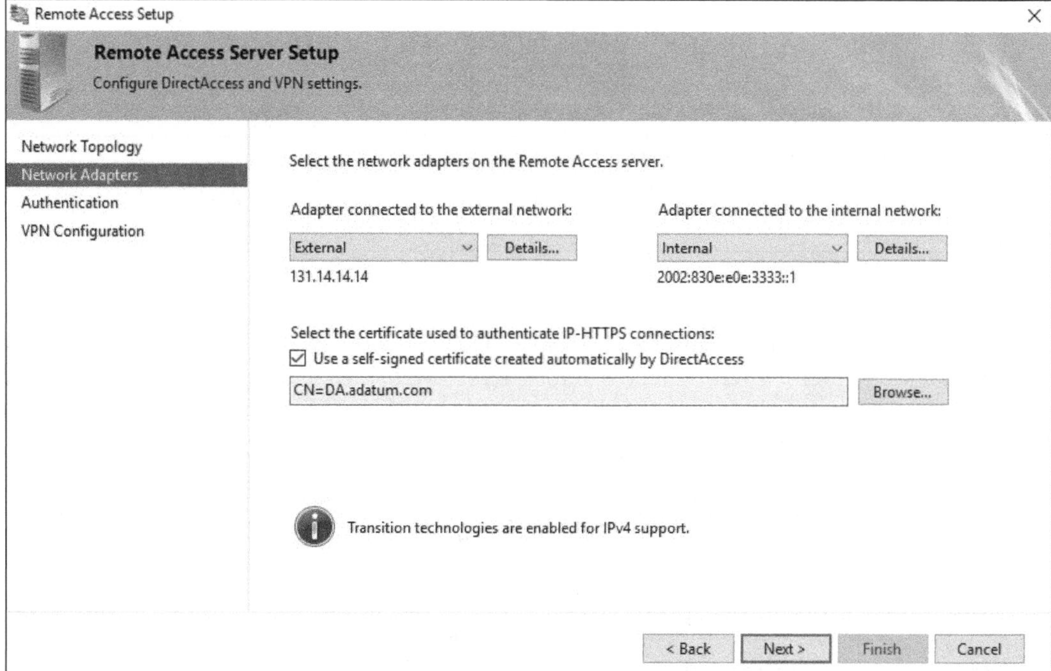

4. Specify the digital certificate that you want to use for HTTPS connections or select the **Use a self-signed certificate created automatically by DirectAccess** check box. Click **Next.**
5. On the Authentication page, specify whether you want to use **Active Directory credentials (username/password)** or **Two-factor authentication.** If you choose Two-factor authentication, you can select **Use OTP.**
6. If desired, you can use computer certificates. If you select the **Use computer certificates** option, you have to choose the **root** or **intermediate certification authority (CA).** If you decide to use intermediate certification authority, you need to select the **Use an intermediate certificate** option.

7. If you want to allow Windows 7 clients, enable the **Enable Windows 7 client computers to connect via DirectAccess** option.
8. Click **Next.**
9. On the VPN Configuration page, you can specify which addresses will be assigned from a static address pool. For now, click **Finish.**

IMPLEMENTING INFRASTRUCTURE SERVERS

After the DirectAccess server is configured, you need to configure the infrastructure servers to support DirectAccess. For example, you need to configure the DNS servers and you need to specify your management servers, such as your WSUS servers.

To configure a Network Location Server, install IIS on a Windows server. Then, for a website, bind a name such as nsl.contoso.com and associate an NLS DNS name to the IP address. Finally, you should make sure that this server is highly available. To do so, use technology such as Network Load Balancing and make sure you have redundant hardware.

To ensure that DirectAccess clients can correctly detect when they are on the Internet, you can configure the IIS server to deny connections from Internet-based clients with the IP and Domain Restrictions Web Server (IIS) role service. Alternatively, you can ensure that the CRL distribution point location in the certificate being used for network location cannot be accessed from the Internet.

CONFIGURE THE DIRECTACCESS INFRASTRUCTURE SERVERS

GET READY. To configure the DirectAccess infrastructure servers, perform the following steps.

1. Continuing with the Remote Access Setup page, under Step 3, Infrastructure Server, click **Configure.** The Infrastructure Server Setup Wizard starts. If you are changing the current configuration, click **Edit.**
2. On the Network Location Server page (see Figure 9-26), type the URL of the network location in the appropriate box. Click **Next.**

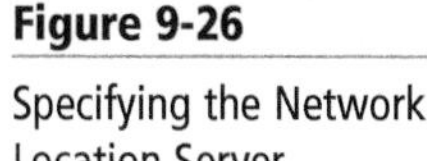

Figure 9-26

Specifying the Network Location Server

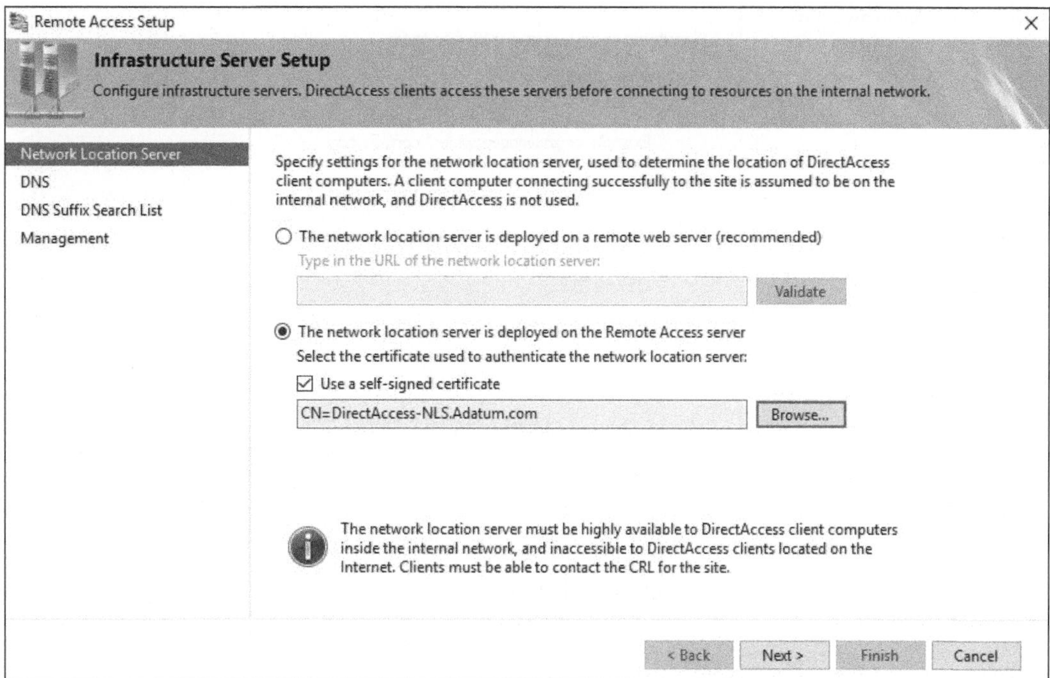

3. On the DNS page (see Figure 9-27), verify the DNS suffixes and internal DNS servers. Then, click **Next.**

Figure 9-27

Specifying the DNS servers

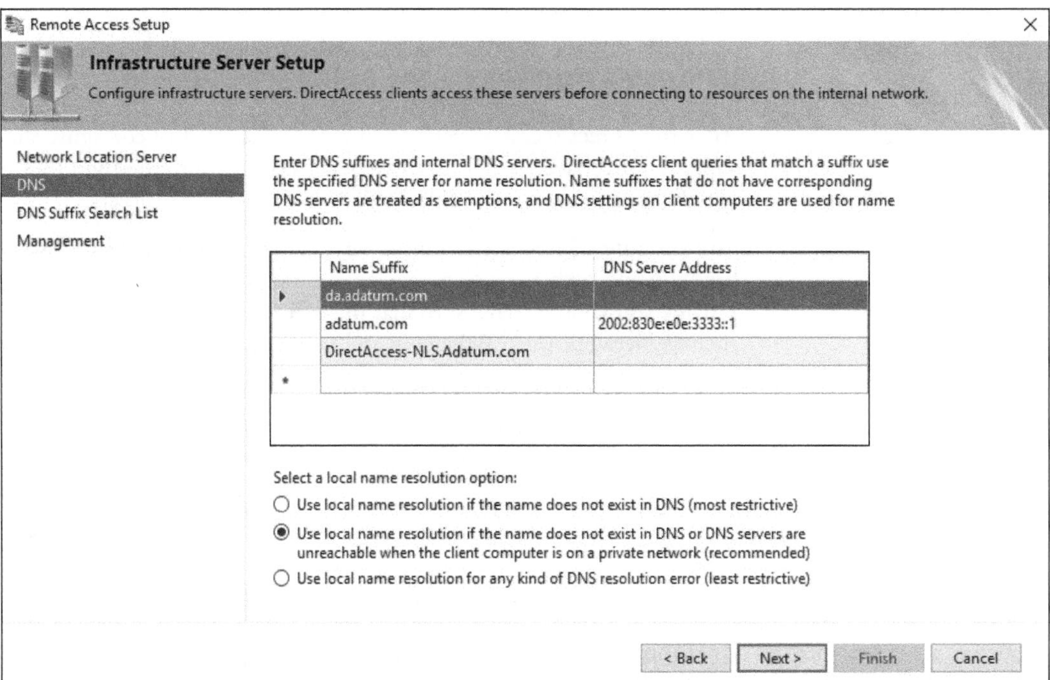

4. On the DNS Suffix Search List page, verify the domain suffixes (such as Adatum.com) and click **Next.**
5. On the Management page, double-click the first line of the Management Servers box.
6. In the Add a Management Server dialog box (see Figure 9-28), add the names of your Management Servers, such as your Windows Update Server. Click **OK.**

Figure 9-28

Adding a Management Server

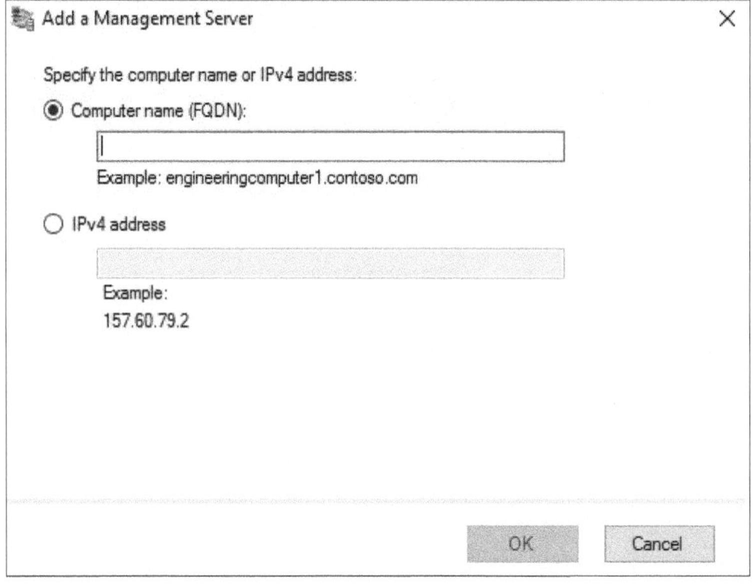

7. Click **Finish.**

CONFIGURING THE APPLICATION SERVERS

As mentioned earlier, you can add an extra level of authentication and encryption to those servers that you must protect at all costs. Using the DirectAccess Application Server Setup Wizard, you select those servers.

CONFIGURE APPLICATION SERVERS FOR DIRECTACCESS

GET READY. To configure the application servers for DirectAccess, perform the following steps.

1. Continuing with the Remote Access Setup Configuration page, under Step 4, Application Servers, click **Configure.** The DirectAccess Application Server Setup Wizard starts. If you are changing the current configuration, click **Edit.**
2. On the DirectAccess Application Server Setup page (see Figure 9-29), if you want to add an additional layer of authentication and encryption between the DirectAccess clients and selected internal application servers, click the **Extend authentication to selected application servers** radio button.

Figure 9-29

Specifying the DirectAccess application servers

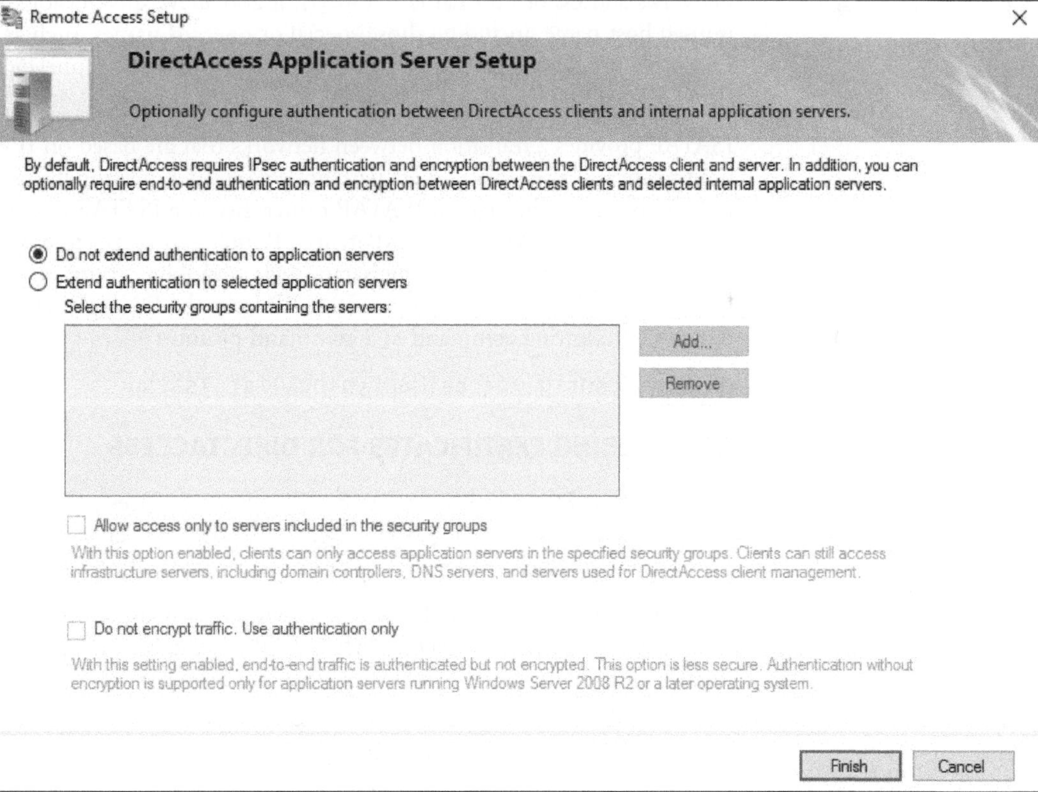

3. If you selected to extend authentication, click **Add.** Then, type the name of the server you want to extend authentication to and click **OK.**
4. Back on the DirectAccess Application Server Setup page, click **Finish.**
5. At the bottom of the Remote Access Management console, click **Finish** to apply all of the changes for Steps 1 through 4.

Preparing for DirectAccess Deployment

Before installing and configuring DirectAccess, there is some work that needs to be completed. You need to make sure that you have IPv6 and any transitional IPv6 technologies in place. You need a certificate server and you need to have external and internal DNS entries.

CONFIGURING DNS FOR DIRECTACCESS

As a VPN technology that has internal resources and external clients, DirectAccess requires internal and external DNS. DirectAccess requires two external DNS A records, both of which point to the first of your two consecutive IP addresses that you specified for the DirectAccess server. These are:

- DirectAccess server, such as directaccess.contoso.com
- Certificate Revocation List (CRL), such as crl.contoso.com

Internally, DNS needs the DNS records for the NLS server and one for the CRL.

The dynamic update feature of DNS makes it possible for a DNS client computer to register and dynamically update the resource records with a DNS server whenever a client changes its network's address or host name. However, it also allows any authorized client to register any unused host name, including those special or reserved names, such as Web Proxy Automatic Discovery Protocol (WPAD) and the Intra-Site Automatic Tunnel Addressing Protocol (ISATAP).

ISATAP provides a transition between networks that are based on IPv4 to IPv6, which is used to encapsulate IPv6 packets with an IPv4 header, making it possible for the IPv6 packets to be transmitted through an ISATAP router. Because ISATAP does not support automatic router discovery, ISATAP hosts a Potential Router List (PRL) to discover available ISATAP routers. The host name would be isatap, such as in isatap.contoso.com. Therefore, if you need to use ISATAP, you need to remove ISATAP from the DNS global query block list by executing the following command at a command prompt:

```
dnscmd /config /globalqueryblocklist isatap
```

CONFIGURING CERTIFICATES FOR DIRECTACCESS

To implement DirectAccess, you need a Certificate Services public key infrastructure (PKI), which requires installing an Active Directory Certificate Services (AD CS) role and Certificate Authority (CA) role. The CA has to be configured as an Enterprise Root CA.

Each DirectAccess client needs to have a computer certificate to establish the IPsec connection to the DirectAccess server and IP-HTTPS connection. The computer certificates are usually assigned using the Microsoft Certificate Server via Group Policy–based computer certificate auto-enrollment.

The DirectAccess server requires the following certificates:

- The IP-HTTPS listener on the DirectAccess server requires a website certificate, and the DirectAccess client must be able to contact the server hosting the CRL for the certificate. If the CRL check fails, the IP-HTTPS connection fails. It is recommended you use a third-party commercial certificate for the IP-HTTPS listener.
- The DirectAccess server requires a computer server to establish the IPsec connections with the DirectAccess clients.

CONFIGURE CERTIFICATE REQUIREMENTS

GET READY. To configure the certificate requirements on the domain controller with the CA (Enterprise CA), perform the following steps.

1. Log on to LON-DC1 as **adatum\administrator** with the password **Pa$$w0rd.**
2. If necessary, open **Server Manager.**
3. Click **Tools > Certificate Authority.** The Certification Authority console opens.
4. Right-click the server and choose **Properties.**
5. In the Properties dialog box, click the **Extensions** tab.
6. On the Extensions tab, click **Add.**
7. In the Add Location dialog box, in the Location text box, type **http://crl.adatum.com/crld/.**
8. Select the **CAName** variable and click **Insert.**
9. Select the **CRLNameSuffix** variable and click **Insert.**
10. Select the **DeltaCRLAllowed** variable and click **Insert.**
11. At the end of the text in the Location text box, add **.crl.** When you are finished, the Add Location dialog box should look like Figure 9-30.

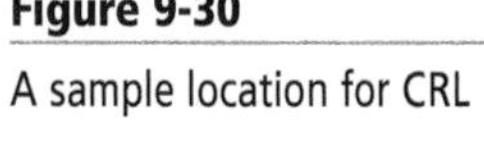

Figure 9-30

A sample location for CRL

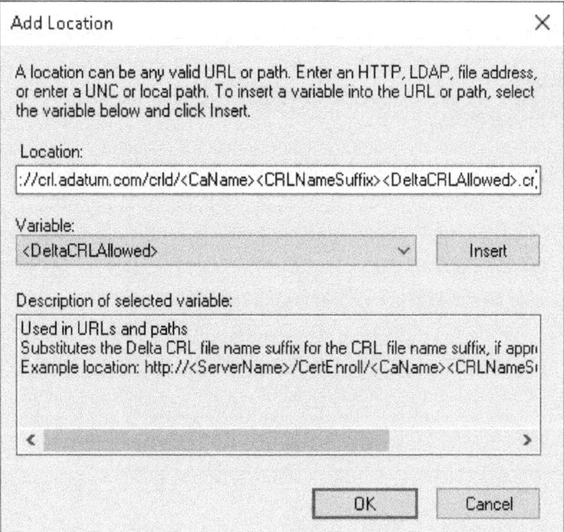

12. Click **OK** to close the Add Location dialog box.
13. Select the **Include in CRLs. Clients use this to find Delta CRL locations.** and the **Include in the CDP extensions of issued certificates** check boxes.
14. Click **Add.**
15. In the Add Location dialog box, in the Location text box, type **\\LON-RTR\crld-ist$\.**
16. Select the **CAName** variable and click **Insert.**
17. Select the **CRLNameSuffix** variable and click **Insert.**
18. Select the **DeltaCRLAllowed** variable and click **Insert.**
19. After you insert **DeltaCRLAllowed**, at the end of the text in the Location text box, add **.crl.**

20. Click **OK** to close the Add Location dialog box.
21. Click **OK** to close the Properties dialog box.
22. When you are prompted to restart Active Directory Certificate Services, click **Yes**.
23. In the Certificate Authority console, right-click **Certificate Templates** and choose **Manage.** The Certificate Templates console opens.
24. Right-click the **Web Server** template and choose **Duplicate Template**.
25. In the Properties of New Template dialog box (as shown in Figure 9-31), click the **General** tab.

Figure 9-31

Opening the properties of a new certificate template

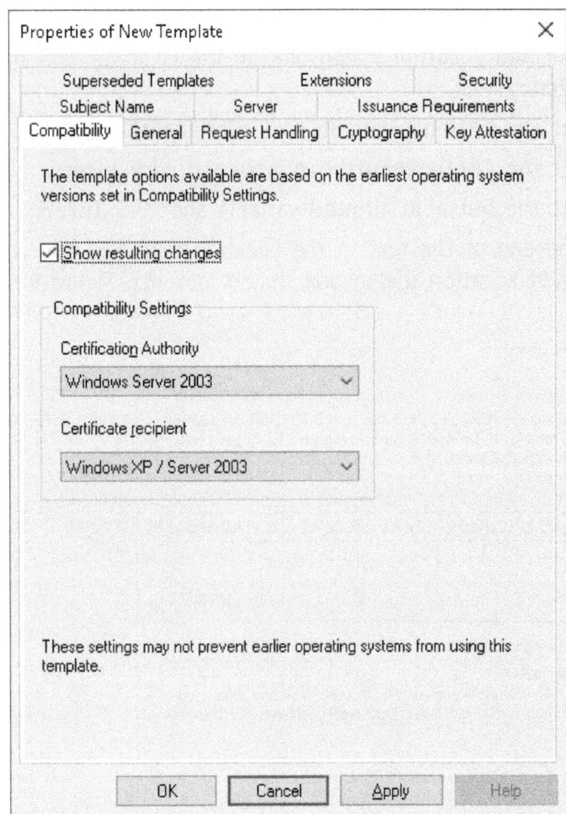

26. On the General tab, in the Template display name text box, type **Adatum Web Server Certificate.**
27. Click the **Request Handling** tab.
28. On the Request Handling tab, select the **Allow private key to be exported** option.
29. Click the **Security** tab.
30. On the Security tab, make sure **Authenticated Users** is selected. Then, under the Allow column, click **Enroll**, as shown in Figure 9-32.
31. Click **OK** to close the Properties of New Template dialog box.
32. Close the Certificate Template console.
33. In the Certification Authority console, right-click **Certificate Templates** and choose **New > Certificate Template to Issue.**
34. Select the **Adatum Web Server Certificate** and click **OK.**
35. Close the Certification Authority console.
36. In Server Manager, click **Tools > Group Policy Management.**
37. In the Group Management console, right-click **Forest: Adatum.com\Domains\Adatum.com\Default Domain Policy** and choose **Edit.**

Figure 9-32

Specifying the permissions assigned to the certificate template

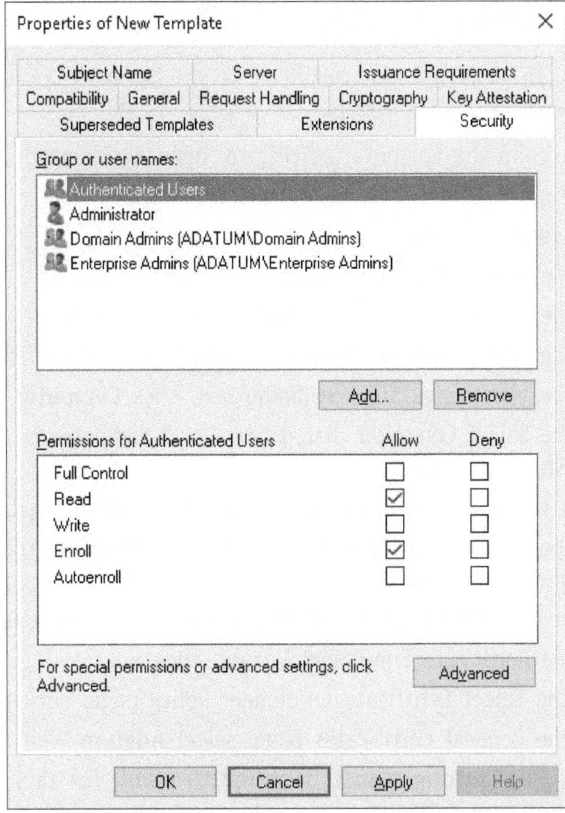

38. In the Group Policy Management Editor, navigate to **Computer Configuration\Policies\Windows Settings\Security Settings\Public Key Policies.**
39. Right-click **Automatic Certificate Request** and choose **New > Automatic Certificate Request.**
40. In the Welcome to the Automatic Certificate Request Setup Wizard, click **Next.**
41. On the Certificate Template page (see Figure 9-33), click the **Computer** certificate template to select it and click **Next.**

Figure 9-33

Specifying which certificates are automatically requested

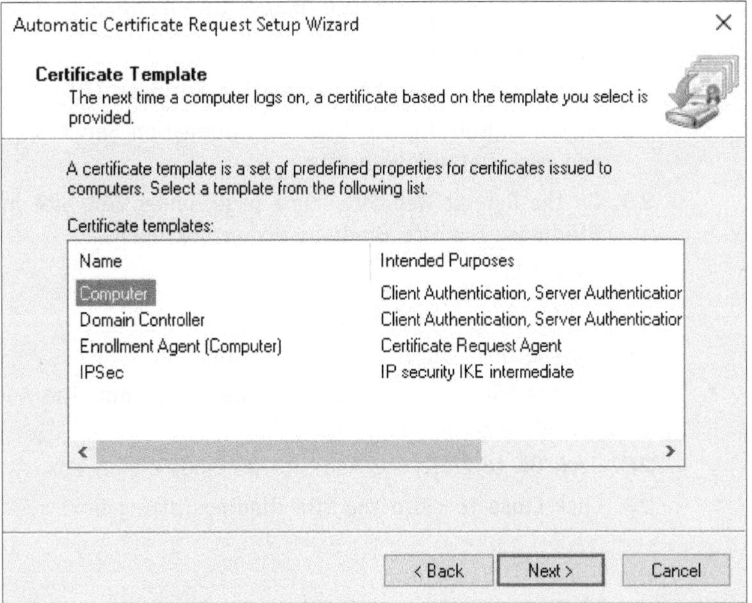

42. When the wizard is complete, click **Finish.**

INSTALL A DIGITAL CERTIFICATE ON THE NETWORK LOCATION SERVER

GET READY. To install a digital certificate on the Network Location Server, perform the following steps.

1. To acquire the Computer certificate, open a command prompt and execute the following command:

   gpudate /force
2. At the command prompt, execute the **mmc** command.
3. In the console, click **File > Add/Remove Snap-in.**
4. In the Add or Remove Snap-ins dialog box, double-click **Certificates.**
5. In the Certificates Snap-in dialog box, click **Computer account.**
6. In the Select Computer dialog box, Local computer is already selected. Click **Finish.**
7. Click **OK** to close the Add or Remove Snap-ins dialog box.
8. In the console, navigate to **\Personal\Certificates.** You should see the Computer certificate.
9. Right-click **Certificates** and choose **All Tasks > Request New Certificate.**
10. In the Certificate Enrollment Wizard, click **Next.**
11. On the Select Certificate Enrollment Policy page, click **Next.**
12. On the Request Certificates page, select **Adatum Web Server Certificate.**
13. Click **More information is required to enroll for this certificate. Click here to configure settings.**
14. In the Certificate Properties dialog box, for the Type, select **Common name.**
15. In the Value text box, type **nls.adatum.com.** Click the top **Add** button. The CN = nls.adatum.com value should appear on the right side of the dialog box.
16. Click **OK** to close the Certificate Properties dialog box.
17. Back on the Request Certificates page, click **Enroll.**
18. When the certificate installation succeeds, click **Finish.** The certificate appears in the Personal\Certificates folder.
19. Close the console window. If you are prompted to save settings, click **No.**
20. Open **Server Manager.**
21. Click **Tools > Internet Information Services (IIS) Manager.**
22. In the console tree of Internet Information Services (IIS), expand the **Sites** node and click **Default Web site.**
23. On the Default Web Site home page, under Edit Site in the Actions pane, click **Bindings.** The Site Bindings dialog box opens.
24. Click **Add.**
25. For the Type, select **https.**
26. For the Host name, type **nls.adatum.com.**
27. For the SSL certificate, select **nls.adatum.com.** The Add Site Binding dialog box should look similar to Figure 9-34.
28. Click **OK** to close the Add Site Bindings dialog box.
29. Click **Close** to close the Site Bindings dialog box.

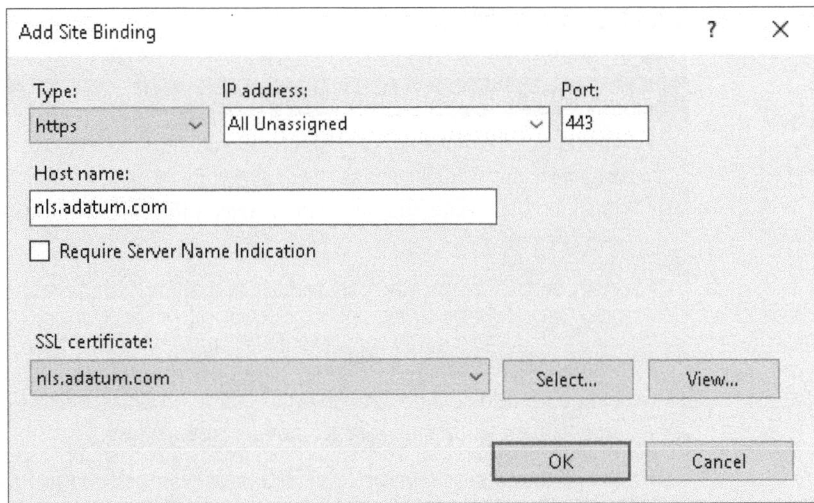

Figure 9-34

Configuring an IIS site binding

30. Close the Internet Information Services (IIS) Manager console.

Troubleshooting DirectAccess

Because DirectAccess is a new technology and it depends on several components, it is easy to have problems with it. Of course, you should first verify that you have system requirements.

CERTIFICATION READY
Troubleshoot DirectAccess
Objective 4.2

When troubleshooting DirectAccess, you should check the following:

1. The DirectAccess client computer must be running Windows 10, Windows 8, Windows 7 Ultimate, or Windows 7 Enterprise edition.
2. The DirectAccess client computer must be a member of an Active Directory Domain Services (AD DS) domain and its computer account must be a member of one of the security groups configured with the DirectAccess Setup Wizard.
3. The DirectAccess client computer must have received computer configuration Group Policy settings for DirectAccess.
4. The DirectAccess client must have a global IPv6 address, which should begin with a 2 or 3.
5. The DirectAccess client must be able to reach the IPv6 addresses of the DirectAccess server.
6. The DirectAccess client on the Internet must correctly determine that it is not on the intranet. You can type the `netsh dnsclient show state` command to view the network location displayed in the Machine Location field (Outside corporate network or Inside corporate network).
7. Use the `netsh namespace show policy` command to show the NRPT rules as configured on the Group Policy.
8. Use the `netsh namespace show effectivepolicy` command to determine the results of network location detection and the IPv6 addresses of the intranet DNS servers.
9. The DirectAccess client must not be assigned the domain firewall profile.
10. The DirectAccess client must be able to reach the organization's intranet DNS servers using IPv6. You can use Ping option to attempt to reach the IPv6 addresses of intranet servers.
11. The DirectAccess client must be able to communicate with intranet servers using Application layer protocols. If File and Printer Sharing is enabled on the intranet server, test the Application layer protocol access by typing `net view \\IntranetFQDN`.
12. Use the DirectAccess Connectivity Assistant on computers running Windows 7 and Network Connectivity Assistant on computers running Windows 8 or later to determine the intranet connectivity status and to provide diagnostic information.

SKILL SUMMARY

In this lesson you learned:

- Virtual private networks (VPNs) link two computers or network devices through a wide area network (WAN) such as the Internet. Because the Internet is a public network and is considered insecure, the data sent between the two computers or devices is encapsulated and encrypted.
- VPN connections provide encapsulation, authentication, data encryption, and data integrity.
- A site-to-site VPN connection connects two private networks. Site-to-site VPN connections can be used to connect branch offices to an organization's primary site, or to connect one organization to the network of another organization.
- The remote access (dial-up or VPN) allows clients to connect to this server through a secure virtual private network connection.
- To provide constant connectivity, you use Internet Key Exchange version 2 (IKEv2), which automatically establishes a VPN connection when Internet connectivity is available. Only Windows 7, Windows Server 2008 R2, and later support VPN Reconnect.
- In Windows Server 2016, there are several ways to create a VPN connection. They include the Network and Sharing Center Set Up a Connection or Network Wizard, the Windows Server 2016 Settings, and the Connection Manager Administration Kit (CMAK). This book focuses on the Network and Sharing Center and CMAK because you cannot configure all of the options using the Windows Server 2016 Settings.
- DirectAccess is a feature introduced with Windows 7 and Windows Server 2008 R2 that provides seamless intranet connectivity to DirectAccess client computers when they are connected to the Internet. Different from the traditional virtual private network (VPN) connections, DirectAccess connections are automatically established and they provide always-on seamless connectivity.
- DirectAccess clients use the Network Location Server (NLS) to determine their locations. The Network Location Server is an internal web server. If the client computer can connect with HTTPS to the URL specified, the client computer assumes it is on the intranet and disables DirectAccess components. If the client cannot reach the NLS, it assumes it is on the Internet.

■ Knowledge Assessment

Multiple Choice

Select the correct answer for each of the following questions.

1. Which VPN protocol should be used to use VPN Reconnect?
   a. PPTP
   b. L2TP
   c. IKEv2
   d. SSTP

2. As an administrator for an organization, you want to make a server running Windows Server 2016 into a VPN server. However, the networking team allows only HTTPS through the firewall. Which VPN protocol should be used?
   a. PPTP
   b. L2TP
   c. IKEv2
   d. SSTP
3. Which authentication protocol should be used to start using smart cards with the VPN?
   a. PAP
   b. CHAP
   c. MS-CHAPv2
   d. EAP
4. Which authentication protocol is the least secure and, therefore, should *not* be used?
   a. PAP
   b. CHAP
   c. MS-CHAPv2
   d. EAP
5. Which of the following allows split tunneling?
   a. Open Advanced TCP/IP Settings and select Use default gateway on remote network.
   b. Open Advanced TCP/IP Settings and deselect Use default gateway on remote network.
   c. Open Advanced TCP/IP Settings and select Don't use default gateway on remote network.
   d. Open Advanced TCP/IP Settings and deselect Don't use default gateway on remote network.
6. Which of the following is the easiest way to set up a VPN client on a computer for a nontechnical user?
   a. Use PAP.
   b. Type up step-by-step instructions with screen shots to give to the user.
   c. Use a group policy to configure the settings.
   d. Use CMAK to create an executable to install.
7. Which option should be used to make sure that a user can dial in using only her home phone?
   a. Verify Caller ID
   b. Always Callback To
   c. No Callback
   d. Set By Caller
8. Which of the following is the main advantage of using DirectAccess over VPN connections?
   a. Users don't have to manually connect to the remote network.
   b. DirectAccess uses IPv4 rather than IPv6.
   c. DirectAccess supports more operating systems than VPNs.
   d. DirectAccess connections are unidirectional.
9. Which of the following technologies is used to automatically connect to the company network whenever Internet access is available?
   a. BranchCache
   b. VPN Autoconnect
   c. DirectAccess
   d. PEAP

10. DirectAccess relies on which of the following?
    a. CHAP
    b. BranchCache
    c. PEAP
    d. IPv6

11. When configuring DirectAccess on Server1, which step needs to be performed to ensure that Server1 can initiate connections to DirectAccess client computers?
    a. Remote Clients
    b. DirectAccess Server
    c. Infrastructure Servers
    d. Application Servers

12. Which two steps need to be performed on the DNS server so that it can support DirectAccess?
    a. Remove the WPAD from the DNS global query block.
    b. Remove the ISATAP from the DNS global query block.
    c. Add a record for the NSL server.
    d. Add a SRV record for the DirectAccess server.

13. A client configured for DirectAccess is connected to the Internet from home. Which of the following allows you, as the administrator, to verify whether the client can resolve the DirectAccess server called server1.contosol.com?
    a. Run the `netsh.exe dnsclient show state` command.
    b. Run the `ipconfig /all` command.
    c. Run the `netsh connect` command.
    d. Run the `ping server1.contoso.com` command.

14. Which table is used to determine the behavior of the DNS clients when determining the address of internal resources?
    a. NAP
    b. NPS
    c. NRTP
    d. NCA

15. Which tool is available in Windows 8 that allows the diagnosis of DirectAccess connections?
    a. DirectAccess Connectivity Assistant (DCA)
    b. Network Connectivity Assistant (NCA)
    c. DirectAccess Troubleshooter
    d. TestDA

16. Which server is used to determine if the server is connected to the intranet or the Internet?
    a. DNS Validator
    b. DirectAccess Detector
    c. DirectAccess Broadcaster
    d. Network Location Server

17. Which of the following describes why DirectAccess needs certificates? (Choose all that apply.)
    a. To support IPsec
    b. To support PPTP

   c. To support SSTP
   d. To support DNS lookup

18. When establishing a VPN connection, which of the following verifies that data has *not* been modified while in transit?
    a. Encapsulation
    b. Authentication
    c. Data encryption
    d. Data integrity

19. SSTP is enabled on a server called Server1. When a user tries to log on, he receives an error: Error 0x80092013: The revocation function is unable to check revocation because the revocation server was offline. The certificate looks fine. Which of the following actions should be taken to overcome this problem?
    a. Renew the certificate.
    b. Publish the CRL distribution point to a site that is available over the Internet.
    c. Add the RRAS server to the client's personal store.
    d. Upgrade the certificate to V3.

20. When installing and configuring DirectAccess, which of the following topologies should be configured to place the server running Windows Server 2016 connected directly to the Internet?
    a. Edge
    b. Edge (with two network adapters)
    c. Behind an Edge Device (with two network adapters)
    d. Behind an Edge Device (with a single network adapter)

Best Answer

Choose the letter that corresponds to the best answer. More than one answer choice may achieve the goal. Select the BEST answer.

1. A corporation has a main office and 12 branch offices. The users and computers are within a single domain. All servers are Windows Server 2008 R2 and Windows Server 2012. All data must be encrypted by using end-to-end encryption. In addition, instead of using user names and passwords, computer-level authentication should be used. Which of the following is the recommended course of action?
   a. Configure a PPTP connection and MS-CHAPv2.
   b. Configure L2TP with IPsec and EAP-TSL authentication.
   c. Configure L2TP with IPsec and MS-CHAPv2.
   d. Configure SSTP with IPsec and PAP.

2. Which of the following statements describes the most effective reason for deploying DirectAccess connectivity for remote users?
   a. Remote users' computers can be easily managed and kept up to date.
   b. Remote users' computers connect automatically.
   c. Remote computers connect via encrypted links over the Internet.
   d. Remote users can access corporate resources.

3. Which one of the Remote Access Management interfaces provides the most control?
   a. The Remote Access Management console
   b. The Enable DirectAccess Wizard
   c. The Remote Access Setup Wizard
   d. The command-line `dnscmd.exe` command

Matching and Identification

1. Identify the correct VPN protocol (PPTP, L2TP, SSTP, or IKEv2) for the following items.
   ____ **a)** Uses MPPE for encryption
   ____ **b)** Requires UDP port 500, UDP port 1701, and UDP port 4500
   ____ **c)** Supports VPN Reconnect
   ____ **d)** Requires only UDP port 500
   ____ **e)** Requires port 1723
   ____ **f)** Uses a certificate or pre-shared key and is combined with IPsec for encryption
   ____ **g)** Uses port 443
2. Identify the correct authentication protocol (PAP, CHAP, MS-CHAPv2, and EAP-MS-CHAPv2) for the following items.
   ____ **a)** Used in older network devices and uses a challenge-response method with MD5 hashing
   ____ **b)** Allows you to change an expired password during the connection process
   ____ **c)** Required when using smart cards
   ____ **d)** User name and password are sent in plaintext
   ____ **e)** Encapsulates the EAP within an encrypted and authenticated Transport Layer Security tunnel

Build List

1. Specify the correct order of steps necessary to configuring a VPN server. Not all steps will be used.
   ____ Run the Configure and Enable Routing and Remote Access wizard.
   ____ Configure VPN parameters using server properties in RRAS.
   ____ Create a VPN connection on the client.
   ____ Enable the VPN Service.
   ____ Install RRAS.
   ____ Install the VPN console.
   ____ Install the VPN Service.
2. Specify the correct order of the process of a DirectAccess client connecting to a DirectAccess server.
   ____ Connects to the server using IPv6 and IPsec, or an IPv6 transitional technology
   ____ Tries to connect with IP-HTTPS to encapsulate IPv6 traffic
   ____ Determines whether the client passes health validation
   ____ Determines whether it is connected to the Internet or the intranet
   ____ Tries to contact the intranet DNS server and domain controllers for authentication
   ____ Establishes an IPsec tunnel to resources on the intranet

■ Business Case Scenarios

Scenario 9-1: Installing a VPN Server

You are an administrator for a sales organization and your manager requests that you install a VPN server so that users can access internal network data while they are off-site with sales customers. Your manager wants you to make the VPN server as secure as possible with the VPN technologies that appear in this lesson. Describe how to configure the server.

Scenario 9-2: Understanding DirectAccess

You are an administrator with the Contoso Corporation, which has about 1,100 users. Of those 1,100 users, 200 users use VPN to connect to the organization network when they are not in the office. You are having trouble keeping the clients updated and performing other maintenance tasks as needed because these clients are often not connected to the network. Describe your recommended course of action.

Scenario 9-3: Installing DirectAccess

As the administrator for a company, you are installing DirectAccess on an internal server. You need to configure the Network Location Server (NLS), but, first, your manager needs you to explain NLS and describe its requirements.

Implementing Network Policy Server (NPS)

70-741 EXAM OBJECTIVE

Objective 4.3 – Implement Network Policy Server (NPS). This objective may include but is not limited to the following: Configure a RADIUS server, including RADIUS proxy; configure RADIUS clients; configure NPS templates; configure RADIUS accounting; configure certificates; configure connection request policies; configure network policies for VPN and wireless and wired clients; import and export NPS policies.

Lesson Heading	Exam Objective
Configuring a Network Policy Server • Configuring a RADIUS Server • Configuring Multiple RADIUS Server Infrastructures • Configuring RADIUS Clients • Configuring RADIUS Accounting • Configuring NPS Authentication Methods	Configure a RADIUS server, including RADIUS proxy Configure RADIUS clients Configure RADIUS accounting Configure certificates
Configuring NPS Policies • Configuring Connection Request Policies • Configuring Network Policies • Configuring and Managing NPS Templates	Configure connection request policies Configure network policies for VPN and wireless and wired clients Configure NPS templates Import and export NPS policies

KEY TERMS

access client
authentication, authorization, and accounting (AAA)
authorization
connection request policy
network policy
Network Policy Server (NPS)
NPS policy
NPS templates
RADIUS accounting
RADIUS clients
RADIUS proxy
RADIUS templates
Remote Authentication Dial-In User Service (RADIUS)

Configuring A Network Policy Server

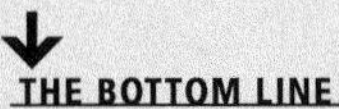

Remote Authentication Dial-In User Service (RADIUS) is a networking and client/server protocol that provides centralized ***authentication, authorization, and accounting (AAA)*** management for computers that connect and use a network service. It can be used in wireless and remote access connection technologies, 802.1x switches, and Remote Desktop Services Gateway.

RADIUS is defined in the Internet Engineering Task Force (IETF) RFCs 2865 and 2866. The Microsoft RADIUS server is ***Network Policy Server (NPS)***. By installing and configuring RADIUS, you can create and enforce organization-wide network access policies for client health, connection request authentication, and connection request authorization.

As mentioned before, RADIUS is used for authentication, authorization, and accounting. ***Authorization*** is the process that determines what a user is permitted to do on a computer system or network. After a client or device is authenticated, the client or device must be authorized to access any type of network resource. The authorization controls which resources an authenticated user can and cannot access. Finally, accounting keeps track of which resources a user has accessed or attempted to access.

When you implement RADIUS, Windows Server 2016 computers running Routing and Remote Access Services and/or wireless access points can forward access requests to a single RADIUS server (see Figure 10-1). The RADIUS server then queries the domain controller for authentication and applies NPS network policies to the connection requests.

TAKE NOTE*

RADIUS clients (also referred to as access servers) are servers (such as servers running RRAS) and devices (such as wireless access points and 802.1X switches) that forward RADIUS requests to a RADIUS server. An ***access client*** is a computer or device that contacts or connects to a RADIUS client, which requires authentication and authorization to connect.

Figure 10-1

Looking at RADIUS servers and clients

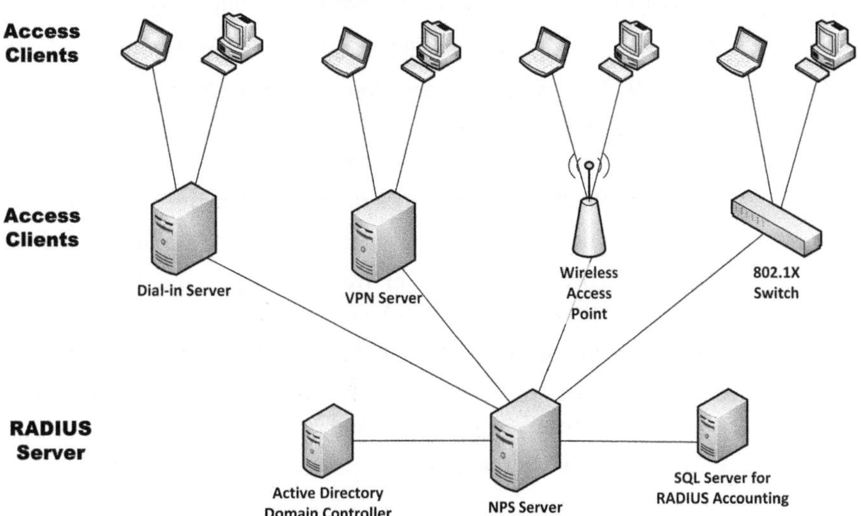

When NPS is used as a RADIUS server, authentication, authorization, and accounting follows these steps:

1. When an access client accesses a VPN server or wireless access point, a connection request is created that is sent to the NPS server.
2. The NPS server evaluates the Access-Request message.
3. If required, the NPS server sends an Access-Challenge message to the access server. The access server processes the challenge and sends an updated Access-Request to the NPS server.
4. The user credentials are checked and the dial-in properties of the user account are obtained by using a secure connection to a domain controller.
5. When the connection attempt is authorized with both the dial-in properties of the user account and network policies, the NPS server sends an Access-Accept message to the access server. If the connection attempt is either not authenticated or not authorized, the NPS server sends an Access-Reject message to the access server.
6. The access server completes the connection process with the access client and sends an Accounting-Request message to the NPS server, where the message is logged.
7. The NPS server sends an Accounting-Response to the access server.

RADIUS has been officially assigned UDP ports 1812 for RADIUS Authentication and 1813 for RADIUS Accounting by the Internet Assigned Numbers Authority (IANA). However, before IANA officially allocated ports 1812 and 1813, ports 1645 and 1646 were used for authentication and accounting. Although Microsoft RADIUS servers default to port 1812 and 1813, others can still use 1645 and 1646. Therefore, if the RADIUS server is separated by a firewall, you should open all four ports.

Configuring a RADIUS Server

CERTIFICATION READY
Configure a RADIUS server, including RADIUS proxy
Objective 4.3

Installing NPS is a simple process, which is done with Server Manager. After NPS is installed, you then use the Network Policy Server console to configure NPS.

INSTALL NETWORK POLICY SERVER

GET READY. To install NPS, perform the following steps.

1. Log on to LON-SVR2 as **adatum\administrator** with the password of **Pa$$w0rd.**
2. Click **Start** and click **Server Manager.**
3. In Server Manager, at the top, click **Manage > Add Roles and Features.** The Add Roles and Feature Wizard opens.
4. On the Before You Begin page, click **Next.**
5. Click **Role-based or feature-based installation** and then click **Next.**
6. Click **Select a server from the server pool**, click the name of the server to install Network Policy and Access Services to, and then click **Next.**
7. On the Server Roles page, click **Network Policy and Access Services** and click **Next.**
8. When you are prompted to add features that are required for Network Policy and Access Services, click **Add Features.**
9. Back on the Select Server Roles page, click **Next.**
10. On the Select Features page, click **Next.**
11. On the Network Policy and Access Services page, click **Next.**
12. On the Confirm Installation page, click **Install.**
13. When the installation is complete, click **Close.**

After the NPS is installed, it can be configured using the Network Policy Server console (see Figure 10-2).

Figure 10-2

Opening the Network Policy Server console

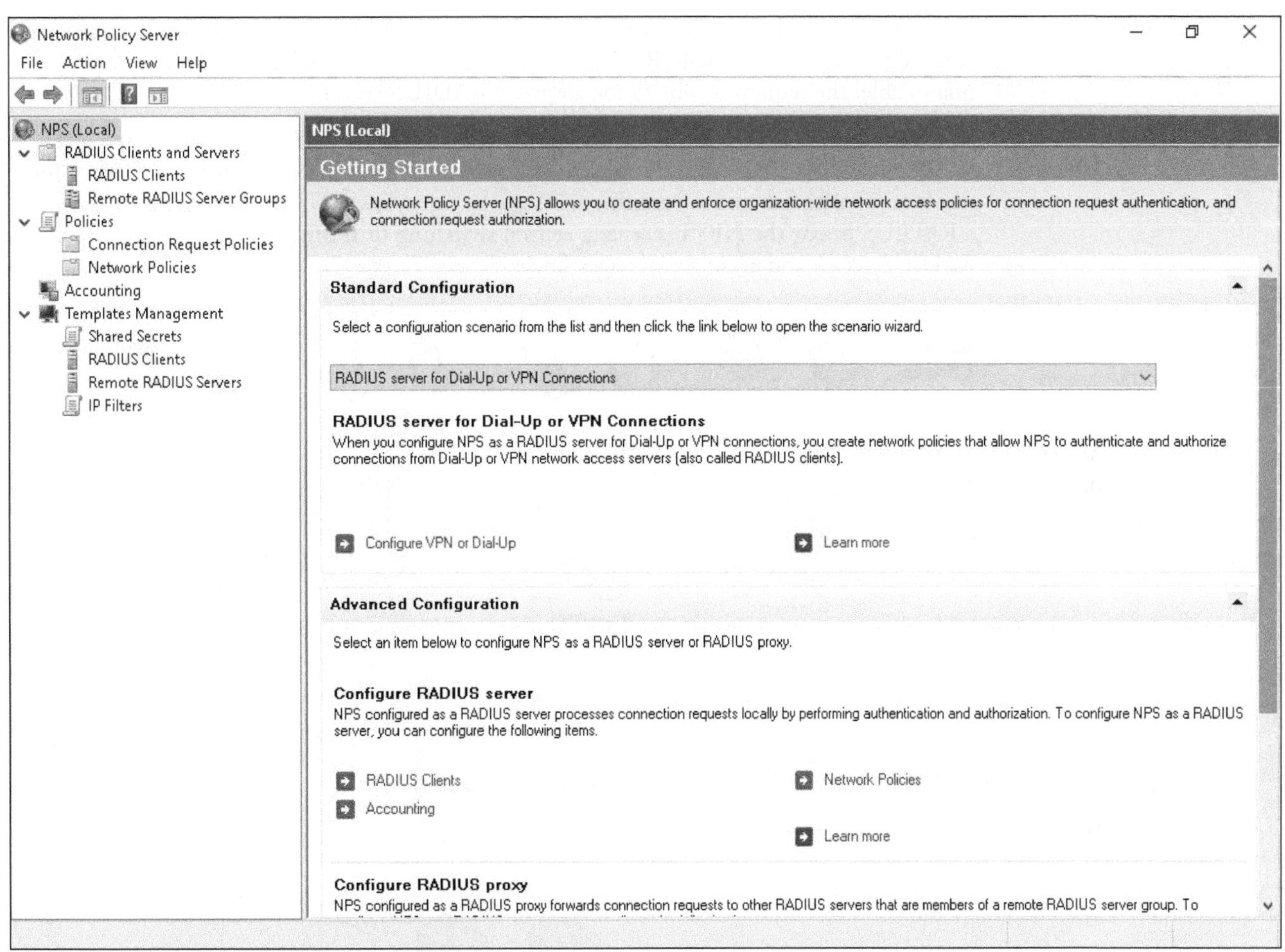

USING WINDOWS POWERSHELL

You can manage RADIUS settings using the following Windows PowerShell cmdlets:

- **`Add-RemoteAccessRadius`:** Adds a new external RADIUS server for VPN authentication, accounting for DirectAccess and VPN, or one-time password authentication for DirectAccess
- **`Get-RemoteAccessAccounting`:** Displays the accounting configuration for Remote Access, such as the different types of accounting that are enabled and the respective configuration
- **`Get-RemoteAccessRadius`:** Displays the list of RADIUS servers, including RADIUS for VPN authentication, RADIUS for DirectAccess and VPN Accounting, and RADIUS for one-time password authentication for DirectAccess
- **`Remove-RemoteAccessRadius`:** Removes an external RADIUS server from being used for VPN authentication, accounting for both DirectAccess and VPN, or one-time password authentication for DirectAccess
- **`Set-RemoteAccessAccounting`:** Sets the enabled state for inbox and RADIUS accounting for both external RADIUS and Windows accounting, and configures the settings when enabled
- **`Set-RemoteAccessRadius`:** Edits the properties associated with an external RADIUS server being used for VPN authentication, accounting for DirectAccess and VPN, and one-time password authentication for DirectAccess

Configuring Multiple RADIUS Server Infrastructures

So far, only a simple installation of NPS has been discussed. However, for larger and more complex organizations, you will most likely have multiple RADIUS servers so that you can provide enhanced performance and redundancy.

If you have multiple RADIUS servers, you can configure RADIUS clients to use a primary RADIUS server and alternate RADIUS servers. If the primary RADIUS server becomes unavailable, the request is sent to the alternate RADIUS server.

Another multiple RADIUS server infrastructure is to place a ***RADIUS proxy*** between the RADIUS server and the RADIUS clients (as shown in Figure 10-3). A RADIUS proxy forwards authentication and accounting messages to other RADIUS servers. When NPS is a RADIUS proxy, the NPS becomes a central switching or routing point through which RADIUS access and account messages flow.

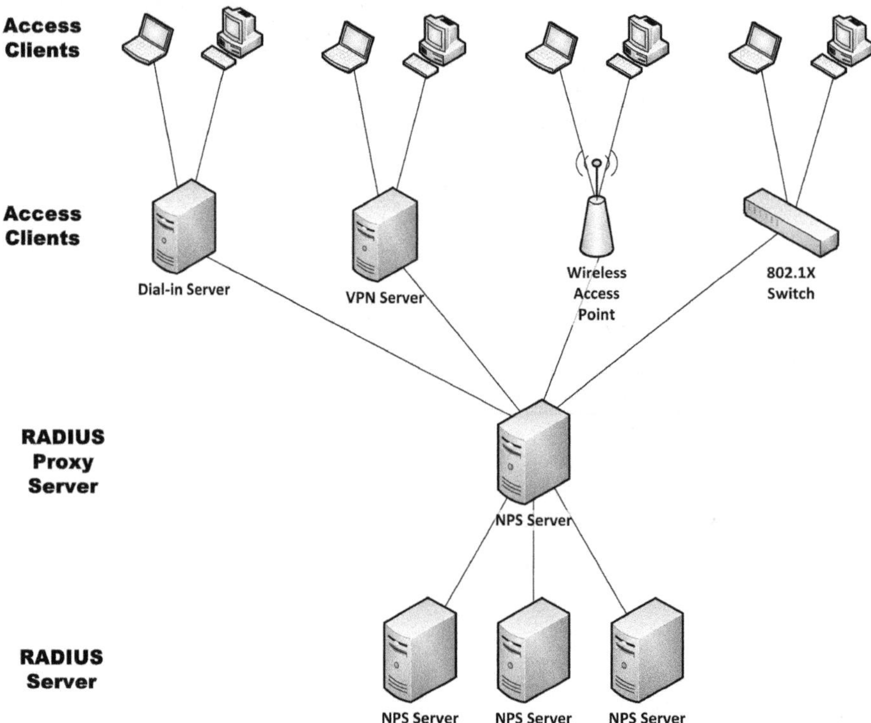

Figure 10-3
Using a RADIUS proxy server

When you configure NPS as a RADIUS proxy, you create a new connection request policy that NPS uses to determine which connection requests to forward to other RADIUS servers. In addition, the connection request policy is configured by specifying a remote RADIUS server group that contains one or more RADIUS servers, which tell NPS where to send the connection requests that match the connection request policy.

To configure load balancing, you must have more than one RADIUS server per remote RADIUS server group. Based on load and resources, you can configure the following:

- **Priority:** Priority specifies the order of importance of the RADIUS server to the NPS proxy server. The lower the number, the higher priority the NPS proxy gives to the RADIUS server. If a RADIUS server is assigned the highest priority of 1, the NPS proxy sends connection requests to the RADIUS server first. If the server is not available, it then sends connection requests to RADIUS servers with priority 2, and so on. You can assign the same priority to multiple RADIUS servers, and then use the Weight setting to load balance between them.

- **Weight:** NPS uses this Weight setting to determine how many connection requests to send to each group member when the group members have the same priority level. Weight setting must be assigned a value between 1 and 100, and the value represents a percentage of 100%. If two servers are assigned the same priority and weight, the connection requests are distributed evenly between the two servers.
- **Advanced settings:** If the remote RADIUS server is unavailable, you can start sending connection requests to other group members. The Advanced settings determine when it considers the server is not available and sends the requests to the next RADIUS server.

ADD A REMOTE RADIUS SERVER GROUP

GET READY. To add a remote RADIUS group, perform the following steps.

1. Log on to LON-SVR2 as **adatum\administrator** with the password of **Pa$$w0rd.**
2. Open **Server Manager.**
3. Click **Tools > Network Policy Server.** The Network Policy Server console opens.
4. In the console tree, double-click **RADIUS Clients and Servers**, right-click **Remote RADIUS Server Groups** and choose **New.** The New Remote RADIUS Server Group dialog box opens.
5. In the Group name text box, type a name for the remote RADIUS server group, such as **RADIUSSERVERGROUP** (see Figure 10-4).

Figure 10-4

Creating a new RADIUS server group

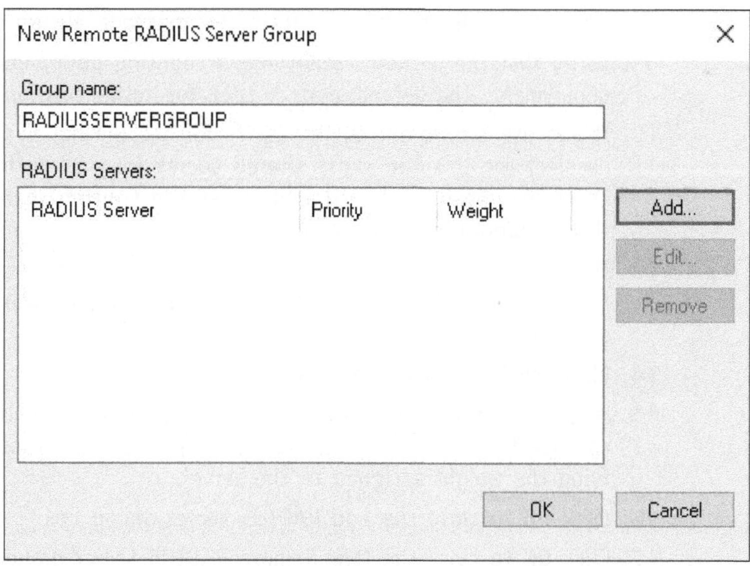

6. Click **Add.** The Add RADIUS Server dialog box opens.
7. Type the IP address of the RADIUS server that you want to add to the group or type the fully qualified domain name (FQDN) of the RADIUS server, such as **LON-RTR.**
8. Click the **Authentication/Accounting** tab. The Authentication/Accounting tab is shown in Figure 10-5.

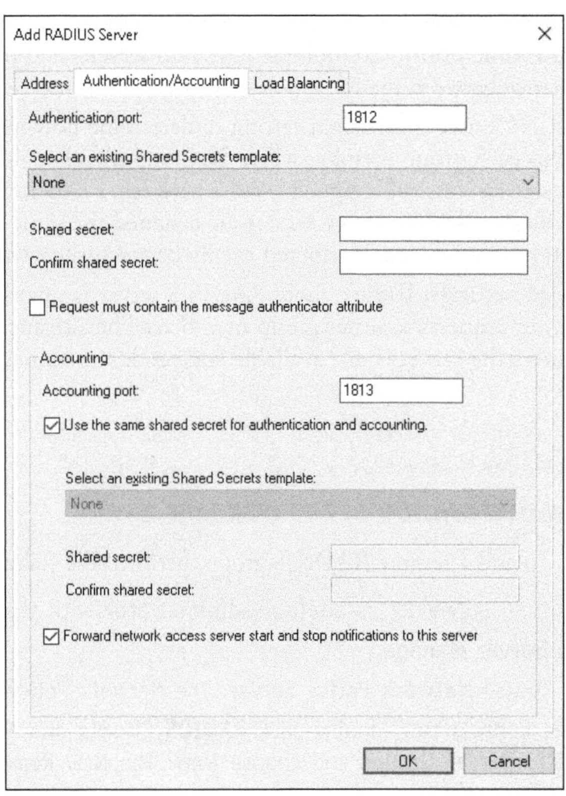

Figure 10-5

Configuring authentication and accounting for a RADIUS server

9. In the Shared secret and Confirm shared secret text boxes, type the shared secret that you used for the RADIUS server, such as **Pa$$w0rd.**
10. If you are not using Extensible Authentication Protocol (EAP) for authentication, select the **Request must contain the message authenticator attribute** check box.
11. Verify that the authentication and accounting port numbers are correct for your deployment. The default port is 1812 for authentication and 1813 for account.
12. If you use a different shared secret for accounting, in the Accounting section, deselect the **Use the same shared secret for authentication and accounting** check box. Then, in the Shared secret and Confirm shared secret text boxes, type the accounting shared secret.
13. If you do not want to forward network access server start and stop messages to the remote RADIUS server, deselect the **Forward network access server start and stop notifications to this server** check box.
14. Click the **Load Balancing** tab.
15. When you want to perform load balancing between multiple RADIUS servers, you can specify how often requests are sent to a specific server in a group by specifying the weight assigned to the server.
16. Click **OK** to close the Add RADIUS Server dialog box.
17. Click **OK** to close the New Remote RADIUS Server group.

Configuring RADIUS Clients

To configure NPS as a RADIUS server, you can use either standard configuration or advanced configuration in the NPS console or in Server Manager.

CERTIFICATION READY
Configure RADIUS clients
Objective 4.3

The standard configuration includes:

- RADIUS server for dial-up or VPN connections
- RADIUS server for 802.1X wireless or wired connections

When you configure NPS as a RADIUS server for dial-up or VPN connections, you create a network policy.

CONFIGURE NPS FOR RADIUS SERVER FOR VPN CONNECTIONS

GET READY. To configure NPS for RADIUS server for VPN connections, perform the following steps.

1. Log on to LON-SVR2 as **adatum\administrator** with the password of **Pa$$w0rd.**
2. Open **Server Manager.**
3. Click **Tools > Network Policy Server.** The Network Policy Server console opens.
4. In the main pane, under the Standard Configuration, click **RADIUS server for Dial-Up or VPN Connections.**
5. Click **Configure VPN or Dial-Up.** The Configure VPN or Dial-Up Wizard opens.
6. On the Select Dial-Up or Virtual Private Network Connections Type page, click **Virtual Private Network (VPN) Connections** (see Figure 10-6). Click **Next.**

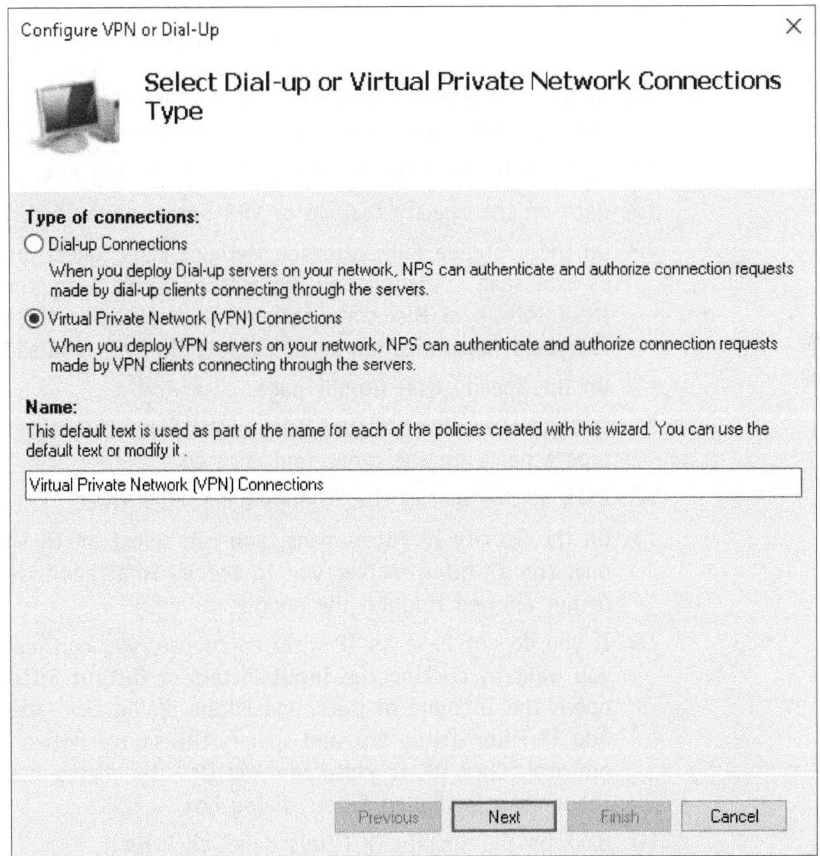

Figure 10-6
Specifying connections on the Select Dial-Up or Virtual Private Network Connections Type page

7. On the Specify Dial-Up or VPN Server page, click **Add.**
8. In the New RADIUS Client dialog box (see Figure 10-7), in the Friendly name text box, type a friendly name for the RADIUS client.
9. In the Address (IP or DNS) text box, type the address of the remote access server, such as **172.16.0.200.**

Figure 10-7

Adding RADIUS clients

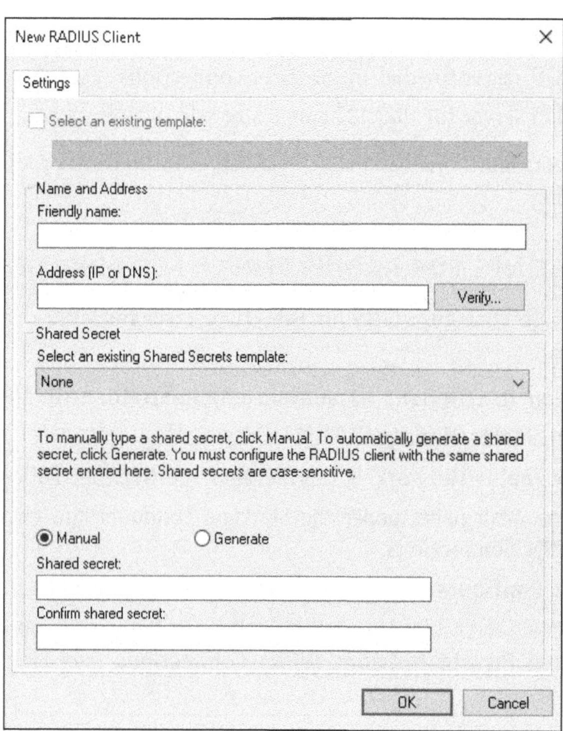

10. At the bottom of the dialog box, in the Shared secret and Confirm shared secret text boxes, type a shared secret password to be used for RADIUS setup, such as **Pa$$w0rd.**
11. Click **OK** to close the New RADIUS Client dialog box.
12. Back on the Specify Dial-Up or VPN Server page, click **Next.**
13. On the Configure Authentication Methods page, select an authentication method, such as Extensible Authentication Protocol, Microsoft Encrypted Authentication version 2 (MS-CHAPv2), or Microsoft Encrypted Authentication (MS-CHAP). By default, Microsoft Encrypted Authentication version 2 (MS-CHAPv2) is already selected. Click **Next.**
14. On the Specify User Groups page, click **Add.**
15. In the Select Group dialog box, in the Enter the object name to select text box, type a name for the group and click **OK.**
16. Back at the Specify User Groups page, click **Next.**
17. On the Specify IP Filters page, you can select an IP Filter template if you have one. (An IP filter enables you to specify what addresses or protocols are allowed or not allowed through the remote servers.)
18. If you do not have an IP filter to choose, you can manually specify the filters you want by clicking the **Input Filters** or **Output Filters** for IPv4 or IPv6, which opens the Inbound or Outbound Filters dialog box. Then click **Add** to open the Add IP Filter dialog box and specify the source network, destination network, and protocol. Click **OK** to close the Add IP Filter dialog box and click **OK** to close the Inbound or Outbound Filters dialog box.
19. Back on the Specify IP Filters page, click **Next.**
20. On the Specify Encryption Settings page, by default, Basic encryption (MPPE 40-bit), Strong encryption (MPPE 56-bit), and Strongest encryption (MPPE 128-bit) are selected. Deselect the encryption that you don't want to support and click **Next.**
21. On the Specify a Realm Name page, if you need to specify a realm (a user account location, such as a domain name or server name), specify the realm name in the appropriate text box. For now, type **adatum.com.** Click **Next.**
22. When the wizard is complete, click **Finish.**

CONFIGURE NPS FOR 802.1X WIRELESS CONNECTIONS

GET READY. To configure NPS for 802.1X wireless or wired connections, perform the following steps.

1. Log on to LON-SVR2 as **adatum\administrator** with the password of **Pa$$w0rd.**
2. Open **Server Manager.**
3. Click **Tools > Network Policy Server.** The Network Policy Server console opens.
4. In the main pane, under Standard Configuration, click **RADIUS server for 802.1X Wireless or Wired Connections.**
5. Click **Configure 802.1X.** The 802.1X Wizard opens.
6. On the Select 802.1X Connections Type page, click **Secure Wireless Connections** (see Figure 10-8). Click **Next.**

Figure 10-8

Selecting the 802.1X connections type

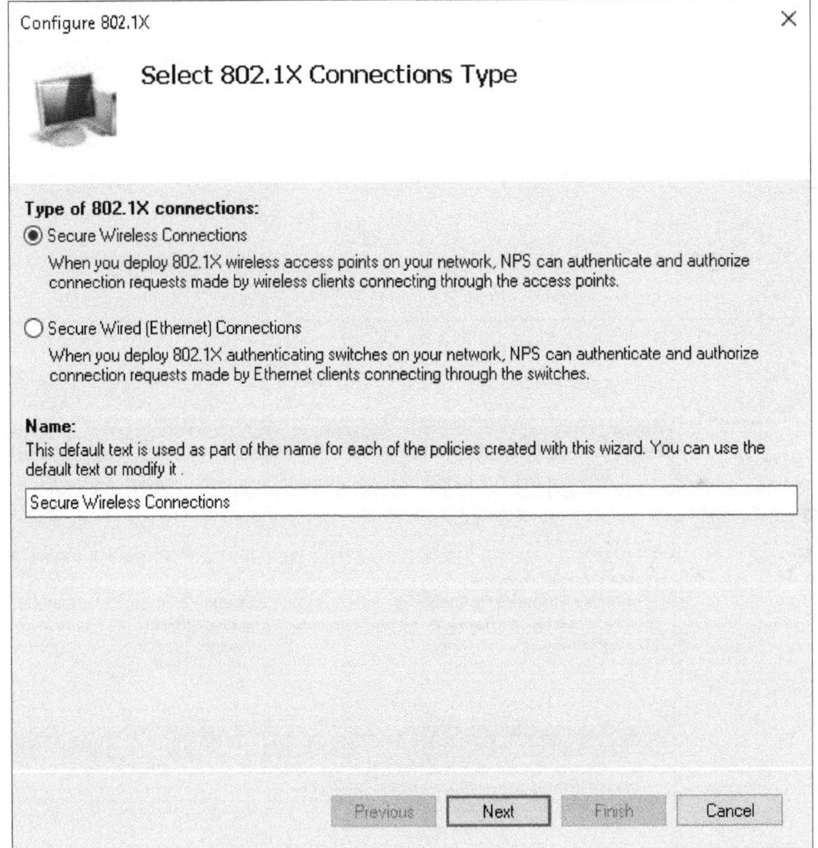

7. On the Specify 802.1X Switches page, click **Add.**
8. In the New RADIUS Client dialog box, in the Friendly name text box, type a friendly name for the RADIUS client.
9. In the Address (IP or DNS) text box, type the address of the remote access server.
10. At the bottom of the dialog box, in the Shared secret and Confirm shared secret text boxes, type a shared secret password to be used for RADIUS setup.
11. Click **OK** to close the New RADIUS Client dialog box.
12. Back on the Specify 802.1X Switches page, click **Next.**

13. On the Configure Authentication Methods page, choose one of the following authentication methods and click **Next:**
    - Microsoft: Smart Card or other certificate
    - Microsoft: Protected EAP (PEAP)
    - Microsoft: Secured password (EAP-MSCHAPv2)
14. On the Specify User Groups page, click **Add.**
15. In the Select Group dialog box, in the Enter the object name to select text box, type a name for the group and click **OK.**
16. Back at the Specify User Groups page, click **Next.**
17. On the Configure Traffic Controls page, you can specify traffic control attributes, which are sent to the RADIUS server with authentication and authorization requests, by clicking the **Configure** button. When you are finished, click **Next.**
18. When the wizard is complete, click **Finish.**

If you want more control in the configuration, use NPS Advanced Configuration. You can modify the RADIUS clients, network policies, and accounting. To modify a network policy, expand Policies in the NPS tree and click Network Policies. Figure 10-9 shows the network policy that was created for the Virtual Private Network (VPN) Connections and the Secure Wireless Connections.

Figure 10-9

Looking at network policies

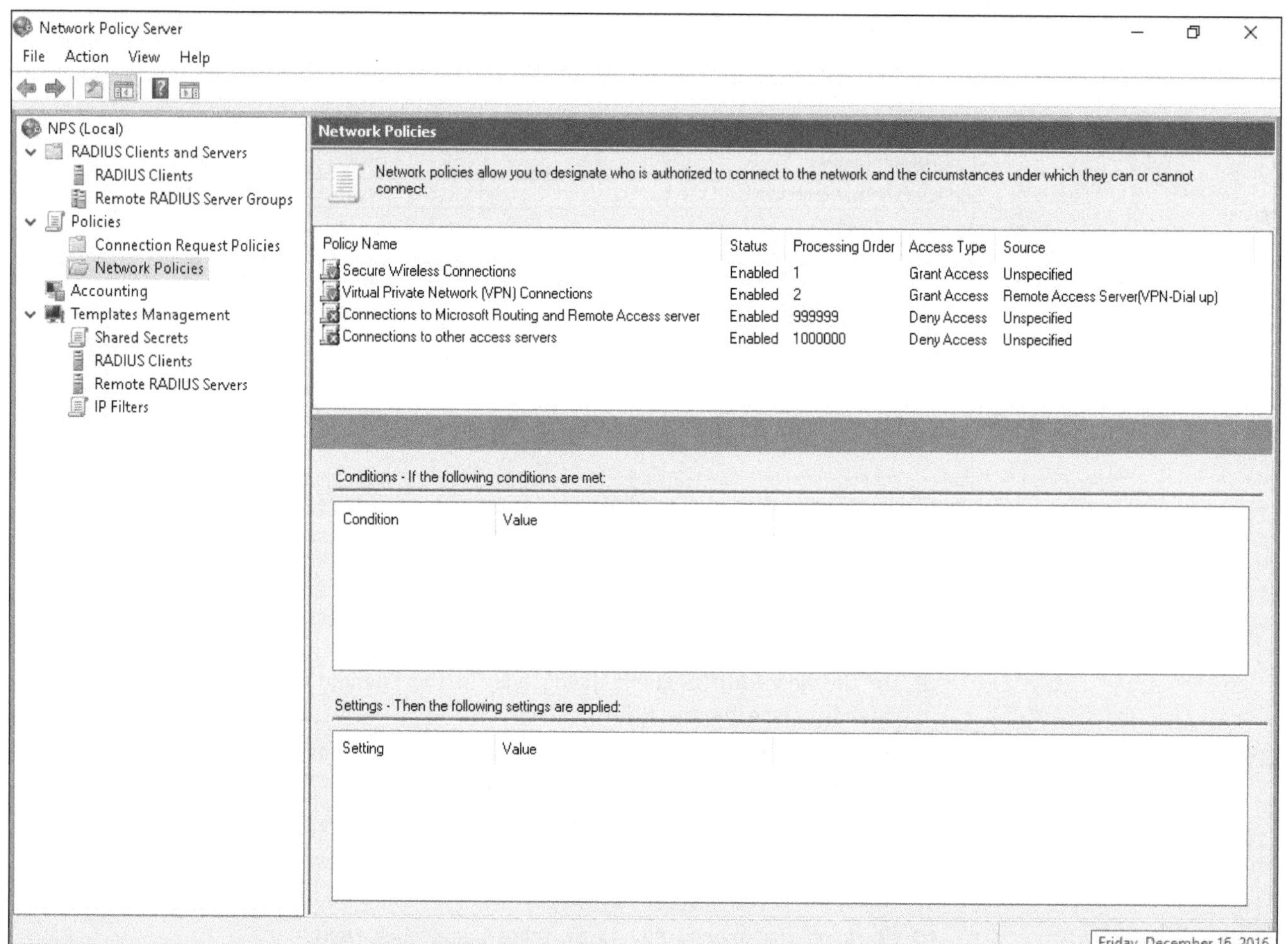

Configuring RADIUS Accounting

NPS supports ***RADIUS accounting***, which you can use to track network usage for auditing and billing purposes.

CERTIFICATION READY
Configure RADIUS accounting
Objective 4.3

When configured for accounting, NPS can log accounting data to a text log file and/or a SQL Server database. When accounting is enabled, at the start of the service delivery, the NPS server generates an Accounting-Start message describing the type of service being delivered and the user it is being delivered to, which is sent to the RADIUS Accounting server. The RADIUS Accounting server sends back an acknowledgment to the RADIUS client. At the end of service delivery, the client generates an Accounting-Stop message that describes the type of service that was delivered and optional statistics, such as elapsed time, input and output octets, or input and output packets. It then sends that data to the RADIUS Accounting server, which sends back an acknowledgment to the RADIUS client.

ENABLE AND CONFIGURE ACCOUNTING ON NPS

GET READY. To enable and configure accounting on NPS, perform the following steps.

1. Log on to LON-SVR2 as **adatum\administrator** with the password of **Pa$$w0rd.**
2. Open **Server Manager.**
3. Click **Tools > Network Policy Server.** The Network Policy Server console opens.
4. On the NPS tree, click **Accounting.** The Accounting pane is shown in Figure 10-10.
5. In the Accounting section, click **Configure Accounting.**

Figure 10-10

Looking at the Accounting configuring options

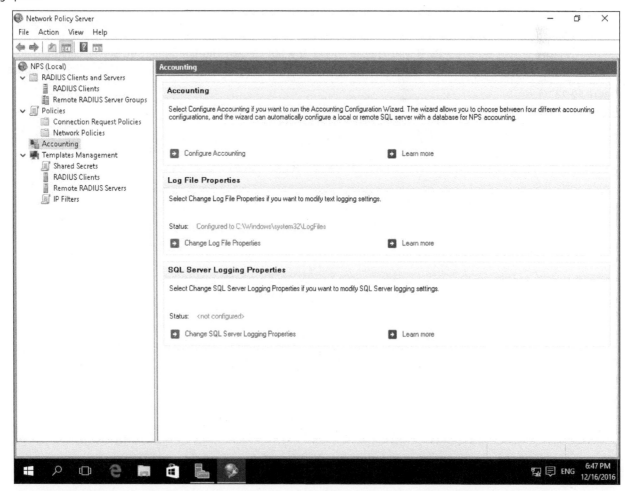

6. In the Accounting Configuration Wizard, click **Next.**
7. On the Select Accounting Options page (as shown in Figure 10-11), click the accounting option that you want to use and click **Next.**

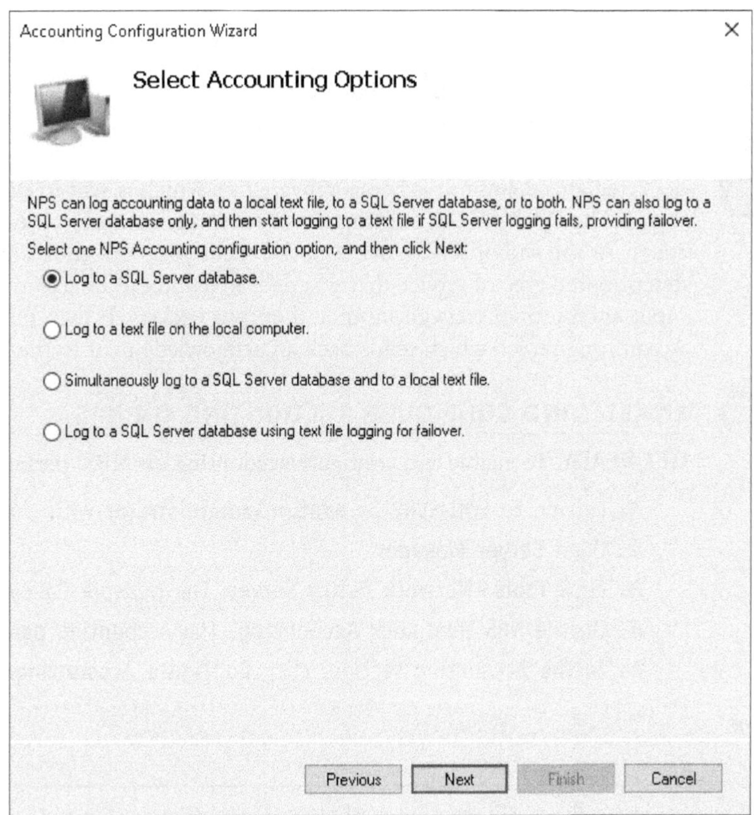

Figure 10-11
Selecting Accounting options

8. If you choose to use the SQL Server, the Configure SQL Server Logging page appears (see Figure 10-12). To configure the SQL connection, click **Configure.**

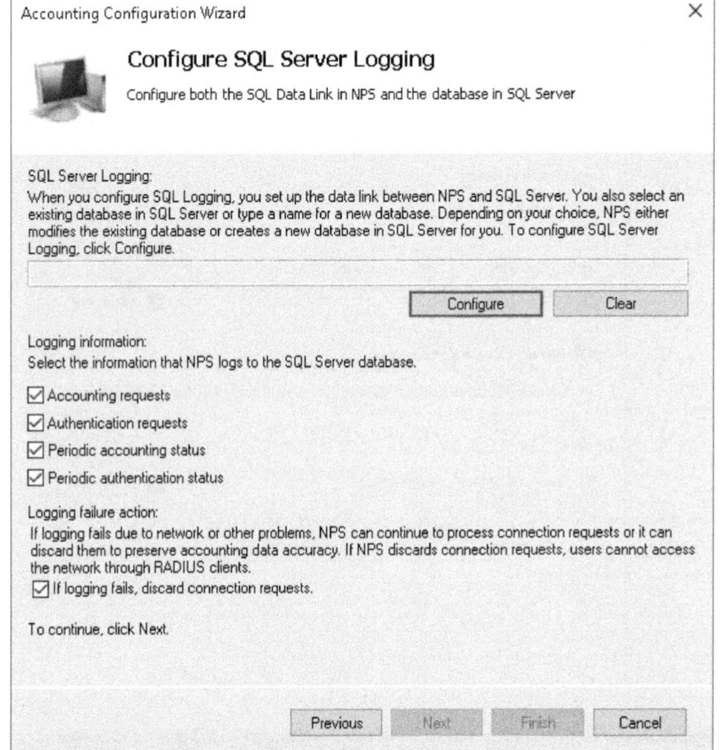

Figure 10-12
Configuring SQL Server logging

9. In the Data Link Properties dialog box, in the Select or enter a server name text box, specify the name of the SQL server and click **Refresh**. Then, specify the user name and password that has access to the SQL server database that you want to log to. Select the database using the Select the database on the server drop-down list. To verify the SQL connection, click **Test Connection**. Click **OK** to close the Data Link Properties dialog box.
10. If you select to save the data into a local text file, the Configure Local File Logging page appears. Notice the path of the log file is C:\Windows\System32\LogFiles. Click **Next**.
11. On the Summary page, click **Next**.
12. On the Conclusion page, click **Close**.

After you run the Accounting Configuration Wizard, you can click the Change Log File Properties or the Change SQL Server Logging Properties to make changes without rerunning the wizard. The Change Log File Properties dialog box opens the Log File Properties. If you choose the Log Files, make sure that the C drive is large enough to hold the logs or move the log files to a drive that is large enough.

When selecting which RADIUS attributes to record, you should include the RADIUS Class attribute, which is used to track usage and simplify the identification of which department or user to charge the usage. It should be noted that if a request is lost, a duplicate request may be sent. Therefore, to accurately track usage, you need to delete duplicate requests.

Configuring NPS Authentication Methods

As already stated throughout the lesson, NPS authenticates and authorizes a connection request before allowing or denying access when a user attempts to connect to a network through a network access server such as a VPN server. NPS must receive proof of the identity of the user or computer.

Authentication is usually broken down into the following categories:

- Password-based credentials
- Certificate-based credentials

When you deploy NPS, you can specify the required type of authentication method for access to your network.

USING PASSWORD-BASED AUTHENTICATION

When a user uses password-based credentials, the network access server passes the user name and password to the NPS server, which verifies the credentials against the user account database, either a domain database or a local server database. Unfortunately, password-based authentication is not considered strong security. As a result, certificate authentication or multi-factor authentication are recommended.

However, if you do use password-based authentication, it is processed from the most secure (Microsoft Challenge Handshake Authentication Protocol v2 or MS-CHAPv2) to the least secure (unauthenticated access) of those enabled options. If you are using only Microsoft clients, you should only allow MS-CHAPv2. However, if you have some non-Microsoft clients, you might need to enable CHAP. Of course, Password Authentication Protocol (PAP) is never recommended because the user name and password are sent in plaintext.

CERTIFICATION READY
Configure certificates
Objective 4.3

USING CERTIFICATES FOR AUTHENTICATION

To provide strong security for authenticating users and computers and eliminate the need for less secure password-based authentication methods, you can use certificates with the NPS. Certificates are customized using certificate templates and are issued using a certificate authority.

When you customize the template, you specify how certificates are issued (how long a certificate is good for and who can receive a certificate) and their purpose. For example, the Computer template is used to define the template that the CA uses to assign certificates to computers, which, by default, includes the Client Authentication purpose and the Server Authentication purpose in EKU extensions.

If you decide to use smart cards for authentication, you need certificates that include the Smart Card Logon purpose and the Client Authentication purpose. When using NPS, you can configure NPS to check certificate purposes before granting network authorization. NPS can check additional EKUs and Issuance Policy purposes, also known as certificate policies.

If you decide to use Protected Extensible Authentication Protocol Microsoft Challenge Handshake Authentication Protocol v2 (PEAP-MS-CHAPv2), Protected Extensible Authentication Protocol Transport Layer Security (PEAP-TLS), or Extensible Authentication Protocol Transport Layer Security (EAP-TLS) as the authentication method, the computers need a digital certificate installed, and the NPS server must use a server certificate that meets the minimum server certificate requirements.

AUTOMATICALLY ADD WORKSTATION AUTHENTICATION CERTIFICATES TO ALL WORKSTATIONS

GET READY. To automatically add workstation authentication certificates to all workstations, perform the following steps.

1. Log on to LON-DC1 (the server that has the Certificate Authority) as **adatum\administrator** with the password of **Pa$$w0rd.**
2. Open **Server Manager.**
3. Click **Tools > Certification Authority.** The Certification Authority console opens.
4. Expand the server. Then, right-click **Certificate Templates** and choose **Manage.** The Certificate Templates console opens.
5. Right-click the **Workstation Authentication** template and choose **Duplicate Template.** The Properties of New Template dialog box opens.
6. Click the **General** tab.
7. In the Template display name text box, type a new name for the certificate template.
8. Click the **Security** tab.
9. In Group or user names section, click **Domain Computers.**
10. Under Allow, select the **Enroll** and **Autoenroll** permission check boxes.
11. Click **OK** to close the Properties of New Template dialog box.
12. Close the Certificate Templates console.
13. In the Certification Authority console, right-click **Certificate Templates** and choose **New > Certificate Template to Issue.** The Enable Certificate Templates dialog box opens.

14. Click the name of the certificate template you just configured and then click **OK.**
15. Close the Certification Authority console.
16. In Server Manager, click **Tools > Group Policy Management console.** The Group Policy Management console opens.
17. Right-click the **Default Domain Policy** and choose **Edit.** The Group Policy Management Editor opens.
18. Expand the console tree and navigate to **Computer Configuration\Policies\Windows Settings\Security Settings\Public Key Policies.**
19. Double-click **Certificate Services Client – Auto-Enrollment.** The Certificate Services Client – Auto-Enrollment dialog box opens.
20. For the Configuration Model, click **Enabled.**
21. Select the **Renew expired certificates, update pending certificates, and remove revoked certificates** check box.
22. Select the **Update certificates that use certificate templates** check box.
23. Click **OK** to close the Certificate Services Client – Auto-Enrollment dialog box.

AUTOMATICALLY ADD RAS AND IAS SERVER CERTIFICATES TO ALL WORKSTATIONS

GET READY. To automatically add RAS and IAS server certificates to all workstations, perform the following steps.

1. Log on to LON-DC1 as **adatum\administrator** with the password of **Pa$$w0rd.**
2. On the server that has the certificate authority, open **Server Manager.**
3. Click **Tools > Certification Authority.** The Certification Authority console opens.
4. Expand the server, right-click **Certificate Templates** and choose **Manage.** The Certificate Templates console opens.
5. Right-click the **RAS and IAS** template and choose **Duplicate Template.** The Properties of New Template dialog box opens.
6. Click the **General** tab.
7. In the Template display name text box, type a new name for the certificate template.
8. Click the **Security** tab.
9. In Group or user names section, click **RAS and IAS Servers.**
10. Under Allow, select the **Enroll** and **Autoenroll** permission check boxes.
11. Click **OK** to close the Properties of New Template dialog box.
12. Close the Certificate Templates console.
13. Back on the Certification Authority console, right-click **Certificate Templates** and choose **New > Certificate Template to Issue.** The Enable Certificate Templates dialog box opens.
14. Click the name of the certificate template you just configured and then click **OK.**
15. Close the Certification Authority console.

Configuring NPS Policies

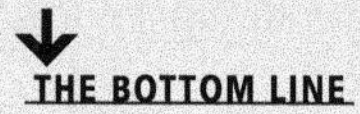

THE BOTTOM LINE

An ***NPS policy*** is a set of permissions or restrictions that are used by remote access authenticating servers that determine who, when, and how a client can connect to a network. With the remote access policies, connections can be authorized or denied based on user attributes, group membership, time of day, type of connection, and many other variables.

NPS provides two types of policies:

- ***Connection request policy:*** A policy that establishes sets of conditions and settings that specify which RADIUS servers perform the authentication, authorization, and accounting of connection requests received by the NPS server from RADIUS clients. It can also be used to designate which RADIUS servers are used for RADIUS accounting.
- ***Network policy:*** A policy that establishes sets of conditions, constraints, and settings that specify who is authorized to connect to the network and the circumstances under which they can or cannot connect.

Configuring Connection Request Policies

Connection request policies determine which RADIUS servers will perform the authentication and authorization of connection requests of RADIUS clients for servers running NPS. It can also be used to specify RADIUS accounting.

CERTIFICATION READY
Configure connection request policies
Objective 4.3

Connection request polices are applied to NPS as a RADIUS server or as a RADIUS proxy. The policies are based on a range of factors, such as:

- The time of day and day of the week
- The realm name in the connection request
- The type of connection requested
- The IP address of the RADIUS client

When you create a connection request policy, you define the following parameters:

- Type of network access server such as remote access server (VPN dial-up)
- Condition that specifies who or what can connect to the network based on one or more RADIUS attributes
- Settings that are applied to an incoming RADIUS message, such as authentication, accounting, and attribute manipulation

RADIUS Access-Request messages are processed or forwarded by NPS only if the settings of the incoming message match at least one of the connection request policies configured on the NPS server. If the policy settings match and the policy requires that the NPS server processes the message, NPS acts as a RADIUS server, authenticating and authorizing the connection request.

Connection request policy conditions, as shown in Table 10-1, are one or more RADIUS attributes that are compared with the attributes of the incoming RADIUS Access-Request message. If there are multiple conditions, all of the conditions in the connection request message and in the connection request policy must match in order for the policy to be enforced by NPS.

The default connection request policy uses NPS as a RADIUS server and processes all authentication requests locally. If you do not want the NPS server to act as a RADIUS server and process connection requests locally, you can delete the default connection request policy.

Table 10-1

Conditions Used in Connection Request Policies

Group	Attribute	Description
Username	User Name	Designates the user name (including the realm/domain name and a user account name) that is used by the access client in the RADIUS message.
Connection Properties	Access Client IPv4 Address	Designates the Internet Protocol version 4 (IPv4) address of the Access client that requests access from the RADIUS client.
	Access Client IPv6 Address	Designates the Internet Protocol version 6 (IPv6) address of the Access client that requests access from the RADIUS client.
	Framed Protocol	Designates the type of framing for incoming packets, such as Point-to-Point Protocol (PPP), Serial Line Internet Protocol (SLIP), Frame Relay, and X.25.
	Service Type	Designates the type of service requested, such as framed (for example, PPP connections) and login (for example, Telnet connections).
	Tunnel Type	Designates the type of tunnel that is created by the requesting client, such as Point-to-Point Tunneling Protocol (PPTP) and Layer Two Tunneling Protocol (L2TP).
Day and Time Restriction	Day and Time Restriction	Designates the day of the week and the time of day a connection can be made.
Identity Type	Identity Type	Restricts the policy to only clients that can be identified through the special mechanism, such as NAP statement of health (SoH).
RADIUS Client Properties	Calling Station ID	Designates the phone number used by the caller (the access client). This attribute is a character string. You can use pattern-matching syntax to specify area codes.
	Client Friendly Name	Designates the name of the RADIUS client computer that requests authentication.
	Client IPv4 Address	Specifies the IPv4 address of the RADIUS client that forwarded the connection request to NPS.
	Client IPv6 Address	Specifies the IPv6 address of the RADIUS client that forwarded the connection request to NPS.
	Client Vendor	Specifies the name of the vendor of the RADIUS client that sends reconnection requests to NPS.
Gateway	Called Station ID	Specifies a character string that is the telephone number of the network access server (NAS).
	NAS Identifier	Specifies a character string that is the name of the NAS.
	NAS IPv4 Address	Designates the IPv4 address of the network access server (the RADIUS client).
	NAS IPv6 Address	Designates the IPv6 address of the network access server (the RADIUS client).
	NAS Port Type	Specifies the type of media used by the access client, such as analog phone lines, Integrated Services Digital Network (ISDN) tunnels, VPN connection, IEEE 802.11 wireless, and Ethernet switches.

To configure a server running NPS to act as a RADIUS proxy and forward connection requests to other NPS or RADIUS servers, you must configure a remote RADIUS server group in addition to adding a new connection request policy that specifies conditions and settings that the connection requests must match.

CREATE A CONNECTION REQUEST POLICY

GET READY. To create a connection request policy, perform the following steps.

1. Log on to LON-SVR2 as **adatum\administrator** with the password of **Pa$$w0rd.**
2. Open **Server Manager.**
3. Click **Tools > Network Policy Server.** The Network Policy Server console opens.
4. Double-click **Policies** in the NPS tree.
5. Right-click **Connection Request Policies** and choose **New.** The New Connection Request Policy Wizard (Figure 10-13) opens.

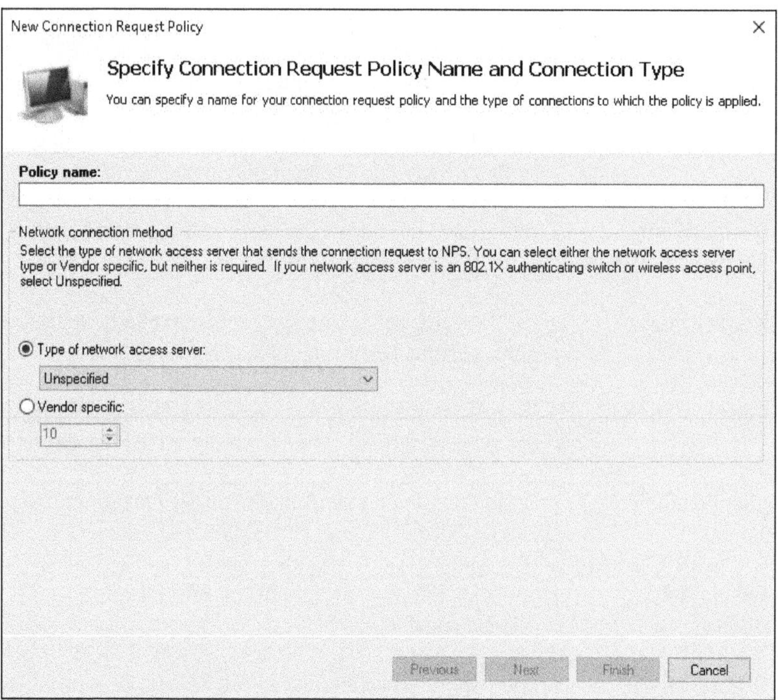

Figure 10-13

Defining the policy name

6. In the Policy name text box, type a meaningful name to identify the policy.
7. If desired, select the type of network access server from the drop-down list—Remote Desktop Gateway, Remote Access Server (VPN-Dial up). Click **Next.**
8. On the Specify Conditions page, click **Add.**
9. In the Select condition dialog box (Figure 10-14 shows some of the conditions available), click the desired condition, such as **Tunnel Type**, and then click **Add.**
10. If you select Tunnel Type, for example, a Tunnel Type dialog box opens (see Figure 10-15). Select the check box for the desired tunnel type and click **OK.**
11. Repeat the process of adding conditions as desired. After the conditions have been added, click **Next.**
12. On the Specify Connection Request Forwarding page (see Figure 10-16), click **Authenticate requests on this server** or **Accept users without validation credentials.** If you have a remote RADIUS server group, you can click the **Forward requests to the following remote RADIUS server group for authentication** option and specify the group. Click **Next.**

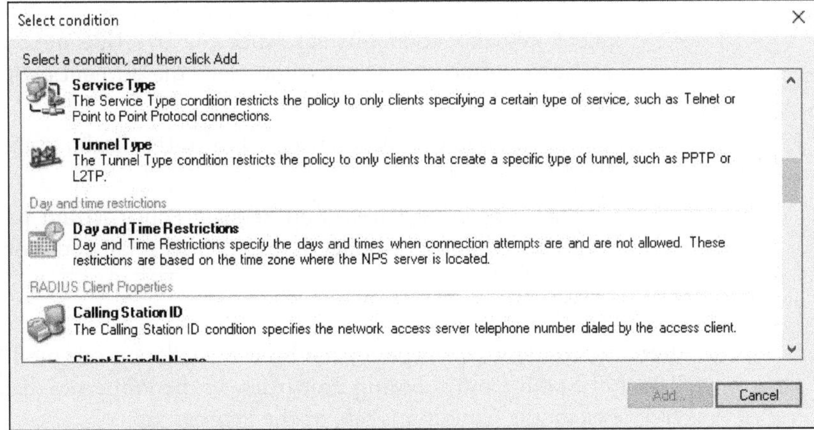

Figure 10-14

Selecting a condition

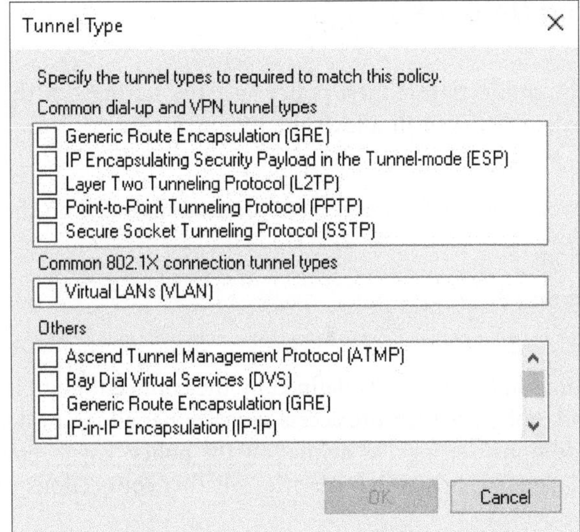

Figure 10-15

Selecting a tunnel type

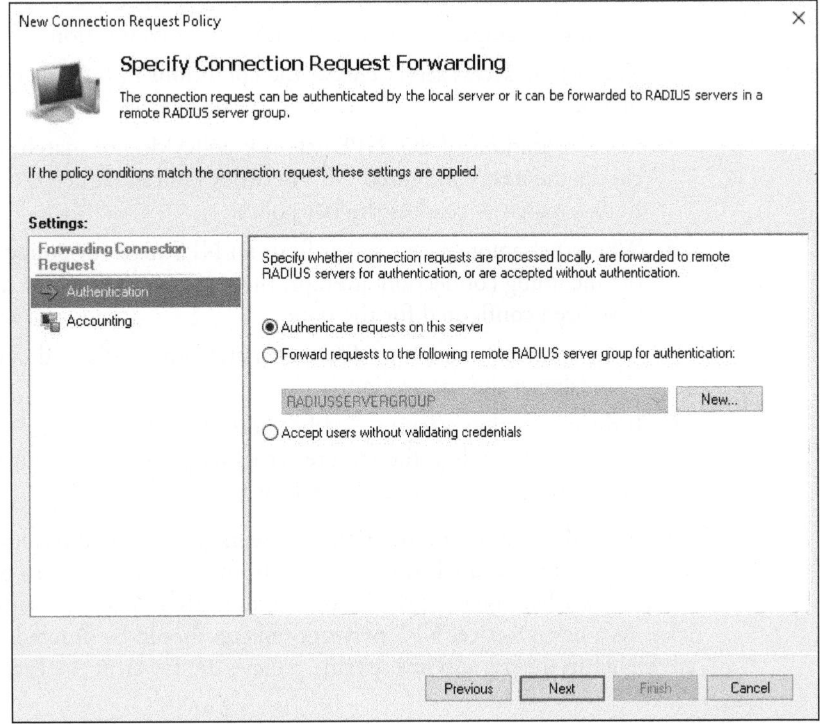

Figure 10-16

Specify Connection Request Forwarding page

13. On the Specify Authentication Methods page, if you want to override the network policy authentication settings, click the **Override network policy authentication settings** option and select or deselect the authentication methods as desired. Click **Next.**
14. On the Configure Settings page, specify the Realm name or RADIUS attribute. Click **Next.**
15. On the Completing Connection Request Policy Wizard page, click **Finish.** When created, the network policy is listed in the Network Policies pane.

After a connection request policy has been created, you can modify the policy by right-clicking the policy and choosing Properties. In the Properties dialog box, you then select the Overview tab, the Conditions tab, or the Settings tab.

Configuring Network Policies

Whereas the connection request policy specifies settings for the RADIUS server, the network policy allows or disallows the remote access.

CERTIFICATION READY
Configure network policies for VPN and wireless and wired clients
Objective 4.3

An NPS network policy evaluates remote connections based on the following three components:

- Conditions
- Constraints
- Settings

If the conditions and constraints defined by the connection attempt match those configured in the network policy, the remote access server either allows or denies the connection and configures additional settings, as defined by the policy. Every remote access policy has an Access Permissions setting, which specifies whether connections matching the policy should be allowed or denied.

When a user attempts to connect to a remote access server, the following process takes place:

1. The user attempts to initiate a remote access connection.
2. The remote access server checks the conditions in the first configured NPS network policy.
3. If the conditions of this NPS network policy do not match, the remote access server checks the next configured NPS network policies. It keeps checking each policy until it finds a match or reaches the last policy.
4. When the remote access server finds an NPS network policy with conditions that match the incoming connection attempt, the remote access server checks any constraints that have been configured for the policy.
5. If the connection attempt does not match any configured constraints, the remote access server denies the connection.
6. If the connection attempt matches both the conditions and the constraints of a particular NPS network policy, the remote access server allows or denies the connection, based on the access permissions configured for that policy.

Of course, if you have multiple NPS network policies, you have to specify the order in which the policies are evaluated from top to bottom. It is important to place these policies in the correct order because once the RRAS server finds a match, it stops processing additional policies. As a best practice, NPS network policies should be ordered so that more specific policies are higher in the list and less specific policies are lower in the list.

CREATE A NETWORK POLICY

GET READY. To create a network policy, perform the following steps.

1. Log on to LON-SVR2 as **adatum\administrator** with the password of **Pa$$w0rd.**
2. Open **Server Manager.**
3. Click **Tools > Network Policy Server.** The Network Policy Server console opens.
4. Double-click **Policies** in the NPS tree.
5. Right-click **Network Policies** and choose **New.** The New Network Policy Wizard opens.
6. In the Policy name text box, type a meaningful name to identify the policy.
7. If desired, select the type of network access server—Remote Desktop Gateway or Remote Access Server (VPN-Dial up). Click **Next.**
8. On the Specify Conditions page, click **Add.**
9. In the Select condition dialog box (see Figure 10-17), select the desired condition, such as **Windows Groups**, and click **Add.**

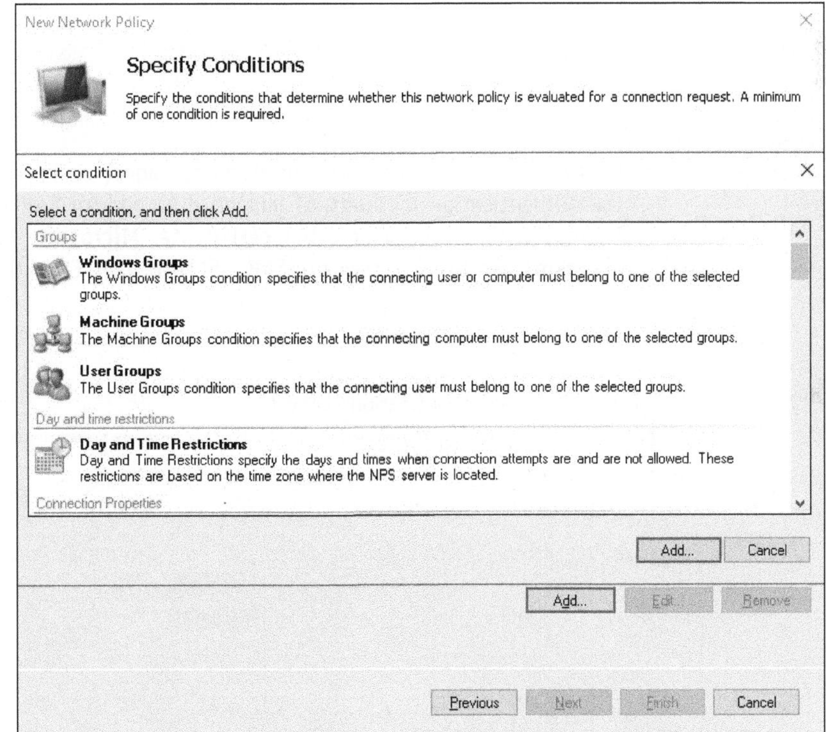

Figure 10-17
Selecting conditions

10. If you select Windows Groups, for example, a Windows Groups dialog box opens. Click **Add Groups.** In the Select Group dialog box, type the name of the desired group and click **OK.**
11. Repeat the process of adding conditions as desired. After the conditions have been met, click **Next.**
12. On the Specify Access Permissions page (see Figure 10-18), click **Access granted**, **Access denied**, or **Access is determined by User Dial-in Properties.**

Figure 10-18

Specifying access permissions

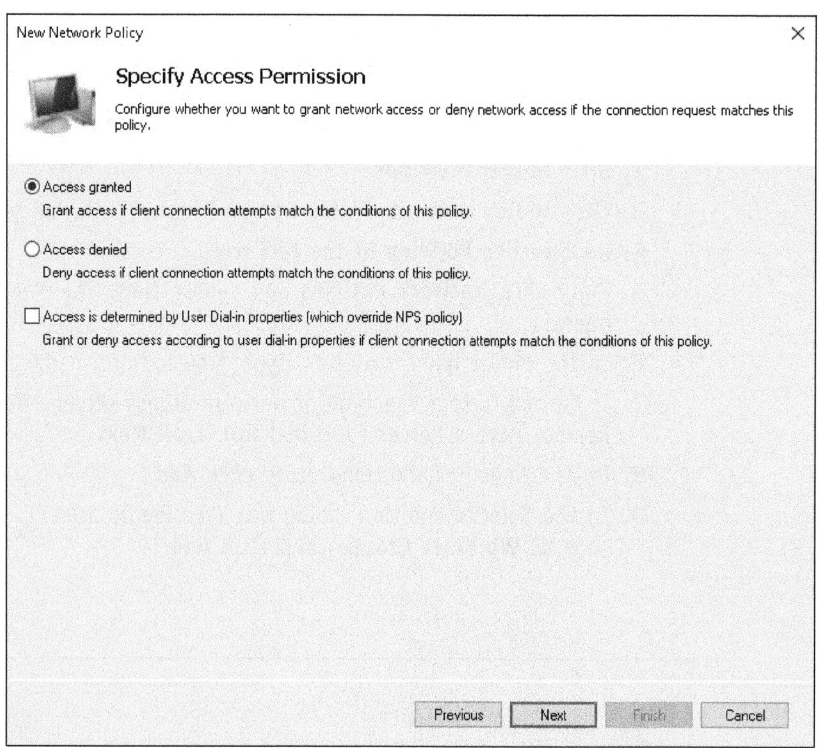

13. On the Configure Authentication Methods page (see Figure 10-19), select or deselect the authentication methods. If you need to add an EAP type, click **Add to specify Microsoft: Smart Card or other certificate**, **Microsoft: Protected EAP (PEAP)**, or **Microsoft: Secured password (EAP-MSCHAP v2)**. Click **OK** and then click **Next.**

Figure 10-19

Configuring authentication methods

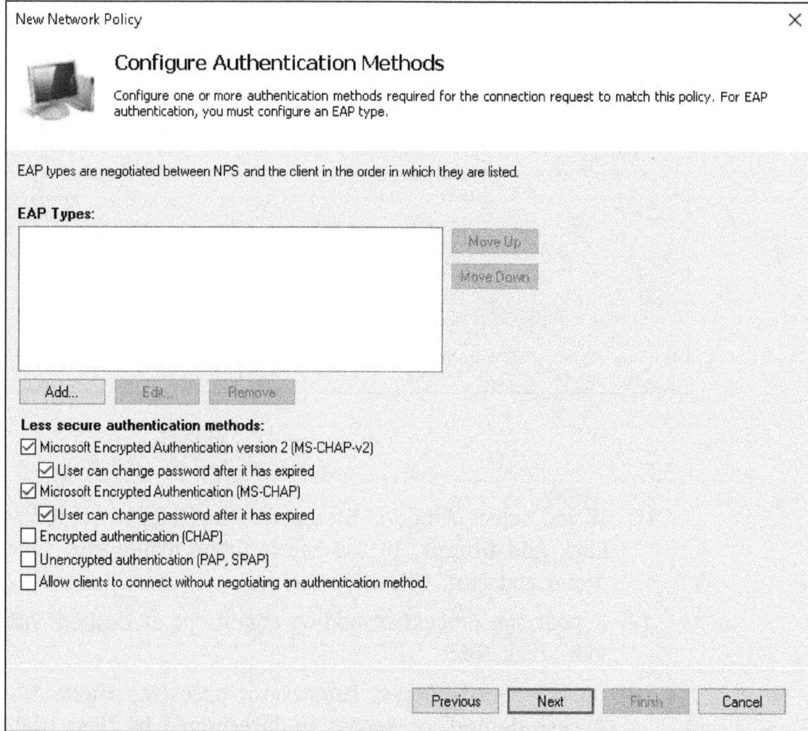

14. On the Configure Constraints page, specify the Idle Timeout, Session Timeout, Called Station ID, Day and time restrictions, and NAS Port Type. Click **Next.**
15. On the Configure Settings page, specify RADIUS attributes and Routing and Remote Access settings. Click **Next.**
16. On the Completing New Network Policy page, click **Finish.** When created, the network policy is listed in the Network Policies pane.

After the network policy has been created, you can modify the network policy by right-clicking the network policy and choosing Properties. In the Properties dialog box, you can then select the Overview tab, Condition tab, Constraints tab, and Settings tab.

MULTILINK AND BANDWIDTH ALLOCATION

When ISDN was introduced, ISDN included multiple channels, which allowed simultaneous voice and data communications. With multilink and Bandwidth Allocation Protocol (BAP) settings, you can specify whether multiple connections form a single connection to increase bandwidth. In addition, you can specify how BAP determines when these extra lines are dropped.

IP FILTERS

The IP filters allow you to control which packets are allowed through the network connection based on IP address. By clicking the Input Filters or Output Filters for IPv4 or IPv6, you can specify to permit or not permit packets. You then use the New button to specify the source network or destination network.

ENCRYPTION

The Encryption settings enable you to specify the supported encryption used with network connections. The available encryption options include:

- **Basic Encryption (MPPE 40-Bit):** For dial-up and PPTP-based VPN connections, MPPE is used with a 40-bit key. For L2TP/IPsec VPN connections, 56-bit DES encryption is used.
- **Strong Encryption (MPPE 56-Bit):** For dial-up and PPTP VPN connections, MPPE is used with a 56-bit key. For L2TP/IPsec VPN connections, 56-bit DES encryption is used.
- **Strongest Encryption (MPPE 128-Bit):** For dial-up and PPTP VPN connections, MPPE is used with a 128-bit key. For L2TP/IPsec VPN connections, 168-bit Triple DES encryption is used.
- **No Encryption:** This option allows unencrypted connections that match the remote access policy conditions. Clear this option to require encryption.

IP ADDRESSING

The last setting in the Routing and Remote Access section is IP settings, which specify how IP addresses are assigned. IP settings include the following options:

- Server Must Supply an IP Address.
- Client May Request an IP Address.
- Server Settings Determine IP Address Assignment (the default setting).
- Assign a Static IP Address.

The assigned IP address is typically used to accommodate vendor-specific attributes for IP addresses.

Configuring and Managing NPS Templates

NPS templates, also known as ***RADIUS templates***, enable you to create RADIUS configuration elements that can be reused on local NPS servers and can be exported to other NPS servers.

CERTIFICATION READY
Configure NPS templates
Objective 4.3

Much like the use of other templates, RADIUS templates (especially RADIUS clients and remote RADIUS servers) are designed to reduce the amount of time and cost that it takes to configure RADIUS on one or more servers. Creating a RADIUS template does not affect the functionality of NPS. It affects only the NPS server when the template is selected and applied when configuring RADIUS. The RADIUS templates are available (see Figure 10-20) for configuration in Templates Management.

Figure 10-20

Looking at template configuration options in the NPS console

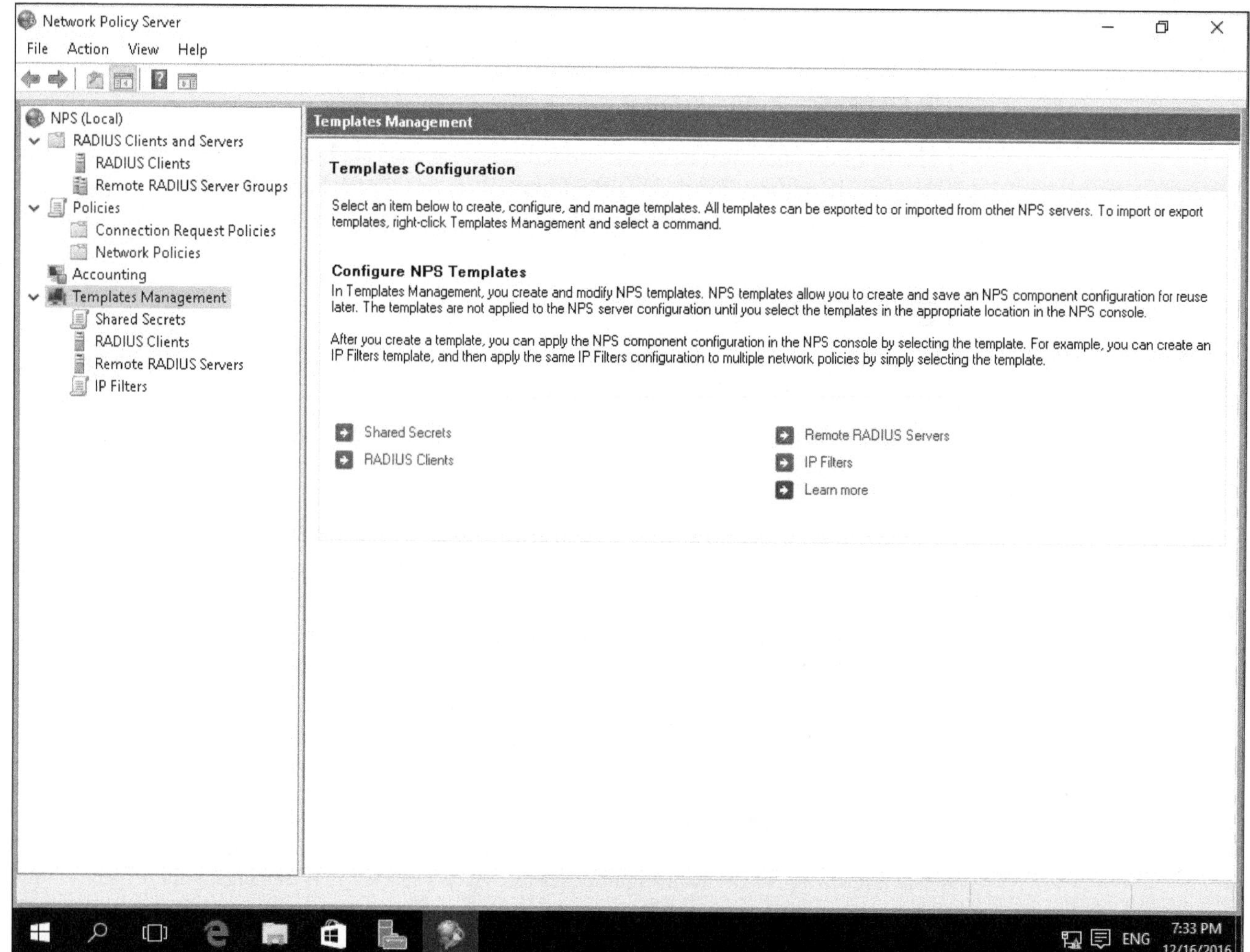

The following NPS template types are available for configuration in Templates Management:

- Shared Secrets
- RADIUS Clients

- Remote RADIUS Servers
- IP Filters

To create a template, right-click a template type in the NPS console tree, such as RADIUS Clients, and then choose New. A New RADIUS Client dialog box opens that allows you to configure your template. Creating a template does not affect the functionality of NPS. It affects only the NPS server when the template is selected and applied when configuring RADIUS. For example, if you right-click RADIUS Clients in the RADIUS Clients and Servers group and choose Properties, you can apply the RADIUS template that was previously created.

EXPORTING AND IMPORTING TEMPLATES

CERTIFICATION READY
Import and export NPS policies
Objective 4.3

To copy templates from one NPS server to another, you can export the templates to a file on the source server and import them into the target NPS server. To export templates so that they can be used on other NPS servers, perform the following steps:

1. To export NPS templates, in the NPS console, right-click **Templates Management** and choose **Export Templates to a File**.
2. To import NPS templates, in the NPS console, right-click **Templates Management** and choose **Import Templates from a Computer** or **Import Templates from a File**.

EXPORTING AND IMPORTING THE NPS CONFIGURATION, INCLUDING NPS POLICIES

You can export the entire NPS configuration, including RADIUS clients and servers, network policy, connection request policy, registry, and logging configuration, from one NPS server for import on another NPS server by using the `netsh` command.

EXPORT AND IMPORT THE NPS CONFIGURATION

GET READY. To export and import the NPS configuration, perform the following steps.

1. Open a command prompt on the source server.
2. Type **netsh** and then press **Enter**.
3. At the netsh prompt, type **nps** and then press **Enter**.
4. At the netsh nps prompt, type **export filename="path\file.xml"exportPSK=YES**, where *path* is the folder location where you want to save the NPS server configuration file, and *file* is the name of the XML file that you want to save. Press **Enter**.
5. When the export is complete, close the command prompt.
6. Copy the XML file to the destination NPS server.
7. Open a command prompt on the target server.
8. At a command prompt on the destination NPS server, type **netsh nps import filename="path\file.xml"** and then press **Enter**. A message appears indicating whether the import from the XML file was successful.
9. When the import is complete, close the command prompt.

WARNING! Do not use this procedure if the source NPS database has a higher version number than the version number of the destination NPS database. You can view the version number of the NPS database from the display of the `netsh nps show config` command.

SKILL SUMMARY

IN THIS LESSON YOU LEARNED:

- Remote Authentication Dial-In User Service (RADIUS) is a networking and client/server protocol that provides centralized authentication, authorization, and accounting (AAA) management for computers that connect and use a network service. It can be used in wireless and remote access connection technologies, 802.1x switches, and Remote Desktop Services Gateway.
- The Microsoft RADIUS server is Network Policy Server (NPS). By installing and configuring RADIUS, you can create and enforce organization-wide network access policies for client health, connection request authentication, and connection request authorization.
- A RADIUS proxy forwards authentication and accounting messages to other RADIUS servers. When NPS is a RADIUS proxy, the NPS becomes a central switching or routing point through which RADIUS access and account messages flow.
- NPS supports RADIUS accounting, which you can use to track network usage for auditing and billing purposes.
- An NPS policy is a set of permissions or restrictions that are used by remote access authenticating servers that determine who, when, and how a client can connect to a network. With the remote access policies, connections can be authorized or denied based on user attributes, group membership, time of day, type of connection, and many other variables.
- NPS templates, also known as RADIUS templates, enable you to create RADIUS configuration elements that can be reused on local NPS servers and can be exported to other NPS servers.

■ Knowledge Assessment

Multiple Choice

Select the correct answer for each of the following questions.

1. Which of the following ports are used by NPS for authentication and accounting? (Choose four answers.)
   a. 389
   b. 1812
   c. 1813
   d. 80
   e. 1645
   f. 1646
2. Several VPN servers are configured using RRAS. Which of the following is the best way to collect information on when and how long a user is connected through the VPN?
   a. Health policies
   b. RADIUS Accounting
   c. System health validators (SHVs)
   d. Connection request policy
   e. Windows Accounting provider

3. Which of the following can be used to provide central authentication of VPN and wireless connections on the network?
   a. Use an NPS server.
   b. Use an HRA.
   c. Use CMAK.
   d. Use RRAS.
4. Which of the following are access clients? (Choose all that apply.)
   a. Domain controller
   b. VPN server
   c. Dial-up server
   d. 802.1X server
5. Which of the following is used to save a configuration so that it can be reused on other NPS servers?
   a. Filter
   b. Shared secrets
   c. Templates
   d. Health policy
6. Which two locations can NPS log to? (Choose two answers.)
   a. Oracle database
   b. SQL server
   c. Text file
   d. XML repository
7. Which of the following are used with NPS templates? (Choose all that apply.)
   a. Remote RADIUS servers
   b. RADIUS passwords
   c. RADIUS proxy
   d. RADIUS clients
8. The Microsoft RADIUS server is known as which of the following?
   a. Network Policy Server
   b. Routing and Remote Access Server
   c. Network Access Policy Server
   d. AAA Server
9. Which of the following tracks network usage for auditing and billing purposes?
   a. RADIUS Authorization
   b. RADIUS Access
   c. RADIUS Accounting
   d. RADIUS Auditing
10. Which of the following is the default location for the log files if text files are used for RADIUS accounting?
    a. C:\Temp
    b. C:\Windows\System32\LogFiles
    c. C:\Logs
    d. C:\RADIUS\Logs
11. Which types of policies are available on the Network Policy Server (NPS) on Windows Server 2016? (Choose all that apply.)
    a. Health policies
    b. Network policies
    c. Connection request policies
    d. Accounting policies

12. Which policy is used to establish sets of conditions and settings that specify which RADIUS servers perform the authentication, authorization, and accounting of connection requests received by the NPS server from RADIUS clients?
   a. Health policies
   b. Network policies
   c. Connection request policies
   d. Accounting policies
13. Which policy establishes sets of conditions, constraints, and settings that specify who is authorized to connect to the network?
   a. Health policies
   b. Network policies
   c. Connection request policies
   d. Accounting policies
14. Which policy should be used to limit when a user can log on through the VPN?
   a. Health policies
   b. Network policies
   c. Connection request policies
   d. Accounting policies
15. Which of the following can be used to specify which RADIUS server handles authentication for a VPN server?
   a. Health policies
   b. Network policies
   c. Connection request policies
   d. Accounting policies
16. Which of the following can be used to stop an NPS server from acting as a RADIUS server and to stop processing connection requests locally?
   a. Stop the RADIUS Server service.
   b. Stop the RADIUS Client service.
   c. Delete the default network policy.
   d. Delete the default connection request policy.
17. Which of the following can be used to configure an NPS server as a RADIUS proxy? (Choose two answers.)
   a. Define a network policy.
   b. Define a connection request policy.
   c. Configure a RADIUS server group.
   d. Add the computer to the RADIUS proxy group.

Best Answer

Choose the letter that corresponds to the best answer. More than one answer choice may achieve the goal. Select the BEST answer.

1. You administer a server called Server1 that runs Network Policy Server. You install a second server called Server2 that sends all requests to server1. Which of the following should you do next?
   a. Modify health policies.
   b. Modify the RADIUS clients.
   c. Modify the remote RADIUS server groups.
   d. Modify the network policies.

2. You administer a server called Server1 that runs Network Policy Server. Server1 is configured to use SQL logging. You install Server2, which also runs Network Policy Server. You want to make sure that the two servers are configured the same. Therefore, you export the NPS settings from Server1 and import the settings into Server2. Which of the following should you do next?
   a. Create an ODBC data course to Server1.
   b. Create an ODBC data source to a SQL server.
   c. Manually configure the SQL logging settings.
   d. Restart the Server2.
3. When using a RADIUS proxy, which policy is used to determine which connection requests are forwarded to another RADIUS server?
   a. RADIUS proxy policy
   b. Dynamic policy
   c. Proxy forward policy
   d. Connection request policy
4. Which of the following are reasons to use multiple RADIUS servers? (Choose two answers.)
   a. To enable auditing
   b. To provide multiple RADIUS services
   c. To break up the workload when performing authentication
   d. To provide fault tolerance
5. When a computer or device accesses a VPN server and uses RADIUS for authentication, the computer or device is referred to as which of the following?
   a. RADIUS client
   b. Access server
   c. Access client
   d. RADIUS proxy
6. You administer three NPS servers known as Server1, Server2, and Server3. On Server1, you have a Remote RADIUS Server Group that contains Server2 and Server3. Server2 and Server 3 are configured to authenticate remote users. Which of the following actions should you take to configure Server1 to forward RADIUS authentication requests to Server2 and Server3?
   a. Create a network policy.
   b. Create a remediation server group.
   c. Create a connection request policy.
   d. Create a health policy.
7. You are an administrator for the Contoso Corporation where you have a single Active Directory domain and an enterprise root certificate authority. You decide to use NAP to protect the VPN connections. You build the following two servers:

   Server1 NPS, Remediation server, and SHVS
   Server2 VPN server and RADIUS server

   Which of the following actions should you take to ensure that all client computers that attempt a VPN connection have the system health policy applied?
   a. Configure the clients as RADIUS clients.
   b. Add the NAP role to the domain controller.
   c. Reconfigure Server1 as a RADIUS client.
   d. Reconfigure Server2 as a RADIUS client.

8. You administer a server running Windows Server 2016 that is configured as a RRAS server. You want only members of the global group named Sales to connect using a VPN connection. Which of the following steps is necessary for granting access to the Sales group?
   a. Add the Sales group to the RAS and IAS Servers group.
   b. Create a new network policy and define a group-based condition for the Sales group. Set the access permission of the policy to Access Granted. Set the processing order of the policy to 1.
   c. Create a new connection request policy and define a group-based condition for the Sales group. Set the access permission of the policy to Access Granted. Set the processing order of the policy to 1.
   d. Create a new network policy and define a group-based condition for the Sales group. Set the access permission of the policy to Access Granted. Set the processing order of the policy to Default.

Matching and Identification

1. Match the term with the definition.

   ____ **a)** RADIUS clients

   ____ **b)** Access client

   ____ **c)** RADIUS

   ____ **d)** RADIUS proxy

   1. A networking and client/server protocol that provides AAA management for computers and network devices

   2. Servers that use AAA services for central authentication

   3. A workstation that connects to a network through a remote server and requires authentication to connect to the network

   4. A server that provides central switching for RADIUS access and account messages

Build List

1. Specify the correct order of the three As for AAA management. Not all of the answers will be used.

   ____ Accounting
   ____ Authentication
   ____ Allowed access
   ____ Attribute
   ____ Authorization
   ____ Application
   ____ Access control

2. Specify the correct order of steps necessary to using RADIUS authentication.

   ____ The connection attempt is authorized.
   ____ The NPS server sends an Accounting-Response to the access server.
   ____ The request is forward to an NPS server, which evaluates the connection request.
   ____ User credentials are checked and the dial-in properties are obtained.
   ____ The access server sends an Accounting-Request message to the NPS server.
   ____ A client computer accesses a VPN server, and a connection request is generated.

Business Case Scenarios

Scenario 10-1: Supporting Multiple VPN Servers

You administer two VPN servers. One is located at the main corporate office and the second is located at the backup site. You want to provide centralized authentication and logging. Describe your recommended solution.

Scenario 10-2: Securing VPN Connections

Your manager approaches you to discuss implementing VPN for the corporate users. However, he is concerned about security. Describe your recommendation for maintaining the highest level of security.

Scenario 10-3: Defining Policies

You administer two VPN servers. One is located at the main corporate office and the second is located at the backup site. You want to create policies that forward authentication and authorization requests to an NPS server and have the users approved if they are members of the Help Desk, Management, or Sales group. Describe your recommended solution.

Scenario 10-4: Duplicating Servers

You are an administrator for the Contoso Corporation and experienced a recent server failure in which the RADIUS server was down for an extended period of time. You need to create a second NPS server for your organization to provide fault tolerance at the DR site. However, the server will only be used when the first server is not available. Describe the easiest way to duplicate all of the settings of the first NPS server on to the second NPS server and how to further configure the server to provide the specified functionality.

Implementing Distributed File System (DFS) and Branch Office Solutions

70-741 EXAM OBJECTIVE

Objective 5.2 – Implement Distributed File System (DFS) and branch office solutions. This objective may include but is not limited to the following: Install and configure DFS Namespaces; configure DFS Replication targets; configure replication scheduling; configure Remote Differential Compression (RDC) settings; configure staging; configure fault tolerance; clone a Distributed File System Replication (DFSR) database; recover DFSR databases; optimize DFS Replication; install and configure BranchCache; implement distributed and hosted cache modes; implement BranchCache for web, file, and application servers; troubleshoot BranchCache.

Lesson Heading	Exam Objective
Understanding Branch Offices	Install and configure DFS Namespaces
Installing and Configuring DFS Namespace	
• Installing DFS Namespace	
• Configuring DFS Namespaces	
• Managing Referrals	
• Managing DFS Security	
Installing and Configuring DFS Replication	Configure DFS Replication targets
• Configuring DFS Replication Targets	Configure replication scheduling
• Configuring Replication Scheduling	Configure Remote Differential Compression (RDC) settings
• Configuring Remote Differential Compression	Configure staging
• Configuring Staging	Configure fault tolerance
• Configuring Fault Tolerance Using DFS	Clone a Distributed File System Replication (DFSR) database
• Cloning a DFS Database	Recover DFSR databases
• Recovering DFS Databases	Optimize DFS Replication
• Optimizing DFS Replication	
Configuring BranchCache	Install and configure BranchCache
• Installing and Configuring BranchCache	Implement BranchCache for web, file, and application servers
• Implementing Distributed and Hosted Cache Modes	Implement distributed and hosted cache modes
• Troubleshooting BranchCache	Troubleshoot BranchCache

LESSON HEADING	EXAM OBJECTIVE
Configuring Print Services	
• Installing Printers	
• Understanding Printer Properties	
• Configuring Printer Sharing	
• Configuring Branch Office Direct Printing	

KEY TERMS

Branch Office Direct Printing
BranchCache
Conflict and Deleted folder
DFS Namespace
DFS Replication
distributed cache mode
Distributed File System (DFS)
domain-based namespaces
full mesh topology
hosted cache mode
hub/spoke topology
local printer
network printer
print device
printer
printer permissions
referral
Remote Differential Compression (RDC)
replication group
staging folder
stand-alone DFS

Understanding Branch Offices

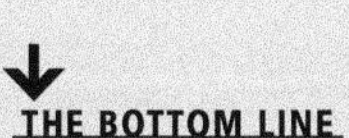

Over the last couple of years, Microsoft has devoted a great deal of attention to branch office computing and the complications that distance and isolation present to IT administrators. However, before branch office administrators can take charge, enterprise administrators must create the policies that the branch offices will follow. One of the biggest factors in Branch Offices is that they connect to the corporate offices with slower WAN links.

What constitutes a branch office? This is a question that can have various answers, even within a single enterprise. For a large organization, a branch office can be a headquarters on another continent, with hundreds or thousands of users. Smaller organizations might have branch offices with only a handful of users. Obviously, these offices have vastly different requirements, and enterprise administrators must distinguish between them in their branch office strategies.

For the purposes of this lesson, imagine an organization with branches in three sizes: a large office with 1,000 users, a medium-sized office with 100 users, and a small office with 10 users. Each office has users that must access resources hosted by the corporate headquarters, but they havev varying amounts of money, equipment, and administrative expertise with which to do that. Table 11-1 lists the basic resources allotted to each branch size. You will learn about the additional resources needed by each as this lesson progresses.

Table 11-1

Branch Office Topology Specifications

Branch Office Size	Large	Medium	Small
Number of users	1,000	100	10
Connection to HQ	44.736 Mbps (T-3)	1.544 Mbps (T-1)	512 Kbps (VPN)
IT support	Full staff	1 administrator	Branch manager
Domain controllers	2	1	0
DNS servers	2	1	1
Global catalog server	1	1	0
Separate site object	Yes	Yes	No

A large branch office running its own domain must have at least two AD DS domain controllers for fault-tolerance purposes, with one or both also functioning as a Domain Name System (DNS) server. It must also have a global catalog server to provide the branch office users with the ability to search other domains in the forest.

A medium-sized office with 100 users should have at least one domain controller, to provide users with local authentication capabilities, as well as a DNS server and a global catalog server. An office of this size should be equipped with a server closet to physically secure the domain controller and other vital components.

Although it might have its own servers for local data storage, the small branch office should generally not have a domain controller, mainly because no one at the location is qualified to maintain it. Small offices also typically lack the physical security needed to protect a domain controller from unauthorized access or theft. Therefore, users must access a domain controller at another location to authenticate.

Installing and Configuring DFS Namespace

Distributed File System improves on the use of the shared folders by enabling you to organize your shared folders and enabling you to distribute shares on multiple servers.

CERTIFICATION READY
Install and configure DFS Namespaces
Objective 5.2

Distributed File System (DFS) is a set of technologies that enable a Windows server to organize multiple distributed SMB file shares into a distributed file system. Although the shares can be on different servers, the location is transparent to the users. Finally, DFS can provide redundancy to improve data availability while minimizing the amount of traffic passing over the WAN links. The two technologies in DFS include:

- DFS Namespaces
- DFS Replication

If you have a site with many file servers and many shared folders, some users will have difficulty finding the files that they need as they have to remember the server name and shared folder name that make up the UNC. ***DFS Namespace*** enables you to group shared folders into a single logical structure. In other words, a DFS Namespace is a shared folder of shared folders (which can be on multiple servers).

DFS is a virtual namespace technology that enables you to create a single directory tree that lists other shared folders. Creating a DFS Namespace allows users to locate their files more easily. See Figure 11-1.

Figure 11-1

Linking to shared folders with DFS Namespace

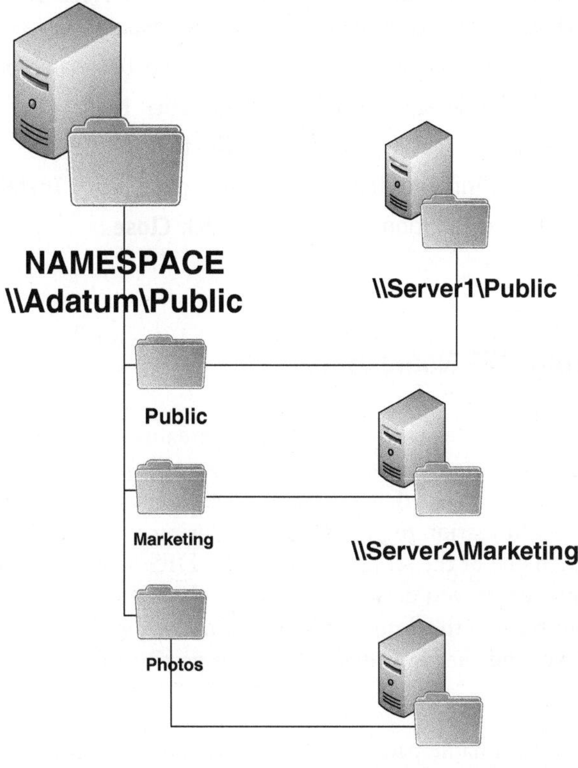

The actual shared folders are referred to as the targets of the virtual folders in the namespace. DFS can be combined with DFS Replication, which increases availability and automatically connects users to shared folders in the same Active Directory site, when available, instead of connecting to another folder connected over a slower WAN link.

Installing DFS Namespace

Installing DFS Namespace is a simple process of adding the appropriate role using Server Manager. However, you should also install the File Server service so that you can create file shares.

The DFS Management Tools installs the DFS Management snap-in, the DFS Namespace module for Windows PowerShell, and command-line tools.

INSTALL DFS NAMESPACE

GET READY. To install DFS Namespace, perform the following steps.

1. Log on to LON-SVR1 as **adatum\administrator** with the password of **Pa$$w0rd.**
2. Click **Start** and click **Server Manager.**
3. At the top of Server Manager, click **Manage > Add Roles and Features.** The Add Roles and Feature Wizard opens.
4. On the Before You Begin page, click **Next.**

5. Click **Role-based or feature-based installation** and then click **Next.**
6. Click **Select a server from the server pool**, click the name of the server to install DFS to, and then click **Next.**
7. Scroll down and expand **File and Storage Services** and then expand **File and iSCSI Services.** Click **File Server** and **DFS Namespace.**
8. When you are prompted to add features to DFS Namespace, click **Add Features.**
9. Back on the Select Server Roles page, click **Next.**
10. On the Select Features page, click **Next.**
11. On the Confirm Installation Selections page, click **Install.**
12. When the installation is complete, click **Close.**

Configuring DFS Namespaces

There are two types of DFS Namespaces: domain-based namespace and stand-alone namespace. With ***domain-based namespaces***, the configuration is stored in Active Directory, which means that you don't have to rely on a single server to provide the namespace information to your clients. By using a domain-based namespace, if you change the name of the server that runs the DFS Namespace service and the name of the server changes, you do not have to change the namespace. The namespace changes only if you rename the domain. With ***a stand-alone DFS***, the configuration is stored on the server and the server name becomes part of the main path to the namespace.

When you create a namespace, the Windows Server 2008 mode is selected by default, which supports up to 50,000 folders with targets per namespace and access-based enumeration. Access-based enumeration means that users can see only the folders and files that they have permission to access. If a user does not have permission to the folder or file, the folder or file does not even show in a directory listing. To use Windows Server 2008 mode, Active Directory must use the Windows Server 2008 domain functional level. If you deselect the Windows Server 2008 mode, you will use the Windows 2000 Server mode, which supports only up to 5,000 folders.

CREATE A DFS NAMESPACE

GET READY. To create a DFS Namespace, perform the following steps.

1. Log on to LON-SVR1 as **adatum\administrator** with the password of **Pa$$w0rd.**
2. Open **Server Manager.**
3. Click **Tools > DFS Management** to open the DFS Management console (see Figure 11-2).
4. In the left-pane, right-click **Namespaces** and choose **New Namespace.** The New Namespace Wizard starts.
5. On the Namespace Server page (see Figure 11-3), in the Server text box, type in the name of the server that hosts the DFS Namespace. Click **Next.**
6. On the Namespace Name and Settings page, in the Name text box, type the name of the namespace. The name appears after the server (stand-alone namespace) or domain name (domain-based namespace). Click **Next.**

Figure 11-2

Using the DFS Management console

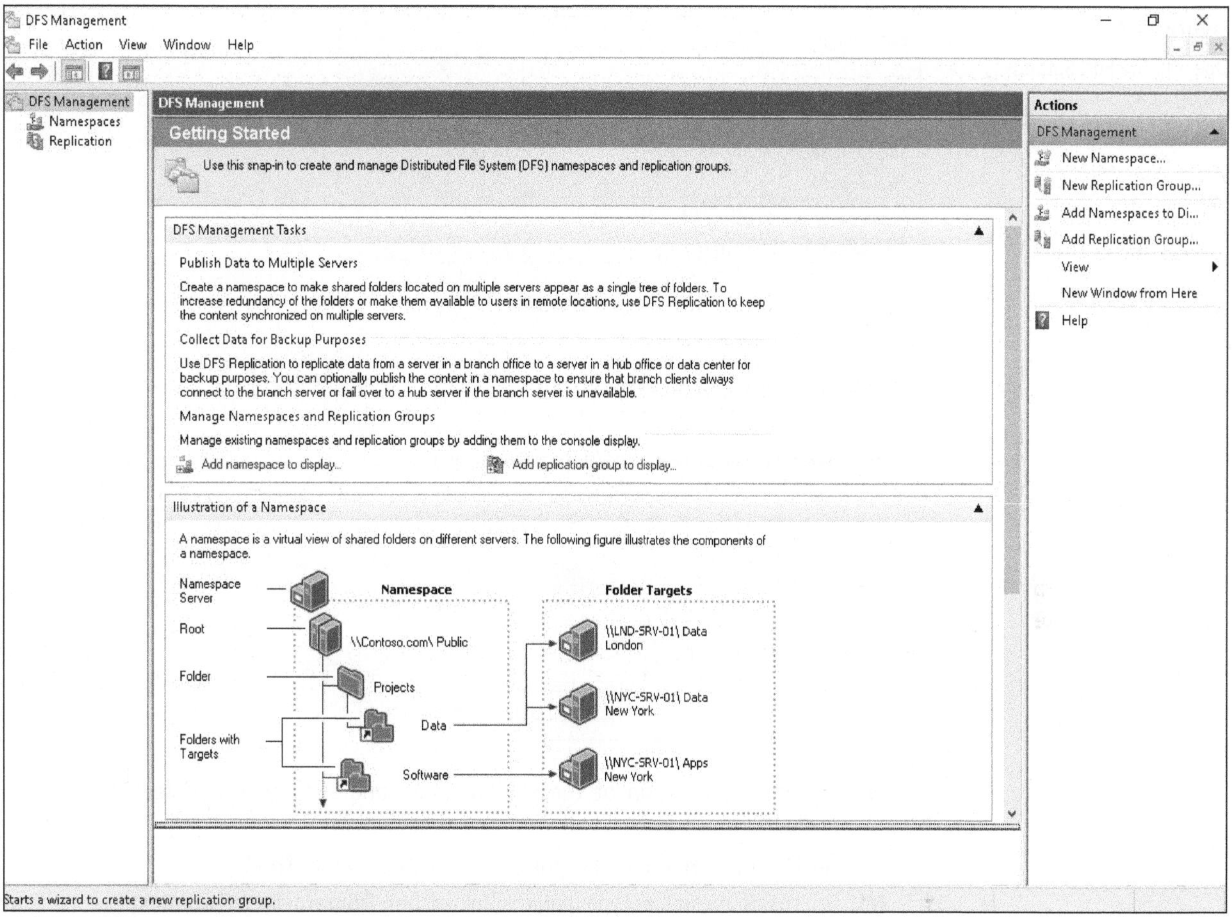

DFS Management
File Action View Window Help
DFS Management
Namespaces
Replication
DFS Management
Getting Started
Use this snap-in to create and manage Distributed File System (DFS) namespaces and replication groups.
DFS Management Tasks
Publish Data to Multiple Servers
Create a namespace to make shared folders located on multiple servers appear as a single tree of folders. To increase redundancy of the folders or make them available to users in remote locations, use DFS Replication to keep the content synchronized on multiple servers.
Collect Data for Backup Purposes
Use DFS Replication to replicate data from a server in a branch office to a server in a hub office or data center for backup purposes. You can optionally publish the content in a namespace to ensure that branch clients always connect to the branch server or fail over to a hub server if the branch server is unavailable.
Manage Namespaces and Replication Groups
Manage existing namespaces and replication groups by adding them to the console display.
Add namespace to display...
Add replication group to display...
Illustration of a Namespace
A namespace is a virtual view of shared folders on different servers. The following figure illustrates the components of a namespace.
Namespace Server
Root
Folder
Folders with Targets
Namespace
\\Contoso.com\ Public
Projects
Data
Software
Folder Targets
\\LND-SRV-01\ Data London
\\NYC-SRV-01\ Data New York
\\NYC-SRV-01\ Apps New York
Actions
DFS Management
New Namespace...
New Replication Group...
Add Namespaces to Di...
Add Replication Group...
View
New Window from Here
Help
Starts a wizard to create a new replication group.

Figure 11-3

Entering the name of the server on the Namespace Server page

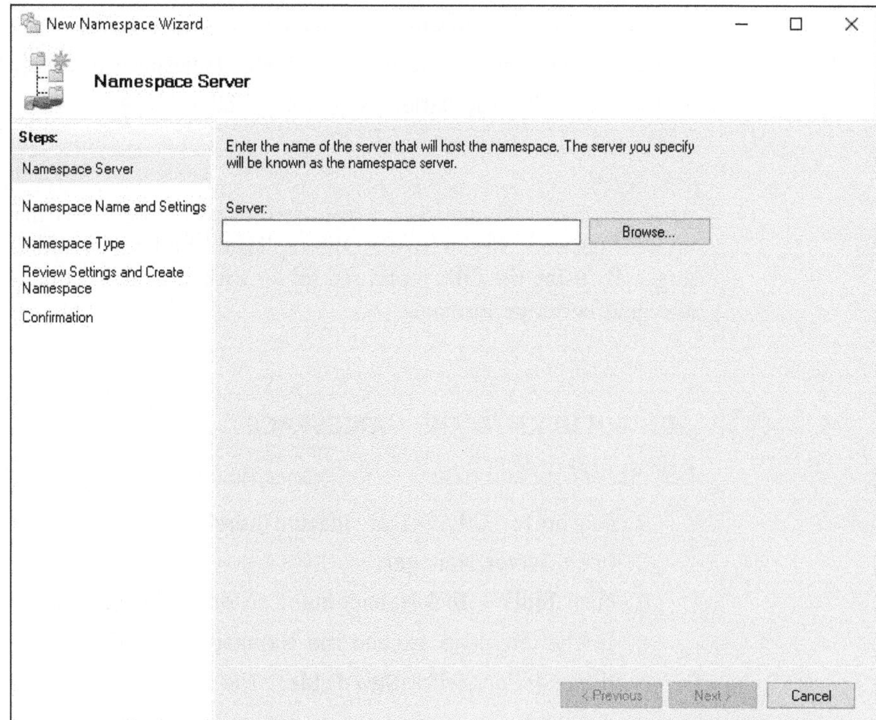

7. To change the location of the shared folder on the server and the shared permissions, click **Edit Settings**. The Edit Settings dialog box opens (see Figure 11-4).

Figure 11-4

Opening the Edit Settings dialog box

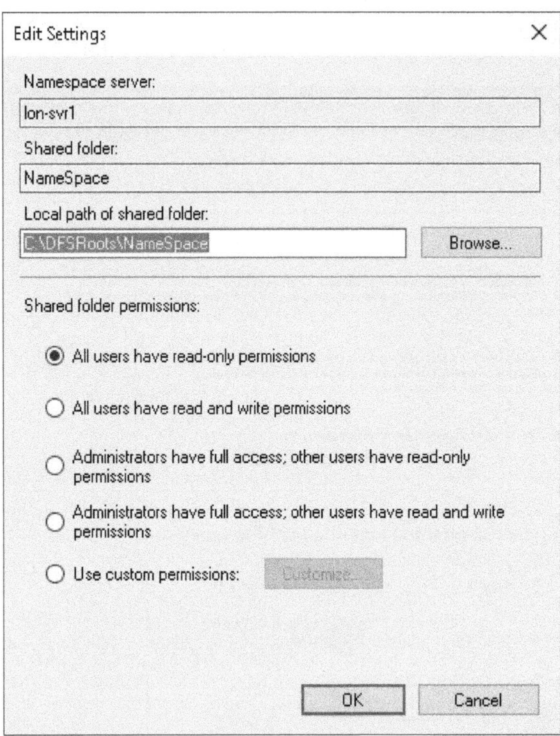

8. Specify the location of the shared folder and specify the Shared folder permissions. Click **OK** to close the Edit Settings dialog box.
9. On the Namespace Name and Settings page, click **Next.**
10. On the Namespace Type page, click either **Domain-based namespace** or **Stand-alone namespace.**
11. Leave the Enable Windows Server 2008 mode option enabled. Notice the entire path of the domain-based namespace. Click **Next.**
12. On the Review Settings and Create Namespace page, click **Create.**
13. When the installation is complete, click **Close.**

After you create the namespace, you need to add folders to it that point to the shared folders on your network. If you have a DFS replicated folder, you add each replicated folder to the target. By using the DFS replicated folder with the DFS Namespace, you provide fault tolerance and better performance.

ADD FOLDERS TO THE NAMESPACE

GET READY. To add folders to the namespace, perform the following steps.

1. Log on to LON-SVR1 as **adatum\administrator** with the password of **Pa$$w0rd.**
2. Open **Server Manager.**
3. Click **Tools > DFS Management** to open the DFS Management console.
4. In the left pane, expand the **Namespaces** folder and select the desired namespace.
5. Under Actions, click **New Folder.** The New Folder dialog box opens (see Figure 11-5).

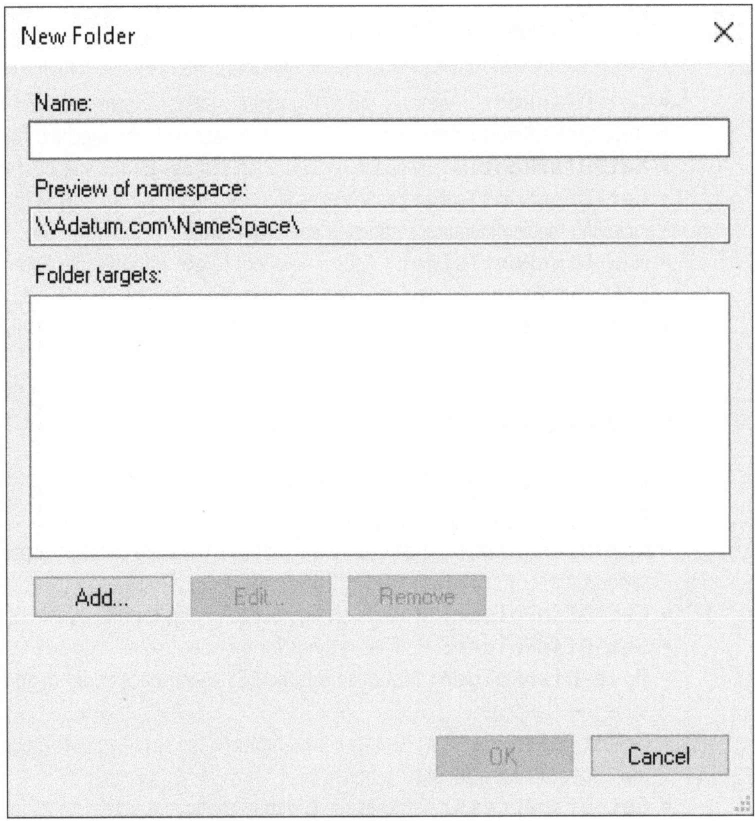

Figure 11-5
Adding a folder to the namespace

6. In the Name text box, type the name of the shared folder. The name should be a descriptive name, but does not have to be the same name as the shared folder that you will be referencing.
7. To specify the shared folder, click **Add.**
8. In the Add Folder Target dialog box, type in the UNC to the desired shared folder. Click **OK.**
9. If you have a DFS replicated folder for your target, add the replicated paths of the folder.
10. Click **OK** to close the New Folder dialog box.

To avoid a single point of failure, you need to have multiple DFS name servers. If the single namespace server goes down, no one can access the data.

ADD NAMESPACE SERVERS TO A DFS NAMESPACE

GET READY. After you install DFS Namespace to LON-SVR2, to add LON-SVR2 to a DFS Namespace, perform the following steps.

1. Log on to LON-SVR1 as **adatum\administrator** with the password of **Pa$$w0rd.**
2. Open **Server Manager.**
3. Click **Tools > DFS Management** to open the DFS Management console.
4. Under the Namespaces node, click a namespace.
5. Click the **Namespace Servers** tab.
6. Under Actions, click **Add Namespace Server.**
7. In the Add Namespace Server dialog box, in the Namespace server text box, type **LON-SVR2** and click **OK.**

USING WINDOWS POWERSHELL

You can manage DFS Namespace using the following Windows PowerShell cmdlets:

- **Get-DfsnRoot:** Retrieves the configuration settings for the specified namespaces
- **New-DfsnRoot:** Creates a new DFS Namespace with the specified configuration settings
- **Set-DfsnRoot:** Modifies the configuration settings for the specified existing DFS Namespace
- **Get-DfsnRootTarget:** Retrieves all the configured root targets for the specified namespace root, including the configuration settings of each root target
- **New-DfsnRootTarget:** Adds a new root target with the specified configuration settings to an existing DFS Namespace
- **Set-DfsnRootTarget:** Sets configuration settings to specified values for a namespace root target of an existing DFS Namespace
- **Remove-DfsnRootTarget:** Deletes an existing namespace root target of a DFS Namespace
- **Get-DfsnServerConfiguration:** Retrieves the configuration settings of the specified DFS Namespace server
- **Set-DfsnServerConfiguration:** Modifies configuration settings for the specified server hosting DFS Namespace(s)
- **New-DfsnFolder:** Creates a new folder in an existing DFS Namespace with the specified configuration settings
- **Get-DfsnFolder:** Retrieves configuration settings for the specified existing DFS Namespace folder
- **Set-DfsnFolder:** Modifies settings for the specified existing DFS Namespace folder with folder targets
- **Move-DfsnFolder:** Moves an existing DFS Namespace folder to an alternate specified location in the same DFS Namespace
- **Grant-DfsnAccess:** Grants access rights to the specified user/group account for the specified DFS Namespace folder with folder targets
- **Get-DfsnAccess:** Retrieves the currently configured access rights for the specified DFS Namespace folder with folder targets
- **Revoke-DfsnAccess:** Revokes the right to access a DFS Namespace folder with folder targets or enumerate its contents from the specified user or group account
- **Remove-DfsnAccess:** Removes the specified user/group account from the Access Control List (ACL) of the DFS Namespace folder with folder targets
- **Remove-DfsnFolder:** Deletes an existing DFS Namespace folder with a folder target
- **New-DfsnFolderTarget:** Adds a new folder target with the specified configuration settings to an existing DFS Namespace folder
- **Get-DfsnFolderTarget:** Retrieves configuration settings of folder target(s) of an existing DFS Namespace folder
- **Set-DfsnFolderTarget:** Modifies settings for the folder target of an existing DFS Namespace folder
- **Remove-DfsnFolderTarget:** Deletes a folder target of an existing DFS Namespace folder

To manage DFS Namespace, you can use the following commands:

- **DfsUtil:** Manages DFS Namespaces, server, and client computers
- **DfsCmd:** Configures DFS folders and folder targets in a DFS Namespace
- **DfsDiag:** Performs diagnostics tests of DFS Namespaces

Managing Referrals

A ***referral*** is an ordered list of servers or targets that a client computer receives from a domain controller or namespace server when the user accesses a namespace root or a DFS folder with targets. After a computer receives a referral, it reaches the first server on the list. If the server is not available, it tries to access the second server. If that server is not available, it goes to the next server.

If you right-click the namespace and choose Properties, you can help choose which server the client uses when you have multiple folders for a shared folder. Figure 11-6 shows the Namespace Properties dialog box. No matter which ordering method is selected, if a client is on the same site as the target, it always chooses the target. Then, by default, it chooses the closest server (lowest cost). You can also select *Random order*, which performs a load balancing for the targets at the other sites. Lastly, you can select the Exclude targets outside of the client's site option, which prevents the clients from accessing targets at other sites.

Figure 11-6

Configuring the referrals for a namespace

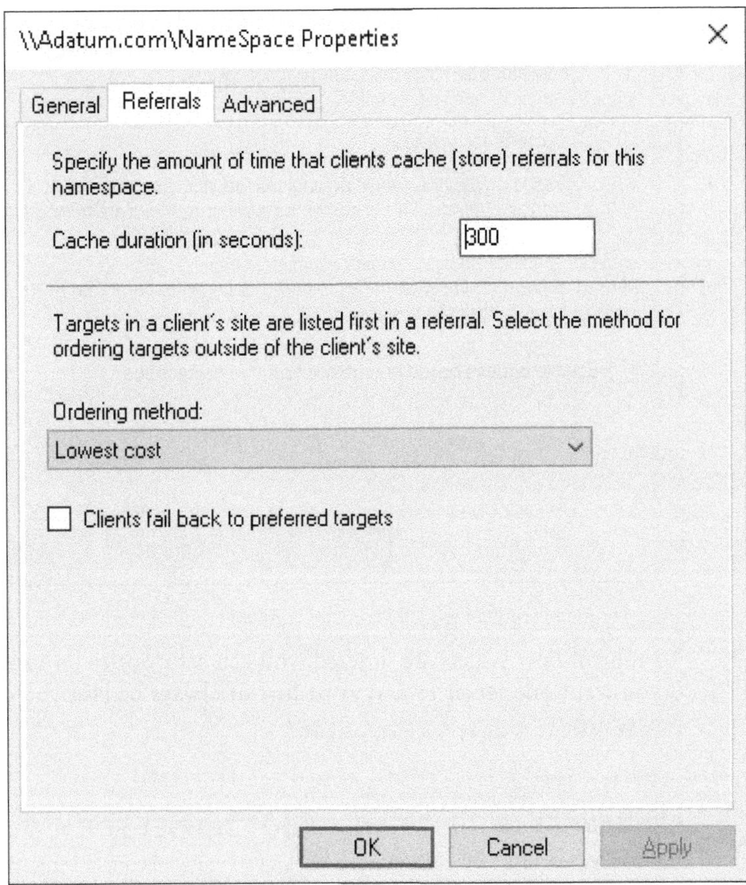

If a server becomes unavailable, you can have a client fail back to targets that were previously unavailable if the server becomes available again and at lower cost than the target the client uses. This is done by selecting the Clients fail back to preferred targets check box.

On the Advanced tab (see Figure 11-7), you can optimize polling. To maintain a consistent domain-based namespace across namespace servers, the namespace servers periodically poll Active Directory Domain Services (AD DS) to obtain the most current namespace data.

By default, the Optimize for consistency option is selected. It causes the namespace servers to poll the PDC emulator each time the namespace changes. If you have more than 16 namespace servers, you should choose the Optimize for scalability option to reduce the load on the PDC emulator. Unfortunately, this option increases the time it requires for changes to the namespace to replicate to all namespace servers, which might cause users to see an inconsistent view of the namespace while namespace changes are replicated to all servers.

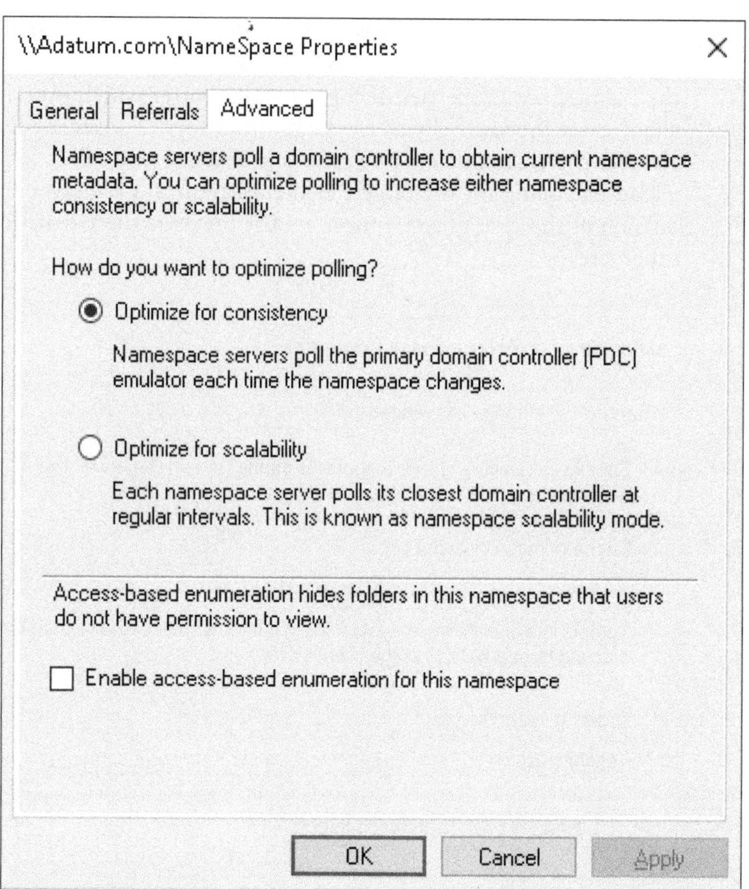

Figure 11-7

Optimizing namespace servers polling options

To control how targets are ordered, you can set priority on individual targets. For example, if you want one server to always be first or always be last, you can use the following procedure.

SET TARGET PRIORITY ON A ROOT TARGET FOR A DOMAIN-BASED NAMESPACE

GET READY. To set the target priority on a root target for a domain-based namespace, perform the following steps.

1. Log on to LON-SVR1 as **adatum\administrator** with the password of **Pa$$w0rd.**
2. Open **Server Manager.**
3. Click **Tools > DFS Management** to open the DFS Management console.
4. In the left pane, expand the **Namespaces** folder and select the desired namespace.
5. In the center pane, click the **Namespace Servers** tab.
6. Right-click the root target with the priority that you want to change and choose **Properties.**
7. In the Properties dialog box, click the **Advanced** tab.
8. Select the **Override referral ordering** check box, as shown in Figure 11-8, and then click the priority that you want:
   - **First among all targets:** Specifies that users should always be referred to this target if the target is available

- **Last among all targets:** Specifies that users should never be referred to this target unless all other targets are unavailable
- **First among targets of equal cost:** Specifies that users should be referred to this target before other targets of equal cost (which usually means other targets in the same site)
- **Last among targets of equal cost:** Specifies that users should never be referred to this target if there are other targets of equal cost available (which usually means other targets in the same site)

Figure 11-8

Optimizing namespace servers via referral ordering options

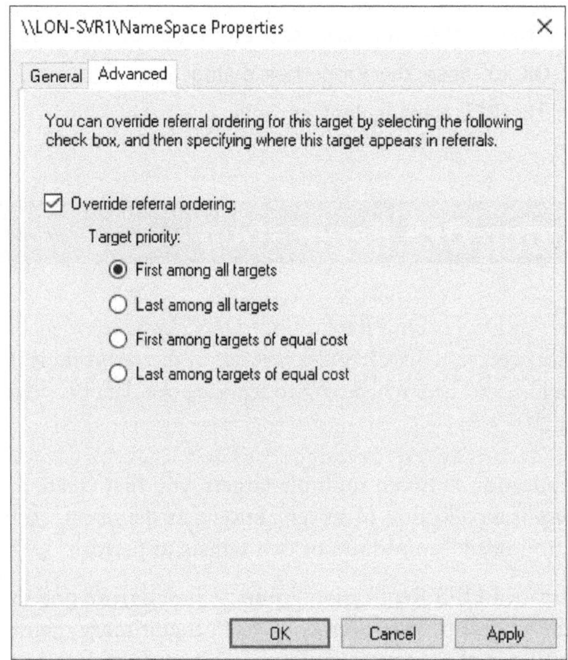

9. Click **OK** to close the Properties dialog box.
10. Close the DFS Management console.

Managing DFS Security

Because DFS Namespace is a specialized shared folder of shared folders, you still secure these folders with share permissions and NTFS permissions. It is recommended that you first configure the share and NTFS permissions on folders that host namespace roots and folder targets before configuring DFS. If you have multiple namespace root servers or if folder target servers will be utilized, you need to manually synchronize permissions between the servers to avoid access problems.

Access-based enumeration hides files and folders that users do not have permission to access. To control access-based enumeration of files and folders in folder targets, you must enable access-based enumeration on each shared folder by using the following procedure.

ENABLE ACCESS-BASED ENUMERATION FOR A NAMESPACE

GET READY. To enable access-based enumeration for a namespace, perform the following steps.

1. Log on to LON-SVR1 as **adatum\administrator** with the password of **Pa$$w0rd.**
2. Open **Server Manager.**
3. Click **Tools > DFS Management** to open the DFS Management console.
4. In the left pane, right-click the namespace and choose **Properties.**
5. Click the **Advanced** tab.
6. Select the **Enable access-based enumeration for this namespace** check box.
7. Click **OK** to close the Properties dialog box.
8. Close the DFS Management console.

■ Installing and Configuring DFS Replication

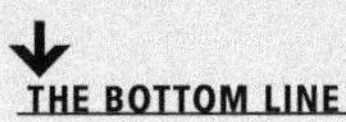

The other part of DFS is DFS Replication. ***DFS Replication*** enables you to replicate folders between multiple servers. To allow efficient use of the network, it propagates only the changes, uses compression, and uses scheduling to replicate the data between the servers.

To enable replication between multiple targets, you first create a replication group. The ***replication group*** is a collection of servers, known as members, each of which holds a target of a DFS folder. You need a minimum of two targets to perform DFS Replication.

When you create a DFS Replication group, you designate one server as the primary member of the replication group. Files then copy from the primary member to the other target servers. If any of the files in the target folders are different, DFS Replication overwrites the other files.

The primary disadvantage of using DFS Replication is that you need to have sufficient storage space available on each server that hosts the DFS replication folders and you need extra space so that DFS Replication can process the replication.

When using DFS Replication, you should keep in mind the following limitations:

- A replication group can have up to 256 members with 256 replicated folders.
- Each server can be a member of up to 256 replication groups, with as many as 256 connections (128 incoming and 128 outgoing).
- A member server can support up to 1 TB of replicated files.
- You can have up to eight million replicated files per volume.

The best method to recover from a disaster is to use backups. DFS Replication can also be used in conjunction with backups to provide a WAN backup solution. For example, if you have multiple sites, it becomes more difficult to perform backups, particularly over the slower WAN links. One solution for this is to set up DFS Replication between the site servers to a central server or servers at the corporate office. Replication occurs when the WAN links are utilized the least, such as in the evenings and during the weekends. You then back up the central computers located at the corporate office.

WARNING! DFS Replication is not a replacement for backups. If a file gets deleted, changed, or corrupted on one target server, it will most likely be deleted, changed, or corrupted on the other target servers. Therefore, you still need to use backups to provide data protection and recovery.

DFS Replication is another server role, similar to DFS Namespace. Therefore, you would use Server Manager to install DFS Replication.

INSTALL DFS REPLICATION

GET READY. To install DFS Replication, perform the following steps.

1. Log on to LON-SVR1 as **adatum\administrator** with the password of **Pa$$w0rd.**
2. Open **Server Manager.**
3. At the top of Server Manager, click **Manage > Add Roles and Features.** The Add Roles and Feature Wizard opens.
4. On the Before You Begin page, click **Next.**
5. Click **Role-based or feature-based installation** and then click **Next.**
6. Click **Select a server from the server pool**, click the name of the server to install DFS to, and then click **Next.**
7. Scroll down and expand **File and Storage Services** and expand **File and iSCSI Services.** Click **DFS Replication.** If File Server is not already installed, select it.
8. If you are prompted to add features to DFS Namespace, click **Add Features.**
9. Back on the Select Server Roles page, click **Next.**
10. On the Select Features page, click **Next.**
11. On the Confirm Installation Selections page, click **Install.**
12. When the installation is complete, click **Close.**
13. Repeat the process for LON-SVR2.

Configuring DFS Replication Targets

When you replicate folders using DFS, you are replicating local folders on a server to another local folder on another server. The folder is most likely shared so that users can access the folder, but this is not necessary.

CERTIFICATION READY
Configure DFS Replication targets
Objective 5.2

By default, replication groups use a ***full mesh topology***, which means that all members replicate to all other members. If you have a simple DFS implementation consisting of two servers, there is some replication traffic between the two servers. However, by adding multiple servers to a replication group, replication traffic increases even more. Therefore, instead of using a full mesh topology, you can use a ***hub/spoke topology*** (in which one server is used to replicate to the other members), thereby limiting the replication traffic to specific pairs of members.

When you configure DFS Replication, you can configure the following settings:

- Bidirectional or unidirectional
- Percentage of available bandwidth
- Schedule when replication will occur

By default, DFS Replication between two members is bidirectional. Bidirectional connections occur in both directions and include two one-way connections. If you desire only a one-way connection, you can disable one of the connections or use share permissions to prevent the replication process from updating files on certain member servers.

Because DFS Replication often occurs over a WAN link, you have to be aware of how much traffic DFS uses and how you can configure it when replication occurs to best utilize the WAN links. Therefore, you can schedule replication to occur only during the night when the WAN links are not used as much or you can specify the bandwidth used by DFS Replication.

CREATE A DFS REPLICATION GROUP

GET READY. To create a DFS Replication group, perform the following steps.

1. Log on to LON-SVR1 as **adatum\administrator** with the password of **Pa$$w0rd.**
2. Open **Server Manager.**
3. Click **Tools > DFS Management.** The DFS Management console opens.
4. Right-click **Replication** and choose **New Replication Group.**
5. On the Replication Group Type page (see Figure 11-9), click **Multipurpose replication group** and then click **Next.**

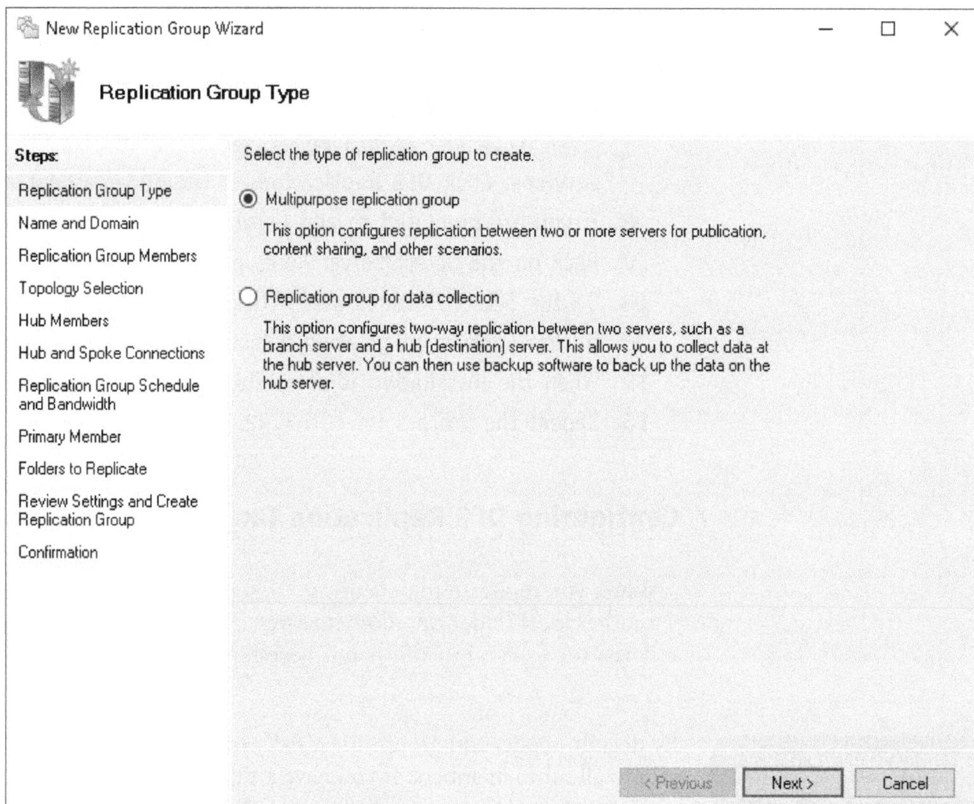

Figure 11-9

Selecting the replication group type

6. On the Name and Domain page, in the Name of replication group text box, type a descriptive name for the replication group. Click **Next.**
7. On the Replication Group Members page, click **Add.**
8. In the Select Computers dialog box, type the name of the first server of the group and click **OK.**
9. Repeat Step 8 until all of the target servers are added to the group.
10. On the Replication Group Members page, click **Next.**
11. On the Topology Selection page, click **Full Mesh** and then click **Next.**
12. On the Replication Group Schedule and Bandwidth page, click one of the following:
    a. **Replicate continuously using the specified bandwidth:** Specify the bandwidth that you want to use. The default bandwidth is **Full.**
    b. **Replicate during the specified days and times:** Then, click **Edit Schedule** to specify which days and time you can replicate and the bandwidth used during those days and time.

    Click **Next.**

13. On the Primary Member page, specify which server acts as the Primary member. Click **Next.**
14. On the Folders to Replicate page, click **Add**.
15. In the Add Folder to Replicate dialog box (see Figure 11-10), specify the local path name of the folder that you want to replicate. Do not type the UNC name.

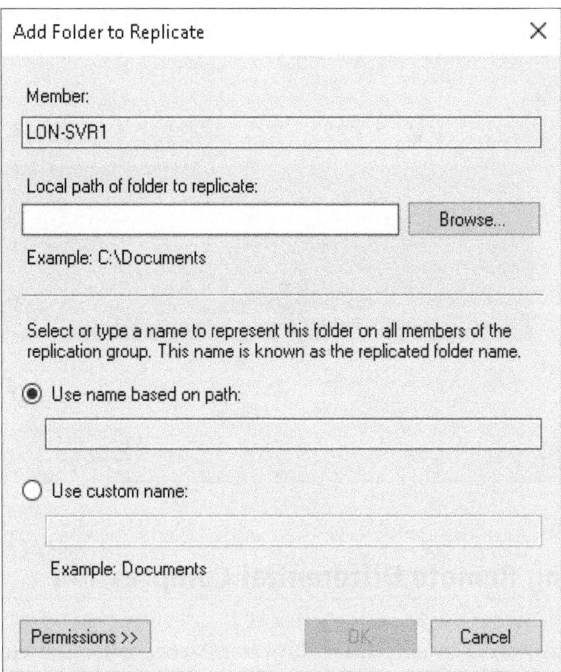

Figure 11-10

Specifying the local folders to replicate

16. Click **OK** to close the Add Folder to Replicate dialog box.
17. Back on the Folders to Replicate page, click **Next.**
18. On the Local Path on Other Members page, select each member server listed and click **Edit.**
19. In the Edit dialog box, click **Enabled** and type the local path on the member server. Click **OK** to close the Edit dialog box.
20. Back on the Local Path on Other Members page, click **Next.**
21. On the Review Settings and Create Replication Group page, click **Create.**
22. When the replication group has been created, click **Close.**
23. If a Replication Delay message appears, click **OK.**

Configuring Replication Scheduling

Depending on network and WAN links and workloads, you might need to modify the maximum bandwidth used by DFS so that it does not consume too much bandwidth. Fortunately, you modify the replication scheduling based on the time of day. For example, you can have one bandwidth during business hours and another bandwidth during nonbusiness hours.

CERTIFICATION READY
Configure replication scheduling
Objective 5.2

When the replication group is created, you can define the scheduled group. You can also modify the schedule after the replication group is created by right-clicking the replication group in the DFS Management console and choosing Edit Replication Group Schedule. In the Edit Schedule dialog box (see Figure 11-11), you can select and deselect a range of time and then select the bandwidth usage.

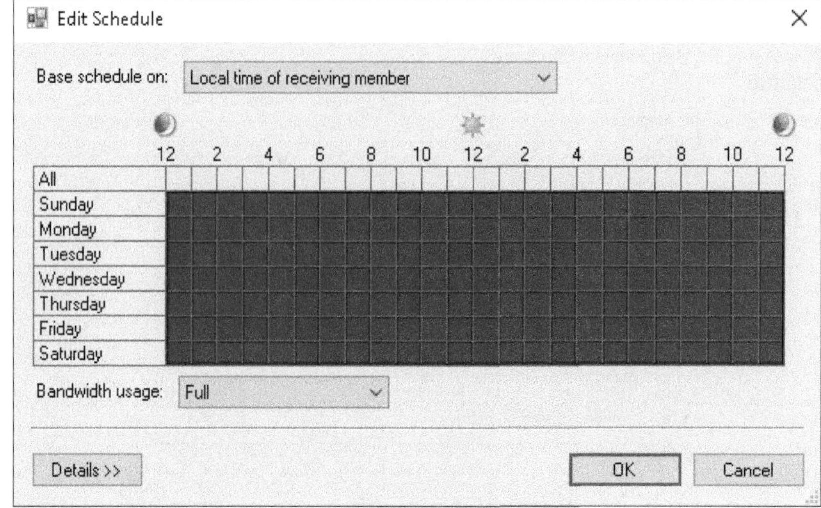

Figure 11-11
Editing a replication schedule

Configuring Remote Differential Compression

DFS Replication is an efficient, multiple-master replication engine that synchronizes DFS folders and replicates the Active Directory Domain Services (AD DS) SYSVOL folder on domain controllers. It replaced the File Replication Service (FRS), which has been deprecated in Windows Server 2012 and still exists in Windows Server 2016. However, to make it more efficient, you should use Remote Differential Compression.

CERTIFICATION READY
Configure Remote Differential Compression (RDC) settings
Objective 5.2

DFS Replication uses a compression algorithm known as ***Remote Differential Compression (RDC)***, which detects changes to the data in a file and replicates only those file blocks that changed instead of the entire file. As a result, not as much data needs to be transferred. If you disable RDC, you can conserve processor and disk input/output (I/O). However, you will, of course, consume much more bandwidth.

DISABLE REMOTE DIFFERENTIAL COMPRESSION

GET READY. By default, RDC is enabled. To disable RDC, perform the following steps.

1. Log on to LON-SVR1 as **adatum\administrator** with the password of **Pa$$w0rd**.
2. Open **Server Manager**.
3. Click **Tools > DFS Management** to open the DFS Management console.
4. In the left pane, expand **Replication** and select the replication group that you want to modify.
5. Click the **Connections** tab.
6. Right-click a connection and choose **Properties** to display the Properties dialog box, as shown in Figure 11-12.

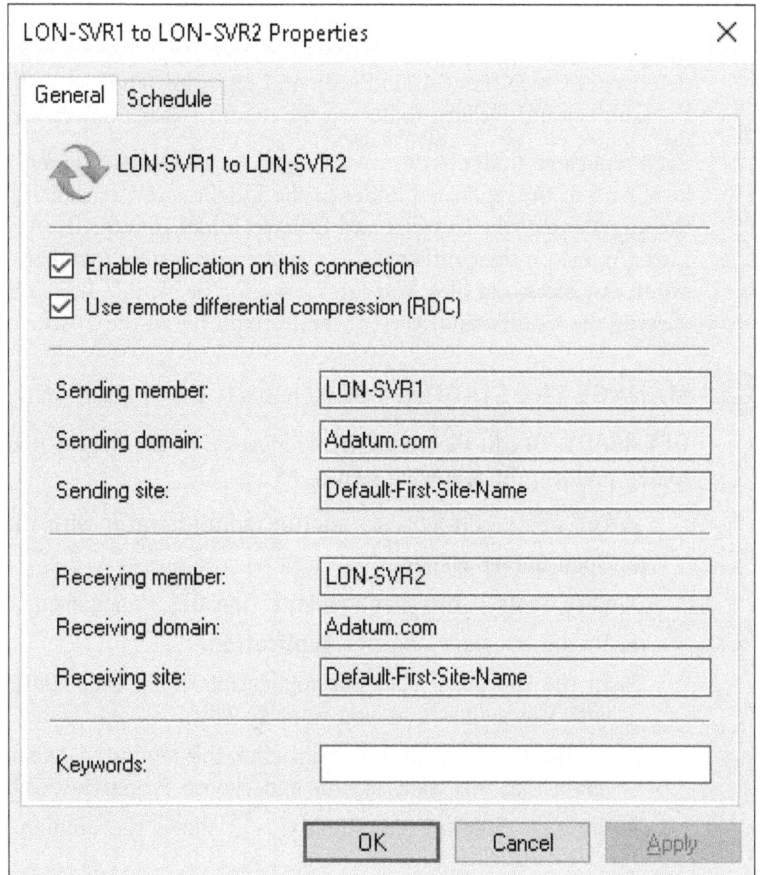

Figure 11-12
Enabling replication and Remote Differential Compression (RDC)

7. Deselect the **Use remote differential compression (RDC)** check box.
8. Click **OK** to close the Properties dialog box.

Configuring Staging

To determine what needs to be replicated, DFS uses staging folders. The ***staging folder*** acts as a cache for new and changed files that need to be replicated. It is also used to compress files that need to be sent. When received on the other end, it is used to decompress the file and install the file into the replicated folder.

CERTIFICATION READY
Configure staging
Objective 5.2

Each replicated folder has its own staging folder, which, by default, is located under the local path of the replicated folder in the DfsrPrivate\Staging folder. The default size of each staging folder is 4,096 MB, which is determined by a quota. When the staging folder reaches 90%, it purges the oldest staged file until it reaches 60%.

It should also be noted that the staging folder quota does not determine the largest file that can be replicated. If a large file is still in the process of being replicated, any cleaning or removal of older files that occurs is retried later after the file has been replicated. You should increase the quota size only if you have multiple large files that change frequently. To keep processor and disk utilization to a minimum, the quota should be configured to the size of the combined nine largest files in the replicated folder.

On occasion, when the same file gets changed at approximately the same time on two different targets, a conflict occurs. DFS Replication uses a last-writer-wins model, which determines which file it should keep and replicate. The losing file is renamed and stored in the Conflict and Deleted folder on the member that resolves the conflict.

Each replicated folder has its own ***Conflict and Deleted folder***, which is located under the local path of the replicated folder in the DfsrPrivate\ConflictandDeleted folder. By default, the quota size of the Conflict and Deleted folder is 660 MB. Although the Access Control Lists (ACLs) on the conflicted files are preserved, only members of the local Administrators group can access the files. You can view a log of conflict files and their original file names by viewing the ConflictandDeletedManifest.xml file in the DfsrPrivate folder.

MANAGE THE STAGING FOLDER AND CONFLICT AND DELETED FOLDER

GET READY. To edit the quota size or location of the staging folder and Conflict and Deleted folder, perform the following steps.

1. Log on to LON-SVR1 as **adatum\administrator** with the password of **Pa$$w0rd.**
2. Open **Server Manager.**
3. Click **Tools > DFS Management.** The DFS Management console opens.
4. In the left pane, expand **Replication.**
5. In the left pane, click the replication group that contains the replicated folder with the quotas that you want to edit.
6. On the Memberships tab, right-click the replicated folder on the member with the quota that you want to edit and choose **Properties.** The Properties dialog box opens.
7. Click the **Staging** tab. Figure 11-13 shows the Staging tab.

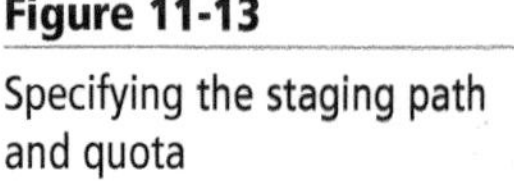

Figure 11-13

Specifying the staging path and quota

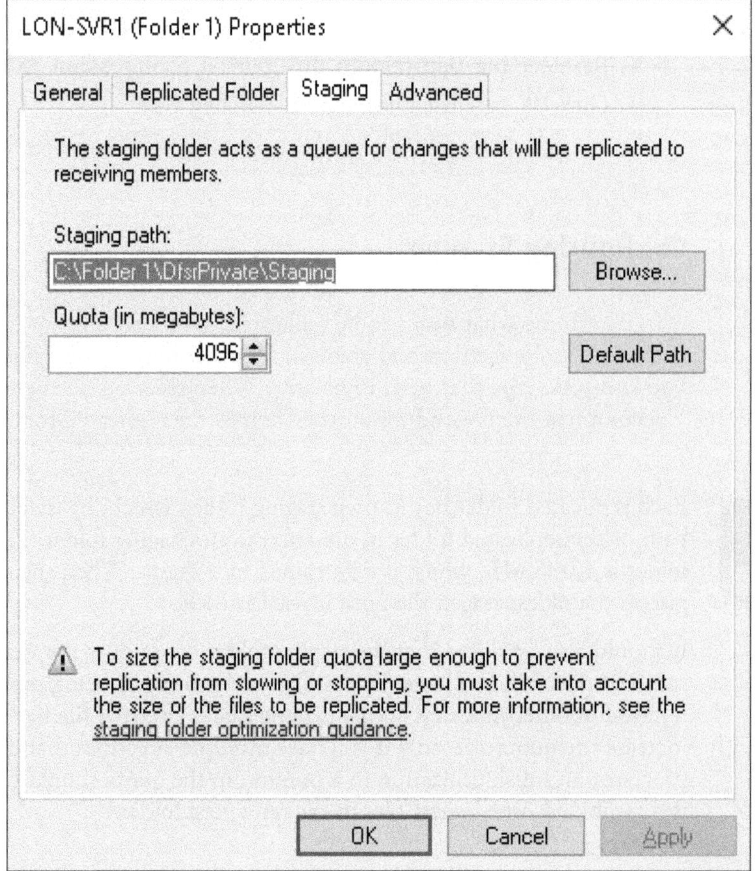

8. Change the Staging path and the quotas as needed.
9. Click the **Advanced** tab.
10. Adjust the Conflict and Deleted folder quota as necessary.
11. Click **OK** to close the Properties dialog box.

Windows Server 2016 includes several tools to help monitor and troubleshoot DFS Replication. To generate a diagnostic report, you can right-click a replication group in the DFS Management console and choose Diagnostic Report. You can also use the DfrsAdmin.exe in a script and schedule the script to run with task scheduler. Finally, you can use DfsrDiag.exe to perform diagnostic tests of DFS Replication.

Configuring Fault Tolerance Using DFS

To make shared files fault tolerant, you need to use both DFS Namespace and DFS Replication.

CERTIFICATION READY
Configure fault tolerance
Objective 5.2

Each technology used in DFS has some impressive capabilities. DFS Namespace offers ease of use when trying to locate a shared folder and DFS Replication replicates files from one server to another. However, when they are combined, they can offer fault tolerance on the network.

To configure fault tolerance using DFS, you would perform the following high-level steps:

1. Create the same folder on multiple servers. Although the folders don't have to have the same name, it makes management easier and cuts down on confusion.
2. Share the folders.
3. Configure DFS Replication between the folders on the various servers.
4. Create a DFS Namespace that includes targets of all target folders for a replication group.

DFS Replication ensures the files are replicated between the servers, providing multiple copies of the files. The DFS Namespace makes the access of the replicated folders transparent to the users when accessing the replicated folder. As far as the users are concerned, they access the DFS Namespace/shared folder, and then they go to one of the replicated folders. If one of the replicated folders is not available, it is rerouted to another replicated folder. When you add a folder to a namespace, you are prompted to create a replication group. Therefore, at this time, you can run the Replication Folder Wizard.

Cloning a DFS Database

If you have a large file repository that you want to replicate to another server, it could take quite a bit of time to synchronize the files. Starting with Windows Server 2012 R2, you can export the DFS database, then preseed the files on the destination server and import the database.

CERTIFICATION READY
Clone a Distributed File System Replication (DFSR) database
Objective 5.2

Before Windows Server 2012 R2, each server records the information in a local database, and then exchanges the information with the remote nodes, stages files, creates hashes, and then transmits the files over the network. If you preseed the files by copying the files to a destination server, and you then implement DFS Replication, DFSR has to go through each file, record the information in a local database, and then exchange the information with the remote nodes. If any differences are found, the two servers reconcile the differences.

For larger repositories, the DFS Replication can take days or even weeks, even if you preseed the data files. If you preseed a server and the database, you can reduce the setup time by approximately 99%.

To preseed a server and database, perform the following steps:

1. On the source computer, create a replication group and replicated folder, but do not add the destination server. Let the initial build complete.
2. Export the cloned database from the source server.
3. Preseed the files to the target server by copying the files using an external drive, from a backup, or over the network.
4. Copy in the exported clone DB files to the target computer.
5. Import the cloned database on the downstream server.
6. Add the target server to the replication group and add the replicated folders.

The DFS Replication database exists on every volume that contains a DRS replicated folder and a single database that contains references for all replicated folders on the volume. To export the DFS database and volume configuration XML file settings for a volume, you can use the `Export-DfrsClone` PowerShell cmdlet. However, you can clone SYSVOL or read-only replicas in Windows Server 2012 R2 and Windows Server 2016.

To export the DFS Replication database clone for the C: volume into the C:\Dfsrclone destination folder and display the associated replicated folders, use the following command:

```
Export-DfsrClone -Volume C: -Path C:\Dfsrclone | Format-List
```

To monitor the export process, use the `Get-DfsrCloneState` PowerShell cmdlet to monitor the export process.

To import a cloned DFS Replication database and volume configuration settings, use the `Import-DfrsClone` PowerShell cmdlet. For example, to clone and import the DFS Replication database and volume configuration XML to the C: volume from the C:\Dfsrclone folder, use the following command:

```
Import-DfsrClone -Volume c: -Path C:\dfsrclone
```

Recovering DFS Databases

Windows Server 2016 has automatic recovery after a loss of power or an unexpected stoppage of the DFS Replication service, which validates the database against the file system and then resumes replication normally.

CERTIFICATION READY
Recover DFSR databases
Objective 5.2

With Windows Server 2008 R2 and higher, the DFS would have to re-enable replication manually by using a Windows Management Instrumentation (WMI) method, unless the SYSVOL folder is the only replicated folder. If SYSVOL is the only replicated folder, replication will automatically start. If a database becomes corrupted, the database will be deleted and a nonauthoritative initial sync process will begin.

When a DFS Replication stops because the DFSR Jet database is not shut down properly and Auto Recovery is disabled, a warning appears in the Event Viewer Applications and Services Logs\DFS Replication.

To manually resume the unexpected shutdown recovery and replication of the replicated folder(s) in a volume, use the following command:

```
wmic /namespace:\\root\microsoftdfs path dfsrVolumeConfig where
volumeGuid="<volume-GUID>" call ResumeReplication
```

To configure older Windows to automatically resume the unexpected shutdown recovery, use the following command:

```
wmic /namespace:\\root\microsoftdfs path dfsrmachineconfig set StopRep
licationOnAutoRecovery=FALSE
```

In Windows Server 2016, when the DFS Replication detects an unexpected shutdown, it automatically triggers a recovery process, which rebuilds corrupt databases using the local file and update sequence number (USN) change journal information. When a file is marked as a normal replicated state, DFS Replication then contacts the partner server and merges the changes. If you don't want the DFSR Replication to resume when a DFS database unexpectedly stops, open the registry and change the HKEY_LOCAL_MACHINE\SYSTEM\CurrentControlSet\Services\DFSR\Parameters\StopReplicationOnAutoRecovery (DWORD) to 1.

Optimizing DFS Replication

Windows Server 2012 R2 and 2016 provide several changes to enhance DFS by supporting larger repositories, file staging tuning, and cross-file RDC disable.

CERTIFICATION READY
Optimize DFS Replication
Objective 5.2

Since DFS was introduced, DFS has been expanded significantly. For example, Windows Server 2003 R2 only supported up to 8 million files and up to 1 TB of data. However, Windows Server 2008, Windows Server 2008 R2, and Windows Server 2012 have the following scalability guidelines:

- Size of all replicated files on a server: 10 TB
- Number of replicated files on a volume: 11 million
- Maximum file size: 64 GB

Windows Server 2012 R2 and 2016 scalability guidelines have been expanded to:

- Size of all replicated files on a server: 100 TB
- Number of replicated files on a volume: 70 million
- Maximum file size: 250 GB

Of course, if you need to replicate large amounts of data over a slower WAN link, you should consider preseeding the data files and import/export the DFS database.

DFS has been limited to supporting about 10 TB of data since Windows Server 2003. With Windows Server 2012 R2 and Windows Server 2016, Microsoft has tested end-to-end deployments that have over 100 TB of data. However, there are a lot of factors to successful replication and your environment might not support a huge data set. If you plan to replicate a large data set over a slow WAN, you should use physical disks that are carried from the source machine to the target machine.

With Windows Server 2016, you have the option to disable cross-file RDC between servers. For servers connected together with fast LAN connections, turning off cross-file RDC may reduce server resource overhead and increase replication performance. However, for slower WAN links, you should keep cross-file RDC enabled between servers.

In Windows Server 2012 and earlier, DFS Replication uses 256-KB file size to determine if a file is to be staged. If the RDC minimum size—which by default is 64 KB—is larger than 256 KB, a file will be staged before it is replicated. When files are staged, the replication time is increased because of RDC operations. With Windows Server 2012 R2 and 2016, you can configure the staging minimum size to range from 256 KB to 512 TB. Increasing the minimum staging size for files can increase the replication performance.

If you are not using RDC or staging, files are no longer compressed or copied to the staging folder, which can increase performance. However, without compression, you do use greater bandwidth.

■ Configuring BranchCache

Branch offices typically have slow connectivity to the central office and typically have limited infrastructure for security servers. When users access files over the slower WAN links, there might be a delay when opening files and when opening large files or many files at the same time, which can cause other programs to be slow or delayed. When using ***BranchCache***, you essentially create a WAN accelerator where information is cached on branch computers or local servers. If the document is cached, it is accessed from the local branch office rather than going across a slower WAN link.

BranchCache improves the performance of applications by reducing network traffic on the WAN connection between branch offices and the central office by locally caching frequently used files on computers in the branch office. BranchCache works in the background by retrieving data from the server as the client requests the data.

BranchCache provides the following additional benefits:

- All data stored in the cache is encrypted.
- By using metadata, you reduce the amount of data traffic traversing the WAN link.
- Users always have access to the current version of the data.

The following represent the types of BranchCache-enabled servers (content servers) that can be configured. You must deploy at least one or more of these types of servers at your main office:

- **Web servers:** Windows Server 2008 R2 or higher running Internet Information Services (IIS) with BranchCache enabled. These servers use the Hypertext Transfer Protocol (HTTP) and Hypertext Transfer Protocol Secure (HTTPS) protocols.
- **Application (BITS) servers:** Windows Server 2012 or higher running the Background Intelligent Transfer Service (BITS) with BranchCache enabled.
- **File servers:** Windows Server 2008 R2 or higher running the File Service server role and the BranchCache for Network Files role service. These servers use the Server Message Block (SMB) protocol to send content.

BranchCache supports the following protocols:

- HTTP or HTTPS
- SMB, including signed SMB traffic
- Background Intelligent Transfer Service (BITS)

BranchCache supports IPv4, IPv6, and end-to-end encryption methods such as SSL and IPsec.

BrancheCache can operate in one of two modes:

- Hosted cache mode
- Distributed cache mode

Although an organization can use both modes, you can configure only one mode per branch office.

With Windows Server 2016, the ***hosted cache mode*** uses one or more dedicated servers to host the cache. If the content is not available in the hosted cache, the content will be retrieved over the WAN link and added to the hosted cache so that clients requesting the same content in the future will benefit. By default, BranchCache allocates 5% of the disk space on the active partition for hosting cache data. However, this size can be changed using Group Policy or the `netsh branchcache set cachesize` command.

Instead of having a centralized cache, ***distributed cache mode*** has the cache distributed among the local Windows 7, 8/8.1, or 10 clients at the local site. Content on an individual client is shared with the other clients at the site. Distributed cache mode is designed for branch offices with fewer than 50 users that do not have a dedicated server in the branch office. BranchCache works across a single subnet only.

Windows 10 clients can be configured through Group Policy as distributed cache mode clients by default. However, the clients will search for a hosted cache server, and if one is found, they will automatically configure themselves into hosted cache mode clients so that they can use the local server.

Installing and Configuring BranchCache

To fully install BranchCache, you need to install the BranchCache feature and the BranchCache for Network Files role service. You then configure BranchCache with Group Policy Objects (GPOs) and enable it for a shared folder.

CERTIFICATION READY
Install and configure BranchCache
Objective 5.2

CERTIFICATION READY
Implement BranchCache for web, file, and application servers
Objective 5.2

To use BranchCache, you perform the following:

- For each web server that you want to cache, you must install the BranchCache feature.
- For each file server, you must install the BranchCache for Network Files role service on the file server that is hosting the data. In addition, you have to configure a hash publication for BranchCache and create BranchCache-enabled file shares.
- For the clients to use BranchCache, you must configure the clients using Group Policy or the `netsh` command.
- If you use the hosted cache mode, you just add the BranchCache feature to the computer running Windows Server 2016 that will be holding the hosted cache.

INSTALL AND CONFIGURE BRANCHCACHE

GET READY. To install and configure BranchCache perform the following steps.

1. Log on to LON-SVR1 as **adatum\administrator** with the password of **Pa$$w0rd.**
2. Open **Server Manager** and then click **Manage > Add Roles and Features.**
3. In the Add Roles and Features Wizard, click **Next.**
4. On the Select Installation Type page, make sure the **Role-based or feature-based installation** option is selected and then click **Next.**
5. On the Select Destination Server page, make sure that the desired server is selected and then click **Next.**
6. On the Select Server Roles page, click **Next.**
7. On the Select Features page, click **BranchCache** and then click **Next.**
8. Click the **Install** button.
9. When the installation is complete, click **Close.**

Alternatively, you can install BranchCache by opening Windows PowerShell and executing the following commands:

```
Install-WindowsFeature BranchCache

Restart-Computer
```

INSTALL BRANCHCACHE FOR NETWORK FILES

GET READY. To install BranchCache for Network Files, perform the following steps.

1. Log on to LON-SVR1 as **adatum\administrator** with the password of **Pa$$w0rd.**
2. Open **Server Manager** and click **Manage > Add Roles and Features.**
3. In the Add Roles and Features Wizard, click **Next.**
4. On the Select Installation Type page, make sure the **Role-based or feature-based installation** option and then click **Next.**
5. On the Select Destination Server page, click the desired server, and then click **Next.**
6. On the Select Server Roles page, under Roles, expand **File and Storage Services** and then expand **File and iSCSI Services.** Click to select the **File Server** and **BranchCache for Network Files** check boxes. Click **Next.**
7. On the Select Features page, click **Next.**
8. On the Confirm Installation Selections page, review your selections and then click **Install.**
9. When installation is complete, click **Close.**

Because all the file servers that participate in the BranchCache infrastructure must have the same hash publication policy, it is best to place all of the servers in the same Active Directory OU and then assign the appropriate Group Policy Object (GPO).

CONFIGURE THE BRANCHCACHE HASH PUBLICATION GROUP POLICY OBJECT

GET READY. To configure the BranchCache hash publication Group Policy Object, perform the following steps.

1. Log on to LON-DC1 as **adatum\administrator** with the password of **Pa$$w0rd.**
2. Open **Server Manager** and click **Tools > Group Policy Management.** The Group Policy Management console opens.
3. Right-click the GPO that is assigned to the OU that the file servers are in and choose **Edit.** The Group Policy Management Editor opens.
4. In the Group Policy Management Editor console, expand the following path: **Computer Configuration > Policies > Administrative Templates.** Click **Network, Lanman Server.**
5. Double-click **Hash Publication for BranchCache.**
6. In the Hash Publication for BranchCache dialog box, click **Enabled** (see Figure 11-14).
7. In the Options section, click **Allow hash publication for all shared folders**, and then click one of the following:
   a. To enable hash publication for all shared folders for all file servers that you added to the OU, click **Allow hash publication for all shared folders.**
   b. To enable hash publication only for shared folders for which BranchCache is enabled, click **Allow hash publication only for shared folders on which BranchCache is enabled.**
   c. To disallow hash publication for all shared folders on the computer even if BranchCache is enabled on the file shares, click **Disallow hash publication on all shared folders.**

Figure 11-14

Configuring Hash Publication for BranchCache using group policies

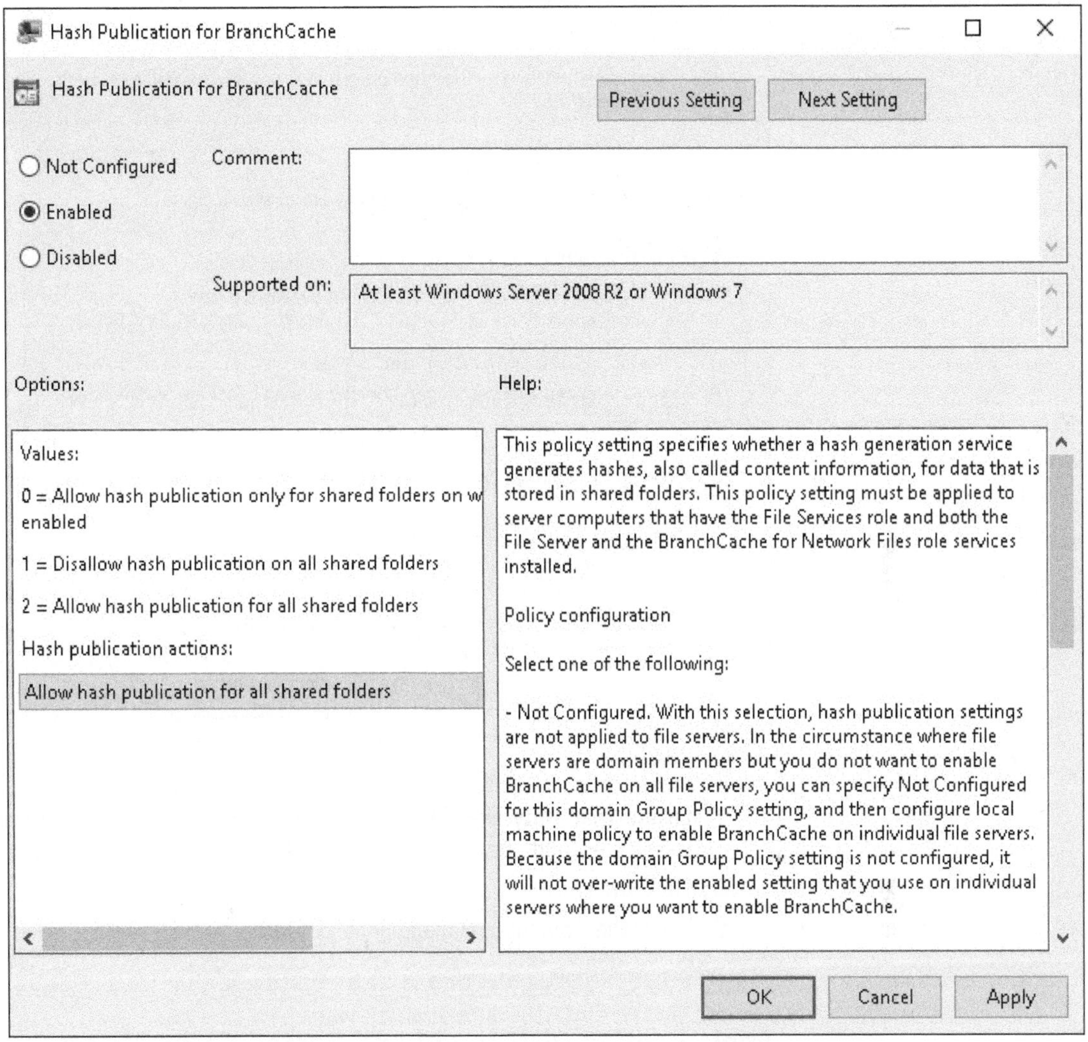

8. Click **OK** to close the Hash Publication for BranchCache dialog box.
9. Close the Group Policy Management Editor.

ENABLE BRANCHCACHE ON A FILE SHARE

GET READY. To enable BranchCache on a file share, perform the following steps.

1. Log on to LON-SVR1 as **adatum\administrator** with the password of **Pa$$w0rd**.
2. Open **Server Manager**.
3. In Server Manager, click **Tools > Computer Management.** The Computer Management console opens.
4. Under System Tools, expand **Shared Folders** and click **Shares.**
5. In the details pane, right-click a share and choose **Properties.** The share's Properties dialog box opens.

6. In the Properties dialog box, on the General tab, click **Offline Settings**. The Offline Settings dialog box opens (see Figure 11-15).

Figure 11-15

Configuring offline settings

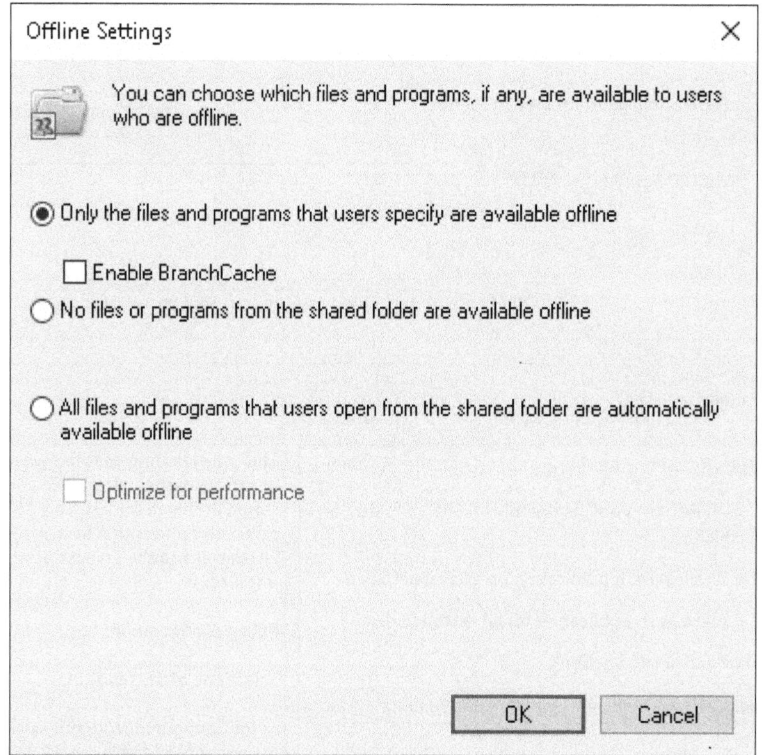

7. Ensure that **Only the files and programs that users specify are available offline** is selected and then select the **Enable BranchCache** check box.
8. Click **OK** twice.
9. Close the Computer Management console.

Implementing Distributed and Hosted Cache Modes

BranchCache is disabled by default on client computers. To enable and configure BranchCache, you need to perform the following steps:

1. Enable BranchCache.
2. Enable the distributed cache mode or hosted cache mode.
3. Configure the client firewall to allow BranchCache protocols.

CERTIFICATION READY
Implement distributed and hosted cache modes
Objective 5.2

To configure BranchCache clients, you must configure the appropriate Group Policy settings, found in the Computer Configuration\Policies\Administrative Templates\Network\BranchCache node of a GPO or in Local Computer Policy. The BranchCache Group Policy settings are as follows:

- **Turn on BranchCache:** Enables BranchCache on the client computer. Enabling this setting along with either *Set BranchCache Distributed Cache mode* or *Set BranchCache Hosted Cache mode* configures the client to use one of those operational modes. Enabling this setting without either one of the mode settings configures the client to cache server data on its local drive only, without accessing caches on other computers.

- **Set BranchCache Distributed Cache mode:** When enabled with the *Turn on BranchCache* setting, configures the client to function in distributed cache mode.
- **Set BranchCache Hosted Cache mode:** When enabled with the *Turn on BranchCache* setting, configures the client to function in hosted cache mode. In the *Enter the location of the hosted cache* field, you must specify the address of the computer that will function as the hosted cache server on the branch office network.
- **Configure BranchCache for Network Files:** When enabled, controls the round-trip network latency value that BranchCache uses to differentiate local from remote servers. The default setting is 80 ms. When you decrease the value, the client caches more files; increasing the value causes it to cache fewer files.
- **Set percentage of disk space used for client computer cache:** When enabled, specifies the maximum amount of total disk space that the computer should devote to the BranchCache cache. The default value is 5%.

Before the clients can use the BrancheCache, you need to enable BranchCache on the clients. To configure BranchCache settings using Group Policy, you open a group policy and navigate to Computer Configuration > Policies > Administrative Templates > Network > BranchCache, as shown in Figure 11-16. You need to enable the *Turn on BranchCache* setting and enable either the distributed cache mode or the hosted cache mode.

Figure 11-16

Configuring BranchCache for clients using GPOs

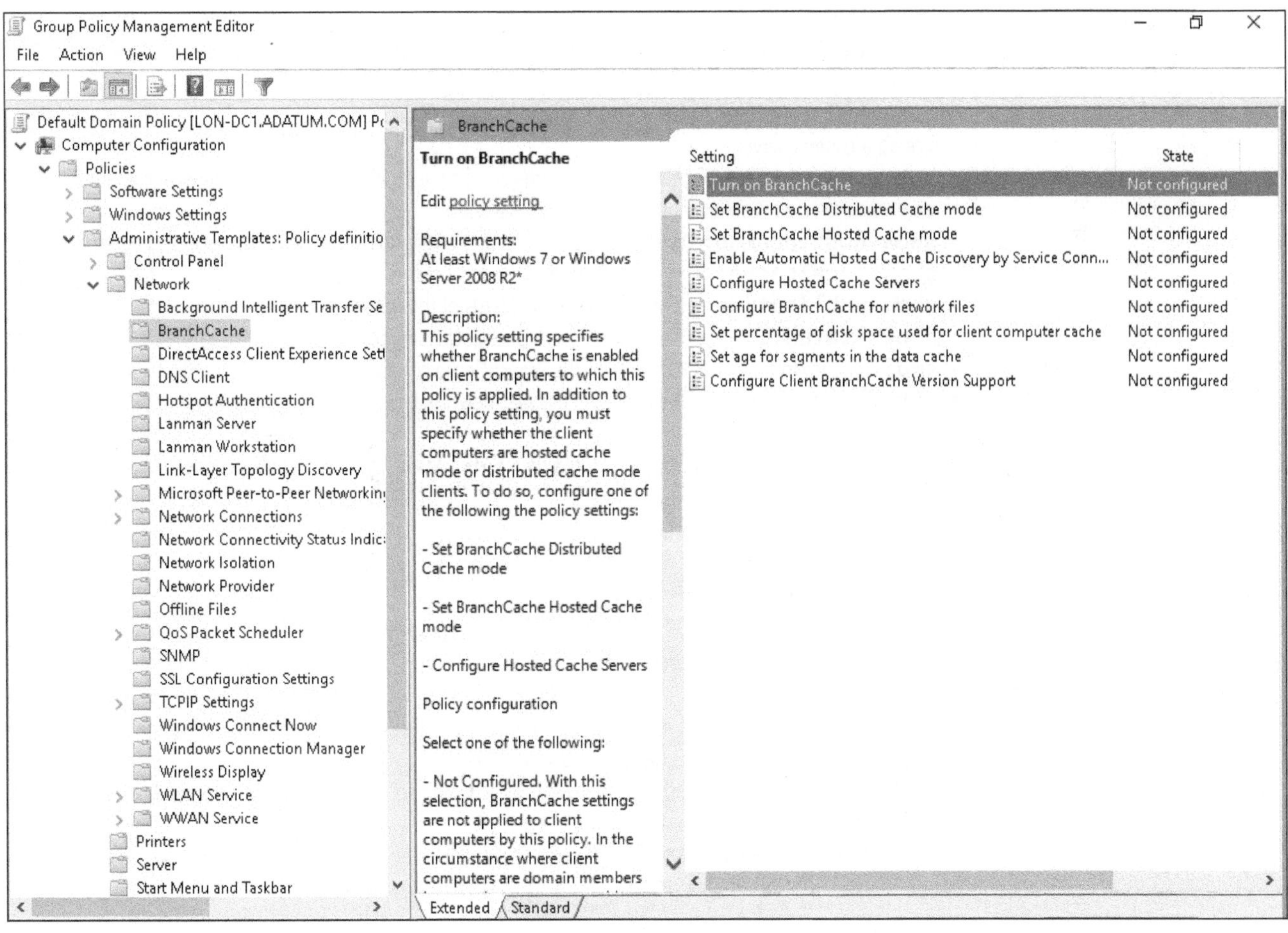

To configure BranchCache settings using the `netsh` command, perform one of the following:

- Use the following `netsh` syntax for the distributed mode:

```
netsh branchcache set service mode=distributed
```

- Use the following `netsh` syntax for the hosted mode:

```
netsh branchcache set service mode=hostedclient location=<Name of
Hosted Cache server>
```

In Windows Server 2016, you can configure and manage BranchCache by using either Windows PowerShell or the Network Shell (`netsch`) commands for BranchCache. Of course, although the `netsh` commands for BranchCache in Windows Server 2016 are identical to Windows Server 2008 R2, 2012, and 2012 R2, it is recommended to move to PowerShell for future versions of Windows.

USING THE NETSH COMMAND

You can configure and manage BranchCache using the `netsh` command with the following options:

- **`Exportkey:`** Exports the key that the BranchCache service uses to publish content and generate content hashes
- **`Flush:`** Deletes the contents of the local BranchCache cache
- **`Importkey:`** Imports a new key from a file that was created by using the `exportkey` command
- **`Reset:`** Resets the BranchCache service and flushes the local BranchCache cache, deleting all content in the cache; all configuration parameters are returned to default values
- **`set cachesize:`** Specifies the size of the local cache as either a percentage of the size of the hard disk where the cache is located or as an exact number of bytes
- **`set key:`** Generates a new key that the BranchCache service uses to publish content and generate content hashes
- **`set localcache:`** Specifies the location of the local cache for the BranchCache service on a client computer
- **`set publicationcache:`** Sets the location of the local publication cache for the BranchCache service on a content server
- **`set publicationcachesize:`** Sets the size of the publication cache on the local computer
- **`set service:`** Configures the BranchCache service
- **`show hostedcache:`** Displays the folder location of the hosted cache on the local computer
- **`show localcache:`** Displays the status of the local cache
- **`show publicationcache:`** Displays the status of the publication cache
- **`show status:`** Displays the status of the BranchCache service
- **`smb:`** Changes to the smb subcontext of the BranchCache context
- **`set latency:`** Specifies the minimum allowed network link latency, in milliseconds, between the branch office and the content source office
- **`show latency:`** Displays the configured minimum link latency value in milliseconds

USING POWERSHELL

You can configure and manage BranchCache using the following cmdlets:

- **`Add-BCDataCacheExtension:`** Increases the amount of cache storage space that is available on a hosted cache server by adding a new cache file
- **`Clear-BCCache:`** Deletes all data in all data and hash files
- **`Disable-BC:`** Disables the BranchCache service
- **`Enable-BCDistributed:`** Enables BranchCache and configures a computer to operate in distributed cache mode
- **`Enable-BCHostedClient:`** Configures BranchCache to operate in hosted cache client mode

- **Enable-BCHostedServer:** Configures BranchCache to operate in hosted cache server mode
- **Enable-BCLocal:** Enables the BranchCache service in local caching mode
- **Export-BCCachePackage:** Exports a cache package
- **Export-BCSecretKey:** Exports a secret key to a file
- **Get-BCClientConfiguration:** Retrieves the current BranchCache client computer settings
- **Get-BCContentServerConfiguration:** Retrieves the current BranchCache content server settings
- **Get-BCDataCache:** Retrieves the BranchCache data cache
- **Get-BCDataCacheExtension:** Retrieves the BranchCache data cache extensions from a hosted cache server
- **Get-BCHashCache:** Retrieves the BranchCache hash cache
- **Get-BCHostedCacheServerConfiguration:** Retrieves the current BranchCache hosted cache server settings
- **Get-BCNetworkConfiguration:** Retrieves the current BranchCache network settings
- **Get-BCStatus:** Retrieves a set of objects that provide BranchCache status and configuration information
- **Import-BCCachePackage:** Imports a cache package
- **Import-BCSecretKey:** Imports the cryptographic key that BranchCache uses for the generation of segment secrets
- **Publish-BCFileContent:** Generates hashes, also called *content information*, for files in shared folders on a file server that have BranchCache enabled and the BranchCache for Network Files role service installed
- **Publish-BCWebContent:** Creates hashes for web content when deploying content servers that are running Windows Server 2016 with the Web Services (IIS) server role installed
- **Remove-BCDataCacheExtension:** Deletes a data cache file
- **Reset-BC:** Resets BranchCache to the default configuration
- **Set-BCAuthentication:** Specifies the BranchCache computer authentication mode
- **Set-BCCache:** Modifies the cache file configuration, including the cache size
- **Set-BCDataCacheEntryMaxAge:** Modifies the maximum amount of time that data can remain in the cache
- **Set-BCMinSMBLatency:** Sets the minimum latency that must exist between client and server before transparent caching functions are utilized

Troubleshooting BranchCache

One way to test BranchCache is to see how long it takes to access a larger remote file that has not been accessed recently. Then, close the file and see how long it takes to access the file on the same machine as well as another machine on the same site. Another way is use the `netsh branchcache` command and Windows PowerShell cmdlet `Get-BCStatus`.

CERTIFICATION READY
Troubleshoot BranchCache
Objective 5.2

You can use the `netsh branchcache show status all` command to display the BranchCache service status. You can also use the Windows PowerShell cmdlet `Get-BCStatus` to provide BranchCache status and configuration information.

If you have problems, you should always look in the logs using Event Viewer. For BranchCache, you should look at the Application logs and the Application and Service Logs\Microsoft\Windows\BranchCache.

Lastly, you can use Performance Monitor to monitor BranchCache performance monitors. You can also use Microsoft System Center Operations Manager after you install the Windows BranchCache Management Pack for Operations Manager.

Configuring Print Services

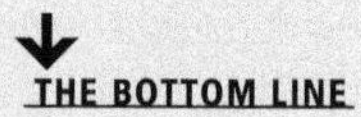

A basic service needed by most enterprise organizations is network printing. When you print a document, the client computer submits print jobs to the print server for delivery to a printer that is connected to the network. In many organizations, a larger network printer is available that can be used by multiple users.

As an administrator, you can install two types of printers: local and network. Today, most local printers are connected using USB ports, although some legacy printers may use parallel or serial ports. Network printers can be shared local printers or printers that connect directly to a network with built-in network cards or expandable jet-direct cards.

When you install a physical printer, which Microsoft calls a ***print device***, you must first connect the printer and turn it on. Next, you need to create a logical printer (Microsoft refers to this as the ***printer***), which provides a software interface between the print device and the applications. When you create the printer, you also load a print driver that acts as a translator for Windows and the programs running on Windows so that they do not have to worry about the specifics of the printer's hardware and printer language.

When you print a document in Windows, the printer uses the logical printer and printer driver to format the document into a form that is understood by the printer, including rendering it into a printer language such as HP's Printer Control Language or Adobe's PostScript to create an enhanced metafile (EMF). The print job is then sent to the local spooler, which provides background printing, allowing you to print and queue additional documents while your first document is being printed.

If a print job is being sent to the local print device, it temporarily saves it to the local hard drive's spool file. When the printer is available, it then sends the print job to the local print device. If Windows determines that the job is for a network print device, Windows sends the job to the print server's spooler. The print server's spooler saves it to the print server's hard drive spool file. Then, when the network print device becomes available, the job prints on the network print device.

Installing Printers

If you have the correct permissions to add a local printer or a remote shared printer, you can use the Add Printer Wizard to install the printer. After the printer is installed, it appears in the Devices and Printers folder as well as in Device Manager.

When you install a printer, you can install one of the following:

- ***Local printer:*** A printer that is connected directly to a computer, usually through a USB port/connection. If your printer is a USB model, Windows should automatically detect it and begin the installation when you connect the printer to the computer.
- ***Network printer:*** A printer that is connected to a dedicated server or network/switch/router device. Anyone who can connect to the printer and has the appropriate permissions can print directly to a network printer.

ADD A LOCAL PRINTER

GET READY. To add a local printer to a system running Windows Server 2016, perform the following steps.

1. Log on to LON-SVR1 as **adatum\administrator** with the password of **Pa$$w0rd.**
2. Right-click **Start** and choose **Control Panel.**
3. Under Hardware, click **Devices and Printers.** The Devices and Printers folder opens, as shown in Figure 11-17.

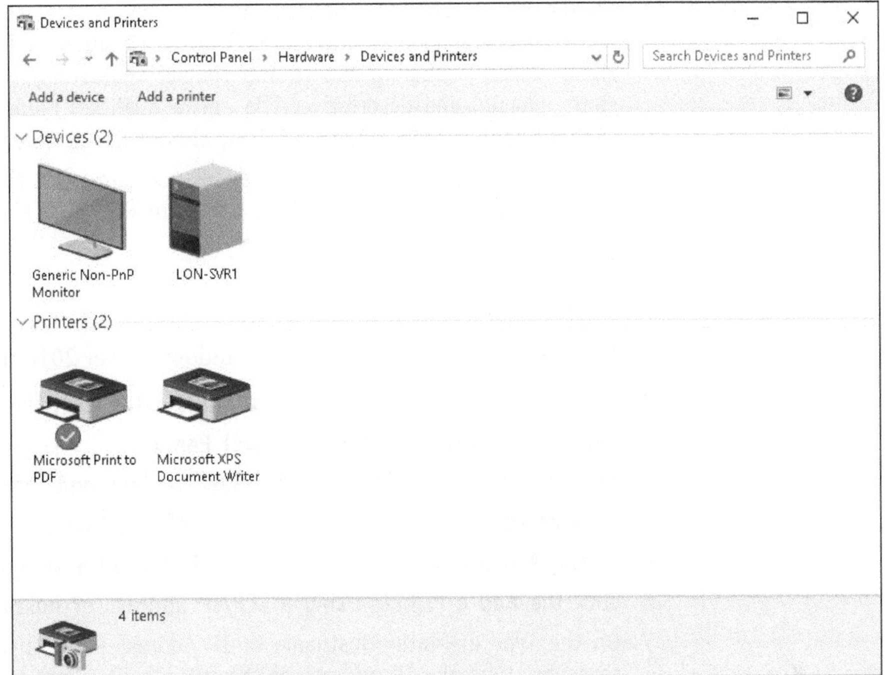

Figure 11-17

Managing devices and printers

4. To start the Add Printer Wizard, click **Add a printer.**
5. If a printer is not found, click the **The printer that I want isn't listed** option.
6. On the Find a Printer by Other Options page, click **Add a local printer or network printer with manual settings** and click **Next.**
7. On the Choose a Printer Port page, do one of the following and click **Next:**
   - For the Use an existing port option, specify the port, such as **LPT1 (Printer Port)**, **COM1 (Serial port)**, or **File (Print to File)**.
   - Click **Create a new port** and click **Next.**
8. On the Install the Printer Driver page, select the manufacturer and printer, as shown in Figure 11-18. If your printer is not listed, click the **Have Disk** button, so that you can navigate to drivers that you have downloaded or received with the printer. Click **Next.**
9. On the Type a Printer Name page, specify the name of the printer. Click **Next.**

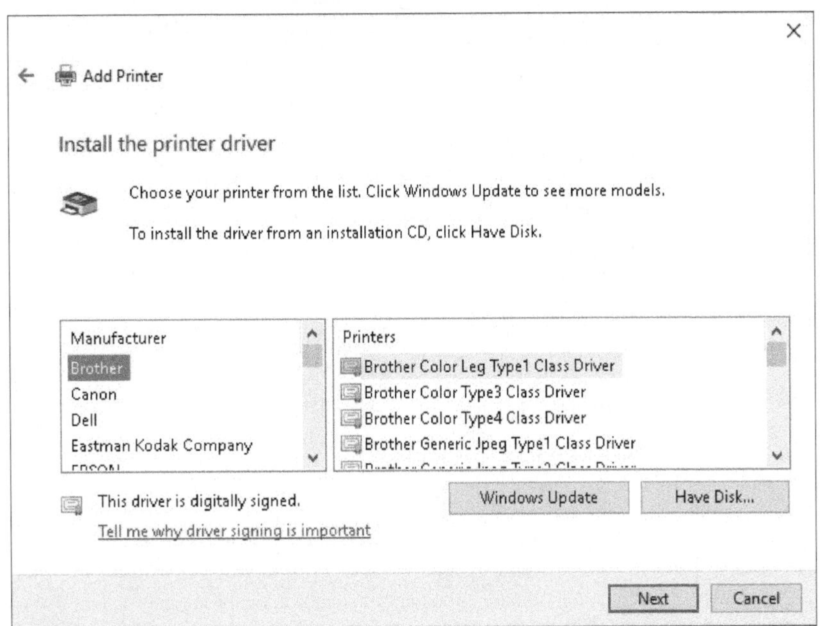

Figure 11-18

Specifying the manufacturer and printer

10. On the Printer Sharing page, specify the share name. You can also specify the Location or Comments. Although Windows 10 supports long printer names and share names (including spaces and special characters), it is best to keep names short, simple, and descriptive. The entire qualified name, including the server name (for example, \\Server1\HP4100N-1), should be 32 characters or fewer.
11. When the printer is successfully added, you can print the standard Windows test page by clicking the **Print a test page** button. Click **Finish**.

ADD A NETWORK PRINTER

GET READY. To add a network printer to Windows Server 2016, perform the following steps.

1. Log on to LON-SVR1 as **adatum\administrator** with the password of **Pa$$w0rd.**
2. Right-click **Start** and choose **Control Panel.**
3. Under Hardware and Sound, click **View Devices and Printers.**
4. To start the Add Printer Wizard, click **Add a printer.**
5. In the Add a Device Wizard, click the **The printer that I want isn't listed** option.
6. Click the **Add a Printer using a TCP/IP address or hostname** option and click **Next.**
7. On the Type a Printer Hostname or IP Address page, in the Hostname or IP address text box, type the IP address of the printer. The Port name will automatically fill in based on what you type in the Hostname or IP address text box.
8. The Query printer and automatically select the driver to use option is already selected. Click **Next.**
9. If the device could not connect to the printer, on the Additional Port Information Required page, select the type of network card that the printer is connected to. Click **Next.**
10. If the correct network card is available, click the **Custom** option and click the **Settings** button to open the Configure Standard TCP/IP Port Monitor dialog box (as shown in Figure 11-19). Then, specify the port protocol (**Raw** or **LPR**) and the port

Figure 11-19

Specifying TCP/IP Port Monitor settings

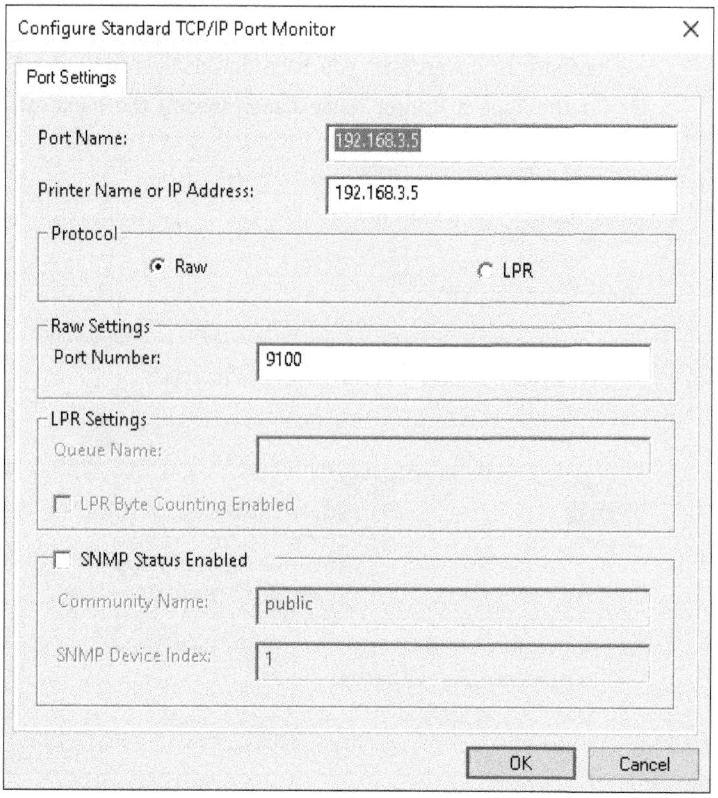

number. The default TCP/IP printer port is port 9100. Click **OK** to close the Configure Standard TCP/IP Port Monitor dialog box. Then, back on the Additional Port Information Required page, click **Next.**

11. On the Install the Printer Driver page, select the manufacturer and printer. If your printer is not listed, click the **Have Disk** button so you can navigate to drivers that you have downloaded or received with the printer. Click **Next.**
12. On the Type a Printer Name page, specify the name of the printer. Click **Next.**
13. On the Printer Sharing page, specify the share name. You can also specify the Location or Comments. Although Windows 10 supports long printer names and share names (including spaces and special characters), it is best to keep names short, simple, and descriptive. The entire qualified name, including the server name (for example, \\Server1\HP4100N-1), should be 32 characters or fewer.
14. When the printer is successfully added, you can print the standard Windows test page by clicking the **Print a test page** button. Click **Finish.**

When you install a printer, the printer that you just added becomes the default printer. To make your printer the default printer, right-click the printer and choose Set as default printer.

Windows can provide a driver to the clients if the driver is loaded on the server. Because Windows 7 through 10 is available in 32-bit and 64-bit editions, many companies have a mix of 32-bit and 64-bit computers. If other Windows clients connect to the printer on your local computer, Windows can provide 32-bit and 64-bit print drivers to those clients.

ADD ADDITIONAL PRINT DRIVERS

GET READY. To add additional print drivers in Windows 10, perform the following steps.

1. Log on to LON-SVR1 as **adatum\administrator** with the password of **Pa$$w0rd.**
2. Right-click **Start** and choose **Control Panel.**
3. Under Hardware and Sound, click **View Devices and Printers.**
4. Click any printer and then click the **Print server properties** option.
5. In the Print Server Properties dialog box, select the **Drivers** tab.
6. Click **Add.** The Add Printer Driver Wizard opens.
7. On the Welcome to the Add Printer Driver Wizard page, click **Next.**
8. On the Processor Selection page (as shown in Figure 11-20), select the appropriate processor (**x64** and/or **x86**) and then click **Next.**

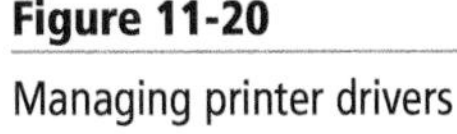

Figure 11-20

Managing printer drivers

Add Printer Driver Wizard
Processor Selection
Each processor uses its own set of printer drivers.
Select the processor of all computers that will be using this driver:
Processor
x64
x86
< Back
Next >
Cancel

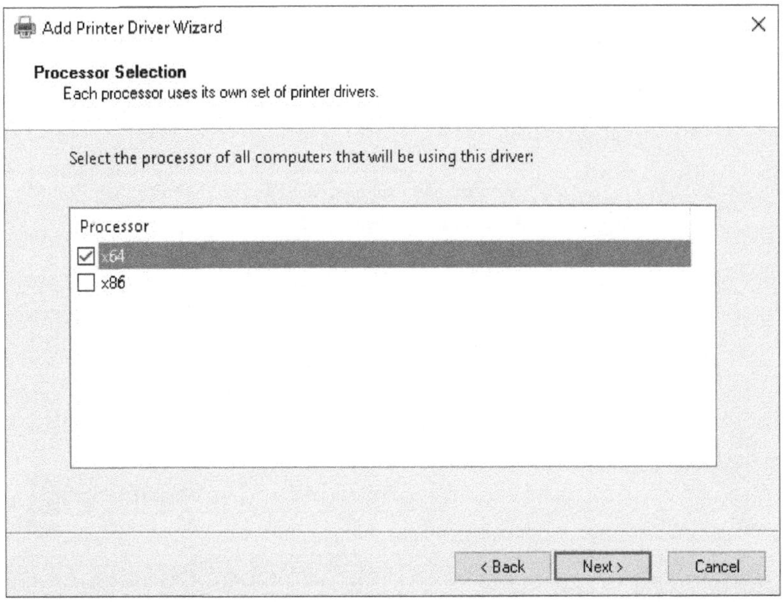

9. On the Install the Printer Driver page, select the manufacturer and printer. If your printer is not listed, click the **Have Disk** button so you can navigate to drivers that you have downloaded or received with the printer. Click **Next.**
10. When the wizard is complete, click **Finish.**

TAKE NOTE*

You can also use Group Policy to install and configure printers.

You can also install and configure printers from Windows 10 Settings, specifically Devices > Printers & scanners. If you don't want the default printer to be the last used printer, you can turn off the appropriate setting.

Understanding Printer Properties

With most printers, you have a wide range of options. Although these options vary from printer to printer, they are easily accessible by right-clicking the printer in the Devices and Printers folder and selecting Printer Properties.

In the Printer Properties dialog box (as shown in Figure 11-21), the following options are available:

- **General tab:** Allows you to configure the printer name, location, and comments and to print a test page. In addition, if you click the Printing Preferences button on the General tab, the default paper size, paper tray, print quality/resolution, pages per sheet, print order (such as front to back or back to front), and number of copies will display. The actual options that are available will vary depending on your printer.
- **Sharing tab:** Allows you to share a printer. You can also publish the printer in Active Directory if you choose the List in the directory option. Because a printer on a server can be used by other clients connected to the network, you can add additional drivers by clicking the Additional Drivers button. When sharing a printer, you are using TCP ports 139 and 445 and UDP ports 137 and 138.
- **Ports tab:** Allows you to specify which port (physical or TCP/IP) the printer will use as well as create new TCP/IP ports.
- **Advanced tab:** Allows you to configure the driver to use with the printer, the priority of the printer, when the printer is available, and how print jobs are spooled.

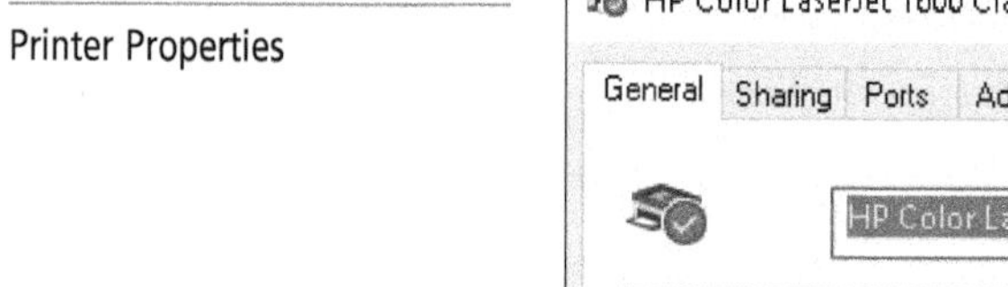

Figure 11-21
Printer Properties

- **Security tab:** Allows you to specify the permissions for the printer.
- **Device Settings tab:** Allows you to configure the trays, font substitution, and other hardware settings.

Some printers may have additional tabs, such as Color Management.

If you right-click a printer and choose Printing preferences, you can specify the following default settings when you print a document:

- Orientation (Portrait or Landscape)
- The type of paper or paper tray
- Black & White or Color

You can click the Advanced button to specify other advanced default settings, such as number of copies, print quality, page order, watermark, and sleep time settings.

Configuring Printer Sharing

Printers are considered objects. Therefore, as with NTFS files and folders, you can assign permissions to a printer so that you can specify who can use the printer, who can manage the printer, and who can manage the print jobs.

When you open the Printer Properties dialog box, you can configure sharing using the Sharing tab. You can change the share name and specify whether you want to render the print jobs on the client computer or not.

To configure the print sharing permissions, click the Security tab, as shown in Figure 11-22. Windows 10 and Windows Server 2016 provide three levels of ***printer permissions***:

- **Print:** Allows users to send documents to the printer
- **Manage this printer:** Allows users to modify printer settings and configurations, including the ACL itself
- **Manage documents:** Provides the ability to cancel, pause, resume, or restart a print job

Figure 11-22

Printer permissions

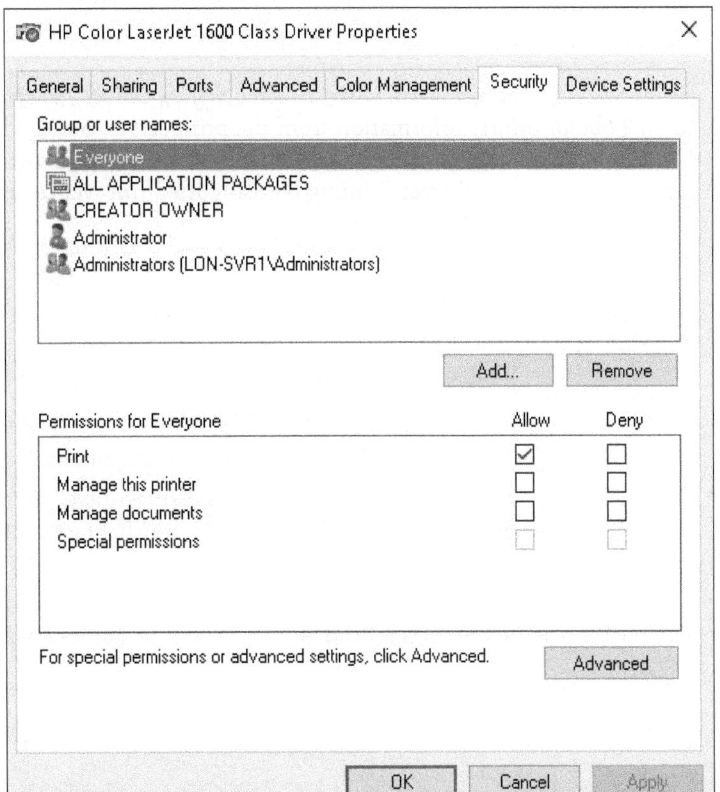

By default, the Print permission is assigned to the Everyone group. If you need to restrict who can print to the printer, remove the Everyone group and add another group or user and assign the Allow print permission to the group or user. Of course, it is still recommended that you use groups instead of users. As with file permissions, you can also deny print permissions.

SHARE A PRINTER

GET READY. To share a printer in Windows Server 2016, perform the following steps.

1. Log on to LON-SVR1 as **adatum\administrator** with the password of **Pa$$w0rd.**
2. Right-click **Start** and choose **Control Panel.**
3. Under Hardware and Sound, click **View Devices and Printers.**
4. Right-click the printer and choose **Printer properties.**
5. To share a printer, click the **Sharing** tab.
6. If you need to share the printer, click the **Share this printer** option, and in the Share name text box, specify the share name of the printer.
7. Click the **Security** tab.
8. To add a group or user, click **Add.**
9. In the Select Users, Computers, Service Accounts, or Groups dialog box, in the Enter the object names to select text box, type the name of the user or group. Click **OK.**
10. Back on the Security tab, select the user or group.
11. Specify the print permissions for the user or group and click **OK.**

Configuring Branch Office Direct Printing

If a printer is installed on a print server at the corporate office, when a user prints from a remote site, the print job travels over the WAN link to the corporate office print server, and then travels back to the branch office. Even if a document is relatively small, the print job could grow many times larger. The print jobs could consume valuable bandwidth.

With Windows Server 2016, when ***Branch Office Direct Printing*** is enabled, Windows clients obtain printer information from the print server, but send the print jobs directly to the printer. The large print jobs stay local, which increases network efficiency. You can configure Branch Office Direct Printing by using the Print Management console or a Windows PowerShell command-line interface.

CONFIGURING BRANCH OFFICE DIRECT PRINTING

GET READY. To share a printer in Windows Server 2016, perform the following steps.

1. Log on to LON-SVR1 as **adatum\administrator** with the password of **Pa$$w0rd.**
2. In Server Manager, click **Tools > Print Management.**
3. In the navigation pane, expand **Print Servers**, and then expand the print server that is hosting the network printer for which Branch Office Direct Printing will be enabled.
4. Click the **Printers** node and then right-click the desired printer and choose **Enable Branch Office Direct Printing**, as shown in Figure 11-23.

Figure 11-23

Enabling Branch Office Direct Printing

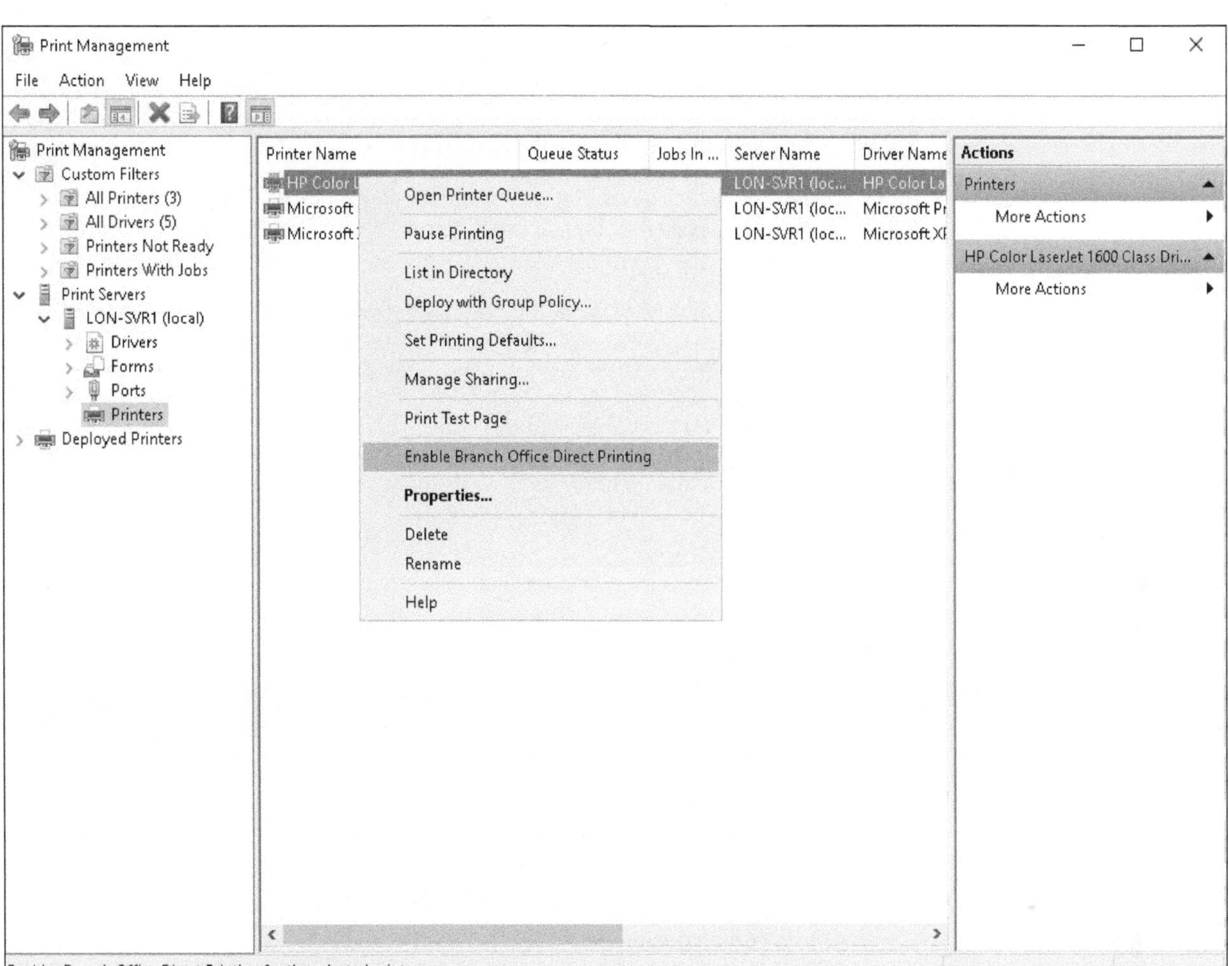

Alternatively, to configure Branch Office Direct Printing by using Windows PowerShell, execute the following cmdlet at a Windows PowerShell prompt:

```
Set-Printer -name "<Printer Name Here>" -ComputerName <Print Server
Name Here> -RenderingMode BranchOffice
```

SKILL SUMMARY

IN THIS LESSON YOU LEARNED:

- Distributed File System (DFS) is a set of technologies that enable a Windows server to organize multiple distributed SMB file shares into a distributed file system. Although the shares can be on different servers, the location is transparent to the users. Finally, DFS can provide redundancy to improve data availability while minimizing the amount of traffic passing over the WAN links.
- A referral is an ordered list of servers or targets that a client computer receives from a domain controller or namespace server when the user accesses a namespace root or a DFS folder with targets.

- DFS Replication enables you to replicate folders between multiple servers. To allow efficient use of the network, it propagates only the changes, uses compression, and uses scheduling to replicate the data between the servers.
- To determine what needs to be replicated, DFS uses staging folders. The staging folder acts as a cache for new and changed files that need to be replicated. It is also used to compress files that need to be sent. When received on the other end, it is used to decompress the file and install the file into the replicated folder.
- When using BranchCache, you are essentially creating a WAN accelerator where information is cached on branch computers or local servers. If the document is cached, it is accessed from the local branch office rather than going across a slower WAN link.
- With Windows Server 2016, the hosted cache mode uses one or more dedicated servers to host the cache. Distributed cache mode has the cache distributed among the local Windows 7, 8/8.1, or 10 clients at the local site. Content on an individual client is shared with the other clients at the site.
- With Windows Server 2016, when Branch Office Direct Printing is enabled, Windows clients obtain printer information from the print server but send the print jobs directly to the printer. The large print jobs stay local, which increases network efficiency.

Knowledge Assessment

Multiple Choice

Select the correct answer for each of the following questions.

1. Which of the following are types of DFS Namespace? (Choose two answers.)
   a. Domain-based namespace
   b. Replicated namespace
   c. Stand-alone namespace
   d. Server-based namespace
2. How many target folders are possible for each namespace in Windows Server 2008 mode?
   a. 1,000
   b. 5,000
   c. 25,000
   d. 50,000
3. Which of the following is an ordered list of servers and targets that a client computer receives from a domain controller or namespace server when a user accesses a namespace root or a DFS folder with targets?
   a. Replication list
   b. Referrals
   c. Target priority list
   d. SID control list
4. Which of the following is the default topology used in DFS Replication?
   a. Site-based topology
   b. Namespace topology

c. Hub/spoke topology
d. Full mesh topology

5. Which of the following is the compression algorithm used in DFS Replication found with Windows Server 2016?
   a. Remote Differential Compression
   b. EFS
   c. BitLocker
   d. FRS
6. Which of the following is the default size of a staging folder?
   a. 1 GB
   b. 2 GB
   c. 4 GB
   d. 8 GB
7. Which of the following is the collection of servers that hold targets of a DFS folder?
   a. Replication group
   b. Replication list
   c. Target list
   d. Referral list
8. Which of the following is a shared folder of shared folders?
   a. DFS Namespace
   b. DFS Linkage
   c. DFS Replication
   d. FRS Replication
9. Which of the following replaced File Replication Services (FRS)?
   a. EFS Replication
   b. Remote Differential Compression
   c. NTFS Replication
   d. AD Dynamic Replication
10. Which of the following is the default quota size of the Conflict and Deleted folder?
    a. 660 MB
    b. 1.2 GB
    c. 2 TB
    d. 4 GB
11. Which Windows Server 2016 server acts as a WAN accelerator?
    a. NFS accelerator
    b. BranchCache
    c. File Server Resource Manager
    d. GPO Cache
12. Which mode in BranchCache allows you to store the cache among multiple computers running Windows 7, Windows 8.1 or Windows 10?
    a. Hosted cache mode
    b. Distributed cache mode
    c. WSCache
    d. WideRanceCache

Best Answer

Choose the letter that corresponds to the best answer. More than one answer choice may achieve the goal. Select the BEST answer.

1. Which of the following is used to create a centralized backup environment of multiple sites?
   a. DFS Namespace
   b. DFS Linkage
   c. DFS Replication
   d. FRS Replication
2. Which of the following is used to prevent oversaturating of a WAN link?
   a. Namespace topology
   b. Referrals
   c. Quotas
   d. Scheduling
3. As an administrator, you discover that two users changed the same file from two different locations that are using DFS Replication, causing a conflict. In which of the following locations is the losing file stored?
   a. In the ConflictandDeleted folder
   b. In the Staging folder
   c. In the Recycle Bin
   d. In the C:\Temp folder
4. An Active Directory domain named contoso.com includes two servers, serverl and server2, which are namespace servers for the \\contoso\.com\DFS1 namespace. Which of the following actions will configure the \\contoso.com\DFS1 namespace so that users only connect to Server2 when Serverl is unavailable?
   a. On the \\contoso.com\DFS1 namespace, modify the referrals settings.
   b. On the \\contosol.com\DFS1 namespace, modify the advanced settings.
   c. From the properties of the \\Serverl\DFS1 namespace servers entry, modify the advanced settings.
   d. From the properties of the \\Server2\DFS1 namespace servers entry, modify the advanced settings.
5. A domain-based namespace called DFS is running Windows Server 2008 Server mode. Which of the following actions ensures users can only see files and folders that they have permission to access?
   a. Modify the Discretionary Access Control List.
   b. Enable access-based enumeration.
   c. Modify the view permissions.
   d. Disable referrals.
6. As an administrator at a corporate office, you have a file server called *Server01*. At a remote site, you installed BranchCache on Server02, which is acting as a BranchCache hosted cache server. To move things along, you decide to preload the data from the file shares on Serverl to the cache on Server02. Which of the following generates the hashes for the file share on Server01?
   a. Use the `Enable-BCCache` PowerShell cmdlet.
   b. Use the `Publish-BCCache` PowerShell cmdlet.
   c. Use the `Export-BCCachepackage` PowerShell cmdlet.
   d. Use the `Set-BCCache` PowerShell cmdlet.

Matching and Identification

1. Match the following terms with the related description or usage.
    ____ **1.** Domain-based namespace
    ____ **2.** Windows Server 2008 mode
    ____ **3.** Windows Server 2000 Server mode
    ____ **4.** Remote Differential Compression
    ____ **5.** Hub/spoke
    ____ **6.** DFS Replication
    ____ **7.** Full mesh
    ____ **8.** Stand-alone DFS
    ____ **9.** Referral

    a. Detects changes to the data in a file and replicates only those changes
    b. An ordered list of servers or targets that a client computer receives from a domain controller or namespace server when a user accesses a namespace root or a DFS folder with targets
    c. A single server that replicates to the other members
    d. Stores information in Active Directory
    e. Supports up to 256 connections
    f. Supports up to 5,000 folders per namespace
    g. Supports access-based enumeration
    h. A topology in which all members replicate to all other members
    i. Information stored on a member server

Build List

1. Specify the correct order of four basic steps necessary when using DFS to create a fault-tolerant shared folder. Not all steps will be used.
    ____ Share the folders.
    ____ Use robocopy to sync the folders.
    ____ Configure DFS Replication between folders on the various servers.
    ____ Run the prime utility.
    ____ Create the same folder on multiple servers.
    ____ Create a DFS Namespace that includes targets of all target folder.
    ____ Take ownership of all files and folders and reset permissions.
2. Specify the correct order of steps necessary to creating a DFS Namespace. Not all steps will be used.
    ____ Type the name of the server.
    ____ Select stage now.
    ____ Specify the location of the shared folder and shared permissions.
    ____ Click Create.
    ____ Type the name of the namespace.
    ____ Select either Windows Server 2000 mode or Windows Server 2008 mode.
    ____ Specify either domain-based namespace or stand-alone namespace.
    ____ Start the New Namespace Wizard.

Business Case Scenarios

Scenario 11-1: Backing Up Remote File Servers

You are an administrator responsible for 10 file site servers connected to the central office with 2,048 Mb/s WAN links. You attempted to run backups over the WAN links, but the backups took too long to execute. Describe your recommended solution.

Scenario 11-2: Protecting Essential File Servers

You administer a file server that has key files that must be accessed from people in multiple sites throughout the country. These files must be accessible 24/7 while keeping performance as high as possible. Describe your recommended solution.

Scenario 11-3: Configuring BranchCache for a Remote Site

You are an administrator for a site (Site1) that has about 20 users. For the last few months, users at Site1 have been complaining about the performance when accessing multiple files at the corporate office, particularly if the files are relatively large. They have no dedicated server to configure DFS Replication. Therefore, describe your recommended solution for improving performance when accessing these files.

Implementing High-Performance Network Solutions

LESSON 12

70-741 EXAM OBJECTIVE

Objective 6.1 – Implement high-performance network solutions. This objective may include but is not limited to the following: Implement NIC Teaming or the Switch Embedded Teaming (SET) solution, and identify when to use each; enable and configure Receive Side Scaling (RSS); enable and configure network Quality of Service (QoS) with Data Center Bridging (DCB); enable and configure SMB Direct on Remote Direct Memory Access (RDMA)–enabled network adapters; enable and configure SMB Multichannel; enable and configure virtual Receive Side Scaling (vRSS) on a Virtual Machine Queue (VMQ)–capable network adapter; enable and configure Virtual Machine Multi-Queue (VMMQ); enable and configure Single-Root I/O Virtualization (SR-IOV) on a supported network adapter.

Lesson Heading	Exam Objective
Implementing High-Performance Network Solutions • Configuring NIC Teaming • Configuring Server Message Block (SMB) Multichannel • Configuring Quality of Service (QoS) • Configuring Network Quality of Service with Data Center Bridging (DCB) • Enabling Remote Direct Memory Access (RDMA) with Switch Embedded Teaming (SET) • Optimizing Network Performance	Enable and configure Receive Side Scaling (RSS) Enable and configure virtual Receive Side Scaling (vRSS) on a Virtual Machine Queue (VMQ)-capable network adapter Implement NIC Teaming or the Switch Embedded Teaming (SET) solution, and identify when to use each Enable and configure network Quality of Service (QoS) with Data Center Bridging (DCB) Enable and configure SMB Direct on Remote Direct Memory Access (RDMA)-enabled network adapters Enable and configure Single-Root I/O Virtualization (SR-IOV) on a supported network adapter Enable and configure SMB Multichannel Enable and configure Virtual Machine Multi-Queue (VMMQ)

KEY TERMS

Common Internet File System (CIFS)
converged network
Data Center Bridging (DCB)
dynamic VMQ
IPsec task offloading
Network Direct
NIC Teaming
Packet Direct
Quality of Service (QoS)
Receive Side Scaling (RSS)Remote Direct Memory Access (RDMA)
Server Message Block (SMB)
Server Message Block (SMB) 3.0
Single-Root I/O Virtualization (SR-IOV)
SMB Direct
Switch Dependent Mode
Switch Embedded Teaming (SET)
Switch Independent Mode
Virtual Machine Multi-Queues (VMMQs)
Virtual Machine Queue (VMQ)

Implementing High-Performance Network Solutions

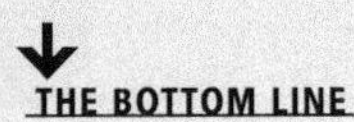

In Lesson 1, you learned how to configure IP settings, including the IP address, default gateway, and DNS settings. To configure the IP settings for a network adapter, you must first load the appropriate driver for the adapter. Fortunately, Windows includes many drivers, which Windows usually loads automatically when it detects the adapter.

CERTIFICATION READY
Enable and configure Receive Side Scaling (RSS)
Objective 6.1

CERTIFICATION READY
Enable and configure virtual Receive Side Scaling (vRSS) on a Virtual Machine Queue (VMQ)–capable network adapter
Objective 6.1

When you open Network and Sharing Center and then open the properties for a network adapter, you can configure the following settings (see Figure 12-1):

- **Client for Microsoft Networks:** Allows your computer to access resources in a Microsoft network.
- **File and Printer Sharing for Microsoft Networks:** Allows your computer to share files and printers in a Microsoft network.
- **Internet Protocol Version 4 (TCP/IPv4):** Allows you to communicate with other computers over an IPv4 network. Unless you are using DHCP, you must specify the IP address, subnet mask, gateway, and other network information.
- **Internet Protocol Version 6 (TCP/IPv6):** Allows you to communicate with other computers over an IPv6 network. Unless you are using DHCP, you must specify the IP address, subnet mask, gateway, and other network information.
- **Link-Layer Topology Discovery Mapper I/O Driver and Link-Layer Topology Discovery Responder:** Allows you to discover and display your home network map.

TAKE NOTE* Based on the adapter, you might see additional settings available to configure. For example, Figure 12-1 shows QoS Packet Scheduler, Microsoft Network Adapter Multiplexor Protocol, and Microsoft LLDP Protocol Driver.

Figure 12-1

Configuring the properties of an Ethernet adapter

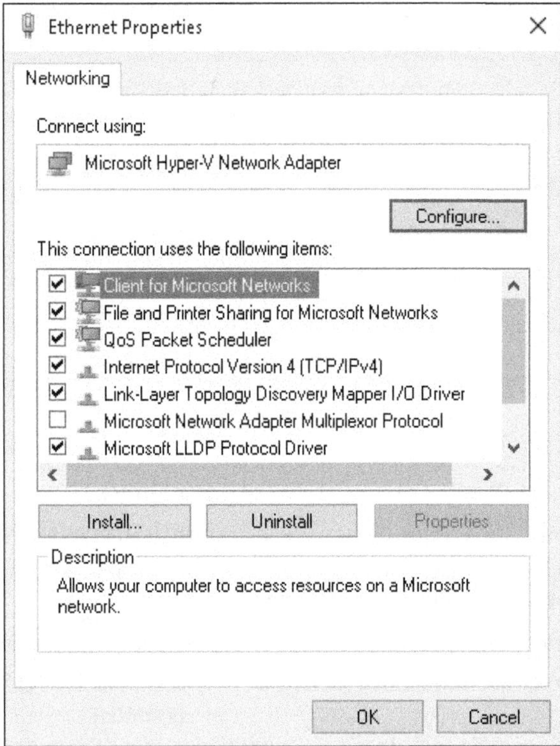

When you click the Configure button, the network adapter properties display, as shown in figure 12-2. The Advanced tab allows you to configure speed settings, MAC address, performance, and power consumption settings. Although these settings vary from adapter to adapter and driver to driver, some of the common settings include:

- **Adaptive Inter-Frame Spacing:** Enables a time gap between packets to help compensate for excessive Ethernet packet collisions on the network.
- **Flow Control:** Helps increase the efficiency of traffic regulation for connections that both support flow control frames. These frames are sent by an adapter when the receive queues reach a predefined limit, to signal the sending station to pause transmission so the adapter does not drop the packets.
- **IPv4 Checksum Offload:** Enables the adapter to compute the IPv4 checksum of packets instead of the host OS, which can help increase adapter performance while also reducing CPU utilization.
- **Jumbo Frames/Jumbo Packet:** Increases the standard Ethernet frame size of 1,514 bytes, such as to 4,088, 9,014, or 16,128 bytes. The larger sizes can increase throughput and decrease CPU utilization. However, to use the larger sizes, all devices across the network must have the same settings. Furthermore, the Jumbo Frames functionality might not work well across different vendors.
- **MAC Address:** Enables you to enter a MAC address for the adapter, overriding the default MAC address.
- ***Network Direct (Remote Direct Memory Access [RDMA]):*** Allows the network adapter to transfer data directly to or from the application memory, without any work being done by the processor, which allows high-throughput, low-latency networking.
- **Offload TCP Segmentation:** Allows the adapter to perform any necessary TCP segmentation of outgoing packets instead of the host OS, which can help increase transmission performance while also reducing CPU utilization.
- ***Packet Direct:*** Replaces the Network Driver Interface Specification (NDIS), which has been the standard network driver interface for the last 20 years, and was not designed for 100-GB network speeds. Packet Direct enables compliant applications to tell the network what they need, thereby increasing the efficiency of the network stack.
- **QoS Packet Tagging:** Enables the adapter to send and receive 802.1p QoS and 802.1Q VLAN indications.
- **Receive Buffers/Receive Buffer Size:** Specifies the buffer size of system memory that can be used by the adapter for received packets, which can be increased to help improve the performance of outgoing network traffic, but it consumes system memory.
- ***Receive Side Scaling (RSS):*** Enables the distribution of incoming network processing across multiple processor cores in multi-core computers, which can help increase performance.
- **Speed and Duplex:** Allows you to select the desired speed (such as 10 Mbps, 100 Mbps, 1 Gbps, or 10 Gbps) and duplex (half-duplex or full-duplex). Half-duplex communication transmits data in both directions but not at the same time. Full-duplex transmits data in both directions at the same time. The default setting is usually auto-negotiation.
- **TCP Checksum Offload:** Allows the adapter to compute the TCP checksum of outgoing packets rather than the host OS, which can help increase transmission performance while also reducing CPU utilization.
- **Transmit Buffers/Send Buffer/Send Buffer Size:** Specifies the buffer size of system memory that can be used by the adapter for sending packets, which can be increased to help improve the performance of outgoing network traffic, but it consumes system memory.
- **UDP Checksum Offload:** Enables the adapter to compute the UDP checksum of outgoing packets instead of the host OS, which can help increase transmission performance while also reducing CPU utilization.
- **Wake on Magic Packet:** Enables you to remotely power on the computer from sleep, hibernation, or when fully powered off by using the magic packet of the Wake-on-LAN feature.

Figure 12-2

Configuring the advanced properties of an adapter

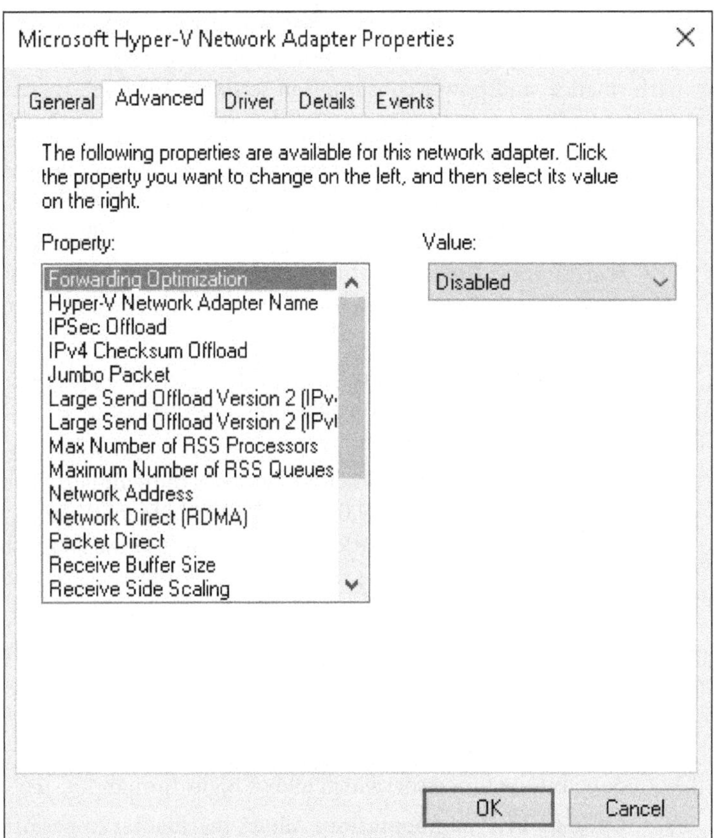

Configuring NIC Teaming

NIC Teaming, also called bonding, balancing, and aggregation, is a Windows feature that enables administrators to join multiple network adapters into a single entity, for performance enhancement or fault-tolerance purposes. Hyper-V virtual machines can also take advantage of NIC Teaming, but they are limited to teams of only 2, as opposed to the host operating system, which can have teams of up to 64 NICs.

CERTIFICATION READY
Implement NIC Teaming or the Switch Embedded Teaming (SET) solution, and identify when to use each
Objective 6.1

To use NIC Teaming in Hyper-V, you must complete three basic tasks, as follows:

1. Create the NIC team in the Windows Server 2016 host operating system.
2. In Hyper-V Manager, create an external virtual switch using the NIC team.
3. Configure the network adapter in a virtual machine to connect to the virtual switch representing the NIC team.

NIC Teaming in Windows Server 2016 supports two modes:

- ***Switch independent mode:*** All of the network adapters are connected to different switches, providing alternative routes through the network. Static teaming and LACP are switch dependent modes.
- ***Switch dependent mode:*** All of the network adapters are connected to the same switch, providing a single interface with their combined bandwidth.

In switch independent mode, you can choose between two configurations. The active/active configuration leaves all of the network adapters functional, providing increased throughput. If one adapter fails, all of the traffic is shunted to the remaining adapters. In the active/standby configuration, one adapter is left offline, to function as a failover in the event the active adapter fails. In active/active mode, an adapter failure causes a performance reduction; in active/standby mode, the performance remains the same before and after an adapter failure.

In switch dependent mode, you can choose static teaming, a generic mode that balances the traffic between the adapters in the team, or you can opt to use the Link Aggregation Control Protocol (LACP) defined in IEEE 802.3ax, assuming that your equipment supports it. When you select the *static teaming* mode, you manually configure both the switch and the host to identify which links form the team.

There is one significant limitation to NIC Teaming. If your traffic consists of large TCP sequences, such as a Hyper-V live migration, the system will shun using multiple adapters for those sequences, to minimize the number of lost and out-of-order TCP segments. You do not, therefore, realize any performance increase for large file transfers using TCP.

You can create and manage NIC teams using Server Manager or Windows PowerShell. In the following exercise, you learn how to create a NIC team using Server Manager.

CREATE A NETWORK TEAM ON WINDOWS SERVER 2016

GET READY. To create a network team on Windows Server 2016, perform the following steps.

1. Log on to a computer running Windows Server 2016 with an administrator account, such as **adatum\administrator** with the password of **Pa$$w0rd.**
2. If Server Manager is not open, click **Start** and then click **Server Manager.**
3. Click **All Servers** and then click the server that you want to create the team on. Then, right-click the server and choose **Configure NIC Teaming.**
4. In the NIC Teaming window, in the Teams section, click **Tasks > New Team.**
5. In the NIC Teaming dialog box, in the Team name text box, type **Team1.**
6. Select two adapters.
7. To show the Additional properties, click the **Additional properties** option (as shown in Figure 12-3). The Additional options allow you to specify the teaming mode, load balancing mode, and standby adapter.

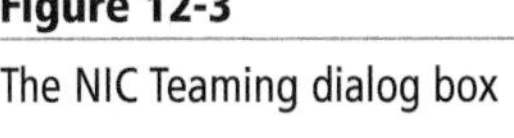

Figure 12-3

The NIC Teaming dialog box

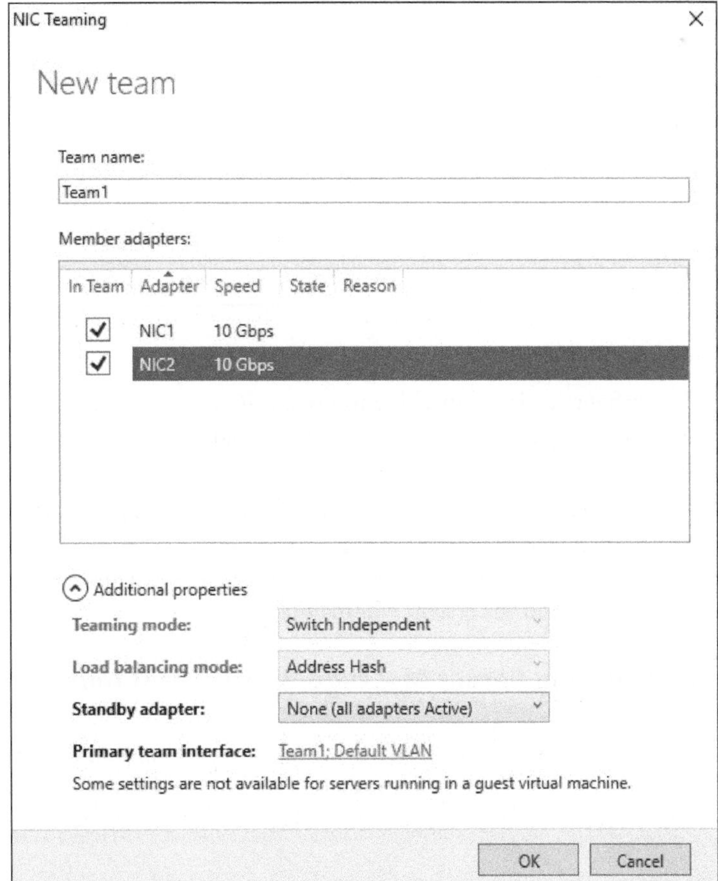

8. To define a VLAN, click the **Primary team interface** link. If you need to specify a VLAN, click the **Specific VLAN** option, and type the VLAN ID. Click **OK**.
9. Click **OK** to close the NIC Teaming dialog box.

Once you have created the NIC team, you can open Hyper-V Manager, open Virtual Switch Manager, and create a new virtual switch by selecting the External network option and choosing Microsoft Network Adapter Multiplexor Driver from the drop-down list, as shown in Figure 12-4.

Figure 12-4

The Virtual Switch Properties settings for a NIC team switch

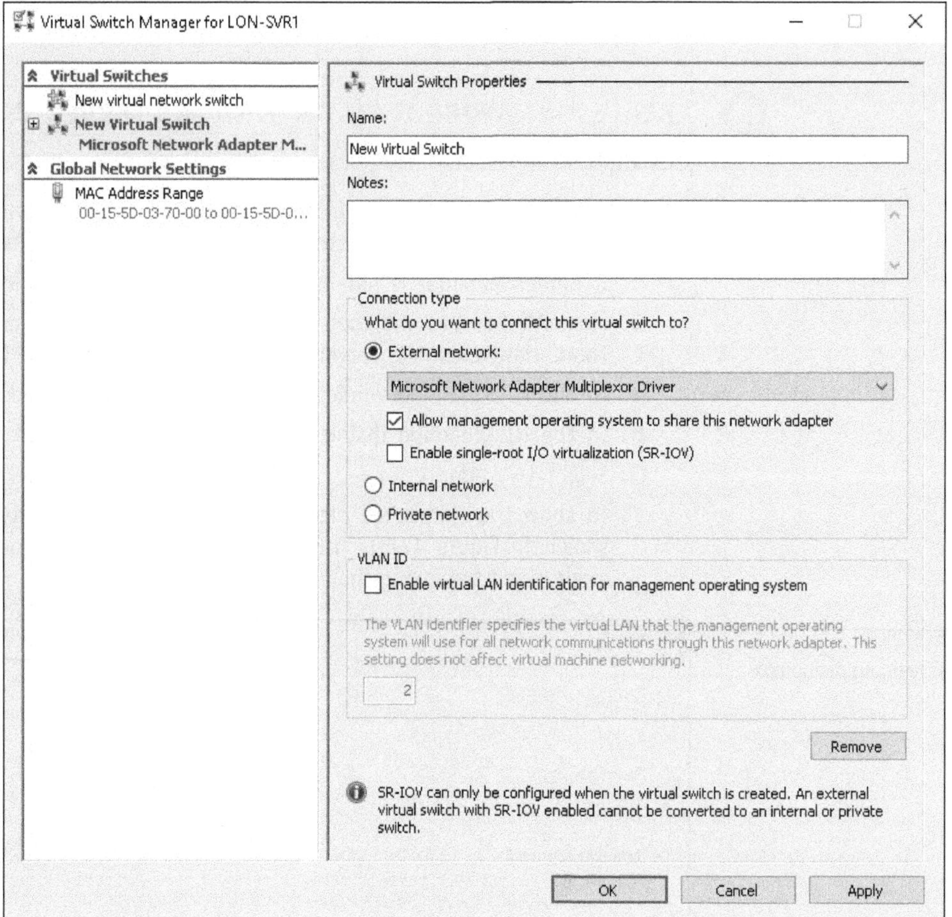

To configure a virtual machine to use a NIC team, you must use the Settings dialog box to modify the properties for a virtual network adapter, configuring it to use the team switch you created in the previous section, as shown in Figure 12-5.

Finally, you must open the Advanced Features page for the network adapter and select the *Enable the network adapter to be part of a team in the guest operating system* check box. At this point, the NIC team is operational for the virtual machine. You can unplug one of the network cables, and the system will maintain its connection to the network.

Configuring Server Message Block (SMB) Multichannel

Server Message Block (SMB), also known as ***Common Internet File System (CIFS)***, is a client/server file-sharing protocol that was created in 1984 by Microsoft. Through the years, there have been different versions, as shown in Table 12-1.

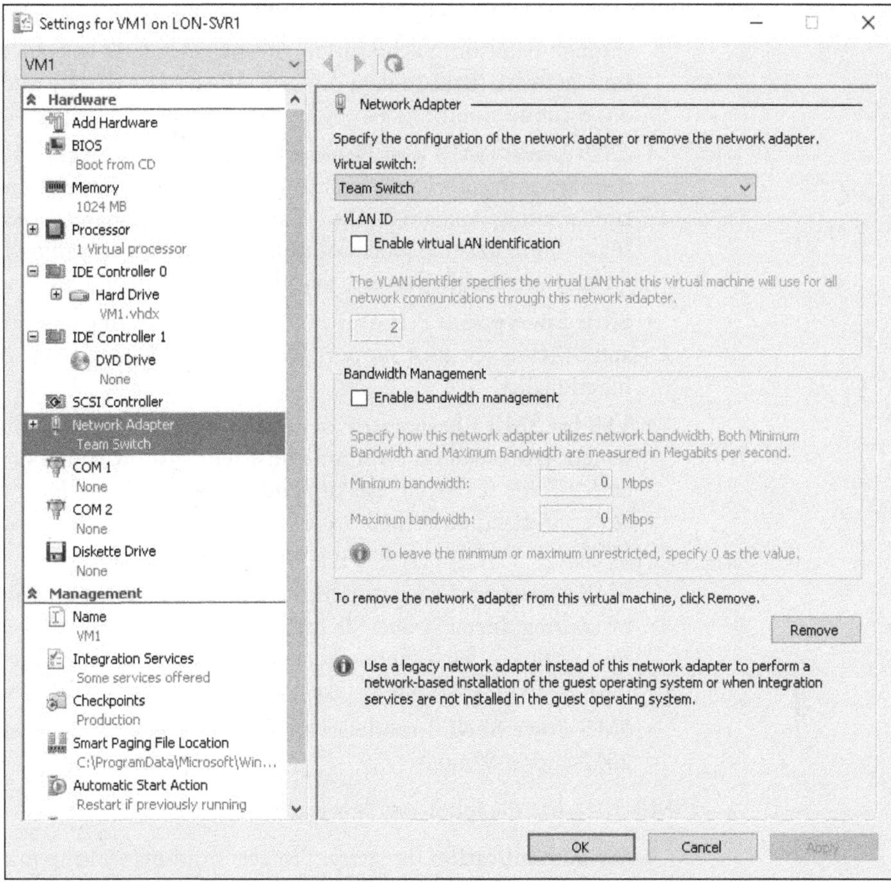

Figure 12-5

The Network Adapter settings for a NIC team adapter

Table 12-1

SMB Versions

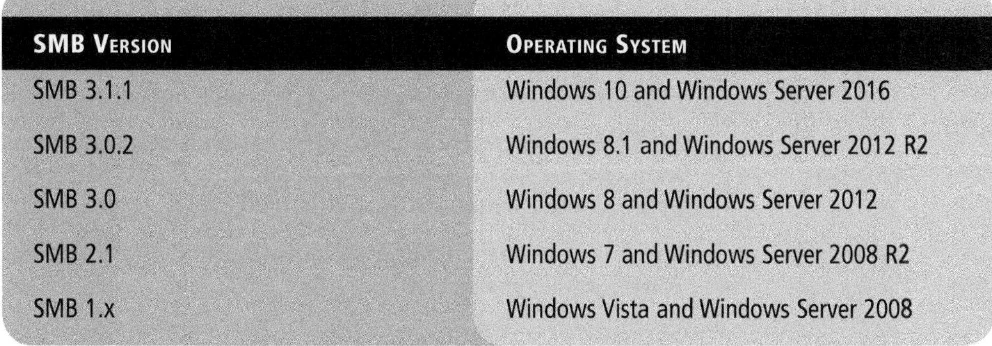

SMB Version	Operating System
SMB 3.1.1	Windows 10 and Windows Server 2016
SMB 3.0.2	Windows 8.1 and Windows Server 2012 R2
SMB 3.0	Windows 8 and Windows Server 2012
SMB 2.1	Windows 7 and Windows Server 2008 R2
SMB 1.x	Windows Vista and Windows Server 2008

Server Message Block (SMB) 3.0 was introduced with Windows 8 and Windows Server 2012. It brings significant changes to add functionality and improve performance, particularly in virtualized data centers.

SMB 3.0 has the following additional features:

- **SMB Transparent Failover:** Provides continuously available properties that allow SMB 3 clients to not lose an SMB session when failover occurs. Both the SMB client and SMB server must support SMB 3.0 to take advantage of the SMB Transparent Failover functionality.
- **SMB Scale Out:** Allows users to scale shared bandwidth by adding cluster nodes. Both the SMB client and SMB server must support SMB 3.0 to take advantage of the SMB Scale Out feature. SMB 1.0 clients do not contain the required client functionality to access SMB scale-out file shares and receive an "Access Denied" error message when they try to connect to a scale-out file share. SMB 2.x clients can connect to SMB scale-out file shares but do not benefit from the SMB Transparent Failover functionality.

- **SMB Multichannel:** Uses multiple network interfaces to provide both high performance through bandwidth aggregation and network fault tolerance through the use of multiple network paths to data on an SMB share. SMB 1.0 and SMB 2.x clients use a single SMB connection.
- ***SMB Direct*** **(SMB over Remote Direct Memory Access [RDMA]):** Enables direct memory-to-memory data transfers between servers, with minimal CPU utilization and low latency, using standard RDMA-capable network adapters (iWARP, InfiniBand, and RoCE). It also minimizes the processor utilization when performing large file I/O operations. SMB Direct functionality requires that the SMB client and SMB server support SMB 3.0.
- **SMB Encryption:** Performs encryption by selecting a check box. Both the SMB client and SMB server must support SMB 3.0 to take advantage of the SMB Encryption functionality.
- **VSS for SMB file shares:** Extends the Windows Volume Shadow Copy Service infrastructure to enable application-consistent shadow copies of server application data stored on SMB file shares, for backup and restore purposes. Both the SMB client and SMB server must support SMB 3.0 to take advantage of the Volume Shadow Copy Service (VSS) for SMB file shares functionality.
- **SMB Directory Leasing:** Reduces the latency when accessing files over slow WAN links by caching directory and file metadata for longer periods, which reduces the associated round-trips to fetch the metadata from the server. Both the SMB client and SMB server must support SMB 3.0 to take advantage of the SMB Directory Leasing functionality.
- **SMB PowerShell:** Introduces SMB PowerShell management cmdlets in Windows Server 2012 and in Windows 8.

SMB 3.1.1 has the following new features:

- **Pre-authentication integrity:** Protects from man-in-the-middle attacks by using a Secure Hash Algorithm 512 (SHA-512) hash to verify packet contents during session setup
- **SMB encryption improvements:** Improves SMB encryption so that it now defaults to AES-128-GCM encryption algorithm, which has better performance than AES-128-CCM, which was used in SMB 3.0.2
- **Cluster dialect fencing:** Supports rolling upgrades of Scale-Out File Server clusters

In Windows Server 2016, SMB Multichannel is enabled by default; you do not have to install additional roles, role services, or features. The SMB client automatically detects and uses multiple network connections when the configuration is identified.

If you want to disable SMB Multichannel on the server side, execute the following Windows PowerShell command:

```
Set-SmbServerConfiguration -EnableMultiChannel $false
```

To disable SMB Multichannel on the client side, execute the following Windows PowerShell command:

```
Set-SmbClientConfiguration -EnableMultiChannel $false
```

To enable SMB Multichannel, you just have to reissue the commands but use `$true`.

Configuring Quality of Service (QoS)

A ***converged network*** shares a single network infrastructure that handles storage, data, voice, video, cluster, and management traffic. ***Quality of Service (QoS)*** is a collection of technology that ensure high-quality performance for critical applications. It measures network bandwidth, detects changing network connections, such as congestion or availability of bandwidth, and then prioritizes or throttles network traffic.

CERTIFICATION READY
Enable and configure network Quality of Service (QoS) with Data Center Bridging (DCB)
Objective 6.1

QoS management in Hyper-V takes the form of controls that enable you to specify the minimum and maximum input/output operations per second (IOPS) for a disk. To configure storage QoS, open the Settings dialog box for a VM, expand a hard drive component, and select Quality of Service. After selecting the Enable Quality of Service management check box (as shown in Figure 12-6), you can specify minimum and maximum IOPS values for the disk to throttle its throughput in 8-KB increments.

Figure 12-6
Storage Quality of Service controls in Hyper-V Manager

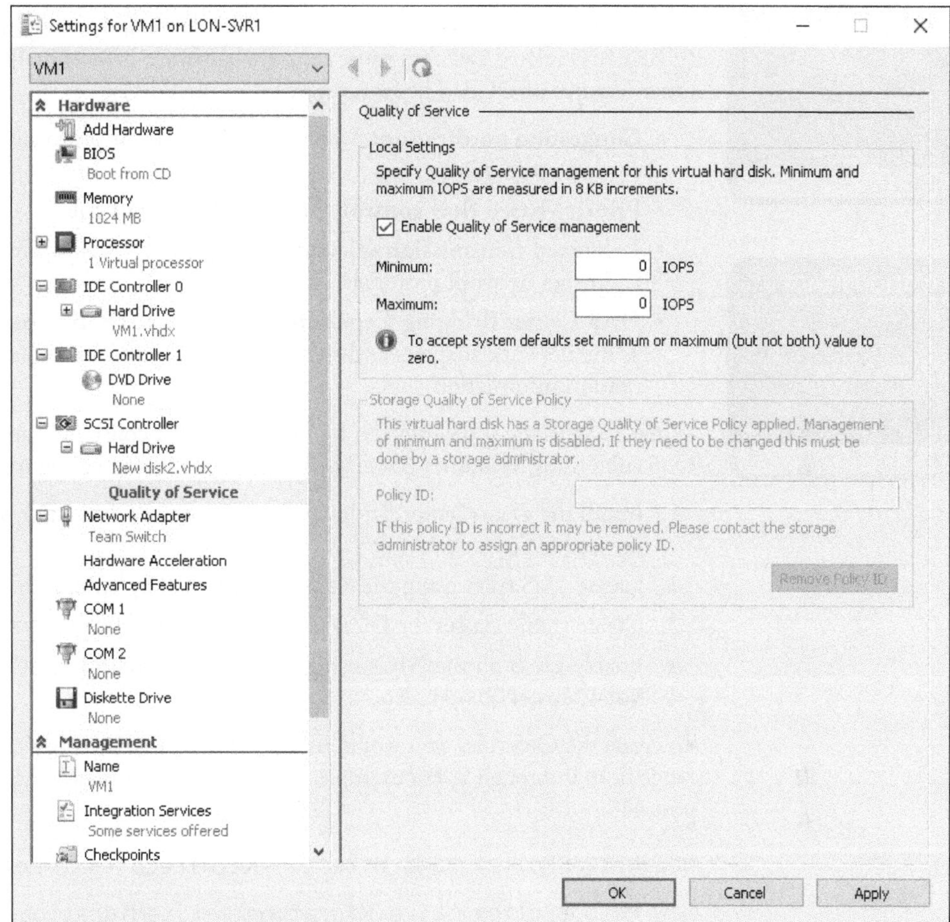

ENABLE QUALITY OF SERVICE

GET READY. To enable Quality of Service for a virtual disk, perform the following steps.

1. Log on to a computer running Windows Server 2016 with an administrator account, such as **adatum\administrator** with the password of **Pa$$w0rd.**
2. If Server Manager is not open, click **Start** and then click **Server Manager.**
3. Click **Tools > Hyper-V.**
4. Right-click a virtual machine and choose **Settings.**
5. In the Settings dialog box, navigate to and expand a virtual disk node and click **Quality of Service.**
6. Select the **Enable Quality of Service management** check box.
7. In the Minimum and Maximum IOPS text boxes, specify the appropriate values.
8. Click **OK** to close the Settings dialog box.

Configuring Network Quality of Service with Data Center Bridging (DCB)

Data Center Bridging (DCB) is a suite of Institute of Electrical and Electronics Engineers (IEEE) standards that supports converged networks so network traffic can get sufficient bandwidth allocation, while maintaining reliability.

CERTIFICATION READY
Enable and configure network Quality of Service (QoS) with Data Center Bridging (DCB)
Objective 6.1

CERTIFICATION READY
Enable and configure SMB Direct on Remote Direct Memory Access (RDMA)-enabled network adapters
Objective 6.1

For you to use DCB, the converged network adapters, dedicated iSCSI host bus adapters (HBA), and related switches must support hardware-based Quality of Service (QoS) and other features of DCB. The features of DCB include:

- **Congestion notification:** Manages congestion for protocols that do not have built-in control mechanisms
- **Priority-based flow control:** Controls the flow of data
- **Enhanced transmission selection:** Enables the system to reserve bandwidth for iSCSI and other network protocols
- **Data Center Bridging Capabilities eXchange (DCBX) protocol:** Enables devices such as the network adapters and switches to communicate and share capabilities and configuration information

When establishing QoS enforced by DCB, you first configure the switches and then create the QoS rules using Windows PowerShell. The four steps in configuring the QoS rules include:

1. Install the Data Center Bridging feature with the `Install-WindowsFeature` cmdlet or Server Manager.
2. Create QoS rules using the `New-NetQoSPolicy` cmdlet that will classify protocols.
3. Create traffic classes for DCB using the `New-NetQoSTrafficClass` cmdlet.
4. Enable DCB on the NICs using the `Set-NetQosDcbxSetting` and `Enable-NetAdapterQos` cmdlets.

To create the QoS rules, you would use the `New-NetQoSPolicy` cmdlet. The priorities can range from 0 through 7. For example, the following command classifies SMB Direct that uses port 445:

```
New-NetQoSPolicy "SMB Direct" -NetDirect 445 -Priority 2
```

```
New-NetQosPolicy "Live Migration" -LiveMigration -Priority 5
```

The `New-NetQoSTrafficClass` cmdlet creates a class that matches the higher-level QoS rule. The command requires that you name the class, use a priority to pair the QoS rule, specify the fair ETS algorithm, and specify the minimum bandwidth weight. Enhanced Transmission Selection (ETS) is a transmission selection algorithm (TSA) that is specified by the IEEE 802.1Qaz draft standard.

Examples of using New-NetQoSTrafficClass include:

```
New-NetQosTrafficClass "Live Migration" -Priority 5 -Algorithm ETS
-Bandwidth 30
```

```
New-NetQosTrafficClass "SMB Direct" -Priority 2 -Algorithm ETS
-Bandwidth 40
```

On each server, you can enable the DCB settings with the following command:

```
Set-NetQosDcbxSetting -Willing $false
```

Lastly, you can enable DCB on the RDMA-capable NICs (rNICs). For example, to enable rNIC1, execute the following command:

```
Enable-NetAdapterQos "rNIC1"
```

Enabling Remote Direct Memory Access (RDMA) with Switch Embedded Teaming (SET)

A converged network allows for different types of communication within a single network, such as storage, video, and data communication. You can form a converged network by combining Switch Embedded Teaming (SET) with Remote Direct Memory Access (RDMA), which allows you to utilize fewer network adapters in your servers.

CERTIFICATION READY
Implement NIC Teaming or the Switch Embedded Teaming (SET) solution, and identify when to use each
Objective 6.1

An alternative to NIC Teaming is to use SET. ***Switch Embedded Teaming (SET)*** allows you to use a Hyper-V virtual switch to team up to eight physical Ethernet adapters located on the same Hyper-V host into one or more software-based virtual network adapters. The virtual network adapters provide fast performance and fault tolerance in the event of a network adapter failure.

To use any RDMA over converged Ethernet, you must install the Data Center Bridging (DCB) Windows feature, which allows Ethernet-based RDMA technologies to work better. RDMA does not function on NIC Teaming. DCB can be installed with the following Windows PowerShell command:

```
Install-WindowsFeature Data-Center-Bridging
```

To create a SET team, you have to create the Hyper-V virtual switch with the `New-VMSwitch` Windows PowerShell command, by including the `EnableEmbeddedTeaming` parameter in your command syntax. For example, to create a new virtual switch called Team2Switch, execute the following command:

```
New-VMSwitch -Name Team2Switch -NetAdapterName "NIC 1","NIC 2"
-EnableEmbeddedTeaming $true
```

If you want to create a SET-capable switch with a single team member so that you can add a team member at a later time, use the `EnableEmbeddedTeaming` parameter:

```
New-VMSwitch -Name TeamedvSwitch -NetAdapterName "NIC 1"
-EnableEmbeddedTeaming $true
```

To add host vNICs and make them RDMA-capable, use the following commands:

```
Add-VMNetworkAdapter -SwitchName SETswitch -Name SMB_1 -managementOS

Add-VMNetworkAdapter -SwitchName SETswitch -Name SMB_2 -managementOS

Enable-NetAdapterRDMA "vEthernet (SMB_1)","vEthernet (SMB_2)"
```

Optimizing Network Performance

CERTIFICATION READY
Enable and configure Single-Root I/O Virtualization (SR-IOV) on a supported network adapter
Objective 6.1

First, you need to make sure that the physical network infrastructure is using at least 1-GB or faster links. As stated earlier in this book, it is recommended that you use the standard network adapters because they are faster than the legacy network adapters and can reduce CPU overhead. You can also use VLANS, which help isolate networks, use bandwidth management to control the amount of traffic at one time, and use NIC Teaming to provide larger bandwidth pipes. In addition, you can access network adapter hardware acceleration to enable Virtual Machine Queue, IPsec task offloading, and Single-Root I/O Virtualization.

CERTIFICATION READY
Enable and configure SMB Multichannel
Objective 6.1

For those machines that need additional performance, some network adapters support features that assist specifically with virtualization and iSCSI storage, including:

- ***Virtual Machine Queue (VMQ)*** uses hardware packet filtering to deliver data directly to virtual machines from an external network, reducing the overhead of routing packets from the management operating system to the virtual machine. Only Hyper-V-specific network adapters support this feature.

CERTIFICATION READY
Enable and configure Virtual Machine Multi-Queue (VMMQ)
Objective 6.1

- ***IPsec task offloading*** enables IPsec task offloading at the machine level, reducing the demands on the virtual machine's CPU by using a dedicated processor on the physical network adaptor. This feature is only supported on Hyper-V-specific network adapters.
- ***Single Root I/O Virtualization (SR-IOV)*** allows a device, such as a network adapter, to distribute access to its resources among PCI Express hardware functions. You can configure a maximum number of offloaded security associations from 1 to 4,096. This feature is supported only on Hyper-V-specific network adapters.

In Windows Server 2016, network performance has been enhanced by ***Virtual Machine Multi–Queues (VMMQs)***, where traffic is spread across multiple queues per virtual machine.

OPTIMIZE NETWORK PERFORMANCE IN HYPER-V

GET READY. To optimize network performance for Hyper-V virtual machines running on Windows Server 2016, perform the following steps.

1. If Server Manager is not open, click **Start** and then click **Server Manager**.
2. Click **Tools > Hyper-V**.
3. Right-click the VM and choose **Settings**.
4. In the Settings dialog box, expand a network adapter node and click **Hardware Acceleration**, as shown in Figure 12-7.

Figure 12-7

Configuring Hardware Acceleration

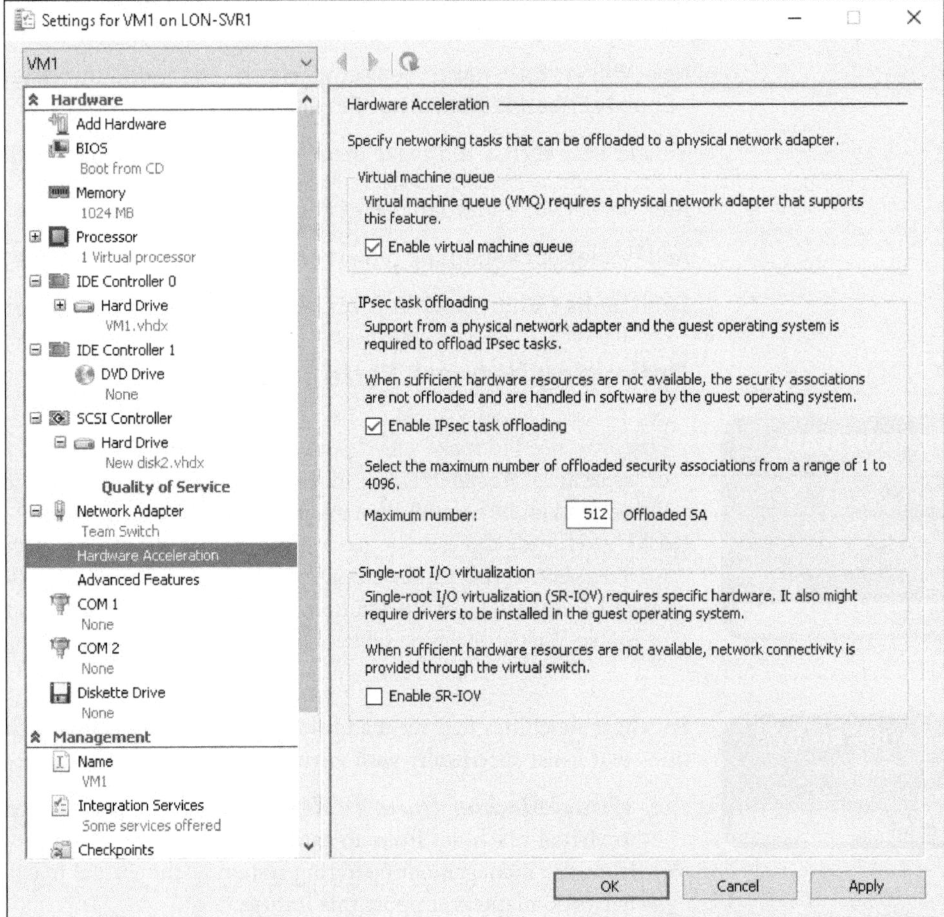

5. By default, the Enable virtual machine queue and Enable IPsec task offloading check boxes are enabled. The default maximum number of IPsec tasks is 512. You can change the number of IPsec tasks by specifying a number from 1 to 4,096.
6. To enable Single-Root I/O Virtualization, select the **Enable SR-IOV** check box.
7. Click **OK** to close the Settings dialog box.

Dynamic VMQ dynamically distributes incoming network traffic processing to physical host CPU cores based on processor usage and network load. When there is heavy network load, dynamic VMQ automatically employs more processors. When the network load is light, dynamic VMQ relinquishes processors. It also spreads interrupts for network traffic across the available processors.

To use Dynamic VMQ, the host computer needs to have network adapters that support Dynamic VMQ. Dynamic VMQ is enabled by default in Windows Server 2016. To view the status of dynamic VMQ, use the following Windows PowerShell command:

```
Get-NetAdapterVmq
```

You can enable or disable it by using the Windows PowerShell cmdlets. For example, to enable a network adapter (NIC1), use the following Windows PowerShell command:

```
Enable-NetAdapterVmq NIC1
```

To disable the same network adapter, use:

```
Disable-NetAdapterVmq NIC2
```

Dynamic VMQ and RSS are very similar. Although VMQ is more automatic, RSS can better avoid a ping-pong effect that has a processor perform work, which generates a lot of network traffic, which then makes the work jump to another processor. By jumping to another processor, a lot of network traffic is generated by the work, which then causes the workload to be moved back to the original processor.

SKILL SUMMARY

IN THIS LESSON YOU LEARNED:

- To configure the IP settings for a network adapter, you must first load the appropriate driver for the adapter. Fortunately, Windows includes many drivers, which Windows usually loads automatically when it detects the adapter.
- NIC Teaming, also called bonding, balancing, and aggregation, is a Windows feature that enables administrators to join multiple network adapters into a single entity, for performance enhancement or fault-tolerance purposes.
- A converged network shares a single network infrastructure that handles storage, data, voice, video, cluster, and management traffic.
- Quality of Service (QoS) is a collection of technology that ensure high-quality performance for critical applications. It measures network bandwidth, detects changing network connections, such as congestion or availability of bandwidth, and then prioritizes or throttles network traffic.
- An alternative to NIC Teaming is to use SET. Switch Embedded Teaming (SET) allows you to use a Hyper-V virtual switch to team up to eight physical Ethernet adapters located on the same Hyper-V host into one or more software-based virtual network adapters.
- Virtual Machine Queue (VMQ) uses hardware packet filtering to deliver data directly to virtual machines from an external network, reducing the overhead of routing packets from the management operating system to the virtual machine.

■ Knowledge Assessment

Multiple Choice

Select the correct answer for each of the following questions.

1. Which option increases the Ethernet frame size so that throughput can be increased and CPU utilization can be decreased?
   a. Packet Direct
   b. Offload TCP Segmentation
   c. Flow Control
   d. Jumbo Frames
2. Which option distributes an incoming network processor across multiple processors?
   a. Network Direct
   b. QoS Packet Tagging
   c. TCP Checksum Offload
   d. Receive Side Scaling
3. Which of the following allows the aggregation of multiple networks so that bandwidth and fault tolerance can be increased?
   a. Converged network
   b. NIC Teaming
   c. SMB Direct
   d. Virtual Machine Multi-Queues
4. Which of the following describes SMB Direct?
   a. SMB Transparent Failover
   b. SMB Scale Out
   c. SMB over Remote Direct Memory Access
   d. SMB Multichannel
5. Which type of network supports storage, data, voice, and video data?
   a. Converged network
   b. Data Center Bridging
   c. Single-Root I/O Virtualization
   d. Multipath network
6. Which of the following is used to ensure that voice and video are delivered to a client without latency and jitter on a converged network?
   a. QoS
   b. SMB Direct
   c. Packet Direct
   d. Dynamic VMQ
7. Which of the following is used to deliver data directly to virtual machines from an external network?
   a. RSS
   b. Virtual Machine Queue (VMQ)
   c. SR-IOV
   d. IPsec task offloading

Best Answer

Choose the letter that corresponds to the best answer. More than one answer choice may achieve the goal. Select the BEST answer.

1. Which of the following can provide the best network performance for virtual machines?
   - **a.** NIC Teaming
   - **b.** SET with RDMA
   - **c.** SMB 3.0
   - **d.** QoS

Build List

1. Specify the correct order of steps necessary to establishing QoS enforced by DCB.
   ____ Create traffic rules.
   ____ Enable DCB on the NIC.
   ____ Create traffic classes.
   ____ Install Data Center Bridging.

■ Business Case Scenarios

Scenario 12-1: Making VMs Fault Tolerant

You are an administrator at an organization that uses a Hyper-V host with 20 virtual machines. You need to make sure that the machines are reasonably fault tolerant. Therefore, you purchased and installed dual power supplies and uninterruptible power supplies for the host and you are using RAID. Describe additional steps you can take to make these more fault tolerant while maintaining high performance.

To make the network connections more fault tolerant, you can combine multiple network connections into an aggregated connection. If the network interface or cable goes down, you will remain connected through the remaining connections. To get the best performance, you should use Switch Embedded Teaming (SET), with Remote Direct Memory Access (RDMA).

Determining Scenarios and Requirements for Implementing Software-Defined Networking (SDN)

70-741 EXAM OBJECTIVE

Objective 6.2 – Determine scenarios and requirements for implementing Software-Defined Networking (SDN). This objective may include but is not limited to the following: Determine deployment scenarios and network requirements for deploying SDN; determine requirements and scenarios for implementing Hyper-V Network Virtualization (HNV) using Network Virtualization Generic Route Encapsulation (NVGRE) encapsulation or Virtual Extensible LAN (VXLAN) encapsulation; determine scenarios for implementation of Software Load Balancer (SLB) for North-South and East-West load balancing; determine implementation scenarios for various types of Windows Server Gateways, including L3, GRE, and S2S, and their use; determine requirements and scenarios for distributed firewall policies and network security groups.

Lesson Heading	Exam Objective
Introducing Virtual Machine Manager	
Understanding Software-Defined Networking (SDN)	
• Determining Deployment Scenarios and Network Requirements for Deploying SDN	Determine deployment scenarios and network requirements for deploying SDN
• Determining Requirements and Scenarios for Implementing Hyper-V Network Virtualization (HNV)	Determine requirements and scenarios for implementing Hyper-V Network Virtualization (HNV) using Network Virtualization Generic Route Encapsulation (NVGRE) encapsulation or Virtual Extensible LAN (VXLAN) encapsulation
• Implementing Network Controller	
• Determining Scenarios for Implementation of Software Load Balancing (SLB) for North-South and East-West Load Balancing	Determine scenarios for implementation of Software Load Balancing (SLB) for North-South and East-West load balancing
• Determining Implementation Scenarios for Various Types of Windows Server Gateways	Determine implementation scenarios for various types of Windows Server Gateways, including L3, GRE, and S2S, and their use
• Determining Requirements and Scenarios for Distributed Firewall Policies and Network Security Groups	Determine requirements and scenarios for distributed firewall policies and network security groups

KEY TERMS

Datacenter Firewall
Distributed Firewall Manager
dynamic IP addresses (DIPs)
East-West traffic
Hyper-V Network Virtualization (HNV)
Network Controller
network security groups (NSGs)
Network Virtualization Generic Route Encapsulation (NVGRE)
Northbound API
North-South traffic
SLB Multiplexer (MUX)
Software-Defined Networking (SDN)
Software Load Balancing (SLB)
Southbound API
Virtual Extensible LAN (VXLAN)
virtual IP addresses (VIPs)
Virtual Machine Manager Administrator console
VMM command shell
VMM library
VMM management server
Windows Server Gateway

Introducing Virtual Machine Manager

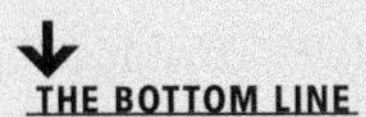

System Center 2016 Virtual Machine Manager (VMM) enables centralized management of virtualized workloads. VMM allows you to manage the virtualized data center infrastructure, increase physical server utilization (including providing simple and fast consolidation of the virtual infrastructure), perform virtual-to-virtual (V2V) migration, and perform intelligent workplace placement based on performance data and user-defined business policies.

In VMM, a cloud is an on-premises logical grouping of resources, such as storage, networks, hosts, load balancers, and libraries. To help delegate administration in VMM, VMM provides four administrative profiles, which assign permissions based on responsibility.

To simplify the management of Hyper-V physical hosts, VMM allows you to manage multiple Hyper-V physical hosts within the same console. You can also use VMM to manage VMware ESXi and Citrix XenServer.

To simplify the process of deploying servers, VMM includes the following features:

- You can use virtual machine templates for common server configurations.
- Using VMM and Microsoft System Center 2016 Service Manager, you can create virtual machine (VM) self-service portals that enable end users to provision approved servers and applications automatically, without assistance from the system administration team. For example, if you have a lab or development team that often needs new virtual machines, the lab personnel or development team can use the self-service portals to provision the servers.
- VMM uses bare-metal Hyper-V provisioning to automatically provision new Hyper-V hosts and bring them into the VMM environment to be managed.

The VMM deployment consists of the following components:

- VMM management server
- VMM Administrator console
- VMM database
- VMM library
- VMM library server
- VMM command shell

The ***VMM management server*** is the computer that runs the VMM service. It processes commands, transfers files, and communicates with the VMM database, library server, and virtualization hosts (including Microsoft Hyper-V, VMware ESX and ESXi, and Citrix XenServer). Because it is considered the hub of a VMM architecture, it should be the first VMM server installed.

The ***Virtual Machine Manager Administrator console*** allows you to centrally view and manage the VMM management server and related components, including the physical and virtual resources. It allows you to:

- Create, deploy, and manage virtual machines
- Monitor and manage hosts and library servers
- Manage global configuration settings

The VMM Administrator console is installed after the VMM server. It can be installed on the same computer as the VMM server or on a different computer. You can also install the console on multiple computers for easy management of any VMM server. However, you can only connect to and manage one VMM server at a time.

The VMM configuration information is stored in a Microsoft SQL Server database. When you install the VMM server, you specify the VMM database. You can access this information and configure VMM by using the VMM Administrator console or by using the Windows PowerShell - Virtual Machine Manager command shell.

The ***VMM library*** is a catalog of resources that can be used to deploy virtual machines and services. It includes virtual hard disks, ISO images, templates, profiles, PowerShell scripts, answer files, and virtual machines. The library server hosts shared folders that are used to store the file-based resources in the VMM library.

By default, the VMM server is also the default library server. If you are managing a large number of hosts, you should set up additional VMM library servers.

Lastly, VMM includes Windows PowerShell via the ***VMM command shell***. The command shell allows you to run commands to perform all functions that you can perform within the VMM Administrator console.

Understanding Software-Defined Networking (SDN)

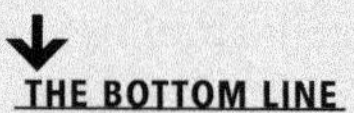

Software-Defined Networking (SDN) allows you to centrally configure and manage physical and virtual network devices, including routers, switches, and gateways in your data center. When creating a virtual infrastructure, you will configure Hyper-V virtual switches, Hyper-V Network Virtualization, and Windows Server Gateway. However, you also need to use and manage physical switches, routers, and other hardware devices and integrate the virtual devices and physical devices together.

By using SDN, you can merge the physical and virtual components that make up a virtual infrastructure. The applications and virtual servers will run on the physical network, and you can virtualize network management by creating virtual IP addresses, ports, and switches. You can also define policies that will manage traffic flow across both physical and virtual networks.

Microsoft has implemented Software-Defined Networking in Windows Server 2012, Windows Server 2012 R2, and Windows Server 2016 Hyper-V by providing the following components:

- **Network Controller:** New to Windows Server 2016, Network Controller provides centralized management, configuration, monitoring, and troubleshooting of both your virtual and physical network infrastructure.

- **Hyper-V Network Virtualization (HNV):** HNV helps you abstract or separate your applications and workloads from the underlying physical network by using virtual networks.
- **Hyper-V Virtual Switch:** Hyper-V virtual switches give you the ability to connect virtual machines to both virtual networks and your physical network. Similar to a physical switch, Hyper-V virtual switches provide security, isolation, and service-level policy enforcement.
- **RRAS Multi-tenant Gateway:** RRAS Multi-tenant Gateway gives you the ability to extend your network boundaries to Microsoft Azure or another provider to deliver on-demand hybrid infrastructure.
- **NIC Teaming:** NIC Teaming allows you to configure multiple network adapters as a team for bandwidth aggregation and traffic failover to guard against network component failure.

Determining Deployment Scenarios and Network Requirements for Deploying SDN

Before you deploy a software-defined network, you need to do some planning. You can start with making sure you can access all of your physical networking components and physical computer hosts.

CERTIFICATION READY
Determine deployment scenarios and network requirements for deploying SDN
Objective 6.2

For the physical network, you must make sure you have access to all of your physical networking components, including virtual LANs (VLANs), routers, and Border Gateway Protocol (BGP) devices. If you are using Remote Direct Memory Access (RDMA) technology, you need to use Data Center Bridging with Enhanced Transmission Selection, and if you are using RDMA over Converged Ethernet (RoCE), you need to use Data Center Bridging with Priority-based Flow Control.

The physical computer hosts are systems running Windows Server 2016 with the Hyper-V role. You also need to have external Hyper-V virtual switches created with at least one physical adapter.

To manage the physical computer host, you must assign a management IP address that is assigned to the management host virtual NIC (vNIC). The management network is used for the Hyper-V hosts to communicate with other Hyper-V hosts. In addition, you should have separate networks for gateways and software load balancers, including the following:

- **Transit logical network:** Allows the RAS Gateway and SLB Multiplexer (MUX) to exchange BGP peering information and North-South (external-internal) tenant traffic.
- **Public virtual IP address (VIP) logical network:** Allows for front-end IP addresses that external clients use to access resources in the virtual network. These addresses need to be Internet routable addresses.
- **Private VIP logical network:** Allows for access from internal cloud clients, via Generic Routing Encapsulation (GRE) gateways or private services. These addresses do not need to be routable outside of the cloud.
- **GRE VIP logical network:** Allows gateway virtual machines running on your SDN fabric to have a server-to-server (S2S) GRE connection type.
- **Logical networks required for RDMA-based storage:** Requires defining a VLAN and a subnet for each physical adapter in your computer and hostage hosts if you are using RDMA-based storage.
- **Routing infrastructure:** Used to advertised by the SLB MUX and HNV Gateways into the physical network by using internal BGP peering. Typically, you configure BGP peering in a managed switch or router as part of the network infrastructure.
- **Default gateways:** Allows the computer hosts to connect to other networks. You can configure only one default gateway on computers, and you usually configure the default gateway on the adapter that is used to reach all the way to the Internet.

Microsoft System Center is a powerful enterprise data center management system that you can use to monitor, provision, configure, automate, and maintain your IT infrastructure.

You can integrate Microsoft System Center with SDN to extend your SDN capabilities. Some of the components that are relevant to SDN are:

- **System Center Operations Manager:** Provides infrastructure monitoring for your data center and both the private and public cloud.
- **System Center Virtual Machine Manager:** Provides tools to manage a virtual infrastructure, which can give you the ability to provision and manage virtual networks.
- **Windows Server Gateway:** Allows you to route data center and cloud traffic between your virtual and physical networks. Windows Server Gateway is a virtual software router and gateway.

When you deploy SDN, you perform the following high-level procedure:

1. Install host networking and validate the configuration.
2. Run SDN Express scripts and validate setup.
3. Deploy a sample tenant workload and validate deployment.

When you prepare the Hyper-V hosts, you need to install the latest network drivers for all NICS, add the Hyper-V role, and create the Hyper-V virtual switch. You would then obtain the VLAN ID of your management VLAN and attach the management vNIC to the virtual switch of the management VLAN. Next, assign a valid IP configuration to the management vNIC of the newly created virtual switch. You also need to deploy a virtual machine to host the Active Directory Domain Services (AD DS) and Domain Name System (DNS) roles and join the Hyper-V hosts to the AD DS domain.

Then, run SDN Express scripts and validate the setup. The scripts can be found at https://github.com/Microsoft/SDN. To run the script, set up your deployment computer by installing Windows Server 2016 on the deployment computer, extract the scripts, and copy the SDNExpress folder from the extracted files to the root of drive C on the deployment computer.

The SDNExpress folder should contain the following subfolders:

- **AgentConf:** Stores copies of schemas used by the SDN Host Agent on each Windows Server 2016 Hyper-V host to program network policy
- **Certs:** Stores certificate files on a temporary basis
- **Images:** Stores your Windows Server 2016 .vhdx image file
- **Tools:** Stores the utilities and tools for troubleshooting
- **TenantApps:** Deploys tenant workloads
- **Scripts:** Stores the deployment scripts

The scripts folder contains the following scripts:

- **SDNExpress.ps1:** A script that deploys and configures the SDN fabric, including the Network Controller virtual machines, SLB/MUX virtual machines, gateway pools, and the HNV Gateway virtual machines corresponding to the pools.
- **FabricConfig.psd1:** A configuration file template for the SDNExpress script, which you customize for your environment.
- **SDNExpressTenant.ps1:** A script that deploys a sample tenant workload on a virtual network with a load-balanced VIP. You can use this script with an Undo option to delete the corresponding configuration.
- **TenantConfig.psd1:** A template configuration file for tenant workload and S2S gateway configuration.
- **SDNExpressUndo.ps1:** A script that cleans up the fabric environment and resets it to a starting state.

- **SDNExpressEnterpriseExample.ps1:** A script that provisions one or more enterprise site environments. You can use this script with an Undo option to delete the corresponding configuration.
- **EnterpriseConfig.psd1:** A script that is a template configuration file.

After you share the C:\SDNExpress folder, edit and configure the SDNExpress\scripts\FabricConfig.psd1 script file by changing the << Replace >> tags with specific values to fit your infrastructure, including:

- Host names
- Domain names
- User names and passwords
- Network information for your networks

In DNS, create a Host A record for:

- The NetworkControllerRestName (FQDN)
- The NetworkControllerRestIP

Then, run the following script as a Domain Admin:

```
SDNExpress\scripts\SDNExpress.ps1
-ConfigurationDataFile FabricConfig.psd1 -Verbose
```

If the script ran without errors, you can proceed to validate the setup:

1. Ensure that the Network Controller Host Agent and SLB Host Agent are running on all Hyper-V hosts by using the `Get-Service NCHostAgent` and `Get-Service SlbHostAgent` cmdlets.
2. Verify network connectivity on the management logical network between all Network Controller node virtual machines and Hyper-V hosts.
3. Use Netstat.exe to check that the Network Controller Host Agent is connected to the Network Controller on TCP:6640.
4. Verify that the dynamic IPs associated with all Hyper-V hosts that are hosting load-balanced tenant workload virtual machines have Layer-3 IP connectivity to the SLB Manager VIP address.
5. Use diagnostic tools to ensure that there are no errors on any fabric resources in the Network Controller. For example, use the `Debug-NetworkControllerConfigurationState` cmdlet.
6. Verify the BGP peering state to ensure that the SLB MUX is peered to the Top-of-Rack switch or RRAS virtual machine (the BGP peer). Run the following cmdlet from a Network Controller node virtual machine: `Debug-SlbConfigState`.

After you have deployed SDN and verified the configuration, you can deploy a sample tenant workload.

When you decide to implement SDN, you first need to decide if you want to use System Center Virtual Machine Manager to manage your SDN infrastructure. If you do, you will set up the SDN infrastructure using VMM using wizards or scripts. The VMM SDN Express scripts are located at https://github.com/manishmsft/SDN/tree/master/VMM/VMM%20SDN%20Express. If you do not want to use VMM, you can deploy the SDN using scripts located at https://github.com/Microsoft/SDN/tree/master/SDNExpress.

Typically, you would install Windows Server 2016 Datacenter edition for Hyper-V hosts and virtual machines (VMs) that run SDN infrastructure servers, such as Network Controller and Software Load Balancing nodes. However, you can run Windows Server 2016 Standard edition for Hyper-V hosts that contain only tenant workload virtual machines that are connected to SDN-controlled networks.

Determining Requirements and Scenarios for Implementing Hyper-V Network Virtualization (HNV)

Hyper-V Network Virtualization (HNV) allows you to create and manage virtual switches. With network virtualization, you can have multiple virtual networks, which can be logically isolated, on the same physical network infrastructure.

CERTIFICATION READY
Determine requirements and scenarios for implementing Hyper-V Network Virtualization (HNV) using Network Virtualization Generic Route Encapsulation (NVGRE) encapsulation or Virtual Extensible LAN (VXLAN) encapsulation
Objective 6.2

As part of SDN, network virtualization provides a layer of abstraction or separation over the physical network. The Hyper-V virtual switch in Windows Server 2016 supports network virtualization by using two IP addresses for each virtual machine. One address is used to connect with virtual networks, and the other is used to connect to the physical network topology. Network virtualization provides the following benefits:

- **Flexible virtual machine placement:** SND allows you to provide abstraction and separates IP addresses used in virtual machines from the IP addresses used on the physical network so that you can group or isolate virtual machines as needed.
- **Multi-tenant network isolation without VLANs:** SDN allows your network infrastructure to support multiple clients or tenants without the use of VLANs or the need to reconfigure physical network switches. When compared with the 12-bit identifier for VLANS, network virtualization uses a 24-bit identifier for virtual networks. In addition, instead of supporting 4,094 VLAN IDs, you can support 16 million virtual networks.
- **IP address reuse:** Because virtual networks are isolated, they can use the same address space without any conflict or issue, which allows virtual machines in different virtual networks to use the same or overlapping IP address space, even when deploying those virtual machines on the same physical network. Virtual networks are isolated, and they can use the same address space without any conflict or issue.
- **Live migration across subnets:** Network virtualization allows you to move virtual machines to different subnets and it can change the IP address to match the new network.
- **Support running virtual machines on a shared infrastructure as a service (IaaS) cloud:** By using network virtualization, you can move the virtual machines between Hyper-V hosts in your data center, between Hyper-V hosts in different data centers, and between Hyper-V hosts in your data center and the shared IaaS cloud.
- **Support for resource metering:** By providing resource metering, you can determine the usage of host and network resources for individual virtual machines, which can be used to charge a customer or tenant based on their actual resource usage.
- **Configuration by Windows PowerShell:** You can use Windows PowerShell to configure the network virtualization and isolation policies, including configuring, monitoring, and troubleshooting network virtualization.

HVN also implements overlay tenant networks using Virtual Extensible local area network (VXLAN) and Network Virtualization Generic Route Encapsulation (NVGRE). VXLAN is the default.

Virtual Extensible LAN (VXLAN) uses a VLAN-like encapsulation technique to encapsulate MAC-based OSI Layer 2 Ethernet frames within Layer 4 UDP packets. By default, VXLAN uses UDP port 4789. VXLAN endpoints, which terminate VXLAN tunnels and may be either virtual or physical switch ports, are known as VXLAN tunnel endpoints (VTEPs).

Windows Server 2016 Hyper-V uses ***Network Virtualization Generic Route Encapsulation (NVGRE)*** to implement network virtualization, which provides the two addresses for each virtual network adapter:

- **Customer address (CA):** The IP address that is configured and used by the virtual machine guest operating system. The CA address is used when communicating with another system. If you migrate a virtual machine to a different Hyper-V host, the CA can remain the same.

- **Provider address (PA):** The IP address that the virtualization platform assigns to the Hyper-V host and is dependent on the physical network infrastructure where the Hyper-V host is connected. When the virtual machine sends traffic on the physical network, the Hyper-V host encapsulates the packets and includes the PA as the source address from where the packets were sent. If you migrate a virtual machine to a different Hyper-V host, the PA changes. NVGRE is used to encapsulate its packets.

You can use network virtualization and policies to move virtual machines between Hyper-V hosts and preserve their network configuration.

Implementing Network Controller

The ***Network Controller*** is a Windows Server 2016 server role that provides two application programming interfaces (APIs): the Southbound API and the Northbound API. The ***Southbound API*** is used to communicate with the network, whereas the ***Northbound API*** gives you the ability to communicate with the Network Controller. For example, using the Network Controller, you can manage the Hyper-V virtual machines and virtual switches, Datacenter Firewall, RAS Multi-tenant Gateways, virtual gateways, gateway pools, and load balancers.

The Southbound API is used to communicate with network devices, services, and components. With it, you can discover network devices, detect service configuration, and gather information about the network.

The Northbound API allows you to gather network information from the Network Controller, which can be used to monitor and configure the network. It uses Windows PowerShell, Representational State Transfer (REST) API, and management applications to configure, monitor, troubleshoot, and deploy new devices on the network.

When you deploy a Network Controller in an AD DS domain, the Network Controller authenticates users and devices with Kerberos. When you deploy a Network Controller in a non-domain environment, you must deploy digital certificates to provide authentication.

You can deploy Network Controller on a server running Windows Server 2016 Datacenter edition. The management client must be installed on a computer running Windows 8/8.1 or Windows 10. You must configure dynamic DNS registration to enable registration of required DNS records for Network Controller.

If the computers or virtual machines running Network Controller or the management client for Network Controller are joined to a domain, you must create the following security groups:

- A security group that holds all the users who have permission to configure Network Controller
- A security group that holds all the users who have permission to configure and manage the network by using Network Controller

In addition, users added to these groups must also belong to the Domain Users group.

CREATE THE REQUIRED AD DS SECURITY GROUPS

GET READY. To create the required AD DS security groups, perform the following steps.

1. Log on to LON-DC1 as **adatum\administrator** with the password of **Pa$$w0rd.**
2. Click **Start** and click **Server Manager.**
3. In Server Manager, click **Tools > Active Directory Users and Computers.**
4. In Active Directory Users and Computers, expand **Adatum.com** and then click **IT.**
5. Right-click **IT** and choose **New > Group.**

6. In the New Object – Group dialog box, in the Group name text box, type **Network Controller Admins** and then click **OK.**
7. In the details pane, double-click **Network Controller Admins**, and in the Network Controller Admins Properties dialog box, on the Members tab, click **Add.**
8. In the Select Users, Contacts, Computers, Service Accounts, or Groups dialog box, in the Enter the object names to select (examples) text box, type **administrator** and then click **OK** twice.
9. Right-click **IT** and choose **New > Group.**
10. In the New Object – Group dialog box, in the Group name text box, type **Network Controller Ops** and then click **OK.**
11. In the details pane, double-click **Network Controller Ops**, and in the Network Controller Ops Properties dialog box, on the Members tab, click **Add.**
12. In the Select Users, Contacts, Computers, Service Accounts, or Groups dialog box, in the Enter the object names to select (examples) text box, type **administrator** and then click **OK** twice.
13. Close Active Directory Users and Computers.

If the system running Network Controller or the management client for Network Controller is not joined to a domain, you must configure certificate-based authentication:

- You must create a certificate for use on the management client that is trusted by the Network Controller.
- The certificate subject name must match the DNS name of the computer or virtual machine holding the Network Controller role, the server authentication purpose is present in enhanced key usage (EKU) extensions, and the certificate subject name should resolve to the IP address of the Network Controller, if Network Controller is deployed on a single computer or virtual machine, or the REST IP address, if Network Controller is deployed on multiple computers, multiple virtual machines, or both.
- The certificate must be trusted by all the REST clients, the SLB MUX, and the southbound host computers that Network Controller manages.

REQUEST A CERTIFICATE FOR AUTHENTICATING NETWORK CONTROLLER

GET READY. To request a certificate for authenticating Network Controller, perform the following steps.

1. Log on to LON-SVR2 as **adatum\administrator** with the password of **Pa$$w0rd.**
2. Right-click **Start** and choose **Run.**
3. In the Run dialog box, type **mmc.exe** and press **Enter.**
4. In the Console1 – [Console Root] window, click **File > Add/Remove Snap-in.**
5. In the Add or Remove Snap-ins dialog box, in the Snap-in list, double-click **Certificates.**
6. Click **Computer** account, click **Next**, and then click **Finish.**
7. Click **OK.**
8. In the navigation pane, expand **Certificates** and then expand **Personal.**
9. Right-click **Personal** and choose **All Tasks > Request New Certificate.**
10. In the Certificate Enrollment dialog box, on the Before You Begin page, click **Next.**
11. On the Select Certificate Enrollment Policy page, click **Next.**
12. Select the **Computer** check box and then click **Enroll.**
13. Click **Finish.**
14. Close the management console and do not save changes.

You can deploy the Network Controller role by following these high-level steps:

1. Install the Network Controller server role.
2. Configure the Network Controller cluster.
3. Configure the Network Controller application.
4. Validate the Network Controller deployment.

DEPLOY NETWORK CONTROLLER

GET READY. To deploy Network Controller, perform the following steps.

1. Log on to LON-SVR2 as **adatum\administrator** with the password of **Pa$$w0rd.**
2. Click **Start** and click **Server Manager.**
3. In Server Manager, in the details pane, click **Add roles and features.**
4. In the Add Roles and Features Wizard, on the Before You Begin page, click **Next.**
5. On the Select Installation Type page, click **Next.**
6. On the Select Destination Server page, click **Next.**
7. On the Select Server Roles page, in the Roles list, select the **Network Controller** check box.
8. Click **Add Features** and then click **Next.**
9. On the Select Features page, click **Next.**
10. On the Network Controller page, click **Next.**
11. On the Confirm Installation Selections page, click **Install.**
12. When the role is installed, click **Close.**
13. Right-click **Start** and choose **Shut down or sign out > Restart.**
14. In the Choose a reason that best describes why you want to shut down this computer dialog box, click **Continue.**
15. After LON-SVR2 has restarted, log on as **Adatum\administrator** with the password of **Pa$$w0rd.**

Alternatively, you can install the Network Controller server role by using the following Windows PowerShell command:

```
Install-WindowsFeature -Name NetworkController -IncludeManagementTools
```

After performing this task, restart your computer or virtual machine.

Configure the Network Controller cluster.

To configure the cluster, complete the following steps:

1. You must create a node object for each computer or virtual machine that is a member of the Network Controller cluster using the Windows PowerShell `New-NetworkControllerNodeObject` cmdlet. For example, to create a Network Controller node object named Node1 on NodeNC.Adatum.com, with Ethernet as the name of the interface on the computer listening to REST requests, use the following Windows PowerShell command:

   ```
   New-NetworkControllerNodeObject -Name "Node1" -Server "NodeNC
   .Adatum.com" -FaultDomain "fd:/rack1/host1" -RestInterface "Ethernet"
   ```

2. To configure the cluster, use the Windows PowerShell `Install-NetworkControllerCluster` cmdlets:

   ```
   $NodeObject = New-NetworkControllerNodeObject -Name "Node1"
   -Server "NCNode1.Adatum.com" -FaultDomain "fd:/rack1/host1"
   -RestInterface "Ethernet"
   Install-NetworkControllerCluster -Node $NodeObject
   -ClusterAuthentication Kerberos
   ```

To configure the Network Controller application, use the Windows PowerShell `Install-NetworkController` cmdlet. For example, to create a Network Controller node object, and then store it in the `$NodeObject` variable, use the following command:

```
$NodeObject = New-NetworkControllerNodeObject -Name "Node01"
-Server "NCNode11" -FaultDomain "fd:/rack1/host1" -RestInterface
Ethernet
```

Then, to get a certificate named NCEncryption, and store it in the `$Certificate` variable, use the following command:

```
$Certificate = Get-Item Cert:\LocalMachine\My | Get-ChildItem | where
{$_.Subject -imatch "NCEncryption" }
```

To create the Network Controller cluster, use the following command:

```
Install-NetworkControllerCluster -Node $NodeObject
-ClusterAuthentication None
```

In a test environment with a single node, there is no high-availability support; the Network Controller employs no authentication between the cluster nodes, between the REST clients and Network Controller. The command specifies the `$Certificate` to encrypt the traffic between the REST clients and Network Controller:

```
Install-NetworkController -Node $NodeObject -ClientAuthentication None
-RestIpAddress "10.0.0.1/24" -ServerCertificate $Certificate
```

After you have deployed the Network Controller, you can validate the deployment by adding a credential to the Network Controller and then retrieving the credential.

Complete this task by performing the following steps:

1. Open Windows PowerShell (Admin), and then run the following commands:

```
$cred=New-Object Microsoft.Windows.Networkcontroller
.credentialproperties

$cred.type="usernamepassword"

$cred.username="admin"

$cred.value="abcd"

New-NetworkControllerCredential -ConnectionUri https://
networkcontroller -Properties $cred -ResourceId cred1
```

2. To retrieve the credential that you added to Network Controller, run the following command:

```
Get-NetworkControllerCredential -ConnectionUri https://
networkcontroller -ResourceId cred1
```

Determining Scenarios for Implementation of Software Load Balancer (SLB) for North-South and East-West Load Balancing

If you have large workloads, you can try to divide the workload by distributing network traffic among virtual network resources. Windows ***Software Load Balancing (SLB)*** evenly distributes tenant and tenant customer network traffic among the virtual network resources. Like Network Load Balancing (NLB), Windows Server SLB enables multiple servers to host the same workload, providing high availability and scalability.

CERTIFICATION READY
Determine scenarios for implementation of Software Load Balancing (SLB) for North-South and East-West load balancing
Objective 6.2

When looking at network traffic patterns within a data center, you can divide traffic into two types. The ***North-South traffic*** is traffic between servers and clients. The ***East-West traffic*** is traffic between servers. SLB can be used in both types of traffic.

To provide load balancing, SLB maps ***virtual IP addresses (VIPs)*** to ***dynamic IP addresses (DIPs)***, which are part of a cloud service set of resources in the data center. Clients connect to a server via the VIP, which then translates to the appropriate DIP. The VIPs are in the ***SLB Multiplexer (MUX)***, which uses Border Gateway Protocol (BGP) to advertise each VIP on routers.

Network Controller hosts the SLB Manager and performs the following actions for SLB:

- Processes SLB commands that come in through the Northbound API
- Calculates policy for distribution to Hyper-V hosts and SLB MUXs
- Provides the health status of the SLB infrastructure

The Network Controller role can be used with SLB to distribute traffic based on the policies defined in the load balancer:

- Layer 4 load balancing for North-South and East-West network traffic
- Internal and external network traffic
- Dynamic IP addresses
- Health probes

Determining Implementation Scenarios for Various Types of Windows Server Gateways

A ***Windows Server Gateway*** is a virtual machine (VM)–based software router and gateway that allows cloud service providers (CSPs) and enterprise organizations to enable data center and cloud network traffic routing between virtual and physical networks, including the Internet.

CERTIFICATION READY
Determine implementation scenarios for various types of Windows Server Gateways, including L3, GRE, and S2S, and their use
Objective 6.2

To deploy Windows Server Gateway, you must use VMM. The Windows Server Gateway router uses a limited set of Border Gateway Protocol (BGP) configuration options, including Local BGP IP Address and Autonomous System Numbers (ASN) and List of BGP Peer IP Addresses. Although Windows Server Gateway supports IPv4 and IPv6, when you configure Windows Server Gateway with Network Address Translation (NAT), only NAT4 is supported. Windows Server Gateway supports Level 3 (L3) protocols, Generic Routing Encapsulation (GRE), and server-to-server (S2S) communications.

When you implement network virtualization with Hyper-V, the virtual switches operate as routers between different Hyper-V hosts in the same infrastructure. You can define network virtualization policies to define how packets are routed from one host to another. However, the virtual switch cannot route to networks outside the Hyper-V server infrastructure when using network virtualization. If you connect the virtual machine to an external switch and you do not use network virtualization, the virtual machine connects to the same network as the host machine.

Windows Server Gateway allows you to connect the virtualized networks to the Internet with a multi-tenant-aware mechanism so that traffic to external networks is routed correctly to the internal addresses that the virtual machines use. In addition to connecting to internal resources, you can also connect to external networks, including the Internet.

When you implement Windows Server Gateway, you can use one of three configurations:

- Multi-tenant-aware virtual private network (VPN) gateway
- Multi-tenant-aware NAT gateway
- Forwarding gateway for internal physical network access

With the multi-tenant-aware virtual private network (VPN) gateway, you configure Windows Server Gateway as a VPN gateway that is aware of the virtual networks deployed on the Hyper-V hosts. You can connect to the Windows Server Gateway by using a site-to-site VPN from a remote location. You can also configure individual users with VPN access. If you have multi-tenants, you can have multiple virtual networks with overlapping address space located on the same virtual infrastructure.

Multi-tenant-aware NAT gateway provides access to the Internet for virtual machines on virtual networks. As the name implies, it translates addresses that connect to the Internet to addresses used on the virtual networks using NAT. This configuration allows Windows Server Gateway to be multi-tenant aware while allowing all virtual networks behind the gateway to connect to the Internet, even if they use overlapping address spaces.

The forwarding gateway for internal physical network access has the Windows Server Gateway provide access to internal network resources that are located on the physical network. This allows connection to physical servers that are not part of the virtualized environment.

Determining Requirements and Scenarios for Distributed Firewall Policies and Network Security Groups

The Network Controller's ***Datacenter Firewall*** allows you to configure and manage firewall access control rules for both East-West and North-South network traffic in your data center. The Datacenter Firewall is a stateful, multi-tenant firewall. When deployed, tenant administrators can install and configure firewall policies to help protect their virtual networks from unwanted traffic from Internet and intranet networks, and between tenants. A stateful firewall looks at the state of current connections and allows inbound connections based on the outbound response for a connection.

CERTIFICATION READY
Determine requirements and scenarios for distributed firewall policies and network security groups
Objective 6.2

The firewall is enforced at the VMSwitch as traffic attempts to ingress or egress from a connected vNIC. Like other firewalls, the firewall uses a set of policies that define Access Control Lists (ACLs), which are distributed from a component called the ***Distributed Firewall Manager***. The Distributed Firewall Manager is part of the Network Controller. The ACLs are applied to a virtual subnet or a network interface.

Network security groups (NSGs) allow you to define rules to segment your virtual environment into virtual subnets, which support multitiered environments. An NSG contains Access Control List rules that either allow or deny traffic to or from a virtual subnet or virtual machine.

Each rule will have the following:

- A name
- Fire-tuple set (destination port range, destination IP range using CIDR notation, source port range, source IP range using CIDR, and protocol, such as TCP, UDP, or *)
- Type (inbound or outbound)
- Priority (101–65,000 for user ranges)
- Action (allow or deny)

The default rules have lower priorities (high number).

The Datacenter Firewall provides a highly scalable and manageable solution that can be offered to multiple tenants. It also allows you to move tenant virtual machines to different hosts while keeping the firewall configuration for the tenant. Because the firewall policies are applied to a subnet or network interface, the protection is applied regardless of the tenant guest operating system.

For tenants, the Datacenter Firewall provides the ability to:

- Define firewall rules that can help protect Internet-facing workloads on their virtual networks.
- Define firewall rules that can help protect traffic between virtual machines on the same L2 virtual subnet and also between virtual machines on different L2 virtual subnets.
- Define firewall rules that can help protect and isolate network traffic between tenant on-premises networks and their virtual networks at the service provider.

SKILL SUMMARY

IN THIS LESSON YOU LEARNED:

- Software-Defined Networking (SDN) allows you to centrally configure and manage physical and virtual network devices, including routers, switches, and gateways in your data center.
- By using SDN, you can merge the physical and virtual components that make up a virtual infrastructure. The applications and virtual servers will run on the physical network, and you can virtualize network management by creating virtual IP addresses, ports, and switches. You can also define policies that will manage traffic flow across both physical and virtual networks.
- The Network Controller is a Windows Server 2016 server role that provides two application programming interfaces (APIs): the Southbound API and the Northbound API. The Southbound API is used to communicate with the network, whereas the Northbound API gives you the ability to communicate with the Network Controller.
- The Windows Software Load Balancing (SLB) evenly distributes tenant and tenant customer network traffic among the virtual network resources. Like Network Load Balancing (NLB), Windows Server SLB enables multiple servers to host the same workload, providing high availability and scalability.
- A Windows Server Gateway is a virtual machine (VM)–based software router and gateway that allows cloud service providers (CSPs) and enterprise organizations to enable data center and cloud network traffic routing between virtual and physical networks, including the Internet.
- The Network Controller's Datacenter Firewall allows you to configure and manage firewall access control rules for both East-West and North-South network traffic in your data center. The Datacenter Firewall is a stateful, multi-tenant firewall. When deployed, tenant administrators can install and configure firewall policies to help protect their virtual networks from unwanted traffic from Internet and intranet networks, and between tenants.

■ Knowledge Assessment

Multiple Choice

Select the correct answer for each of the following questions.

1. Which of the following provides a single platform to manage virtual machines across multiple Hyper-V hosts?
   a. Northbound API
   b. Network Controller
   c. SLB Multiplexer
   d. Virtual Machine Manager

2. Which of the following allows for centrally configuring and managing physical and virtual network devices, including routers, switches, and gateways in a data center?
   a. Northbound API
   b. VMM library
   c. Software-Defined Networking
   d. SLB Multiplexer
3. When deploying SDN using Hyper-V, which of the following scenarios should be used? (Choose two answers.)
   a. On a converged Ethernet network
   b. On multiple Hyper-V stand-alone hosts
   c. With Virtual Machine Manager managing multiple Hyper-V hosts
   d. Using Software Load Balancing
4. Which of the following is the easiest way to create SDN on Hyper-V hosts?
   a. Download and use scripts.
   b. Run the Create SDN Wizard on a domain controller.
   c. Run the Create SDN Wizard on a Network Controller.
   d. Install Virtual Machine Manager.
5. When using Network Virtualization Generic Route Encapsulation, which address is configured and used on the virtual machine guest operating system?
   a. VXLAN address
   b. SLB address
   c. Provider address
   d. Customer address
6. Which of the following is used to manage Hyper-V virtual machines, Datacenter Firewall, RAS Multi-tenant Gateways, virtual gateways, and gateway pools?
   a. SLB Multiplexor
   b. Network Controller
   c. Virtual Extensible LAN
   d. Windows Server Gateway
7. Which traffic is between servers and clients?
   a. North-South
   b. East-West
   c. North-East
   d. South-West
8. Which of the following allows defining rules to segment the virtual environment into virtual subnets via the Datacenter Firewall?
   a. Northbound API
   b. Southbound API
   c. Network security group
   d. SLB Multiplexer

Best Answer

Choose the letter that corresponds to the best answer. More than one answer choice may achieve the goal. Select the BEST answer.

1. In Windows Server 2016, which of the following provides a VM-based software router and gateway?
   a. SLB Multiplexor
   b. Network Controller

c. Virtual Extensible LAN
d. Windows Server Gateway

2. Several virtual machines are load balanced with an SLB Multiplexer. Which of the following addresses is accessed when connecting with the virtual workload?
a. Virtual IP addresses
b. Dynamic IP addresses
c. Customer address
d. Provider address

Matching and Identification

1. Specify the correct order of the steps necessary to deploying SDN.
____ Run the SDN Express scripts.
____ Install host networking and validate the configuration.
____ Validate setup.
____ Install the Hyper-V host.
____ Validate workload deployment.
____ Deploy a sample tenant workload.

2. Specify the correct order of steps necessary to deploying a Network Controller.
____ Configure the Network Controller application.
____ Create at least two AD DS security groups.
____ Validate the Network Controller deployment.
____ Configure the Network Controller application.
____ Create a certificate for the Network Controller.
____ Install the Network Controller server role.
____ Configure the Network Controller cluster.

■ Business Case Scenarios

Scenario 13-1: Making Workloads Highly Available and Scalable

As an administrator for a corporation, you have a new employee application that will run on virtual machines and will be available to corporate employees. Because this application will be used by most employees, you need to make sure that a single virtual machine does not get overworked and that it is highly available. Describe the actions you should take to make sure the application is highly available and supports load balancing.

Scenario 13-2: Making Tenant VMs Secure from Other Tenants

The corporation where you are an administrator has a Hyper-V virtual environment that hosts servers for several clients that run on multiple Hyper-V hosts. To ensure you have the highest security, you need to make sure that VMs for one client cannot access VMs from another client, although they are running on the same Hyper-V host. Describe your recommended solution.

Index

J

K

L

M

N

T

Z